THE MAKING OF CHINA

THE MAKING OF

Edited by
Chun-shu Chang
The University of Michigan

CHINA

MAIN THEMES IN PREMODERN CHINESE HISTORY

PRENTICE-HALL, INC., Englewood Cliffs, New Jersey

Library of Congress Cataloging in Publication Data

CHANG, CHUN-SHU, 1934–   comp.
   The making of China.

   Bibliography: p.
   CONTENTS: The pattern of Chinese history: Chang, Chun-shu. The periodization of Chinese history: a survey of major schemes and hypotheses.—Ancient China: from prehistory to the classical age: Bodde, D. Myths of ancient China. Chang, Kwang-chih. From archaeology to history: the Neolithic foundations of Chinese civilization. Walker, R. L. Interstate relations during the Ch'un-Ch'iu period. Hsü, Cho-yun. The transition of ancient Chinese society. Graham, A. C. The place of reason in ancient Chinese philosophical tradition. [etc.]
   1. China—History—Early to 1643.   2. China—History—Ch'ing dynasty, 1644–1912.   I. Title.
DS735.C365   951   75-1045
ISBN   0-13-545640-1

The Making of China: Main Themes in Premodern Chinese History
Edited by Chun-shu Chang

© 1975 by Prentice-Hall, Inc., Englewood Cliffs, New Jersey

All rights reserved. No part of this book may be reproduced in any form or by any means without permission in writing from the publisher.

Printed in the United States of America

10   9   8   7   6   5   4   3   2   1

Prentice-Hall International, Inc., *London*
Prentice-Hall of Australia, Pty. Ltd., *Sydney*
Prentice-Hall of Canada, Ltd., *Toronto*
Prentice-Hall of India Private Limited, *New Delhi*
Prentice-Hall of Japan, Inc., *Tokyo*

Foreword

I am pleased to see the second reprinting of this small volume. While the book is still a good supplementary text for courses in Chinese history from the prehistoric period to the eighteenth century, it needs extensive revision and updating. My present research schedule, however, does not permit me to do this urgent task. But I believe that the reader can do part of this work by consulting three recent bibliographical masterpieces: John K. Fairbank, *China: A New History* (Cambridge, Mass: Harvard University Press, 1992), pp. 437-490; Charles W. Hayford, *China: New Edition* (Santa Barbara, CA: Clio Press, 1997); and Endymion Wilkinson, *Chinese History, A Manual* (Cambridge, Mass: Harvard University Press, 1998).

For the reader's convenience, I have added to this reprint a new "Chronology of Major Dynasties and Periods" in Chinese history. It serves to correct some of the serious mistakes in the 1975 version.

Chun-shu Chang
Ann Arbor, Michigan
January 5, 2000

To Shelley Hsueh-lun

CONTENTS

Preface, ix

Acknowledgments, xi

Chronology of Major Dynasties and Periods, xiii

I The Pattern of Chinese History, 1

CHUN-SHU CHANG, The Periodization of Chinese History:
A Survey of Major Schemes and Hypotheses   3

II Ancient China: From Prehistory to the Classical Age, 13

DERK BODDE, Myths of Ancient China   15

KWANG-CHIH CHANG, From Archaeology to History:
The Neolithic Foundations of Chinese Civilization   38

RICHARD L. WALKER, Interstate Relations During the Ch'un-Ch'iu Period   46

CHO-YUN HSÜ, The Transition of Ancient Chinese Society   62

A. C. GRAHAM, The Place of Reason in Ancient Chinese Philosophical Tradition   72

III Early Imperial China: 221 B.C.–A.D. 220, 85

YÜ-CH'ÜAN WANG, The Central Government of the Former Han Dynasty	87
LIEN-SHENG YANG, Great Families of Eastern Han	116
H. G. CREEL, The Eclectics of Han Thought	140

IV Middle Imperial China: A.D. 221–959, 157

ARTHUR F. WRIGHT, Domestication of Buddhism in China	159
EDWARD H. SCHAFER, The Glory of the T'ang Empire	171
E. G. PULLEYBLANK, The Economic Background of the Rebellion of An Lu-shan	199
GUNGWU WANG, The Military Governors and the Decline of the T'ang Dynasty	211
CH'AO-TING CHI, Key Economic Areas in Chinese History: From the Huangho Basin to the Yangtze Valley	230

V Late Imperial China: A.D. 960–ca. 1795, 249

E. A. KRACKE, JR., Sung Society: Change Within Tradition	251
JAMES T. C. LIU, Reform in Sung China: Wang An-shih and His New Policies	258
W. THEODORE DE BARY, A Reappraisal of Neo-Confucianism	266
JUNG-PANG LO, The Emergence of China as a Sea Power During the Late Sung and Early Yüan Periods	287
PING-TI HO, Social Composition of the Ming-Ch'ing Ruling Class	298
T'UNG-TSU CH'Ü, The Gentry and Local Administration in Ch'ing China	310
PING-TI HO, The Population of China in Ming-Ch'ing Times	330

Bibliographical Note, 346

ACKNOWLEDGMENTS

This volume grew out of a set of selected articles originally used as supplementary readings for my classes in traditional Chinese history. My students' enthusiastic response to the selections, and the lack of any such supplementary text, encouraged me to make the selections available in published form.

The publication of this volume would have been impossible without the encouragement and assistance of many friends. My thanks go to Professor Albert Feuerwerker of the University of Michigan for his encouragement. I am also indebted to Dr. Donald E. Thackrey, of the Editorial Office at the University of Michigan Office of Research Administration, for his efficient editing on a very short notice.

Some of the materials used in this volume are taken from two of my works under preparation, which have received support from the Center for Chinese Studies at the University of Michigan, the Social Science Research Council, and the American Council of Learned Societies. To all these institutes go my special gratitude.

The manuscript for this book was completed some five years ago. When I recently reviewed the edited manuscript before its long-delayed publication, I made a few minor changes and updated, to a limited extent, the bibliographical suggestions in my introductions to the various selections. I would like to take this opportunity to thank Brian Walker, of Prentice-Hall, for his interest in the book. I am most grateful to Carolyn Davidson, also of Prentice-Hall, for her thoughtful and careful work in preparing the manuscript for publication.

My wife Shelley has helped in every way in preparing this volume: indeed, many of the points expressed herein are hers. Without her assistance this book could never have been published. To her, my deepest thanks and affection.

A volume of this nature can never be satisfactory even to the editor, because new research results continually come out and because some of the materials that might have been included are not available for a variety of reasons. However, there is always the chance of revision. Since this is the first such reader of selected articles on premodern China, I can best describe my feeling by quoting a popular Chinese expression: "P'ao-chuan yin-yü," literally, "May the brick I here cast attract jade from others."

CHINA
Major Dynasties and Periods

I. **The Classical Age (Ancient China)**

    The Hsia (Xia) Dynasty   Ca. 1900-1600 B.C. (trad. 2200-1766 B.C.)
    The Shang Dynasty   Ca. 1600-1100 B.C. (trad. 1766-1122 B.C.)
    The Chou (Zhou) Dynasty   Ca. 1100-256 B.C. (trad. 1122-256)
        Western Chou   ca.1100-771 B.C.
        Eastern Chou   770-256 B.C.
            The Spring and Autumn (Ch'un-ch'iu) Period: 722-468 B.C./770-404 B.C.
            The Warring States (Chan-kuo) Period: 403-221 B.C.

II. **The Imperial Period (Imperial China)**

                    EARLY IMPERIAL
    The Ch'in (Qin) Dynasty   221-207 B.C.
    The Ch'u-Han Transition   206-202 B.C.
    The Western (Former) Han Dynasty   202 B.C.-A.D.8
    The Hsin (Xin) Dynasty   9-23
    The Eastern (Latter) Han Dynasty   25-220

                    MIDDLE IMPERIAL
    The Three Kingdoms
        Shu (Shu-Han)   221-263
        Wei   220-265
        Wu   222-280
    The Chin (Jin) Dynasty   265-280-420
        Western Chin   265-317
        Eastern Chin   317-420

    The Southern Dynasties
        The Fomer (or Liu) Sung (Song) Dynasty   420-479
        The Southern Ch'i (Qi) Dynasty   479-502
        The Southern Liang Dynasty   502-557
           (The Latter Liang Dynasty   555-587)
        The Southern Ch'en Dynasty   557-589

    The Northern Dynasties
        The Northern Wei Dynasties   386-535/534
        The Eastern Wei   534-550
        The Western Wei   535-557
        The Northern Ch'i (Qi) Dynasty   550-577
        The Northern Chou (Zhou) Dynasty 557-581

    The Sui Dynasty   589-618
    The T'ang (Tang) Dynasty   618-907
    The Five Dynasties
        Later Liang   907-923
        Later T'ang   923-936

Later Chin (Jin)	936-947
Later Han	947-950
Later Chou (Zhou)	951-960

LATER IMPERIAL

The Sung (Song) Dynasty	960-1279
Nothern Sung	960-1126
Southern Sung	1127-1279
The Liao (Khitan) Dynasty	907-916-1125
The Hsi-Hsia (Xi Xia, Tangut Tibetan) Dynasty	990-1032-1227
The Chin (Jin, Jurchern) Dynasty	1115-1234
The Yuan (Mongol) Dynasty	1279-1368
The Ming	1368-1644
The Southern Ming	1645-1662 (1683)
The Ch'ing (Qing, Manchu) Dynasty	1644-1911/1912

III. The Republic   1912---

THE MAKING OF CHINA

1

THE PATTERN
OF CHINESE HISTORY

CHUN-SHU CHANG

The Periodization of Chinese History: A Survey of Major Schemes and Hypotheses

Like the histories of all other countries, the history of China clearly follows a certain pattern, in one sense, and yet in another sense it defies all attempts at imposing any single pattern. Scholarly preference depends upon one's standpoint of historical analysis and upon the degree of generalization employed in that analysis. Because historians have applied different standpoints and different degrees of generalizations, they have reached different conclusions regarding patterns of Chinese history. In general, historians have emphasized one of three patterns: repetitive dynastic or periodic cycles, continuous developments, and stagnation. All of these views have been reflected in different periodization schemes applied to Chinese history.

The periodization of Chinese history has been a subject of discussion for centuries, particularly within China, but also outside China in modern times. Many schemes and views of Chinese history have been presented in various Western-language works.

The tradition of dividing Chinese history into stages stems from Confucius (551–479 B.C.), the first Chinese thinker whose views on historical stages can be documented. In modern times, K'ang Yu-wei (1858–1927) and Liang Ch'i-ch'ao (1873–1928) were among the first to discuss the problem. In a book entitled *Li-yun chu (The Li-yun Annotated)*, K'ang proposed in 1884–85 a three-division scheme of Chinese history: the Age of Order—the periods from Yao and Shun to Hsia, Shang, and (Western) Chou; the Age of Disorder—from Ch'un-ch'iu to the unification of China under the Ch'in; the Age of Order—from Ch'in to his time (nineteenth-century China); and the Age of Great Peace—a new age of Grand Unity he proposed that China enter through reforms. It is a well-known fact that this division of Chinese history follows the famous theory of the "Three Ages," a concept developed by Yen An-lo (first century B.C.), a third-generation disciple of Tung Chung-shu (179–104 B.C.), and Ho Hsiu (129–182 A.D.). This concept was included in their commentaries on the *Kung-yang Commentary* on the *Ch'un-ch'iu (Spring and Autumn Annals)*. K'ang's contribution was to set forth his scheme in terms of the theory of the "Three Ages" and the idea of Grand Unity in the *Li-yun* section of the *Book of Rites*. Political and social conditions are evidently the primary criteria in this periodization. The adoption of the idea of Grand Unity was aimed at easing the Chinese and non-Chinese, par-

Reprinted with minor changes from *The Bulletin of the Institute of History and Philology, Academia Sinica*, Vol. XLV, Part I (1973), 157–79. By permission of the author. Footnotes omitted.

ticularly the Manchu, conflicts of interest. The unique feature of Grand Unity points to the Utopian nature of the proposal.

Turning to the twentieth century, Liang Ch'i-ch'ao (1873–1928), K'ang Yu-wei's pupil, seems to have been the first Chinese scholar to discuss the problem of periodization of Chinese history. In 1901, following conventional European divisions, he proposed a three-division scheme. The ancient period lasted from high antiquity (the Yellow Emperor) to the end of Chan-Kuo, and was characterized by aristocratic political structure and self-development of the Chinese people; the medieval period, from the founding of the Ch'in in 221 B.C. to the end of the reign of Ch'ien-lung of the Ch'ing in 1795, was characterized by autocratic government and keen competition of the Chinese with other Asian peoples; the modern period, initiated since the Ch'ien-lung period, has witnessed China's transformation into the modern age, with modern government and increasing contact and competition among China, other Asian countries, and the West. In 1922, Liang revised his scheme by changing the beginning of the ancient period to the time of the legendary sage ruler Yü of Hsia, and by changing the lower limit of the medieval period to the end of the Ch'ing dynasty in 1911. This change added the factor of cultural growth to the two primary criteria used for the first scheme: the pattern of political structure, and the development of the Chinese people as a nation and its relations with other peoples of the world.

In 1913–14, a more systematic scheme of periodization was proposed by Chang Ch'in (1880–1931). Using the criteria of political and cultural developments, Chang divided Chinese history into four periods: the ancient period, from prehistory to the end of Chan-kuo in 221 B.C.; the medieval period, from the founding of the Ch'in in 221 B.C. to the end of the T'ang in 907 A.D.; the early modern period, from the beginning of the Five Dynasties in 907 to the end of the Ming in 1644; and the modern period, the Ch'ing dynasty. The major contribution of this scheme is its suggestion of the Five Dynasties as the starting point of the early modern period, a view that, as will be shown later, has been agreed upon by contemporary researchers.

In 1918 Fu Ssu-nien (1896–1950) suggested still another scheme of periodization. Focusing on the history of the growth of the Chinese people as a nation, and its interactions with the various groups of northern nomads of Inner Asia, Fu periodized Chinese history as follows:

I. Ancient Period: First China—China of the Han people
   Subperiod I: pre-770 B.C.
   Subperiod II: 770–221 B.C.
   Subperiod III: 221 B.C.–A.D. 317
   Subperiod IV: 317–589: Beginning of barbarian influence in China
II. Medieval Period: Second China—China under Nomads' penetration and influence
   Subperiod I: 589–959: China under strong influence of northern barbarians
   Superiod II: 960–1279: Revival of the Han spirit
III. Modern Period: China of Nomads' predominance
   Subperiod I: 1279–1364: Mongol rule
   Subperiod II: 1364–1661: Revival of the Han rule from the founding of the Wu State (Chu Yüan-chang) to the Ming, and to the end of the Southern Ming
   Subperiod III: 1661–1911: Manchu rule
IV. Contemporary Period: 1912–

Fu's view is a major contribution in its suggestion that the end of the Sung dynasty in 1279 was the starting point of the modern period in China. He is among the first to have made such a suggestion.

The topic of periodization became a subject of heated debate during the "Controversy on the Social History of China" in the late 1920s and early 1930s. Various schemes of division were advanced in this period. Among the notable ones are those of Kuo Mo-jo, T'ao Hsi-sheng, Li Chi, Mei Ssu-p'ing, Hu Chi'iu-yüan, Wang Li-hsi, and Ku Meng-yü. Three of these are sketched here to show the variety of views and approaches.

Writing in 1928, Kuo Mo-jo, following a Marxist interpretation of history, divided Chinese history into the following major stages:

I. Primitive Communism: Pre-Chou period—classless clan society
II. Slave Society: Western Chou—nobles versus commoners and slaves
III. Feudal Society: From the Ch'un-ch'iu period to the mid-nineteenth century—well stratified class society
IV. Capitalist Society: From the mid-nineteenth century to the 1920s—capitalists versus proletarians

As Kuo clearly notes, his sole criterion is the mode of production and the social structure generated by it.

T'ao Hsi-sheng's view changed a few times during the period of the "Controversy," but by 1935 his periodization scheme had emerged in definitive form, as follows: ancient society from the fifth century B.C. to the third century A.D., during which China passed from a clan society in the Chou period to a slave society; medieval society from the third to the ninth century, during which manorial economy and aristocratic government prevailed; and modern society from the tenth to the nineteenth century, during which China saw autocratic government and a new monetary, market- and handicrafts-economy with expansion of domestic and foreign trade—a type of economy T'ao had previously termed "proto-capitalistic."

Taking the mode of production as his sole criterion, Li Chi periodized Chinese history in a novel way. He termed the periods of the legendary Yao and Shun as the era of a primitive communist mode of production, the period from Hsia through Yin as the era of an Asiatic mode of production, the Chou period as the era of a feudal mode of production, the period from Ch'in to the eve of the Opium War as the era of a proto-capitalistic mode of production, and the period from the Opium War to the 1930s as the era of a capitalistic mode of production.

The "Controversy on the Social History of China" brought about three new fronts on the periodization of Chinese history. First, Chinese historians turned to a broad and penetrating investigation of the economic and social factors affecting major stages of Chinese history. Second, new views on periodization were advanced at this time to form a new framework for Chinese historical studies. Third, periodization schemes proposed by scholars outside China were introduced; among these were the Naitō hyopthesis and Karl A. Wittfogel's theory of "hydraulic society." Above all, periodization has since become a major field of interest in contemporary Chinese historiography. Different schemes and views have been advanced. In 1936 Lei Hai-tsung (1902–1962) made a unique proposal. He first questioned the applicability of the conventional European divisions—ancient, medieval, and modern—to the periodization of Chinese history. He divided China's past into two major cycles, "Classical China" from antiquity to 383 A.D., and "Synthetic China" from 383 A.D. to date. He pointed out that the history of "Classical China" followed, in general, the same growth pattern as other great civilizations—from feudal age to empire and the decline of classical culture—but the history of the second cycle is unique; no other nations have been able to create a synthetic culture on the basis of several foreign influences, racial and cultural, as did China during this long period. Like Fu Ssu-nien, Lei also took the national factor as his main criterion for the growth of Chinese civilization. In the first cycle, the creator of culture was mainly the Han Chinese, but in the second, the creator was the mixed Han-Tartar Chinese with a strongly Buddhist-influenced mind. Similar to Lei's basic attitude but different from Lei's views was the proposal made by Ch'ien Mu in 1939. Ch'ien held that it is incorrect to study Chinese history in terms of European history, and that division schemes of European history are naturally not applicable to Chinese history. In the end, he divided China's past into eight parts: the period of prehistory and Hsia–Shang–Chou, the period of Ch'un-ch'iu and Chan-kuo, and six other periods arranged by dynastic groupings, i.e., Ch'in-Han, Wei-Chin and Nan-pei-ch'ao, Sui-T'ang and Wu-tai, Sung, Yüan-Ming, and Ch'ing.

One significant concept advanced further in the post-"Controversy" periodization schemes is "incipient capitalism" *(tzu-pen chu-i meng-ya)*, a concept that played a key role in Chinese historiography of the 1950s and 1960s, when a great number of works were written on this problem in Chinese history. Although the concept had already been developed by Wang Chih-jui, T'ao Hsi-sheng, and Li Chi, and had been termed *Shang-yeh tzu-pen* (commercial capitalism), *hsien tzu-pen chu-i* (proto-capitalism), and *ch'ien tzu-pen chu-i* (proto-capitalism), respectively, Chou Ku-ch'eng in 1939 proposed a periodization scheme which included "incipient capitalism" as a major stage of Chinese history. His five-part division follows the order of (1) a tribal society before 770 B.C.; (2) an era of formation of private ownership of land, from 770 B.C. to 9 A.D.; (3) a high feudal age from 9 to 960; (4) continuation of the feudal society from 960 to 1840; and (5) an era of "incipient capitalism" from 1840 to the 1920s.

The discussion of periodization schemes assumed a new vigor during the "Debates on the Periodization of Chinese History" in Mainland China in the fifties, and was continued, but with less vigor, into the early sixties, until the coming of the Great Cultural Revolution in 1966. Over 350 articles and a number of books dealing with the various aspects of periodization were published. About one-third of the articles were edited into seven impressive volumes. While it is not feasible to reproduce here the diversified views of these works, we can discuss a few of their common features or grounds. They follow, for the most part, the Marxist view that the only deciding factors in history are (1) the mode of production, (2) the class struggle, and (3) the principal contradictions within a society. But a unique factor in the context of Chinese history that has been added to these elements is "nationalism," a factor depicted in struggles between the Han Chinese and northern nomads before modern times, and between the Chinese as a whole and Europeans since the nineteenth century. As we have seen already, the application of nationalism as a major factor in periodizing Chinese history is traditional; it dates back to Liang Ch'i-ch'ao and Fu Ssu-nien. It is a product of the political nationalist movement in modern China.

The second common feature of the Marxist interpretation of history is that histories of all countries follow a single universal course: from primitive communism, to ancient slavery, to medieval feudalism, to modern capitalism, to socialistic society. But in the special context of China three additional conceptions, "incipient capitalism," "semi-colonial" *(pan ch'ih-min-ti)*, and "semi-feudal" *(pan feng-chien)*, have come to play a major role in historical periodization. In the various periodization proposals, "incipient capitalism" is used to describe the later feudal age or to replace the era of "capitalism" in the Marxist model, and a "semi-colonial" or "semi-colonial and semi-feudal" age replaces "capitalism," denoting China as under "imperialist" influences since 1840. The periodization scheme of Fan Wen-lan, one of the leading and at one time one of the most influential historians in Mainland China, is a good illustration of this point. Fan holds that the period before Hsia was the age of primitive communes; the periods of Hsia and Shang represented China's slave society; the feudal age lasted from Western Chou to the time of Opium War; and a semi-colonial and semi-feudal society existed from 1840 to 1949. Fan also maintains that "incipient capitalism" began in the Ming period, but it was never strong enough to shake the feudal economy and society.

While a small minority have dissented from the general Marxist normative stages of societal development by simply stating that the present state of research on Chinese history does not warrant periodization efforts, the majority of historians in Mainland China have followed the pattern. But this does not make analysis of their schemes any easier. They have disagreed about the presence of some stages following feudalism in Chinese history; for example, some have rejected the stage of "incipient capitalism." Further, even though they have agreed on the order of stages of the system, very often they have disagreed with one another on the timing of shifts from one stage to another. It is this latter issue that has greatly divided Mainland Chinese historians. Most of the controversies in this regard have centered around two questions. One concerns when the slave age ended and the feudal age began; the other, assuming the existence of "incipient capitalism," concerns when this period began. For the former, Chou Ku-ch'eng proposed in 1950 that China's feudal age started after A.D. 9, while the period from the Shang through the Former Han to A.D. 9 was the slave age. Kuo Mo-jo suggested in 1952 that the transition from Ch'un-ch'iu to Chan-kuo was the transition from the slave age to the feudal age. Yang Hsiang-k'uei proposed in the same year that the Western Chou represented the beginning of the feudal age; his view was shared by T'ung Shu-yeh, Ts'en Chung-mien, Hsü Chung-shu, Fan Wen-lan, Lü Chen-yü, and many others. Li Yan-nung's studies of 1953 contended that the collapse of the Western Chou in the eighth century B.C. marked the ending of China's slave age.

As has been discussed above, the issue of "incipient capitalism" in the problem of periodization in Chinese historical studies is an old one. But the political factor has brought about a new wave of enthusiasm for a most intensive and extensive investigation of the issue. Numerous works on the problem have produced an amazing amount of new materials, secondary and primary, for the study of Chinese economic and social history. Disagreement on when "incipient capitalism" began in China, however, remains as wide as ever. Ten possible periods have been proposed, namely, T'ang (618–907), Sun (960–1279), Southern Sung (1127–1279), early Yüan (13th century), early Ming (14th century), middle Ming (the 15th to the 16th century), the early sixteenth century, late Ming (the late 16th and the early 17th centuries), the early seventeenth century, and early Ch'ing to the eighteenth century. But, like the very existence of the issue itself, none of these is conclusive.

In contrast with their mainland colleagues, historians of Nationalist China have been relatively inactive with regard to the problem of periodization. Only a few works have been written; none has been able to raise controversy. Influenced by Ott Franke, Liang Ch'i-ch'ao, Fu Ssu-nien, and Lei Hai-tsung, in 1957 Yao Ts'ung-wu proposed using the development and influence of Confucian cosmopolitanism and the growth of the Chinese nation as the main criteria for periodizing Chinese history. In general, Professor Yao contends that the history of imperial China (221 B.C.–A.D. 1912) should be divided into two major periods: one prior to the fall of the T'ang dynasty in 907, and one after this date. Each constitutes an independent cycle in terms of the development of Confucian cosmopolitanism and the growth of the Chinese nation. Specifically, he suggests a four-part division: (1) Shang to the end of Han; (2) Wei to the end of T'ang; (3) the Five Dynasties to the end of Yüan; and (4) Ming and Ch'ing, each witnessing a complete cycle of racial mixing of the Chinese and northern nomads. He also holds that China of today is in the process of the fifth such cycle. The striking feature of this view is its strong nationalist inclination and an absence of such conventional European labels as "feudalism," "modern," and the like.

Taking into consideration the complexity of the periodization problem, Lao Kan suggests three ways to look at the issue. Viewing political history and the tools used in different ages, he divides Chinese history into (1) a stone age—palaeolithic and neolithic; (2) a bronze age from Shang through Ch'un-ch'iu—feudal society; (3) an iron age from Chan-kuo to the end of the Tao-kuang reign (1821–1850) of the Ch'ing dynasty—agricultural empire with bureaucratic government; and (4) a machine age since Tao-kuang. Viewing stages of cultural progress, Lao proposes a four-part division: (1) a period from the Ch'in to the Eastern Han (221 B.C.–A.D. 25), marked by mutual influences and the growth of Confucianism and Taoism; (2) a period from the Eastern Han through the T'ien-pao era (742–756) of the T'ang dynasty, marked by great cultural progress and strong Buddhist influence; (3) a period from the end of T'ien-pao to the Tao-kuang era of the Ch'ing dynasty, marked by dominance of Neo-Confucianism, development of popular novels and stories and dramas, increasing political authoritarianism, and rigid civil service examinations; and (4) a period since Tao-kuang, an era of transformation. Viewing the periodic recurrence of internecine wars, Lao divides imperial China into three cycles: Ch'in to the end of the Southern and Northern dynasties (221 B.C.–A.D. 589); Sui through the Sung dynasty (589–1279); and Yüan to the end of Ch'ing (1279–1912), with each going through a cycle of cultural and political creative periods, an era of peace and prosperity, and a period of social and institutional disintegration and wars.

It is clear that Lao's schemes stem from three early sources. The first is influenced by one of the conventional European divisions; the second is based on the works of Liang Ch'i-ch'ao, Fu Ssu-nien, Lei Hai-tsung, and others; and the third is a revision of a system first formulated by Li Ssu-kuang in 1931.

Another scheme of Chinese historical divisions was suggested by Lo Hsiang-lin in 1953. Based primarily on the evolution of four factors—the role of family in Chinese society, the predominance of agricultural economy, the influence of Confucian principles, and the overall configuration of Chinese society, which he termed "olive-shape" society, Lo's scheme divides the long history, or more properly the history of the evolution of Chinese society, into four major periods: (1) the tribal society (3000–1401 B.C.), in which a confederate head ruled over various supporting tribes; (2) the feudal society (1400–221 B.C.), in which the king ruled over the feudal princes; (3) the selective-system society (221 B.C.–617 A.D.), in which the centralized power of the sovereign ruled the country by the force of a bureaucracy recruited through a recommendation-selection system; and (4) the civil service examination system society (617–1911 A.D.), in which the ruling class of the society was the elite who passed the civil service examinations. Lo makes careful analyses of the characteristic developments of the aforementioned four major factors in each of the four periods. It seems clear that his periodization of Chinese history provides some insights into the evolution and dynamics of change of Chinese society, although the system itself is not entirely original.

Outside China, many different periodization schemes and views concerning the developmental stages of Chinese society and history have also been suggested. While some of these are duplicates of the models mentioned above, the others present new theories. A few representative ones may be briefly sketched here. In Japan, Naitō Torajirō (1860–1934) suggested in 1922 that the late T'ang and the Five Dynasties marked the transition to China's "modern age," which started with the Sung, while the period from the end of the Han through the middle T'ang constituted China's "middle ages," and the period of the Han and prior to that lay in China's "ancient society." Miyazaki Ichisada proposed in 1950 to divide Chinese history into four major ages: an ancient empire—from high antiquity to the end of the Han; an aristocratic society—from the Three Kingdoms to the end of the Five Dynasties; a period of autocratic government—from the unification of the Sung to the Opium War; and the age of modernization—since the Opium War. Like Naitō, he also maintained that the dividing line between China's medieval period and the modern age was the late T'ang. A theory quite different from the above two, which have been followed by a considerable number of scholars in Japan, was advanced by Maeda Naonori (1915–1949) in 1948. According to him, the periodization of Chinese history must be considered together with that of all other East Asian countries, such as Japan and Korea. Secondly, the Five Dynasties period after the T'ang dynasty was the beginning of China's medieval, feudal society, while the T'ang and before constituted the ancient period, a society marked by slavery. This new hypothesis has since aroused strong interest among a number of scholars. New research trends thus have resulted from their efforts to test its applicability to Chinese history and the histories of other East Asian countries. Among these researchers are Japan's leading scholars on Chinese economic and social history, such as Nishijima Sadao and Sudō Yoshiyuki. In 1953 Hamaguchi Shigekuni, a leading Japanese expert on Chinese socio-economic and military history, proposed a different line of division: China's ancient society lay in the period from high antiquity through the Ch'un-ch'iu and Chan-kuo periods, and her middle ages lasted from the Ch'in to the end of the Ch'ing in 1912. He thus maintains that the differences in socio-economic and cultural developments between the Ch'in and Han, the Wei and Chin and the Southern and Northern Dynasties, and the Sui and T'ang are merely those between the various subperiods of a long stage of history; therefore the period from the Ch'in and the Han to the middle T'ang is China's early middle age, in which some of the elements of ancient society still functioned, and the period since the middle T'ang represents China's high middle age in which all medieval elements reached maturity.

In the West, various periodization schemes and views have been advanced. A few significant ones may be briefly stated. Following the Marxist theory of Oriental Society and control of water resources as his main concern, Karl A. Wittfogel considers imperial China a "complex hydraulic (Oriental)" society which never underwent basic changes and therefore needs little periodization. Chou and pre-Chou China are termed "simple hydraulic" and "semi-complex hydraulic" societies, respectively, in terms of governmental forms. From a standpoint of sociological characteristics, Wolfram Eberhard sees no merit in the concept of basic differences between East and West, and suggests retaining the conventional European tri-partite division. Thus he periodizes Chinese history as (1) antiquity—a period of feudalism, from Shang to the mid-third century B.C.; (2) medieval time—a period of gentry society, from the mid-third century B.C. to the tenth century A.D.; and (3) modern time—a period of the middle class, from the tenth century onwards. Influenced by the Naitō proposal and, like Naitō, focusing major attention on socioeconomic and intellectual changes, Edwin O. Reischauer and John K. Fairbank suggest that the late T'ang marked the transition from "classic" to "early modern" China. They regard the late T'ang and Sung as a period of renaissance that showed a decided shift in the basic values of culture and the establishment of new patterns. Along the same line, noting a "great divide" taking place in the late T'ang, James T. C. Liu proposes a "neo-traditional period" from about 800 to 1900 A.D., which signifies a selective continuity of the old tradition as well as a reintegration of the old heritage and the new ingredients into a new tradition that in turn imposes its own set bounds.

Somewhat different from the two suggestions just mentioned is Earl H. Pritchard's theory of "Six Ages," proposed in 1964. He divides Chinese history into six major periods. The first two are "The Stone Age" and "The Archaic Bronze Age," which are contemporaneous, existing in different parts of China from ca. 2000 B.C. to 770 B.C. or 500 B.C. for the Archaic Bronze and Stone Ages, respectively. During the Archaic Bronze Age a fully developed civilization emerged, while elementary forms of society and different styles of economic life evolved during the Stone Age. The Classical Age lasted from 700 B.C. to 220 A.D., during which the dominant ideology ultimately became Confucianism; the Cosmopolitan Age, from 220 to 1127 A.D., possessed Buddhism as its dominant ideology, with Confucianism and Taoism of secondary importance; the Neo-Classical Age, from 1127 to 1911 A.D., was dominated by Neo-Confucianism; and the Sino-Western Age, which continues to date, has as its dominant ideology a mixture of Chinese and Western ideas. It is of interest to note Pritchard's use of "dominant ideology" as his main criterion in periodizing Chinese history, although factors of other kinds have also been taken into consideration. Pritchard also notes in his scheme three occurrences of the same cycles: (1) an "Interim-Empire" period: a period of division and internal disorder preceding a powerful empire, such as the Eastern Chou, the Three Kingdoms and Six Dynasties, the Chin, the Hsi-Hsia, and the Southern Sung, etc.; and (2) "Empires" made up of (a) a short-lived conquest dynasty such as the Ch'in, the Sui, and the Yüan; (b) a strong, long-lived dynasty such as the Western Han, the T'ang, and the Ming; (c) an "Interim-dynasty" such as the Hsin (Wang Mang), the Five Dynasties, the Ming-Ch'ing transition; and (d) another strong, long-lived dynasty such as the Eastern Han, the Northern Sung, and the Ch'ing.

Complementing these considerations of evolutionary movements is the theory of cycles, which, as our foregoing discussion has indicated, can be classed as periodic cycles and dynastic cycles. Chi Ch'ao-ting's division of Chinese history from 255 B.C. to A.D. 1912, based on the shifting of key economic areas, into five cycles of *unity and peace* and *division and struggle* represents the former; and Edwin O. Reischauer and John K. Fairbank's analysis of the cyclical pattern of the Han dynasty illustrates the latter. The whole problem of dynastic configurations in Chinese history was further refined by Professor Lien-sheng Yang in 1954.

The periodization schemes discussed above fall into three broad models: that of unique Chinese historical process, that of European history, and that of the Marxist normative stages of societal development. As already stated, historians of the last group hold that like the histories of all other countries, Chinese history follows a single universal course as prescribed by the Marxist scheme of historical stages. The only cause of disagreements and disputes between them is the dating of the different stages within this single universal course.

Historians of the second group recognize the applicability of conventional periodization schemes of European history in analyzing Chinese historical stages. Their arguments emphasize the effects of economic and political development, with the focus of attention on the difference between preindustrial and industrial societies.

The first model rejects the usefulness of Marxian concepts of historical process and the general model of European history in periodizing Chinese history; it assumes, instead, that the course of Chinese history is unique, that foreign concepts cannot fit in, and that new views of history and new methods of periodization must be created on the basis of unique characteristics of Chinese historical process, including the unique pattern of cultural growth, the pattern of relations between the northern barbarians and the Chinese, the image and influence of China in Asia, the developmental stages of Chinese national character, and the pattern of dynastic relations.

These differences in asserting the pattern of Chinese history, in general, can be understandably attributed to different stands based upon the cultural values and political beliefs of the historians. Specifically, they can be understood in terms of the intellectual climate and historiographic trends of the times in which the historians lived in the past, or now live. The majority of the historians of the first group, for example, are all renowned Chinese nationalists; their schemes of periodization were advanced during the height of the Chinese nationalist movement, in which the climate of opinion in almost every kind of intellectual pursuit was dominated by a strong nationalistic spirit.

It is significant to note that the frequency

of proposals of periodization schemes and the intensity of interest in making such proposals are correlated with, among other elements, the general state of academic enterprise in China and of Chinese studies in countries outside China. For example, the highest frequency of writings on periodization in Mainland China was in the mid- and late-fifties, which was also the most active period of the mainland academic world under the relatively free atmosphere of *Po-chia cheng-ming* (let the one hundred schools of thought contend). On the other hand, the relative lack of attention to the periodization problem in Nationalist China may be explained by the fact that the academic world there had been in general less active until the 1960s, due to a complex of factors.

The search for patterns of Chinese history signifies a broad dimension of persistent efforts of historians in particular and scholars in general for an in-depth understanding of the configuration and salient phases of Chinese society and civilization. Besides constituting an integral intellectual discipline, such an understanding has direct contemporary relevance. For those historians and scholars outside China, this effort is part of their research on China's past and its relevance to the present, and constitutes a significant part of the meaning of their profession for their respective societies. For historians and scholars in China, such an effort is both part of the Chinese intellectual tradition and representative of the contemporary design of rewriting China's past in terms of current value systems and political ideologies. Looking into the long history of Chinese historical writings, we note a long, recurrent tradition that after a dynastic transition or during great political changes historians and scholars chose or were induced to devote their intellectual efforts to examining the pattern and course of history. As a result, new historical writings based on new views were produced. The reasons for this phenomenon were manifold. First of all, the great changes, dynastic or otherwise, produced new ages which, in turn, gave rise to new ways of evaluating the past. Furthermore, the need to preserve the records of the past after the changes generated and directed new intellectual efforts in historiographic pursuit. Thirdly, political changes increased the desire and need to examine the historical course of the past to find the right course of action for the future, and to reinterpret the past to affirm the legitimacy and authority of the present institutions. An examination of the timing of and ideologies behind the historiographic endeavors throughout Chinese history can fully testify to these views. For example, of the twenty-six Dynastic Histories, twenty-two were compiled in the first years of a new dynasty, and eight of these are not even the history of the preceding dynasty of the regimes under which they were compiled. The tremendous amount of historical and quasi-historical works (over eleven hundred, according to a contemporary record) produced during the Ming-Ch'ing transition, which examined from both the standpoint of dynastic changes and general Chinese history the causes of the fall of the Ming and the rise of the Ch'ing, is another good illustration of these points. Therefore, one may conclude that increased Chinese historiographic efforts in contemporary times—the upsurge in efforts to explore the pattern of Chinese history in both specific and general terms—is quite in line with a recurrent model of Chinese traditional historiography, i.e., the review and re-evaluation of past experiences after great political changes, for political, intellectual, and historiographic purposes.

II

ANCIENT CHINA FROM PREHISTORY TO THE CLASSICAL AGE

DERK BODDE

Myths of Ancient China

The intense historical-mindedness of the Chinese, together with the Confucian tendency to reject supernatural explanations for the universe, prevented their myths from being recorded in mythological form. As a result, the Chinese transformed what were once myths and gods into seemingly authentic history and human beings.

In the following article, Dr. Derk Bodde, Professor of Chinese at the University of Pennsylvania, discusses the problem of ancient Chinese myths under three main headings: euhemerization,[1] fragmentation and language, and chronology. He points out that in the first place our search for myth must go beyond the Confucian-dominated classics to the writings of the several non-Confucian schools. Secondly, he notes that the characteristics of fragmentation and euhemerization in the ancient myths that appeared in Chou literature contrasted markedly with the characteristics of the myths recorded in Han times. In Han times, these myths became so fantastic and prolific that one may fairly ask whether many of them are not simply the fanciful creation of their authors rather than based upon actual popular belief. Confronted with these two very different bodies of literature, Professor Bodde has proposed to apply a methodology which includes both Barnhard Karlgren's historical approach and Wolfram Eberhard's sociological approach.[2]

Following this methodology, Dr. Bodde presents his study of five examples of cosmogonic myth and offers his general observations about them. One of the most

"Myths of Ancient China" by Derk Bodde from the book MYTHOLOGIES OF THE ANCIENT WORLD, edited by Samuel N. Kramer. Copyright © 1961 by Doubleday & Company, Inc. Reprinted by permission of the copyright owner.

[1] As commonly used by writers on Chinese mythology, *euhemerization* denotes the process of the transformation of what were once myths and gods into seemingly authentic history and human beings.

[2] It is pertinent that following an anthropological-historical approach, Chang Kwang-chih has made comparable new excellent contributions to the study of the mythology of ancient China; see his articles in *Chung-yang yen-chiu yüan min-tsu yen-chiu so chi-k'an* (Bulletin of the Institute of Ethnology, Academia Sinica), nos. 8 (Autumn 1959), 14 (Autumn 1962), and 16 (Autumn 1963), each of which carries both Chinese and English versions. Along the same lines as Chang, Wen Ch'ung-i has recently done a comprehensive analysis of the myths in the *Ch'u-tz'u* (The Songs of the South or Ch'), a main source for the study of pre-Ch'in mythology. Using both literary and supplementary archeological sources, in many respects Wen's study throws new light on the whole horizon of ancient Chinese mythology; see his *Ch'u wen-hua yen-chiu* (Aspects of the Culture of Ch'u) (Taipei, 1967), pp. 119–61, esp. 119–35; English summary on p. 169.

interesting observations, particularly from a historiographical point of view, is that the "historical age" of a myth usually stands in an inverse ratio to its "literature age." In other words, the earlier the purported age of a myth, the later is its actual appearance in literature.

Myth and myth-making are all a significant component of Chinese civilization. They had a special place in traditional Chinese political structure. Almost all imperial houses and ruling groups, Chinese and alien, had myths either creating or propagating their divine origins and powers; the great culture heroes, whose study is beyond the scope of Dr. Bodde's article, were believed to be true historical figures, and their deeds and virtues often provided rulers with precedents for the implementation of new institutional measures and not infrequently served as norms of activities to check the improper use of the ruler's unlimited powers. Hence the study of the motives of myth-making and the practical functions of myths in traditional—and to some extent in modern—China is a significant task for Chinese historians.[3]

I. Introduction

The student of Chinese religion quickly learns that there is a world of difference between the gods of classical China (ending with the fall of the Han dynasty in A.D. 220) and those of post-classical times. The latter are large in number, diverse in origin (Buddhist, Taoist, or numerous local cults), have clearly defined anthropomorphic traits, and belong to a spiritual hierarchy which, in its gradations, closely parallels the terrestrial hierarchy of bureaucratic imperial China. These gods are portrayed for us in art, described in religious literature, and even satirized in works of fiction such as the great sixteenth-century novel *Hsi yu chi* (translated by Arthur Waley as *Monkey*). It is notable that relatively few of them are known as early as the classical period. This means that though several compendia have been published under such generalized titles as "Chinese mythology," they are of little relevance for the study of *ancient* Chinese myth since, despite their titles, they limit themselves very largely to these later gods.

The gods of ancient China, by comparison, are fewer in number, appear very rarely or not at all in art, and are commonly described so vaguely or briefly in the texts that their personality, and sometimes even their sex, remains uncertain. Side by side with them, on the other hand, appear a good many figures who, at first sight, seem to be human beings, yet on closer examination are found to display more than ordinary human qualities. They are gods or demigods who, through a process to be discussed presently, have been largely stripped of their divine attributes and transformed into men.

It would be tempting but erroneous to conclude from this that there are no myths in ancient China. More accurate would be the statement that individual *myths* certainly do occur, but not a systematic *mythology*, meaning by this an integrated

---

[3] This subject is treated in detail in my forthcoming work, *History, Religion, and Society in Ancient China*, Chapter III.

body of mythological materials. On the contrary, these materials are usually so fragmentary and episodic that even the reconstruction from them of individual myths —let alone an integrated *system* of myths— is exceedingly difficult. Before discussing the myths themselves, we shall in the following section elaborate on some of the factors which may throw light on this peculiar situation. First of all, however, some definitions and explanations are in order.

In this essay we shall confine our attention to the field covered by what Stith Thompson calls a "minimum definition" of myth. "Myth," he has written (in an article appearing in *Myth: A Symposium, 1955*), "has to do with the gods and their actions, with creation, and with the general nature of the universe and of the earth. This is a minimum definition." Even within this minimum definition, moreover, reasons of space will compel us to limit ourselves still further to myths of a cosmogonic nature. This means that, aside from their mention in connection with cosmogonic phenomena, we shall be obliged to disregard the much larger category of ancient Chinese *hero* myths: those of the culture hero who enjoys supernatural birth, is sometimes aided by protective animals, becomes a sage ruler or otherwise performs great deeds for mankind, and so on.

Chronologically, our attention will be focused for the most part on myths believed to have existed during the pre-imperial epoch of Chinese "feudalism," in other words, during the Chou dynasty (ca. 1027–221 B.C.). (For the preceding Shang dynasty, trad. 1766–ca. 1027, the extant inscriptional material is unfortunately too limited to be serviceable for our subject.) This means that whenever possible we shall base ourselves on texts belonging to the Chou dynasty itself. Because, however, these are often inadequate, we shall in case after case supplement them with the more abundant sources dating from the Han dynasty (206 B.C.–A.D. 220)—an age of empire which, though still forming a part of China's "classical" period, differs in many respects from the pre-imperial Chou dynasty. The question of textual chronology is an exceedingly complicated one, on which we shall have more to say in a later section (II, 3).

Finally, a word about the seemingly precise dates given for many of the personages to appear in these pages. These dates, when marked as "trad." (traditional), should not, of course, be accepted literally, nor even as necessarily signifying that the personages in question ever historically existed. They derive from the traditional chronology formulated by Chinese historians of a later time, and as such are indicative of that same euhemerization about which we shall speak in a moment. We give them here, therefore, simply to show how the Chinese historians have tried to fit their ancient traditions into a chronological framework.

II. The Problems

Though ancient Chinese myths have been studied by some of the best known scholars of East and West alike, the nature of the available data has prevented anything like a generally accepted consensus from emerging. What we have, instead, are diverse theories which, though often ingenious, are rarely conclusive and sometimes exceedingly fanciful. In writing a brief essay such as this, therefore, we are at once confronted by an almost impossible task: that of synthesizing and simplifying where no really reliable basis exists for so doing; of compressing into a few pages what would ideally require a good-sized volume of analysis and exposition. The manifold factors responsible for this situation can perhaps be summarized under three main headings: those of euhemerization, of fragmentation and language, and of chronology.

1. The Problem of Euhemerization

The theory to which Euhemerus has given his name maintains that the origin of myth is to be found in actual history, and that the gods and demigods of mythology were, to start with, actual human beings. As commonly used by writers on Chinese mythology, however, "euhemerization" denotes precisely the opposite process: the transformation of what were once myths and gods into seemingly authentic history and human beings. Unquestionably, a fair amount of what purports to be early Chinese history has been subjected to this kind of euhemerization, the literal acceptance of which by most people until recent years led to gross misunderstandings concerning the beginnings of Chinese civilization. Not infrequently, to be sure, the literalists might encounter certain mythological elements not wholly concealed beneath their euhemerist dress, but when this happened, these could always be explained as mere later accretions to what in essence was genuine history. Henri Maspero, in the opening paragraph of his notable study, "Légendes mythologiques dans le *Chou king*" (1924), has vividly described the situation as follows:

> Chinese scholars have never known more than one way of interpreting legendary accounts, that of euhemerization. Under the plea of recovering from such accounts their historical kernel, they eliminate those elements of the marvellous which seem to them improbable, and preserve only a colorless residue, in which gods and heroes are transformed into sage emperors and sage ministers, and monsters into rebellious princes or evil ministers. Such are the lucubrations which, placed end to end according to a sequence imposed upon chronology by various metaphysical theories, especially that of the five elements, constitute what is called the history of Chinese origins. In this there is nothing but the name of history; actually there are only legends, sometimes mythological in origin, sometimes coming from the ancestral temples of the great families, sometimes emanating from local religious centers, sometimes the accounts—more or less learned—which have been elaborated to explain a rite, sometimes simple stories borrowed from folklore, etc. All these phantoms ought to disappear from the history of China, whose origins they encumber; rather than persist in the search for a nonexistent historical basis beneath the legendary form, we should seek to recover the mythological basis or the popular story beneath the pseudo-historical account.

It should be added that since 1924, when this was written, the Chinese scholars themselves have done wonders along these lines. In many cases, indeed, they have been more iconoclastic toward their own early history than have the Western scholars—sometimes, one might add, overly iconoclastic.

That euhemerization was already a recognized process in Chou dynasty China, and that it was then viewed with skepticism by some, is clearly indicated by several amusing anecdotes preserved in literature ranging from the fourth to around the first century B.C. In all of them, significantly, Confucius (551–479 B.C.) is made the exponent of euhemerism. The first story (contained in *Ta Tai li-chi*, ch. 62; compiled i cent. B.C. from earlier materials) concerns the legendary sage ruler Huang Ti, the "Yellow Lord" or "Yellow Emperor" (trad. xxvi cent. B.C.). "Was the Yellow Lord a man or was he not a man?" asks a disciple of Confucius. "How is it that he reached (an age of) three hundred years?" To which

Confucius is made to reply that this is a misunderstanding: what is actually meant is that during the Yellow Lord's own life of one hundred years, the people enjoyed his benefits; during the first hundred years after his death, they revered his spirit; and during the next hundred years after that, they continued to follow his teachings. "And this is why there is mention of three hundred years."

The next anecdote, also about the Yellow Lord, is based on a double meaning of the word *mien*, primarily signifying "face," but also meaning a "side, direction, quarter." In a passage from the fourth century B.C. *Shih-tzu* (now missing from the text, but quoted in a later encyclopedia), another disciple asks Confucius: "Is it true that the ancient Yellow Lord had four faces [*ssu mien*]?" To which Confucius replies that this is not at all true. What is meant is that the Yellow Lord used four officials to govern the four quarters (*ssu mien*) of his empire, so that he was "four faced" in the sense that the four "faces" or "sides" of his empire were controlled by these officials on his behalf.

The third anecdote again rests on a double meaning, this time of the word *tsu*, ordinarily meaning "foot" but in some contexts meaning "enough." This anecdote (recorded in *Han Fei-tzu*, ch. 33, and *Lü-shih ch'un-ch'iu*, XXII, 6; both iii cent. B.C.) has to do with a curious being called K'uei. In the euhemerized histories he is the human Music Master of the sage ruler Shun (trad. xxiii cent. B.C.), but from other scattered references we can see that he was actually a mythological creature having only one foot. In the story, the ruler of Confucius' native state of Lu is made to ask Confucius: "I have heard that K'uei was one-footed [*i tsu*]. Is this really so?" To which Confucius replies: "K'uei was a man, so why should he have one foot?" Then he goes on to explain that because K'uei's royal master Shun was greatly pleased with K'uei's musical ability, he once exclaimed of him: "As to K'uei, one (like him) is enough [*i erh tsu*]." By later people, however, this saying came to be misconstrued as meaning that K'uei had but one foot (*i tsu*).

These anecdotes are surely apocryphal, yet the fact that they all center around Confucius is no accident. For it is precisely the Confucianists who, more than any other school of thought, were historically minded and assumed prime responsibility for conserving and editing the ancient texts which eventually became the Chinese classics. In so doing they were, on the one hand, always intensely interested in the search for historical precedents which would confirm their own social and political doctrines; on the other hand, their strong humanism tended to make them either indifferent toward supernatural matters, or to seek to explain them in purely rationalistic terms. The results have been disastrous for the preservation of early Chinese myth, for they mean that it is precisely in those classical texts which might otherwise be expected to be prime repositories of myth, that such myth has either vanished entirely or (more probably) suffered grievous distortion.

Obviously, therefore, our search for myth must go beyond the Confucian-dominated classics to include the writings of the several non-Confucian schools. Among such writings, those of the Taoists, because of their iconoclasm toward Confucian tradition, their greater interest in popular beliefs, and their richly imaginative mode of expression, are by far the most promising. Here again, however, there is a limitation imposed by the philosophical assumptions of Taoism: its denial of teleology and anthropocentrism, and insistence upon a natural rather than a supernatural explanation for the universe. This in practice means that though mythological allusions abound in Taoist writings, they are introduced as a rule only for philosophical or literary effect, and not because the Taoist authors actually believe in them themselves. Rarely, therefore, do these authors bother to narrate at length the myths to which they allude. Rather, they take from them those elements which can be used for allegories of their own invention, thereby to express the philosophical ideas in which they themselves are interested.

A good example is the conversation in the seventeenth chapter of the *Chuang-tzu* (iii cent. B.C.) between a centipede and that same K'uei whom we have just encountered in Confucian dress. There is no doubt that Chuang Tzu's K'uei is a mythological creature, for he is made to complain to the centipede about his own difficulties in hopping around on one foot, and to ask the latter how he succeeds in controlling those many feet of his. The allegory's purpose, however, is not at all mythological but philosophical. From it we learn the Taoist moral that every creature should be satisfied with his own native endowment, but nothing whatsoever concerning the K'uei himself, other than the basic fact that he is one-footed.

2. The Problems of Fragmentation and of Language

Not only does pre-Han literature lack any separate genre which might be called myth, but within any single literary work it is not easy to find a myth recorded in consecutive entirety. All that we have are casual references and tantalizing fragments, widely scattered among texts of diverse date and ideological orientation. No wonder then that scholars can rarely agree as to how to fit these pieces into some kind of unity.

This fragmentation is characteristic even of what is probably the richest single storehouse of Chou mythological lore: the anthology of imaginative and sensuous poems known as the *Ch'u-tz'u* or *Songs of Ch'u* (wherein, however, are to be found Han as well as Chou poems). A striking example, to which we shall refer many times, is the *T'ien wen* or "Heavenly Questions" (prob. iv cent. B.C.), whose 185 lines are packed with mythological allusions, all, however, presented in the form of enigmatic riddles. Typical are the following lines (as translated by David Hawkes, *Ch'u Tz'u, the Songs of the South,* Oxford, 1959, pp. 49, 56):

Where is the stone forest? What beast can talk?
Where are the hornless dragons which carry bears on their backs for sport? (11. 47–48)
P'eng Chien made a drink-offering of pheasant's broth. How did the Lord eat of it?
He received the gift of long-lasting life. Why then was he still sad? (11. 171–72)

Other than that P'eng Chien may be identified with fair certainty as the Chinese Methuselah, P'eng Tsu, practically nothing is known of what is here alluded to (aside from the very uncertain guesses of much later commentators).

The difficulties produced by such fragments are enhanced by linguistic difficulties inherent in the Chinese classical language. In the first place, its many homophones and characters easily confused for one another make very tempting the search for new readings and identifications, usually based on such arguments as: character X of text A appears as character Y of text B; character Y appears in turn as character Z in text C; hence character X of text A and character Z of text C are equivalents. This kind of work, brilliantly performed by a long line of Chinese scholars, has done wonders in elucidating the ancient texts. On the other hand, conducted too exuberantly it can lead to quite startling results.

In the second place, the telegraphic brevity of classical Chinese, coupled with its inflectional inability (without the use of added words) to indicate gender, number, or tense, makes it often possible to translate a small fragment in several ways, with no assurance as to which is correct unless a larger clarifying context can be found. A good example is the fifty-sixth line of the *T'ien-wen* poem, wherein most scholars see an allusion to the myth of the shooting of the ten suns by Archer I (see III, 4 below), and therefore translate: "Why did I shoot down the suns? Why did the ravens shed their wings?" Bernhard Karlgren, however (in his encyclopedic "Legends and Cults in Ancient China," 1946, p. 268), believes that the motif of *ten* suns came to be associated with Archer I only in Han times. Therefore he translates in the singular: "Why did I shoot at [and not "down"] the sun? Why did the raven shed its feathers?" Either translation is grammatically possible; which one we accept, however, determines our entire decision as to whether or not the two themes originally formed a single myth.

3. The Problem of Chronology

The year 221 B.C., because it saw the final unification of "feudal" China into a truly centralized empire, is the great watershed of early Chinese history. Before that year, the country was divided into mutually warring, independent states, each ruled by a hereditary house and divided in turn into lesser domains also held by noble families. Politically, most of this pre-imperial age was covered by the Chou dynasty (ca. 1027–221 B.C.). Following 221, on the other hand, the next several centuries saw the consolidation of a new form of centralized empire, in which an official bureaucracy which was nonhereditary and centrally appointed took the place of the landed aristocracy of Chou times. The patterns of empire then laid down remained the norm until the present century, but the classical phase of Chinese history came to an end with the disintegration of the Han dynasty (206 B.C.–A.D. 220).

Culturally speaking, the Chou dynasty was the creative age of China's great classical and philosophical literature, whereas the Han dynasty, though also notably creative, was at the same time the first age when the writings of the past were systematically collected, edited, and commented upon. It was likewise the epoch which saw the appearance (ca. 100 B.C.) of China's first "universal" history. To what extent the Han scholars changed the texts they edited, sometimes introducing (perhaps quite unconsciously) ideas reflecting their own environment, and to what extent they may even have forged works which they then attributed to Chou or earlier times, still remains a subject of great controversy. Fortunately, much has been done by Chinese and Western scholars alike in recent decades to clarify the situation. Nonetheless, many points of uncertainty still remain.

In the field of mythology, the differences between the two dynasties are equally striking. Thus what, in the Chou literature, is fragmented and frequently euhemerized, often becomes, in Han times, so greatly elaborated that though the personages in the myths remain in large part the same, what is said of them may be totally new. It would seem, in many cases, that the Han writers were tapping new sources of living popular tradition, hitherto neglected by the more aristocratically oriented writers of the Chou. Likewise, for the first time, a very few of the mythological figures are portrayed in sculptured reliefs. A notable example of the new imaginative trend is the *Shan-hai ching* or *Classic of Mountains and Seas* (trad. ascribed in part to the Chou, but probably all of Han date), wherein not only the lands of China proper, but those extending to the far reaches of the earth, are populated by hundreds of strange new gods and monsters. So fantastic and prolific, indeed, are the beings of this book that one may fairly ask whether many of them are not simply the fanciful creations of their author (or authors), rather than based upon actual popular belief.

On the other hand, we can also often see the Han scholars manfully grappling with a body of older tradition which apparently has lost its living reality. They strive to reconcile seeming differences, to fill in lacunae, to put into order (according to their own ideological preconceptions) matters that they no longer truly understand. These efforts are particularly conspicuous in the disagreements often found among the Han commentators on the Chou classics.

All these developments, it should be kept in mind, are entirely distinct from the phenomenon noted at the very beginning of this essay: the gradual fading, in post-Han times, of most of the ancient gods from popular consciousness, and their replacement by a new and more clearly defined pantheon (no doubt stimulated in part by the advent of Buddhism).

What, then, is the scholar of early Chinese myth to do when confronted by these two very different bodies of literature? Two general approaches are possible, one of which we may term the "historical," the other the "sociological." As respective examples of these approaches, let us briefly contrast the theories of Bernhard Karlgren (expressed in his large "Legends and Cults in Ancient China," 1946), and of Wolfram Eberhard (expressed in several works, notably his two-volume *Lokalkulturen im alten China*, 1942, which, however, covers much else besides myth proper).

According to Karlgren, the main reason for the recording of ancient Chinese traditions in Chou literature is the fact that the personages in these traditions were regarded by the many grandee houses of Chou times as their ancestors. As a consequence, their memory was kept alive in the ancestral cults maintained by these houses. This, Karlgren believes, explains why they are portrayed neither as outright gods nor yet quite as ordinary mortals, but rather as "supermen," that is to say, as cultural heroes who are definite historical figures, but who at the same time possess something more than purely human characteristics. With the destruction of the old social order at the end of the third century B.C., however, the ancestral cults of these grandee houses lost their social significance, with the result that the memory of the ancient legends and heroes became divorced from living tradition. Thus was the way paved for the fanciful elaborations or antiquarian speculations of the Han writers.

In discussing these legends and heroes, therefore, Karlgren distinguishes sharply between what he calls the "free" texts of Chou times (texts in which the legends and heroes appear casually, without any tendentious purpose), and the fanciful or "systematizing" texts of Han times (in which materials are arranged according to set systems and theories, notably that of the five elements; among these "systematizing" texts Karlgren would also include a few late Chou works). For the study of genuinely early myth and legend, therefore, Karlgren believes that only the pre-Han "free" texts have any real validity.

Eberhard, on the other hand, sees the rise of Chinese civilization as resulting from the interaction and intermixture of various cultural components which, he believes, were in early times ethnically and regionally distinct from one another. Therefore, though by no means indifferent to the problem of historical development, his main interest lies in trying to isolate (regionally rather than chronologically) what he believes to be these basic cultural components. For his purposes, therefore, what is recorded in a Chou text, and what may be said by a writer many centuries or even a millennium later, may both be valid provided they both point toward a common cultural cluster. Basing himself on this standpoint, Eberhard, in a lengthy review (1946), has severely criticized Karlgren's methodology on several counts, two of which in particular may be mentioned:

(1) The mere fact that version A of a given myth happens to appear in an older text than version B, does not necessarily mean that *developmentally* speaking version A is the earlier or more primitive. On the contrary, as Eberhard points out, the Han writers could and did utilize long-existent popular oral tradition to a greater extent than did the more aristocratically oriented writers of the feudal age. (2) Karlgren's belief that most of the beings in the myths were originally human heroes, who only later, in some cases, acquired the attributes of gods or even animals, is at variance with modern ethnological and sociological theory. "If this opinion were correct, Chinese mythology would be the greatest exception hitherto known in the whole field of ethnology: the Chinese would first have created heroes and later only have made them into gods or even animals!"

Karlgren's strictly historical approach does indeed seem overly mechanical when, for example, he accepts or rejects a text simply according to whether it happens to have been written before or after the dividing line of 221 B.C., instead of evaluating, in each case, the particular ideology and other individual circumstances of the text itself. Furthermore, his rigid approach would seem to overlook the possibility of persistence or recurrence of a given motif (perhaps in varying forms) over a very long period of time.

On the other hand, Eberhard's use of chronologically widely separated data for reconstructing an ancient myth (in contrast to his main endeavor, that of isolating a cluster of long-term cultural components) has its obvious dangers. No doubt Eberhard is correct in asserting that "a myth reported only in a later text, may very well represent a form reflecting quite an early stage of development." However, as he himself then goes on to say, "Of course, we have to prove this in every single case." Unfortunately, the proofs presented by followers of this methodology are by no means always convincing, nor are they sometimes even seriously attempted. In many cases, indeed, they can never be really convincing, simply because the data themselves make this impossible.

In what follows, therefore, we shall try to steer a middle course: that of limiting ourselves (save for the first myth, which is a special case) to those myths for which at least *some* factual basis can be found in the Chou literature. However, we shall not hesitate to add to this what the Han writers have to say, in every instance being careful to warn the reader accordingly.

III. The Myths

The following are five examples of cosmogonic myth; as explained earlier, space does not permit us to discuss, more than incidentally, those having to do with cultural heroes, unless (as in the fifth myth) they also have cosmogonic significance.

1. The P'an-ku Creation Myth

In the *San-wu li-chi* (Record of Cycles in Threes and Fives), an obscure work of the third century A.D. now known only through quotations in later encyclopedias, there appears the following story (here paraphrased):

Heaven and Earth were once inextricably commingled (*hun-tun*) like a chicken's egg, within which was engendered P'an-ku (a name perhaps meaning "Coiled-up Antiquity"). After 18,000 years, this inchoate mass split apart, what was bright and light forming Heaven, and what was dark and heavy forming Earth. Thereafter, during another 18,000 years, Heaven daily increased ten feet in height, Earth daily increased ten feet in thickness, and P'an-ku, between the two, daily increased ten feet in size. This is how Heaven and Earth came to be separated by their present distance of 90,000 *li* (roughly 30,000 English miles).

Other texts, probably somewhat later in date, add the further information that after P'an-ku died, his breath became the wind and clouds, his voice the thunder, his left and right eyes the sun and moon respectively, his four limbs and five "bodies" (fingers?) the four quarters of the earth and five great mountains, his blood the rivers, his muscles and veins the strata of the earth, his flesh the soil, his hair and beard the constellations, his skin and body-hair the plants and trees, his teeth and bones the metals and stones, his marrow gold and precious stones, and his sweat the rain. The parasites on his body, impregnated by the wind, became human beings. In graphic portrayals of much later date, he is often shown as a horned demiurge who, with hammer and adze, chisels out the universe.

Here, in these works of the third century A.D. and later, we find China's *only* clearly recognizable creation myth. Most Chinese scholars believe it to be of non-Chinese origin and link it to the ancestral myth of the Miao and Yao tribal people of South China (also first recorded in the third century), in which these tribes trace their origin to a dog named P'an-hu. This dog, a pet of the Chinese legendary ruler Ti K'u (trad. ca. 2400 B.C.), succeeded in bringing to his imperial master the head of a certain troublesome barbarian general, and in accordance with a previously promised reward was given the emperor's own daughter as wife. The dog then carried her off to the mountain fastnesses of South China, where the progeny of the two became the ancestors of the present Miao and Yao tribes. Aside from the phonetic similarity between the names P'an-ku and P'an-hu, however, and the fact that both cults seem to have been centered in South China, where they were sometimes confused with one another, there is little apparent similarity between the myths.

Similarities to the P'an-ku story do appear, however, if we look farther afield, for example at India and ancient Sumer. Thus the *Rig Veda* tells us that the cosmic waters were originally restrained within a shell, but that the fashioner god, Tvaṣṭr, created Heaven and Earth, who in turn engendered Indra. By drinking the soma, Indra became strong and forced Heaven and Earth apart, himself filling up the space between them and also slitting open the cover within which lay the cosmic waters, so that they could issue forth. Another later story in the *Rig Veda* also tells us that when Purusa was sacrificed by the gods, the parts of his cut-up body became the sun, sky, atmosphere, earth, four quarters, four social classes of mankind, and so forth.

In Sumer, similarly, it was believed that there first existed the primeval sea, which engendered the cosmic mountain, consisting of Heaven and Earth in undivided form. They in turn produced the air-god Enlil, who separated Heaven from Earth, carried off Earth for himself, and through union with his mother Earth set the stage for the organization of the universe.

Though in China itself the P'an-ku myth does not appear before the third century, Eberhard (in his *Lokalkulturen*, II, 467 ff.) would relate it conceptually to what he believes to be a much earlier Chinese idea: that of a primeval egg or sac, the splitting of which permits its undifferentiated contents to assume form as an organized universe. In its sophisticated version, this conception may well underline the astronomical theory, current in Han times, according to which Heaven and Earth are shaped like an egg, Earth being enclosed by the sphere of Heaven just as the yolk of an egg is enclosed by its shell.

The first of our texts, it will be remembered, says that Heaven and Earth were once inextricably commingled (*hun-tun*) like a chicken's egg. In late Chou and Han philosophical texts, the same onomatopeic term *hun-tun* is used to designate the state of undifferentiated chaos before an organized universe came into being. Curiously enough, the term appears again in modern Chinese parlance as the name for a small *sac*-like dumpling (a thin shell of dough enclosing chopped-up meat), used as the basic ingredient of the popular *hun-tun* soup served in Chinese restaurants.

In the *Shan-hai ching* or *Classic of Mountains and Seas* (bk. 2), of Han date, Hun-tun is personified as a being living southwest of the Mountain of Heaven (T'ien Shan), who has six feet and four wings, is the color of fire, lacks a face or eyes, and is *shaped like a sac*. Among Chou dynasty texts, the *Tso-chuan* history (iv cent. B.C., with later additions), under the year 618 B.C., euhemerizes Hun-tun as the evil son of an early sage ruler. Describing his undesirable characteristics, it says, among other things, that he "screens [i.e., covers over or bottles up] righteousness." The best-known Chou reference to Hun-tun, however, is the charming allegory in the seventh chapter of the Taoist work *Chuang-tzu* (iii cent. B.C.). There we are told that Hun-tun or Chaos was the Ruler of the Center, and that he lacks the usual seven openings of other men (eyes, ears, nostrils, and mouth). Therefore his friends, Shu and Hu, having been well treated by him, decided to bore such openings in him. Each day they bored one hole, but on the seventh day Hun-tun died.

Such are the scattered data from which we must decide whether or not the cosmogonic *conception* underlying the P'an-ku myth (and not, of course, the myth as such) possibly goes back to early times. Marcel Granet, for his part (in his *Danses et légendes de la Chine ancienne*, 1926, p. 546 ff.), would link the *hun-tun* idea to another mythical theme in which, though the term *hun-tun* itself does not appear, a leather sack plays a central role. It concerns King Wu-i (trad. reigned 1198–95 B.C.), one of the last evil rulers of the Shang dynasty, who made a human figure which he called the Spirit of Heaven (T'ien Shen), and played a game of counters with it, which he won. To show his contempt, he then hung up a leather sack filled with blood and shot at it with arrows, saying that he was shooting at Heaven. Soon afterward, while hunting, he was killed by lightning. The same theme recurs almost a millennium later in connection with the last king of Sung, a state which in Chou times was ruled by descendants of the Shang royal house. This king too hung up a leather blood-filled sack and shot at it, saying that he was shooting at Heaven. Shortly afterward, in 282 B.C., he was attacked by a coalition of other states, killed, and his state annihilated.

Possibly Granet is correct in believing that this theme is related to the *hun-tun* conception. On the other hand, a parallel has also been suggested between it and the theme of Archer I's shooting at the sun (see III, 4 below).

2. *The Fashioning Deity Nü-kua*

Nü-kua, the 'Woman Kua," though fairly prominent in Han times, appears only twice in earlier literature. Despite her name, it is only in the first century A.D. that her sex is positively stated. At about the same time she also becomes identified as either the sister or consort of the much better known Fu-hsi (Subduer of Animals), a sage (trad. ca. 2800 B.C.) said to have taught men how to hunt and cook, to make nets, and so on. On the stone reliefs of the Wu Liang offering shrines (ca. A.D. 150), Fu-hsi and Nü-kua appear together; their upper bodies are human, but merge below into serpent tails that are intertwined with one another. Fu-hsi holds a carpenter's square in his hand and Nü-kua a compass, apparently as symbols of their constructive activities. The constructive work of Fu-hsi, however (other than as inventor and ruler), has not come down to us, and we may wonder whether the purported association between him and the fashioning deity Nü-kua really goes back before Han times.

The best account of the latter's activities occurs in the sixth chapter of the Han Taoist work, *Huai-nan-tzu* (ii cent. B.C., a work rich in mythological materials):

In very ancient times, the four pillars [at the compass points] were broken down, the nine provinces [of the habitable world] were split apart, Heaven did not wholly cover [Earth], and Earth did not completely support [Heaven]. Fires flamed without being extinguished, water inundated without being stopped, fierce beasts ate the people, and birds of prey seized the old and weak in their claws. Thereupon Nü-kua fused together stones of the five colors with which she patched together azure Heaven. She cut off the feet of a turtle with which she set up the four pillars. She slaughtered the Black Dragon in order to save the province of Chi [the present Hopei and Shansi provinces in North China]. She collected the ashes of reeds with which to check the wild waters.

The text goes on to say that thereafter there was universal harmony: the seasons followed their due course, beasts sheathed their claws and teeth and serpents hid their poison, the people lived lives of undreaming sleep and uncalculating wakefulness.

The "four pillars" mentioned in this myth belong, of course, to the cosmological belief, found in many cultures, that Heaven is supported on pillars or some other kind of foundation. In China (where the pillars were thought of as mountains), the earliest mention is that in the *T'ien-wen* poem (iv cent. B.C.), which, however, speaks not of four but of eight pillars. The same poem, as well as the Kung-kung story below (and other texts as well), further makes mention of the *wei* or "cords" of Earth. As a technical term, *wei* designates the cords which, on a chariot, secure its canopy to the frame or body. By analogy, therefore, the *wei* of Earth (sometimes stated to be four in number) must likewise serve to attach the canopy of Heaven to Earth below. (The comparison of Heaven to a chariot's canopy and Earth to its body is a common one in the texts.) Just how the *wei* function in relation to the (four or eight) pillars of Heaven is, however, unstated.

The story of Nü-kua is by several Han writers linked to the cosmic struggle between Chuan-hsü (legendary ruler, trad. xxv cent. B.C.) and Kung-kung (euhemerized in Chou writings as a human "rebel," but in late Han times described as a horned monster with serpent's body). Wang Ch'ung (A.D. 27–ca. 100), for example, in his *Lun heng* or *Critical Essays* (chs. 31 and 46), says that anciently, when Kung-kung fought unsuccessfully with Chuan-hsü to become ruler, he blundered in his rage against Mount Pu-chou (in the northwest quarter), thereby causing the pillar of Heaven and the cord of Earth to break off at that point. It was then that Nü-kua patched up Heaven with melted stones and cut off a turtle's feet to hold it up. Nonetheless, Heaven and Earth have since that time sloped toward one another in the northwest, but have tilted away from one another in the opposite direction. This is why the astral bodies of Heaven continue to this day to move in a westerly direction, whereas the rivers (of China) on Earth flow toward the ocean (in the east). In the *T'ien wen* there is already mention of the gap in the southeast between Heaven and Earth, from which we may infer that at the time of this poem the story of Kung-kung was already current.

We may question, however, whether this story and the Nü-kua myth properly belong together. In the *Huai-nan-tzu* (ch. 3), for example, the Kung-kung story appears alone, without any mention of Nü-kua at all, and though the two are joined in the fifth chapter of *Lieh-tzu* (a Taoist work, trad. Chou but prob. Han), their order is there reversed (the story of Nü-kua given first, followed by that of Kung-kung). This, of course, destroys any logical connection between them.

In a passage (now known only through later quotation) from the *Feng-su t'ung-i* (Comprehensive Meaning of Customs), by Ying Shao (ca. 140–ca. 206), Nü-kua is also portrayed as the creator of mankind:

It is popularly said that when Heaven and Earth had opened forth, but before there were human beings, Nü-kua created men by patting yellow earth together. But the work tasked her strength and left her no free time, so that she then dragged a string through mud, thus heaping it up so as to make it into men. Therefore the rich and the noble are those men of yellow earth, whereas the poor and the lowly —all ordinary people—are those cord-made men.

Another passage from the same work (likewise now known only in quotation) tells us further that Nü-kua is prayed to as the goddess of marriage, because it is she who first instituted marriage. (In other words, having created men, she taught them how to propagate.)

Finally, we are told in the *Shan-hai ching* (bk. 16) that beyond the northwest sea there are ten spirits, called "Nü-kua's intestines," because (after she died) they were transformed into spirits (from her intestines).

Whether or not Nü-kua as the creator of mankind represents simply a popular addition to the primary theme of Nü-kua as the repairer and organizer of the world, it is evident that neither theme constitutes a true creation myth (in the sense of the P'an-ku myth), since both take place in an already existing universe. We might assume the entire Nü-kua cult to be a Han creation, were it not for two bare references to her occurring in Chou literature. The more important of these is one of the riddles in *T'ien-wen:* "Nü-kua had a body. Who formed and fashioned it?" This certainly suggests that Nü-kua's fashioning activities were already known in Chou times if, as seems reasonable, it should be interpreted as meaning: Nü-kua was a fashioner of other things. Who then fashioned her?

3. The Separation of Heaven and Earth

We have already encountered the theme of the separation of Heaven and Earth in the P'an-ku myth. It crops up again, though in a very different context, in two texts of Chou date. The first is one of the major classics, the *Shu-ching* or *Classic of History* (sect. *Lü-hsing,* trad. x cent. B.C., but prob. some cents. later). There we are told that the Miao (a tribe or confraternity, notorious as troublemakers during the reigns of Yao and Shun, trad. xxiv–xxiii cent. B.C.) created oppressive punishments which threw the people into disorder. Shang Ti, the "Lord on High" (name of the most prominent ancient divinity), surveyed the people and found them lacking in virtue. Out of pity for those who were innocent, the August Lord (surely another name for Shang Ti, though the euhemerizing commentators interpret him as either Yao or Shun) had the Miao exterminated. "Then he charged Ch'ung and Li to cut the communication between Heaven and Earth so that there would be no descending and ascending [of spirits and men between the two]." After this had been done, order was restored and the people returned to virtue.

The second much more detailed account —actually an early exegesis of the foregoing—is that in the *Kuo-yü* or *Narratives of the States* (iv cent. B.C. with later additions; sect. *Ch'u yü,* II, 1). In it King Chao of Ch'u (515–489), puzzled by the *Shu-ching*'s statement about the separating of Heaven from Earth, asks his minister: "If it had not been thus, would the people have been able to ascend to Heaven?" To which the minister, after making denial, supplies his own metaphorical explanation:

Anciently, men and spirits did not intermingle. At that time there were certain persons who were so perspicacious, single-minded, and reverential that their understanding enabled them to make meaningful collation of what lies above and below, and their insight to illumine what is distant and profound. Therefore the spirits would descend into them. The possessors of such powers were, if men, called *hsi* (shamans), and, if women, *wu* (shamannesses). It is they who supervised the positions of the spirits at the ceremonies, sacrificed to them, and otherwise handled religious matters. As a consequence, the spheres of the divine and the profane were kept distinct. The spirits sent down blessings on the people, and accepted from them their offerings. There were no natural calamities.

In the degenerate time of Shao-hao (trad. xxvi cent. B.C.), however, the Nine Li (a troublesome tribe like the Miao) threw virtue into disorder. Men and spirits became intermingled, with each household indiscriminately performing for itself the religious observances which had hitherto been conducted by the shamans. As a consequence, men lost their reverence for the spirits, the spirits violated the rules of men, and natural calamities arose. Hence the successor of Shao-hao, Chuan-hsü, charged Ch'ung, Governor of the South, to handle the affairs of Heaven in order to determine the proper places of the spirits, and Li,

Governor of Fire, to handle the affairs of Earth in order to determine the proper places of men. "And such is what is meant by 'cutting the communication between Heaven and Earth.'"

Still later, however, the Miao, like the Nine Li before them, stirred up new disorders, obliging the ruler Yao to order the descendants of Ch'ung and Li to resume the tasks of their forebears. Since that time members of the same two families have continued to maintain the proper distinctions between Heaven and Earth. Under King Hsüan of Chou (827–782), one of them remarked of the two ancestors: "Ch'ung lifted Heaven up and Li pressed Earth down."

A detailed comparison of these two texts is unnecessary, other than to say that the first telescopes events which by the second are placed in two different periods (the troubles caused by the Nine Li during the reigns of Shao-hao and Chuan-hsü, and the similar troubles caused by the Miao during that of Yao); that both accounts are in part euhemerized; but that this is especially evident of the second, with its added "human" details and metaphorical explanation of what, in the first text, might be understood as a literal separating of Heaven from Earth. However, the second text also reveals the real state of affairs in its significant final quotation: "Ch'ung lifted Heaven up and Li pressed Earth down."

The idea that Heaven and Earth were once joined together, thereby permitting free communication between men and the divine powers, but later became separated, is extremely widespread among many cultures. It and related concepts have been brilliantly analyzed by Mircea Eliade in his two books, *The Myth of the Eternal Return* ([New York] 1954; first published in French in 1949) and *Le chamanisme et les techniques archaïques de l'extase* ([Paris] 1951).

In the former (p. 12 ff.) he discusses the concept of an *axis mundi*. This cosmic symbol, widely found among Asian peoples, may take the form of a mountain, a sacred temple, palace or city, or a tree or a vine; its distinguishing characteristic is that it is believed to occupy the center of the world and to connect Earth with Heaven. Concerning the ideas underlying this belief, Eliade writes further (p. 91):

... the myths of many peoples allude to a very distant epoch when men knew neither death nor toil nor suffering and had a bountiful supply of food merely for the taking. *In illo tempore*, the gods descended to earth and mingled with men; for their part, men could easily mount to heaven. As the result of a ritual fault, communications between heaven and earth were interrupted and the gods withdrew to the highest heavens. Since then, men must work for their food and are no longer immortal.

In his *Le chamanisme*, Eliade has also discussed at length what it is that motivates the shaman when he enters his ecstatic trance. It is his desire to be able thereby to ascend to Heaven and thus momentarily restore, in his own person, that contact between Heaven and Earth which had more generally existed prior to the "fall."

It can hardly be doubted that our two Chinese texts are reflections of these widespread concepts. For in them, too, the cutting of communication between Heaven and Earth follows upon a "ritual fault," and the second text, in particular, describes in some detail the male and female shamans who enjoy contact with the spirits.

There is, however, also an important shift of emphasis: the fact that in the Chinese story it is the shamans only, and not the people as a whole, who originally enjoyed communication with the spirits, and that the usurpation of this prerogative by other persons then constituted the "ritual fault" leading to the cutting of communication between Heaven and Earth. Conceivably this shift in emphasis is not, after all, deeply significant, for it may be merely an attempt on the part of the author (or of the minister whose speech he is ostensibly recording) to enhance the prestige of the shamans by emphasizing their dominant role in earliest times. We cannot really know. (In his *Le chamanisme*, pp. 396–97, Eliade has also discussed this second text, basing himself, however, on an inexact translation which has led to certain misunderstandings on his part.)

The Miao, it will be remembered, are mentioned in both texts as one of the two groups responsible for the ritual disorder. Maspero ("Légendes mythologiques," pp. 97–98) has already pointed out that in the *Shan-hai ching* (bk. 17) these Miao are described as winged human beings living in the extreme northwestern corner of the world, while in a still later text they are said to have wings but to be unable to fly. Here, perhaps, is a symbolic expression of the "fall": the fact that the Miao had once been able to communicate with Heaven, but lost this power when, because of their ritual fault, the Lord on High exiled them to their distant region and ordered the (shamans) Ch'ung and Li to sever the communication between Heaven and Earth.

Are there other passages in Chinese literature expressive of a paradisal era followed by a "fall"? The Taoists often write about man's state of innocence before the rise of human institutions, but it is hard to know whether this is simply a Taoist philosophical abstraction, or may be inspired, at least in part, by popular traditions concerning a primordial paradise. The latter hypothesis, however, seems quite reasonable.

Among such passages, one of the most vivid is that in the eighth chapter of *Huai-nan-tzu*, describing the era of Great Purity, when men were genuine and simple, sparing of speech and spontaneous in conduct. "They were joined in body to Heaven and Earth, united in spirit to the *yin* and *yang* [the negative and positive cosmic forces or principles], and in harmonious oneness with the four seasons." At that time wind and rain brought no calamities, sun and moon equably distributed their light, the planets did not deviate from their courses. But then came the era of decline: men began to mine the mountains for minerals, to make fire with the fire drill, to fell trees for houses, to hunt and fish, and to do the many other things which destroyed their original purity.

A later passage in the same chapter is even more suggestive of an ancient Chinese Garden of Eden: In ancient times men entrusted their children to birds' nests and left the grain in the fields. Without fear of injury, they could freely grasp the tails of tigers and panthers and tread upon serpents. Then, however, came the inevitable decline. It is notable that nowhere here or elsewhere do the Taoists provide a mythological explanation for the "fall"; it is simply, for them, the inexorable concomitant of the rise of human civilization.

4. Sun Myths

Anciently there existed not one but ten suns, each of which would appear in succession on each day of the Chinese ten-day week. Once, however, at a time usually placed in the reign of Yao, all ten suns, through some confusion, appeared simultaneously, so that it seemed as if the world were about to burn up. At this climactic point the Chou texts (*Chuang-tzu*, ch. 2; *Lü-shih ch'un-ch'iu*, XXII, 5; etc.) leave off; for the denouement we must turn to the *Huai-nan-tzu* (ch. 8). There we are told that when the suns appeared, a certain I (or Hou I), famous as an archer, shot down all but one, thus rescuing the world and leaving the single sun which moves in the sky today. At Yao's bidding he also killed a number of destructive monsters (described in gory details in works like *Shan-hai ching*). So overjoyed were the people by this happy ending that (somewhat inconsequentially, as we might think) they thereupon established Yao as their ruler.

There is an ambiguous line in the *T'ien-wen* which, as usually translated, reads: "Why did I shoot down the suns? Why did the ravens shed their feathers?" Here we have the earliest reference to the belief that in the sun (or in each individual sun) there is a raven. (In *Huai-nan-tzu*, ch. 7, it is said to be three-legged.) From this line one might also conclude that the story of Archer I's shooting at the ten suns goes back at least to the fourth century B.C.

Karlgren, however, believes the story to have originated only in Han times, and therefore, as we have seen (II, 2 above), would translate the line in the singular: "Why did I shoot at the sun? Why did the raven shed its feathers?" His main reason for so doing is the chronological difficulty that, in other Chou texts, I appears as a great but arrogant hunter who lived in the early part of the Hsia dynasty (a century or more after Yao), and who, after usurping the throne, came to a bad end. I's shooting at a *single* sun (and not ten of them) is, therefore, as interpreted by Karlgren, simply "a sacrilegious act," expressive of I's hubris, but having nothing to do with the threatened burning up of the earth; he compares it with the act of the two kings (see III, 1 above) who shot at a leather sack filled with blood, calling it Heaven.

There are several arguments, however, which—at least to this writer—speak in favor of the more usual interpretation. In the first place, I's shooting at the ten suns provides a necessary conclusion to a myth which otherwise—quite literally—would leave the several suns dangling in mid-air. In the second place, is it really fair to look for strict chronological and thematic consistency in what, after all, is not history but myth? It seems to have been the focus of several cycles of story. There is no real reason to be surprised, therefore, if he appears as a hero in one cycle, but as a villain in another.

Thirdly, and perhaps most important, the theme of saving the world from multiple suns is by no means peculiarly Chinese. On the contrary, as shown by Eduard Erkes ("Chinesisch-amerikanische Mythenparallelen," 1926), it has many parallels on both sides of the Pacific. Among the Battaks of Sumatra and the Semangs of Malaya, for example, the sun is believed to be the parent of several children suns, but is tricked by the moon into devouring them when they threaten to burn up the world. Among the Shasta Indians of California it is the coyote who slays nine of ten brother-suns (a striking numerical agreement with the Chinese myth). And among the Golds of eastern Siberia there is even a national hero who, in the manner of the Chinese story, shoots down two of three suns when they make the world unbearably hot.

Returning to China, we find considerable lore concerning the daily course taken by the sun (or suns) across the sky. Perhaps the earliest source is the opening chapter of the *Shu-ching* (*Classic of History*), which, as usual for this work, is considerably euhemerized:

He [the sage Yao] then charged Hsi and Ho, in reverent accordance with august Heaven, to calculate and delineate the sun, moon, stars and constellations, and respectfully to give the people the seasons. He separately charged the younger Hsi to reside among the Yü barbarians, [at the place] called the Valley of Light (Yang-ku), there to receive the rising sun as a guest and regulate its activities in the east. . . . He further charged the younger Ho to reside in the west, [at the place] called the Valley of Darkness (Mei-ku), there respectfully to see off the setting sun and regulate the completion of its work in the west. . . . He further charged the youngest Ho to reside in the Northern Region (Shuo-fang), [at the place] called the City of Obscurity (Yu-tu), there to supervise its operations in the north.

Other Chou texts make it evident that the two sets of three brothers, here spoken of as supervising the movements of the sun and other heavenly bodies, are in actual fact mere multiplications of a single person, Hsi-ho. (The multiplication was no doubt motivated by the desire to provide enough brothers to take care of all celestrial operations in all quarters of the sky.) As pointed out by Karlgren, Hsi-ho appears in the Chou texts simply as an ancient cult-master (sex unspecified) who observes the heavenly bodies, creates the calendar, prognosticates by means of the sun, and controls the sun in its movements.

In the *Shan-hai ching* (bk. 15), on the other hand, Hsi-ho for the first time becomes the mother of the sun or suns (for ten are specifically mentioned). She lives beyond the Southeast Sea, in the midst of the Sweet Waters (Kan-shui), where she bathes the suns one by one in the Sweet Gulf (Kan-yüan). The same work (bks. 9 and 14) tells us further that in the eastern Valley of Light (already mentioned in the *Shu-ching*) there grows a tree known as the Fu-sang (Supporting Mulberry; other names for it appear in other texts). Its trunk reaches a height of 300 *li* (about 100 miles), yet its leaves are no bigger than mustard seeds. It is in the branches of this tree that the suns (personified, it will be remembered, as ravens) rest when they are not crossing the sky; as soon as one of them returns from its journey, another starts forth.

The daily itinerary of the sun (or suns) is best described in the third chapter of *Huai-nan-tzu* (though several of its place names also occur in other texts, both of Chou and Han time). At dawn, we are told, the sun first emerges from the Valley of Light and bathes in the Hsien Pool (presumably the same as the Sweet Gulf mentioned in *Shan-hai ching*, and identified in some texts as a constellation). Maspero points out ("Légendes mythologiques," pp. 26–27) that at the Chou royal court there was a Hsien Pool Dance, the details of which are uncertain, but which is said to have been performed at the summer solstice on a square outdoor altar in the middle of a pond.

The *Huai-nan-tzu* goes on to say that after bathing, the sun ascends the Fu-sang tree and from there crosses the sky, passing en route a dozen or more places of which we know little more than the names. Finally it arrives at Yen-tzu, said to be a mountain in the extreme west of the world. There, at its setting place, grows another mythological tree known as the Jo tree, the flowers of which shine with a reddish glow. It has been suggested by modern scholars that these flowers symbolize either the glow of sunset or the twinkling of stars as they appear after sunset.

The *Ch'u-tz'u* anthology contains a poem, probably of the third century B.C., called *Tung-chün* (Lord of the East), which, though it never mentions the sun by name, seems to be a hymn sung in its praise. From it we may infer that the sun uses a chariot when it traverses the sky, for the poem's opening lines read (as translated by David

Hawkes, *Ch'u Tz'u, the Songs of the South*, Oxford, 1959, p. 41):

*With a faint flush I start to come out of the east,
Shining down on my threshold, Fu-sang.
As I urge my horses slowly forward,
The night sky brightens, and day has come.*

The last two lines of this hymn give us the one and only hint in all early Chinese literature as to how, after setting, the sun makes its way (perhaps under the earth?) back to its eastern starting point:

*Then holding my reins I plunge down to my setting,
On my gloomy night journey back to the east.*

5. Flood Myths

Of all the mythological themes of ancient China, the earliest and by far the most pervasive is that of flood. It appears in writings belonging to the beginning of the Chou dynasty (*Shih-ching* or *Classic of Poetry* and *Shu-ching*), and thereafter the references are too numerous to be listed here. Though it crops up in localized form in conjunction with several minor figures (including Kung-kung, whom we have already encountered in connection with Nü-kua in III, 2 above), its really universal version is that in which Yü, together with his father Kun, play the major roles. The former is renowned in history not only as conqueror of the flood, but also as founder of China's first hereditary dynasty, that of Hsia (trad. in 2205 B.C.). Though Yü and his father are portrayed in the orthodox accounts as human beings, the written graphs for their names betray their non-human origin: that for Kun contains the element meaning "fish," and that for Yü is written with an element often found in the names of reptiles, insects, and the like.

The euhemerized version of the Kun-Yü myth, notably as found in the early chapters of the *Shu-ching*, may be summarized as follows:

"Everywhere the tremendous flood waters were wreaking destruction. Spreading afar, they embraced the mountains and rose above the hills. In a vast flow they swelled up to Heaven. The people below were groaning." In response to their appeals, a being who in the *Shu-ching* is referred to simply as Ti, "Lord," rather reluctantly (because he had reservations about his ability) commanded Kun to deal with the flood. (By the commentators this "Lord" is equated with the sage ruler Yao; in all probability, however, he was none other than the supreme divinity, Shang Ti, the "Lord on High.")

For nine years Kun labored without success to dam up the waters. At the end of that time either Yao or his successor Shun (the texts differ) had Kun executed at the Feather Mountain (Yü-shan), and ordered Kun's son, Yü, to continue the task. The latter, instead of trying to dam up the waters in the manner of his father, adopted the new technique of channeling passages for them to drain off to the sea. In this way he eventually conquered the flood and made the land fit for habitation. As a reward, he was given the throne by Shun and became founder of the Hsia dynasty.

In contrast to this "historical" account, we can, by piecing together the fragments found both in Chou and Han literature, produce another version which is much more "mythological":

On being ordered to deal with the flood, Kun stole from the Lord the "swelling mold" (*hsi-jang*)—a magical kind of soil which had the property of ever swelling in size. With this he tried to build dams which, through their swelling, would hold back the waters. When his efforts failed, the Lord, angered by his theft, had him executed at Feather Mountain, a sunless place in the extreme north. There his body remained for three years without decomposing, until somebody (unspecified) cut it open with a sword, whereupon Yü emerged from his father's belly. (One tradition says that Yü was born from a stone, which would apparently signify that Kun's body had turned to stone.) Following Yü's birth, Kun became transformed into an animal—variously said to be a yellow bear, black fish, three-legged turtle, or yellow dragon—and plunged into the Feather Gulf (Yü-yüan). A cryptic line in the *T'ien-wen* poem, however, suggests that he subsequently managed to get to the west, where he was restored to life by a shamanness.

Yü, we are told, "came down from on high" to continue his father's work. He was helped by a winged dragon which, going ahead of him, trailed its tail over the ground and thus marked the places where channels should be dug. For some eight or ten years Yü labored so intensely that, though several times passing the door of his home, he had no time to visit his family within. He wore the nails off his hands, the hair off his shanks, and developed a lameness giving him a peculiar gait which in later times came to be known as the "walk of Yü." Nonetheless, he eventually succeeded in draining the great rivers to the sea, expelling snakes and dragons from the marshlands, and making the terrain fit for cultivation. So great, indeed, were his achievements, that the *Tso-chuan* history, under the year 541 B.C., reports a noble as exclaiming: "Were it not for Yü, we would indeed be fish!"

There are many other stories about Yü, for example, that he used the same "swelling mold" which had brought disaster to his father to build China's great mountains. Or again, we read that he ordered two of his officials (presumably after he became ruler) to pace off the dimensions of the world from east to west and north to south. In this way they determined it to be a perfect square, measuring exactly 233,500 li (roughly 77,833 miles) and 75 paces in each direction. Yü himself also traveled extensively. His itinerary included mythological places like that of the Fu-sang tree (where, as we have seen, the sun comes up), as well as the lands of the Black-teeth People, the Winged People, the Naked People, and many more; among the latter he even stripped himself naked so as to accord with local custom. Furthermore, Yü was a mighty warrior who conquered notorious rebels and gained the allegiance of ten thousand states. On one occasion he held a great assembly on a mountain consisting, in its euhemerized version, of dependent nobles, but elsewhere described as an assembly of spirits.

One curious episode concerns Yü's wife, the Girl of T'u, whom he met and married in the course of his flood labors. Later, while digging a passage through a certain mountain, he was changed (for unexplained reasons) into a bear. His wife, seeing him, ran away and herself became changed to stone. She was pregnant at the time, and so when Yü pursued her and called out, "Give me my son!" the stone split open on its north side and a son, Ch'i, came forth. It should be added that the name of this son (who succeeded Yü as second ruler of the Hsia dynasty) means "to open."

Of the foregoing episodes, most are already attested by the Chou texts. Some, however—notably Kun's theft of the "swelling mold," Yü's use of it to build the great mountains, and the measuring of the world by his two officials—are known only from Han works (primarily *Huai-nan-tzu* and

Shan-hai ching). Of still later date, moreover, is the story of Ch'i's birth, which first appears only in a seventh-century A.D. commentary, where it is claimed, quite erroneously, to come from the *Huai-nan-tzu*. At first sight the story appears to be nothing more than the clumsy repetition of two already attested themes, since in it Ch'i (like his father Yü) is born from a stone, and Yü (like his father Kun) is changed into a bear. Yet it would be unwise to dismiss it simply as a late and deliberate literary invention, for already in 111 B.C., according to the sixth chapter of *Han-shu* (History of the Han Dynasty), Emperor Wu of that dynasty issued an edict in which he said: "We have seen the mother-stone of the Hsia sovereign Ch'i." This can only mean that at that time the belief that Ch'i was born from a stone was already current.

The story of Kun's transformation into an animal also raises a problem: the fact that in its Chou version (see *Tso-chuan* under the year 535 B.C.) the animal in question is a bear, whereas in other much later versions it is variously described as a fish, turtle, or dragon. Kun's close associations with water make any one of these latter interpretations much more plausible. Nevertheless, the earlier bear version cannot be rejected out of hand, since its context is a story in which a noble, having dreamed that he was visited by a bear, is told that this is none other than Kun's spirit.

The fact that the bear is associated both with Kun and Yü (if the story of the latter's change into a bear can be accepted as more than literary invention) has been adduced as evidence for an ancient (and possibly totemistic) bear cult in China. Certainly it accords very poorly with the otherwise overwhelmingly aquatic associations of Kun and Yü alike. This contradiction, together with other thematic disparities, suggests that the Kun-Yü myth (aside from its central theme of flood) is by no means a homogeneous entity, but rather an amalgam of several cultural components which, originally, may have been geographically and perhaps ethnically quite distinct from one another. Just how these diverse cultural components should be interpreted and localized, however, is by no means an easy question. To cite only two of several hypotheses: both Maspero ("Légendes mythologiques," pp. 70–73) and Eberhard (*Lokalkulturen* I, 365; II, 380–81, etc.) believe that the Kun-Yü myth originally had two major centers of development. Maspero, however, would locate these in North China (along the upper and lower reaches of the Yellow River), whereas by Eberhard they would be placed much farther south (very roughly along a west-east axis extending from eastern Szechuan to coastal China).

In closing, let us repeat (in slightly expanded form) two conclusions already suggested by Maspero: (1) The flood motif is by no means uniquely Chinese, for it is widely found among other peoples of East and Southeast Asia. Hence it could not have been inspired by the localized memory of any particular flood, whether along the Yellow River or elsewhere. (2) Between the Chinese and the Biblical or other Near Eastern flood stories there is this basic difference: in the Chinese version the flood is not inflicted as divine retribution for human sin, but simply epitomizes the condition of the world before there yet existed an organized human society. What is emphasized, therefore, is not the flood as such. Rather it is the task of draining the land and rendering it fit for settled human life. In essence, therefore, the Chinese myth is one about the origins of civilization, in which a divine being, Yü, descends from on high, creates a habitable world for mankind, and founds the first civilized state, the perpetuation of which he ensures by marrying a human mortal.

IV. Conclusions

1. The fragmentary and episodic nature of China's ancient myths suggests that they are not homogeneous creations, but rather the amalgams—still incomplete at the time of their recording—of regionally and perhaps ethnically diversified materials.

2. The intense historical-mindedness of the Chinese—displayed already in very early times—together with their tendency to reject supernatural explanations for the universe—caused them to "humanize" or "euhemerize" much of what had originally been myth into what came to be accepted as authentic history. No doubt this trend was encouraged by the eagerness of the noble houses of feudal China to find convincing genealogies for themselves among the shadowy figures of ancient tradition. So early did the process begin, in relationship to the development of written literature, that it largely prevented the myths from being recorded in this literature in their pristine mythological form. This situation is perhaps well-nigh unique among the major civilizations of antiquity.

3. Chinese scholars of the past few decades—notably the historian Ku Chieh-kang—have devoted much energy to the problem of the chronological stratification of early Chinese myth. In so doing they have demonstrated a widespread phenomenon: the fact that the "historical age" of a myth (the period of history to which it purports to belong) usually stands in inverse ratio to its "literary age" (the period when it is first actually recorded in the literature). In other words, the earlier the purported age of a myth, the later is its actual appearance in the literature.

This phenomenon quite possibly reflects the gradual geographical expansion of Chinese civilization, in the course of which it absorbed the cultural traditions—including myths—of peoples originally lying outside the Chinese orbit. As these myths were thus successively acquired, the historically minded Chinese tried to fit them into a chronological sequence, in which each new acquisition had to be dated earlier than its predecessor, since the lower chronological levels had already been pre-empted. Confirmation of this phenomenon is in general supplied by the five myths we have studied (aside from the fourth, that of the ten suns), as shown by the following table (in which, of course, the dates under the middle column are traditional only).

Of these five examples, the flood myth of Yü, indubitably the oldest in literary age, also has by far the greatest hold on the Chinese consciousness. That of P'an-ku, on the other hand, is both the youngest and

Myth	Historical Age	Literary Age
P'an-ku	Beginning of creation	iii cent. A.D.
Nü-kua	Fu-hsi (2852–2738)	Only two pre-Han references (one of iv cent. B.C.)
Separation of Heaven and Earth	Chuan-hsü (2513–2436)	First half of Chou
Ten suns	Yao (2357–2256)	Second half of Chou
Flood	Yü (2295–2198)	Early years of Chou

the most obviously alien (unless, which is far from certain, it can be *conceptually* linked with the possibly Chou-time notion of the primordial universe as an egg or a sac).

4. It is rather striking that, aside from this one myth, China—perhaps alone among the major civilizations of antiquity—has no real story of creation. This situation is paralleled by what we find in Chinese philosophy, where, from the very start, there is a keen interest in the relationship of man to man and in the adjustment of man to the physical universe, but relatively little interest in cosmic origins.

5. Violence and drama, boisterous humor or morbid macabreness, a frank concern with sex or the other bodily functions: all these are traits often found in other mythologies, but softened or absent in the myths we have examined. No doubt the selectivity of these myths—the fact that they are cosmogonic rather than intimately "human" in their subject matter—is partly responsible for this situation. Yet there also seems to be a reflection here of a broader phenomenon: the didactic tone and concern for moral sensibility found in much early Chinese literature. It is striking, nonetheless, that when it comes to actual human history, the writers of ancient China could, if need be, record quite unflinchingly the raw facts of life.

6. That the themes of ancient Chinese myth are by no means peculiar to China is demonstrated by the outside parallels noted by us for four out of our five examples (all save that of Nü-kua).

7. Virtually the only texts recovered in original form from pre-Han China are the short and restricted inscriptions on Chou bronze vessels or the even shorter and more restricted inscriptions of Shang divination bones. Almost none of the more extensive literature written on bamboo slips has come down to us physically, owing to the North China climate. This fact, coupled with the rarity of anthropomorphic portrayal in pre-Han art, makes it unlikely—though prophesy is admittedly dangerous—that future archaeology will add very greatly to what we already know about the myths of ancient China from traditional literary sources.

KWANG-CHIH CHANG

From Archaeology to History:
The Neolithic Foundations of Chinese Civilization

There was in China a continuous development of man and his cultural traditions from the Paleolithic to the Neolithic periods. In the late Neolithic period the foundations of the historic Shang civilization developed in the middle Yellow River valleys and on the North China plains. The nucleus of this development was approximately where the modern provinces of Honan, Shansi, and Shensi join. The two major cultures that constitute these foundations are those of Yang-shao and Lung-shan, with the last being the forerunner of the Shang.

At the time of the beginning of the historical period, the regions outside the middle and lower Yellow River in China, from Shantung to Sinkiang and from Manchuria to Kwangtung and Yunnan and Szechwan, saw the growth and spread of mixed and less-developed cultures that depended on either hunting or fishing or both as their major economic pattern.

In the following selection, Dr. Kwang-chih Chang, Professor of Archeology at Yale University, discusses three main problems in the emergence of China's first historic civilization. First, he draws a clear, systematic picture of Neolithic China as a whole. He then examines the various types and basic cultural elements of different Neolithic cultures. Second, he analyzes the transition from archeology to history, that is, from the Neolithic period to the historic Shang, and its profound implication in Chinese history. Third, he focuses his attention on the problem of whether the first historic civilization of the Shang was influenced by cultural elements coming from areas outside China, such as the Near East. By a systematic and comprehensive examination of the numerous Shang cultural elements in terms of continuity and discontinuity from the Neolithic traditions of North China and of other factors, he argues that on the whole the Shang civilization was an indigenous development, while acknowledging that sources of certain elements of it remain open to question.

Dr. Chang has not only provided us with a systematic picture of Neolithic China and its transition to the historical age; he has also clarified many problems regarding the origins of the Shang, generally misunderstood in the past.

Reprinted from Kwang-chih Chang, *The Archaeology of Ancient China* (New Haven, Conn.: Yale University Press, 1963), pp. 126–29, 133–42. By permission of the Yale University Press. Footnotes omitted.

From Archaeology to History: The Neolithic Foundations of Chinese Civilization

Neolithic China [1]

It is clear that the hunting-fishing Mesolithic populations continued to occupy their original habitat after the Neolithic ways of life began in the Nuclear Area of North China, but that they gradually adopted the technology of ceramic making and stone polishing from the Huangho Neolithic and from other Neolithic sources outside of China. It is also clear, then, that their remains are best described as sub-Neolithic. Agriculture and animal domestication, furthermore, were introduced into some of these regions, and the Neolithic transformation process took place gradually. The whole process and pattern of cultural assimilations can be elaborated and clearly understood when some of the early cultural history of the regions adjacent to China is taken into consideration. While a lengthy discussion of these adjacent regions is not possible in this volume, some general remarks will prove helpful.

The northern Asiatic regions to the west and north of the Huangho valley and immediately adjacent to it can be grouped on the basis of vegetation and topography into three groups: the steppe-desert zone of Central Asia, Sinkiang, Mongolia, and southwestern Siberia; the taiga zone around Lake Baikal and the Upper Lena, the Selenga, and the Amur; and the Pacific coast from the Okhotsk down to the coast of Korea. Sub-Neolithic and Neolithic cultures in these regions more or less follow similar subdivisions. The taiga culture may be omitted from discussion for the present, for the reason that the region directly adjacent to it, northernmost Manchuria, which is separated from Lake Baikal by the Khingan Mountains, is archaeologically unexplored.

[1] Subheading added by the editor.

The available archaeological evidence from central Manchuria in the Sungari valley . . . indicates more direct affiliations with the Pacific coast than with the taiga zone to the north.

The northwestern part of China, extending from the eastern Mongolia through Sinkiang, is the eastern portion of the steppe-desert belt that consists of Russian Turkestan and eastern European steppes as well as Northwest China, and the Microlithic cultural assemblages from the latter region resemble the Kelteminar complex to the west. This complex is characterized by microblade implements which show considerable elaboration but which are rarely retouched bifacially, and seems to suggest a whole series of local cultures adapted to a similar natural environment. According to A. A. Formozov, the "best witness for the ethnic diversity of this large culture area is the variation of pottery types found within it." In the Chinese peripheries, pottery elements in association with microlithic implements can be classified into three groups: those that show connections with the Huangho valley, such as some of the painted pottery and the *li* and *ting* tripods; those that show connections with the Kelteminar complexes in southwestern Siberia and Khazakstan, such as the combed and some of the incised pottery; and those that show affiliations with neither, such as the brownish and plain-surfaced wares of eastern Mongolia. This may lead to the conclusion that the Microlithic assemblages in the northern frontiers of China, instead of belonging to a single cultural complex (such as the so-called "Gobi Culture"), may represent a series of local survivals of the Upper Palaeolithic hunting-fishing cultures, which adopted ceramic and other neolithic technological traits compatible with their local environment and cultural ecology from

China and from their northern and western neighbors. Some of these groups in more favorable environments had even adopted agriculture and animal domestications. This process as observed in northern frontiers of China is parallel, for example, to that seen in the eastern Caspian areas where pottery and food-production were introduced from the Nuclear Area of Iran, leading to a series of food-producing assemblages such as the Jeitun Culture of Jeitun-Tepe and Anau near Ashkabad. The steppe zone undoubtedly also served as a route of cultural movement and diffusion between the high cultural centers in the East and in the West. In the current archaeological record, we see two radiating centers, one in the Iraq-Iran area and the other in the Huangho, which spread their influence across the intervening steppes from opposite directions and made scattered contacts. We do not see, however, that the steppe zone during the sub-Neolithic and the Neolithic stages served as a route of cultural transmission from one of the high culture centers to the other.

The influence of the steppe culture phase tapers off toward the east and is only weakly felt in southern and central Manchuria, which may legitimately be classed, during the sub-Neolithic and Neolithic stages, with the Pacific coast traditions. During the several millennia before the Christian era, the regions in northeastern Asia in Manchuria, Korea, and the Maritime Province of the U.S.S.R. can probably be said to belong to a single culture area characterized by flat-bottomed and straight-walled pottery, shell collecting, fishing, and sea-mammal hunting, as well as a distinctive complex of bone artifacts such as barbed and (occasionally) toggle harpoons, bone armors, and needle cases made of bird bones. This phase of culture is of considerable antiquity on the islands off the coast and in scattered areas on the coast. The sub-Neolithic cultures in the Sungari and in the Tumen valley appear to be the interior phases of this same cultural tradition. It is upon such a tradition of culture that the Neolithic farmers' cultural influences were imposed from the Huangho valley to the southwest. Farming, however, seems to have been introduced only into the Upper Sungari, where ecology was permissible, while elsewhere in central and eastern Manchuria the archaic hunting-fishing cultures persisted into historic periods.

In South China, the early Recent period hunter-fishers were apparently part of the widespread population whose cultural remains, discovered throughout all of mainland Southeast Asia, bear striking resemblances from region to region, and which have been named the Hoabinhian after their type region. It has been suggested that in northern Indo-China the Hoabinhian horizon, characterized by crude pebble choppers, was followed by a Bacsonian horizon, a continuation of the previous Hoabinhian but with the addition of ceramics and partially polished stone implements. Skeletal remains from Hoabinhian and Bacsonian strata, similar to those found in southwest China, bear Oceanic Negroid features. Lungshanoid farmers coming down from the Huangho valley not only assimilated or replaced the hunting-fishing-collecting population of Southwest China, but also may very well have been responsible for the emergence of agriculture in a large part of Southeast Asia. Furthermore, the Neolithic cultural distributions in Southeast Asia suggest further extensions into the South Seas, following the subdivision of Neolithic cultures of South China. Shouldered axes and corded ware are characteristic of the Indo-Chinese Neolithic as well as the Chinese Southwest, whereas rectangular stone axes, stepped adzes, and many other cultural traits are common to both southeastern China and the eastern part of Malaysia and some parts of Oceania.

. . .

From History to Archaeology

In the archaeological record, this major societal transformation is clearly defined. The stage of primary village-farming efficiency is known in North China as the Yangshao, and, following it, the Lungshanoid stage represents stratified village-farmers. The Shang, which follows the Lungshanoid in Honan, marks the earliest stage of Chinese civilization that is known archaeologically. Figuratively speaking, the Shen-nung Age is similar to the Yangshao stage, and the Age of Huang-ti comes to a peak with the beginning of the Shang. In legendary history, however, Shang was not the first dynasty of the Huang-ti Age, which was initiated by Huang-ti himself and passed through several legendary epochs and a major dynasty, the Hsia, before arriving at the Shang. The problems encountered by one who tries to tie legendary accounts and archaeological sequence together center around these questions: Should the epochs of Huang-ti and other legendary heroes and the Hsia Dynasty be sought in an initial Bronze Age antedating the Shang and as yet undiscovered, or should they be looked for among remains of the Lungshanoid stage? Or are some of them attributable to the former and some others to the latter?

To a volume such as this, which is archaeologically oriented, these problems are somewhat irrelevant. But an archaeologist has to face them sooner or later, and I do not think that the legendary history should be completely ignored. Archaeology and history merge at these points, and if they should be complementary when doing so it would prove mutually beneficial. In any case, several points regarding these problems are self-evident. In the first place, the archaeological sequence in the northern Honan area is reasonably complete in showing that the Shang civilization in that region was derived from the Lungshanoid culture, and that there was no major break in the sequence. Unless this is a strictly local phenomenon (which is not at all impossible, considering that for other areas the record for this stage is incomplete), it is likely that the legendary history from Huang-ti through the Hsia Dynasty is included in the time span of the Lungshanoid. Secondly, the Lungshanoid stage of Chinese Neolithic cannot be considered to have achieved the kind of civilization that has been attributed to Huang-ti through Hsia. This need not, however, worry us particularly, for a strong political organization certainly appeared during the Lungshanoid stage, probably along with some other items of civilization such as incipient metallurgy, intensified industrial specialization, and intensified status differentiation. On the other hand, we need not regard the Huang-ti through Hsia interval as necessarily having achieved a full-fledged civilization, as recorded in the traditional history, for this part of the tradition must have been tempered considerably in accordance with the historical perspectives of these early times. It is possible, therefore, that the Hsia Dynasty was one of the local cultural groups immediately preceding the Shang Dynasty. Finally, this identification may never be certain unless and until some archaeological finds belonging to the late Lungshanoid stage are identified by means of written records as having been left during the Hsia Dynasty. Since we are still uncertain about the early history of Chinese writing, it is impossible to say at this stage whether or not this is a likely prospect.

In any case, prior to the Shang Dynasty there are two kinds of prehistories of the Chinese, namely, archaeological sequence and legendary history. The former is certainly the more reliable of the two, but an archaeologist must also bear the latter in mind constantly for future reference and clarification which will undoubtedly prove useful to the study of both kinds of prehistories. With the emergence of the Shang civilization, there is a fusion of archaeology and history.

. . .

Neolithic Foundations of the Shang Civilization

With the coming of the Shang Dynasty, the absolute chronology of the cultural history of early China can, for the first time, be determined in terms of centuries and even decades, if not years. Traditional sources place the founding of the dynasty by T'ang in 1766 B.C. This may not be quite reliable, but Tung Tso-pin of the Academia Sinica, a student of oracle bone inscriptions for more than thirty years, is convinced that P'an-keng moved his capital city to An-yang in 1384 B.C. and that the last Yin king, Ti-hsin (or Chou), was overthrown by the invading Chou in 1111 B.C. Tung's An-yang chronology is not accepted by all authorities, some of whom prefer to place the downfall of the Yin at as late a date as 1027 B.C. But this argument, in my opinion, has little relevance to the major trends of Chinese cultural growth.

Whichever chronological scheme we may choose, the fact is that the known beginning of civilization in China is approximately a millennium and a half later than the initial phases of Near Eastern civilization. We can also take note of the fact that many essential elements of Chinese civilization, such as bronze metallurgy, writing, the horse chariot, human sacrifice, and so forth, had appeared earlier in Mesopotamia. Here, then, is the problem of East–West relationships all over again. And again, the problem must be resolved in two parts. First, did some of the civilizational elements of the Shang Dynasty originate in North China or did they come from the Near East? Second, were these, if coming from the West, responsible for the emergence of civilization in North China? The first question must obviously be answered piecemeal, and for many of the elements, there is no definite evidence one way or the other. As to the second question, many scholars argue that civilization came to China as a result of stimulus diffusion from the Near East, principally because they think it came suddenly and without previous foundation.

Descriptions of the Lungshanoid stage of Chinese Neolithic have shown that the Shang civilization did not evolve out of a vacuum. A number of Lungshanoid elements foreshadowed the subsequent birth of civilization in the Huangho valley: (a) The permanent settlement and the large area of the farming villages, and the advancement of agriculture. (b) The specialization of industries which had been considerably developed, as shown by the appearance of wheel-made pottery in some of the areas. (c) The village fortifications indicating the need for defense, and hence the frequency of warfare between settlements. (d) The oracle bone, the prone burial, and the concentration of jade objects in certain places within the village,

From Archaeology to History: The Neolithic Foundations of Chinese Civilization

which may imply an intensification of the differentiation of individual status. (e) The regional variation of styles and the possible importance of the residential group at the community-aggregate level which foreshadowed, if it did not indicate, the formation of urban networks and the beginning of regional states. One of these local states eventually succeeded in expansion and conquest, and is subsequently known as the Yin-Shang.

The Yin-Shang civilization was indeed a new phenomenon in the Huangho valley, an outcome of a quantum change, which put a full stop to the Neolithic way of life in the area of Shang's distribution, and in doing so prefaced a new book which has the title of Chinese history instead of prehistory. But the main stream of this new civilization was evidently handed down from the previous Neolithic substratum. There were, in the Shang culture, new elements of culture and new systems of organization for new and old elements of culture, but this does not necessarily mean that the Shang civilization was not a native growth. Table 1 shows, in a preliminary fashion, the Neolithic heritage of the Yin-Shang Bronze Age Culture and its innovations. From this enumeration it becomes apparent that the "suddenness" of the emergence of the Yin-Shang civilization has been

Table 1[1]
North China Neolithic–Bronze Age Continuities and Discontinuities

Continuities	Discontinuities
A. Formation of village-aggregate	a. Mature urbanism and related institutions (especially the formation of settlement groups)
B. Raid and warfare	b. Class differentiation
C. Industrial specialization	c. New government and economic patterns (conquest, tribute, redistribution, etc.)
D. Differentiation of status and prone burials	d. Wider trade, currency
E. The elaborate ceremonial complex (more lineage-ancestral than community agricultural)	e. New war patterns (capture of slaves and use of chariots)
F. Cultivation of millet, rice, kaoliang, wheat, hemp	f. Chamber burials and human sacrifices
G. Domestication of dog, pig, cattle, sheep, horse, chicken	g. Domestication of water buffalo
H. Stamped-earth structures	h. Highly developed bronze metallurgy
I. Semisubterranean houses and lime-plastered floors	i. Writing
J. Scapulimancy	j. Advanced stone carvings
K. Some pottery forms (especially ritual forms with ring feet and lids)	k. New pottery forms
L. Some decorative motifs	
M. Some stone implements and weapons (especially semi-lunar knife, sickle, arrowhead, adze, axe, hoe, spade, perforated axe, halberd)	
N. Shell and bone craft	
O. The cord-marked pottery tradition	
P. Silk	
Q. The jade complex	

[1] Table 6 in the original work.

unduly exaggerated by past scholarly writing. In fact, few Yin-Shang eco-social and stylistic elements did not have a Neolithic basis. Thus, one thing can be considered as settled, namely, that the Chinese civilization, on the whole, was built upon the Chinese Neolithic foundation. With this basic question out of the way, three problems still confront us: (a) the origins of the cultural elements that appeared during the Shang Dynasty for the first time, and the extent to which these new elements can be considered responsible for the appearance of the civilization; (b) the new structure and configuration of the Shang civilization which distinguish it from the Neolithic, continuities in cultural elements notwithstanding; and (c) the regional phase of the Lungshanoid stage that is directly ancestral to the Shang. The second problem will be discussed at length in subsequent sections. Evidence pertaining to the first and the third problems is still meager, but the following remarks may be of some help.

Most of the new features that appeared during the Shang Dynasty and serve to mark it off from the Neolithic are largely developmental and functional in nature. Urbanism, class distinctions, political systems, and the like are poor indications of historical relationships; the use of currency, patterns of warfare, and many ceremonial practices can apparently be said to be concomitant with particular functional contexts. Only bronze metallurgy, the use of writing, and the horse chariot are, therefore, of possible historical significance. Unfortunately, the history of these elements and their occurrence in China has yet to be studied. Horse bones have been found from some of the Lungshanoid sites. It is widely accepted that during the Shang Dynasty, horses were used only for drawing chariots, and were neither ridden nor used for food. There is no reason to suppose that horses during the Lungshanoid stage, if domesticated, were employed for purposes other than warfare. Since the riding of horses during the Lungshanoid is highly unlikely, we might even be tempted to conclude that the horse chariot appeared during that period, but the ground for this conclusion is dangerously thin. In the first place, horse bones have been found only rarely at Lungshanoid sites, and the zoological characteristics of those that have been found remain to be specified. Secondly, chariot warfare does not seem to fit the Lungshanoid context satisfactorily. Thirdly, remains of chariots have never been found at Lungshanoid sites. A great number of excavations and comparative studies of horse and chariot remains in China and in Mesopotamia must be made before we can be certain about the origin of the horse chariot in the Shang Dynasty.

The history of writing in China is another unknown factor. Palaeographers are agreed that a stage of writing existed in China prior to the period of the Shang Dynasty when An-yang was the capital. The scripts during this pre–An-yang stage were supposedly more representational and elaborate than the An-yang oracle bone inscriptions which were highly simplified and conventionalized. Such archaic characters have been found in An-yang bronzes and oracle bones, along with the simplified and conventionalized form, probably for artistic and ceremonial usage. Archaeologically, however, this archaic writing has not been found from a stratigraphic context demonstrably earlier than the An-yang period. Past efforts to link the early Chinese writing to ancient Sumerian and Egyptian writing have proved to be futile. Chinese writing was probably an independent invention, but its early history is still unknown.

The history of bronze metallurgy in China is now better known than previously, although it is not yet a solved problem. In 1949, Max Loehr states that:

> An-yang represents, according to our present knowledge, the oldest Chinese metal age site, taking us back to ca. 1300 B.C. It displays no signs of a primitive stage of metal working but utter refinement. Primitive stages have, in fact, nowhere been discovered in China up to the present moment. Metallurgy seems to have been brought to China from outside.[1]

Regardless of its apparent validity at the time, this statement has been rendered obsolete by findings in China since 1949. Based on these findings, the following points can be made: (a) An-yang does not represent the oldest Chinese metal age site; the existence of bronze metallurgy during the Shang Dynasty before the period of An-yang has been established. Even the possibility that metallurgy began to appear in North China toward the end of the Lungshanoid stage of the Neolithic cannot be ruled out. (b) At Cheng-chou, where bronze artifacts have been unearthed from a pre–An-yang stratigraphic context, bronzes are few and less refined than those at An-yang, although metallurgical details are not yet available. It is not impossible that this marks one of the "primitive stages" that Loehr spoke of as lacking. (c) An intensive investigation into the metallurgical techniques of the Chinese Bronze Age has convinced Noel Barnard that, showing little similarity to Western bronze metallurgy, bronze foundry in China was invented independently *in situ*. (d) Deposits of copper and tin ores, according to the studies of Amano Motonosuke and Shih Chang-ju, are abundant in North China, and were easily accessible from northern Honan. This indicates that, given appropriate necessity and stimulus, the opportunity for independent metallurgical invention was available to the first Chinese bronze workers. (e) It is generally agreed that the Shang craftsmen used bronze as a new medium for working the traditional artifactual forms; in other words, the Shang bronzes manifested the traditional forms and functions by means of a new kind of raw material and technology. Considering all of these points, we could say that much new light has been thrown upon the problem of the origin of bronze metallurgy in China, which renders likely the possibility of independent invention of this new technology in China. Much more information, to be sure, is required to transform this possibility into certainty, but the trend of available data is clear, and we are more sure of the various areas in which intelligent questions can be asked.

Furthermore, some new light has also been thrown upon the problem pertaining to the transition from the Lungshanoid to the Shang. The fact that the Lungshanoid culture was the forerunner of the Shang civilization is certain. But as yet we have to pin down the exact region where this transition took place, and—still more difficult—to determine the exact process of how it took place. Cheng-chou in northern Honan offers the first tangible clue toward the solution of these problems. A long stratigraphical sequence has been established for the area of Cheng-chou, ranging from an early phase of the Shang when metallurgy was poorly represented, if at all, to the final phase of the Shang. The earliest

---

[1] Max Loehr, *Amer. Jour. Arch.*, 53 (1949), 129.

phase, represented by the sites at Shang-chieh, Nan-kuan-wai, and the lower strata of Lo-ta-miao, Tung-chai, and Ko-ta-wang, is actually on the borderline between the Lungshanoid and the Shang. It has many ceramic, stone, and bone features characteristic of the later phases of the Shang, but its many artifacts and pottery forms are indistinguishable from the inventory of the Lungshanoid sites in the same area. It still has some pocket-shaped storage pits, typical of the Lungshanoid, a large number of shell artifacts, which diminished subsequently, oracle scapulae with little trace of advanced preparation, and no actual remains of bronze artifacts. At the Ko-ta-wang site, this early Shang phase lies stratigraphically above a Lungshanoid stratum, and the culture was apparently continuous from one layer to the next. We might be tempted to conclude that the transition from the Lungshanoid to the Shang took place principally in the Cheng-chou area. But since similar early Shang phases have not yet been found widely in other areas in Honan, much more work remains to be done before we can be sure that what took place in Cheng-chou was not simply a local manifestation of a widely occurring phenomenon, nor the result of cultural assimilation, with the major centers of radiation being located elsewhere. Furthermore, Lungshanoid-Shang similarities have been noted in western Honan and southwestern Shansi, and allegedly early Shang bronzes have been turned up in the Hanshui valley in Hupei. It is likely that the Shang civilization was derived directly from the Honan phase of the Lungshanoid horizon, but it will probably be some time before we can rule out other possibilities, and before we can pin down an exact location, if there was one, where the actual cultural transformation took place.

RICHARD L. WALKER

Interstate Relations During the Ch'un-ch'iu Period

The decline of the Chou dynasty witnessed the rise of a multi-state system within the loose framework of Chou feudalism. The patterns of interstate intercourse during Ch'un-ch'iu times (722–468 B.C.) did to some extent originate in feudalism. However, interstate relations and diplomacy were in the main dictated by the security interests of the states rather than by the former feudal rank. And there was a growing body of custom that developed as contacts and commerce

Reprinted by permission of the publishers from Richard L. Walker, *The Multi-State System of Ancient China* (Hamden, Conn.: The Shoe String Press, 1953), pp. 73–95. Footnotes omitted.

increased among states or within the leagues of states. These conditions were an expression of the transitional society that marked the close of Chou feudalism and the preparation of a unified empire.

In the following selection, Dr. Richard L. Walker, Professor of Chinese History and International Relations at the University of South Carolina, discusses the patterns of interstate relations during the Ch'un-ch'iu period. He is interested not only in describing the patterns but also in emphasizing the divergences from these patterns and the reasons for them.

Professor Walker points out that the only important uniformity in state behavior in this period is a central regard for state power. Thus, although this multi-state system provided a hope for peace and the establishment of interstate intercourse based on law, such a hope remained unrealized when the power considerations of the states weighed most heavily and when several large sovereign states were constantly struggling for superiority.

Let us turn now in somewhat more detail to the actual conduct of relations among the Ch'un-ch'iu states. It was to be expected that certain patterns should develop for the carrying on of these relations. Such patterns created a greater ease in maintaining the relations, and facilitated the flow of trade and information. There were advantages involved for every state which adhered to the pattern, a mutual benefit to be derived for all—up to a certain point. These patterns naturally created certain uniformities which are fairly easy to discern, and these uniformities taken as a whole constituted a system of state behavior expectations which enabled a state to make at least a rough assessment of its situation at any particular time and to forecast the consequences of its actions with a fair degree of accuracy.

These uniformities in interstate relations during the Ch'un-ch'iu have been most intensively studied. From Han times the Chinese traditionalists fastened upon some of these uniformities as a further proof of the unity under the Chou empire. This led to their preoccupation with the morality of the actions of the various Ch'un-ch'iu states, rather than with an analysis of the rationale of state actions. Thus, for example, the greater part of the Kung-yang and Ku-liang commentaries upon the *Ch'un-ch'iu* chronicle is concerned with whether or not the events recorded fit in with the elaborate system of rules which supposedly existed under the Chou Empire. The three ritual works in the Chinese Classics, the *Li-chi*, the *I-li*, and the *Chou-li*, set up an elaborate system of administration, ceremonies, ranks of officials, methods of intercourse, and behavior standards which also supposedly formed the model for the Chou Empire. While these works may have had some basis in reality under the early Chou, they are now generally conceded to be, in the main, later fabrications.

Some modern Chinese scholars have studied the uniformities in state behavior during the Ch'un-ch'iu under the title of "Interstate Law of Ancient China," and indeed there is little reason for us to doubt that the patterns of interstate intercourse which developed did constitute a rudimentary system of interstate law. Yet it must be pointed out that most of these modern students have been none too careful in their utilization of the early sources, drawing without hesitation on such works as the *Chou-li* to prove their points. There can be little doubt, as we have pointed out above, that the bald chronicles and *unsystematizing pre-Han* texts constitute the most reliable basis upon which to reconstitute the system of interstate law as it developed in Ancient China.

The patterns of interstate intercourse during the Ch'un-ch'iu did to some extent originate in the feudalism which existed in a limited area under the Western Chou. There were, however, other sources of equal importance. There was a growing body of custom which developed as contacts and commerce increased; there were the increasing number of treaties which were signed during the period and to which appeal was frequently made; and there were the patterns and rules set up within the leagues of states. In one of the recent works on the interstate law Hung Chün-p'ei states his belief that "the greater part of the interstate law of the Ch'un-ch'iu period was produced in the league headed by Chin."

It is, of course, necessary, in our discussion of the multi-state system of the Spring and Autumn times, to take account of this system of interstate law which developed. We are, however, less interested in the formal aspect—the listing of the many rules and forms—than in the effectiveness of the law. When did the states adhere to the pattern, when did they not, and why? It is perhaps typical of most of the students of the interstate law of the Ch'un-ch'iu that they have ignored these questions. In their eagerness to find and catalogue the various rules they have failed to realize that those cases where the rules did not hold were probably of greater significance. Thus,

for example, Dr. Ch'en Shih-ts'ai points out a general rule to the effect that a state should not conquer another state whose ruler had the same surname, and adds that on this score all three of the commentaries to the *Ch'un-ch'iu* condemn Wei's conquest of Hsing in 635 B.C. We are more interested in the reasons why Wei, a relatively small state, should ignore a commonly accepted canon at this time at the risk of general distrust and ill will on the part of those states which accepted it. The *Ch'un-ch'iu* and *Tso-chuan* report other actions by Wei at this time to increase its power and consolidate its position, including an alliance with Lu. This undoubtedly was because of the growing threat of the superior power of Chin under the inspired leadership of Duke Wen. Wei's actions in this case were of little use, for Chin did temporarily take over the state in 632 B.C. to safeguard its flank in preparing for the battle of Ch'eng-p'u. At the time of its action in 635 B.C., however, Wei felt that the absorption of Hsing offered a better guarantee of its security than adherence to an otherwise generally accepted rule. But let us turn to a more general consideration of some of these laws of interstate behavior.

A great many of the canons of interstate law in the Ch'un-ch'iu concerned diplomacy among the states—diplomacy in the more narrow sense of the term: the actual conduct of relations. We have seen that with the exception of the states which from time to time assumed the role of leaders in their various areas, the states, in general, dealt with each other on a footing of equality. Within a few years after the beginning of the Ch'un-ch'iu the ranks of the rulers of the various states as derived from the former feudal system were without any practical significance. Diplomacy and the fruits which it bore, such as alliances, treaties, and economic aid, were in the main dictated by the security interests of the states rather than by former feudal rank. The *free* Chinese sources record the various diplomatic activities under such terms as *ch'ao*, a court visit paid by one ruler to another; *hui*, meetings of officials or nobles of different states; *p'in*, missions of friendly inquiries sent by the ruler of one state to another; *shih*, emissaries sent from one state to another; *shou*, hunting parties where the representatives of different states combined business with pleasure; etc. Such activities are recorded with increasing frequency by the *Ch'un-ch'iu* and *Tso-chuan*; this, of course, was a logical consequence of the increasing area of contact.

A realization had developed by Ch'un-ch'iu times that the continued existence of a state depended quite as much upon its external policies—its ability to attract allies, to pick the winning side, etc.—as on its internal strength. The group of officials whose duties involved relations with other states became ever larger and more complex within the more powerful states. In the early years of the Ch'un-ch'iu, the rulers of the various states were the most important personages in the conduct of external affairs. They soon came to rely on their *hsing-jen* or messengers to carry on most of the preliminary work in any matters of importance. These *hsing-jen* were usually officials of fairly high rank within the state who carried out these commissions on a temporary basis. There were also the ambassadors, *shih*, who carried out more and more of the ceremonial duties of the ruler outside his state. During the first half of the Spring and Autumn period the rulers themselves usually had to be present at the signing of any agreements which committed their states to any action.

A most interesting perceptible trend in the conduct of external affairs in Ancient China was the changing role played by the *hsiang* or prime ministers—perhaps "chancellor" is a better translation of the term. We have noted that these officers increasingly directed the affairs of the state, usually in the name of the rulers. At first their attention was directed toward the internal consolidation of state power and the elimination of the power of the powerful hereditary families within the states. As time went on, however, they also came to realize the importance of external alignment in determining the strength not only of their states but also of their positions. They, therefore, assumed an even more active role in diplomacy. As it became more apparent that a struggle for state survival was in progress, their attention and time were turned almost exclusively outside the borders of their own states. An indication not only of the growing power of the *hsiang* but of their concern with external affairs was the fact that the prime ministers of several states were able to, and did with great haste, repudiate a covenant which had been signed in 506 B.C. by the rulers of their various states. The covenant, based mainly on dynastic interests, cut across traditional alliance patterns and threatened to upset the security policies on which the ministers had been working. The culmination of this trend was reached later in Chan-kuo times when the pattern of the struggle for the control of the whole China area is even more clearly perceptible. By that time, the conduct of external affairs and the establishment of an external policy for security had become almost the exclusive concern of the prime ministers.

In an age and culture where ceremonies played an extremely important part in everyday life, it was to be expected that there should be a great amount of ritual in the relations between the states. Although the greater part of the content of the three ritual classics is now conceded to be the work of later writers, when read in conjunction with the other free pre-Han texts, they do at least give some indication of the importance of the ceremonial aspect of interstate life. The *I-li*, for example, lays down many formal rules for the ceremonies for the reception of a mission from another state, including the manner in which the officials are to be housed and even the number of dishes to be served at the banquet given for them by the ruler of the state to which they were sent. Tso [Ch'iu-ming] confirms many of these ceremonial aspects as reported in the *I-li* but not in such meticulous detail. Many of the ceremonies were derived from the former feudalism, others developed with the increasing contacts. What is important from our point of view is that the states strove to outdo each others developed with the increasing contacts. that their ability to put on a rich ceremonial front frequently determined their position among their associates.

Such a determination was not entirely without a practical basis for at least two reasons. In the first place, the extent to which elaborate ceremonies could be carried on for visiting dignitaries depended in large measure upon the economic strength of the state. Large outlays were required even to the extent of erecting special houses for the envoys. Secondly, since the rigidity of ceremonial forms required a great amount of discipline, their observation provided an indication of the efficiency of the current regime. The *Yen-tzu Ch'un-ch'iu* reports that "Duke P'ing of Chin wanted to invade Ch'i and sent Fan Chao to investigate the political situation there." Fan Chao, pretending to be drunk, attempted in various ways to have Yen-tzu and other officials act contrary to the ceremonies, but did not succeed. On this basis he reported back to Duke P'ing that Ch'i could not at that time be successfully invaded.

The accent on ceremonies led to an extreme formality in diplomatic relations. Each emissary had to go through a rigid pattern in presenting to the ruler of the state where he had been sent, his proper credentials, *chieh*. He could not accept any gifts for himself, he must not accept any ceremonies to which his rank did not entitle him, and he must conduct himself at all times in a very formal manner. The envoys also had to be able to respond in proper manner to the toasts given at the banquets in their honor. This usually involved the ability to select for the occasion a fitting verse from the well known songs of the time. Tso reports in many places the precise verses recited by the various diplomats at these banquets.

Although there were no permanent legations maintained in Ch'un-ch'iu times, the frequency of diplomatic intercourse even from the earliest years provided almost the equivalent. The ceremonies accorded to an envoy made it necessary for him to remain for a quite a period of time, and the number of occasions which required the sending of a mission led even to overlapping. For the purposes of our discussion here, the reasons for diplomatic activity might be listed under the following headings: dynastic, economic, security, and legal; the categories are by no means exclusive.

Practically all the major events in the life of a ruling family required some sort of diplomatic representation from the other friendly states. The assumption of the throne, burial of the former ruler six months after his death, marriage of a ruler to a daughter of another ruler: all these events brought, for ceremonial purposes at least, gatherings of diplomatic representatives at the court in question. On these occasions, when the proper ceremonies had been dispensed with, interstate affairs were frequently discussed and settled. Most of the earlier entries in the Confucian chronicle are concerned with activities of this nature. These missions in turn required missions of acknowledgment, so that each of the dynastic reasons for diplomatic activity usually required at least two missions. For example, many representatives of friendly states were present in Lu when Duke Wen assumed the throne in 626 B.C. The *Ch'un-ch'iu* also records that year a mission of friendly inquiries from Lu to Ch'i. Tso, in commenting on this entry, states the general rule that on "the accession of princes of States, their ministers should go everywhere on such friendly missions, maintaining and cultivating old friendships, and forming external alliances of support." Likewise, the various rulers sent envoys to commiserate with friendly sovereigns whose lands were suffering the misfortunes of flood, drought, fire or famine; and again to participate in such joyous occasions as the building of a new palace, a new capital or a like venture.

With the formation of the different leagues of states and the declining significance of the feudal families in charge of the various states, these more formal exchanges constituted an even smaller proportion of the diplomatic activity. By 493 B.C., Legge, paraphrasing one of the commentaries on the *Tso-chuan*, observes "according to 'the rules of propriety,' the interchange of court visits between the princes should have been more frequent. 'The rules of propriety' gave place to 'the way of the world.' Great states gave up those visits altogether, and small ones observed them by constraint not willingly." The meetings of the various members of the leagues, and the diplomacy called for the leagues constituted the main reason why diplomatic activity not only continued at a high rate but actually increased. Even the earliest alliance of the Chou states under the leadership of Duke Huan of Ch'i called for a great amount of diplomatic activity. A modern Chinese student of the Ch'un-ch'iu period, Li Tung-fang, lists 24 meetings, bilateral and multilateral, called by the Ch'i ruler between 681 and 644 B.C.

A certain amount of the diplomatic activity of the Ch'iun-ch'iu times was also carried on for economic reasons. The chronicles report many missions for the purpose of buying agricultural goods such as in 666 B.C., when a Lu minister went to Ch'i to buy grain to make up for a deficiency in Lu's crop of the former year. State missions were also sent to arrange for trade agreements. The greater part of the commerce between the states, however, was carried on by the merchants who were free to travel from state to state without many encumbrances.

By far the greatest part of the diplomatic activity of Ch'un-ch'iu times was occasioned by the quest for security or attempts to increase power on the part of the various states. This was especially true during the latter half of the period. Princes or ministers of the states met to plan military expeditions or to discuss mutual problems which might someday call for military action. The rulers of Lu and Ch'i met in 664 B.C., to plan an attack against the Jung barbarians; ministers of Lu and Chin met in 616 B.C., to discuss the possible repercussions of several of the smaller states formerly loyal to Chin having gone over to the side of Ch'u. Representatives met with greater frequency to plan mutual defense, to strengthen ties of friendship, or to keep each other posted on their activities. It was a general rule that a state should notify its allies of any military expeditions which it contemplated, whether it needed their help or not; and the state also sent a mission to announce the result of the expedition. Thus, for example, in 565 B.C. a Chin officer came to Lu to announce to the duke of Lu, Chin's intention to make an invasion of Cheng which was leaning toward the side of Ch'u.

One of the most interesting diplomatic episodes recorded in the *Ch'un-ch'iu* and *Tso-chuan* was carried on to bring the growing state of Wu into alliance with the Chou states under Chin's leadership. Relations started in 584 B.C., when Chin sent a military mission to Wu to instruct the Wu armies in the latest methods of warfare which Chin had developed. Shortly after this, at the initiative of Chin, representatives from Lu and some of the smaller states started cultivating relations with Wu, and finally Chin itself arranged a full-fledged military alliance with Wu against Ch'u. Interestingly enough, although in the traditional Chou-centered view Wu was one of the rude barbarian tribes and not worthy of dealing with the Chou states on a footing of equality, when it came to matters of security there was no hesitation about entering into an alliance with it. There is nothing in either the *Ch'un-ch'iu* or *Tso-chuan* to indicate that the negotiations leading to the alliance in question were in any way different from those carried on among the Chou states.

The legal reasons for the diplomatic activity which was carried on by the Ch'un-ch'iu states were for the most part derived from custom. Thus it could be considered almost a legal requirement that the states send envoys to each other to acknowledge more formal missions. Failure to do so was considered a serious breach of propriety. Likewise treaties signed with the leaders of the leagues required a fixed number of missions to their courts over a fixed period of time, and failure to send these missions was the frequent occasion for punitive expeditions. It was a fairly well-fixed rule after the time of Duke Huan of Ch'i that the member states of the leagues must send a minimum of one mission every three years to the court of the league president, usually Chin, and that the rulers themselves pay a court visit at least every five years.

The pattern which these diplomatic missions frequently followed was the exchange of missions between two states followed usually by a treaty. A good illustration is recorded in the *Ch'un-ch'iu* starting in 566 B.C. That year a Lu officer went to Wei on a mission of friendly inquiries and to talk over mutual problems. This was followed the same year by a mission of a Wei officer to Lu both to acknowledge the Lu mission and to continue the discussions. This resulted in a treaty which was in effect a renewal of a treaty of 588 B.C. between Lu and Wei. Such treaties were also an important part of the interstate life of Ch'un-ch'iu times, and it is important that we discuss them in some detail; but let us first point out one other form of diplomatic activity which is frequently recorded in the early texts.

We refer to the sending of diplomatic notes or reports in writing from one court to another. Frequently a well composed note from a high official was more effective in achieving the desired result than the dispatch of a minor official. Therefore, the chief ministers of the states would use the minor officials to carry their own personal proposals and messages. We have already noted the success with wihch Tzu-ch'an utilized this form of diplomacy, and his exchanges of letters with Shu Hsiang. Almost three-quarters of a century earlier in 610 B.C., another Cheng minister, Tzu-chia, utilized this form to communicate with Chin. He carefully reviewed past relations between Chin and Cheng in order to convince Chin of his state's complete loyalty, thus forestalling a Chin invasion. Such messages were also used for propaganda purposes. In 578 B.C., for example, the ruler of Chin sent a message to the court of Ch'in which in effect broke off relations between the two states—war usually followed quickly after such a formal breakoff—but he also utilized the opportunity to review in great detail the relations between Chin and Ch'in over a long period of time. This "white paper" was certainly not a fair representation of the past, yet facts and dates were cited in such a way as to make Ch'in appear the obvious villain. Presumably it was intended for the consumption of the representatives of the other states who were at the Ch'in court when Chin's messenger read it aloud to the chief minister of Ch'in.

The most formal documents involved in the relations between the states of the Ch'un-ch'iu period were the treaties. These are designated in the chronicles by the word *meng* which is perhaps more literally translated *covenant*. The term usually refers to the whole of the ceremony by which states joined in a pact, rather than to the pact itself. After long discussions about the terms of the treaties to be signed, the representatives participated in a very solemn ritual in which an animal—usually a calf—was sacrificed at some holy spot outside the walls of a city. The left ear of the sacrificial victim was cut off and it was used to smear with blood both the document bearing the articles of agreement, and the lips of the principals. One copy of the document was buried with the sacrificial beast and each of the signatories kept a copy.

The texts of these treaties were couched in brief but solemn language and usually involved three parts: the statement of purpose, the articles of agreement, and an oath invoking the wrath of the most important deities upon anyone who transgressed the agreements. Most of the treaties expressed many lofty aspirations and high ideals; and had but a small fraction of those recorded been carried out, there would be little interstate conflict to record here. In all, more than 140 treaties are recorded in the *Ch'un-ch'iu*. Of these 72 were bilateral.

Bilateral treaties were concluded for many purposes: mutual defense, trade, marriage alliance, and for the sake of traditional friendship. The bilateral pacts predominate in the early years of the Ch'un-ch'iu, but with the hegemony of Duke Huan of Ch'i the states came to rely more upon the meetings of the leagues to settle their problems; and the greater number of the recorded treaties became multilateral. It was only with the decline of Chin power toward the close of the sixth century B.C. that a system of bilateral alliances again became predominant. Perhaps an extreme example of the bilateral type of treaty was the abortive attempt in 579 B.C. to bring about peace between the traditional rivals Chin and Ch'u. As in the general disarmament attempt thirty-five years later, a statesman from Sung was the instigator; this time it was a minister by the name of Hua Yüan. He managed to persuade the rulers of Chin and Ch'u to sign a treaty of friendship and mutual aid the provisions of which read:

1. Ch'u and Chin shall not go to war with each other.

2. They shall have common likings and dislikings.

3. They shall compassionate States that are in calamity and peril, and be ready to relieve such as are unfortunate.

4. Chin shall attack any that would injure Ch'u, and Ch'u any that would injure Chin.

5. Their roads shall be open to messengers that wish to pass with offerings from the one to the other.

6. They shall take measures against the disaffected, and punish those who do not appear in the royal court.

Whoever shall violate this covenant, may the intelligent spirits destroy him, causing defeat to his armies, and a speedly end to his possession of his state.

This treaty was concluded with all the formal and religious ceremonies, and by its wording we would expect that there should be no further enmity to record between Chin and Ch'u.

But this was flying in the face of reality: Chin and Ch'u as leaders of powerful leagues of states were bound to be rivals. Why then did they even bother with this scrap of paper? We know the reason in Chin's case, and we also know that it was not taken too seriously by Ch'u. Chin was willing to conclude the pact in hopes of securing its left flank against Ch'u for an attack which it planned and carried out against Ch'u in the next year, 578 B.C. That Ch'u regarded the pact as hardly more than a temporary measure can be seen in the fact that three years later, in 578 B.C., it dispatched a military force to the north against Chin. Before the decision to attack was made, at least one Ch'u official wondered, "Is it not improper to violate the covenant which we made so recently with Chin?" It was at this time that the Ch'u general Tzu-fan made the statement which we have quoted above: "When we can gain an advantage over our enemies, we must advance, without any consideration of covenants."

Note that despite the idealistic phrasing of the treaty, Chin was still identified as the enemy state.

Not all the bilateral pacts, however, were treated so lightly. When they were concluded between states whose positions made them, so to speak, natural allies, the provisions were carried out with great rigor; and the treaties were renewed many times. The Lu chronicle reports, for example, in 588 B.C., that the Duke of Lu renewed two covenants that year, one with Chin which had been concluded in 590 B.C., and one with Wei which had been signed in 602 B.C. It is interesting to note that on this occasion Chin sent a minister of 3rd degree while Wei sent one of 1st degree in rank. There was some question as to which of the two treaties of renewal should be signed first. The Lu officers advised giving precedence to the minister from the stronger state, regardless of rank.

Most of the multilateral treaties recorded in the Ch'un-ch'iu period were signed in connection with a meeting of one of the leagues of states. They usually carried more weight with the individual states because there were provisions for joint action on the part of the other signatories against any state which violated the provisions. Thus, for example, Chin, Sung, Wei, and Ts'ao signed a treaty in 579 B.C., to the effect that "they would compassionate states which were in distress and punish those which were disaffected." The covenant signed by the Chou league under the direction of Duke Wen of Chin in 632 B.C., read:

We will all assist the royal house, and do no harm to one another. If any one transgresses this covenant, may the intelligent spirits destroy him, so that he shall lose his people and not be able to possess his State, and, to the remotest posterity, let him have no descendant old or young.

That mutual enforcement was understood can be seen in the fact that all the signatories except Cheng met the next year to plan an attack against Cheng, whom they felt to be violating the pact by leaning toward Ch'u.

The covenant of mutual aid which was signed in 562 B.C. by twelve of the Chou states included perhaps as many states of the Chou league as any treaty recorded in the *Ch'un-ch'iu;* and its wording was accordingly impressive:

All we who covenant together agree
1. Not to hoard up the produce of good years
2. Not to shut one another out from advantages
3. Not to protect traitors
4. Not to shelter criminals
5. To aid one another in disasters and calamities
6. To have compassion on one another in seasons of misfortune and disorder
7. To cherish the same likings and dislikings
8. To support and encourage the royal House.

Should any prince break these engagements, may He who watches over men's sincerity and He who watches over covenants, (the spirits of) the famous hills and the famous streams, the kings and dukes of our predecessors, the whole host of Spirits, and all who are sacrificed to, the ancestors of our 12 States with their 7 surnames: —may all these intelligent Spirits destroy him, so that he shall lose his people, his appointment pass from him, his family perish, and his State be utterly overthrown.

In times when religious superstitions still weighed heavily in the conduct of affairs, the oath recorded in this treaty was indeed a formidable one. Yet the very next year there is a record of hostilities between two of the states which signed the pact, Chü and Lu.

If ever the most solemn of agreements were violated in so short a time, what then were the guarantees which the states relied on to keep the treaties in force, and why were they not more effective? In addition to the provisions for mutual enforcement which we have noted in the multi-partite treaties, and the solemn oaths whose importance should not be underestimated, there were other systems of guarantees in use. In some cases the states posted a bond for their conformance to treaty provisions. In 571 B.C., for example, the Chou states held the city of Hu-lao, which belonged to Cheng, as a bond for Cheng's good faith in carrying out treaty provisions. A more common practice was the exchange of hostages, *chih*. This was the method for guaranteeing the enforcement of a great number of the bilateral treaties. Important persons from each state were sent to the other state, to be put to death if faith were broken. Most commonly these hostages were the sons of the rulers. In 643 B.C., the eldest son of the ruler of Chin was sent to Ch'in as a hostage. Another example occurred in 610 B.C., when Chin and Cheng exchanged hostages.

Another type of hostage, of course, was the daughter or son from an outside state who was married to a child of the ruler. These marriage alliances were frequently used to buttress treaty arrangements. There was a danger, however, that the outside state might support the claims to the throne of any offspring of such a marriage and thus succeed in setting up a satellite or puppet government. The rulers of the Ch'un-ch'iu period appreciated the value of supporting claimants to power in other states on even the most tenuous ground; and, indeed, the use of satellite parties and puppet regimes was one of the most important strategies for state expansion. The contemporary scholar Chao Ch'ih-tzu has pointed out thirty-six cases in Ch'un-ch'iu times in which the expanding power relied upon such fifth columns within the territory of its victim. In some cases indirect support to the claimant was sufficient, but more often a fostered civil war was combined with invasion.

There was another factor which worked in favor of the enforcement of treaties, and that was the desirability of having a reputation for good faith. Such a reputation was important in attracting allies or in gaining the support of one of the great powers in a treaty of mutual assistance. The great powers themselves were especially anxious for a reputation of good faith, for it could sometimes be the basis on which the in-between states chose between them and their rivals. Thus, although this factor of interstate morality did rest upon the principle of self-interest, it nevertheless frequently worked for the maintenance of good faith in interstate relations. We have noted the important part it played in the solid backing which the Chou states gave to Duke Wen of Chin.

In general, the leagues of states were the most effective means of enforcement, not only of the treaties but also of the rules of interstate law in Ch'un-ch'iu times. These leagues or alliances of states came to play an increasingly important role in interstate life from the formation of the first Chou league in 680 B.C., until near the end of the Ch'un-ch'iu period. The sources which have been preserved limit our knowledge of these leagues mainly to two groups, the Chou states and the states which united under the banner of Ch'u. But there are indications that Ch'in was a consistent center of power and leader of a league of states in the West and that in the latter half of the Ch'un-ch'iu, Wu headed a league of states in the southeast. Although when one league confronted another, wars were bound to become larger in scope, yet they occurred less frequently because for the sake of security and solidarity, the members of a league were obliged to maintain as much harmony within their area as possible. This meant that the members of a league had to conform as much as possible to the laws, either as agreed upon mutually, laid down by the leader, or handed down by custom.

The position of leader of a league involved both advantages and disadvantages to the state which filled it. Among the advantages were the facts that the smaller member states sent tribute to the court of the leader, the leader could effectively direct the general policies and alignments of league members, and the state of the leader was usually protected from the devastations of military incursions because it was surrounded with the buffer of satellites. Disadvantages included the fact that the league leader usually had to maintain a large fighting force and come to the aid of the league members on all sides.

These leagues of states served many functions besides the main one of collective security for which they were organized. One type of activity in which they aided was the peaceful settlement of disputes between their members. The *Ch'un-ch'iu* reports many cases of mediation, arbitration and even intervention within both the Chou and Ch'u leagues. These methods of settlement developed to prevent disputes which might have weakened the power of either league. In most cases the court of the league leader served as the high tribunal. Occasionally, however, in the Chin league, most members of which gave ritual allegiance to the Chou court, the Chou ruler rather than the hegemon served as a tribunal for the settlement of disputes. Most of the works on the interstate law of the Ch'un-ch'iu which we have listed above discuss in great detail the examples of pacific settlement of disputes. A few cases should suffice for purposes of illustration.

In 587 B.C., a dispute arose between Cheng, which was at that time closely allied to Ch'u, and little Hsü, over a tract of land at their borders. Ch'u sent its general Tzu-fan to prevent any outbreak of hostilities; "and the earl of Cheng and the baron of Hsü sued each other, Huang Shu pleading the case for the earl. Tzu-fan could not determine the matter in dispute, and said, 'If you two princes will go before my ruler, then he and some of his ministers will hear together what you want to prove and the merits of your case can be known.'" The following year the rulers of Cheng and Hsü appeared at the Ch'u court and the case was settled there in Hsü's favor. Cheng, unhappy with the decision, started once again to lean in favor of the Chou league. Again, a dispute about who was to blame for an armed clash which had occurred between men of Chu and Lu was settled at the Chin court in 519 B.C.

In case of a dispute between the league leader and one of the member states, usually a third member of the league offered to mediate the dispute. In 625 B.C., Wei and Chin were having a serious dispute which threatened to lead to war. Wei was in a position from which it could not retreat with any dignity, and yet a war against the powerful armies of Chin would have been disastrous. Accordingly, Wei requested Ch'en to mediate the dispute, which it did, successfully. The following year, 624 B.C., the *Ch'un-ch'in* records that the Wei ruler himself went to Ch'en to thank that state for its mediation. An example of mediation by the Chou court occurred in 636 B.C., when the Chou king was mediator in a dispute between Cheng and the little state of Hua.

Occasionally the league leader would call for forceful intervention by one of the member states to settle a dispute which seemed to threaten the security of the league. It was considered a grave breach of interstate and league rules for one of the states to assume such a responsibility without first having the permission of the league leader. In fact, any military action inside a league without prior assent of the president of covenants, *meng-chu*, was a serious offense. In 605 B.C., Lu and Ch'i intervened with force to settled a dispute between Chü and T'an which had been disturbing the peace in the East. At this time, Chin was actively engaged against Ch'in, and Ch'i had taken upon itself active leadership of the eastern states for a few years. The later critics nevertheless condemn the action as contrary to the rules. In 569 B.C., it obtained permission from Chin to undertake a military action against Tseng, and again in 544 B.C., a Lu diplomat received the hegemon's permission to continue its expansion against the eastern state of Chi. Before the decision on the latter application of Lu for permission to undertake military operations there was some discussion at the Chin court as to whether Lu was not too ambitious and was not becoming too strong. A Chin officer, friendly to Lu, carried the day with the following argument, which illustrates some of the points which we have made with reference to relations between league leaders and members:

Chi is a remnant of (the House of) Hsia, and has assimilated the wild tribes to the east. The princes of Lu are the descendants of the duke of Chou, and are in most friendly relations with Chin; if we should confer all Chi on Lu, we should not be doing anything strange, so that there is nothing to make to do about (in the present matter). In its relations with Chin, Lu contributes its dues without fail; its valuable curiosities are always arriving; its princes, ministers and great officers come, one after another, to our court. Our historiographers do not cease recording; our treasury is not left empty a month. Let such a state of things alone.

Why should we make Lu thin in order to fatten Chi?

One of the fields of interstate law in which the rules did undergo some changes during the Ch'un-ch'iu period as a result of the growing importance of the leagues was that concerned with the right of asylum. In his study of the first twenty years of the Ch'un-ch'iu Roswell Britton points out that there was "a general acknowledgment of a right of asylum among the nobility of the northern states." This rule continued to carry some weight, but opposed to it were the growing number of treaty clauses providing for extradition of criminals and traitors, as, for example, clauses three and four in the multilateral treaty quoted above. It became even more difficult for the political refugees to find a safe place of refuge; from the point of view of his state he was both a traitor and a criminal. If he wished to find a haven, it would have to be outside the confines of league territory. Thus through the Spring and Autumn period we find more and more examples of political refugees being captured by league members for other league members. This is especially true of refugees from Chin, most of the time leader of the league of Chou states. Many commentators treat the right of asylum as something which remained rather constant throughout the period, and merely comment upon those occasions where it did not hold. The extent to which the rule of extradition of political criminals had replaced the right of asylum is indicated by the fact that Chin returned the viscount of the Man-Jung to its rival Ch'u in 491 B.C. In doing so, the Chin ruler made allusions to the Covenant of 546 B.C., most of the provisions of which had long since been violated. Dr. Legge observes here, "The act of Chin in this matter is held to have been disgraceful to it. The right of asylum for refugees seems to have been accorded by the States to one another; and one which had played such a part as Chin ought to have maintained it with peculiar jealousy."

Another indirect service which the leagues undoubtedly performed was to stimulate trade, communications, and cultural interchange. From the first meeting of the states under Duke Huan of Ch'i in 681 B.C., the members of the Chou league of states averaged two meetings in every three years until the end of the Ch'un-ch'iu. These meetings were not small affairs. A delegation with its retainers often numbered over one hundred members; and merchants from the same state frequently went along to the meeting to trade with members of the other delegations. This meant that most of the meetings of the states had to be held in the larger cities, and these cities profited greatly from the extended stay of so many visitors. The frequent passage of these large delegations also served to stimulate road building and to improve the means of communication, since each delegation attempted to keep in close touch with its home territory.

A word must be added about the place of Chou itself in the league which paid at least lip service to its superior place. After the first few meetings of the league under Ch'i's leadership, it became customary for the Chou king to send a representative to be present at the meetings. The various presidents of the league welcomed these representatives, for they gave an air of legitimacy to the leaders' claims to superiority. The support of the Chou ruler encouraged the smaller states to existence. The Ch'un-ch'iu, however, leaves us in no doubt that Chou was just another weak member. It even records instances in which the Chou representative signed covenants resulting from conferences on a footing of equality with the other states. Whenever possible the league president utilized the symbol of allegiance to Chou as a buttress for his own position; but if circumstances demanded, there was no hesitation about ignoring the wishes of the Chou king. Thus, in the Chou area at least, the league organization aided to a limited extent in state preservation.

In the southern league under Ch'u's leadership, this air of legitimacy was very obviously lacking. This perhaps accounts for the fact that Ch'u had to place more reliance upon military forces to hold its allies and was more frequently obliged to extinguish the states in its area. There was no moral restraint placed upon its treatment of its allies, and this was probably Ch'u's chief element of weakness. Ch'u did borrow upon Chou's prestige for a short time following the conference of 546 B.C., when members of the Chou league under Chin and Ch'u's member states paid visits to the courts of both league presidents. Even though this arrangement lasted but a few years, it must have had an important part in increasing contacts between league areas.

The various leagues of states, then, did play an important role not only in creating and enforcing rules of interstate intercourse but also in providing a certain uniformity in state behavior patterns. These patterns were, however, little more than patterns of convenience in a power struggle; and it now behooves us to examine some of the cases where they did not hold up, and to offer some sort of an answer to the question "Why?" These cases where the interstate law did not hold up were after all the important cases. In view of the weight attached to the slightest ceremonial details, it would hardly be expected that the law would be violated in matters which were not important.

In general, the rules which governed the intercourse among the states of the Ch'un-ch'iu period prevailed only where they were mutually beneficial. In the very first years, when most of the rulers of the states were still relatively insecure in their positions, the right of asylum was uniformly granted because few rulers were sure that they might not someday be political refugees themselves. Again, it was similarly mutually beneficial to grant diplomatic immunity. Throughout the period, there was the overall expectation that the state which adhered closely to the rules had a better than even chance against another state of comparatively equal power which violated them. A few years after the conference of 546 B.C., a statesman of Cheng expressed to Shu Hsiang, the leader of a Chin embassy which was passing through Cheng on its way to the Ch'u court, apprehension about the plans of Ch'u. "The extravagance of the king of Ch'u is excessive; you must be on your guard against it," he warned. Shu Hsiang's reply probably fairly represents the attitude of those who placed faith in adherence to the law as a main prop of security:

His excessive extravagance, replied Shu Hsiang, will be calamitous to himself, but how can it affect others? If we present our offerings, and be careful of our deportment, maintaining our good faith, and observing the rules of propriety, reverently attentive to our first proceedings and thinking at the same time of our last, so that all might be done over again; if we comply (with his requirements) so as not to lose our decorum, and, while respectful, do not lose our dignity; if our communications be according to the lessons (of wisdom), our service be performed according to the laws of antiquity, and our duty be discharged according to (the rules of) the ancient kings, and regulated by a consideration of (what is due to) our two States, however extravagant he be, what can he do to us?

Such a statement of expectations was easy for a Chin representative to make. Chin was not only a match for Ch'u in power, but if it were thus attentive to the rules, it could count on the moral support of Chou. If, on the other hand, Chin itself showed ambitious designs in its relations with Ch'u, it might cause some of the smaller states on its fringes to transfer their loyalty to Ch'u. In its dealings with the smaller states well within its own orbit, however, Chin did not have to be so careful; and, indeed, it was not. For example, in 580 B.C., Chin detained the ruler of Lu at its court and kept him a virtual prisoner. Again in 519 B.C., it seized the Lu ambassador Shu-sun She and held him prisoner for a while. In both these cases it violated the accepted rule of diplomatic immunity; but it had little to fear from the state of Lu, and the results achieved outweighed any possible distrust aroused among other members of the league each time. In general, the great powers could and did act with less consideration of rules. Adherence to the law in any instance usually involved a power calculation by the state in question. *If the penalties for non-adherence outweighed the advantages to be gained by non-adherence, then the law was obeyed.* This was usually the case mainly for the lesser powers.

In their struggles with each other, the big powers seldom found it more advantageous to hold to the rule. For example, they frequently violated the rule that a state should not be invaded in the year in which a ruler had died or in which there had been an insurrection within the state. In 560 B.C., Wu invaded Ch'u whose ruler had died; and again in 515 B.C., it took advantage of the confusion caused by the death of a Ch'u king to invade that land. In 571 B.C., Chin led a force into Cheng the ruler of which, Duke Ch'eng, had just died. This was at a time when Chin needed every possible advantage in its struggle with Ch'u. Since Chin was acting for the Chou states, the traditional commentaries have little to say on this breach of interstate law. In 676 B.C., Pa took advantage of an insurrection in Ch'u to invade it. At that time Pa was the great rival of Ch'u in the southwest.

An excellent example of a case where rules and treaties had little weight in the struggles between the powers occurred in 627 B.C. At that time a Chin minister noticed that there was a great amount of dissatisfaction among the people of Ch'in. ". . . This is an opportunity given us by Heaven. It should not be lost," he said. The Chin ruler objected to this statement, pointing out that Ch'in had helped to put the former Chin ruler Duke Wen on the throne and was by treaty a friendly power. Yet the minister insisted that Ch'in was the natural enemy. "Ch'in has shown no sympathy with us in our loss (the death of Ch'ung-erh). . . . It is Ch'in who has been unobservant of propriety; what have we to do with former favors? I have heard that if you let your enemy go a single day, you are preparing the misfortunes of several generations." Accordingly Chin did attack Ch'in and won the engagement.

Still another violation of rules by Chin is recorded by Tso in 582 B.C. "In autumn, the earl of Cheng went to Chin, the people of which, to punish him for his disaffection, and inclining to Ch'u, seized him in T'ung-ti. Luan-shu then invaded Cheng which sent Po-chüan to go and obtain peace. The people of Chin, however, put him to death, which was contrary to the rule;—during hostilities messengers may go and come between the parties."

These few examples of cases where expectations of state behavior, based upon interstate law, broke down should be sufficient to point out what was actually the only important uniformity in state behavior in the Ch'un-ch'iu period; that is, a central regard for state power. With respect to the law, even adherence to the most minor rules of interstate intercourse depended upon a power calculation. In diplomacy, we have seen that the former system (if it actually did exist) of ranking states by the title of their rulers gave place to a system of precedence by power. Again, we have noted that the supposedly superior Chou states did not hesitate in their struggle with Ch'u, to deal with Wu on a footing of equality.

Even in those cases where the legal methods of settlement seemed to work, the power considerations of the states weighed most heavily. In 614 B.C., when Lu mediated successfully for Wei and Cheng at Chin, it is not sufficient, as the students of Ch'un-ch'iu interstate law mentioned above have done, merely to note that this was a case where mediation worked. It is necessary to note also that at that time Chin was probably only too happy to have its difficulties with Wei and Cheng settled, since it was being forced to guard its borders against Ch'in.

Thus in the Spring and Autumn times, under such a system, the greatest hope for peace and the establishment of interstate intercourse based upon law would seem to have been to expand the area of mutual benefit where the advantages of obedience to the law consistently outweighed those of breaking the law. This was generally the case within the leagues; and for the short time after 546 B.C., the area expanded to include both the Chin and Ch'u controlled states—an unplanned result of a disarmament conference. But in a time when several large sovereign states were struggling for superiority, such a hope remained unrealized. Some of the great men of the Ch'un-chiu, such as Tzu-ch'an, recognized the situation for what it was and tried to ameliorate it in their own time.

Another group of individuals, the philosophers, sought for an overall answer to the problem of conflict which continued on through the Chan-kuo times. Some of these philosophers sought the answer in institutions; Confucius through an idealization of former Chou unity; the legalists through a rigid system of laws. Others turned to an examination of man's basic nature: those who followed Confucius, and especially Mencius, declared that man's nature was fundamentally good and could be turned from conflict under the ideal Chou system of exemplary rule; those who followed the legalist argument, influenced by Hsün-tzu, declared it to be fundamentally evil and that stringent measures and harsh control were required to prevent conflict. It took a combination of both approaches to bring the peace and unity which came under the Han dynasty, in the second century before the Christian era.

CHO-YUN HSÜ

The Transition of Ancient Chinese Society

The fall of its western capital Hao (near modern Sian, Shensi Province) in 771 B.C., after a series of crises, marked the beginning of the final breakdown of the long-standing Chou feudal order in China. In the following year, the Chou court was reestablished at Lo-i (modern Loyang in Honan Province). In this new environment, the supreme lord of all vassals, the Chou king, then King P'ing, found himself in a somewhat alien soil. By abandoning his rich, fertile land and base in the west, the king lost much of his economic and military power. This fact, together with the debacle in which his father lost not only the western capital to the Jung barbarians but also his own life, diminished the king's prestige among the feudal states. Thus, economically, militarily, and politically, the king had now lost to a great extent his ability to command his vassals. Worse than that, he even had to live on the mercy of some of his close and powerful feudal lords. These circumstances marked the end of the ancien regime *and the beginning of a new phase in Chinese history, an age of drastic political, social, economic, intellectual, and military changes.*

In terms of the degree of these changes, the period following the removal of the court was divided into two main subdivisions, Ch'un-ch'iu (722–468 B.C.) and Chan-kuo (403–221 B.C.).[1] *During these periods the political structure of China underwent fundamental changes. The feudal order, based on "familialistic" relationships, was succeeded by the bloody struggles among independent states that led to the final reunification under a bureaucratic empire in 221 B.C. The analysis of the causes for this change has become a fundamental topic in the study of Chinese history ever since that period.*

Different interpretations of the change have resulted from different approaches. Generally speaking, the various approaches may be grouped under the labels of political, economic, ideological, cultural, and social, and combinations of any of these.

In the following article, Dr. Cho-yun Hsü, Professor of History at the University of Pittsburgh, takes an ideological view in interpreting this very significant

Reprinted by permission of the International Association of Historians of Asia and the author. *Second Biennial Conference Proceedings* (Taipei, 1962), pp. 13–25. Footnotes omitted.

[1] Other different conventional datings of these two periods are 770 for the beginning of Ch'un-ch'iu; 481, 476, 464, and 404 for the ending of Ch'un-ch'iu; 481, 475, 468, 463, and 453 for the beginning of Chan-kuo; and 222 for the ending of Chan-kuo.

change in Chinese history. *He singles out the change of the concept of social relationship from familialistic to contractual as the prime cause for all other types of changes during the Ch'un-ch'iu and Chan-kuo periods.*[2] *His article improves our understanding of the making of Chinese history in this transitional period.*

This paper is a case study of ideological influence in ancient Chinese society of the Ch'un-ch'iu (722–464 B.C.) and Chan-kuo (463–222 B.C.) periods. These transitional periods mark the close of Chinese feudalism and the preparation for a unified empire. This paper will attempt to deal with a single aspect of ideology, the concept of social relationship.

In the Ch'un-ch'iu period, society was predominantly structured in what Henry Maine calls "familial relationships." By this is meant that society is an aggregation of families, rather than a collection of individuals. In such a society the individual finds himself fixed within a constellation of kinship connections which provides a conventionalized pattern for all social relationships. The nature of his life is determined largely by the status into which he is born, a status that can be altered very little by his own initiative. The whole noble class in Ch'un-ch'iu China, from the Chou King downward to the lowest knight, constituted a vast kinship network. Those who had the same royal surname recognized the royal house as the principal stem of the family tree while ducal houses and the families of nobles of lower rank were secondary branches, tertiary branches, or lower. In addition to this, nobles who had surnames other than that of the Chou royal house were woven into this network by means of marital ties. Thus the Chou King addressed dukes of his own surname as paternal uncles, and dukes of other surnames as maternal uncles. The same system was used by a duke to address his ministers.

Some twelve surnames have been identified as those of noble families in ancient China. The Chi surname was that of the Chou royal house and of the ducal houses of a number of states including Lu, Wei, and Chin. The ducal house of Sung (descended from the Shang kings) had the surname Tzu. Chiang was the surname of the rulers of the great state of Ch'i and the small state of Hsü. The marital interrelationships between these families are epitomized by the tradition that the founder of the Chi family, the royal Chou house, was born after a supernatural conception by a woman of the Chiang family. The custom of intermarriage between these particularly illustrious families is referred to in one of the *Odes*, which reads:

Why, in taking a wife,
  Must we have a Chiang of Ch'i? . . .
Why, in taking a wife,
  Must we have a Tzu of Sung?

---

[2] For a comprehensive treatment of the whole period in terms of social mobility, see Cho-yun Hsü, *Ancient China in Transition, An Analysis of Social Mobility, 722–222* B.C. (Stanford, Ca.: Stanford University Press, 1965; paper edition, 1968). For a recent and different treatment of the same topic, see Barry B. Blakeley, *Regional Aspects of Chinese Socio-political Development in the Spring and Autumn Period: Clan Power in a Segmentary State* (Ann Arbor, Mich.: University of Michigan, Ph.D. dissertation, 1970; University Microfilms Publication, No. 71-75,097).

Chart 1 is an ideal scheme showing marital ties in successive generations between the Chou royal house and the ruling houses of dukedoms.

Chart 2 shows the network of relationships that linked the noble ministerial houses of the state of Lu with each other; all of these families were either sprung from the ducal house or connected with it by marital ties. Chart 3 shows the repetitive marital relationships that linked the ducal family of Lu, which had the Chi surname, with ruling houses having other surnames in other states; the ruler of Lu took wives from, and sent daughters in marriage to, these other ruling families.

Just as the younger sons of dukes established secondary branch families, the process of family sub-division continued further. The main line in a ministerial house consisted of generations of ministers. The subordinate lines were composed of ministers of lower grades, and from these there branched off families of "knights" (*shih*) who served the ministers in the same way that ministers served dukes. This process of familial subdivision was not conceived as a weakening, but rather as a strengthening of the family; each new branch remained a subordinate part of the main familial group. A noble, in general, yielded to his feudal master not only as his superior in lord–vassal relationship, but also as the head of the family from which his own branch sprang. The familial network embraced all of China with the feudal structure as the

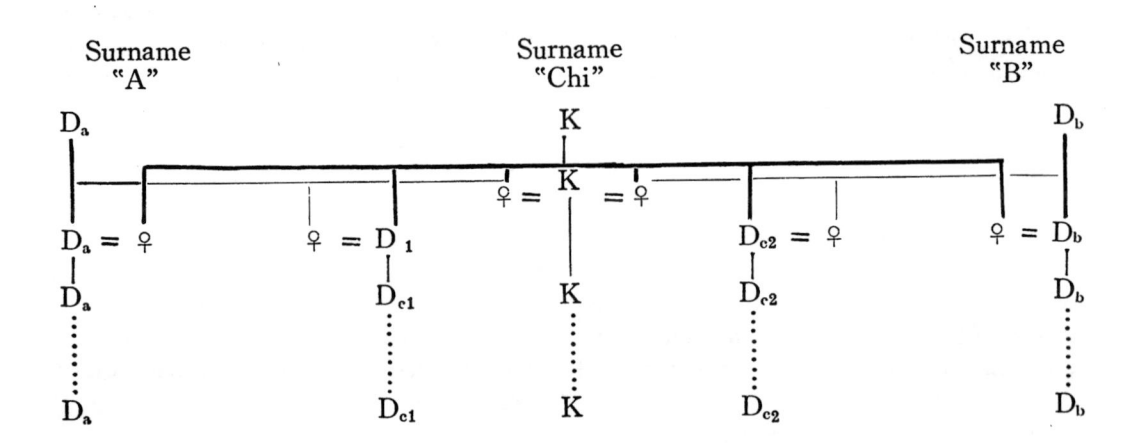

Legend:

K = Kings
D_a = Dukes of Clan A
D_b = Dukes of Clan B
D_{c1}, D_{c2} = Dukes of the Chi in different states.
♀ = female

Chart 1

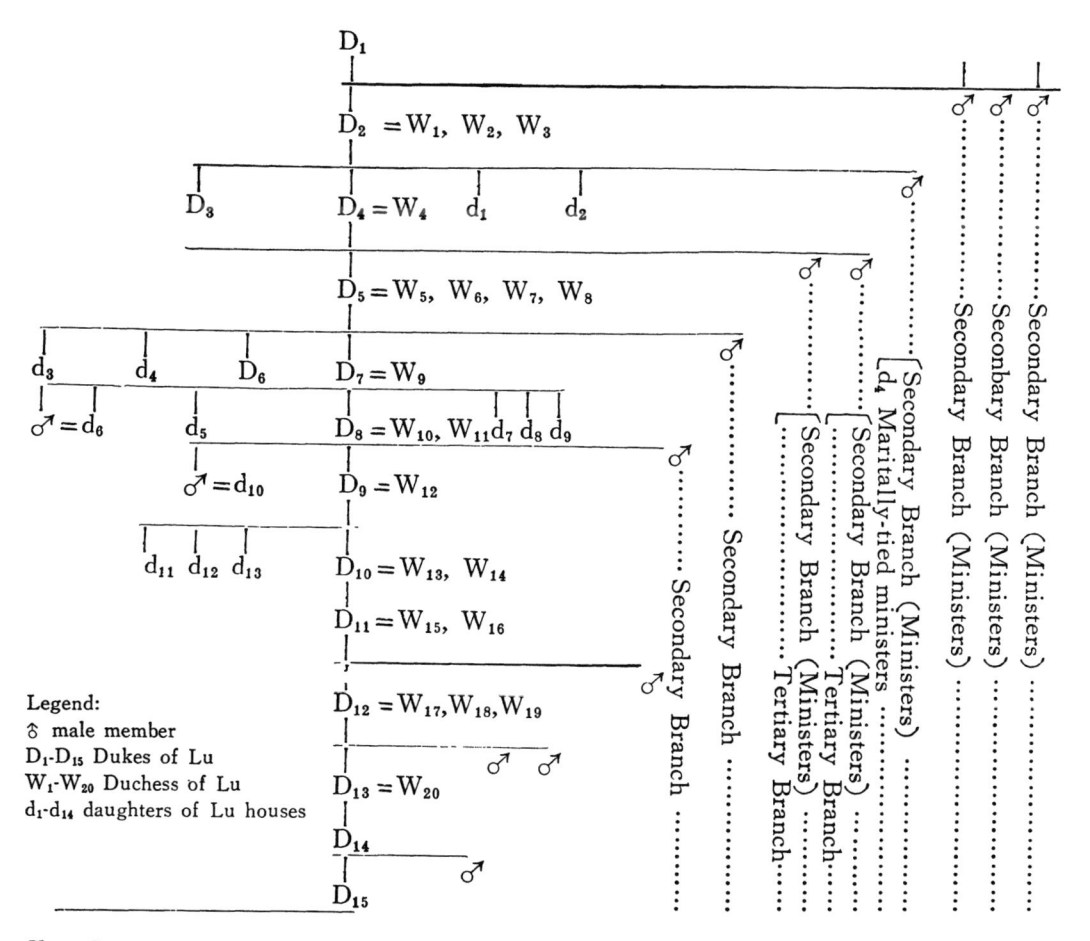

Chart 2

Legend:
♂ male member
D_1-D_{15} Dukes of Lu
W_1-W_{20} Duchess of Lu
d_1-d_{14} daughters of Lu houses

political counterpart of the family structure.

Though the Chou royal house lost the actual control of the semi-independent dukedoms, the familial concept still dominated inter-state relationships. It even found its way into the language of an agreement signed by several dukes. An inter-state agreement made at a meeting called by Duke Huan of Ch'i contains such injunctions as "Slay the unfilial; change not the son who has been appointed heir, exalt not a concubine to be the wife." These provisions, dealing with familial affairs, would seem to lie beyond the normal concern of an inter-state agreement.

The familial concept was not limited to relations among nobles; it extended also to ruler–subject relationships, as is well illustrated by the words of a learned man of that period who once said: "A good ruler will reward the virtuous and punish the vicious; he will nourish his people as his children, overshadowing them as heaven, and supporting them as the earth. Then

Surname	State	Wives from	Daughters to
Tzu	Lu		d_4
Tzu	Sung	W_1, W_2, W_3	d_5, d_{10}, d_{11}
Chiang	Ch'i	$W_4, W_5, W_6, W_9, W_{10}, W_{12}, W_{13}$	d_8, d_{12}
Chiang	Chi		d_1, d_2
Ssu	Ch'i	W_{14}, W_{20}	d_3, d_6

Chart 3

the people will maintain their ruler, love him as a parent, look up to him as the sun and moon, revere him as they do spiritual beings, and stand in awe of him as of thunder."

It is clear from this how much the relationship between ruler and subject resembled that between parents and children and how the state was conceived of not as a political unity but as an enlarged household.

Taking the ruler–minister relationship for illustration, a minister enters his government post because it is his inherited privilege as well as obligation. The ruler has not hired him and, hence, is not able to discharge him. The minister can be neither degraded nor promoted drastically from his post. Moreover, the Ch'un-ch'iu mind did not approve of any change in the established order. The so-called six instances of insubordination are "the mean stand in the way of the noble; or the young presume against their elders; or distant relatives cut out those who are near; or new friends alienate from the old; or a small power attacks a great one; or lewdness defeats righteousness. If a ruler followed such improper courses he followed the way to accelerate calamity."

Closely associated with familial relationships is a strong reverence for the past. Since each past generation serves as the link between extant families, the solidarity of members today depends on the tie established by forefathers yesterday. The natural consequence of this is that tradition exercises heavy pressure on members of the community. Thus we read in the *Shih-ching:*

Erring is nothing, forgetful of nothing
Observing and following the old statutes.

Innovation and novelty indeed are seldom acclaimed in the Ch'un-ch'iu period. Such conditions resemble those subsumed in the concept of Gemeinschaft; a social order based upon consensus of wills, resting on harmony and developed and ennobled by folkways, mores, and religion. No legislation was needed. Tradition determined the criterion of propriety, which in Ch'un-ch'iu China was called *li*. Thus we read in the *Tso-chuan*, "It is *li* which governs states and clans, gives settlement to the tutelary altars, secures the order of the people, and provides for the good of one's future life."

The familial concept did not encourage the development of commercial activities. Affection, genuine or alleged, eliminates the possibility of coldly calculated pursuit of profit. Without such pragmatic thinking, commerce lacks fertile soil in which to grow. Moreover, the role of merchant was not one of high social status, with the political sphere monopolizing all the recognized high status roles. Even when a merchant had become rich, he still was not allowed to use a chariot more precious than one with a "plain wood frame and hide cover."

Thus in the Ch'un-ch'iu period, a successful merchant was not very highly regarded. He was merely a "small man." This attitude certainly would not encourage people to go into business. Perhaps these are the reasons why there is such scarcity of information on commercial activities in the *Tso-chuan*. Lack of commerce may explain the fact that almost all the Ch'un-ch'iu cities are either fortresses or capitals. Commercial cities have apparently not yet emerged.

Social mobility along the channel of government service was very limited. This has been brought out in my research on this subject. I pick up 516 persons who appear in *Tso-chuan* from the name list, "Ku Chin Jen Piao," of Pan Ku's *Han-shu,* while state rulers and women are excluded from this group. Among them 68 were sons of rulers; 335 were ministers. Now 41 percent of the 335 Ch'un-ch'iu ministers were from a few of the most eminent noble houses; less than 16 percent of the ministers may have risen from obscurity. At least 68 percent of the remaining 113 persons have no possible connections with families of higher status. This sharp contrast indicates that the barrier between the upper and lower social strata was very hard to pass. It indeed substantiated the concept that the mean should not stand in the way of the noble.

Therefore, we may accept the opinion that the familial conception of the Ch'un-ch'iu period influenced other factors of social change, encouraging respect for tradition, creating mental obstacles to rational business, and limiting social mobility.

However, though the familial concept shuts the door on open competition among family members, many ambitious individuals sought after the satisfaction of their personal interests by means of power struggles in the courts and on the battlefield. Violence is the extremity to which people were driven when no other recourse was available. Thus we see that from the record of the *Tso-chuan* only 38 of 259 years of the Ch'un-ch'iu period are relatively peaceful. The phenomenon of extensive conflicts among states starts about the middle of the seventh century B.C., and one century later the number of conflicts has been raised to an all time high. Hundreds of dukedoms are brought to an end by their strong neighbors, even though they claim to be kinsmen. The power struggle within particular states is equally bloody. Influential ministerial households extinguish each other by means of *coups d'etat* or mere family feuds. Near the close of the Ch'un-ch'iu period a few noble households took control of entire states. In the state of Chin, as an example, more than twenty old noble houses were reduced to four powerful ones.

As a consequence, family organization disintegrated. The former seemingly solid network of Chou clans was shattered. Whenever a main family collapsed the relationships that had existed through it came to an end. Branches that had been subordinate became independent families, no longer linked to each other through the main stem. This is demonstrated by the adoption of branch names or secondary branch names to replace old surnames. Here we have a social change, the appearance of independent families, as the consequence of changes in the political sphere, resulting from the power struggle among nobles.

The status of an individual was no longer clearly defined by the pattern of his familial ties. Men came to establish their relationships with each other through voluntary association based on either market exchange, or self-interest, or through adherence to a set of common absolute values. This was not the product of emotional or affectional interests; it was the calculated outcome of a certain "cause." Hence, contractual relationships were established on the basis of consensus of parties involved to achieve some mutually-benefiting goal with an understood exchange of services or of profits.

The introduction of legislation heralds the end of the reign of familial relationships. Law should have no part in a Gemeinschaft order; tradition dictates propriety on a categorical and personal basis. But when the status of the individual can no longer be determined on categorical grounds, specific arrangements to settle issues between individuals on the basis of general and impersonal principles become necessary. This need arose in the Ch'un-ch'iu society after the sixth century B.C.

In 536 B.C. a law code was published in the state of Cheng, being cast on a metal tripod; this was not an unusual way to record important documents. A noble of the state of Chin sharply criticized the prime minister of Cheng for his action in setting up laws. These, he said, challenged the authority of the traditional models of conduct, which should be the only standard for judgment. The Cheng minister, replying to his conservative friend, wrote: "My object is to save the present age."

This incident is one of many indicators which show that the tradition was on the road to collapse, even though the conservatives still defended it strongly, and that social relationships, after the weakening of the familial concept, would be regulated according to new principles. These tendencies did not reach their culmination in the dominance of consciously recognized contractual relationships until the Chan-kuo period, but the casting of this law code in 536 B.C. was a harbinger of the change. Soon there was to be a social order of the Gesellschaft type which, being based upon a union of rational wills, rests on convention and agreement and is safe-guarded by political legislation.

When the relationship between the ruler and his officials was familial, each party took his position to be an obligation. When the ruler began to give offices to persons because of their ability, an employer–employee relationship was set up, even though such persons may have been kinsmen to the ruler. The official might regard his post as a source of wages. Mencius said, "Office is not sought on account of poverty; yet there are times when one seeks office on this account." The new contractual relation was naturally looser than the obligatory relationship between the two kinds of ministers: the high ministers who are nobles and relatives of the prince, and those who are of a different surname. For the former, Mencius said, "If the prince has great faults, they ought to remonstrate with him, and if he does not listen to them after they have done this again and again, they ought to leave the state." By "ministers of a different surname" Mencius must have meant persons such as himself, newly advanced subjects, who served temporarily and on an employee basis.

Since they were not obliged to stay in any particular state, they were relatively free to offer their services to any ruler who could or would use them. There developed a concept of reciprocity which Mencius described as follows:

When the prince regards his ministers as his hands and feet, his ministers regard their prince as their belly and heart; when he regards them as his dogs and horses, they regard him as any other man; when he regards them as the ground or as grass, they regard him as a robber and an enemy.

Such a radical statement would have astonished a loyal Ch'un-ch'iu minister, but Mencius in the Chan-kuo period said this to the king of Ch'i as if it were a self-evident truth.

Han-Fei-tzu stated the same ideas even more unequivocally when he discussed the uselessness of the familial concept of the state:

In human nature, nothing surpasses the affection of parents. However if both parents show love for their children, order will not necessarily result. Similarly, even though the ruler deepens his love for his subjects, how could one expect an immediate end to disorder? Therefore since the love of the early kings for the people matched the love of parents for their children, yet since under such conditions the children would not be necessarily orderly, then how can one expect the people to be so easily ordered?

The remedy given in the *Han-Fei-tzu*, for the error of relying on familial relations to keep order, is to understand that the first concern of any individual is his own interest.

The *Han-Fei-tzu* also defined the reciprocity between master and hired hand as such that no love existed between them, but the employee, expecting good food and generous wages from his employer, would work hard, and the master, expecting good service from the hired man, would treat him well.

The services of the people were bought by the ruler with wages, as was made clear in the *Han-Fei-tzu:* "The sovereign sells ranks and offices; the ministers sell wisdom and strength." According to the *Han-Fei-tzu* a state can be kept in good order when the ruler and his subjects realize that the familial relationship should be supplanted by calculations for mutual profit.

The principal idea in the theory of Shen Pu-hai is that the ruler is to "bestow office according to the capacity of the candidate; demand actual performance in accordance with the title of the office held; to hold fast the handles of the power of life and death; and to examine into the abilities of all his ministers." Reward or punishment from the ruler and service from the ministers are the items of exchange, i.e., the price and the commodity. Inspection and examination are necessary to ensure a satisfactory exchange; according to Shen Pu-hai, the whole process resembles a bargain.

A passage of the *Han-Fei-tzu* (I, 21) even uses such words as "covenants" and "warrants" in explaining the relationship between ruler and minister, as follows:

Whenever an action is performed pursuant to a statement, the ruler holds its covenant. Whenever any task is performed, he holds to its warrant. And on the basis of coincidence and discrepancy between covenant and action, and warrants and performance, reward and punishment are born. Therefore the ministers set forth their statements, and the ruler assigns them tasks and demands performance according to the task. When the performance matches the task and the task matches the statement, there is reward; when they do not match, there is punishment.

The employer–employee relationship was also reflected in the salary system of the Chan-kuo officials which the *Mo-tzu* and the *Mencius* both mentioned.

The effect of such change on social relationships is manifold. When the rewards or salary of the ruler were exchanged for the service of the officials on a barter basis, the relation of officials to the ruler appears to have been voluntary, but it also appears far less definite and less constant than the obligatory relationship among family members bound together by kinship. Hence the contractual relationship made for free social mobility within the channel of government service.

Numerous persons rose from obscurity to high posts because they excelled in one way or another. Again, from the "Ku Chin Jen Piao" of *Han-shu* I pick up 197 Chan-kuo persons who appear in pre-Ch'in literature and whose dates are definite. Because the social structure of the Chan-kuo period is different from that of Ch'un-ch'iu period, it is no longer possible to distinguish the group of hereditary ministers. Therefore, after taking away the twenty sons of rulers found on this list, I counted and found that 60 percent of those 177 persons remaining were of obscure origin, according to the definition used in establishing the figures for the Ch'un-ch'iu period. The percentage of persons of obscure origins among the total 448 Ch'un-ch'iu persons (516 minus 68 sons of rulers) was 32 percent. Thus the rate of social mobility in the Chan-kuo period appears to have been twice that of the Ch'un-ch'iu period.

The individual emancipated from "status" controls can be more critical of tradition. In the Chan-kuo period, we see an accelerating reformation of old institutions and the creation of new ones. New philosophies were proposed and advocated; new kinds of government, new ways of warfare, all had chances to be tested against practical reality. Denunciation of tradition echoes in royal courts whenever new ideas are discussed.

The profit-oriented mind seems to have facilitated the development of commerce. Max Weber points out that in regard to the rise of capitalism in the West as soon as accountability is established within the family community and economic relations are no longer communities, there is an end of the naive piety and its repression of the economic impulse. This can be applied also to China.

One index of commercial activity in ancient China is provided by the quantity of bronze coinage that has been discovered. The earliest date at which metal coins were used in China is a subject of much debate. There seems to be no doubt, however, that by around 400 B.C. both the bronze coins known as "spade-money" and those known as "knife-money" were widely disseminated in the areas in which each type was dominant. Numismatic research has shown that about 99 percent of the "spade-money" coins known were minted after 400 B.C. Of the "knife-money" coins, those minted after 430 B.C. far outnumber earlier coins among those now extant. Moreover, coins of particular denominations circulated over remarkably extensive areas in the Chan-kuo period. It is not unusual for a coin to be discovered more than two hundred miles from where it was minted. A type of coin known as *ming-knife* (because it bears the character *ming*) has been found in North China, South Manchuria, and Korea. This clearly indicates a flourishing and extensive commerce.

Another indication of the flourishing state of this commerce is the appearance of large commercial cities. In the Ch'un-ch'iu period, cities were mostly political centers or military fortresses. The fall of a city meant the fall from influence of the noble household that ruled it. In Chan-kuo times, a city included within its walls not only political institutions but also a large population and a large variety of different professions. Among the Chan-kuo cities, Lin-tzu of Ch'i was one of the most well known, populous, prosperous and noisy. Its population is said to have reached several hundred thousand souls who found their livelihood in numerous occupations.

A Ch'un-ch'iu city had a population of no more than three thousand families, while an average city of the Chan-kuo period might reach ten thousand families. Moreover, cities of such size were located "within sight of one another." Archeological evidences have verified this statement. We know that the central section of one Chan-kuo city, Han-tan, covered an area of about two square kilometers. No doubt, its total area was many times the size of the central section, which served primarily as palace grounds for the ruler and his staff. The ruin of Hsia-tu, a city in the state of Yen, has an area more than eleven times that of Han-tan. Chan-kuo cities were usually located at the junctions of crossroads or on the important waterways. Also, many of these Chan-kuo cities had mints. Large numbers of coins have been discovered in the ruins of these ancient cities.

All these things indicate that the Chan-kuo cities possessed the characteristics of commercial centers. These new cities had developed to such an extent that some of them were chosen as new political capitals, when the states in which they were located were attempting to strengthen their positions in the contemporary interstate power struggle. In turn, the prosperity of these also indicates the flourishing state of trade.

Certainly the flourishing of commercial activities in the Chan-kuo period is related to non-ideological factors such as the use of coins *per se*, better transportation when a centralized government in a state of larger area could provide security and maintain good roads and reduced inconvenience when there are few borders to be crossed and less tariff to be exacted. Yet, the contractual concept is the indispensable predecessor of these material and physical changes. The development of commercial activities, in turn, leads to other social changes, such as the emergence of commercial centers, increased division of labor, regional inter-dependency and the appearance of a group of *nouveaux riches* who are "lords without sceptre, kings without throne."

In summary, we see that ideological transformation rooted in political change in this instance precedes social mobility and economic development. The transition from a familial concept of social relationship to the contractual concept seems not the result, but one of the conditions, of changes in social structures as well as economic and other conceptual changes.

A. C. GRAHAM

The Place of Reason in Ancient Chinese Philosophical Tradition

The greatest creative period of classic Chinese philosophy is the late Ch'un-ch'iu (722–468 B.C.) and Chan-kuo (403–221 B.C.) eras. During these periods, rapid and drastic social changes called for the attention of the thinkers of the time. The ancient thinkers, facing all the problems of a transitional society, concerned themselves mainly with the conduct of the individual and the organization of society. With a few exceptions, they were not interested in constructing metaphysical systems. Their humanistic or ethical approach leaves many people doubtful whether their thought truly deserves the name of "philosophy."

In the following selection, Dr. A. C. Graham, Lecturer in Chinese at the University of London School of Oriental and African Studies, examines the degree to which the ancient Chinese thinkers appealed to reason rather than to tradition or intuition. He emphasizes the importance of the social conditions that influenced the Chinese thought of the period.

The selection that follows includes only Dr. Graham's discussion of classic Confucianism, Mohism, Taoism, and Legalism before the reunification of China in 221 B.C. Particularly interesting are his comparison of the place of reason in the four different schools of thought and his explanation of the special social conditions responsible for the differences. In the end, the dominant respectable schools were Confucianism and Taoism, both of which utilized reason while maintaining higher values—the former custom and precedent, the latter an intuitive conformity with nature.

After Chinese philosophy became known in Europe in the seventeenth and eighteenth centuries Confucianism greatly interested the thinkers of the Enlightenment as an example of a humanistic ethic independent of revealed religion. More recently Taoism and Zen Buddhism have attracted a different kind of audience, the connoisseurs of the mystical "perennial philosophy." Yet Chinese thought continues to puzzle Western readers, even to leave many of them doubtful as to whether it truly de-

From Raymond Dawson, ed., *The Legacy of China* (Oxford University Press, 1964), pp. 29–49. Reprinted by permission of the Clarendon Press, Oxford. Footnotes omitted.

serves the name "Philosophy." The great Chinese thinkers are moralists, mystics, and political theorists, concerned with the conduct of the individual and the organization of society, but seldom interested in constructing metaphysical systems. By itself this fact may not deter readers today as much as a generation ago, metaphysics being at present rather out of fashion; but it is far from obvious to many people that Chinese thinkers can be credited with thinking rationally at all. Admittedly they are not religious prophets and do not appeal to divine revelation, but the two more influential documents, the *Analects* of Confucius and the *Tao te ching* ascribed to Lao-tzu, do not appeal to reason either. To what extent was the Greek discovery of rational discourse paralleled in China?

We must consider Chinese thought from two sides, the social situation which gave rise to its problems, and the degree to which thinkers appealed to reason rather than to tradition or intuition as authority for their solutions. The great creative period covered three centuries, from Confucius (551–479 B.C.) to Han Fei (died 233 B.C.). This was a time of rapid and drastic social change without equal in Chinese history before the present century. The emperors of the Chou Dynasty (?1027–256 B.C.) had already by the time of Confucius lost all their power; the great fiefs had become independent states which continued to prey upon each other until the final victory of the state of Ch'in and the reunification of China under the Ch'in Dynasty in 221 B.C. At some time about 600 B.C. bronze, in China as elsewhere a near-monopoly of the nobles, gave way to the more plentiful and easily worked iron. Later merchant and artisan classes developed; within the states bureaucracies of varied social origin began to supersede the old aristocracies; serfs evolved into peasant owners and tenants. Confucius and his successors found themselves in a world in which traditional methods of government and standards of conduct were ceasing to apply. They looked back with regret to the stable feudal order of the early Chou, in which there had been an accepted code of *li*, "rites," "manners," regulating on the one hand the relations of lord and vassal, father and son, on the other the service of Heaven, of mountains, rivers, and other natural phenomena, and of ancestral spirits. This traditional way of behaving was the "Way of the ancient kings," and the recovery of the *Tao* or Way became the central theme of Chinese philosophy.

The Chou tradition survived best in the small state of Lu, originally the fief of the duke of Chou, brother of the king Wu (?1027–?1025 B.C.) who established the dynasty by overthrowing the preceding Shang. Lu was the home of Confucius, the first Chinese known to have gathered disciples and set himself up as a teacher of the Way. Confucius, like Socrates and Jesus, is known to us only by later reports of his sayings, and like them has an individual and impressive voice which sounds through the records even when we are least certain of their authenticity. He conceived his mission as purely conservative, to be the guardian and restorer of the deteriorating culture and manners of Chou, "a transmitter and not an originator, trusting in and loving the ancients." His collected sayings, the *Analects*, give us glimpses of him overwhelmed by his first hearing of an ancient piece of ceremonial music on a visit to the state of Ch'i, and scandalized when the governing family of Lu usurps the prerogatives of the Chou emperor by using eight rows of dancers in a rite and by performing the sacrifice on Mount T'ai. A striking illustration of his conservatism is his attitude to the growing tendency of rulers to counter the decay of unwritten custom by codifying laws. In 513 B.C. the state of Chin inscribed its laws on a tripod. "The people will look to the tripod," Confucius objected. "What reason will they have to honour the nobles? And what special function will there be for nobles to guard? Without degrees of noble and mean, how can one govern a state?"

But if the decay of the *li* impresses Confucius with the importance of conserving them, it also forces him to reflect on their significance. "In applying the rites," he says, "harmony is to be valued most. By the way of the former kings it is this which is most honoured, and followed in all matters great or small. But it cannot be applied everywhere. It cannot be applied by harmonizing from a knowledge of harmony, without regulating according to the rites." This shows Confucius both clinging to the traditional manners and seeking a principle behind them which can be used in the increasingly numerous cases where they cannot be directly applied. The main work of Confucius, although he did not know it himself, was quite original, the development of a conception of moral goodness (*jen*) and of the gentleman (*chün-tzu*, literally "lord's son") which he supposed to be implicit in the poetry, ceremonies, and music of the early Chou, and which was to dominate the moral consciousness of China from the victory of his school in the second century B.C. down to the present century. "If a man is not good," he asks, "what do rites matter? If a man is not good, what does music matter?" Confucius is the discoverer for China of the Golden Rule and of the principle that love for others is the basis of morality:

When Fan Ch'ih asked about the good man, the Master answered: "He loves others."
What you do not like yourself do not do to others.
The good man wishing himself to stand helps others to stand, wishing himself to arrive helps others to arrive; the ability to recognize the parallel to one's own case may be called the secret to goodness.

This conception of the basis of morality, developed into a doctrine of universal love, became the central tenet of the earliest rivals of the Confucians, the Mohist school founded by Mo-tzu (*c.* 480–*c.* 390 B.C.). Mo-tzu's teaching survives in a series of treatises on his characteristic doctrines, most of them preserved in three versions apparently derived from different branches of his school. "The sage," the treatise on *Universal Love* begins, "is one whose business it is to govern the Empire. He can govern it only if he knows from what source disorder arises, he cannot govern it if he does not; he is like a physician curing a man's sickness, who can cure only if he knows from what source the sickness arises." If we examine the types of disorder, we find that all derive from lack of mutual love. "Disloyalty of minister to ruler and son to father is what one calls a disorder. Sons love themselves more than their fathers, and therefore deprive their fathers to benefit themselves; and younger brothers do the same to elder brothers and ministers to rulers." All other disorders, oppression by rulers and fathers, robbery, sedition, aggressive war, have the same source, loving oneself more than others, and the same cure, mutual love. "If we regard father, elder brother, and ruler as we regard ourselves, what scope shall we have for disloyalty? . . . If we regard other men's houses as we regard our own, who will steal? If we regard other men's persons as we regard our own, who will do violence?"

Laid down in these uncompromising terms, the principle which for Confucius gives meaning to the traditional conventions turns into a weapon against these conventions. Confucians always accused Mo-tzu of outraging filial piety by teaching sons to love other people's parents as much as their own. It is not likely that he went as far as this, but certainly he was a fierce critic of various customs which Confucians counted among the major duties. The Mohist *Economy in Funerals* points out that defenders and critics of mourning customs both appeal to ancient authority, and proposes this test for judging between them: "If fine funerals and prolonged mourning can really enrich the poor, increase population, replace peril and disorder by safety and order, then they are good and right, and a duty for loyal sons" but otherwise they are not. Since extravagance in mourning wastes goods, interferes with productive work, and damages the health of mourners, this test is sufficient to discredit it. It is objected: "If fine funerals and prolonged mourning are really not the Way of the sage kings, why is it that gentlemen throughout the civilized world never fail to perform and uphold them?" Mo-tzu answers that "this is what one calls 'mistaking the familiar for the suitable and the customary for the right,'" and points out that barbarous peoples are equally convinced of the rightness of customs which horrify the Chinese.

But if a custom is wrong, who is to reform it? The people with effective power were the rulers of the states, who had progressively won themselves complete independence from the Chou emperor and full authority within their territories, rather in the manner of the despots of sixteenth- and seventeenth-century Europe. For Confucians there was still a traditional Way which the rulers and the emperor himself were morally obliged to follow. But Mo-tzu affirms the independence of rulers from every authority except the will of Heaven, which they can discover by listening to him. In his view people accept a ruler with the purpose of escaping the primitive anarchy in which each man has his own idea of right, and they achieve this purpose only by "conforming to those above," subjects taking their judgments of right and wrong from the ruler and the ruler from Heaven. Another issue on which Mo-tzu supports the new absolute monarchs against feudal institutions is the question of "the advancement of worth and employment of ability." The essay *Advancement of Worth* recommends that men be appointed to high office on grounds of personal worth alone, irrespective of wealth, rank, family, and connexions, even if they are peasants or craftsmen.

The sayings of Confucius never show him defending a position by consecutive argument. This is as one would expect; he is the interpreter of a code not yet openly questioned although increasingly disregarded in practice, and is not aware that there are novelties in his interpretation. But Mo-tzu has opinions of undisguised originality on many political, moral, and practical topics, and the pressure of controversy forces him to give reasons. According to the essay *Against Fatalism*, "One must set up criteria. Affirming something without criteria is like marking East and West on a turning potter's wheel." There are three such standards for judging an opinion: "On what should one base it? Base it on the past deeds of the ancient sage kings. By what should one test it? Test it by examining what nowadays the eyes and ears of ordinary people find real. What use is it? Apply it in administration and observe whether it benefits the people of the civilized states."

Applying these criteria, Mo-tzu disproves fatalism by quotations showing that the ancient kings disbelieved in it; by the absence of witnesses who have seen or heard this being called Destiny; and by the moral dangers of supposing that one's conduct will not affect one's fortune. It is the last consideration which counts most with Mo-tzu. He cares only for theories with practical consequence, and his first concern is whether the consequences are beneficial or harmful. He accepts the authority of the ancients without reserve, but he also finds a pretext for ignoring it whenever it conflicts with his utilitarian test. Confucius had appealed to a genuine tradition, that of the Chou Dynasty at its prime, which he considered greater than the earlier Hsia and Shang. Mo-tzu is the first to take advantage of the fact that little was known about the institutions of the earlier dynasties. "You model yourselves on Chou and not on Hsia," he remarks to the Confucian Kung Meng. "Your antiquity is not antiquity at all." The essay *Against the Confucians* defends innovation explicitly: "The Confucians say 'To be a good man a gentleman must assume the opinions and dress of the ancients.' My reply is that what we call ancient opinions and dress were all new once, so that the most ancient of the men who expressed these opinions and wore this dress were not gentlemen. Is it suggested that to be a good man one must assume the opinions and dress of the ungentlemanly?"

There is a further difference between Confucianism and Mohism which is surprising at first sight. Mo-tzu's ultimate sanction for moral conduct is reward and punishment by Heaven and the spirits. He therefore insists on the personality of Heaven and the existence of spirits. Confucius had always put aside such topics, as irrelevant to the conduct of ordinary life; he recommended "respect for the spirits while keeping them at a distance," and dismissed an inquiry about death with the question: "Until you understand life, how can you expect to understand death?" Throughout most of its history Confucianism has combined dogmatism concerning rules of government and conduct, and meticulousness in dress and manners, with the utmost latitude on such trivial questions as whether we survive death and whether Heaven is a personal God of impersonal power or, in neo-Confucianism, a principle of order running through all things. Mo-tzu, arguing with a certain Ch'eng-tzu, accuses the Confucians of calling down the wrath of Heaven and the spirits by maintaining that "Heaven is without consciousness and the spirits are not divine"; and he indicts Kung Meng for the contradiction of holding both that spirits do not exist and that it is a duty to sacrifice to them. The latter position, held for example by Hsün-tzu in the third century B.C., has never seemed self-contradictory to Confucians. My father's spirit may or may not exist; the important point is that my performance of the rite should fully express the reverence due to him. Confucius himself is described in the *Analects* as "sacrificing to the spirits *as though* the spirits were present."

Why is it the traditionalists who on this issue take the side of skepticism? Part of the answer is that Confucianism, being a refinement of the accepted aristocratic code, needs no sanction except the self-respect of the man who does not wish to be shamed before his peers. The aristocrat's sense of fitness is independent of religion and may clash with it, as happened in Christian

Europe over such issues as duelling and amorous intrigue. Mo-tzu, preacher of a new morality, threatens offenders, not with the contempt of neighbours who are more likely to agree with the Confucians, but with the anger of invisible beings whom he presumes to agree with himself. Psychologically, this is the shift from shame to guilt. Mo-tzu's attitude, rare in China, resembles that of the great religions of Western Asia, Judaism, Christianity, and Islam. But unlike the prophets of these religions he does not claim any personal mission or revelation from the spirits. The essay *Explaining the Spirits* is a rational demonstration using Mo-tzu's three criteria; spirits exist because the ancient sages said they do, because many people have seen them, and because people behave better if they think that the spirits will punish their sins. It is interesting that the Chinese Communists, coping with the same task of converting the masses to a new and rationalistic moral code, have resorted to the apparatus of guilt, confession, repentance, and forgiveness which successive generations of Christian missionaries had failed to implant in the "shame culture" of traditional China.

Mo-tzu's method of criticizing accepted morality in terms of the resulting benefit and harm was a weapon which could be used in other hands for other purposes. In the fourth century B.C. we find people beginning to use it to defend the claims of private against public life. The struggle for power, as war between the states increased in frequency and savagery, was becoming murderously competitive; just why, people were beginning to ask, do we take it for granted that wealth and power are worth the perils of contending for them? The conviction grew that external possessions, which are replaceable, are less important than the safety and health of one's body, which is not. The individualists flattered themselves that they had risen above the vulgar infatuation with wealth and power to a truer understanding of benefit and harm; but both Confucians and Mohists treated them as shirkers too selfish to serve the community by taking office. The most famous individualist, Yang Chu (*c.* 350 B.C.), has left no authentic writings. He seems to have held that no one should injure his body, even by the loss of a hair, for the sake of any possession, even the whole empire; but his enemies seized on the implication that he would not take the opportunity to benefit the whole empire by good government at the least cost to himself. A fragrant surviving in a late book, *Lieh-tzu* (*c.* A.D. 300), shows us Yang Chu debating with Mo-tzu's disciple Ch'in Ku-li, who embarrasses him by pressing him to say whether he would give a hair to benefit the whole world. A disciple recovers the offensive by forcing Ch'in Ku-li to admit that, in spite of the chance to do good, he would not accept a state in exchange for the loss of an arm.

The corrosion of traditional morality by the utilitarian test provoked a Confucian counter-attack from Mencius (*c.* 390–*c.* 305 B.C.). Mencius, like Confucius, is a conservative who expects a restoration of the institutions of Chou to cure all ills; he remains a believer in hereditary rank, and approves of promoting social inferiors only in cases of exceptional merit. He abhors the utilitarian test, and in the very first episode of his book we find him protesting when a king asks him for something which will profit his country: "Why must Your Majesty speak of profit? I have nothing for you but goodness and right." In the context of his time this amounts to a refusal to expose Confucian morality to any rational test whatever. Yet the rival schools were pulling

Confucians into controversies which gave them no choice but to prove themselves better reasoners than their opponents. When, for example, a certain Hsü Hsing asserts that rulers should plough the land with their subjects, Mencius argues in detail that division of labour and exchange of products is to the good of all, and that those who work with their minds deserve to be fed by those who work with their hands. However much Mencius hates appeals to utility, he cannot escape the necessity of showing that the restoration of Chou institutions will indeed benefit the community. Confucius, when asked how to rule a state, advised the use of the Hsia calendar, the Shang coach, and the Chou ceremonial cap; in the same position, Mencius recommends lenient punishments, low taxes, and no forced labour at times when workers are needed on the land.

The type of Mohist argument which condemns wasting on one's father's funeral goods which could be better used in the service of the community merely convinced Confucians that utility is one thing and morality quite another, and so opened the way to a kind of moral intuitionism. Mencius, with his contemporary and rival Kao-tzu, is among the first Chinese to turn attention inwards, to consider moral feelings as well as moral conduct, and to raise the question whether morality is internal or external, the product of nature or of training. Kao-tzu defined human nature as "the inborn," identified it with hunger and sexual desire, and pronounced it morally neutral. But the Confucian view that everything outside our control is the work of Heaven, a benevolent even if impersonal power, leads Mencius to the conclusion that human nature is good, and that we can discover whether a course of action is good by looking inside ourselves. He insists that the feelings developed by moral education are present in us without our being taught them. "Now if anyone suddenly notices a child about to fall into a well, he will have a feeling of alarm and distress. It is not that he expects it to win him favour with the child's parents, or praise from friends or neighbours; nor does it come about because he dislikes a bad reputation."

Towards the end of the fourth century B.C. the virtuosity of debaters of the rival schools began to breed sophists interested in argument for its own sake. The only surviving writings of the sophists are some essays ascribed to Kung-sun Lung (*c.* 320–*c.* 250 B.C.), of which all but one are of doubtful authenticity or interpretation. The exception is a demonstration in dialogue form that "A white horse is not a horse," a piece of pure sophistry which assumes that "A white horse is a horse" affirms identity and not class membership. Among sayings known by quotation the most interesting are a set of ten ascribed to Hui Shih (late fourth century B.C.), of which the last is: "Love the myriad things indiscriminately; heaven and earth are one body." The preceding nine are paradoxes evidently designed, like Zeno's, to prove that the universe is one body by showing that it is self-contradictory to make divisions. We can make guesses of varying plausibility as to the nature of Hui Shih's arguments. Spatial divisions lead to the paradoxes that the universe both must be and cannot be infinite ("The South has a limit and has no limit") and that a quantity is an aggregate of its smallest parts, which however being infinitely small will add up to nothing ("What has no bulk cannot be accumulated, but its size is a thousand miles"). Temporal divisions imply moments at which the sun is both at noon and declining and at which the dying are both still alive and already dead ("The sun is declining when it is at noon, a creature is dead when it is alive"), and entitle me, if I cross the frontier between two countries at the moment between one day and the next, to say both that I left there today and that I reached here yesterday ("I go to Yüeh today and arrived yesterday").

Philosophers reacted in opposite ways to the sophists, by a total disillusionment with reason or by a new logical rigour. The greatest Chinese anti-rationalist is the Taoist Chuang-tzu (c. 365–c. 290 B.C.), a friend and critic of Hui Shih. The argument of Hui Shih that all distinctions involved self-contradiction comes dangerously near to discrediting analytic reasoning altogether, and Chuang-tzu takes this further step. His *Treating Things as Equal* denies the consistency of affirming even that all things are one, with an argument used at almost the same time by Plato in the *Sophist*: " 'The myriad things and I make one'—With them already making one, can I still say something? But having called them one, have I avoided saying something? One and the words make two, two and one make three. . . ."

The fruitless debates of Confucians and Mohists, each side starting from its own unproved premisses, lead Chuang-tzu to an uncompromising relativism. Every doctrine is right from one standpoint and wrong from another, just as "this" at one position is "that" from another position. If you and I disagree, no third party can judge between us because he will have authority only for one side, will need another judge to judge himself, and so on indefinitely. Chuang-tzu's scepticism arises from disputed questions of value, but makes no distinction between these and questions of fact. *Treating Things as Equal* shows throughout the shock of the discovery, stupefying to those who first made it, that a name has only a conventional relation with a thing. "Speech is not blowing wind," says Chuang-tzu, "it is about something; it is simply that what it is about is not fixed. Is it really about something or never about anything? If you think it is different from the twittering of chicks can you or can't you show the difference?" There is no need of sophistry to prove that a horse is not a horse; it is a horse if you choose to name it so, not if you give the name to something else. A curious dialogue between Hui Shih and Chuang-tzu shows the latter's extreme relativism, gives an interesting glimpse of Hui Shih proving a point, and illustrates how the Chinese language sometimes gives an argument a twist difficult to catch in English translation:

Chuang-tzu and Hui Shih were strolling on the bridge above the Hao. "The dace swim out in their free and easy way," said Chuang-tzu, "you can tell that the fish are happy."

"You are not a fish. How [literally "From where"] do you know the fish are happy?"

"You are not me. How do you know that I do not know that the fish are happy?"

"Not being you, admittedly I do not know you; all the more obvious then that you, who are admittedly no fish, do not know whether the fish are happy."

"Let us go back to where we started. You said: '*From where* do you know the fish are happy?' You questioned me already knowing that I knew it. I knew it from up above the Hao."

Hui Shih plays according to the rules, Chuang-tzu kicks over the board. But his last reply is more than a stupid pun. He sees in the use of the word "where an admission that a request for reasons is merely a request to define the standpoint from which a judgment is the right one. The stroke of wit at the end is a way of saying that an intellectual position is as arbitrary as a position in space from which some things are "this" and others "that."

Chuang-tzu's relativism commits him to rejecting tradition without any of the Mohists' reservations. Times change, what was good for our ancestors is not good for us. But this contempt both for reason and for ancient authority does not imply despair of finding the Way; on the contrary his destructive criticism is inspired by the conviction that it is self-consciousness, analysis, and conformity with conventions which separate us from the Way. Chuang-tzu is deeply interested in types of ordinary behaviour which thinking inhibits and types of knowledge which cannot be verbally expressed. A player winning while the stakes were low pauses to think when the stakes are raised, and loses his knack; a woman discovers she is beautiful and ceases to be beautiful. Hitting on the Way is a skill like swimming or handling a boat or catching insects with a rod and line. We can no more put it into words than an old carpenter can explain to his son how to use a chisel neither too fast nor too slow. Chuang-tzu guides us towards the development of this dexterity by humour, poetry, aphorism, and parable, using reason only to discredit reason.

In taking this position, Chuang-tzu is among the originators of the new conception of the Way or *Tao* which has come to be known specifically as "Taoism." This conception implies insight from another direction into the distinction which a European might describe as that between laws of nature and moral laws. Heaven and Earth pursue a consistent course through the cycles of the seasons and of the heavenly bodies, a Way which earlier thought had never distinguished from that prescribed for man, and which later Confucianism was to moralize even more explicitly, seeing Heaven's kindness in the growth of spring and justice in the destruction of autumn. But the Taoist sees this order as indifferent both to our morality and to our selfish ambitions, although he still conceives it as in some way prescriptive, obliging us to side with it against morality and ambition. The author of the *Tao te ching*, who wrote perhaps a little earlier in the fourth century B.C., shared Chuang-tzu's assumptions about the Way but drew different practical conclusions. His brief collection of aphorisms expresses in bald paradoxes a complicated pattern of insights into the contradictions between the aims and results of action. One of its focal points is the thesis that "Reversion is the movement of the Way"; whatever grows stronger arrives at a point from which it declines into weakness. The ordinary ruler strives to perpetuate strength, and to force other things out of their courses into his own. "The Way of Heaven takes from those with too much and adds to those with too little. The way of man is otherwise; it takes from those with too little in order to make a present to those with too much." The sage ruler on the other hand "does nothing" (*wu-wei*), takes the side of weakness instead of strength, acts against a rising power only at the earliest stage before it gathers strength, and otherwise yields until the trend turns in his favour. This is a strategy of government like that of Japanese *judō* wrestling, which it later inspired. It implies that the Way is outside the ruler, whose relation to it, as explicitly paradoxical as every other aspect of the book's many-sided thought, is to use it for his own ends by renouncing those ends: "It is because he has no selfishness that he can make his selfishness succeed." What Chuang-tzu teaches, on the other hand, is the ordered spontaneity of the mystic and poet, in the perfection of which human action accords with the Way like the natural processes of Heaven and Earth, because it is itself a natural process undisturbed by reflection. His audience, like Yang Chu's, consists of those who wish to live their own lives free from the cares of office, and he offers a *mystique* where Yang Chu could offer only reasons for thinking that the behaviour he advocated was sensible.

The threat of sophistry on the one hand and irrationalism on the other excited the Mohists of the third century B.C. to a closer examination of the definitions of words and the validity of arguments. Earlier thinkers had defined moral terms and such controversial terms as "human nature"; the later Mohists defined "all" ("none not so") and "some" ("not all"), "duration" ("filling different times") and "extension" ("filling different places"). One section of the *Mohist canons* distinguishes different senses of ambiguous words, observing for example that "same," a word which had been used treacherously by philosophers who denied the validity of all distinctions, can mean "identical" or "belonging to one body" or "associated in place" or "of a kind." The same section distinguishes three kinds of names, "all-inclusive," "classifying," and "proper":

"Thing" is all-inclusive; any object must get this name. The naming "horse" is classifying; for what is like the object one must use this name. The naming "Tsang" is proper; this name is confined to this object.

The answers of the later Mohists to the arguments of other schools have a subtlety and precision no doubt anticipated in the lost writings of the sophists, but unprecedented in the extant literature. To the argument that it cannot be a duty to love all men since the number may be infinite, they reply:

If men do not fill the infinite the number of men is finite, and there is no difficulty about exhausting the finite; if they do fill the infinite the infinite is exhaustible, and there is no difficulty about exhausting the infinite.

In passages which seem to be concerned with Chuang-tzu's thesis that from one point of view all statements are right and from another all wrong, they object that "treating all statements as mistaken" and "rejecting rejection" are both untenable, since in the first case "If this man's statement is admissible it is not mistaken, so there are admissible statements," and in the second case "If 'rejection is to be rejected' cannot be rejected, he is not rejecting rejection."

One late Mohist essay, the *Hsiao-ch'ü*, is entirely devoted to distinguishing between types of sound and unsound argument. Its theme is that statements can look perfectly parallel and yet not be. "Inquiring about a man's illness is inquiring about the man; disliking the man's illness is not disliking the man. A man's ghost is not a man; your elder brother's ghost is your elder brother." This deceptive parallelism often leads us into fallacies. Thus it is common to confuse sequences of these three kinds:

i. "A white horse is a horse; riding a white horse is riding a horse."
ii. "Her younger brother is a handsome man; loving her younger brother is not loving a handsome man."
iii. "Cockfights are not cocks; liking cockfights is liking cocks."

Mohists are wrongly derided as sophists for claiming that, although robbers are men, killing robbers is not killing men. (Their motive was no doubt to reconcile execution of robbers with universal love; we could make the point differently by saying that one can kill someone as a robber while loving him as a man.) The claim seems self-contradictory because people assume that it belongs to the first class. But it belongs to the second:

> Having too many robbers is not having too many men, having no robbers is not having no men. . . . The world agrees on this. But if so, there is no more doubt that although robbers are men, loving robbers is not loving men, not loving robbers is not loving men, killing robbers is not killing men.

The pressure of competition with other schools, which had forced Mencius into public debate, drove Hsün-tzu (?298–?238 B.C.) to a much more thorough rationalization of the Confucian position. Although still defending Chou institutions and the prime importance of *li*, "rites," "manners," he no longer follows Mencius in insisting, for example, on hereditary privilege. He freely uses the phrase "advancement of worth and employment of ability" as though forgetting its Mohist origin, and explicitly favours degrading unworthy men of high birth and promoting worthy commoners. A more basic point is that he tacitly accepts what Mencius denied, the Mohist principle that the value of institutions is subject to the test of utility. Hsün-tzu's case for traditional forms and ceremonies is that they do benefit the people. All men desire more than they can get, and are protected from destroying each other only by rules which lay down clearly who is to defer to whom, subject to ruler, wife to husband, younger to elder. His objection to Mo-tzu is simply that he overlooks the utility of degree.

Hsün-tzu is the first and last Confucian to accept the Taoist thesis that Heaven and Earth follow a Way which is indifferent to the desires and the ideals of men. But he sees that this Way imposes no obligation on us to follow it; it is a neutral order which the sage studies for the sake of ordering society in the way which will take most advantage of the seasons of Heaven and the resources of Earth. The "Way of the ancient kings," he says, consists of "rites and duties," and "is not the Way of Heaven nor the Way of Earth; it is what man takes as his Way, what the gentleman takes as his Way." One consequence of this is that Hsün-tzu can no longer accept the faith of Mencius that the nature implanted in us by Heaven must be good. "Man's nature is bad," he declares, "and the good in him is artificial." His opinion is that our nature consists of desires which lead to contention if given free play; it is not quite that they are evil, as understood in the Christian doctrine of Original Sin, but that they share the amorality of all the natural forces which the sage manipulates for the benefit of man. "Someone asks: 'If man's nature is bad, from what were rites and duties born?' The answer is that all rites and duties were born from the sage's artifice and were not originally born from man's nature. . . . The sages thought them out step by step, drilled themselves in artificial habits, and so brought forth rites and duties and established laws and measures."

Hsün-tzu's *Correct Use of Names* considers the relation between names and objects already discussed by the later Mohists. If a thing keeps the same place although changing in appearance there is one object, more than one if there is similarity of appearance but difference of place. The mind, which knows the passions directly, knows objects through the five senses, and finds them similar or different in varying degrees. Similar objects are given the same name, which may be of any degree of generality; we may distinguish "animal" and "bird" or call both "thing." Names are conventional, appropriate if "the convention is fixed and the usage becomes settled." (The shock of this discovery had by now worn off.) Sentences are complex names: "The sentence puts together the names of different objects in order to convey one idea." Errors fall into three types:

i. "Confusing names by misuse of names," refuted by showing that a name does not fulfil its purpose of distinguishing the similar from the different. (Among his examples: "Being insulted does not disgrace," "Killing robbers is not killing men.")
ii. "Confusing names by misuse of objects," refuted by examining the facts. (Example: "There are few genuine [not artificial] desires.")
iii. "Confusing objects by misuse of names," refuted by arguing from something acknowledged. (Example: "A [white] horse is not a horse.")

An attack on a certain Sung Hsing (fourth century B.C.) in another essay, the *Treatise of Corrections,* refutes in detail errors of the first two classes, although unfortunately not of the third. It rejects "Being insulted does not disgrace" on the grounds that the sages used "disgrace" in two senses, social and moral, and that Sung Hsing has no right to use it only in the latter sense; it rejects "There are few genuine desires" on factual grounds.

Down to the third century B.C. many rulers continued, with remarkable patience, to listen to philosophers who travelled from state to state teaching them how to become emperor of a reunited China—Confucians who recommended reversion to an irrecoverable past, Mohists and other moralists who, although more alive to changed conditions, persisted in preaching universal love and the wickedness of aggression against neighbour states. But at the very end of the great period of Chinese philosophy a school appeared which advised rulers to pursue power undistracted by moral considerations. This was the Legalist school which culminated in Han Fei (died 233 B.C.), a former disciple of Hsün-tzu. Han Fei argues that moral considerations can outweigh self-interest only for a minority, and lead to a good government only under the occasional sage; on the other hand a consistent code of rewards and punishments, acting directly on men's interests, will ensure good government except under the occasional tyrant. His explicitly amoral reasoning brings him, remarkably enough, to a conception of law which accords closely with Western ideas of justice. The ruler should reward and punish, promote and dismiss, by comparing his subjects' deeds with his own commands and prohibitions as objectively as though he were weighing on a balance, without favouring or sparing even those closest to himself. It is a system which, although it left a deeper mark on Chinese institutions than could ever be officially acknowledged, offended the Confucians' conviction that duties are primarily to those connected with oneself by family, office, or friendship, as well as their dislike of using the harsh methods of law for anything which can be settled by custom and precedent. The Legalists are new also in sometimes, although not always, plainly acknowledging that their teaching is *not* that of the ancient sages. They have advanced from Chuang-tzu's general observation that times change to noticing connexions between social forms and social changes. Han Fei notes that a man can have five children and live to see twenty-five grandchildren, and that the moral appeals of the ancient sages, which may have been effective in a small community, no longer work with a large population competing for limited natural resources. The Legalist *Book of Lord Shang* distinguishes three phases of organization as population has increased, a primitive anarchy, growth of moral conventions to control increasing competition, and finally division of land and goods and separation of the sexes, requiring the development of government to ensure that each keeps his place.

The state of Ch'in, which patronized Legalism, completed the conquest of all other states and the reunification of China in 221 B.C. Under the Ch'in Dynasty and the succeeding Han (206 B.C.–A.D. 220) a new and stable social system consolidated itself, the old hunting and fighting aristocracy with hereditary fiefs giving way by degrees to a centralized bureaucracy, sedentary and bookish, recruited to an increasing extent by public examinations which in later centuries were gradually opened to almost the whole population. In spite of the practical success of Legalism its ruthless amorality made it unsuitable as a public ideology, and from the second century B.C. the Han Dynasty earned itself the blessing of the ancient sages by patronizing the Confucian school. Confucianism remained for two thousand years the official philosophy, adapting with remarkable success the old forms to new realities. The great creative period of Chinese thought was now over. Taoism was the only survivor among the rival schools, becoming, until it was overshadowed by Indian Buddhism, the favoured philosophy of those who preferred private to public life. For the next two thousand years nearly all new developments outside Buddhism occurred within these two schools, culminating in the neo-Taoism of the third and fourth centuries A.D. and the neo-Confucianism of the Sung Dynasty.

III

EARLY IMPERIAL CHINA:
221 B.C.–A.D. 220

YÜ-CH'ÜAN WANG

The Central Government of the Former Han Dynasty

The establishment of a centralized government was a landmark in Chinese history. The first empire was established in 221 B.C. by the Ch'in dynasty. Thenceforth, this basic government machinery, with some modifications, has functioned for two thousand years of Chinese history. Since the Ch'in dynasty was short-lived, lasting only about fifteen years (221 to 207 B.C.), students of Chinese history have always regarded the imperial government of the Former Han Dynasty (202 B.C.–A.D. 8) as the basic structure for study. The most comprehensive study in English on the Former Han government is by Dr. Yü-ch'üan Wang, who now resides in Peking.

The political institution is never a static object for study; it is always changing and developing. In this study, Professor Wang not only draws a clear, systematic picture of the organizational structure of the Former Han government, but also details the working of this machinery. He lucidly explains the political ideology behind such a governmental setup and examines its effectiveness as a means of political control.

1. Introduction

The governmental machinery which functioned through two thousand years of Chinese history and which was abandoned only in 1911 had its inception in 221 B.C., the year China was unified. Later developments modified many aspects of its organization but never changed the basic structure.

By 221 B.C. the First Emperor of the Ch'in dynasty had overthrown the reigning house of Chou and conquered the other feudal states, abolished feudal political institutions, and created a centralized government. The dynasty was short-lived. The radical social and political changes which the First Emperor enforced after his conquest caused considerable derangement and unrest. He made enemies of the old nobility of the conquered states by depriving them

From *Harvard Journal of Asiatic Studies*, 12 (1949), 134–87. Also reprinted in John L. Bishop, ed., *Studies of Governmental Institutions in Chinese History* (Harvard University Press, 1968). Reprinted by permission of Harvard-Yenching Institute and Harvard University Press. Footnotes omitted.

of their long-established privileges, and failed to make friends with the common people, on whose shoulders rested the main financial burden and the labor service needed for the consolidation of the empire. Widespread rebellions followed the death of the First Emperor in 210 B.C. and his dynasty was overthrown in 207 B.C. In 202 B.C. Liu Pang, the most successful of the rebel leaders, was enthroned. With him the Former Han dynasty was established, which lasted till 8 A.D.

The new dynasty reversed and substantially modified many of the important political institutions of Ch'in; it abandoned centralized control over the Empire and revived the political feudalism of the Chou dynasty. Almost two thirds of the Han territory was divided into *wang-kuo* or "kingdoms" which were bestowed upon the founder's brothers, sons, and meritorious assistants. Each kingdom had the same governmental setup as the domain of the Emperor and possessed full authority over the people within its boundaries. For many years the power of the central government of the Former Han was confined to the Imperial domain comprising modern Shensi, Shansi, Honan, Szechwan, Hupeh, and part of Kansu.

Liu Pang did not parcel out any part of this Imperial domain but controlled it through the administrative mechanism of Ch'in, run by a centralized autocratic bureaucracy. The period from 154 B.C. to 126 B.C. witnessed a struggle between the Imperial government and the semi-independent kingdoms. The outcome was that the Han Emperor was able to reduce the size of the kingdoms, abolish their political sovereignty, and establish central supervision over them. The victory of the Imperial government over the kingdoms enabled it to strengthen itself and to extend the scope of its administration. The power of the Imperial central government reached its zenith in the last quarter of the second century B.C. From the middle of the first century B.C. on, the central government of the Former Han gradually lost its grip over the empire. But this time its growing weakness was caused by social and economic forces of a different nature, which initiated a course of events which was to be repeated many times in the subsequent history of China.

The territory of the Han Empire was extensive, divided into *chün* "provinces" and *wang-kuo* "kingdoms," which, in turn, were subdivided into *hsien* "counties," *hsiang* "districts," and *li* (the smallest administrative unit). By the end of the second century B.C. it had expanded to cover the whole of present-day China proper (except for the extreme southwest), southern Manchuria, northern Korea, and Tonkin. Its population in 2 A.D. was recorded as 12,233,062 households or 59,594,978 individuals, probably with the omission of children below the age of seven. This spectacular growth was acclaimed by the author of the *Han shu* and must have dwarfed the Empire in its early days.

With an empire so extensive and a population so large, the administrative work was bound to be heavy, making administrative machinery imperative. By the end of the first century B.C., government offices, both local and central, were numerous, and the number of functionaries of the central and provincial governments ran as high as 130,285. The regular officials in the Chancellery numbered 382 in 117 B.C., when the dynasty was at the height of its power, and more than three hundred in the period from 15 to 7 B.C. If we add the clerks, who numbered as many as 282 in 117 B.C., the total of the employees in the chancellery that year was 644. The Imperial Secretariat employed 341 functionaries in 110 B.C.; including the clerks the total was well over 500.

Officialdom in the Empire was divided hierarchically into twenty ranks (reduced, after 32 B.C., to sixteen). Each individual was assigned a rank, which determined his status in the official world, his salary, the type of clothes he wore and carriage he used, the privileges accorded him—such as exemption from forced labor and from military service—and which served as a measure in promotion.

Rank was expressed by the official's annual salary in terms of so many *shih* or Chinese bushels, ranging from the ten-thousand-bushel to the one-hundred-bushel rank, the highest being held by the Chancellor, the lowest by the petty officials. Actually the number of *shih* marking the rank of an official did not always correspond to his salary, which was paid partly in grain and partly in cash. Nevertheless this system of rank provides us with a key to the arrangement of the Han bureaucracy.

2. The Emperor

At the head of the central government of Han stood the *Huang-ti* or "Emperor." His predecessor was the *wang* or "king" of the Chou dynasty, who claimed that his authority was of divine origin. The king of Chou shared with the princes, whom he enfeoffed, the responsibility of administering the realm. As the royal court of Chou entered its period of decline the princes usurped the title of "king" and made themselves independent rulers of their respective states. After defeating the royal house and the several feudal states and bringing the whole of the Chinese Empire under his control, the king of the state of Ch'in, later known as the First Emperor of the Ch'in dynasty, was so exuberant at his unprecedented achievement that he felt that the title "king" was no longer adequate to express his "power" and "virtue" (his "mana" or "charisma"), and created himself the title *Huang-ti,* thus elevating himself above previous rulers of "all-under-Heaven" and making himself "the Great King" and "the King of Kings."

With the creation of the title "Emperor" there was instituted for the first time in China a centralized Imperial government, which through its provincial and local administrative agencies directly controlled the whole empire. The local governments and the people looked to the central government for directives in all important political, military, or legal matters.

Such was the power wielded by the central government, which found its personification in the Emperor, since he was the final authority and the source of all laws. He was the head of the state, and so to speak, the state itself. As the Emperor possessed absolute power over state affairs and the people, the government of Ch'in was, to use a modern term, authoritarian in form. The rebellion which overthrew the Ch'in regime naturally brought about many changes in its authoritarian policies, but the administrative machinery was preserved.

Unlike the Emperor of Ch'in, the founder of Han, Liu Pang, came from a family of poor and lowly origin. He had no *shih-yeh* or "historical background" to rely upon and before his revolt against the Ch'in he was only a police chief patrolling a tiny part of a county.

The prevailing conception of the ruler of "all-under-Heaven" at the time was that he must be a man of noble origin, or a man ordained by Heaven, or a man of great wisdom and virtue. The first theory grew directly out of the historical fact that China had been ruled hitherto by the nobility of Chou. The second was an attribute upon which the Chou kings, like the kings of other lands, had based their claim to sovereign rights. The third was a product of the new social and economic changes which in politics found their expression in the Confucian theory of government by the sage and the wise and virtuous man. This last, however, may not have been as intelligible and convincing as the other two for the common people in third century B.C.

Liu Pang was not of noble birth, nor was he, to quote his own words, a man of wisdom and virtue. He was elevated to the throne by his followers and assistants for the following ostensible reasons: first, in overthrowing the Ch'in regime his contribution was considered the greatest; second, he had brought peace to the people, which was a great virtue; and third, he had unselfishly shared the land of the Empire with the various "feudal lords" who had assisted him. In addition, efforts were made to strengthen his claim to the throne by cloaking him with divine attributes.

All the rulers of China before Liu Pang were believed to have been of divine origin. In contemporary folklore even the unpopular house of Ch'in was said to have been descended from a White God. Similar claims were made by most of the founders of succeeding dynasties. The ancient Chinese believed that the benefactors of man should be worshipped, as, indeed, did the Greeks and the peoples of the eastern Mediterranean world of the Hellenistic age.

There are a number of myths which attributed divinity to Liu Pang. One story has it that his mother conceived him by a god in her dream, and at his birth a dragon was seen hovering over her. Another story tells that whenever he slept some strange phenomenon always appeared over his head. His wife told him that she always knew his whereabouts because there always was a cloud of a recognizable shape hovering above him in the sky. By his contemporaries he was regarded as the son of the Red God who battled against the son of the White God, that is, the ruler of Ch'in. When he entered the Han-ku Pass to take the Ch'in capital, five stars converged on the Tung-ching (Gemini) constellation. These different stories all had the one purpose of making Liu Pang appear to be superhuman.

However, the living Han ruler, like the rulers of other dynasties, was not regarded as a god, nor was any worship instituted for him. But it is reasonable to assume that the divine character attributed to Liu Pang must have played an important part in winning the people to his side or of awing them into submission. Unfortunately this did not work with his companions, who had been intimate with him through his campaign to win the throne and had become now ministers of the Han court. As can be easily observed from all histories, authority cannot be preserved and enhanced without the establishment and maintenance of social distance through ritual and conventions between the one who commands and those who obey. Therefore, it was necessary for the new ruler of "all-under-Heaven" to adopt a set of rigid court ceremonies to elevate himself to an unapproachable position. The ceremonies were introduced in 201 B.C. with the aid of a group of Confucian scholars. They greatly enhanced the prestige of the Emperor and saved the Emperor's dignity from being sullied by continued familiar intercourse with his former friends.

As a symbol of the ruling dynasty, the Emperor had his ancestral temples erected throughout the Empire. In 72 B.C. they numbered 168. As Emperor Yüan put it in 40 B.C.: "This was the best expedient by which power was established, subversive intentions eradicated, and the people unified."

Later, in the reign of Emperor Wu (140–

87 B.C.), the most outstanding philosopher of this time, Tung Chung-shu (179–104 B.C.), revived and expounded the theory that the Son of Heaven, i.e., the Emperor, must have received a Heavenly mandate to be ruler of "all-under-Heaven." In 110 B.C. Emperor Wu ascended Mount T'ai, the sacred mountain in present-day Shantung, and performed the ceremonies of *feng* and *shan*, the purpose of which was to report to Heaven that as recipients of the Heavenly mandate he and his ancestors had successfully carried out their mission of ruling the people on earth. The performance of these ceremonies put the Emperor in direct connection with Heaven and placed the final touch upon his divine character. The legitimacy was accorded to the position of the Emperor, to his person as well as to his authority, as being beyond the people and above the people.

These conscious efforts to make the Han Emperor superhuman may have played some part in legitimatizing his authority, but his actual power came directly from the military and political forces which he controlled. Supernatural theories and popular beliefs merely strengthened his position and contributed to its perpetuation.

Unlike the Pharaohs of Egypt and their Ptolemaic and Roman successors, the Great Kings of Persia and the Seleucids, the Han Emperor did not own the Chinese Empire as his private property. He possessed a few Imperial parks, but they were not for production of any kind. His other possessions were limited, as far as historical data tell us, to the products of the mountains and the seas. The income derived from these resources was separated from the government revenue from the Empire.

But the Han Emperor had two great resources which constituted the basis of his power. They were the taxes and the labor of the people. The most important of the taxes were the land tax, the poll tax on adults (*suan-fu*) and that on children (*k'ou-ch'ien*). In 119 B.C. taxes on merchants' property and on handicrafts were introduced, and in about 114 B.C. a tax on livestock was instituted. With the strengthening of the central government, the government monopoly of salt and iron began in 119 B.C. and that of coinage in 115 B.C. From the people who had reached adulthood the Emperor demanded one year's service for military training, one year for garrison duties, and annually one month of service at their home locality.

Out of the taxes he paid the administrative expenses and the salaries of his officials. Military service and forced labor enabled him to maintain an army, of which he was the commander-in-chief, and to carry out large-scale construction work, such as military fortifications, roads, canals, etc., which in one way or another helped to secure his control of the Empire.

In the matter of government personnel the Emperor appointed all officials from the six-hundred-bushel rank up in the central government and the Provincial Governors (*T'ai-shou*), the County Prefects (*Hsien-ling*) and the County Chiefs (*Hsien-chang*) in the local government. In so far as he was the only one who exercised control over all the offices of importance he was the source of all power, honor, and social privileges. This is all the more significant as formerly in China a position in the government meant not only political power but social prestige and wealth as well.

Furthermore the Emperor was the sole legislator. The Han law consisted of the code, the Imperial decrees, the precedents, and the decisions of the Commandment of Justice (*T'ing-wei*). The code was compiled by the Chancellor of State, Hsiao Ho (d.

193 B.C.). To it were later added the laws laid down by various ministers and sanctioned by the Emperors. The Imperial decrees were orders regarding specific matters. The precedents also had to be approved by the Emperor. Only the decisions of the Commandant of Justice did not emanate directly from the Emperor, but since he was appointed by the Emperor, his decisions could not contradict the Emperor's wishes.

In purely civil law cases the Emperor acted as the supreme judge. The lowest law court was the county (*hsien*) administration. Lawsuits which the County Prefect was unable to settle were sent to the Provincial Governor, who, in case of doubt, presented them to the Emperor.

With all these powers in his hands, the Han Emperor exacted absolute obedience from his subjects. To make this more convincing and his rule benign, contemporary political theorists maintained that the Emperor was a son in his relationship to Heaven and a father in that to his people. This interpretation not only explained his divine character in such simple terms that every person could easily understand it, but also enabled him to exact from the people a loyalty and reverence akin to that owed by a son to the *paterfamilias*. As father the Emperor should care for and govern, and as children the people had to respect and obey.

3. The Imperial Cabinet

As shown by the titles of the Imperial ministers (mentioned below) and their primary functions, the Imperial cabinet of the Former Han was the direct descendant of the court of the Chou kings. Its personnel was that of a large household. As China developed from a kingdom into an empire and the administrative work multiplied many times, the empire builders did not devise a new administratve organization, but retained the form of the old royal court and allocated new functions to the original offices.

The Chancellor

Both in the meaning of his title and in administrative duties connected with it, the *Ch'eng-hsiang*, rendered as "Chancellor" for the sake of convenience, was assistant to the Emperor. Next only to the sovereign in rank and power, he topped the entire official hierarchy.

At the beginning of the Han dynasty there was one Chancellor. From 196 to 180 B.C. there were two Chancellors—a Chancellor of the Right and a Chancellor of the Left, the former ranking above the other. From 179 B.C. on only one Chancellor was functioning, though for a while nominally both positions were kept. In 1 B.C. the title of *Ch'eng-hsiang* was changed to *Ta-ssu-t'u*.

In Chapter 19 of the *Han shu,* which treats of government organizations, the functions of the Chancellor are described in the following words: "He assists the Son of Heaven and helps him manage all important matters." Such a terse explanation is inadequate to convey an understanding of the duties and authority of the Chancellor. In order to obtain a fuller picture of his responsibilities, we have to turn to other sources of information. These are: (1) the biographies of the Chancellors in both the *Shih chi* and the *Han shu;* (2) the Imperial directives dismissing incompetent Chancellors; (3) the books on the Han government institutions written in the first and second centuries A.D.

In a directive to his Chancellor, Emperor Ai (6–1 B.C.) said, "The Chancellor is our arms and legs, the one with whom we, succeeding our Ancestors, rule all within the Seas." Confirming the words of the authors of the *Han shu,* Emperor Ai's statement defines the position of the Chancellor as that of an assistant to the throne.

In a directive to his Chancellor, Wang Shang, Emperor Ch'eng (32–7 B.C.) said, "The Chancellor with his virtue cares for the state, and takes charge of all the officials." Emperor Ai once said to his Chancellor, K'ung Kuang, "Sir, in your hands you bear the heavy burden of state affairs and take overall charge of the duties of all officials." Here the Chancellor is described as the head of the officialdom.

As assistant to the Emperor and head of all officials, the Chancellor enjoyed privileges and powers denied to other ministers. Every Chancellor was enfeoffed with a marquisate (*hou-kuo*) and bore the title of Marquis (*Hou*). He was entitled to recommend candidates for the most important positions in the central, as well as in the local governments. He could appoint officials from the six-hundred-bushel rank down without consulting the Emperor. However, inasmuch as he could recommend and appoint officials high and low, he was also held responsible for their conduct of administrative affairs. When the selection of officials was found unwise, the Chancellor naturally was the one to bear the brunt of the criticism. He kept a record of all important officials, particularly the provincial governors, checking upon them constantly. One of his subordinates, entitled *Ssu-chih* ("Director of Rectitude"), investigated the neglect of duties and improper behavior on the part of the officials. In case an official, even one ranking as high as or higher than Provincial Governor, was found to have abused his authority, the Chancellor might mete out punishment without first reporting to the Emperor.

The Chancellor was responsible for the finances of the state, and, in the words of Emperor Ch'eng (32–7 B.C.), had to estimate the amount of the revenue of the state and determine the budget of expenditures. For the same reason the Chancellor was held responsible for the grain supplies provided to the frontier garrisons. Although he was not the commander of the army, his position as assistant to the throne and head of the administration made him responsible for military preparations.

Throughout the Former Han dynasty, important political, military, and religious issues which concerned the Empire were generally transferred to the Court Conference for deliberation before the Emperor made his decision (see below, Court Conference). As head of the Imperial cabinet, the Chancellor seems to have presided at the meeting and directed the discussions, which he then summarized and reported to the throne. Even after 86 B.C., when state affairs were run by a regent, who also participated in the Court Conference, the Chancellor still retained his old honored position.

In addition, the Chancellor had the power to direct and supervise the provincial and, indirectly, also the county administration. As Emperor Ch'eng once said to K'ung Kuang, Chancellor from 36 to 30 B.C., a Chancellor "takes charge of the financial reports and knows the actual situation in the provinces." In his office were kept the registers of land and population, the maps of the empire, the provincial reports on harvests and banditry, and the financial accounts from the provinces. At the end of each year, which legally came at the end of the tenth month (about the end of November), every province sent a delegate to the court to present its annual reports, of which one copy went to the Imperial Secretariat and another to the office of the Chancellor. After looking through them the Chancellor graded the provincial administrators and made recommendations regarding the promotion or demotion of the Provincial Governors. Before the departure of the provincial delegates for their provinces the Chancellor gave administrative instructions to them, which were to be relayed to the Governors. Some of the lawsuits which could not be solved by the Governors were sent to the Chancellor for decision. When special administrative matters arose of which the settlement required a higher authority, he despatched his subordinates to the province. In case the Provincial Governor failed in suppressing outlaw bands, the Chancellor sent out one of his assistants to accomplish the task. All of these duties and powers were the logical result of the fact that the Chancellor was made responsible for the administration of the provinces.

The Imperial Secretary

Next to the Chancellor in position, as well as in power, was the *Yü-shih ta-fu* or Imperial Secretary. In 8 B.C. the title was changed to *Ta-ssu-k'ung*. Four years later the original title was restored. But in 1 B.C. the title of *Ta-ssu-k'ung* was again adopted. The change of title, however, was not accompanied by any change in the official duties associated with it.

Defining the functions of the Imperial Secretary, the author of the *Han shu* states, "He was an associate Chancellor." Therefore, he was also called the Vice-Chancellor, who "outside of the palace assists the Chancellor in the over-all direction of the administration of the empire." When important issues came up, the Chancellor discussed them with him. If they failed to agree, the Emperor was appealed to to make the final decision (though the Chancellor's opinion usually prevailed). Just because he and the Chancellor shared responsibilities in many cases, edicts concerning such matters were issued to both of them to be in turn communicated to the provinces. His office was sometimes regarded as almost as important as that of the Chancellor.

However, this fact should not lead to the belief that the Chancellor and the Imperial Secretary were two ministers for one office, possessing equal power. Chu Po, himself Imperial Secretary from 6 to 5 B.C., explained the functions of his office to Emperor Ai with these words: "The founder of Han set up the Imperial Secretary with a position next only to the Chancellor to take charge of the laws and to rectify their violations. Sharing duties with him [that is, the Chancellor], he maintains a general supervision over all of the officials and sees to it that the superior and the inferior check upon each other." This statement of Chu Po makes it clear that the Imperial Secretary was a Vice-Chancellor, not with regard to the civil administration, but only as far as the supervision of administrative personnel was concerned. His main function was to ascertain that no official neglected his duty or abused his authority. For this reason the Imperial Secretary was also called the *Tien-fa ta-ch'en* (Great Minister in Charge of the Laws). To be sure, these "laws" were not those that applied to the population in general, but specific ones which concerned the officialdom. For instance, it was the duty of the Imperial Secretary to stamp out venality among the officials and to see to it that no official abused his authority, and no Provincial Governor filed an inaccurate annual report on land, population, and taxes. For this reason his office, like the Chancellery, also kept a copy of the records of important officials.

As a Vice-Chancellor he also received the provincial delegates who came to present those reports and gave them instructions on their departure. However, his instructions differed from those of the Chancellor, for they were mostly concerned with disciplinary matters within the provincial administration.

He exercised disciplinary supervision not only over officials below him in rank, but also over the chief executive, the Chancellor. His authority was not merely confined to the inspection of officials in the government offices, but extended over the Emperor's personal attendants, through his subordinate, the *Yü-shih chung-ch'eng* (Palace Assistant to the Imperial Secretary), who had his office inside the Palace.

As the Emperor's secretary, he received and transmitted to the Chancellery, whence they were further despatched to the provinces and kingdoms, some of the Imperial edicts, especially those affecting affairs of the state, such as proclamation of laws, choice of heir apparent, and recommendation of candidates to official positions made by Provincial Governors. In that capacity, too, he presented to the Emperor memorials from the high ministers. Thus, the Imperial Secretary was not only a disciplinary supervisor but also an agent of transmission.

It is pertinent for further clarification of the functions of the Imperial Secretariat to say here a few words about the Palace Assistant of the Imperial Secretary. Like his superior, this official was in charge of disciplinary actions. This is clearly expressed in his original title which was the *Yü-shih chung-chih-fa* or Holder of the Law within the Palace. The difference between him and his superior is that his sphere of action was inside the Imperial Palace, which his superior could not enter except on official business.

Besides maintaining discipline among attendants and eunuchs in the Palace, the Palace Assistant of the Imperial Secretary was also in charge of maps, registers, and sacred books, and moreover, supervised the Attendant Secretaries (*Shih-yü-shih*), who kept a daily record of the Emperor's activities and were said also to be in charge of the execution of laws. Outside the Palace he controlled the Circuit Inspectors (*Pu-tz'u-shih*) whose duty it was to maintain a watch over the activities of the Provincial Governors and to impeach those governors who were found guilty of conduct contradictory to the interests of the people and the state. He received for the Emperor memorials presented by the ministers, and the edicts to the provinces also passed through his hand.

A very significant point in the organization of the Imperial Secretariat is that this ministry was actually made up of two offices, one outside of the palace and the other inside. The reason for this was chiefly that government functionaries were not permitted to stay in the Palace, so that a disciplinary minister had to be set up inside the Palace to supervise the Imperial attendants and the palace ladies. During the later part of the dynasty the Han Emperors distrusted their regular ministers, preferring those close to the Imperial person. The Palace Assistant of the Imperial Secretary, being close to the Emperor, gradually gained power and finally superseded the Imperial Secretary, his superior, thus becoming an independent minister with disciplinary and political powers.

Other Ranking Ministers

Students of government institutions during the Han period are familiar with the terms *San kung* (Three Lords) and *Chiu ch'ing* (Nine Ministers), which comprise all the ministers of importance in the central government. *Kung* was an honorific designation for the three highest officials, the Chancellor, the Imperial Secretary, and the *T'ai-wei* or Grand Commandant. The word *ch'ing* was applied in the same way to the nine ministers who ranked below the three *kung*, and whom we may call ranking ministers.

Before the discussion of the ranking ministers a word must be said about the Grand Commandant. As *Han shu* puts it, he was a minister "in charge of military affairs." And that was his function actually. In formalistic accounts of the Han central government he is always regarded as a regular member of the highest triumvirate of the Three Lords. Since his office was not a permanent one, but was set up whenever the need arose and eliminated when that need disappeared, and since it was finally done away with in 139 B.C., I find it proper not to treat this office as of equal importance with those of the Chancellor and the Imperial Secretary.

The nine ranking ministers were (1) the *T'ai-ch'ang* (Minister of Ceremonies), (2) the *Kuang-lu-hsün* (Supervisor of Attendants), (3) the *Wei-wei* (Commandant of Guards), (4) the *T'ai-p'u* (Grand Servant), (5) the *T'ing-wei* (Commandant of Justice), (6) the *Ta-hung-lu* (Grand Herald), (7) the *Tsung-cheng* (Director of the Imperial Clan), (8) the *Ta-ssu-nung* (Grand Minister of Agriculture), and (9) the *Shao-fu* (Small Treasurer).

Each of them held the rank of the full-two-thousand-bushel (*chung-erh-ch'ien-shih*), and maintained an office of considerable size, divided into various departments. They always participated in the deliberations of the Court Conferences regarding important issues concerned with the welfare of the Empire.

The Minister of Ceremonies is said to have been "in charge of the ceremonies in the Imperial ancestral temples" and "in charge of the worship of Heaven and Earth." He was thus described as a chief priest in the government. But actually his functions went far beyond that. For example, among his subordinates, each one of whom headed a different department, one was called the *T'ai-shih-ling* or Prefect of the Grand Clerks. He was in charge of astronomy, astrology, and the daily records of the Emperor's activities. Another entitled *T'ai-i-ling* took charge of the Imperial physicians.

When the candidates for offices, such as Men of Wisdom and Virtue (*Hsien-liang*) and Men of Letters (*Wen-hsüeh*), recommended by the Provincial Governors, arrived at the Court, the Minister of Ceremonies had to examine them by means of written tests, presenting the results to the Emperor, who then decided upon their appointment or rejection. Before the Master of Documents (*Shang-shu*) employed any clerks, the Grand Clerk, a subordinate of the Minister of Ceremonies, ascertained whether the candidates remembered the nine thousand characters required for such a position.

Most important of all the functions of the Minister of Ceremonies was the supervision he exercised over the Imperial Academy. Following the example of its predecessor, the Han set up a good number of Erudites (*Po-shih*) under the Minister of Ceremonies. They were learned men "who know thoroughly both the past and the present" and "are completely familiar with the institutions of the state," and capable of answering any question of the Emperor. They also took part in the Court Conference. Their number is given as "several tens" and more than seventy during the reign of Emperor Wen (179–157 B.C.). In 124 B.C. fifty students were placed under the instruction of these learned men; thus the *T'ai-hsüeh* (Imperial Academy) was established. The students were selected by either the Minister of Ceremonies himself or recommended to him by the provincial authorities. The minister was also responsible for their examination and reported their eligibility for office to the Emperor. The number of students was increased to one hundred by Emperor Chao (86–74 B.C.), to two hundred by Emperior Hsüan (73–49 B.C.), to one thousand by Emperor Yüan (48–33 B.C.), and even for a time to three thousand during the reign of Emperor Ch'eng (32–7 B.C.). In so far as he supervised the Imperial Academy the Minister of Ceremonies performed the same duties as a Minister of Education in the present Chinese government.

The Supervisor of Attendants was in charge of the *Lang* or Court Gentlemen, who had the duty of guarding the doors of the palaces and halls. The important point is that these Court Gentlemen were not simply guards, but were at the same time candidates for office. They consisted of sons and brothers of officials ranking from the two-thousand-bushel up, men of filial piety and honesty recommended by the Provincial Governors, graduates of the Imperial Academy, men of great wealth, men of special ability, men who had presented an important memorial, and for a time men who made financial contributions to the government. As the Emperor's attendants, some of them were able to maneuver themselves to such a favorable position that their advice was sought in political matters. Every year these Gentlemen were examined and rated by the Supervisor according to their possession of four qualities—simplicity, generosity, modesty, and virtue—and according to their merits they were recommended for offices.

Under the Supervisor of Attendants there were also the Grandee Attendants (*Kuang-lu ta-fu*), who stayed inside the Palace and served as the Emperor's advisors, and the group of Grandees within the Palace who waited upon the Emperor in a similar capacity. Of the latter group the Grandee Remonstrants (*Chien-ta-fu*) admonished the sovereign, and the Internuncios *(Yeh-che)* frequently served as his envoys. When the Ch'i-men Guard (in 138 B.C.) and the Yü-lin Guard were established (ca. 104 B.C.), it was the Supervisor of Attendants who took charge of them.

The Commandant of Guards was "in charge of the garrison soldiers at the gate of the palaces," that is, he was the chief of the Imperial Guards. These guards were adults drafted from among the people, who were required to serve in this capacity for one year. The Imperial Guards numbered twenty thousand before 140 B.C. and were reduced to ten thousand in that year.

The Grand Servant was "in charge of [the Emperor's] chariots and horses." The type of chariots, their number, and number of horses, and the number of the accompanying chariots were all prescribed according to the occasion. It was also his responsibility to see to it that the arrangement was properly carried out. Probably the most important part of his duty, however, was to supervise the government pastures and the horses raised there. After the middle of the second century B.C. one large-scale expedition after another was launched against the Hsiung-nu barbarians in the north, and a great need for horses was felt. According to the *Han-kuan chiu-i* the Han government maintained thirty-six pastures in its northern and western border regions where three hundred thousand horses were kept. Although there might have been reductions in later years, the number of horses still must have been large.

The Commandant of Justice was "in charge of the laws of the state." He accepted and decided all the lawsuits that the Provincial Governors failed to dispose of. The cases which the Commandant of Justice was unable to decide he reported to the Emperor, giving the relevant details and the appropriate articles of the law code that might possibly apply to them. In Han times there was a law code called the Law of the Commandant of Justice. This may have been a compilation of the decisions made by this minister. Moreover, he is said also to have been in charge of the military law. It will have become apparent that there is a duplication in the functions of the Chancellor and of the Commandant of Justice with regard to the execution of justice. This multiplication of legal authorities is a result of the fact that in China in the past all administrative organs possessed judcial powers. We are not clear as to the exact legal procedure in Han times, or which category of lawsuits was handled by which of the aforementioned functionaries.

The Grand Herald is reported to have been a minister "in charge of the barbarians who had returned to righteousness" (that is, offered their submission). This is confirmed by the fact that one of his subordinates was entitled the "Interpreting Official" (*I-kuan*). But historical records show that the functions of the Grand Herald were not so limited. He was a director of ritual when sacrifices were offered to Heaven and at the Imperial ancestral temples, and also was master of ceremonies at the reception of guests by the Emperor. Moreover, the affairs concerning the marquises (enfeoffed meritorious officials) were left in his hands.

As indicated by his title, the Director of the Imperial Clan was in charge of members of the Imperial house. He kept a record of them and received the registers of Imperial relatives prepared and handed up by the provincial authorities.

The last two of the Nine Ministers were officials in charge of finances. The Grand Minister of Agriculture was in charge of the state revenue and disbursement, and the Small Treasurer was manager of the private finances of the Imperial house. The poll taxes on adults, the land tax, the commutation of labor service into cash payment, the profits from the government monopoly of iron and salt, and the income from public land and the profit from the government sale of wine all went to the treasury of the state; while the taxes on mountains, seas, and lakes, which were regarded as the Emperor's property, went to the Palace treasury. The Grand Minister of Agriculture disbursed the expenditures of the government, such as salaries for officials and supplies for the army, while the Small Treasurer provided the necessities for the Imperial household. Thus, in their fiscal administration the government and the Imperial house were formally separated.

In the hands of the Grand Minister of Agriculture rested the administration of government monopolies from the production and sale of iron and salt and the sale of wine. Apart from the economic importance of these sources of revenue they had many political implications. When the government established the Office of Tax Substitutes (*Chün-shu*), which required the taxpayers to offer special local products needed by the government instead of cash or grain, the administration of that office was entrusted to the Grand Minister of Agriculture. When the Office for Equalization (*P'ing-chun*) was instituted to standardize prices by selling commodities in the possession of the state, it was also this minister who directed its work. Besides, he also took direct charge of the granaries in both the capital and the provinces.

The Small Treasurer was rather an official in the personal service of the Emperor. Therefore, among his subordinates are found the Masters of Documents (*Shang-shu*), the Prefect of Tallies and Staffs of Authority (*Fu-chieh-ling*), and the eunuchs. By the end of the dynasty, when the Emperor had more confidence in officials close to his person, the Prefect of the Masters of Documents (*Shang-shu-ling*) attained to a position which superseded that of the Chancellor, and the eunuchs for a while controlled the Empire, a situation which will be discussed in a later section.

4. The Colonel of Censure and the Circuit Inspectors

There are still to be discussed two more types of officials, who, without belonging directly to the body of the central government, yet played a rather important role in assuring the efficacy of the central administration. They were the *Ssu-li hsiao-wei* (Colonel of Censure) and the *Pu-tz'u-shih* (Circuit Inspectors). The nature of their functions was solely disciplinary.

As pointed out in the Introduction, the central government of Han was a large administrative organization. Discipline was maintained by the Imperial Secretary together with his subordinates, and also by the Director of Rectitude functioning under the Chancellor. But both the Imperial Secretary and the Director of Rectitude were officials belonging to the cabinet outside of the Palace—in other words, not close to the Emperor. The office of the Colonel of Censure was instituted to remedy this situation.

A literal rendering of the title *Ssu-li hsiao-wei* should be Colonel Director of Convict-Laborers, *Hsiao-wei* being a military title for an officer ranking below the General (*Chiang-chün*). According to Cheng Hsüan (127–200 A.D.), there had previously been an official called the *Ssu-li*, or Director of Convict-Laborers, whose duty it was "to command the convict-laborers to construct roads and canals." We do not know with certainty whether he also bore the title *Hsiao-wei*; probably he did not. In 91 B.C. there was a large-scale witch hunt in the Empire which caused thousands to be put to death. Inside the Palace many persons were investigated. Even the Heir Apparent was accused of having practised witchcraft against the life of his father, Emperor Wu (140–87 B.C.), an accusation which led to the armed revolt of the Heir Apparent. Defeated, he committed suicide, and a number of the ministers and officials who had sided and sympathized with him fell into disgrace. The Director of Convict-Laborers, the *Ssu-li*, was then promoted and given unusual powers. Carrying the staff of authority and commanding twelve hundred convict-laborers, he was empowered "to seize practitioners of witchcraft and investigate important treacherous elements." His power was extensive. The statement of Wei Hung (fl. [flourished] 25–27) that "no one from the Heir Apparent and the Three Lords (e.g., Chancellor, Imperial Secretary, and Grand Commandant) down was outside his control" is no exaggeration, for Chüan Hsün, Colonel of Censure in 20–19 B.C., speaks of his functions in a memorial as "carrying the Imperial mandate to inspect and investigate all persons from the *kung* and the *ch'ing* (officials holding the rank of the full-two-thousand-bushel) down." He was "mandated minister of the Son of Heaven" to whom even the Chancellor could not give orders. The *Han shu* contains a number of stories which substantiate the statements quoted above.

In 45 B.C. the Colonel of Censure was deprived of the staff of authority. In 9 B.C. his office was abolished altogether. In 7 B.C. the office was re-established, but the title of the holder of the office was reduced to *Ssu-li* without *Hsiao-wei* (Colonel). Depriving him of the staff of authority had limited his power merely to inspecting, investigating, and impeaching.

In many respects the functions of the Colonel of Censure duplicated those of the Chancellor and the Imperial Secretary in exercising a disciplinary supervision over the entire officialdom. But the difference lies in their relation to the Emperor and subsequently in the manner, either direct or indirect, in which the Emperor through them exercised control over the bureaucracy. The Chancellor and the Imperial Secretary were not his personal men and frequently acted against his wishes; while the Colonel of Censure, specially commissioned by the Emperor, was his personal man, receiving orders from him and being responsible to him alone. The Imperial staff of authority which he carried on his missions was the symbol of his power to arrest and punish criminals on the spot just as the Emperor could himself. The establishment of the office of the Colonel of Censure meant a partial transfer of the power of disciplinary supervision over the administrative machine from a regular government setup to the Emperor himself; it also meant the concentration of that power in the hands of the latter.

The control of Provincial Governors through disciplinary officials was a practice of the Ch'in dynasty which the Han inherited and developed. At the beginning of the dynasty certain subordinates of the Imperial Secretary, known as the *Chien-yü-shih,* or the Imperial Secretaries of Inspection, were sent out to check on the Provincial Governors. In the tenth month of every year they went to the Imperial capital to make their reports, and in the twelfth month they returned to their respective provinces. In 167 B.C. some of the Secretaries of Inspection were found delinquent in their duties. As a remedy Clerks (*Shih*) of the Chancellors were sent out to inspect the provincial administration and supervise the Secretaries of Inspection. In 106 B.C. the Empire, except for the areas around the Imperial capital, was divided into thirteen *pu* (circuits). In each of these a disciplinary official was installed with the title of *Pu-tz'u-shih,* or Circuit Inspector. The old system of Secretaries of Inspection was abolished. These new Circuit Inspectors were, according to the *Han shu,* "to investigate the *chou* (divisions, another name for the circuit) in accordance with the items specified in an edict." According to Ts'ai Chih (2nd cent. A.D.) the items consisted of the following:

1. "Whether the land and houses of powerful clans and of magnates have overstepped the regulations, whether these people have made use of their power to oppress the weak, or, relying on their greater number have tyrannized over the few;
2. "Whether the two-thousand-bushels (i.e. Provincial Governors) have failed to observe the Imperial edicts or failed to obey the statutes of the state; whether they have turned their backs on the interests of the state and have

pursued their private interests; or whether they have put aside the Imperial edicts in order to keep their profits; whether they have exploited the people by illegal exactions;

3. "Whether the two-thousand-bushels have failed to give careful attention to doubtful law cases, or have put people to death cruelly; whether they have recklessly resorted to punishment when in anger, or whether they have granted rewards lavishly when in a happy mood; whether they have been so troublesome and tyrannical as to skin the people or cut them into pieces, and are so hated by the people that mountains collapse, rocks crack, strange signs appear, and rumors arise;

4. "Whether the two-thousand-bushels have been unfair in selecting officials, favoring those they like, concealing [from the Emperor] those who are worthy, and tolerating those who are stupid;

5. "Whether the sons and brothers of a two-thousand-bushel, relying upon his prestige and power, have demanded favors from those under his supervision;

6. "Whether the two-thousand-bushels have acted contrary to the public interest and formed factions together with their inferiors, attaching themselves to powerful individuals, accepting bribes, thus invalidating the government ordinances."

One interesting point in connection with the Circuit Inspectorate deserves to be emphasized here. The Circuit Inspectors were under the supervision of the Palace Assistant of the Imperial Secretary, who though a subordinate of the Imperial Secretary was also, by virtue of the location of his office inside the Palace, an official close to the throne. The fact that the direction of these inspectors was not entrusted to the Imperial Secretary or the Chancellor indicates that the Emperor—at least Emperor Wu, who introduced the new system—desired to keep the control of provincial administrators in his own hands.

Another point to be noted is that the Circuit Inspectors inspected the kingdoms as well as the provinces, a right which their predecessors did not possess. As has been stated before, the kingdoms were provinces which had been bestowed upon sons of the Emperor as their fiefs. Before 154 B.C. a king had full authority over the kingdom and over the population living within it. After 154 B.C. the central government forced the kings to forfeit their original rights as a result of the movement of centralization of the Imperial power. The establishment of the Circuit Inspectorate signified not only concentration of disciplinary supervision over the provincial administration in the hands of the Emperor, but also an extension of the supervision over the kingdoms.

It is generally true that any autocratic government, if it is to have its will prevail, must have an efficient supervisory machinery over the local administration. In fact, the power which such a government wields can be judged from the degree of the direct supervision that it can exert over its local agencies. The functions of the Han Circuit Inspector were performed also by the Procurator in the Roman Empire. Though a financial official, the Procurator held an independent mandate from the Roman Emperor and served as a check upon the Legate in an Imperial province and upon the Proconsul in a senatorial province. To check upon the administration of his provincial governors the French king established the *intendant des provinces*. The Roman Procurator was an institution of the Principate, the French Intendant was a creation of the French absolute monarchy, and the Han Circuit Inspector was set up in the days of the greatest centralization in the history of the Han dynasty. The similarity between these phenomena is not accidental.

5. The Emperor and His Cabinet

From all ministerial positions except one, namely that of the Director of the Imperial Clan, the members of the Imperial House were barred. The reason was that the Emperor wanted no person in a privileged position to possess political power, as this might become detrimental to the interests of the throne. But were the commoners who occupied ministerial positions always subservient to the Emperor's wishes? This question leads us to the investigation of the relations between the sovereign and his ministers.

It is true that, formally speaking, the Emperor's word was law and that his authority was unquestioned. But in reality his power also had its limits, as authoritarian power has under any form of autocratic rule. First of all there were the law code, the earlier Imperial orders, the precedents, and the customs, all of which the sovereign was expected to observe, and which constituted obstacles for free action on his part. But the greatest obstacle was the very Imperial Cabinet which he established. The reason is of a practical nature.

Certainly the Emperor possessed absolute power, but this power could be exercised only through the government organ, his cabinet; for no ruler was so familiar with the administrative work and possessed such skill as to enable him to run the government single-handed. Power that is not effective is nominal only. Yet not all the Han Emperors were content to be mere figureheads. Thus the Emperor came to feel jealousy and suspicion with regard to the leading cabinet members who happened to be at variance with him on certain matters. The greater the lust for power and the will to rule in the occupant of the throne, the more serious the conflict became. Emperor Kao, the founder of the Han dynasty, suspected the loyalty of his ablest general, Han Hsin, who was deposed, deprived of his military command, and finally met his death in 196 B.C. Similarly some of his other generals revolted because they resented the jealousy and suspicions of their lord. Out on a punitive expedition against one of his revolting generals in 196 B.C., Emperor Kao conceived doubts of his Chancellor of State, Hsiao Ho, and sent men back to the capital to spy on the activities of the latter. The second able ruler of Han, Emperor Wu, was even more distrustful of his ministers. He deposed and caused the death of no less than five of his Chancellors, sometimes because of suspicion and sometimes on the slightest indication of independent action on their part. Chancellor Li Ts'ai (121–118 B.C.) committed suicide after he was charged with embezzling government land. Chancellor Yen Ch'ing-ti (118–115 B.C.) ended his own life in jail after his chief subordinates had been put to death for their political intrigues. Chancellor Chao Chou (115–112 B.C.) was found guilty of accepting from marquises tribute gold which was deficient in weight; he was thrown into jail, where he committed suicide. Chancellor Kung-sun Ho (103–91 B.C.) died in jail, where he was confined on the charge that he had had sexual relations with Emperor Wu's daughter and had practiced witchcraft against the Emperor's life. Chancellor Liu Ch'ü-li (91–90 B.C.) was punished by having his body cut in two after he was accused of the intention of setting up the King of Ch'ang-i, the Emperor's youngest son, as successor to the throne in the event of his father's demise. Incidents of a similar nature also occurred under other Emperors. Chancellor Wang Chia (4–2 B.C.) even went so far as to return to the Emperor an Imperial edict which he considered improper, an action which by no means could please the absolute ruler. There were cases in which the Emperor was guilty of irresponsible treatment of his subordinates. However, it is not necessary to decide here who was right and who was wrong; I am interested only in pointing out that incidents like those mentioned above were symptomatic of the strained relations between the Chancellors and the Emperor, and increased on the one hand the ruler's distrust of his ministers and on the other the desire on the part of the ministers to seize administrative power in their own hands.

It is needless to say that in the history of Han there were also Emperors and Chancellors who co-operated harmoniously and whose relations were not hostile. This was especially the case when the Emperor was powerless, or the Chancellor subservient in character. The conflict between the Emperor and Chancellor serves to indicate the relations between the Emperor and his other ranking ministers, though here the antagonism was not so pronounced.

On the side of the ministers there were also attempts to restrict the Emperor's power and to reduce him to a mere figurehead. From 194 B.C. to 141 B.C. the empire was ruled by sons and grandsons of the founder of the dynasty with the latter's assistants and friends as their chief ministers. The old ministers treated the rulers as a man's trusted friends treat his children. All that was demanded of the Emperors was respect, and of the ministers devotion. The Emperors of this period did not show much initiative as expressed in political decisions.

From 140 B.C. on, the old type of minister began to be displaced by Confucian scholars. Naturally with their rise to power the political doctrines of Confucianism came to prevail. With regard to kingship (or emperorship) Confucian principles emphasize two points: (1) The ideal ruler of mankind is not a practical administrator but a perfect moral leader who sets himself up as a model for the people to follow; (2) Such a ruler should select "wise and virtuous men" and entrust them with state affairs. This Platonic theory of government is ably expounded by the outstanding scholar and statesman, Tung Chung-shu, in his book entitled *Ch'un-ch'in fan-lu*. When this theory prevails, according to Tung Chung-shu, "the ruler of mankind makes non-action his principle and regards unselfishness as a treasure. If he maintains the position in which he remains non-active and makes use of an officialdom perfect in every respect, the usher will show him the way, without his having to move his own feet; the reception attendant will extend to the guest the speeches in the latter's honor, without his having to open his own mouth; and the ministers will rightly perform their duties [in administering the empire], without his having to think about it himself. Consequently, no one will have seen the ruler do anything; but a successful administration will have been achieved."

How much influence this theory ever actually did exert on Han politics is hard to judge. But its validity has never been questioned either by the rulers or by court ministers.

Besides this doctrine of government by wise and virtuous men, Tung Chung-shu developed another theory which had a much stronger bearing on Han politics. It is the doctrine of the relationship between Heaven and man, or "the mutual response between Heaven and man." In essence it asserts that since Heaven possesses consciousness it never fails to react to the happenings on earth, particularly to the activities of the ruler. Evil done by a ruler finds its reflection in natural phenomena. Thus any anomalous happenings in nature, such as eclipses of the sun or the moon, and any calamities, such as floods, droughts, earthquakes, locusts, were construed as signs of warnings by Heaven toward the misbehavior or misgovernment of the ruler of man. So declared not only Tung Chung-shu and other Confucian ministers at the court, but also the Emperors who were apparently convinced of the validity of the doctrine. Such events frightened the Emperor so much that he would avoid appearing in the main hall of the palace, retire to his inner apartments to ponder over his faults, and issue edicts asking his ministers to discuss frankly whatever mistakes he might have committed and to cast around for appropriate remedies. The significance of the anomalies or calamities of nature was generally interpreted to criticize his conduct or his policy. To the student of history two thousand years later the "theory of calamities and anomalies" appears as if it were a well-conceived device to check the will of the ruler.

Sometimes the Emperor would end his penitence with an open discussion of his faults by his ministers. He even issued edicts commanding his ministers at court and the Provincial Governors to recommend "men of wisdom and virtue and of an upright character" or "men who will speak straightforwardly and admonish unreservedly" so that the people's grievances might be exposed and his own administration criticized.

Out of this theory that a ruler's misbehavior brings about the misfortune of the people there naturally arose the political doctrine that the welfare of the Empire depends upon the proper conduct of the Emperor. To quote Tung Chung-shu: "Therefore the master of men must right himself in order to right the court; right the court in order to right the hundred (i.e., all) officials; right the hundred officials in order to right the ten thousand (i.e., all) people." When all are righted "the principles of the *yin* and the *yang* will be in harmony, and wind and rain will arrive at the desired time." There will be no more anomalies, no more calamities. As far as can be deduced from this premise, an Emperor's main duty is to cultivate his character and rectify his behavior so as to make himself a perfect man. This gave the ministers and the people an opportunity to criticize not only the administration, but also the personal conduct of the Emperor; and they did so.

As for the political significance of the "theory of anomalies and calamities" one has only to read some of the memorials to the throne and answers to the Emperor's queries to realize its extent. In 12 B.C. anomalies and calamities were reported to have occurred more frequently than ever. Emperor Ch'eng sent for Ku Yung's opinion at the time when the latter was about to take up the position of Provincial Governor of a province on the northwestern frontier. This man boldly began his reply with the remark that "the empire is an empire of all the people of the empire; it is not an empire of one man," and he concluded, "One can do good things working with a superior ruler and cannot do bad things with him. One can do bad things working with an inferior ruler and cannot do good things with him." Naturally the actions he suggested in order to counteract the anomalies were all "good things." It was in the hands of Emperor Ch'eng whether he was to be a superior or an inferior ruler. Far from being offended by these remarks from a Provincial Governor, Emperor Ch'eng is said to have been "greatly touched by his words."

The "theory of anomalies and calamities"

alone seems to have served the Han ministers as a handy and efficacious weapon to remedy many a worthless policy, to keep the Emperor's power in check, and to strengthen the body of bureaucrats against an absolute ruler.

6. The Transfer of Administrative Power from the Outer Court (Cabinet) to the Inner Court

After learning about the conflicts between the Han Emperors and their ministers, particularly when a strong personality like Emperor Wu was involved, one would suspect that a change in the government structure was inevitable, and this change came at the end of Emperor Wu's reign, by his creation of a regency which was to become a semi-permanent institution.

The regency was held by a general, such as the *Ta-chiang-chün* (Grand General), the *Tso-chiang-chün* (General of the Left), the *Chü-ch'i chiang-chün* (General of the Chariot and Mount), or the *Wei-chiang-chün* (General of Protection). As a special honor the general holding the regency was invariably granted the title of *Ta-ssu-ma* or Grand Minister of Mount, in addition to the other title. Thus, the Grand General who was regent was called *Ta-ssu-ma-ta-chiang-chün*, and so on. Differing from ordinary generals a regent-general was no longer a purely military officer; he was primarily a political figure. While the regular general maintained only temperory headquarters at his camp, a regent-general had a permanent office with a large staff.

Subordinate only to the Emperor, the nominal head of the state, the regent possessed unlimited powers—although in the official hierarchy his position ranked below that of the Chancellor. The reason was that the Chancellor, however limited his power during the period of the regency, was still the head of the Imperial cabinet, while the regent was merely a personal official of the Emperor.

When an autocratic ruler distrusts his ministers and fears competition in power, the men who can most easily win his confidence are usually his loyal attendants of low or alien origin and his relatives by marriage. These men count no noble personage in their family tree, depend on no wide social and political affiliation for their ascendancy, and can boast of no literary learning for their employment; they attain to power purely through their master's favor, which they always must depend upon and in return they must demonstrate ceaseless devotion. In the history of the Roman Empire the Imperial freedmen, the Germanic generals, and the eunuchs wielded great powers. Analogies can be found in China, in the past as in the present. It is of great interest that we find the two men who held the first regency in the history of Imperial China were Ho Kuang (d. 68 B.C.) and Chin Mi-ti (134–86 B.C.).

Ho Kuang was from a poor and common family and was able to enter Emperor Wu's personal service only through his stepsister, who was born of the same mother as Empress Wei, wife of Emperor Wu. He had been in the Palace and served Emperor Wu for over twenty years before he was made the Grand Minister of Mount–Grand General in 87 B.C. and entrusted by the Emperor with the regency on behalf of his eight-year-old son. Ho Kuang owed his position to his loyal service and to the confidence which Emperor Wu placed in him.

Chin Mi-ti was the co-regent commissioned to assist Ho Kuang. He was the son of Prince Hsiu-ch'u of the Hsiung-nu. Captured in 121 B.C. he became a slave attached to the Palace. He won Emperor Wu's confidence by taking captive a would-be assassin and by his devoted service in the Palace. As the second regent his title was Grand-Minister of Mount–General of Chariot and Mount.

The third regent was Chang An-shih, an old minister at the court who had played a part in the enthronement of Emperor Hsüan in 74 B.C. under the direction of Ho Kuang. Immediately after the regent, Ho Kuang, died in 68 B.C., he was promoted to the post of Grand Minister of Mount–General of Chariot and Mount, in which capacity he was charged with supervising the affairs of the office of the Masters of Documents. He held this position from 68 to 62 B.C.

After Chang An-shih the regency was mostly in the hands of Imperial relatives-in-law, as shown in the table below.

The creation of the regency produced the following significant results: First, the Chancellor and the Imperial Secretary were both relegated to the post of mere administrators and lost their power to influence decisions regarding major state affairs. Second, replacing the Chancellor, an official close to the Emperor was now at the helm of the state. Third, the Imperial Cabinet, or the Outer Court (*Wai-t'ing*) as it was also called, was replaced by the Inner Court (*Nei-t'ing*), and the government was transferred into the Palace.

Another change relevant to the transfer of administrative power from regular cabinet members to officials close to the Emperor was the promotion of the Masters of Documents and the eunuchs, a phenomenon interestingly analogous to the employment and the empowering of the freedmen by the early Roman Emperors.

The Masters of Documents were originally lesser officials attached to the office of the Small Treasurer, the bursar of the Imperial household. They were sent into the Palace to take charge of preparing and keeping state documents. During the time of Emperor Wu their duties were extended to the receiving of memorials presented by officials. Because they worked inside the Palace and were active in preparing the decrees and rescripts, the Emperor frequently consulted them on political issues. As a result of this the Masters of Documents gradually gained political impor-

Name	Duration	Relation to the Imperial House
1. HAN Tseng	61–56 B.C.	Unknown
2. HSÜ Yen-shou	56–53	Brother to the Empress of Emperor Hsüan (73–49 B.C.)
3. SHIH Kao	49–43	Emperor Hsüan's first cousin, once removed
4. WANG Chieh	43–41	Unknown
5. HSÜ Chia	41	Father of the Empress of Emperor Ch'eng (32–9 B.C.)
6. WANG Feng	33–22	Emperor Ch'eng's maternal uncle
7. WANG Yin	22–15	Emperor Ch'eng's maternal uncle
8. WANG Shang	15–13	Emperor Ch'eng's maternal uncle
9. WANG Ken	13–8	Emperor Ch'eng's maternal uncle
10. WANG Mang	8	Emperor Ch'eng's cousin
11. SHIH Tan	7	Unknown
12. FU Hsi	6	Maternal granduncle of Emperor Ai (6–1 B.C.)
13. TING Ming	5–2	Emperor Ai's maternal uncle
14. WANG Mang	A.D. 1–8	See 10

tance. When a high minister, such as the Chancellor, was found abusing his authority, the Prefect of the Masters of Documents was sent to question him. When the post of the Imperial Secretary was vacated, the Prefect of the Masters of Documents had to examine the records of the Ministers ranking at the two-thousand-bushels level and determine which one should fill the vacancy.

In the office of the Masters of Documents there was also kept a list of the meritorious officials in the provincial government for purposes of promotion. When a Circuit Inspector came to the Imperial capital to make reports on the administration of the provinces under his jurisdiction, he for some reason had to see the Prefect of the Masters of Documents.

Such were the powers of the Office of the Masters of Documents. Therefore, Hsiao Wang-chih, General of the Front (*Ch'ien chiang-chün*), said about 46 B.C., "The Office of the Masters of Documents is the foundation of all offices. It is the key organ of the state." It superseded the Chancellery and the Imperial Secretariat and brought them under its control (see below). Just because the office of the Masters of Documents had become extremely important in the latter part of the Han period, the regents were invariably granted the authority of supervising the affairs of this office. Any trusted minister upon whom the Emperor wanted to rely was also allowed this privilege.

According to both the *Han chiu i* and the *Han kuan i*, before 29 B.C. there were four departments in the office of the Masters of Documents. They were:

1. the *Ch'ang-shih-ts'ao*, or Department of Regular Attendance, charged with the affairs of the Chancellery and the Imperial Secretariat;
2. the *Erh-ch'ien-shih-ts'ao*, or Department of Two-thousand-bushels, in charge of the affairs concerning the Circuit Inspectors and the Two-thousand-bushels (Provincial Governors);
3. the *Hu-ts'ao*, or Department of Civil Affairs, in charge of affairs concerning the presentation of memorials by the people;
4. the *K'o-ts'ao*, or Department of Guests, in charge of foreign affairs.

In 29 B.C. Emperor Ch'eng added one more department:

5. the *San-kung-ts'ao*, or Department of the Three Lords, in charge of justice.

The organization of the office of the Masters of Documents clearly shows that it was in itself a complete governmental setup, superseding the regular organization. The Chancellor remained the chief executive of the regular government, and the director of the super-government was the Prefect of the Masters of Documents.

Another group which gained prominence was the eunuchs. These were attendants waiting upon the Emperor and upon other members of his family inside the Palace. Their service was menial, but they could follow the Emperor to places from which ordinary attendants were barred. This proximity to the source of authority offered them unusual advantages as was also the case of their counterparts in the later Roman Empire.

Emperor Wu first used eunuchs to transmit documents. As he liked to enjoy himself in the inner palace, he made some of the eunuchs Palace Masters of Documents (*Chung-shang-shu* or *Chung-shu*), putting them in charge of transferring documents addressed to the throne into the inner palace. These Palace Masters of Documents presumably were headed by a Prefect of the Palace Masters of Documents (*Chung-shu-ling*) as they were in later days. Eunuch officials served in this capacity through the reign of Emperor Chao (86–74 B.C.) and the greater part of the reign of Emperor Hsüan (73–49 B.C.), but they were entrusted with no political powers. In the later part of Emperor Hsüan's reign Hung Kung, a eunuch, was made the Prefect of the Palace Masters of Documents. He is reported to have been well versed in laws, decrees, and institutional precedents, as well as skilled in making useful suggestions, and consequently quite competent in fulfilling his duties. We learn from his story that at least in the second half of the first century B.C. the Prefect of the Palace Masters of Documents had expanded his field of activities to politics. When Hung Kung died in 47 B.C., Shih Hsien, another able eunuch, stepped into his place. Being fond of music and at the same time in poor health, Emperor Yüan failed to attend to political matters, leaving them to Shih Hsien to dispose of. As a consequence, "all matters, big or small, were reported to the throne for decision by Shih Hsien. The esteem and favor [in which the Emperor held him] swayed the whole court. All the officials served [Shih] Hsien respectfully." A eunuch official had become the actual head of the government, and his office had become the "key office" at the Court. In fact, he was so powerful that Hsiao Wang-chih, the former Grand Guardian (*T'ai-fu*) of Emperor Yüan and now the General of the Front supervising the affairs of the Masters of Documents, was outmaneuvered by Shih Hsien, and in the struggle with him Hsiao Wang-chih was compelled to take his own life.

The acquisition of political power by officials close to the Emperor, whether they were the Masters of Documents or eunuch attendants, could mean only one thing: the concentration of power in the Palace or the transfer of power to a faction inside the Palace.

However, a difference between the Masters of Documents and the eunuch attendants should be noted. As far as can be proved from historical data, the Master of Documents owed his ascendancy primarily to his close relations with the throne and his function of handling state documents, while the rise to power of the eunuchs implied more personal and political factors. The reason for Shih Hsien's advancement to a prominent position, as related in the *Han shu,* is that "being a eunuch he was associated with no faction outside the palace, and consequently was devoted to the Emperor and trustworthy." However, as soon as Shih Hsien acquired power, he not only associated himself with an outside faction, but also tried to form a large clique of his own. The significant thing is that, even after Shih Hsien had built up such a clique, Emperor Yüan seems still to have harbored no doubts regarding his reliability. Therefore, a minister's partisan activities at the Court did not necessarily conflict with the interests of the throne so long as the Emperor found his faction instrumental to the realization of his wishes. In fact, the ministers at the Han court were always divided into different factions for political or other reasons. The ruler had to rely on one faction or a combination of factions to maintain his power.

However, the eunuchs in the Former Han period did not enjoy prominence for any length of time. Three years after Shih Hsien's deprivation of power and expulsion from the palace by Emperor Ch'eng in 32 B.C. the office of the Palace Masters of Documents was abolished. As in the Later Roman Empire, the eunuchs gained power only under weak emperors.

7. The Court Conference

Any treatise on the organization and the operation of the central government of the

Former Han dynasty would be inadequate without due emphasis on the Court Conferences. Although the Han Emperor was the sole policy-maker and legislator, he seldom proclaimed a law or established an important policy without first consulting his ministers individually or collectively. The collective consultation was known as the *T'ing'i,* or Court Conference. Among subjects deliberated on at the Court Conference were political problems, such as the enthronement of a new Emperor (in case the previous ruler left no heir), enfeoffment of the Emperor's children, the system of Imperial ancestral temples, the state religion; financial problems, such as the government monopoly of iron and salt, the system of taxation, and the monetary system; legal problems, such as the introduction of new laws, decisions on difficult lawsuits; and foreign policies, such as war or peace with foreign countries.

The enthronement of Emperor Wen (179–157 B.C.) in 180 B.C. and that of Emperor Hsüan (73–48 B.C.) in 74 B.C. were both the outcome of debates by the Han nobles and ministers. Following a decision reached by a Court Conference, an edict was promulgated in 40 B.C. ordering all Imperial ancestral temples in the provinces and kingdoms to be abolished. A decision by a later Court Conference compelled Emperor Yüan to eliminate a number of the Imperial ancestral temples in the capital. In 121 B.C. Emperor Wu ordered his ministers to discuss whether the God of Earth (*Hou-t'u*) should be worshipped; he accepted the affirmative solution arrived at by a Court Conference. The shrine of the God of Earth was then erected in Ho-tung province. Following the majority opinion of fifty to eight at a Court Conference, Emperor Ch'eng in 32 B.C. moved the shrine of the God of Earth from Ho-tung province to the northern suburb of the Imperial capital and instituted the ceremonies of worship for the God of Earth in the northern suburb. In A.D. 5 Emperor P'ing accepted a unanimous decision of a Court Conference (with sixty-seven participants) and resumed the practice inaugurated in 32 B.C. after the shrine of the God of Earth at the capital had been abolished twice previously (16 B.C. and 4 B.C.). Accepting a unanimous decision of a Court Conference of eighty-nine ministers, he officially announced the title of the God of Heaven as *Huang-t'ien-shang-ti* (Supreme God of the Great Heaven) and that of the God of Earth as *Hou-t'u* (Sovereign of Earth).

Financial problems, especially when fraught with political implications, were always an issue of importance both for the government administration and in the people's life. In 81 B.C. Emperor Chao handed the problem of the government control of salt and iron, which had aroused criticism and objections, to an enlarged Court Conference which included a large number of the Men of Wisdom and Virtue and Men of Letters recommended by the provinces. A hot debate ensued. But the administration won a victory. A Court Conference about 44 B.C. advanced the age of the children subject to the head-tax (*k'ou-ch'ien*) from three to seven. A change of the monetary system was an issue of debate in the forties and again during the last decade B.C. At one time it was suggested that cloth and silk replace metal currencies, while on other occasions the advice was offered that tortoise shells and cowrie shells be used as a substitute. The opinion of the majority at the Court Conferences was opposed to these proposals.

Next in importance to civil affairs were the issues concerning peace or war with foreign countries. More than any other problem their decision depended upon the deliberations of the Conference. In 176 B.C. a Court Conference suggested peace with the Hsiung-nu. In the Court Conference of 133 B.C. debating the same question, opinions were divided, while the Emperor Wu first favored peace and then war. In 121 B.C. the Erudite, Ti Shan, stood alone in a Court Conference as opposed to war. He was defeated. In 61 B.C. Chao Ch'ung-kuo, commander-in-chief in an expedition against the Ch'iang people, who were living just beyond the western border of the Han Empire, advised repeatedly that the defense of the western frontier be strengthened by establishing permanent settlements in which the frontier guards would combine farming with military duties and thus defend the border against the Ch'iang tribesmen instead of engaging in continual offensive forays against them. Court Conferences were called to deliberate on his proposal. At the beginning only 30 percent of the participants voiced approval, then 50 percent expressel sympathy with the idea. Eventually Chao's proposal won a victory with a majority of 80 percent of the total participants.

It is unnecessary to continue enumerating events of this kind. Suffice it to say that the Court Conference of the Former Han dynasty served as an organ of deliberation on state politics, whether of a military or civil nature. It constituted an inter-ministerial organization possessing an authority higher than that of the Chancellery and regency. Its decisions were based on the opinion of the majority regardless of the position or rank of the individuals on either side. As a rule they were accepted by the Emperor.

The Conference was always called in the name of the Emperor or the Empress Dowager. The participants in the Conference consisted usually of the Chancellor, the Imperial Secretary, the Generals, the Marquises, ministers ranking as full-two-thousand-bushels, those ranking as two-thousand-bushels, all of the Grandees such as Grandee Remonstrants, Palace Grandees (*Chung-ta-fu*), the Erudites, and the Court Gentlemen-Advisors (*I-lang*). In terms of their relations to the Emperor they can be classified into two groups—the Outer Court members, including all the ranking ministerial officials, and the Inner Court members, including the Grand Minister of Mount, the Generals, the Attendants within the Palace (*Shih-chung*), the Palace Regular Attendants (*Chung-ch'ang-shih*).

For issues of limited importance smaller Court Conferences were called. In this case the participants were reduced to the Chancellor, the Imperial Secretary, ministers ranking as full-two-thousand-bushels, and the ministers in whose domain the particular problem lay. For example, in discussions regarding religious institutions the ministers in charge of ceremonies participated, while in case of judiciary questions the presence of the Commandant of Justice was required.

During the later part of the Former Han period, when the Emperors placed more confidence in their relatives-in-law and close officials than in their ministers, the conference of the Inner Court was called more frequently. This was a result of the ruler's desire to concentrate the power of the state in an inner circle immediately surrounding him. For vital issues, however, a joint conference of the Inner Court and the Outer Court was usually called.

The Chancellor acted as president both at the Outer Court Conference and at a joint conference of the two Courts. The Emperor attended the Conference occasionally; but as a rule he remained absent. After the question at issue was discussed, the

Chancellor summarized the opinion of the Conference and presented a report to the Emperor for his final decision. In case the opinions of the Conference were divided, he presented also the dissenting views and recorded the number of persons of each group.

Caution must be exercised against overestimating the importance of the Court Conference. However prominent the role it played in the deliberations on policies of the Han government, it was merely an advisory body and not a legislative organ. Consequently, its decisions, even if unanimous, were not laws but suggestions. The Emperor was customarily bound to accept them, but was not constrained to do so. Furthermore, the right to convene the Conference was in the hands of the Emperor. Neither its participants nor even its president, the Chancellor, could do so. As far as can be judged from the literary data extant there were no laws or Imperial decress that stipulated the nature of political matters which had to be placed before the Conference for discussion. It is highly problematical whether during the Conference its participants could always express their opinions freely and openly, especially after a hint had been given of the wishes of the Emperor or those of the dominating minister or ministers.

However, the functions and political significance of the Court Conference cannot be questioned or minimized. On the one hand it exerted much restraint on the freedom of action of the ruler; on the other it imposed a check upon any singlehanded action by a dominating minister or group of ministers. It may have mitigated in good part the friction between government departments. It clearly solicited different opinions and gave formal expression to the majority opinion. Above all it strengthened the position of the ministers in their struggle for power with the Emperor. The setting up of the Court Conference of the Inner Court to counter-balance that of the Outer Court is good proof of this fact.

8. The Appointment of the Leading Ministers

Except for the early part of the dynasty, when ministerial positions were filled by aides of the founder of the dynasty during his campaigns to win the throne, the men appointed to head the various ministries of the central government were generally the chief assistants of the ministers, provincial governors who had proved themselves able administrators, or meritorious officials who had been granted the title of Marquis. The only exception was the ministry of the Director of the Imperial Clan, which was always headed by a member of the Imperial house.

To avoid factual enumerations and tedious discussions of each ministry I prefer to offer some brief observations regarding the appointment of the Chancellor and the Imperial Secretary as an example of the selection of the leading ministers in the central government.

In the early days of the Former Han dynasty before 124 B.C., candidates for the Chancellorship were always selected from among the Marquises, who were enfeoffed because of their contributions to the establishment of the dynasty and in accordance with traditions of the older feudal Chou dynasty. It has been a common phenomenon among many peoples that one of the prerogatives of the nobility is to hold public office and thus form an administrative aristocracy. The only difference between the Chou and the Former Han aristocracy was that the former was, generally speaking, an aristocracy of blood and the latter of service to the Emperor.

In 124 B.C. a commoner, Kung-sun Hung, was for the first time made Chancellor. He started his official career by passing a court examination. In keeping with the tradition that a Chancellor had to be a Marquis, Kung-sun Hung was immediately granted the title of Marquis of P'ing-chin. Thus was established the custom of conferring the title of Marquis on each Chancellor on his appointment. The enfeoffment of a commoner who had become the lieutenant to the throne was obviously motivated by the desire to keep the old tradition alive and to grant him a social and political status which would qualify him to be an assistant to the throne and a member of the ruling aristocracy. Even if it had to be enlarged to cope with a new situation, the administrative aristocracy was consciously maintained. This reminds one of the advice of Maecenas to Octavius to give money to an able but poor man in order to fit him out to be a Roman Senator.

In terms of previous office, before 124 B.C. the Marquises who were made Chancellors all had held important positions. In the eighty-two years from 206 B.C. to 124 B.C. there were seventeen Chancellors, and their previous offices ranged from Minister of Ceremonies up to the Grand Minister of Mount, the lowest ranking as a full-two-thousand-bushel. Five of them had held the office of Imperial Secretary. From 124 B.C. on, it became the standard practice to promote the Imperial Secretary to the post of Chancellor. From 124 B.C. to A.D. 8, the year the Former Han fell, there were twenty-nine Chancellors. Of these only six had not held the post of Imperial Secretary before their appointment, and three, though not promoted directly from the post of Imperial Secretary, had previously occupied that position. In 9 B.C. Chu Po, who was the Imperial Secretary (then known as the *Ta-ssu-k'ung*), presented a memorial dealing with the selection of the Chancellor. He said, "The precedent is that . . . a full-two-thousand-bushel (minister holding such a rank) is selected to be the Imperial Secretary, and he, if competent in his duties, is to be made the Chancellor." The practice of the Former Han after 140 B.C. confirms Chu Po's statement.

Thirty-six of the forty-six Chancellors have their personal history recorded in the *Han shu*. Of these, five had ancestors who had held official positions, and four obtained the office because they were relatives-in-law of the Imperial house. Eight are described as being from "poor" or "lowly" families. The family background of the other nineteen is not given—a fact which usually implies that there was nothing in their family history worth recording. Seven of the nineteen began their official careers by passing examinations or by recommendation, and twelve started their careers as small officials in local governments. It was through their ability as administrators that they generally climbed up the hierarchical scale and finally reached the highest position.

Regarding the appointment of the Imperial Secretary, Chu Po states in the memorial quoted above: "The precedent is that the most successful Provincial Governor or Chancellor of a kingdom is selected to be a full-two-thousand bushel (rank of a cabinet minister) and a full-two-thousand bushel is selected to be the Imperial Secretary." This was true only generally speaking. Of the seventy Imperial Secretaries throughout the period, I find only twenty-six who had held the rank of the full-two-thousand-bushel. Among the rest there were twenty-six two-thousand-bushels, four equal-to-two-thousand-bushels, and fourteen whose office and rank are unknown. Basing our conclusion on these numerical observations we may say that only ministers who had held offices with the rank of the two-thousand-bushel were eligible for the post of the Imperial Secretary.

Keeping these numbers in mind and reading the personal histories of the ministers, one cannot escape the impression that in the selection of candidates for the ministerial positions, aside from the administrative ability of the candidate, the rank was the primary consideration and hence the key to the hierarchical structure of Han officialdom. The *Shih chi* and the *Han shu* contain several stories which tell how rapidly able ministers were promoted, finally to be installed in the highest offices of the central government. Their promotions were rapid but seldom exceptional, for this would have broken the hierarchical structure of the bureaucracy. In one memorial dealing with the selection of officials among other subjects, Tung Chung-shu said: [The officials] obtain noble ranks by piling up the days in office and attain to [higher] government positions by accumulating a long period of service." On the whole this statement holds true. Promotion by seniority is characteristic of all bureaucratic organizations.

9. Conclusion

The structure of the central government of the Former Han dynasty was that of an autocracy supported by a bureaucracy. There were times when the Emperor exercised absolute authority, but generally the bureaucracy was the *de facto* authority. In spite of the basic interests of its members, the bureaucracy did not constitute a homogeneous body. It was made up of a number of factions, all struggling for supremacy, which were formed on the basis of personal ambition for power and position or on the basis of the interests of the social group which a particular faction represented. The bureaucracy was maintained by equilibrium of the forces between the various factions or by the domination of one of them.

Servile as they were, the bureaucrats were not always subservient to the wishes of the Emperor, especially when his wishes ran counter to the interests which the dominating faction represented or were detrimental to the personal aspirations of the minister who led this faction. Hence the antagonisms between the Emperor and his cabinet or the minister who headed it. Armed with Confucian political ideology, the bureaucrats constantly combatted and restrained the power of the Emperor and fought for power for themselves.

For the purpose of counteracting this bureaucracy, therefore, the Emperor elevated the position of officials close to him at the Inner Court, fitting them out with power above those of the Outer Court. The establishment of the regency, the enhancing of the office of the Masters of Documents, the employment of relatives-in-law and eunuchs, these were the most important measures adopted by the throne to achieve this purpose. They were measures to substitute a personal rule for an institutional government. But the Emperor was not too successful. As soon as the office of the Masters of Documents grew into a super-cabinet, it stepped out of the Inner Palace and became another organ of the Outer Court, no closer to the person of the Emperor nor more subservient to his wishes than the former Chancellery. The relatives-in-law, if they wanted their power maintained, had perforce to collaborate with one or more factions of the ministers at the Outer Court, who were deep-rooted in the government administration. Even the eunuchs, who had the fewest social and political connections with the ministers outside of the Palace, were no exception. On the other hand, the existence of factions in the official body could strengthen the position of the Emperor. This is probably what happened during Emperor Wu's reign, when those favoring a strongly centralized regime wrested power from those statesmen who advocated a policy of *laissez faire* in the political and economic sense.

Technically, the organization of the central government was highly advanced, competent enough to discharge the tasks of administering a great empire and to serve as a model administrative setup for two thousand years, despite such shortcomings as are commonly shared by all governments of the past as well as of the present. Records of the administrative personnel were kept by both the Chancellery and the Imperial Secretariat, and they served as basis for promotion and demotion. As head of the officialdom and as personnel supervisor respectively, the Chancellor and the Imperial Secretary kept a disciplinary control over the whole body of officials. This duplication of disciplinary functions was complementary, and, in addition, provided a mode of "checks and balances." The principle of checks and balances is also seen in other aspects of the governmental setup, such as the double chancellorship discussed in section 3.

The Han historians proudly stated that after Confucianism was declared the state philosophy and after the establishment of the Imperial Academy in 124 B.C., the officialdom was replaced by "men of letters," i.e., men trained in Confucian learning. Modern scholars, too, are profuse in their praise of the change. There is much truth in this statement, but we must not be led to believe that men with Confucian training were always Confucian statesmen. Tung Chung-shu, the most outstanding Confucian scholar and one of the most brilliant statesmen of his age, who firmly believed in the political principles of Confucianism, and who fought for their realization, winning respect and admiration of his contemporaries and of Emperor Wu, was not even given a position in the central government. On the other hand, Chai Fang-chin, Chancellor from 15 to 7 B.C., was considered a very successful man by his contemporaries. Certainly he was a Confucianist; in fact, he was so important a Confucianist that he was regarded as their leader. But how far his conduct and policy conformed to Confucian ideals is a serious question. Regarding the secret of his success as a minister, the *Han shu* states: "Fang-chin was full of wisdom and ability; he was versed both in [Confucian] learning and the laws. In his administrative work he decorated the laws with Confucian elegance. He was regarded as the most understanding and the wisest Chancellor. The Son of Heaven esteemed him highly. Nine of his requests failed to please the throne." He is also said, however, to have "secretly sought for the hidden desires of the ruler of men in order to secure his position," and was accused of having destroyed a large reservoir used by the people of his native province to irrigate their land when he failed in his request to appropriate the fertile land around it. Both accusations most likely were true, and certainly are in contradiction to Confucian ideals.

The story of Chai Fang-chin is but one of its kind in the history of the Former Han dynasty. It confirms the findings which Lyman Bryson discovered in his studies on

Lincoln in power. Mr. Bryson holds that the qualities that lead to power are not those that make for wisdom in office, that the exercise of wisdom by one in power is made extraordinarily difficult because he must spend a large part of his time in judging and disposing of the ideas of his assistants, instead of conceiving and executing plans of his own, and that a man in power must spend much of his time in maintaining his position of authority. These findings lead him to the conclusion that "no matter how a man may come into office, corrupting forces begin to work on him as soon as he takes control over the destinies of other men."

Though I do not accept Mr. Bryson's conclusion as true of every culture and of every great statesman in the history of mankind, it does help to explain the careers of many outstanding figures in the history of the Chinese bureaucracy. Aside from the points mentioned by Mr. Bryson, there are still two more forces that exercise no less influence in bureaucratizing an administrative machinery. These are the decorum of the officialdom and the play of maneuver and compromise within the administration. The behavior pattern imposed by the decorum of the officialdom is incompatible with integrity, and maneuver and compromise negate political principles.

These reasons serve to explain why Chai Fang-chin, leader of his contemporary Confucianists, used the Confucian principles merely as ornaments for his administrative maneuvers, and tried to satisfy the ruler's hidden wishes rather than put into practice the theories in which he had been trained. These may also explain why Tung Chung-shu and other great men like him failed to achieve success in political careers, and why scarcely any Confucian philosophers are found in the upper hierarchy of the Han bureaucracy or in that of later dynasties. Both Confucius and Plato maintain that for the well-being of the state political power and philosophy have to be united. Yet, kingly qualities and philosophic wisdom are not likely to be combined in any one person, except in a society in which to rule is no longer a privilege of one man or of a few and to govern is not to exercise power over others for exploitation.

LIEN-SHENG YANG

Great Families of Eastern Han

Under the Han imperial system the emperor was the source of power, because he was the final authority and the source of all laws. Thus Han politics consisted chiefly in ways to obtain political influence over the emperor.

Four groups of people had opportunity to be with or close to the emperor, namely, the royal families, the empresses' families, the palace officials and the eunuchs, and the families of high officials. The first three groups can generally be referred to as the "inner court," since their relationship with the emperor was more or less personal. The last group, the influential bureaucrats, can generally be termed the "outer court," since the bureaucrats' relationship with the emperor was more or less in the course of governmental service.

One of the questions of Chinese history is, how was de facto power distributed? Was it wholly concentrated in the legitimate source, the emperor? Did the groups of the inner court have power? The bureaucrats and great families? Chinese historians often advanced the idea that when the government was relatively independent of inner court influence, civil authority advanced; when it came under the domination of the inner court, civil government declined.

In the following study, Professor Lien-sheng Yang, Harvard-Yenching Professor of Chinese History at Harvard University, analyzes the power held by the great families in Eastern Han politics. He describes the reason for their rise and discusses the methods they employed in expanding their political influence, such as the system of "disciples and ex-subordinates" and the system of selecting officials. Inevitably power struggles arose among these great families. When these unrelenting struggles intensified greatly, the empire finally collapsed under the strain.[1]

The great families of Han were the forerunners of the power families of the later period, the Chin and the Southern and Northern dynasties, whose members filled high government posts, owned tremendous amounts of landed property, possessed vassals, and at the same time acquired legal sanction for many special privileges, such as exemption from government taxation.

Reprinted with permission of the American Council of Learned Societies from *Chinese Social History*, trans. and ed. by Sun Zen E-tu and John De Francis (Washington, D.C.: American Council of Learned Societies, 1956), pp. 103–34.

[1] For a recent study of the great families of the Han dynasty, see Ch'ü T'ung-tsu, *Han Social Structure* (Seattle, Wash.: University of Washington Press, 1972), pp. 160–247, 393–506.

An equally important theme examined in this article is the role of eunuchs in traditional Chinese politics. Often a destructive one, it has been a cause of recurrent disastrous political feuds in Imperial China. Perhaps it is an institution that became, for a variety of reasons, inseparable from the traditional Chinese emperor system.[2]

1. Development of Great Families in Western Han

The two Han dynasties, especially Eastern Han, constituted a long gestation period for the rule of powerful families, a development which came about in the Tsin and Northern and Southern dynasties (265–581 A.D.). The great families of Han were the forerunners of the powerful families of the later period, whose members filled high government posts, owned tremendous amounts of landed property, possessed vassals, and at the same time were exempt from government taxation. There was no intermarriage between them and the common people; between the two was an unbridgeable social gap.

Liu Pang, founder of the Han dynasty, defeated the last of the Chou-Ch'in aristocrats, Hsiang Yü. This was highly pleasing to the group of non-aristocratic landlords and merchants, who had already emerged during the Warring States as wealthy but socially inferior and politically impotent persons. But now the old social order was overthrown by an emperor of commoner origin. Everyone was equal under him as to obligations; noble rank now held no special privileges.

In the early years of Han, the central government was occupied with several rebellions. The wealthy people utilized these periods of war to expand their industrial, agricultural, and commercial enterprises. There are accounts in the *Historical Records*, for instance, of high returns on investments, and of private loans to the government. By the time of Emperor Wu (140–87 B.C.), the expansion of the empire in the northwest, coupled with the Yellow River floods, brought the government into financial straits. The moneyed people then began to obtain special privileges, such as exemption from corvée duty, in return for their contributions of money, grain, and slaves to the government.

Pressed by economic difficulties, Emperor Wu began to employ great salt and iron proprietors like K'ung Chin. These persons, though rich, had never had official positions before. Once in power they did not scruple to preserve their own and their friends' fortunes at the expense of the interest of their own class. One by one such policies as inflation and the monopoly on salt and iron

---

[2] For wide-ranging commentaries on the historical role and social world of eunuchs in China, see Taisuke Mitamura, *Chinese Eunuchs: The Structure of Intimate Politics*, trans. by Charles Pomeroy (Rutland, Ver.: Charles E. Tuttle Co., 1970). For special studies of eunuch problems in later dynasties, see John K. Rideout, "The Rise of the Eunuchs during the T'ang Dynasty," *Asia Major*, Vol. I (1949–50), 53–72, Vol. III (1952), 42–58; Robert B. Crawford, "Eunuch Power in the Ming Dynasty," *T'oung Pao*, Vol. XLIX, No. 3 (1961), 115–48; and Charles O. Hucker, "The Tung-lin Movement of the Late Ming Period," in John K. Fairbank, ed., *Chinese Thought and Institutions* (Chicago: University of Chicago Press, 1967), pp. 132–62.

were put into practice. The worst blow to the rich merchant class was the property tax on the merchants, based on property reports returned by the owners. Those who evaded reporting, or reported short, would have their property confiscated. Informers received one-half of the confiscated amount. Merchants were prohibited from owning landed estates, on pain of confiscation. As a result, the government took over enormous amounts of such property, including land, houses, and slaves.

It is reasonable to conclude that at this point many rich people turned from commerce to invest in agriculture. Land was not subject to the property tax. Moreover, a landlord paid a land tax of one-thirtieth to the government, but usually took a 50 percent rent from the tenant farmers. It is likely that this was the situation throughout all of Western Han, as shown by the writings of Tung Chung-shu and Wang Mang. From now on the biggest problem of the Han dynasty was that of land, that is of annexations by the great landlords.

Another Han method of keeping down the wealthy was the moving of their residences, a policy which was inherited from the Ch'in dynasty. The removals were carried out during the reigns of the first seven emperors of Han, and especially during the reign of Emperor Wu, that is in the periods when the central government was strong. Though the first emperor of Han employed the device of dispersing the descendants of the Chou aristocrats, by the time of Emperor Wu the removals were directed against the new great families.

But such temporary restrictions could not prevent the wealthy from gaining strength. When the government gradually weakened after emperors Chao and Hsüan (86–48 B.C.), the great landlords became still more free in their annexations of estates.

As a result, in the reign of Emperor Ai (6–2 B.C.), Shih Tan suggested the need for government limitation of the size of landed property, remarking as follows:

Now that for generations the country has enjoyed peace, the rich people and the officials have been accumulating fortunes amounting to myriads [of cash], while the misery of the poor deepens. In the rule of a superior man, there is esteem for following past practices together with emphasis on instituting reforms. The purpose of instituting changes is to remedy a present emergency. There is no need to be thoroughgoing, but merely to provide some general limitations.

The plan drawn up by the ministers as a result of this plea limited estates of the nobility and officials to thirty *ch'ing* per family; the number of slaves per household was restricted to 200, 100, and 30, according to the rank of the owner. Although the limit of three years in which to achieve the standard does not appear to be severe, many landlords had exceeded the limits of land ownership and were in a panic to sell, so that the price of land and slaves fell precipitously. The plan was vehemently opposed by many landlords who were at the court. Their influence was shown in an edict from the emperor which "postponed" indefinitely the implementation of these restrictions.

Thus, the economic power of the large landlords was already strongly entrenched. Furthermore, on the basis of this economic power, the landlords were seeking political ascendancy. Hence even such a mild reform as Shih Tan had proposed came to nothing. Unexpectedly there appeared a Wang Mang, who "always admired antiquity and knew not the trends of the times," and proceeded to "imperialize" the land. In his edict promulgated after assuming power, he gave a description of the concentration of land in the hands of the rich, and plight of the tenantry, and the inequities of the distribution of the tax burden. Although nominally the land tax was one-thirtieth of the yield, actually the landlords were getting five-tenths from their tenants. Therefore he decreed that henceforth all land was to become crown land, all slaves were to be known as "private retainers" (of the emperor), and both were not to be bought and sold. Persons owning more than the prescribed amount of land, the area of a "well field" per family of less than eight males, must distribute the surplus to their relatives and neighbors, on pain of the death penalty.

Though Wang Mang was able to see the root of the problem, his government was not strong enough to carry out the reforms, which were rescinded after three years. Weakness, corruption, invasion of the Hsiung-nu, and natural calamities threatened the security of the rich and the existence of the poor. The joint forces of landlords and peasants ultimately brought about Wang Mang's downfall.

2. Establishment of the Political Power of Great Families in Eastern Han

The activities of the landlord class, to which belonged the successful Kuang-wu emperor, during the revolutionary regime of Wang Mang, are worth noting.

The home of Kuang-wu was in the Commandery of Nan-yang (in Honan). Wan, one of the great metropolises of Han, was situated in this commandery, and a large number of very wealthy families congregated there. At a time when Nan-yang was suffering from famine, Kuang-wu's family still had grain to sell in Wan. According to a commentary on the *Later Han History*, "At that time there was a drought and famine in Nan-yang, but His Majesty's field alone bore a harvest." This indicates that he must have possessed good land, and a great deal of it, so that there could be surplus grain, since Heaven obviously could not have particularly sought out the future emperor's fields to rain on. On the other hand, the account was probably euphemistic, in which case it actually would be that Kuang-wu had hoarded a lot of grain, and was waiting to sell at a good price. In time of upheaval landlords were all versed in the art of "robbing during a fire."

The maternal grandfather of Kuang-wu, of the house of Fan, was a still greater landlord. The commentary on the *Later Han History* records that the family could "close its gates and become a market in itself."

A more detailed description of the Fan family is given in the *Later Han History*, which shows that it owned more than 300 *ch'ing* (about 30,000 *mou*) of land, and was self-sufficient in all the economic necessities of life. Kuang-wu's sister's husband Teng Ch'en also came of a wealthy family.

The basic armies of the rebelling landlords were composed of family members and household followers. The latter were unemployed vagrants, who depended on the great families for a living in return for services rendered. The status ordinarily was probably like that of a first-class butler, though they were treated with more courtesy by the master when a particular service was required of them, such as, for instance, killing some adversary in a feud. These followers were usually scornful of legal authority. For example, as the result of the conduct of his followers, Liu Hsüan, a cousin of Kuang-wu, once had to pretend death in order to avoid a bad scrape with the authorities.

The majority of household followers dabbled in crime—robbery and such like—when they were hard up. It so happened that when the conduct of his followers became too intolerable, Liu Hsiu, the later Kuang-wu, decided to take them for a trip to Wan. There he met Li T'ung, whose family for generations had been known as great merchants. Li T'ung informed him of an alleged prophecy that "the Liu family shall be restored to the throne with the aid of Li," and the two men decided on an uprising, using their army of family members and followers.

Liu Hsiu's forces were weak at the beginning. He therefore began by cooperating with Liu Hsüan, who headed an army composed mainly of peasants and famine refugees. But the peasant army of Liu Hsüan and the landlord army of Liu Hsiu were uneasy bedfellows, and before long the two forces split. Liu Hsiu obtained a base area on the North China plain, while Liu Hsüan secured his position in Honan and Shensi. Then, without an overall plan and with an army that specialized in plundering, Liu Hsüan was finally defeated by another peasant army, the Red Eyebrows.

The Red Eyebrows had risen in Shantung. According to the *Later Han History*, they "became bandits under pressure of poverty, and lacked any strategic plans for attacking cities or overcoming fortifications." They apparently had no high political ambitions. Though temporarily able to gain hegemony over Liu Hsüan in Shensi, they were ultimately suppressed by Kuang-wu.

The peasant armies were not the only ones that were engaged in plundering; their brutality was quite equalled by that of the landlord armies. Kuang-wu's troops were somewhat less predatory than others and so were relatively more popular. After suppressing the Red Eyebrows, Kuang-wu conquered the forces of other local strong men in Shantung and in the Huai River and lower Yangtse regions. Finally he turned his attention to the west, where the territory was divided and separately controlled by the landed magnates Wei Hsiao, Tou Jung, and Kung-sun Shu. It was only after strenuous campaigns in which he employed alternately his tactics of war and diplomacy and allied with Ma Yüan, the great owner of herds and land, that Kuang-wu was able to suppress them. Ma Yüan's economic power in Pei-ti (in Shensi) consisted of several thousand horses, sheep, and cattle, some hundred thousand pecks of grain, and also several hundred vassal families. Here we see that the household followers could become dependent on the great house in "family" units.

It is the custom of the dynastic histories to describe the famine refugees and vagabonds as "vagrant bandits," but to refer to the strong and wealthy families as "heroes," a practice which enables us to determine the class origins of the leaders of the rebellions. The famine refugees and vagabonds lacked organization and ambition. By themselves they probably would have been unable to overthrow Wang Mang. But the strong and wealthy families were also opposed to the Hsin dynasty (of Wang Mang), and rose together in revolt. When the entire country was torn to pieces, the landlord army of Liu Hsiu was able to gather the fragments together and pacify the people, thus easily gaining political power.

A noticeable feature of the revolts of this time was that the leaders all claimed descent from the ruling house of Han, and the name Liu served to rally popular support for many of them. This was probably an indication of popular longing more for the Han system than for the Liu family.

Kuang-wu revived the one-thirtieth land tax, which was advantageous for the large landlords. But at the same time he succeeded in keeping the political powers of his enfeoffed officials and relatives in check. In order to preserve his own prerogatives he was loath to see other great landlords embark upon unlimited expansion. He held that "proper administration lies in suppressing the strong and supporting the weak," so that "at Court there are no officials with overbearing authority, and in the fiefs there are no powerful heroes." He repeatedly ordered improvement in the treatment of slaves, and decreed the freeing of some common people who had been seized and sold into slavery.

In order to rectify landownership, Kuang-wu ordered a general survey of agricultural land in the country. But the officials returned dishonest measurements, ruthlessly encroaching on the land of the peasants and causing them to rebel. Kuang-wu was even willing to punish a few corrupt officials. A story in the *Later Han History* tells how the emperor one day found out with the help of the twelve-year-old heir apparent that his trusted officials and relatives possessed vast estates near the capital much beyond the limit set by law, and that the reports of the local officials were not reliable. Following this revelation many persons were punished. This story shows that cases of possession of extra-legal properties by powerful officials and imperial relatives were so flagrant that even the twelve-year-old heir to the throne had known about it. It also shows that there were certain regulations regarding the big landlords' property, and that Kuang-wu was desirous of maintaining these regulations. Kuang-wu's whole attitude toward the big landlords was ambivalent, however, and after the first three reigns of Eastern Han, political power began to fall into the hands of eunuchs and the families of empresses, thus bringing about the period of control by the great families.

3. Survey of Great Families in Eastern Han

What is known as a great family did not consist simply of persons of the same name and lineage. It was rather a group centered around an extended patrilineal family, and included many other families or individuals appended to it through political or economic relations. Such was the unit of a great family.

Some of the great families first possessed political positions and afterwards established their economic power. Others first possessed economic power and afterward acquired political positions, which in turn helped to develop further their economic power.

The establishment of the rule of Kuang-wu meant the establishment of the political power of the great landlords, that is, of the great families. Nearly all of his two chancellors and twenty-eight generals came from great families.

Several typical generals among the twenty-eight are known to have maintained large numbers of followers. Other officials, like Teng Ch'en and Ma Yüan, were also rich individuals, as described above. With the founding of the Eastern Han dynasty these great families received high positions and investitures. The great families had thus succeeded in enhancing their political position through economic power.

There were two major categories of great families in Eastern Han. The first consisted of individuals who suddenly gained importance through connections with the central power; these included members of the imperial family, members of the families of empresses, and eunuchs. The other category consisted of individuals who rose gradually through their own efforts; these included high officials and local magnates.

Members of the imperial family were given the rank of Prince; sons of Princes who were not in the line of inheritance became Princely Marquises. According to one estimate, there were sixty-one known Princes and 344 Princely Marquises in Eastern Han. Though rather numerous, these persons enjoyed no real power. In 52 A.D. Kuang-wu executed several thousand followers of the princely households as the aftermath of a case of vendetta warfare in which these persons were engaged on behalf of their masters. The princes were greatly curbed thereafter in their activities. Few new princes were invested after the reign of Emperor Ming (58–76 A.D.).

Many of the relatives of the empresses belonged already to great families. The system for the choice of "Palace Beauties" in the Eastern Han was the selection by palace officials of girls from good families around the capital city of Lo-yang. However, it was easy for these officials to be partisan to the great families either through special connections or bribery. Nine-tenths of the empresses mentioned in the "Chronicle of Empresses" in the *Later Han History* came from great families; some were even daughters of princesses. For instance, Kuang-wu's wife, Empress Yin, was a famous beauty who came of an old wealthy family; her half-brother maintained several thousand followers. Later four members of the Yin family were enfeoffed. The wife of Emperor Ming, Empress Ma, was Ma Yüan's daughter. The powerful Tou and Liang families produced two empresses each. It is known that there were altogether eighty-nine members of empresses' families who were invested as marquises. The political influence of such families far outweighed that of the members of the imperial family.

The growth of eunuchs into great families occurred in the later part of Eastern Han. The first eunuch to be ennobled was Cheng Chung in the reign of Emperor Ho (89–105 A.D.). In 135 A.D. eunuchs were allowed to have adopted sons inherit their rank. This was probably the recognition of a *fait accompli*, since Cheng Chung's adopted son had already inherited Cheng's rank in 114 A.D.

The power and influence of the eunuchs have been described in biographical accounts in the *Later Han History*. For instance, the eunuchs Ts'ao Chieh and Wang Fu were able to place their relatives in many central government positions; aside from possessing official rank and income they also engaged in business dealings which further increased their wealth. They lived sumptuously, and lorded it over their home districts, creating resentment among the people, who, however, dared not remonstrate against them. During the reign of Emperor Ling (168–190 A.D.) the eunuchs became so oppressive that their activities contributed directly to the rebellion of the Yellow Turbans. The Ts'ao family that ultimately usurped the throne was related to the eunuchs of Ts'ao T'eng and Ts'ao Sung. There were altogether seventy-nine members of eunuch families who were given noble ranks.

It is difficult to distinguish the high officials from local great families. The twenty-eight generals mentioned above may be taken as examples of this group of persons. The great families were scattered over the entire country. T'ao Hsi-sheng has enumerated a large number of them in the third volume of his *History of Chinese Political Thought*. Many more can be added. These magnates were powerful enough to ask the princes to intercede for them with the emperor.

Some of the great families maintained their status over several hundred years. For instance, the magnate Lien Fan, who lived during the reign of Emperor Ming, was a descendant of the famous general Lien P'o, who lived about 300 years earlier. Another example was the Lu family of Chiang-tung (i.e. the lower Yangtze region), which began to attain prominence under Kuang-wu and also lasted for about 200 years. Another family, Ts'ui, was active from the reign of Emperor Chao (86–73 B.C.) to the end of Han, a period of approximately 300 years; in the time of Emperor Ling (169–190 A.D.) Ts'ui Lieh was able to purchase with five million cash the position of one of the three prime ministers in the Han government.

4. Great Families and the Economy: Misery of the Common People

Those who became dependents of the great families did so for two reasons, economic and political.

Economic dependency had an early beginning. According to Huan T'an of early Eastern Han, there were already free men who served big merchants and moneylenders as dependents, and shared in the profits. But larger numbers were dependents of great landlords. The case of Ma Yüan's several hundred vassal families is a good example.

Ts'ui Shih, who was active during the reign of Emperor Huan (147–168 A.D.), in his *Discourses on Politics* analyzed with some care the reasons why free men became dependents. The destruction of the ancient system by Ch'in, he said, had encouraged the annexation of estates and the accumulation of wealth. Consequently, the rich amassed enormous property, enjoyed high prestige and unrestrained power, lived like royalty, and tyrannized the countryside, while the poor could hardly maintain themselves. They therefore bowed their heads and with their families went into the service of the rich. After generations of slavery they were still not able to provide for their own subsistence. "Alive," says Ts'ui Shih, "they face a life-time of hard labor; dead, they worry for lack of a decent burial. When the year is poor, they drift about and starve in ditches, they marry off their wives and sell their sons."

This hard lot of the free peasant went back to the time of the Warring States. A contemporary statesman, Li K'uei, once drew up a budget for the small farmer in that period on the basis of 100 *mou* of land with a total yield of 150 *tan* of grain per family of five. After providing for taxes and basic necessities, the farmer was short 450 cash per year, not counting expenses for illness or other emergencies. Another budget was drawn up by Ts'ao Ts'o during the reign of Emperor Wen (179–156 B.C.), also on the basis of 100 *mou* for a family. The plight of the peasant worsened with the increased annexations of estates during the reign of Emperor Yüan (48–32 B.C.), at which time Censor Kung Yü, in describing the farmer's life, pointed out that many would rather leave the land to engage in trade or become bandits.

The small farmer continued to lead a hard life in Eastern Han. In Ts'ui Yin's *On Gamblers*, written during the reign of Emperor Ho (89–106 A.D.), there is a poignant passage describing the gambler's scorn for the farmers:

The gambler came upon a farmer clearing away weeds. He had a straw hat on his head and a hoe in his hand. His face was black, his hands and feet were covered with calluses, his skin was as rough as mulberry bark, and his feet resembled bear's paws. He crouched in the fields, his sweat mixing with the mud. The gambler said to him, "You cultivate the fields in oppressive summer heat. Your back is encrusted with salt, your legs look like burnt stumps, your skin is like leather that cannot be pierced by an awl. You hobble along on misshapen feet and painful legs. Shall I call you a plant or a tree? Yet you can move your body and limbs. Shall I call you a bird or a beast? Yet you possess a human face. What a fate to be born with such base qualities!"

So the farmer was likened to plants or beasts. But even his hard labor was not enough for a livelihood, and he was obliged to make other plans. Of the two alternatives pointed out above by Kung Yü, the first, selling the land and entering trade, was only a pipe-dream for the small farmer, for the price of his land would not even be enough to pay off his debts. The other alternative, becoming a bandit, was quite simple, but there were numerous officials around, and once caught, his life would be unbearable. Therefore the peasant would not choose this alternative unless pressed to desperation. The small farmers generally took two other alternatives: one was to become dependents of the great families; the other was to become displaced persons on government relief, that is, to become a reserve force for bandits.

Throughout the Han dynasty there were large numbers of displaced persons. These consisted chiefly of peasants who were victims of famines or warfare and had to leave their villages. The government had no other alternative but to feed them, which was known as providing "relief," or to send them back to their home districts by some means. According to the "Life of Shih Fen" in the *Han History,* there were over two million displaced persons in the Kuan-tung area in the fourth year of the Yüan-feng period of the reign of Emperor Wu of Western Han (107 B.C.). In the first year of the Yung-hsing period of Emperor Huan of Eastern Han (153 A.D.), there were several hundred thousands of displaced families.

A number of edicts of the emperors Chang and Ho indicated that there were various kinds of corrupt practices connected with the relief administration, and that the displaced persons had become a major problem of the state. According to official records, during the seventeen-year reign of Emperor Ho it was necessary to give relief and loans to people in several prefectures and several score commanderies, covering nearly all parts of the country. Despite these government efforts, the number of such persons increased steadily. It was reported in the reign of Emperor An (107–126 A.D.) that in Lo-yang the number of the "idlers" was a hundred times that of farmers. Those of the "idlers" who had some skill were engaged in light handicrafts, such as the making of toys. But that did not constitute long-range livelihood, as the majority were peasants who had left their villages. They were probably not very different from the displaced persons living on relief, who played a crucial role in the Yellow Turban uprising.

5. Great Families and the Economy: Wealth and Extravagance of the Magnates

The second way out for the small peasants was to become dependents of great families: Chung-ch'ang T'ung, who lived at the end of Eastern Han, described a number of great families in his work *Frank Words:*

The magnate, without being the head of even one platoon, commands the services of a thousand families and entire townships. He lives more lavishly than a prince, and has more power than a district magistrate. . . . The magnate's mansion contains hundreds of rooms. His rich fields extend across the land. His slaves are counted by the thousands, and his dependents by the tens of thousands. He trades by land and by water in all parts of the country. His bulging warehouses fill the city, his huge dwellings overflow with treasure, his horses, cattle, sheep, and pigs are too numerous to be contained in the mountain valleys.

The individual small peasant was unable to produce enough to meet his own needs. The outcome became different, however, when land was concentrated under the management of large landlords and was worked by the dependent small peasant. This was because with a vast land area and abundant labor supply all sorts of facilities in production and distribution became available. There would be no lack of ploughing oxen and seeds, and it would also be possible to choose the crop according to the quality of the land. In the description of the great landlords in Ts'ui Shih's *Book of the Months* (fragments collected in *Complete Writings of Later Han*), for instance, it is recorded that aside from such crops as glutinous millet, ordinary millet, rice, and wheat, some scores of other crops were also planted, including linseed, large and small varieties of onions and garlic, clover, turnips, melons, squash, celery, mallow, legumes, water-pepper, mustard, indigo plant, chives, and so forth. Among the trees were bamboo, varnish tree, tung, *catalpa ovata*, pine, cedar, and various others. The landlords were also able to experiment in agricultural methods, such as, among others, the "rotation" method of Chao Kuo (flourished ca. 140–86 B.C.), and the "block planting" method of Fan Sheng-chih (flourished ca. 32–6 B.C.). Moreover, the water mill has been very important in agriculture since the time of Wei and Tsin (3rd–4th centuries A.D.). This new production tool was perhaps already invented in Eastern Han, but the records are unfortunately incomplete, so that the details cannot be traced. The only evidence is found in a passage in the Sung dynasty encyclopedia *T'ai-p'ing yü-lan*, chapter 829, quoting Huan T'an's *New Discourses:*

An Hsi devised the pestle and mortar, thus benefiting myriads of people. Later on others added to the design; they devised a tread mill which utilized the weight of the body to grind the grain. The profit became tenfold. Further, a machine was installed which employed donkeys, mules, oxen, and horses as well as water to grind the grain. The profit became a hundredfold.

Huan T'an lived at the beginning of Eastern Han, so that the great landlords of that period must certainly have utilized the watermill. Further, in chapter 117 of the *Later Han History* mention is made of "using canals for irrigation, water-grinding, and grain transportation." "Water-grinding," according to the commentary of Li Hsien, Prince Chang-huai (of T'ang), is "milling by water." This seems to be further proof.

Another advantage of the great landlords was their ability to engage in trade as well as in agriculture. Although the Han government prohibited people from taking part in two professions, actually the restriction was probably not effective. The great landlords were not only simultaneously great merchants, but also great pastoral lords, thus constituting a trinity of economic power. The *Book of the Months* also contains accounts of the great landlords' hoarding of goods, buying cheap and selling dear. From the second to the eleventh month of the year the landlord was active in some business transaction in every month except the ninth. His business activities were concerned with the staple goods of food or clothing. For instance, cloth was bought during the summer and sold during the winter, which of course brought in large profits. Grain was sold in large quantities in the spring, but the winter wheat was purchased immediately on being harvested in the fourth month of the year (ca. May–June of the solar calendar). The considerable surplus of cloth produced in the landlord's own household and of foodstuffs from his own fields was probably also sold.

Agricultural work was done chiefly by the male members of the landlord's family and the dependent small peasants. The majority of the slaves worked in handicrafts, such as cloth-weaving, but few took part in agriculture. It is estimated that the proportion between the number of handicraft and domestic slaves and that of the dependent people was probably one to ten. Slaves were not free men, and could be bought and sold; the dependents were semi-free.

With a huge income and the command of the labor of slaves and dependents, the life of the magnates reached a high state of luxury. For the wedding of a daughter of the Yüan family in Lo-yang it is recorded in the *Later Han History* that the dowry of the bride included one hundred silk-clad slave girls. Funerals also were occasions for an even more lavish display of wealth, from expensive coffins and burial articles to splendidly constructed mausolea and family shrines. These phenomena were also described and criticized by Ts'ui Shih in his *Discourses on Politics*. Excessive sumptuousness at funerals occasionally brought forth restrictions from government authorities.

6. Great Families and Politics: Disciples and Ex-subordinates

The great families led a luxurious life, but politically they did not always have influence. Although they were able to purchase for themselves the status of "exemptees," their slaves and dependents still could not evade obligations to the government. What the magnates wanted was the total exemption of their dependents from taxation and labor service, that is an increase in the magnates' political power in order to further their own economic interests, as was done later in the Tsin period. However, while the Han system still ruled, it was not possible to bring about this radical change. As a first step toward the acquisition of political power, therefore, the great families began to establish connections with the government, and to influence the selection of officials.

To acquire political influence meant the obtaining of official positions. There were three major ways in which one attained the latter in Han.

(a) *National selection:* This was done through the recommendation of the authorities in commanderies in accordance with the various government classifications, which consisted of two major categories, the fixed and the non-fixed. For the "Filial and Incorrupt" class in the fixed group, for instance, the general rule was one candidate per 200,000 population. In thinly populated areas, however, the ratio was sometimes changed to one per 100,000, and for some areas with a population of less than 100,000 the recommendation was to be made for one candidate once every three years. Another class, the "Abundant Talents," called for one candidate per year for each commandery, though it is not known whether or not this was made in proportion to the population figure. As for the non-fixed group, the candidates for various classifications were recommended by the local authorities after special decrees were issued by the emperor, at times when men of talent were needed.

The selected candidates were often persons who had already had minor official careers, and all were probably given examinations in order to determine their official rank. The examinations were sometimes personally presided over by the emperor. Usually the responsibility for the determination of rank rested with either the Secretary of State or with the three Grand Ministers, between whom there was serious rivalry over this right of patronage. The power rested most of the time with the Secretary of State.

(b) *Ministerial selection:* This was done locally to staff the administrative offices of the metropolitan ministers and of the commandery and prefectural governments. In the prefectural governments, for example, there were ten bureaux: Finance, Memorials, Judicature, Police, Criminal Affairs, Criminal Executions, Military Affairs, Coinage, and Public Granaries. Persons selected to posts in the prefectural governments could look forward only to minor local positions. But those selected by the metropolitan ministerial offices could, with the help of the right personal relations with the superiors, hope to advance into high positions in the central government. There were cases in which the same individual was selected simultaneously by a number of Ministries.

(c) *Appointment of sons:* This system resembled inheritance of rank, and dated from early Western Han. Every official with an annual salary of 2,000 piculs (i.e. of the rank of Prefect) and up, and who had had three years' service, was entitled to name one son or full brother as a *lang,* the expectant rank waiting for appointment to various lavels of office. It was very likely that a large number of porsons utilized this special privilege. In Eastern Han the grandsons of the Grand Minister were sometimes appointed in a similar fashion. Thus, there were those who entered officialdom on the strength of the influence of their fathers, brothers, or grandfathers, and were placed on an equal footing with the officially selected personnel.

The above methods led to the prevalence of the system of "disciples and ex-subordinates." Thus, especially close relations often arose between the selected candidate and the official who selected him. Chou Ching, a well-known Prefect of Eastern Han, was famous for his specially cordial relations with the official candidates he selected. Chou usually gave in his own residence several banquets in honor of each "Filial and Incorrupt" candidate, and regarded the latter as his son. He often made later selections from among the candidate's close relatives. On the other extreme, there was Han Yin, the Prefect of Ho-nei (in Honan), who would give his candidate only one farewell interview, and did not extend the favor of selection to members of the candidate's family.

Persons who held positions under a particular superior developed a relationship of specific loyalty to the latter. Even if the superior were later transferred to another post, the subordinate still considered himself his "ex-subordinate," and on this basis the superior–subordinate relationship was continued. At the death of the superior, the ex-subordinates often erected memorial tablets for him on which were inscribed their own names as testimony to the relationship. Ex-subordinates often wore mourning for the superior up to three years. This practice, occurring at a time when the period of mourning for parents was not yet finally fixed, demonstrated the importance attached to the relationship with one's superior official.

Candidates ministerially selected but not yet appointed to substantive positions were originally not to be considered as ex-subordinates of the selector. But as time went on, the tendency toward dependency on powerful personages overrode early scruples, so that by the end of the Eastern Han these candidates were also considered as ex-subordinates of their selectors.

Another method of dependency took the form of "disciples." This did not mean that one actually had to receive instruction from any person of influence. The word "disciple" was the cover used for the establishment of a dependent relationship with an influential person in the hope of receiving appointments. Originally, "disciple" denoted one who had studied under the direct pupils of a certain teacher. Ku Yen-wu (1613-1682) holds that, according to Han usage, the "pupils" were people who received instruction, and the "disciples" were those who attached themselves to a well-known personage because of his position and influence. For instance, Great General Tou Hsien, the brother of Empress Tou, and Wang Fu, a eunuch, were both said to have had disciples; obviously they could not have had disciples by way of teaching. Chao I (1727-1814) is of the opinion that, because those who generally followed the same school of thought were considered "disciples" of a master, as distinguished from "pupils," the practice had grown up whereby all who became dependents of a person out of consideration not for his knowledge but for his power came also to be known as disciples. This in later ages developed into the corrupt practice of gathering personal disciples and followers.

Such great families of Eastern Han as the Yüan of Ju-nan (in Honan) and the Yang of Hung-nung (in Honan) had attained the rank of Grand Minister through four successive generations, and their disciples and ex-subordinates were scattered over the whole country. Take for instance the disciples of the Yang family. When Yang Chen, due to slandering by others, was dismissed as Grand Commandant and went back to his home commandery, he was still followed by a large number of disciples. Before he committed suicide out of extreme chagrin, his disciples heard his will together with his sons. After his death, two of his disciples "went to prosecute his case at the capital, and the people at Court all praised their loyalty [to Yang Chen]."

Yang Chen probably had four sons. . . . They were Mu, Jang, Pin, and Feng. Mu's son, T'ung, and Jang's son, Chu, never became high officials. But Tz'u, the son of Pin, and Piao, the son of Tz'u, both became Grand Commandants. Later Ts'ao Ts'ao killed Piao's son, Yang Hsiu, out of jealousy of this great family. The story that he did it out of personal jealousy of Yang Hsiu's talent probably did not tell the whole truth. Yang T'ung also had disciples, although his official position was low. The memorial tablet of Yang Chen was erected by Yang T'ung's disciples. Thus, the disciples not only served one person, but also the entire family. Not only did they have to erect a tablet for the master's grandfather, but also they had to do it for the master's son. The "Tablet on Fortunate Youth" in the collection of inscriptions *Li-shih* was erected by disciples. On the memorial tablet of Yang Chu, who had been the magistrate of Kao-yang (in Hopei), were inscribed these words among the names of the erectors: "disciples of the Second Lord," and "disciples of Sir P'ei." The *Li-shih* notes: " 'Sir P'ei' was Yang T'ung, the Chancellor of P'ei; 'The Second Lord' was Yang Pin, the Grand Commandant. The latter was called 'Second,' because Yang Chen had held that post before him. Thus 'Sir P'ei' was Chu's cousin, and 'the Second Lord' was his younger paternal uncle."

It is quite likely that very few of the

Yang family in the above-mentioned generations did not have disciples. That was precisely one of the major reasons why the Yang became a famous clan of Eastern Han.

7. Great Families and Politics: Selection and Requests for Positions

In order to increase their political power, the wealthy great families became active in influencing the selection of officials. As early as the beginning of Eastern Han "dishonest selection" had become an issue.

Upon his accession to the throne in 58 A.D., the second emperor of Eastern Han issued a decree condemning dishonest practices as well as the meddling of powerful families in official selections, and calling for reports on malpractices. This was clear proof that the great families had already taken root in politics. It also became obvious that Emperor Ming's desire to correct the situation did not bear fruit, as was demonstrated by a decree of his successor, Emperor Chang, one year after the latter's accession (77 A.D.). Here again irregularities in the selection of officials were condemned: local officials were said to name the "Abundant Talent" and "Filial and Incorrupt" classes by the hundred every year, despite the fact that these were not actually all men of the right qualifications for official duties. The emperor invoked as an example the good system of past ages, in which men of talent, albeit of rustic background and unconnected with the great families, could expect to be chosen for government careers.

In the fifth year (93 A.D.) of the next reign, Emperor Ho, having killed the members of the dictatorial Tou family, again issued a decree against current practices. He pointed out that the reforms were not carried out in the selection of officials, with the result that "the wrong persons occupy official positions, and the common people suffer from maladministration." This shows that Emperor Chang before him had also been unable to effect any reform in the system.

Another noticeable irregularity was the selection of a large proportion of young persons, in the hope that they might in the future amply repay the selector. This phenomenon also appeared early in Eastern Han, for during the reign of Kuang-wu a memorial from Fan Shu, the son of the great landlord Fan Hung, specifically mentioned the practice of selecting young candidates at the expense of men of mature experience and renown.

Thus, the Court was not able to eradicate dishonest practices in official selection through several reigns. By the time of Emperor Shun (126–145 A.D.), politics had reached such a corrupt stage that certain literati could not tolerate it further. Tso Hsiung, for instance, proposed a method of age restrictions, which for a time resulted in some improvement of the situation. First he described in a memorial the injustices involved in official selections, and the resultant oppression in government; but the strongly entrenched power of the eunuchs prevented the emperor from taking effective steps. Then he made the proposal that "those under forty years of age should not qualify for selection as 'Filial and Incorrupt' candidates," and that there should be exceptions only in cases of men of extraordinary talent. Opponents to this plan, such as Hu Kuang, also memorialized the emperor, quoting incidents in ancient times to prove that age was no determinant of ability. However, they failed to move Emperor Shun's decision for reform.

Tso Hsiung was then the Grand Secretary of State. He soon successfully disqualified an under-forty candidate who classified himself as one of extraordinary talent, therefore entitled to exemption from the age regulations. Thenceforth selection practices became stringent. During the ten-odd years of his Secretaryship the number of candidates drastically decreased, and the system was put in some order. Among the small number of selected candidates were persons like Ch'en Fan, Li Ying, and others, who later figured prominently in the political inquisition owing to their anti-eunuch stand. Furthermore, Tso Hsiung invited well-known scholars as instructors, and encouraged advanced studies by ambitious and upright young men, so that the number of students in the capital greatly increased. Tso Hsiung, in fact, was becoming a leader of the scholar's party.

The utterly ridiculous practices in official selection before Emperor Shun's reign can be illustrated by the following story from the "Life of Chung Sung" in the *Later Han History:*

At first [Chung Sung] was a minor government clerk in the district office. At that time Wang Tan, nephew of the Ho-nan magistrate T'ien Hsin, was known for his ability to judge personalities. [T'ien] Hsin said to him, "It is now time to recommend six 'Filial and Incorrupt' candidates. I have already received written requests from powerful personages for most of the quota, and it is better that I do not reject them. But I want to select one scholar of my own choice, in order to repay our country. Do help me to find such a man." The next day, as [Wang] Tan was seeing some guests off at Ta-yang Gate, he saw [Chung] Sung from a distance, and was powerfully impressed. Upon his return he told [T'ien] Hsin, "I have found the candidate for you. He is right at hand, a minor government clerk in Lo-yang."

It was evidently unusual even to have one candidate out of six chosen without special requests. This testifies to the political influence enjoyed by the great families. Moreover, such influence could not be stemmed by temporary corrective measures, such as that initiated by Tso Hsiung.

The great families made requests not only to the local authorities, but also to the central government. After Tso Hsiung's time the authority of the central government rested with either the empresses' families or with the eunuchs, both of which groups themselves comprised great families. Local great families began to establish connections with them, and the selection of officials worsened. The situation at the end of Han was described by [a contemporary] Wang Fu, in his *Discourses of a Hermit,* as follows: ". . . Name corresponded not with actuality, desire matched not the recommendations. The rich relied on their wealth, the powerful brandished their weight and influence. The possession of much money constituted virtue, and unyielding hardness became a superior quality." A contemporary doggerel quoted in the "Book on Examination of Officials" in the fourth century work *Pao-p'u-tzu* ran:

The "Chosen Scholar" thinks learning's a bother,
The "Filial and Incorrupt" lives apart from his father,
Poverty and purity are considered not smart,
Grandees and generals are like chickens at heart.

With such selection, and such officials, it is not difficult to imagine the degree of corruption in politics. The common people of course were the victims of such government, but the more law-abiding great families—usually the relatively less wealthy—and the scholars who aspired to government positions were also frustrated in their objectives. Thereupon they united their forces, and took action against the corrupt government before the common people had begun to stir.

8. Political Control by Families of Empresses and Eunuchs

Political authority in late Eastern Han rested in the hands of the eunuchs and families of the empresses. These comprised two sorts of great families; their influence had a particularly close relation with the central government. In general, the empresses' families were already great families, but suddenly underwent particular expansion after obtaining power in the central government. The eunuchs were originally not great families, but with their ascendancy to power large numbers of people began to gather under them as dependents, and with further development the eunuchs too became especially great families.

The empresses' families and eunuchs were known as "lucky risers." This was especially true of the eunuchs, whose rise was a sudden over-night phenomenon. The two groups were for the most part untrained in letters. Their elders, "riding on dragons and flying with phoenixes," did not need to study; those of the younger generation were pampered from infancy and did not know how to study. They lacked political insight, not to mention political experience. They were ignorant of the principle "keep by right methods that which was first obtained by wrong," and thought only of even more rapid expansion of their suddenly acquired power. Therefore, aside from exploiting the common people, they had to strike at other great families and rob the latter of their property and rank. As the large fish finds that eating small fish is more nourishing than eating shrimp, so did the empresses' families and eunuchs find the above a very convenient method of expansion.

The sudden rise to power of empresses' families and eunuchs roused dissatisfaction on the part of the conservative group of great families. Many persons among these were high officials and leaders of the intelligentsia. They knew their Classics, and understood the axiom of Mencius: "If close-meshed nets are not allowed in pools and ponds, the supply of fish and turtles will be inexhaustible." Therefore in addition to their feelings of insecurity resulting from the selfish attitudes of the newly risen great families, they also were opposed to the latter's policy of "drying the lake to get the fish." They realized that, if the newly risen were given a free hand, the rule of the Han dynasty would be threatened. Thereupon a sense of loyalty and righteousness suddenly asserted itself. Motivated by a combination of public spirit and self-interest, they started to resist the newly risen families.

There was no very clear-cut distinction between the newly risen and conservative groups, nor did the distinction appear suddenly. That they were each able to form a separate group was due to the fact that owing to their connections with relatives, household followers, disciples, and ex-subordinates, they had already evolved into great-family units. Because of common interest, great families began to unite themselves for the struggle; the more fierce the struggle, the greater the unity.

It has been argued that the struggle between the newly risen and the conservatives represented one between metropolitan and local great families. This is partly true, but it does not tell the whole story. For, although the empresses' families and eunuchs were the metropolitan great families, they could not have swallowed all local magnates at one gulp. With some of the local magnates they had established friendly connections, and the natural tendency was for them to ally themselves with similar great families and overrun others that were antagonistic.

The empresses' families and eunuchs were "wealthy but quite ignorant," while the intelligentsia were "learned but not very wealthy." Polarization gradually developed between these two groups. However, not all empresses' families were "wealthy but quite ignorant"; occasionally they also united with the intelligentsia. Hence we cannot call the struggle between the two groups one of empresses' families and eunuchs against the intelligentsia. The intelligentsia often considered themselves the "pure ones." Therefore let us call the "learned and not very wealthy" (i.e. the conservatives) the "Pure Group," and the "wealthy but quite ignorant" ones (i.e. the newly risen) the "Turbid Group." Political struggle intensified with the widening of the gulf between the Pures and the Turbids.

The influence of the Turbids was due to their control of the sovereign. And the authority of the sovereign resulted from the centralization of power from the time of Emperor Kuang-wu on. Actually the centralization of power did not begin with Kuang-wu, but went back to Emperor Wu of Western Han. However, Kuang-wu made the system more definite. Chung-ch'ang T'ung has given the following clear account of the causes and effects of Kuang-wu's centralization:

Emperor Kuang-wu, angry at the loss of [imperial] power during the preceding reigns, and incensed by the usurpation of the [Heavenly] mandate by strong officials, went to the other extreme and never delegated administrative authority to subordinates. Although the three Grand Ministers were installed, matters were actually entrusted to the Grand Secretary of State. Henceforth, the function of the Grand Ministers consisted of no more than the staffing of their own offices. . . . Power then shifted to the empresses' families, and imperial favor was granted to personal attendants.

The centralization of power was indeed a double-edged sword. Under an able emperor it could be used to curb the great families; but under an incompetent emperor it could be grasped by the great families and used by them to control the emperor.

In looking for a reliable force to wield this sword for him, an ignorant and weak ruler naturally thought his relatives would be the most trustworthy. During Eastern Han many an emperor died young and, like as not, left no heir. His widow, fearful of the future, often chose to supervise the rule of the heir, who was generally adopted from a feudatory house, thus placing real authority in the hands of her own relatives. In this way power was transferred to the empresses' families.

As a result of imperial grants, these empresses' families were already extremely wealthy, but with the assumption of power they became even more acquisitive. For example Tou Hsien, as the Empress Dowager's relative, controlled the government during the reign of Emperor Ho (89–106 A.D.). The Tou family had been magnates for many generations, first achieving prominence as an empress' family in the time of Emperor Wen (179–156 B.C.) in Western Han. Their tremendous wealth and power at the beginning of Eastern Han is described in the *Later Han History*. Tou Hsien's sister was the wife of Emperor Chang. On the strength of the sister's position Tou Hsien once even tried to seize an estate belonging to a princess, but was temporarily curbed by Emperor Chang, who called him a stinking rat. After the death of the emperor, Empress Dowager Tou supervised the reign of Emperor Ho, whereupon Tou Hsien had the control of the government in his hands. After his successful campaign against the Hsiung-nu he was invested with the title of Great General, ranking above the Grand Ministers, and his followers filled official posts in all parts of the country. Ultimately he overreached himself. He was killed and his party suppressed by the careful planning of the emperor, who allied himself with eunuchs in the venture. This was the first instance of the eunuch's interference in politics. Thereafter their influence steadily increased and they constantly plotted to usurp power. They did so sometimes in alliance with the empresses' families, sometimes in opposition to them.

Another case of the empress' family assuming power occurred in the reign of Emperor Huan (147–168 A.D.). The Empress Dowager Liang came of a magnate's family that dated back to Western Han. Her brother Liang Chi was also invested as Great General, with 30,000 dependent families to his fief; in addition, other members of the family also received large grants. But the Liangs and their followers were not satisfied, and frequently used various methods to augment their wealth. For instance, Liang Chi himself confiscated, on the basis of trumped-up charges, the entire property of some 170,000,000 [cash] that belonged to a miserly magnate, T'u-sun Fen. Many of Liang Chi's own men were also placed at Court, and he became so overbearing in his conduct that the emperor, like Emperor Ho before him, again sought the aid of the eunuchs and suppressed the Liang group in a coup in which thousands lost their lives. Liang's property was auctioned and brought in over 3,000,000 [cash] to the government treasury. Again the fortunes of the empress' family were ruined by the eunuchs.

All five eunuchs who helped to organize the coup were ennobled on the same day, and henceforth were known as the "Five Lords." Their fiefs ranged from 20,000 to 13,000 families each, and money grants from 15,000,000 to 13,000,000 cash each. The leading person, Tan Ch'ao, died soon after, but the other four lorded it over the country unchecked. Contemporary epithets described them individually as follows: "Tso [Kuan] can turn heaven upside down; Chü [Yüan] sits on peerless heights; Hsü [Huang] is like a recumbent tiger; T'ang [Heng] rains evil upon us." Sons were adopted to inherit their ranks, and relatives were given official posts. Thus, though without lineal heirs, the eunuchs still succeeded in founding great families with their dependents. These were an utterly unlettered group, very turbid indeed. The Pures could not tolerate them and directly attacked them with the Pures' own dependent groups. The frontal clash between the Pures and the Turbids constituted the two "political inquisitions" of Eastern Han.

9. Rise of Great Families of the Intellectuals

Though economically not as strong as the Turbids, the Pures nevertheless had large numbers of dependents who followed them for the fame that could be derived from such connections and the moderately well-to-do intellectuals, such as the Fellows of the National Academy, originated what was known as "public opinion" in Eastern Han. The interpretation of Chang Ping-lin (1868–1936) that they were "representatives" of public opinion, who aided the administration of local governments, is probably far-fetched. Nevertheless, according to some extant stone inscriptions dating to Eastern Han, the term *i-jen,* or *i-min* referred to corvée-exempt privileged persons, and presumably denoted those who expressed opinions on public affairs and also occupied positions of prestige in society.

Many persons resorted to deceitful devices in order to create favorable local opinion of themselves and facilitate selection to officialdom. Some succeeded, as for instance Hsü Wu and his two younger brothers, all of whom displayed the proper fraternal behavior under conditions of stress and succeeded in winning candidacies. Others failed, as in the case of Chao Hsüan, who first won a reputation as a filial son who lived for twenty years at his mother's tomb, but later was punished when it was found out that five sons were born to him during his period of mourning, which should have been a period of continence.

In response to the demand for local evaluation of personality, "censurers" appeared. For example, Hsü Shao at the end of Eastern Han was director of official selection at Ju-nan. He and his cousin Hsü Ching were both fond of censuring the local people, and published their comments once every month. Once, pressed for an opinion by Ts'ao Ts'ao before the latter had gained power, Hsü Shao had commented "You are a villain in times of peace and a hero in times of trouble," which despite the obvious barbs greatly pleased Ts'ao Ts'ao. Relations were not friendly between Hsü Shao and Hsü Ching; other censures had a low estimate of the former, owing, very likely, to unfavorable comments on him from Hsü Ching.

Another famous censurer and contemporary of Hsü Shao was Kuo T'ai (127–169), leader of the National Academy Fellows. At that time the Academy Fellows were restless, and spent their time in criticizing current affairs or political personages. Kuo's policy was never to speak against others, but always to confine himself to favorable comments when he did express his opinion. His fame was prodigious. On one occasion when he left Lo-yang for his home district the scholars who came to bid farewell arrived in several thousand chariots. When among all these multitudes Li Ying, the Pure magistrate of Ho-nan, alone was allowed to cross the river with him, the others envied Li for such immortal honor.

The Grant Ministers often solicited advice from censurers before reaching decisions on the selection of officials. This opened the way for opportunists and imposters, such as the two self-styled censurers Chin Wen-ching and Huang Tzu-ai. They began by striking an impressive pose, thus winning the admiration of many high officials at Court, but they were exposed as frauds by Fu Jang, disciple of the aforementioned Li Ying. Chin and Huang fled Lo-Yang *sans* honor and *sans* fame. Since his delineation of their character had turned out to be correct, Fu Jang was able to reap further honors out of this episode as a censurer.

The National Academy was actually an avenue to officialdom. At first fifty fellowships were created by Emperor Wu of Western Han. The Fellows were selected by the Minister of Rites, or recommended by local officials, and all were exempt from labor service. Examinations were held once a year, out of which a number of Fellows were sent to fill official posts. Gradually the number of Fellows was increased, until it reached three thousand in the time of Emperor Yüan (48–32 B.C.). Extra quotas were added in the reign of Emperor P'ing (1–6 A.D.) for sons of officials of the *yüan-shih* rank. Placements through examination thenceforth were divided into three classes, with a total of one hundred per year.

In the early years of Eastern Han the scholarly traditions of the former period were maintained in the Academy, but the spirit of learning declined sharply after the reign of Emperor An. The professors neglected their teaching, the Fellows neglected their studies, and the Academy premises were turned into a vegetable garden. Later Emperor Shun, following the advice of high officials, restored and expanded the physical plant of the Academy, which now possessed 240 buildings with a total of 1,850 rooms. The Fellows at this time numbered some 30,000, ten times that of Western Han.

Most of the Fellows probably came not to learn the Classics but to seek entrance into officialdom. Actually contemporary scholarship in the Classics was probably not very interesting. It merely involved extremely detailed textual commentaries; sometimes a ten-thousand word study was made to explain one word. Therefore the Academy Fellows paid scant attention to the Classical texts, but concentrated on frivolities, political discussions, and the making of social connections. They can be considered as a kind of public opinion makers, who often voiced their criticism of political affairs and personalities. Some high officials, fearing their unfavorable comments, personally sought them out for friendship. The Fellows were glad of this opportunity to establish connections with those in high places, and called themselves the latter's friends or disciples. Such persons as Kuo T'ai and Chia Piao, for instance, became leaders of the 30,000 Academy Fellows, and together with people like Li Ying mutually sang each other's praises. The fellows coined seven-word slogans for every person whom they esteemed. . . .

Thus, the Academy Fellows became united with the Pure ministers into a clique, and later were banned from official employment due to their strife with the eunuchs. However, the political inquisitions did not originate in the Eastern Han period. On the contrary, they had made their initial appearance, at the latest, during the reign of Wang Mang. It is recorded in the "Biography of Yun Ch'ang" in the *Early Han History:*

Yün Ch'ang, styled Yu-ju, was a native of P'ing-lin [in Hopei]. He studied under Wu Chang of the same district, who was a specialist on *The Book of History* and an Academy professor. . . . Being a famous scholar of the time, [Wu] Chang was exceedingly popular as a teacher, having under him over one thousand pupils. [Wang] Mang considered them a villainous clique deserving to be banned entirely from official employment. Thereupon his pupils named others as their teachers.

([Yen] Shih-ku comments: The pupils changed to other teachers, and avoided mention of [Wu] Chang as their teacher.)

The eunuchs of Eastern Han probably were merely following the example of Wang Mang.

The formation of the Northern and Southern factions in Kan-ling Commandery (in Shantung) probably marked the beginning of political cliques in Eastern Han. Chou Fu, a native of Kan-ling, had tutored Emperor Huan when the latter was still a prince. Upon the latter's accession Chou Fu was raised to the office of Secretary of State. At that time Fang Chih, the magistrate of Ho-nan who also came from Kan-ling, was a man of renown in the government. The friends and relatives of Fang Chih then began to circulate the saying: "Fang Po-wu (i.e. Fang Chih) sets an example of good for the country; Chou Chung-chin (i.e. Chou Fu) is appointed for his connections as tutor," which was somewhat disrespectful toward Chou Fu. Thereupon the followers of these two families began to jeer at and attack each other, each rounding up its own group, and a feud gradually developed. Kan-ling was thus divided into the opposing Northern and Southern factions. "Faction" meant "clique," which shows the importance of the role played by the followers and disciples in the ranks of each camp.

The keeping of household followers prevailed in Eastern Han. These persons still maintained a degree of the sense of personal loyalty that had marked their counterparts during the Warring States. Like the disciples and ex-subordinates, they were often willing to risk their lives for their masters, as several episodes show. The episodes involving Li Ku's disciple Kuo Liang and Tu Ch'iao's ex-subordinate Yang K'uang during the time of Liang Chi's control of government is a case in point. The Pures, then, encouraged by the prospects of fame and supported by loyal followers, charged into the field and gave battle to the overwhelmingly powerful Turbids, thereby touching off the earth-shaking political contest that followed.

10. Internal Strife among Great Families: The First Political Inquisition

The eunuchs ennobled by Emperor Huan after his coup against Liang Chi brought the tyranny and rapacity of their conduct to a new height. Some of their followers actually practised highway robbery, not to speak of the more refined methods of extortion and oppression. Their first major setback was suffered in 165 A.D., when Grand Commandant Ch'en Fan, who succeeded Yang Chen, was able to force the suicide of two of the eunuch leaders and bring about the demotion or dismissal of many of their relatives and followers from official posts. A few years before, however, three Pure officials—Li Ying, magistrate of Ho-nan; Feng K'un, Governor of a jail; and Liu Yu, Minister of Agriculture—had been sentenced to hard labor because of their actions against the interests of influential eunuchs. They were only pardoned upon the vigorous intercession of Garrison Commander Ying Feng.

In 166 A.D. Li Ying was appointed a Garrison Commander. Within ten days of his taking office he tried and executed Chang So, a tyrannous magistrate who happened also to be the brother of the eunuch Chang Jang. Thereafter the eunuchs conducted themselves with extreme caution, and upon the emperor's query tearfully answered that they "feared Commander Li."

Meantime, other Pure officials also were exerting themselves in the suppression of eunuch agents within their jurisdictions. For instance, Fan Pang, personnel director at Ju-nan, had the support of his superior Tsung Tzu, the Prefect of Ju-nan, in his stand against pressure from eunuchs. Ch'ing Chin, personnel director at Nan-yang, also was trusted completely by Ch'eng Chin, the Prefect of Nan-yang. Both Ch'ing Chih and Liu Chih, Prefect of T'ai-yüan, resorted to confiscation of property and execution of eunuchs or their followers, after the latter had already received formal pardons. Chang Chien, a famous scholar who was Post Inspector of Shan-yang (in Shantung), once impeached the eunuch Hou Lan because "he forcibly seized others' property to the amount of 381 houses and 118 ch'ing of land. He built sixteen mansions . . . and robbed graves. . . ." Failing to receive orders for action, Chang Chien proceeded on his own, confiscating Hou's property and destroying his home. Many other cases involving prominent eunuchs also occurred in the years 165 and 166. In the latter year, as a result of pressure brought to bear on Emperor Huan by the eunuchs, the first political inquisition took place against outstanding anti-eunuch officials who were members of the Pure Clique. In the autumn of 166, Ch'eng Chin and Liu Chih both died in prison. In the winter of the same year, Li Ying and some two hundred others were imprisoned on grounds of being Pure men. Emperor Huan initiated this mass imprisonment on charges lodged against them in 165 by Lao Hsiu, disciple of the charlatan Chang Ch'eng, who bore a grudge against Li Ying. In his charge Lao Hsiu said Li Ying and others "maintained Academy Fellows and errant scholars . . . and formed themselves into factions and cliques. They criticized the government and disturbed the public morals."

Arrests were carried out, and a man-hunt was begun for those who escaped. Grand Commandant Ch'en Fan, however, refused to put his signature to the order for imprisonment, saying: "All those who are about to be investigated are persons highly regarded throughout the country as loyal and public-spirited officials; they deserve to be pardoned even if their descendants should be criminals for ten generations to come. How can we round them up in prison before their offense has been defined?" This further incensed the emperor, who summarily jailed Li Ying and others. Ch'en Fan advised against it, but to no avail. Instead, he himself was dismissed by the emperor on the grounds that he had proved himself incompetent in the selection of officials.

Among those imprisoned was Fan Pang, who proved to be an outspoken leader of the jailed scholars. Asked at their trial why they had organized into a clique, Fan Pang replied, "To bring good persons together so as to magnify their goodness and bring about a united effort to eliminate evil persons." On another occasion he said, "In olden times people were good so as to increase their own fortune. Nowadays people who are good invite catastrophe. . . . I have a clean record and a clear conscience. . . ."

There were some among the Pure clique who were more cautious. Seeing that the inquisition was calamitous and involved large numbers of persons, they began to appeal for help from the Empress Tou's relatives and other high officials. Moreover, Li Ying and others also named some of the eunuchs' followers as members of the Pure Clique, which intimidated the eunuchs. Prompted by the latter's importunities, the emperor decreed a general amnesty in 167 A.D. The members of the clique were banished to their home districts and were forbidden to have official employment as long as they lived. Thus ended the first political inquisition.

11. Internal Strife among the Great Families: The Second Political Inquisition

The first political inquisition was but a prologue to the serious frontal clash that was to occur later.

Emperor Huan died without heir in 167 A.D. Ch'en Fan, Tou Wu, and others placed a minor on the throne as Emperor Ling, and the Empress Dowager Tou supervised the reign. The Tou family had retained a good deal of power. Tou Wu, the brother of the Empress Dowager, had already established good relations with the Academy Fellows and the Pure party. For instance, the Academy Fellows had chosen as the Three Esteemed ones Tou Wu, Ch'en

Fan, and Liu Shu, the last-named being a member of the imperial house. With the accession of Emperor Ling, Tou Wu became invested as Great General, and Ch'en Fan became Assistant Grand Tutor. Under them people like Li Ying, Wang Ch'ang, and many other Pures received official appointments. Besides the Three Esteemed Ones, the Academy Fellows also had a series of four gradations of eight persons each, denoting succeeding levels of esteem for each person. Among these figured Fan Pang, Chang Chien, Ch'ing Chih, and others, all of whom, with only minor exceptions, were officials.

There was thus a total of thirty-five Pure leaders who had the support of the Academy Fellows and were in a position to eradicate the Turbids. However, though the political views of the Pures differed from those of the Turbids, they were none the less also out to seek political power for themselves. Now that this had been largely achieved, especially for Tou Wu and his family, the urge to act became dulled. Despite repeated promptings by Ch'en Fan for action against the eunuchs, Tou Wu and the Empress Dowager continued to procrastinate.

Then in 168 the news leaked out that Ch'en and Tou were determined to kill the eunuchs. The latter forestalled them with a coup d'état, took the imperial seal from the Empress Dowager, and placed it in the hands of the twelve-year old Emperor Ling. On hearing of this Ch'en Fan rushed to the palace with a group of eighty-odd armed disciples, but they were overpowered and Ch'en was murdered in prison that night. In the meantime, Tou Wu succeeded in rallying a few thousand metropolitan Guards to fight an equivalent force commanded by Wang Fu and other eunuchs. But the Guards, used to fearing the authority of the eunuchs, failed Tou Wu, who thereupon committed suicide. The Ch'en and Tou families, together with their followers, were convicted and sentenced. The families were sent into exile and the disciples and ex-subordinates were barred from official employment. This was the beginning of the second political inquisition, which was marked by the destructon of the Ch'en and Tou families.

In 169, in an attempt to curry favor with the eunuch Hou Lan, someone informed the emperor against Chang Chien and twenty-four others on grounds of "plotting against the state." Emperor Ling thereupon ordered the imprisonment of over one hundred scholars, including Li Ying and Fan Pang. Li died of torture in prison. Fan Pang, on hearing that the government agent assigned to arrest him was instead closeting himself at home with the warrant and weeping, went and delivered himself to the local magistrate. The latter advised him to flee, but Fan Pang refused; later he too died in prison together with some hundred others.

Chang Chien, on the contrary, fled from the authorities and went beyond the Great Wall. All along his route of escape entire families were exterminated by the eunuch's agents for giving him aid and comfort. Altogether a large number of families were directly or indirectly involved in this inquisition, and six or seven hundred persons were permanently barred from further employment.

However, there were some cautious elements among the Pures who were able to escape the upheaval. For instance, Kuo T'ai secretly lamented the deaths of the scholars, but did not openly express any opinion on the subject. He had been listed in one of the categories of esteemed persons by the Academy Fellows, but had been careful not to offend any quarters in his daily utterances. Now the Academy Fellows were the only remaining force of the Pure group. The Fellows had had a long history of participating in political affairs; their first intercession went back to the end of Western Han, and several others occurred previous to the first political inquisition. On each occasion, as when they interceded for the Prefect of I-chou in 153, their efforts were met with some success. It did not appear that the Fellows themselves had suffered great losses in the two inquisitions just described. Yet the eunuchs were aware that the Fellows were seething with unrest. In 170 the Empress Dowager Tou, who had lived under surveillance of the eunuchs since the coup of 168, died. Shortly afterward someone scrawled various accusations on the Palace gate, charging the eunuchs with murdering the Empress Dowager, the high officials with accepting sinecures and being disloyal, and Hou Lan with killing Pure men. After this incident over one thousand Fellows were thrown into prison by imperial order. Thereafter misfortune became the lot of whoever spoke in favor of the Pures. The eunuchs and their Turbid faction lorded it over the entire country, staffed the government at all levels with their own men, and wantonly killed off all opponents. It was not until 184 A.D. that a slightly more enlightened eunuch, Lu Ch'iang, advised Emperor Ling to rescind the order banning the Pures from government employ, so as to prevent them from collaborating with the Yellow Turbans. By that time the revolt of the Yellow Turbans was already a year old.

To sum up the political contest of the two decades: Despite the fact that the actual conditions were quite complex, this was nothing but an unrelenting struggle for power between the Pures and the Turbids. Both were supported by family members, household followers, disciples, and ex-subordinates. The martyrs showed to a high degree a sense of loyalty and righteousness, but the object of such loyalty was not so much the country and sovereign as their own superiors and teachers. Nevertheless, the fact that they were able to fight showed that they could unite in one purpose; it also showed that the political influence of great families was already strong. Such unity of great families was further evidenced during the upheavals of the Three Kingdoms period, as described in the *Records of the Three Kingdoms* and the *Tsin History*. With the granting of legal recognition to the special privileges of the great families, the rule of powerful families during the two Tsin and Northern and Southern dynasties was initiated.

H. G. CREEL

The Eclectics of Han Thought

As the Han imperial system became the basic structure of a unified and centralized government in traditional China, there had been a tendency to glorify the civil and military achievements of the Han Dynasty. The so-called triumph of Confucianism under the Han Emperor Wu (Han Wu-ti, r. 140–87 B.C.) was one of the myths in the service of that tendency. The fact is that this Confucianism was only a convenient façade for the Legalistic operations of the government. Even within the school of Han Confucianism, a great variety of conceptions of other schools were adopted. The obvious example is Tung Chung-shu (179–104 B.C.), one of the great Confucianists, if not the greatest, of the Han period. In Tung's cosmological theory, which sought symmetries in natural phenomena, one can easily detect the influence of Taoism and Mohism, and probably the theory of the Five Elements.[1]

In the following selection, Dr. H. G. Creel, Martin A. Ryerson Distinguished Service Professor of Chinese History at the University of Chicago, examines the eclectics of Han thought from the origin of the dynasty to the social and political circumstances that influenced its development. He points out that three human factors should be given particular attention: the rulers, the scholars, and the mass of the people.

Professor Creel compares the intellectual environment in China's feudal independent states from the sixth century to the unification in 221 B.C. with that of the unified Chinese empire. In the days of Confucius (551–479 B.C.), Mencius (372–289 B.C.), and Han Fei Tzu (d. 233 B.C.), if one did not like one state, he could go to another, but under a centralized unified empire, there was no place for the

---

Reprinted from *Chinese Thought from Confucius to Mao Tse-tung* by H. G. Creel, by permission of The University of Chicago Press. © 1953 by H. G. Creel. All rights reserved. Footnotes omitted.

[1] Recent studies have questioned that Tung Chung-shu made any reference to the theory of the Five Elements. The *History of the Former Han Dynasty (Han-shu)* by Pan Ku (32–92), the most authentic source on Tung Chung-shu, never mentions Tung's interest in the "Five Elements," and the parts of the *Ch'un-ch'iu fan-lu* or *Luxuriant Dew from the Spring and Autumn Annals* (traditionally attributed to Tung Chung-shu) dealing with the "Five Elements" are not authentic. See, for example, Tai Chün-jen, "Tung chung-shu pu-shuo wu-hsing k'ao" (Tung Chung-shu Never Discussed the Five Elements), *Bulletin of the National Central Library*, vol. 2, no. 2 (Oct. 1968), 9–19. The arguments supported by numerous documents are quite convincing. Reexamination and revision of this part of Tung Chung-shu's thought has thus become necessary.

dissatisfied to go. In the former days philosophers had rebuked rulers with impunity, but in the unified empire one might be put to death if he merely acted discourteously toward some worthless favorite of the emperor. It is no wonder that under such circumstances men's minds were not very creative. The result of such an intellectual climate is the emergence of an expedient, eclectic way of thinking that avoids conflicts and stresses compromise. This is the climate of opinion that gave birth to the electics of Han thought.

In the West we do not usually think of government and philosophy as being intimately related. In China, however, they have commonly been linked quite closely. Most of the Chinese philosophers we have considered held government offices of some sort, and those who did not were very much interested in the way government was carried on. The connection between government and philosophy became especially apparent in the last centuries before the Christian Era.

In 213 B.C., under the short-lived Ch'in dynasty, almost all the philosophical literature was proscribed, and discussion of the classics that were particularly in vogue among the Confucians was forbidden. Legalism was in the saddle. A few years later, after the founding of the Han dynasty, the situation as regards philosophies was fluid. When we come to the time of the Emperor Wu, who reigned from 140 to 87 B.C., students of Legalist writings were barred from official positions, an imperial university was established for the study of the Confucian classics, and considerable strides were made in the development of the examination system. Since that time, a large proportion of Chinese officials have normally been appointed on the basis of examinations in the Confucian classics.

Thus, in the space of less than a century, the full swing was made from the situation under Ch'in, in which Legalism was the officially sanctioned doctrine, to that under the Han Emperor Wu, in which we have what is commonly called "the triumph of Confucianism."

The nature of Confucian orthodoxy, and the position that it has occupied in China during the last two thousand years, were profoundly affected by its so-called "triumph" in Han times. Many attempts have been made to explain this event. Some scholars have sought to interpret it as solely the consequence of the political and economic circumstances of the age, moving along inevitable lines to a predictable result. Others have gone to the other extreme and tried to explain it as due simply to the predilections of certain rulers and their close advisers. Still others—and there are many of these—have said that the Emperor Wu adopted Confucianism as the official philosophy of his government because Confucianism emphasized the subservience of subjects to the ruler, and enhanced the power and prestige of the emperor and the ruling class.

Whatever else may be right or wrong about them, all these generalizations are much too simple. If we are really to understand what took place, we must try to forget preconceived theories and examine with care what actually happened. We must of course consider the political and economic circumstances, for they are an important part of the data. Particular attention needs to be paid, however, to three human factors: the rulers, the scholars, and last but not least the mass of the people.

Anciently the aristocrats could almost ignore the ignorant masses. But the masses had become far less ignorant. The founder of the Han dynasty was so poor as a young man that his wife—later a reigning empress of supreme and terrible power—worked in the fields with her own hands. But at the same time his younger brother studied philosophy with a disciple of Hsün Tzu. We have already noticed that as early as the days of Confucius and Mencius the common people of eastern China had come to enjoy such importance that certain great families cultivated their favor, and found it useful in promoting their political ambitions.

This was not equally true in the relatively uncultured state of Ch'in. We have some evidence that its people did not enjoy the severe repression that their government exercised, any more than a horse likes to be beaten, but like the horse they were used to it and made little protest. One of the greatest mistakes that the First Emperor of Ch'in made was to suppose that the whole Chinese people could long be confined within the strait jacket of savage discipline to which the people of his native state submitted meekly.

Only a few years passed before a peasant began the rebellion, in the east, and he was immediately joined by all sorts of men, including a number of Confucians and Moists. As one of his chief advisers he had the direct heir of Confucius in the eighth generation. The peasant leader seems to have believed that Confucianism had propaganda appeal to the masses. He and the descendant of Confucius were killed together after a few months, but this did not stop the revolution, which had spread like wildfire. The Ch'in imperial regime virtually collapsed of itself as the result of palace intrigues; but after it had been overthrown, it was still necessary to decide who should found a dynasty to replace it. War continued for several years, between the two most able of the revolutionary generals.

One of the generals, Hsiang Yü by name, was the very type of the hereditary aristocrat. His ancestors had held fiefs, and had been distinguished as generals, for generations. In the field he was so skilful that it is said he never lost a battle of which he was personally in command. His manner was so imposing that, it is reported, men instinctively fell to their knees at his approach, and even the war horses of his adversaries neighed and fled in terror when he bent his piercing gaze upon them. As befitted one so highly bred, he had a very low regard for humanity in general, and enjoyed nothing so much as to boil or burn a captured enemy alive, or order his soldiers to slaughter every man, woman, and child in a captured area.

Since Hsiang Yü was always successful in battle, it may seem a little surprising that he lost the war. He himself was completely baffled by the fact that, although he led his men to victory after victory, his armies slowly melted away until finally he had to commit suicide.

His adversary, who founded the Han dynasty, was the first man of plebeian birth to sit on the Chinese throne. For convenience we may call him by the name that history has given him, Han Kao Tsu. The son of a farmer, he accidentally broke one of the Ch'in laws and had to flee for his life. He became a bandit chief, and when the revolution came emerged as one of the leading generals. It was not as a strategist that he excelled, however, but as a leader of men, one who could select capable strategists and men with other skills and get them to exert themselves in his service.

His self-control was almost incredible. On one occasion, when his army was drawn up opposite that of his enemy, he met Hsiang Yü in full sight of both armies for a parley. Hsiang Yü drew a hidden crossbow and shot him in the chest. Han Kao Tsu was seriously wounded. If his soldiers, who were looking on, had realized this, they would have been dangerously discouraged. Without a moment's hesitation Han Kao Tsu picked up his foot and cried out, "Oh, this villain has shot me in the toe!"

He was ruthless. He fought by every means, fair or foul, that promised success. He pledged his word and violated it as served his purpose. He was capable of sacrificing the lives of thousands of men and women, and even the lives of his own children, to save his own life.

If this were all, he would have been only another intelligent and ruthlessly ambitious man. But Han Kao Tsu was far more. He was a profound student of psychology. He knew that he could not afford to appear ruthless. Therefore, whenever he could do so without injuring his cause, he was conspicuously generous. He gave his subordinates full credit for all his accomplishments and said that his only merit was that he had appreciated and used their abilities. When some of his followers plotted rebellion he first had them arrested, then pardoned them and restored them to posts of honor. He even treated his common soldiers well, which was unheard of.

Once Kao Tsu was emperor, a genealogy was of course made for him, proving that he was descended from the mythical emperor Yao. We might expect that he would have disowned, if not disposed of, all those who had known him as a common man. On the contrary, he gave offices to some of his early associates and exempted his home town from taxation. Furthermore, he returned there on one occasion and feasted all his old friends and acquaintances for some days, personally singing and dancing to entertain them.

Kao Tsu was no snob. In this he was sincere, but it was also policy. Homer H. Dubs has written: "Kao-tsu's generous and kindly treatment of the people thus brought to him the fellow-feeling of the people. They realized that he was one of them. More than once the leaders of the people came to him with important advice. His lack of manners and use of churlish language towards even his most distinguished followers probably accentuated the kindly feeling of the people to him. He won because he manipulated public opinion in his favor; that feeling was so strong two centuries later that, at the downfall of his dynasty, only another Han dynasty with the same surname could gain the throne."

Kao Tsu not only sought the people's favor by proclaiming amnesties, remitting taxes, freeing slaves, and so forth. He also, early in his struggle for power, gave the people a very limited voice in the government, by arranging that his officials should regularly consult with representatives of the people to ascertain their wishes. When he was made emperor, he said that he was accepting the title only "for the good of the people." Even after he was emperor he did not act arbitrarily, but only with the advice and consent of his ministers.

Gradually this practice achieved the force of unwritten law, so that decisions of his successors, if not ratified by their ministers, were considered illegal. Dubs says that "the accession of Kao-tsu marks the victory of the Confucian conception that the imperial authority is limited, should be exercised for the benefit of the people, and should be founded upon justice, over the legalistic conception of arbitrary and absolute sovereignty. While Kao-tsu and his successors technically remained absolute sovereigns, in practice their powers were much limited by custom." Here, then, we have a government that to some extent agrees, in theory, with Confucius' idea of what a government should be: a government run *for* the people, *by* ministers selected by a ruler who leaves the administrative authority in their hands. Obviously, it was still far from Confucius' ideal, but it is surprising that a burly ruffian like Han Kao Tsu should have even approximated it.

Kao Tsu was no partisan of the Confucians. He considered them pompous bookworms and liked nothing better than to humiliate them with very vulgar practical jokes. Nevertheless he had some Confucians, including his own younger brother, among his intimate advisers, and they did all they could to Confucianize him, even writing a book for the purpose. Becoming disgusted with the rowdy manners of his rough companions in the court, Kao Tsu called upon a Confucian to devise a simple court ceremonial to be followed. Beyond doubt, however, what chiefly moved this shrewd statesman in favor of Confucianism was its popularity among the people.

It is often supposed that in Han times Confucianism was primarily the doctrine of aristocrats and wealthy landed gentry. This was not the case. Even as late as the first century B.C., after many of them had been made more prosperous by government subsidies, their enemies described the Confucians as a class of poverty-stricken scholars living on poor farms and in mean alleys, wearing plain clothing and torn sandals. As a group, they seem to have remained in economically depressed circumstances throughout the Han period. This very fact, however, kept them in touch with the people, and therefore influential with them.

Han Kao Tsu recognized this and exploited its propaganda value. During his struggle for power he preached a "crusade" against his adversary, Hsiang Yü, in Confucian language appearing frequently in his edicts. In 196 B.C. he ordered that his officials throughout the empire should recommend all virtuous and capable men to the throne, so that they might be honored and given positions. This practice, continued and elaborated by his successors, developed into the characteristically Confucian institution that we know as the Chinese examination system.

Nevertheless, Kao Tsu's court was neither exclusively nor predominantly Confucian. Taoism, with its large ideas and sweeping generalizations, naturally appealed to adventurers. Increasingly it was becoming amalgamated with the popular superstitions, which caused it to appeal to the masses. Since many of Kao Tsu's followers were adventurers of plebeian birth, it is not surprising that Taoism attracted them.

Neither was Legalistic thought by any means dead. Although the Confucians firmly believed that they should hold the principal offices in the government, they were too much occupied with questions of ritual, metaphysics, and literature to be bothered with the mundane problems of keeping house for the empire; they thought that such matters were unworthy of gentlemen anyway. But the Han state was a huge political and economic organization, that imperatively demanded complex administrative techniques and officials able to use them. Only the officials left from the Ch'in empire possessed these skills, and the Han emperor had to employ them. They were essentially Legalist in outlook.

The fourth Han sovereign, Emperor Wen, who reigned from 179 to 157 B.C., conformed in many respects to the ideal of what a Confucian ruler should be. He considered the imperial office a stewardship, having for its purpose the welfare of the people. He reduced taxes to the minimum, freed government slaves, discouraged official corruption, reduced the severity of the law until capital punishment became a rare occurrence, and set up pensions for the aged. He repealed the laws forbidding criticism of the emperor, saying that he wished to hear about his faults. He proposed that he should, in accord with Confucian principles, not leave his throne to his son but, instead, seek out the most virtuous man in the empire and make him his heir; his officials persuaded him, however, that this would not benefit the empire, but endanger it. He lived frugally, and when he died he asked that mourning be limited to the absolute minimum, in order not to trouble the people.

This was not hypocrisy; Emperor Wen was a genuine paragon of Confucian virtue and one of the most benevolent monarchs in all history. Nevertheless he was very superstitious, and was repeatedly imposed upon by adventurers who claimed to possess magic powers. Among the scholars at his court who were officially appointed to study philosophy, all the various doctrines were represented; at first there was only one Confucian among them. Furthermore, when Wen came to choose a tutor for his heir, he chose a man who was a Legalist.

Despite this fact, the Confucians were again dominant at court when the Emperor Wu, the sixth ruler of the dynasty, succeeded to the throne in 140 B.C. It is rather generally held that Emperor Wu was a sincere if perhaps misguided patron of Confucianism, that Confucians were influential at his court, and that Confucianism "triumphed" during his reign.

Yet if we look carefully at the facts that history has preserved for us, it is difficult to avoid the following conclusions: First, while Emperor Wu may have been a Confucian when he first inherited the throne, as a boy of fifteen, he quickly outgrew this phase; during his long adult life he was in fact a Legalist, who made an elaborate pretense of being a Confucian for reasons of policy. Second, the advisers who carried real weight in framing the policies of his government were outspokenly Legalistic and anti-Confucian. Those nominally Confucian officials who held high office at Wu's court were in fact not very good Confucians, and in any case Wu paid almost no attention to their advice on matters of real importance. Finally, if we agree that Confucianism "triumphed" in the reign of the Emperor Wu, this can be only in a very limited sense. The fact is that in the process Confucianism was perverted and distorted in a manner that would have horrified Confucius, Mencius, and Hsün Tzu, as in fact it horrified genuine Confucians of Emperor Wu's own day.

It has often been remarked that if we look at the overt acts of Emperor Wu, they correspond remarkably well with the prescriptions of such Legalists as Han Fei Tzu. Confucian scholars complained that he used the totalitarian method of registration of the population that had been devised by Shang Yang. The severe laws of the Ch'in dynasty had never been wholly repealed and under Wu they were expanded into a strict and detailed legal code that was enforced without mercy. For trifling crimes men were compelled to pay heavy fines, condemned to serve in the army, or made slaves of the government, so that merchants and the middle class were ruined. Wu's Legalist advisers urged that he confiscate the more profitable industries; he did so, and the manufacture of salt, iron, and fermented liquors was made a government monopoly. To provide labor for these monopolies alone, it appears that more than one hundred thousand persons were condemned to slavery. To pay for his military adventures he taxed heavily and debased the coinage. Punishments were so frequent and severe that men feared to hold government office; a plan was then devised whereby those appointed to office might make a payment to buy themselves free of the dubious "honor"; this further enriched the treasury.

The Legalists emphasized warfare, and so did Wu. At the beginning of his reign there was a genuine threat from the neighboring barbarian tribes; but after this had been removed, his taste for conquest became boundless. His armies pushed far into Central Asia; on one occasion he sent more than one hundred thousand men to Ferghana in order to secure a rare breed of horses. It is impossible to calculate how many tens of thousands of lives were lost in these incessant expeditions, but we know that they ruined the country economically. Nevertheless, Wu greatly expanded China's territories; this fact undoubtedly helped to make his repressive measures slightly less unpalatable to the people at large.

Emperor Wu no longer left the administration of government in the hands of his ministers, as Confucius had long ago recommended and as had been the practice, generally speaking, since the founding of the Han dynasty. Instead he held the reins of government himself, and seems to have refrained from confiding really effective power to any of his ministers or advisers, exactly as Han Fei Tzu had recommended. No longer was it lawful, as it had been under the Emperor Wen, to criticize the emperor; such impertinence was punished severely. Nevertheless there was much criticism, especially in Confucian circles, and in 99 B.C. a rebellion broke out. Significantly, it centered around the region of Confucius' birthplace. When it was suppressed, more than ten thousand persons were executed.

Not only did Emperor Wu act like a Legalist and have Legalists as his most influential advisers. As more than one scholar had noted, there is considerable reason to believe that he consciously modeled himself after the First Emperor of the Ch'in dynasty. And in his edicts he occasionally quoted from Legalist works, including the *Han Fei Tzu,* showing that he was acquainted with them, although he was too prudent to name his sources. How, then, did such an emperor ever get the reputation of being a sincere, if perhaps somewhat misguided, patron of Confucianism? In a very interesting manner.

When he became emperor at the age of fifteen, the court was dominated by certain Confucian ministers. Since the boy ruler's studies had inclined him toward Confucianism, these ministers had no difficulty in getting him to sign a decree barring from office students of certain Legalist works, including those of Shang Yang and Han Fei Tzu. Apparently this decree was never formally rescinded, but the young emperor's genuine enthusiasm for Confucianism was short-lived. His grandmother, the powerful Grand Empress Dowager, was an ardent Taoist, and she quickly curbed the power of his Confucian advisers.

The emperor soon found that Confucians were not to his liking. They had not enough respect for his august position and criticized him quite impertinently. Furthermore, he complained (and here the emperor was quite right), they were utterly impractical. They not only opposed needless war but even argued against any reasonable preparedness against the incursions of the savage nomad hordes that ravaged the borders. If the emperor would only meet them with virtue, the Confucians asserted, these barbarians would submit of their own accord. In government too, they said, only virtue and a knowledge of the classics were necessary. Such vulgar trivia as arithmetic and administrative methods were, in their opinion, utterly unworthy of gentlemen.

These men could not possibly have successfully administered Wu's vast and complex empire. Yet they believed themselves entitled to do so, and they were popular with the people. The fate of the Ch'in dynasty had shown that it was dangerous to offend them. Wu had started his reign with the reputation of being a friend of Confucianism, and he was careful never to lose it. He constantly referred to the Confucian classics in his edicts. He gave positions of high honor—but no power—to two descendants of Confucius. While multiplying the laws and making punishments more savage, he asserted: "My endeavor is to decrease punishments that evil may become less." While wringing the last ounce of tribute from the people, he repeatedly issued edicts proclaiming the anguish which he felt for their sufferings. For his most predatory schemes he alleged ingeniously plausible motives of the purest benevolence.

For some time it had been the practice for scholars, recommended from their home districts, to go to the court and be examined by the emperor. A famous Confucian named Tung Chung-shu took such an examination early in Wu's reign. In his examination paper he accused the emperor point-blank of using the Legalistic methods of the Ch'in dynasty, and asserted that his officials were grinding down the people.

The Ch'in First Emperor would have made a martyr of Tung Chung-shu, but Emperor Wu was much more clever. He appointed him as a high minister at the court of a swashbuckling vassal who hated pedants and had the habit of executing ministers who annoyed him. However, Wu's reasonable expectations were disappointed, for Tung Chung-shu became a favorite of his new master. The emperor tried again, sending him to the court of a still more murderous vassal. This time Tung Chung-shu resigned, as he said, "for reasons of health," and spent the rest of his life in retirement. During his later years the emperor would from time to time send one of his courtiers to Tung Chung-shu "to ask his advice." In this way Wu obtained, and still enjoys, the reputation of being a patron of the Confucian scholar, Tung Chung-shu.

A little later than the examination of Tung Chung-shu, another was held in which one of the hundred scholars examined was a certain Kung-Sun Hung. As a young man he had been a jailer; possibly this gave him the interest in Legalism that he showed later. Discharged for some fault, he became a swineherd, and late in life studied one of the Confucian classics. He was in his sixties when he wrote an examination for the emperor. His reply, although it had the necessary Confucian façade, was in fact distinctly Legalistic. He said that the emperor must energetically set forth the laws, and use *shu,* "methods" (it will be recalled that this is a Legalist term). Further, the emperor must "monopolize the handles that control life and death" (this paraphrases a passage in the *Han Fei Tzu*) and keep strong personal control of the government.

The scholars who graded the papers were scandalized at this and graded Kung-Sun Hung's paper last among the hundred. When the papers reached the emperor, he moved it up to first place. Here at last was the "Confucian" he needed. He heaped Kung-Sun Hung with honors and soon made him prime minister. The emperor kept him in this position until he died of old age. The government was actually run by the emperor and a small group of Legalistically inclined advisers. The prime minister provided, as another official of the emperor's court tells us, a convenient Confucian façade for the Legalistic operations of the government.

Look up Kung-Sun Hung in almost any history, and you will read that he was a Confucian scholar, a former swineherd whom Emperor Wu honored so greatly for his knowledge of the classics that he made him his prime minister and ennobled him as a marquis. We may be quite sure that the emperor planned that history should read in this way.

He richly rewarded those nominal Confucians who applauded him and punished those who criticized. Though control was strict, Tung Chung-shu was once condemned to death for writing a "stupid" book, but the emperor pardoned him. Wu made co-operation with the government attractive by founding the imperial university, in which fifty Confucian students were supported by the state. Offices in the government were increasingly awarded to scholars who performed satisfactorily in the government examinations on the Confucian classics; these examinations gave the emperor a matchless opportunity to influence the direction of Confucian thought and studies.

Because much of the literature had been destroyed in the Ch'in period, scholars were greatly interested in recovering old books, especially the classics. The emperor encouraged this interest in texts, which from his point of view was greatly preferable to the accent that Confucius and Mencius had placed on the criticism of social and political practices.

Around this time there began the great period of the production of commentaries, to explain the ancient books. In these explanations, Han scholars interpreted all the classical literature in terms of the thought of their own day. It is largely in terms of these commentaries that the classics are still studied and translated in the twentieth century, despite the fact that the Han thinking they set forth is very different from that of the time when the early classics were written.

It is human to want to do things in the easiest way. Few of us will add a column of figures when an adding machine is at hand or think out a difficult problem when a satisfactory short cut makes this unnecessary. We saw that Confucius believed that each individual must think things out for himself, but that almost immediately after his death Confucians began to rely more on authority, and to seek easier ways to solve problems.

Once such method, divination, had been used in China from remote antiquity. An ancient diviner's manual, the *Book of Changes,* came in Han times to be considered one of the Confucian classics, despite the fact that Confucius and all the great early Confucians had scorned the practice of divination. Ten appendixes to the *Book of Changes* were also written; they set forth a method of understanding and even controlling events by means of a mystical science of numbers. These appendixes were probably written by Confucians who were deeply influenced by Taoism. The appendixes pretended, however, to quote Confucius and were even ascribed to his authorship.

Another idea, which possibly began its rise in the fourth century B.C., was that all things may be classified as partaking of the *yin* or negative principle, or the *yang* or positive principle. Everything was classified under these categories. *Yin* is female, *yang* is male. Heaven, the sun, and fire are *yang;* earth, the moon, and water are *yin*. If you want proof, a burning-glass will draw fire from the sun, while a mirror left out at night will collect dew, that is, water, from the moon. It should be noted, however, that this was not a dualism of the Occidental sort, like that between good and evil or spirit and matter. On the contrary, *yin* and *yang* complemented each other to maintain the cosmic harmony, and might transform into each other; thus winter, which is *yin*, changes into summer, which is *yang*.

Another very important conception that appears to have arisen about the same time is that of the so-called "Five Elements." The Chinese term might better be translated as the "Five Forces." They were: wood, fire, earth, metal, water. With these were correlated five directions, the center being added to the four cardinal points. Five seasons were also found to correspond to them, by adding a center season between summer and autumn and calling it "earth," the name of the center force. There were also added five colors, flavors, odors, numbers, organs of the body, etc., almost ad infinitum.

In philosophy the sequences of these forces are very important. Wood produces (that is, can support) fire; fire produces earth (that is, ashes); earth produces metal; metal produces water (dew deposited on a metal mirror); water produces (that is, makes possible the growth of) wood. The order of their destruction is: water extinguishes fire; fire melts metal; metal cuts wood; wood penetrates earth (either by the roots of trees or by the wooden plow); and earth soaks up or dams the course of water; thus the cycle is again completed.

By means of such divination techniques as those of the *Book of Changes,* and the theories of numerology, *yin* and *yang,* and the five forces, there was developed a vast and intricate system for the analysis and control of phenomena. If the theories had been stated tentatively and checked by experiment, they might well have developed into true science. But since this theorizing was almost completely dogmatic and nonexperimental, it never rose above the level of an elaborate pseudo-science.

We have already noted that Taoism early took over a great deal of popular superstition. These pseudo-scientific ideas were also adopted and cultivated in Taoist circles. The First Emperor of the Ch'in dynasty heavily subsidized Taoist magicians, who undertook to obtain for him the elixir of immortality. In the Han dynasty Emperor Wu married his eldest daughter to a magician who promised to obtain for him this elusive drug; when the magician failed to deliver, Wu had him cut in two at the waist.

During the reign of Emperor Wu a certain prince, who studied various philosophies but inclined chiefly toward Taoism, had a book compiled by philosophers whom he supported as his guests; it has come down to us under the name of *Huai Nan Tzu*. It is generally Taoistic in nature but shows the strong tendency to eclecticism that is characteristic of Han thought. Its first chapter says: "Unfold the *Tao* and it fills the universe; and yet it can be contained in a tiny scroll that does not fill the hand! . . . It is the very axle of the universe, and the vessel that contains the *yin* and the *yang*.

It binds all space to all time, and illumines the sun and moon and stars." A later chapter says:

Heaven has the four seasons, five forces, nine cardinal points, and three hundred sixty-six days. Man similarly has four limbs, five viscera, nine apertures, and three hundred sixty-six joints. Heaven has wind, rain, cold, and heat, and man has the activities of taking and giving, joy and anger. Thus the gall bladder corresponds to clouds, the lungs to air, the liver to wind, the kidneys to rain, and the spleen to thunder. In this way man forms a trinity with Heaven and Earth, and his heart is master. For this reason his ears and eyes play the parts of the sun and moon, and the blood and breath of the wind and rain. There is a three-legged bird in the sun, and a three-legged toad in the moon. If the sun and the moon get off their courses, the result is an eclipse and darkness. If wind and rain occur unseasonably, there is destruction and disaster. If the five planets get off their courses, whole states and even continents suffer calamity.

Chapter 13 begins by saying that anciently emperors did not display pomp, nor inflict punishments, nor collect taxes. Instead, they treated the people kindly and bestowed wealth upon them. The people responded by appreciating their virtue. "At this time the *yin* and the *yang* were in harmony, wind and rain were seasonable and moderate, and all things flourished. Crows and magpies were so tame that men could reach into their nests and handle them; wild animals could be led on the leash." This passage is obviously Taoist, but with Confucian overtones. The chapter goes on to develop the point that practices have been changed and, indeed, must be changed with changing times. It ascribes the fall of the Hsia and Shang dynasties to an obstinate "refusal to change their methods." This is, of course, thoroughly Legalist.

There follows a lengthy discourse that is both Taoist and Legalist, which criticizes both Confucians and Moists by name. Yet at the same time the First Emperor of Ch'in is criticized for his repressive methods and his excessive militarism. And the same chapter includes some very Confucian sentiments, of which neither a Legalist, nor a Taoist in the early sense of that term, could possibly approve. For instance: "If the ruler of a badly governed state seeks to enlarge his territory but neglects humanity and justice, and seeks to enhance his position but neglects the Way and virtue, he is discarding that which could save him and paving the way for his downfall."

The fact that the *Huai Nan Tzu* includes ideas chosen from various schools does not, of course, prove that its authors were necessarily confused. On the contrary, they sometimes seem uncommonly level-headed, seeking to strike a balance between the militarism and despotism of the Legalists on the one hand and the pacifism and too complete trust in the power of virtue of the Confucians on the other.

The Confucians were not less eclectic. In fact, it is difficult to find what we may call a "pure" Confucian in Han times. One of the longest and most important of the so-called Confucian classics, the *Records on Ceremonial*, was compiled during the first century B.C. from documents of varying age. Although it has always held a high place of honor in Confucianism, it contains much that is transparently Legalist and Taoist, as well as incorporating the theories of *yin* and *yang* and the five forces. One lengthy section of this work explains what activities must be carried on (especially by the emperor), what colors must be used, and so forth, during each month of the year, and what dire calamities would befall if this were not done. Punishments, for instance, such as the death penalty, should be inflicted in autumn; if they were inflicted in spring, "there would be great floods and cold waves, and attacks by plundering raiders." Something more than a century after the publication of the *Records on Ceremonial* it was ordered, by imperial decree, that such punishments must henceforth always normally be carried out in the autumn.

This same work quotes Confucius as having made various statements involving the mystical significance of numbers and as saying that a true ruler must be able to predict the future. Some parts of this sacred Confucian text quote Confucius as speaking like a complete Taoist and attacking the very cardinal principles of Confucianism. Nor do its various portions agree; in one section we find it prescribed, in the Confucian manner, that one should make antiquity his sole study, while elsewhere we find this principle condemned in the manner of the Legalists. There is a good deal of Legalist influence. Whereas Confucianism commonly deplored harsh punishments, we find here many crimes that are said to have been punished, in the ideal times of old, by death without mercy; they include using licentious music, being hypocritical, studying false doctrines, and wearing strange clothing. If one studies the *Records on Ceremonial* closely, he is compelled to conclude that the Confucians of Han times must have been somewhat confused.

Tung Chung-shu has frequently been called the greatest Confucian of the Han period. A number of examples of his thought have come down to us; the chief of these is the work called *Luxuriant Dew from the Spring and Autumn Annals*. The following passage from its forty-second chapter illustrates the manner in which he used Taoist and other conceptions in developing his moral and political philosophy:

Heaven has five forces, namely, wood, fire, earth, metal, and water. Wood is first and water last, with earth in the middle. This is their Heaven-ordained sequence. Wood gives birth to fire, fire gives birth to earth [ashes], earth gives birth to metal, metal gives birth to water, and water gives birth to wood. This is their father–son relationship. Wood occupies the left, metal the right, fire the front, water the rear, and earth the center. This is the order in which, as fathers and sons, they receive from and transmit to each other. Thus wood receives from water, fire from wood, earth from fire, metal from earth and water from metal. As transmitters they are all fathers, as receivers, sons. Constantly to rely upon one's father in order to provide for one's son is the way (*tao*) of Heaven.

Therefore wood, living, is nourished by fire; metal, when dead, is buried by water. Fire delights in wood and nourishes it by means of the *yang* [solar?] power; water overcomes metal [its "father"], yet mourns it by means of the *yin* power. Earth in serving Heaven, shows the utmost loyalty. Thus the five forces provide a pattern of conduct for filial sons and loyal ministers. . . .

The sage, by understanding this, is able to increase his love and lessen his severity, to make more generous his support of the living and more respectful his performance of funeral rites for the dead, and so to conform with the pattern established by Heaven. Thus as a son he gladly cares for his father, as fire delights in wood, and mourns his father, as water overcomes metal. He serves his ruler as earth reverences Heaven. Thus he can be called a man of "force." And just as each of the five forces keeps its proper place according to their established order, so officials corresponding to the five forces exert themselves to the utmost by employing their abilities in their respective duties.

Three centuries earlier Mo Tzu had declared that natural calamities were the expression of Heaven's displeasure at improper conduct on the part of the ruler. This same idea appears, as we have seen, in the *Records on Ceremonial*. Tung Chung-shu reduced it to a science. He based his system on the *Spring and Autumn Annals*, one of the classics which is a skeletonized history of Confucius' native state for the years 722–481 B.C. and which was erroneously attributed to the authorship of Confucius. Tung made an exhaustive analysis of natural phenomena occurring in that work, together with political events that preceded them. On this basis, he said, whenever in his own day there was a large fire, a flood, a famine, or any such phenomenon, it was only necessary to search the *Spring and Autumn Annals* to find the reason and the remedy.

Thus in the Han period a great variety of pseudo-scientific and even magical practices were grafted onto Confucianism. And this new kind of Confucianism became, as Hu Shih has said, "a great synthetic religion into which were fused all the elements of popular superstition and state worship, rationalized somewhat in order to eliminate a few of the most untenable elements, and thinly covered up under the disguise of Confucian and Pre-Confucian Classics in order to make them appear respectable and authoritative. In this sense the new Confucianism of the Han Empire was truly the national religion of China." In some Han works we find Confucius described as a god, the son of a certain mythical Black Emperor. At his birth, it is recounted, spirits and dragons hovered in the air over the scene of the nativity.

All this is different enough from the teachings of the scholar of Lu, but there is another aspect of Han Confucianism that would have disturbed Confucius, if he would have known of it, even more. We saw that in the Confucian authoritarianism of Hsün Tzu there was already an insistence upon the stratification of society, although the strata were not fixed by heredity. The scholars, Confucian and otherwise, had a strong tendency to consider themselves an elite composed of something far better than common clay. Thus Tung Chung-shu, in arguing against Mencius' idea that human nature is good, says that this is obviously not the case, for otherwise the masses of the people would not be called "the blind," by which he apparently means "the stupid." "Heaven," he says, "endowed the common people with the raw material of goodness, but they could not make themselves good. For this Heaven established the king, to make them good; this was Heaven's intention. . . . The king is charged by Heaven with the duty of teaching the people to bring out the potential goodness that is in them." Having been given this responsibility by Heaven, the ruler looks upon Heaven as his father, and thus it is most fitting that he is called the "Son of Heaven."

It was almost inevitable that Han metaphysics, as an ideology tailored to fit the centralized Han empire, should thus have given to the emperor this supernatural support for his position, which Confucius had been careful to withhold from the ruler. It was equally inevitable that this should have played into the hand of monarchical despotism. Thus we find a non-Confucian official of Emperor Wu's court declaring that it is the Confucian doctrine that the emperor must take the lead, and his ministers must follow. It is not unnatural, therefore, that some scholars have concluded that Emperor Wu favored Confucianism because it was an aristocratic doctrine favorable to autocratic rule.

Certainly, from this time forward, Confucianism was often exploited by despots, seconded by complaisant ministers, to forward their selfish designs. But this is not the whole, or the most important part, of the story. Despots always find, or distort, or create, an ideology to condone their tyranny. And although Confucianism was misused in this manner, its total effect has been far more to eliminate or at least to modify despotism. Tung Chung-shu's method of arguing from analogies in the *Spring and Autumn Annals* was devised as a check on the autocracy of the emperor, and it was actually used in this way by later Confucians. Tung also advocated that taxes should be lightened, that the amount of land which might be held by a private owner should be limited, and that slavery should be abolished.

We do find, in fact, that in Han times even very high nobles were punished for mistreating slaves, and the circumstances leave no doubt that this was in large measure the result of Confucian humanitarianism. From Han times onward, Confucianism has sometimes been dragged at the chariot wheels of despotism, but can hardly be said to have been its willing handmaiden. The best Confucians have always spoken out fearlessly for what they believed to be right, whether the cost might be exile, prison, or death.

By Han times, ideas peculiar to each of the major philosophies may be said to have won a certain triumph. Beyond doubt, the Han imperial system was in very large degree the child of philosophy, or rather of the various philosophies. Yet the situation was such that the philosophies must have found themselves in the position of the man who, having at last attained success, wonders why he valued it so highly.

Certainly Legalism had triumphed in large measure, for the actual administration of the state was Legalistic. But it was not nominally so, and after Wu many emperors were to a large extent Confucian in fact as well as in name. Ministers were selected, in theory at least, on Confucian principle, for their learning and virtue. Most abhorrent of all to Legalism, these ministers were given power. In fact, both the Former Han and the Later Han dynasties were terminated by supremely powerful ministers who supplanted their rulers.

Taoism had come far. Indeed, the so-called Confucianism of Han times was in large part Taoism. Taoism itself was greatly in favor in aristocratic circles, and much of the time at the court. But the emphasis on military aggression under Wu, the oppression of the people, and the downright stupidity of much that was called Taoism in Han times would not have pleased the authors of the *Lao Tzu* and the *Chuang Tzu*.

It might seem that Moism had been forgotten. Yet there was a considerable sense of hierarchy in Han times, which would have pleased Mo Tzu. Furthermore, the ideas propounded by Tung Chung-shu, that natural phenomena are the warnings of Heaven and that the emperor is Heaven's vice-regent on earth, became increasingly popular, and it will be remembered that Mo Tzu had preached both of them. It is obvious, however, that the state of the world would have pleased him no more than it would the Taoists.

And finally, Confucianism. It had triumphed, but at the cost of such transformation that one wonders whether it can still properly be called Confucianism. The very fact that the Han political system was called Confucian caused Confucianism to be held responsible for the repressive despotism that functioned under the cover of its name. The criticisms of its enemies—and they were many—make it clear that Confucianism was increasingly thought of as a system of hidebound traditionalism, meaningless ritualism, and abject subservience to despotic authority.

If we may generalize concerning Han thought from around 100 B.C. up to the time the Later Han dynasty fell in A.D. 220, it appears that it was often disturbed, frequently apathetic, but seldom vigorous in the sense of being forward-looking and original. Of the Confucians of the time of Emperor Wu, Hu Shih has said: "They were groping in the dark for some means whereby to check the absolutism of the rulers of a united empire from which there was no means of escape." Étienne Balázs describes the thought of the second century A.D. as characterized by "a certain uneasiness, an irresolution, an uncertainty among the best minds." And he analyzes this as being due to the fact that Chinese philosophy, no matter how metaphysical it may seem, is at base a social and even a political philosophy, so that Chinese thinkers find it difficult to be at ease in a world that is manifestly out of joint.

The Confucians in particular found it impossible to ignore the distress of the world, partly because most of them were poor and shared in it. Finally, in the latter half of the second century A.D., the Confucians became so open in their attacks upon the aristocracy and the eunuchs, who had pushed them from power, that many of the Confucians were exterminated by their enemies. Yet, although the Confucians took up the cudgel to right the wrongs of the people, they had become too much identified with the oppressive government to be able decisively to control popular favor.

In a sense the dream of the philosophers had come true. China was united, under a sovereign who ruled in the *name* of the good of the people and repeated the slogans beloved of the philosophers. But the dream proved a nightmare, and the sage emperor, at his worst, a Frankenstein's monster. What could be done? Unless one had influence at court, very little. In the days of Confucius and Mencius and Han Fei Tzu, if one did not like one state he could go to another, but now there was nowhere to go. In those days philosophers had rebuked rulers with impunity, but now one might be put to death if he merely acted discourteously toward some worthless favorite of the emperor. We need scarcely be surprised that men's minds were not very creative or if they took refuge in such pastimes as a kind of elaborate and abstruse repartee, and in what Balázs calls "nihilism," an attempt to flee from reality.

We have noted that for a long time there had been a tendency to seek easier and easier formulas to solve problems. This reached a high point in the sort of magical procedures proposed by men like Tung Chung-shu. There was a reaction against his ideology which took various forms, and some of them were remarkably refined and subtle. On the whole, however, the critics were not very original, and they themselves proposed easy formulas.

The Confucians said, in words that sounded like those of Mencius, that it was only necessary to return to the ways of antiquity and to restore the reign of *li* and justice. The Taoist said that all would be well if everyone would just be natural; they sometimes seem almost to be reciting from the *Lao Tzu* and the *Chuang Tzu*. Some thinkers turned, to find the way out, to Legalism, but they seem to have considered its practice to be a far easier thing than Han Fei Tzu ever did; some of them conceive of "law" as almost a metaphysical principle which, if espoused, will solve all problems as if by magic. These latter-day Legalists insist that the trouble is that men look to the past and do not recognize that new times need new measures; but in making this very point they often seem to be content to parrot Han Fei Tzu almost verbatim.

These are generalizations, to which there are always exceptions. An outstanding exception was Wang Ch'ung, who lived from A.D. 27 to about 97. Unlike most scholars of the day, he did not merely study and memorize one or a few classical texts but read widely. Being a poor boy he could not buy books, but browsed constantly in bookshops, and it was said that he could repeat from memory whatever he had read. Being given a small official post he tried, like the very bright young man that he was, to instruct his colleagues and superiors concerning their mistakes. Very soon he had to resign. He wrote several books, of which one long work called the *Lun Heng* or *Critical Essays* has survived.

They certainly were critical. If we consider the environment in which they were produced, it may be doubted whether any other literary work in human history shows a more independent spirit. Wang attacks the entire mode of classical study, saying that it is too narrow. In writing, he says, one should not just comment on the classics, nor imitate what has been done before, but should express one's own ideas, in clear and understandable language. Although he considers history important, he asserts that modern times are quite as worthy of study as antiquity, and declares that much of what is accepted as history is manifestly false.

Although Wang apparently considers himself a Confucian, he does not fear to criticize even Confucius himself, accusing him of speaking obscurely, vacillating in his opinions, contradicting himself, and even acting improperly. Much of the trouble sprang, he says, from the fact that Confucius' disciples did not question him or criticize him enough. All students ought to argue with their teachers, he says, and to accept nothing that the teacher does not prove.

Wang makes a detailed attack on thousands of the superstitions that were believed even by the learned. It was believed —and is to this day believed by the ignorant—that the bore in the Ch'ien-t'ang River was caused by the spirit of a minister who had been put to death and thrown into the river in the fifth century B.C. Wang makes fun of this and correctly explains that the bore is caused by the entrance of tidal waters into a constricted channel; he also says that tides are correlated with the phases of the moon.

To a large extent Wang is a tough-minded mechanist, and therefore a determinist. Heaven and Earth do not produce man purposely, but accidentally. Heaven has no intelligence or will power, and it cannot bless the good or punish the evil. Natural phenomena are just that, not warnings from Heaven. Neither divination as to the future nor pills to prolong life have any effect. Men die when the circumstances cause them to do so, and when they are dead that is the end; there are no ghosts.

All this sounds astonishingly modern. Yet since Wang Ch'ung was not superhuman he could not entirely escape the beliefs of his age. Although he refuted many superstitions, he solemnly averred that a variety of miracles recorded by tradition had indeed taken place. His criticisms are often as pedantic and ill-grounded as the propositions he attacks, and he is often inconsistent. Furthermore, as Fung Yu-lan has well said, he is so predominantly a destructive critic, and offers so little of his own that is constructive, that in fact his thought is not as important as many contemporary scholars suppose it to be.

What was his influence on Han thought? A number of scholars of the present day have held that he strongly affected the reaction against the traditional Confucianism in the second century A.D. But this seems doubtful. The very fact that much of Wang Ch'ung's thought appears so reasonable to us indicates that it would probably have seemed absurd, if not incomprehensible, to many of his contemporaries. There seems to be no evidence that the *Critical Essays* was even known in scholarly circles until long after Wang was dead. The book was discovered in Wang Ch'ung's native district on the southeast coast, about a century after it was written, by a scholar who did not publish it but, instead, kept it secret and used it to embellish his conversation, pretending that the ideas he borrowed from it were his own. Again in the third century, the book is said to have been discovered in Wang's native district by an official who used it in the same way, but did at length make it public. This does not sound as if Wang Ch'ung's book was well known at an early date.

The great new influence on Chinese thought, which began to make itself felt in Han times, was Buddhism. And it pointed in a direction almost diametrically opposed to that of the thought of Wang Ch'ung.

IV

MIDDLE IMPERIAL CHINA:
A.D. 221–959

ARTHUR F. WRIGHT

Domestication of Buddhism in China

The decline of the Han Empire was followed by a long period of disunion in China. The steady erosion of central power and the gradual refeudalization of local forces by great families invited barbarians to come to China. Finally, in the early fourth century, the weakening central government collapsed and the whole of North China was lost to northern barbarians. For nearly three hundred years thereafter, the country was politically divided between successive unstable Chinese dynasties in the south and an aggregate of non-Chinese states controlling all or part of the north.

Under such conditions Buddhism began to find its way into China, just as Christianity found its way into Western Europe during the Dark Ages. But Buddhism did not arrive without challenge: its two principal opponents in China were Taoism and Confucianism. Although both proved inadequate and unsatisfactory in a stricken, insecure society, Confucianism and Taoism had deep roots in China and had become too much a part of the culture and life of the Chinese to be ignored. Thus we find that Buddhism entered China under the mode of neo-Taoism, was adapted by the Confucianists, and finally developed a new kind of culture that was not pure Buddhism, pure Taoism, or pure Confucianism.

In the following selection, Dr. Arthur F. Wright, Charles Seymour Professor of Chinese History at Yale University, examines the coming of Buddhism and its adaptation to two evolving cultures with different needs, one in the north and one in the south. Buddhism not only adapted well to these two different environments but also was important in reducing their differences, thus laying the foundations of the united, and eventually Confucian, society that was to come.

And, Sir, the last Emperor—so they say—fled from Saragh [Loyang] because of the famine, and his palace and walled city were set on fire. . . . So Saragh is no more, Ngap [the great city of Yeh, further north] no more!

In these words a Sogdian merchant, writing back to his partner in Samarkand, recorded the destruction of the Chinese capital—an imposing city of 600,000—and

Reprinted from *Buddhism in Chinese History* by Arthur F. Wright with the permission of the publishers, Stanford University Press. © 1959 by the Board of Trustees of the Leland Stanford Junior University. Footnotes have been omitted, except for those of a substantive nature.

the shameful flight of the Son of Heaven before the oncoming Huns. The year was 311, and it marks a turning point in Chinese history comparable, as Arthur Waley has suggested, to the sack of Rome by the Goths in 410. Within the next few years, the Chinese had lost their second capital and the whole of North China—the heartland of their culture—to the Huns. The steady erosion of the central power and the refeudalization which was both its cause and its corollary had progressively weakened Chinese control of the northern and central provinces. The effete aristocrats who served the enfeebled throne had neither the will nor the talent to reverse the tide. Wang Yen, the last Prime Minister—he of the jade-white hands and the addiction to the neo-Taoist principle of *le néant*—was taken prisoner and protested to his captors that he had never been interested in politics. The rude chief of the barbarian forces is said to have rebuked him, saying, "You took office when you were quite young, made a name for yourself everywhere within the Four Seas, and now hold the highest office. How can you say that you have never had political ambitions? If any one man is responsible for the ruin of the Empire, it is you."[1]

After the catastrophic loss of the north, members of the Chinese elite fled in large numbers to the area south of the Yangtze, and for nearly three hundred years thereafter the country was politically divided between unstable Chinese dynasties with their capital at Nanking and a succession of non-Chinese states controlling all or part of the north. In the south the Chinese developed a new culture. They clung tenaciously and defensively to every strand of tradition that linked them with the past glory of the Han. Yet they lived and worked in an area that had been a colonial province of the Han— a land whose aboriginal peoples were only gradually converted to Chinese culture. In climate, landscape, crops, diet, and architecture and in many other ways, it contrasted sharply with the northern plains on which their ancestors had begun to shape a distinctive Chinese civilization. Those ancestral plains were now the scene of wars between rival barbarian chiefs, of a succession of institutional experiments designed to perpetuate the rule of alien minorities and keep the Chinese in their place. Thus in this period Buddhism had to be adapted not to one but to two evolving cultures, one in the north and one in the south, with different needs. In the following pages we shall examine these two patterns of interaction from the beginning of the age of disunion to the sixth century, when they converged and culminated to usher in the great period of independent growth.

The South

When we speak of the area of the Yangtze valley and below in the period of disunion, we must banish from our minds the picture of the densely populated, intensively cultivated South China of recent centuries. When the aristocrats and the remnants of the Chin ruling house fled to the Nanking area early in the fourth century, the south contained perhaps a tenth of the population of China. There were centers of Chinese culture and administration, but

---

[1] The above is drawn from Arthur Waley, "The Fall of Loyang," *History Today*, No. 4 (1951), pp. 7–10. The contemporary Sogdian letter, found in the ruins of a watchtower west of Tun-huang, was translated by W. B. Henning. The account of Wang Yen's interview with the Hun chief Shih Lo is found in *Chin-shu chiao-chu*, ch. 43, p. 25; the rebuke may well have been attributed to Shih Lo by later historians moralizing on the loss of the north.

around most of these lay vast uncolonized areas into which Chinese settlers were slow to move.

The old provincial families of the Yangtze valley tended to be conservative; they clung to the traditions of Confucian learning which the northern aristocrats had long since discarded in favor of neo-Taoist speculation. Indeed, some southerners blamed the pursuit of "naturalness" among northern statesmen for the catastrophe which had befallen the empire. Tension between the southern Chinese and the immigrants from the north arose quickly and persisted for several generations, but in the end both contributed to an elite southern culture. In this culture the literary traditions of the Han were continued and developed; Confucian learning was preserved to provide links with the proud past and an ideology of dynastic and cultural legitimacy which in a measure reassured those who now controlled only the periphery of a once great and united empire. The supremacy of birth over talent, a concept which had gained ground in the last years of the Han, was here affirmed as the social basis of the only remaining "Chinese" state. At the same time the Neo-Taoism brought in by the northern émigrés fitted congenially into the picturesque and dramatic scenery of the Yangtze valley and found devotees among those aristocrats whose shaken confidence was not to be restored by hollow claims that they were the "legitimate" masters of the "Central Kingdom"; these were men who sought something immutable in a time of disaster, or perhaps an escape into nature from a human scene they found intolerable. It was in this cultural milieu that a characteristic southern Buddhism developed in the period of disunion.

This Buddhism was initially molded—in its concepts, its centers of speculative interest, its vocabulary—by neo-Taoism. Much of the discussion of Buddhist ideas was carried on in neo-Taoism's favored mode: the dialogue or colloquy known as *ch'ing-t'an*. As we have seen, the philosophic vitality of neo-Taoism was already a thing of the past, and *ch'ing-t'an* had been transformed from a speculative instrument into the drawing room pastime of an effete and disillusioned aristocracy. But despite the philosophical failures of its devotees, neo-Taoism had broken the anachronistic shell of Han Confucianism and widened and deepened the speculative range of Chinese thought. It had gone on to raise questions which could not be answered by reference to the poetical images of its favorite texts, the *Chuang-tzu* and the *Lao-tzu*.

The Chinese converts to Buddhism who began to move among the salons of the southern capital and then to Buddhist centers as these became established throughout the south were men of a certain definable type. Demiéville has suggested that Hui-yüan (334–416) was typical of the Chinese literati who turned to Buddhism. His early training was in Confucian classics, and he taught for a time at a Confucian school. But along with this he developed a strong intellectual interest—or problem interest—in the *Lao-tzu* and the *Chuang-tzu* and achieved a mastery of these texts. Then one day when he heard a famous monk lecture on the Prajñā-pāramitā, Hui-yüan exclaimed that Confucianism, Taoism, and all other schools were but chaff compared with Buddhism. He became a monk, studied, and began to preach. In both his teaching and his writing he relied heavily on Taoist terms and concepts to expound, and thus to modify, the Buddhist ideas that he presented.

Another famous monk who contributed to the spread of Buddhism in the south was

Chih-tun (314–66). He was brilliant, witty, and personable, and a great favorite among the émigré aristocrats at Nanking. He spoke the language of neo-Taoism, and he excelled in the light repartee so esteemed in *ch'ing-t'an* circles. He selected certain ideas from the available Buddhist sutras and related them to the problems of neo-Taoism. Thus, for example, he made a spirited attack on an authoritative commentator who saw in Chung-tzu's parable of the phoenix and the cicada the meaning that the secret of personal liberty (*hsiao-yao*) lay in conforming to one's lot in the universal order. Chih-tun affirmed that one could and should escape into the infinite like the phoenix and like the Buddhist who frees himself from worldly ties.

Demiéville traces to Chih-tun certain philosophic innovations which were to have far-reaching effects in the subsequent development of Chinese thought. One of these was investing the old Chinese naturalistic notion of *li*, "order," with a new metaphysical meaning drawn from Mahayana philosophy; in this new sense the term came to mean the transcendental absolute principle as opposed to the empirical data of experience, and this form of dualism—new to China—was to appear centuries later as the central conception of a new Confucianism.

Again, one finds in Chih-tun's works, and more fully expressed in the writings of Chu Tao-sheng (365–434), an important polarization which had been prefigured in earlier Chinese thought but only now became explicit. The two poles were gradualism (*chien*) and subitism (*tun*). Chu Tao-sheng and his contemporaries were troubled by the apparently conflicting formulas of salvation offered in the Hinayana and Mahayana texts that had by now been translated. The former appeared to prescribe an age-long and arduous accumulation of positive karma leading to ultimate release into nirvana. The Mahayana texts, on the other hand, offered the seeker after salvation the help of Buddhas and Bodhisattvas and the possibility of a single and sudden moment of enlightenment. Chinese Buddhists thus felt that they discerned in Buddhism two paths to truth and liberation. Gradualism (*chien*) was an approach to the ultimate reality (*li*) by analysis, the accumulation of particulars, long study; it also implied a sense of reality which presupposed plurality, a set of spatially and temporally defined aspects of reality to which a succession of graded methods provided the key. Gradualism, though elaborated with a subtlety unknown to pre-Buddhist China, is basically akin to the native Confucian tradition with its prescriptions for the slow accumulation of knowledge and wisdom. Subitism (*tun*), on the other hand, meant the one as opposed to the multiple, totality as opposed to particulars, the complete apprehension of reality in a sudden and complete vision. Subitism, in Demiéville's view, was clearly associated with the indigeneous Taoist tradition; at the same time it was a peculiarly Chinese reaction—found among many who studied Buddhism—against the prolixity of Buddhist writings, their attenuated chain reasoning, and their scholastic rigor of demonstration. This polarization was later to be the center of controversy within the school of Ch'an (*Zen*), and still later characterized the principal division within a revived Confucianism.

In addition to such developments in the philosophic realm, Buddhist monks in the south introduced certain practical and doctrinal innovations that were in keeping with the intellectual climate of their time. Hui-yüan, by reason of his versatility, exemplified in his career many of these innovations. He and men like him did not merely cater to the capital aristocrats but built their own centers of devotion and teaching, often in a mountain fastness. They attracted lay patrons, and the number of temples steadily increased. Hui-yüan was the first to teach the attainment of salvation through faith in Amitābha and thus laid the foundations for the great Pure Land sect, which was eventually to become the most popular form of Buddhism in eastern Asia. While his own writings are full of Taoist thought and terminology, he was indefatigable in his search for a sounder and fuller understanding of Indian Buddhist ideas. To this end he sent disciples to Central Asia to bring back texts, and was in touch with at least six foreign translators.

Hui-yüan was also called upon to defend the Buddhist clergy against the threat of government control or suppression. In his defense one can discern many of the points of conflict between Chinese views of life and society and the principles of the imported faith. Hui-yüan was not militant; he sought a *modus vivendi,* and, by dexterous appeals to the Taoist classics, he managed to make a far better case than he would have been able to make if Confucianism had maintained its erstwhile authority. He argued strongly that a subject who becomes a monk cuts his ties with the world of material gain and personal reward; since he does not seek to benefit from the arrangements maintained by secular authority, he should not be obliged to pay homage to the reigning prince. But, he conceded, lay Buddhists do seek worldly goals and owe secular authority full respect:

Those who revere the Buddhist teaching but remain in their homes are subjects who are obedient to the transforming power of temporal rulers. Their inclination is not to alter prevailing custom, and their conduct accords with secular norms. In them there are the affections of natural kinship and the proprieties of respect for authority. . . . The retribution of evil karma is regarded as punishment; it makes people fearful and thus circumspect. The halls of heaven are regarded as a reward; this makes them think of the pleasures of heaven and act accordingly. . . . Therefore they who rejoice in the way of Śākya invariably first serve their parents and respect their lords. . . .[2]

Buddhism was interpreted by Hui-yüan as acquiescent in the political and social arrangements of a world of illusion: Buddhism ameliorates and assuages but it does not seek reform. Yet Buddhists worked hard and skillfully to win the favor of the southern rulers, offering them not only the hope of personal salvation but new, potent, and colorful rituals invoking the help of Buddhist divinities for the well-being of the realm, for the warding off of evil. The treasure-trove of Buddhist legend also offered a new model for kingly behavior—that of the Indian Cakravartin-rāja, the king who rules well and successfully through devotion to Buddha and his teaching—and the related model of the munificent donor, the Mahādānapati, whose gifts to the Buddhist order for the benefit of his fellow creatures make of him something akin to a living Bodhisattva. These models had a strong appeal to monarchs whose life and power were always uncertain, whose claims to "legitimate" descent from the Han were scant reassurance after decades of political instability.

Among the monarchs who embraced and promoted Buddhism, the best known is Emperor Wu of the Liang (reigned 502-49). He himself took the Buddhist vows and on several occasions literally "gave himself" to a Buddhist temple, requiring his ministers to "ransom" him with huge gifts to the

[2] *Hung-ming chi* 5, in *Taishō*, LII, 30. My translation differs somewhat from that of Hurvitz, " 'Render unto Caesar' in Early Chinese Buddhism," *Sino Indian Studies*, 1957, p. 98.

temple. On the Buddha's birthday in 504 he ordered the imperial relatives, the nobles, and the officials to forsake Taoism and embrace Buddhism. In 517 he decreed the destruction of the temples of the Taoists —whose religion had steadily grown in power and influence (partly through its selective borrowing from Buddhism)—and ordered the Taoist adepts to return to lay life. He patterned himself after the new Buddhist model of kingly behavior, and his efforts won him titles which suggest the fusion of Chinese and Buddhist political sanctions. He was called Huang-ti p'u-sa (Emperor Bodhisattva), Chiu-shih p'u-sa (Savior Bodhisattva), and P'u-sa t'ien-tzu (Bodhisattva Son of Heaven).

Yet neither wealth nor political power in the south was concentrated in the throne. Rather the great territorial families came to control and manipulate the throne, and to monopolize the selection of officials. Among these great families and among the less well-to-do but literate families Buddhism gradually attracted a large following. The metropolitan officials and the leaders of the intellectual and social life of the capital were greatly impressed by Vimalakīrti, central figure in one of the most influential Buddhist scriptures of the time. He was not a naked ascetic but a rich and powerful aristocrat, a brilliant talker, a respected householder and father, a man who denied himself no luxury or pleasure yet possessed so pure and disciplined a personality that he changed all whom he met for the better. Here was a new model for aristocratic lay Buddhists who were attracted by the ideals of Buddhism but had no desire to renounce their worldly pleasures. There was also, for the rich and powerful, new satisfaction in the lavish building of temples and retreats in the developing style of Chinese Buddhist architecture. Here was an opportunity for display, for "conspicuous consumption," which had the added charm of accumulating merit toward future salvation. And, in many cases, the temples built and endowed by the rich served both as their personal retreats and as shrines for the perpetual performance of their family rites.

Others among the literate were deeply moved by the new Buddhist vision of reality and salvation, became the disciples of certain noted monks, and entered the order. Still others took orders simply out of disgust with the corrupt political life which denied them the satisfaction of a public career, or out of disillusionment with the threadbare formulas of neo-Taoism. As Buddhism became more and more generally accepted, the literate monks found in it counterparts of those scholarly and cultural satisfactions which their ancestors had found in Confucianism. Many collected books; some became noted calligraphers or writers in a particular genre. Others became antiquarians or historians of Buddhism or specialists in one or another Buddhist text, just as in an earlier day they might have specialized in one of the Confucian classics. A life of devotions and scholarship in some temple set in the midst of lovely scenery not only offered satisfactions which the troubled world outside could scarcely provide, but was fully sanctioned by the Bodhisattva ideal of renunciation and work for the salvation of all creatures. This conception of the monastic vocation—withdrawal, gentle contemplation, scholarship, and speculation—proved perennially attractive to literate Chinese in the centuries that followed.

Of popular Buddhism in the south we know far less than we know of the Buddhism of the elite. There is evidence of a sharp clash in the countryside—often cast as a contest of charismatic and magical powers —between the Buddhist clergy and the Taoist adepts. The Taoists had established roots in parts of the south from the time of the Yellow Turban uprising, and in these places Buddhism had to struggle to win a mass following. Monks from various temples would spend part of each year working among the populace. Their rituals and charms, their promise of salvation cast in simple terms, perhaps driven home by one of the stories which dramatized the working of karmic law, undoubtedly won them adherents. As often as possible, in both south and north, they deftly introduced Buddhist elements into the old village associations which existed for the support of fertility rites or other observances. Many commoners attached as hereditary serfs to the growing landholdings of the Buddhist temples must have increased the number of Buddhists among the masses. So perhaps did the increasingly large and diversified class of artisans which catered to the needs of the temples and monasteries.

As Chinese colonists slowly moved into the old aboriginal areas, they brought Buddhism with them, often in the person of officials or incoming gentry who combined Buddhism as a personal religion with old Confucian-rooted ideas and techniques for bringing Chinese civilization to "the natives." Buddhism was seen as a "civilizing" competitor against native shamanistic rites —a field of competition in which Confucianism was ill-equipped.

In the south, then, we find Buddhism adjusting to elite and popular culture, interacting with southern philosophical and literary traditions, developing its beliefs and practices in response to a society which was inadequately served by the traditions it had inherited from the dying Han empire. Let us now consider the concurrent progress of Buddhism in North China.

The North

The area north of the Yangtze which was relinquished to alien rule in 317 was not, we should remind ourselves, the North China of today. For Chinese of that time it *was* China, referred to in their writings not only as "the central plain" (*chung-yüan*) but by the historic and value-laden term *chung-kuo*, "the Central Kingdom." It was the scene of the great cultural achievements of the Chinese people, the homeland of their philosophers, the land on which the great empires of Ch'in and Han had first given political unity to the people of China. The loss of this land to despised barbarians reduced the émigré aristocrats of Nanking to tears of remorse and self-pity. Their relatives who remained in the north—and they were an overwhelming majority of the literate class—endured a succession of alien regimes which outdid one another in tyranny, rapacity, and incompetence. Chinese invariably served these regimes, partly out of self-interest—the protection of family property— but partly in the hope that they could meliorate the harshness of the barbarians and work toward the reestablishment of a Confucian polity and society.

The society of North China, in the early years of disunion, was a deeply divided one. The fissures ran in many directions. The alien minorities—generally, at first, horsemen contemptuous of farmers—were shortly divided into two groups: those who favored different degrees of Sinization and those who clung to the traditions of their steppe ancestors. Often before they had resolved this difference they were overwhelmed by new invaders from beyond the Great Wall. Racial hatred between one non-Chinese group and another was ferocious, and between the Chinese and the alien intruders it often broke into violence and mass slaughter. Endless wars laid waste the land; levy after levy tore the peasant from his fields. The great landed magnate of today would be killed tomorrow, and those who had sought his protection would become the slaves of a stranger. It is against this background of tension and insecurity that Buddhism began to find its way into this society.

The pioneer missionary in the north was a Kuchan, Fo-t'u-teng. He was on his way to the Chin capital of Loyang, probably with the aim of becoming a translator in one of the imperially supported temples there. Instead he arrived just as the great capital was sacked and burned, and he found himself in the camp of a rude, illiterate Hun who was on his way to control of most of North China. The instinct of the true missionary was equal to the occasion. "He knew that Lo (the Hun chieftain) did not understand profound doctrines but would only be able to recognize magical power as evidence of the potency of Buddhism. . . . Thereupon he took his begging bowl, filled it with water, burned incense, and said a spell over it. In a moment there sprang up blue lotus flowers whose brightness and color dazzled the eyes." Lo was deeply impressed, and for the next two decades he was an ardent patron of Buddhism.

Throughout the north the initial foothold was won for Buddhism by the demonstration to credulous barbarians of its superior magical power, the charisma of its monks which helped to win battles, bring rain, relieve sickness, and assuage the spasms of remorse which overcame the simple barbarian chiefs after some particularly ghastly slaughter. With the favor thus won Buddhist monks began to establish centers, to teach, and to spread their religion throughout the north. In the long run this foreign religion commended itself to alien rulers on a number of grounds besides that of its superior magical power. First of all, it was a religion alien to China. When the barbarian chiefs learned enough to know that their own tribal ways would not long sustain them in control of North China, they were reluctant to adopt the Confucian principles urged on them by wily Chinese advisers; this course might well mean the loss of cultural identity, the cession of a fatal amount of power to the subject Chinese. Buddhism provided an attractive alternative, and its monks—many of them foreigners—seemed, in their total dependence on the ruler's favor and their lack of family networks, to be useful and trustworthy servants. A further point in favor of Buddhism was that its ethic was universalistic, applicable to men of all races, times, and cultures; it thus seemed the very thing to close some of the social fissures that plagued these regimes and to contribute to the building of a unified and pliable social body.

These apparent advantages won for Buddhism the support and protection of a succession of autocratic rulers and, through this support, an unequaled opportunity to spread throughout the whole of society. From the mid-fourth century onward, we find extraordinary expansion at all levels. At the topmost level the rulers and their families became lavish patrons of the Buddhist church, making munificent gifts of treasure and land to the clergy, building sumptuous temples and monasteries, supporting such great works of piety as the cave temples of Yun-kang. In many of the great temples, regular official prayers were said for the welfare of the ruling house and for the peace and prosperity of the realm. Upper-class Chinese followed the pattern of their counterparts in the south: a substratum of solid Confucian training at home, unsatisfying experiments with neo-Taoism, and then conversion to a faith which seemed to explain the ills of a stricken society and to offer hope for the future. It is from this class that the great thinkers and teachers of northern Buddhism in this period were recruited.

The grandees—alien, Chinese, or of mixed stock—took as much delight in lavish building as the southern aristocrats. Some sought to expiate past crimes, others to win spiritual credit, others to impress the populace or their pious overlords. There was a veritable orgy of temple-building, monasteries were heavily endowed, new Buddhist statues and paintings were commissioned, and the sacred texts were copied and recopied with loving care. Many of these buildings and pious works reflected a family interest, and Buddhist monks became the priests of the ancestor cults of their patrons.

Among the masses, both alien and Chinese, Buddhism found a wide following. As in the south, it was often grafted onto existing rural cults. But in the north, at least in the early part of this period, Buddhist monks did not have the competition of an entrenched religious Taoism, and the peasantry were converted *en masse*. The Buddhist clergy not only offered the consolation of a simple faith, but, as favored instruments of government, often brought into the rural areas medicine, relief grain, and other practical benefits which in an earlier day might have been provided by local officials or rural gentry. The great monasteries, as Gernet has shown, became entrepreneurs; at first they were given relatively infertile highlands, often in localities which were economically undeveloped or in decline. Later, however, they expanded and developed their holdings into the lowlands, and, in addition to bringing more land under cultivation, they developed water mills, oil presses, and local manufactures. They increased their wealth by establishing pawnshops, holding auctions, and sponsoring temple fairs. Often they came to control villages or clusters of villages, whose people became hereditary serfs of the temple.

In many respects the Buddhist faith in North China cut across class lines and helped to unite a divided society. The local maigre feast, held on a Buddhist holiday, was an occasion of community fellowship in which social frictions were forgotten. Contemporary inscriptions show that Chinese and alien officials, local notables, the Buddhist clergy, and commoners often collaborated in building temples, making votive images, and other pious works. Moreover, Buddhist inscriptions—from the monumental cave-temples of Yün-kang and Lung-men to the crudest images—testify to the fact that Buddhism was everywhere reconciled to and interwoven with the family cult. A typical inscription of the period might read: "We respectfully make and present this holy image in honor of the Buddhas, Bodhisattvas, and pray that all living creatures may attain salvation, and particularly that the souls of our ancestors and relatives [names given] may find repose and release." The favored object of faith and devotion was more and more the Buddha Amitābha, who presided over the Western Paradise.[3]

The growing strength of the Buddhist faith and its organizations inevitably caused the rulers of North China some misgivings.

[3] Tsukamoto Zenryū, tables in Mizuno and Nagahiro, *Ryūmon sekkutsu no kenkyū* ("A Study of the Buddhist Cave-Temples at Lung-men" (Tokyo, 1941), following p. 449. Although these tables record only changes in the objects of devotion in the Lungmen caves, there is reason to believe that the trend toward Amitābha worship was general.

These misgivings were deepened by widespread abuses of clerical privilege, by mass retreat into holy orders to escape the corvée and taxation, and by the wholesale and often fraudulent transfer of land-titles to the tax-exempt monasteries and temples. There were further grounds for uneasiness in the rise of uneducated and undisciplined village clergy who often in their preaching exploited the apocalyptic vein in Buddhism for subversive purposes.

The two principal opponents of Buddhism were quick to point out these abuses. The clergy of religious Taoism, who invaded the north in the fifth and sixth centuries, hoped thereby to undermine state support of Buddhism and wrest control of the populace from their Buddhist rivals. Chinese officials, striving always to persuade their alien masters to reconstitute a Confucian state in which the educated gentry would have the key role, drew on the arsenal of argument in their own tradition of political economy; they argued with increasing conviction that the Buddhist church was parasitic and subversive, a blight and an anomaly.

The efforts of these two groups, playing upon the fears of the rulers, brought two developments in Buddhist–state relations that are characteristic of the north. One was the setting up of a clerical bureaucracy whose head was responsible to the throne for all matters relating to ordination standards, conduct of the clergy, and the management of Buddhist property. This system of control, modeled on the Chinese civil bureaucracy and guided by similar rules of procedure and organization, was to persist until recent times. The other principal development was an attempt, made in 446–52 and again in 574–78, to impose drastic restrictions on Buddhist organizations and activities. These two attempts were made in different circumstances, but they have some common features which are worth noting. The considerations which led to both were mainly political and economic; the instigators in both cases were Taoists and Confucians in uneasy alliance against their common rival; the suppressions were both ineffective, and both were followed by the rehabilitation of Buddhism and dramatic expiatory acts on the part of the rulers who succeeded the would-be suppressors. Both illustrated northern Buddhism's heavy dependence on the favor of autocratic rulers, but the aftermaths of both demonstrated that Buddhism had become too much a part of the culture and life of the north to be eliminated by imperial edict.

The northern Buddhist solutions to the problem of the relation between secular and religious powers were notably different from those advocated in the south by Hui-yüan and his successors. The southerners had to reconcile Buddhism with an aristocratic state and society, while the northerners had to deal with an autocracy. In the Northern Wei the simple proposal had been made to regard the reigning emperor as a Buddha incarnate and thus resolve the conflict of loyalties. In arguing for the suppression of Buddhism in 574, one group maintained that it was not the Buddhist religion but the church that was bad, and that if the church were eliminated, the state would become one vast and harmonious temple—(P'ing-yen ta-ssu)—with the ruler presiding over his believing subjects as a Buddha. Northern Buddhism was, in sum, far closer to Caesaro-papism than that of the south, where Buddhists had been content to make of the politically feeble emperors great lay patrons (mahādānapati) and wielders of kingly power for the good of the faith in the manner of the Indian Cakravartin-rāja.

The north, in these years, was the major center of translation and of the dedicated pursuit of a deeper understanding of Buddhism. Despite its political instability, the north was more open to foreign missionaries arriving from Central Asia than the relatively isolated south. These great missionaries came in increasing numbers through the fourth and fifth centuries, and more and more learned Chinese joined with them in the immense effort to translate Buddhist ideas into Chinese terms. One of the great Chinese monks was Tao-an (312–85), a disciple of the pioneer missionary monk Fo-t'u-teng. Tao-an worked indefatigably with foreign translators, and it was he who developed a mature theory of translation which recognized the danger that Buddhist ideas might be dissolved beyond recognition into the neo-Taoist concepts first used to translate and interpret them.

The emancipation of Buddhist ideas from Taoism, which was still incomplete at Tao-an's death, was to be furthered by Kumārajīva, the greatest of the missionary translators and perhaps the greatest translator of all times. Kumārajīva arrived at Ch'ang-an in 401 after learning Chinese during a long captivity in northwest China, where the local warlord had held him for his charismatic power. Fortunately he found a royal patron, and Chinese monks were assembled from far and near to work with him in translating the sacred texts. This was a "highly structured project," suggestive of the cooperative enterprises of scientists today. There were corps of specialists at all levels: those who discussed doctrinal questions with Kumārajīva; those who checked the new translations against the old and imperfect ones; hundreds of editors, subeditors, and copyists. The quality and quantity of the translators produced by these men in the space of eight years is truly astounding. Thanks to their efforts the ideas of Mahayana Buddhism were presented in Chinese with far greater clarity and precision than ever before. Śūyatā— Nāgārjuna's concept of the void—was disentangled from the Taoist terminology which had obscured and distorted it, and this and other key doctrines of Buddhism were made comprehensible enough to lay the intellectual foundations of the great age of independent Chinese Buddhism that was to follow.

Toward the end of the period of disunion we have been considering, the cultures of north and south were tending to influence each other and thus to reduce the differences which had developed in the course of their separate evolution over nearly three centuries. Buddhist monks from the north migrated to the south, and southern monks went north. The great translations made in the north were soon circulating in the temples of the south. Buddhists of north and south thus developed common philosophical and textual interests and styles of Buddhist art in north and south began to affect one another.

Socially and politically the north tended, toward the end of this period, to become more and more Sinicized. Rulers of alien stock still occasionally asserted their separateness and insisted on their dominance, but intermarriage had broken down many of the barriers between Chinese and barbarian, and the rehabilitation of China's agricultural system had made the Chinese increasingly indispensable to the alien rulers. Most important of all, many of these rulers dreamed of conquering the south and reuniting China under their sway. To this end they schooled themselves in Chinese history, political ideology, and statecraft, and in so doing they inevitably came to adopt Chinese ideas and attitudes in these spheres. Yet cultural and institutional differences in the late sixth century were still many and great. Buddhism played an important role in reducing these differences and thus in laying the foundations of the unified, and eventually Confucian, society that was to come.

EDWARD H. SCHAFER

The Glory of the T'ang Empire

Although the names of Han and T'ang have been paired as the two golden ages of the Chinese Empire, it was perhaps under the T'ang (618–907) that the Chinese empire reached her most glorious height. The T'ang brought the Chinese into direct contact with the borderlands of Indian and Near Eastern civilizations. Never again until the twentieth century was China to prove so responsive to foreign influences.

One sign of the close contact with the outside world was the large number of foreign residents in China. In early T'ang, Ch'ang-an (Changan), the greatest walled city ever built by men, was literally crowded with foreigners—hundreds of members of the official embassies came periodically from all over Asia, and still larger numbers of merchants, soldiers, monks, and jugglers and other entertainers were attracted to the greatest metropolis of the world.

The open, cosmopolitan spirit of early T'ang gradually faded into a narrower, more exclusively China-centered and introspective attitude. Yet the scope of the imitation of the T'ang model abroad, of which Japan is one example, proves that this very cosmopolitanism of T'ang culture had already had a deep impact on world history. Never before and never again did such a large proportion of mankind look to China as the paramount political and military power of the world and as the obvious model for government and culture.

In the following selection, Dr. Edward H. Schafer, Professor of Oriental Languages at the University of California, Berkeley, gives us a fascinating account of the glittering world of the T'ang empire. He presents a picture of the kaleidoscope of T'ang cosmopolitan cities and commerce, of which the foreign flavor is most characteristic. Students of history may find Professor Schafer's treatment of for-

From *The Golden Peaches of Samarkand* by Edward H. Schafer (Berkeley: University of California Press, 1963), pp. 7–39. Reprinted by permission of The Regents of the University of California. Footnotes omitted.

eigners in T'ang China especially interesting, since detailed description of this type is rare in general historical works or textbooks, which usually focus on the civil and military achievements of the T'ang empire.

Historical Matters

The tale is of the T'ang empire, ruled by dynasts of the Li family, famous throughout Asia in the Middle Ages, and still famous retrospectively in the Far East. Let us look at it hurriedly. The three centuries of the empire's formal existence were not all alike: we must distinguish them somehow, and fashion a chronological skeleton on which to hang the flesh of our story, acknowledging readily that the framework is arbitrary, taking too much of what is radically changed, and too little of what remains the same, or is changed only subtly. Fortunately, since we care chiefly about commerce and the arts, we can make easy divisions, roughly according to century. These fit the facts not too badly.

The seventh century was the century of conquest and settlement. First, the Li family subverted the Chinese state of Sui and destroyed equally ambitious rivals, then subjected the Eastern Turks in what is now Mongolia, the kingdoms of Koguryŏ and Paekche in what are now Manchuria and Korea, and finally the Western Turks, suzerains of the ancient city-states of Serindia, that is, of Chinese Turkestan. Chinese garrisons in these regions made possible the steady flow of their men and goods onto the sacred soil. For the most part it was a century of low prices and of economic stabilization, made possible by the distribution of plots of farm land to the peasants and by the institution of a firm new tax system, the famous triple system of grain tax paid by each adult male, family tax in silk cloth or in linen woven by the women of the household (with a portion of silk floss or hemp), and *corvée,* a period of service at public works, again by the men of the family. It was an age of movement, when settlers migrated in great numbers into what are now central and south China, as lands of new opportunity and possible fortune but also to escape conscription, floods, and barbarian invasions in these underdeveloped areas. It was an age of social change, in which the new provincial gentlemen from the south were established in positions of political power *via* the official examination system, at the expense of the old aristocracy of the north with its traditional ties to Turkish culture. This revolution reached its climax with the reign of the Empress Wu and her transitory empire of Chou in the last decades of the seventh century. It was an age when Indian culture made great inroads, when Buddhist philosophy, accompanied by the Indian arts of astronomy, mathematics, medicine, and philology, permeated the higher levels of Chinese life. It was an age, finally, when a taste for all sorts of foreign luxuries and wonders began to spread from the court outward among city dwellers generally.

The eighth century includes the "Fullness of T'ang" of the literary critics (Tu Fu, Li Po, and Wang Wei), extending until about 765, and also most of "Middle T'ang," a period of slow recovery from many disasters, running until the second decade of the ninth century, and culminating in a real revival of literature (Han Yü, Po Chü-i, and Liu Tsung-yüan). Great changes took place after mid-century, and truly the century can be divided into equal halves, the first climactic and magnificent, the second convalescent and eccentric. The first of these halves, the "Fullness of T'ang," corresponds to the glorious reign of Hsüan Tsung, a long epoch of wealth, safety, and low prices, when "there was no costly thing in the Subcelestial Realm," when one could ". . . visit Ching or Hsiang in the South, go to T'ai-yüan or Fan-yang in the North, or go to Szu-ch'uan or Liang-fu in the West, and everywhere there were shops and emporiums for supplying merchant travelers. Though they should go as far as several thousand li, they need not carry even an inch-long blade." Mules and horses were available to travelers on these secure roads, and an intricate system of canals devised to provide water transport for tax silks from the mouth of the Yangtze River to the capital was now so improved that it could also be used to bring luxury goods from foreign countries. Fine highways and waterways fostered overseas trade, but so did a change in the taste of the young sovereign Hsüan Tsung, who, at the beginning of his reign had an immense pile of precious metals, stones, and fabrics burned on the palace grounds to signalize his contempt for such expensive trifles. But a few years later, seduced by the tales of wealth from abroad accumulating in Canton, the emperor began to relish expensive imports, and to watch jealously over the condition of foreign trade. The old natural economy, under which pieces of taffeta were the normal measure of value and could be used for the purchase of anything from a camel to an acre of land, creaked and finally gave way, in 731, to an officially recognized money economy, the result of unprecedented prosperity, especially at commercial centers like Yang-chou and Canton. Cash was the oil of commerce, and its acceptance was a boon to the rising merchant class. It was inevitable that the tax system of the seventh century should be superseded: in 780 the new "Double Tax" reform went into effect, replacing the taxes in kind and labor with a semiannual tax payable in cash. This change too was in response to the developing money economy, and the merchant class was vastly encouraged by it. The new world of finance represented not only the heyday of businessmen and entrepreneurs but also the collapse of the independent farmers, and the disappearance of the little fields granted them at the foundation of the dynasty. Therefore, beyond its midpoint, the century was an age of landless men and hapless tenants replacing free farmers and set against wealthy landowners and great manors. This was the result of war, the corvée, and the weight of taxes.

The reign of Hsüan Tsung had been a time of triumph for the new literary class, exemplified by the phenomenal career of the statesman Chang Chiu-ling, a native of the tropical south, an enemy of soldiers and aristocratic politicians, a friend of southerners and merchants. But in the same reign came the final triumph of the privileged classes, with the dictatorship of Li Lin-fu, supported by the monarch's hopes for a strong administration. On his death, the dictator's client, Rokhshan "the Bright," encouraged by families of "pure" Chinese blood in Hopei, set himself against a new upstart government, and led his veterans from the northeastern frontier into the valley of the Yellow River, and the loot of the two capitals. So the second half of the century was also an age of decline and death, and enormous reduction of population. It was a century too of change on the frontiers; warriors of the new state of Nan-chao (later Yünnan Province) straddled the direct western route to Burma and India, and would not give up their independence. The Uighur Turks rose to power on the northwestern frontier in mid-century as haughty friends and rivals of the Chinese. In Manchuria the burgeoning race of Khitans (not a great menace for two centuries to come) sapped the strength of the Chinese garrisons. The Tibetans harassed the trade routes to the West, until put down by the great general Kao Hsien-chih, of Korean origin. But in 751 this hero saw his armies in turn dissolve under the onslaughts of the Abbāsid hosts by the Talas River. Then the Muslims took control in Central Asia, and indeed they began to appear in every quarter: Arab troops aided in the government in the suppression of Rokhshan the Bright, and (contrariwise) Arab pirates were involved in the sack of Canton a few years later. It was a century of tolerated foreign faiths, when Buddhists of every sort, Nestorians of Syrian origin, and Manichaeans of Uighur nationality performed their mysteries and chanted their prayers in their own holy places, protected by the government within the cities of China.

The cultural and economic resurrection following the harrying of the north by the well-beloved Rokhshan lasted into the first two decades of the ninth century. That century begins, for our purposes, about 820, and ends with the obliteration of the dynasty in 907. The period of deflation following the promulgation of the Double Tax law was followed by an era of gradually rising prices, beginning in the third decade of this unhappy century. Natural calamities, such as droughts and plagues of locusts, along with disasters of human origin, led to a scarcity of essential goods and costly imports alike, and to universal suffering. Most fatal of the human disasters of this century was the rebellion of Huang Ch'ao, who ravaged the whole country in the seventies and eighties, but was especially calamitous in his massacre of the foreign merchants in Canton in 879, thus doing serious injury to trade and cutting off the revenues derived from it. It was an age of shrinking Chinese authority among erstwhile tributary and client states, and of the appearance of new rivals, such as the men of Nan-chao, invaders now of the ancient Chinese protectorate in Vietnam, and the Kirghiz, conquerors of the powerful and sophisticated Uighurs. The decline of the Uighurs left their religion, Manichaeism, defenseless in China, and in 845 it suffered with Buddhism during the great persecution of foreign faiths, aimed at the secularization of the clerical classes for tax purposes, and at the conversion of a multitude of holy bronze images into copper coins. These economic motives could only be effective in a generation of fear and attendant xenophobia. It was also a century when the power of the state was fatally weakened by centrifugal forces. The headquarters of the great provincial warlords became royal courts in miniature, and finally, in the tenth century, the house of Li and its great state of T'ang disappeared.

Foreigners in T'ang

Into this wonderful land, during these three kaleidoscopic centuries, came the natives of almost every nation of Asia, some curious, some ambitious, some mercenary, some because they were obliged to come. But the three most important kinds of visitors were the envoys, the clerics, and the merchants, representing the great interests of politics, religion, and commerce. Greatest among the envoys was Pērōz, son of King Yazdgard III and scion of the Sāsānids, a poor client of the Chinese sovereign in the seventh century. But there were many lesser emissaries, like him soliciting favors to the advantage of the dynasties, rising or declining, which they represented. There were Indian Buddhists in abundance, but also Persian priests of varying faith: the Magus for whom the Mazdean temple in Ch'ang-an was rebuilt in 631; the Nestorian honored by the erection of a church in 628; the Manichaean who proposed his outlandish doctrines to the court in 694. Turkish princelings pondered the ways of gem dealers from Oman; Japanese pilgrims stared in wonder at Sogdian caravaneers. Indeed, hardly any imaginable combination of nationality and profession was absent. All these travelers brought exotic wares into China, either as sovereign gifts or as salable goods, or simply as appendages to their persons. In return, some found glory there, as the Sogdian merchant who was designated Protector of Annam. Some found riches, as the Jewish merchant of Oman who brought back a vase of black porcelain, gold-lidded, in it ". . . a golden fish, with ruby eyes, garnished with musk of the finest quality. The contents of the vase was worth fifty thousand *dinars*." Some came, possibly more humbly, in search of wisdom, as did the aristocratic Tibetan youths sent by their fathers for reliable interpretations of the Chinese classics.

Ships and Sea Routes

There were two ways to China: overland by caravan, overseas by argosy. Great ships plied the Indian Ocean and the China Seas, carrying eager Westerners to the glittering Orient. In the north, the art and trade of navigation was chiefly in the hands of the Koreans, especially after the destruction of the kingdoms of Packche and Koguryŏ by Silla during the 660's. Then ambassadors, priests, and merchants from the victorious state, and refugees from the vanquished nations too, came in quantity. The Korean vessels usually coasted around the northern edge of the Yellow Sea, and made port on the Shantung Peninsula. This was also the normal route of ships frm Japan, setting sail from Hizen, at least until the end of the seventh century, when Japan and Silla became enemies. In the eighth century the Japanese were forced to come across the open sea from Nagasaki, avoiding Silla, heading for the mouth of the Huai or of the Yangtze River or even for Hang-chou Bay. But in the ninth century, to avoid these voyages, which had proved exceedingly dangerous, Japanese pilgrims and emissaries preferred to take better navigated Korean ships and come via Shantung to the mouth of the Huai, or even to risk Chinese ships, which made land further south in Chekiang and Fukien, instead of at Yang-chou. Though the ships of Silla dominated these waters, merchant vessels of the Manchurian state of P'o-hai, culturally dependent on T'ang, also navigated them, and there were government inns for the accommodation of the ambassadors of P'o-hai, as well as those of Silla, at Teng-chou in Shantung. But the Koreans were in the majority; indeed, they formed a significant alien group on Chinese soil, living in large wards in the towns of Ch'u-chou and Lien-shui, on the system of canals between the Yangtze and the Yellow rivers, enjoying, like other foreigners, some extraterritorial rights.

But most of China's overseas trade was through the South China Sea and the Indian Ocean, and it was governed by the periodic shifts of the monsoon. Ships outbound from Canton sailed before the northeast monsoon, leaving in late autumn or winter. The northeast monsoon was also the wind of departure from the great ports of the Persian Gulf, thousands of miles to the west of China, and even before the merchant vessels were leaving Canton, the ships of Islam were under way: if they left Basra or Sīrāf in September or October, they would be out of the Persian Gulf in time for the fair monsoon of winter to carry them across the Indian Ocean, and could expect to catch the stormy southwest monsoon in June to carry them northward from Malaya across the South China Sea to their destinations in south China. The rule, both east and west, was "southward in winter, northward in summer."

From the seventh to the ninth century, the Indian Ocean was a safe and rich ocean, thronged with ships of every nationality. The Arabian Sea was protected by the power of Islam, and after the Abbāsid capital was moved from Damascus to Baghdad at the head of the Persian Gulf, the eastern trade flourished greatly. Basra, an Arab city, was the port nearest to Baghdad, but it could not be reached by the largest ships. Below Basra, at the head of the Gulf, was Ubullah, an old port of the Persian Empire. But richest of all was Sīrāf, on the Persian side of the Gulf, below Shīrāz. This town owed all its prosperity to the Eastern trade, and it dominated the Gulf until destroyed by an earthquake in 977. Its inhabitants were Persians in the main, but there were also Arab pearl divers, and merchant adventurers who came from Mesopotamia or from Oman to take ship for India and China. The decline of Sīrāf was a disaster for the trade with the Far East, already reduced by the sack of Basra and Ubullah by revolted African slaves in the 870's.

From these ports, then, the ships of many nations set sail, manned by Persian-speaking crews—for Persian was the *lingua franca* of the Southern Seas, as Sogdian was the *lingua franca* of the roads of Central Asia. They stopped at Muscat in Oman, on the way out into the Indian Ocean; maybe they risked the coastal ports of Sind, haunted by pirates, or else proceeded directly to Malabar, and thence to Ceylon, also called "Lion Country" and "Island of Rubies," where they purchased gems. From here the route was eastward to the Nicobars, where they bartered, perhaps with naked savages in canoes for coconuts or ambergris. Then they made land on the Malay Peninsula, in Kedah it is thought, whence they cruised the Strait of Malacca toward the lands of gold, Suvarnabhūmi, the fabulous Indies. Finally, they turned north, impelled by the moist monsoon of summer, to trade for silk damasks in Hanoi or Canton, or even farther north.

The sea-going merchantmen which thronged the ports of China in T'ang times were called by the Chinese, who were astonished at their size, "Argosies of the South Seas," "Argosies of the Western Regions," "Argosies of the Man-Barbarians," "Malayan Argosies," "Singhalese Argosies," "Brahman Argosies," and especially "Persian Argosies." But it is by no means certain that Chinese vessels of this age made the long and hazardous voyage to Sīrāf. The great ocean-going ships of China appear some centuries later, in Sung, Yüan, and early Ming. But in T'ang times, Chinese travelers to the West shipped in foreign bottoms. When the Arab writers of the ninth and tenth centuries tell of "Chinese vessels" in the harbors of the Persian Gulf, they mean "ships engaged in the China trade," as when we speak of "China clippers" and "East Indiamen"; the cinnamon and sandalwood of Indonesia were called "Chinese" by the Arabs and Persians because they were brought from lands near

China, or possibly in Chinese vessels. Similarly, the "Persian Argosies" of the Chinese books must often have been only "ships engaged in trade with the Persian Gulf," often with Malay or Tamil crews.

Chinese sources say that the largest ships engaged in this rich trade came from Ceylon. They were 200 feet long, and carried six or seven hundred men. Many of them towed lifeboats, and were equipped with homing pigeons. The dhows built in the Persian Gulf were smaller, lateen-rigged, with their hulls built carvel-fashion, that is, with the planks set edge to edge, not nailed but sewed with coir, and waterproofed with whale oil, or with the Chinese brea which sets like black lacquer.

Caravans and Land Routes

The wealth of the Oriental nations was brought by land too, from the North and East, from the Northwest, and from the Southwest, in carriage or on camel, by horse or by ass. The products of the peoples of Manchuria and Korea came through the forests and plains of Liao-yang, where Tungusic and proto-Mongolic tribes lived, and down the coast of the Gulf of P'o-hai to the critical spot where the Great Wall ends at a narrow passage between mountains and sea. Here was a township named "Black Dragon" (Lu lung), and a stream named Yü, which has disappeared since T'ang times; and here were a Chinese frontier fortress and a customs station.

The great silk roads, leading in the end to Samarkand, Persia, and Syria, went out from the northwestern frontier of China, along the edge of the Gobi Desert. Beyond the Jade Gate there were alternative roads, none of them attractive. The caravan route could sometimes be identified by the skeletons of men and pack animals. Such was the terrible road direct from Tun-huang to Turfan, which crossed the White Dragon Dunes, part of the salt crust left by the ancient lake Lop-nor. This absolute desert was also haunted by goblins, so that caravan leaders preferred to take the road through I-wu (Hami), so reaching Turfan by a northerly detour. From Turfan the traveler could go westward through the lands of the Western Turks, north of the Mountains of Heaven, or cut southwestward, south of those mountains, and proceed through Kucha and the other oasis cities of Chinese Turkestan. Then there was the parallel road from Tun-huang, the Southern Road, along the northern edge of the mysterious K'un-lun Mountains, and so through Khotan to the Pamirs. These roads were passable only because of the peculiar virtues of the Bactrian camel, which could sniff out subterranean springs for thirsty merchants, and also predict deadly sandstorms:

When such a wind is about to arrive, only the old camels have advance knowledge of it, and they immediately stand snarling together, and bury their mouths in the sand. The men always take this as a sign, and they too immediately cover their noses and mouths by wrapping them in felt. This wind moves swiftly, and passes in a moment, and is gone, but if they did not so protect themselves, they would be in danger of sudden death.

Another overland trade route, very old, but little used in pre-T'ang times, passed from Szechwan, through what is now Yünnan Province, split into two roads through the frightful chasms of the upper Irrawaddy in Burma, and led thence into Bengal. Yünnan was then a region of barbarians, whom the T'ang government tried in vain to subdue. The efforts to reopen this ancient route to Burma were finally frustrated by the rise of the new state of Nan-chao in the eighth century, friendlier to the border-raiding Tibetans than to the Chinese. But after Nan-chao had invaded Tongking in 863, the Chinese were finally able to break its military power. By then the foreign trade of China was declining, so that what was won could be little used. One of these Burma roads passed near the amber mines of Myitkyina, not far from the locality where, in modern times, the popular jadeite of kingfisher hue was mined. This too was sent back over the old route through Yünnan to the lapidaries of Peking.

Finally, Buddhist pilgrims sometimes took the circuitous and difficult route through Tibet to India, usually descending by way of Nepal.

Foreign Settlements in T'ang

Let us now look at the cities and towns of China where foreigners congregated, and at the roads they traveled when moving about within the country. We shall begin in the south. Before T'ang, seafarers coming up the South China Sea usually made port in Tongking, in the vicinity of modern Hanoi. But after the T'ang settlement the merchants of Arabia and the Indies pointed their argosies at Canton or even further north. At this time Chiao-chou was the seat of the Chinese protectorate over the betel-chewing Annamese in Tongking, and its port was Lungpien. Though the overseas trade of Chiao-chou fell off with the rise of Canton in the seventh century, it never became entirely extinct. It even increased somewhat after the middle of the eighth century, and during the final decades of that century, because of the exactions of rapacious officials and agents in Canton, foreign traders preferred to go to Chiao-chou.

But of all the cities of the south, and of all the towns where foreign merchants congregated, none was more prosperous than the great port of Canton, the Khanfu of the Arabs, the "China" of the Indians. Canton was then a frontier town, on the edge of a tropical wilderness populated by savages and wild beasts, and plagued with unpleasant diseases, but handsomely set among lichees, oranges, bananas, and banyans. During the reigns of the T'ang emperors it became a truly Chinese city, even though a large part of its population of 200,000 was "barbarian." It was a wealthy city, but a flimsy one: its triple wall surrounded a crowded mass of thatch-roofed wooden houses, which were repeatedly swept by disastrous fires, until, in 806, an intelligent governor ordered the people to make themselves roofs of tile. In the estuary before this colorful and insubstantial town were ". . . the argosies of the Brahmans, the Persians, and the Malays, their number beyond reckoning, all laden with aromatics, drugs, and rare and precious things, their cargoes heaped like hills." In exchange for their fragrant tropical woods and their almost legendary medicines, these dark outlanders sought bales of silk, boxes of chinaware, and slaves. They enriched the Chinese businessmen who were willing to give up the comforts of the north for the profits of the south, and made possible the high state of the governor of the town and province, ". . . who carries six yaktails, with an army for each yaktail, and who in his majesty and dignity is not to be distinguished from the Son of Heaven."

Many of these visitors settled in the foreign quarter of Canton, which by imperial sanction was set aside south of the river for the convenience of the many persons of diverse race and nationality who chose to remain in Canton to do business or to wait for favorable winds. They were ruled by a specially designated elder, and enjoyed some extraterritorial privileges. Here citizens of the civilized nations, such as the Arabs and Singhalese, rubbed elbows with less cultured merchants, such as the "White Man-barbarians and the Red Man-barbarians." Here the orthodox, such as the Indian Buddhists in their own monasteries, whose pools were adorned with perfumed blue lotuses, were to be found close to the heterodox, such as the Shī'ah Muslims, who had fled persecution in Khurāsān to erect their own mosque in the Far East. Here, in short, foreigners of every complexion, and Chinese of every province, summoned by the noon drum, thronged the great market, plotted in the warehouses, and haggled in the shops, and each day were dispersed by the sunset drum to return to their respective quarters or, on some occasions, to chatter loudly in their outlandish accents in the night markets.

This thriving town had a mottled history, spotted with murders, pirate raids, and the depredations of corrupt officials. Such evils tended to be self-perpetuating, since one gave rise to another. For instance, in an otherwise placid century, the captain of a Malayan cargo vessel murdered the governor Lu Yüan-jui, who had taken advantage of his position to plunder him. This was in 684. The central government appointed a virtuous man to succeed the wretch, but in the years which followed many other silk-robed exiles from the gay life of the capital repaid themselves fully for their discomfort at the expense of the luckless merchants. It was precisely for the purpose of bringing some order and discipline to Canton, and to ensure that the court got its luxuries and the government its income, that, early in the eighth century, the important and sometimes lucrative post of "Commissioner for Commercial Argosies," a kind of customs officer in that difficult city, was established. This was done partly at the instance of the plundered foreigners who had addressed complaints to the throne. But the agents of the city's misfortunes were not always Chinese: in 758 it was raided by a horde of Arabs and Persians, who expelled the governor, looted the warehouses, burned dwellings, and departed by sea, perhaps to a pirate haven on the island of Hainan. This disaster made the city negligible as a port for half a century, and foreign vessels went instead to Hanoi.

Another difficulty which plagued this jeweled frontier town was the practice, which developed during the second half of the eighth century, of appointing eunuchs from the imperial palace to the crucial post of "Commissioner for Commercial Argosies," a custom which led to the evil then euphemistically called "palace markets," that is, interference in trade by these haughty palatines. In 763, one of the gorgeous rascals went so far as to rebel against the throne. The eunuch's insurrection was quelled only with great difficulty. Meanwhile trade had come to a virtual standstill. The poet Tu Fu remarked in two poems the discontinuance of the flow of luxury wares northward from Canton at this time: "about the luminous pearls of the South Seas, it has long been quiet," and "recently the provision of a live rhino, or even of kingfisher feathers, has been rare." Even an honest governor like Li Mien—who ruled the port for three years beginning in 769 without mulcting the hapless foreigners, so that the amount of overseas trade increased tenfold under his administration—could not prevent lesser officials from looting. Small-scale robberies multiplied a thousand times, with an occasional great robber clothed in the robes of office—like Wang O, who, in the last years of the eighth century, collected a private as well as a public tax, and sent endless boxes of ivory and pearls to his family in the north, so that his own resources surpassed those of the public treasury. These chronic and acute diseases led to the diversion of some of the city's commerce to Chiao-chou in the south, and some to Hai-yang, the port of Ch'ao-chou, further north. But somehow the city and its prosperity could not be permanently destroyed: there were governors of rectitude and intelligence in the early decades of the ninth century, and things went fairly well until, in the final quarter of the century, the death throes of the dynasty began. In 879 the prince of rebels, Huang Ch'ao, sacked the city, slaughtered the foreign traders, destroyed the mulberry groves which fed the silkworms, producers of the nation's chief export, and so brought about the great decline of Canton's wealth and prestige, which, despite a brief rejuvenation at the end of the century, she never completely recovered. Under the Sung empire, the argosies from the South China Sea began more and more to turn to the ports of Fukien and Chekiang, and although Canton remained important, her monopoly was broken forever.

An Indian monk or a Javanese ambassador or a Cham merchant who wished to journey northward from Canton to the fabulous capital of China or to some other great city had a choice of two ways to cross the mountain barrier to the north. One possibility was to travel due north on the Chen River, now called "North River," until he reached Shao-chou, whence he turned to the northeast, crossed the "Mountain Pass of the Plum Trees," and descended into the valley of the Kan River, by which he could easily proceed through what is now Kiangsi Province, through Hung-chou, where many Persians were to be found, and on to the Long River, the great Yangtze, and so arrive at the commercial city of Yang-chou, or elsewhere in the heart of China. The way over the pass could not accommodate the greatly increased trade and traffic of early T'ang, but the great minister Chang Chiu-ling, himself a southern parvenu with bourgeois sympathies, had a great new road built through the pass as a stimulus to overseas trade and the development of Canton city. This great work was achieved in 716.

The other possibility, less used though very old, was to take a northwesterly course up the Kuei ("Cassia") River, through the eastern part of modern Kwangsi Province, and follow it to its source at an altitude of less than a thousand feet. Here is also the source of the great river Hsiang, which carried the traveler northward through T'an-chou (Ch'ang-sha) in Hunan Province, and on into the watery lowlands of central China. At its source, the Hsiang is called the Li River, and it is actually connected with the source of the Kuei by an ancient canal, no longer identifiable as such by T'ang times, so that the sources of the northward- and southward-flowing rivers are now identical. It was therefore possible for small boats to travel continuously from Canton to the great waterways of central and north China, and even all the way to the capital.

Both of these routes are referred to in a couplet by the ninth-century poet Li Ch'ün-yü:

*Once we were moored on the Cassia River—
 there was rain by the deep bank;
And again, there, at the Plum Pass—
 our homeward course was blocked.*

But whichever route he took, the traveler could proceed with ease through the great lakes south of the Yangtze, propelled by sail or by sweep or even, from the late eighth century, by paddle wheel, toward his destination, which usually was the magnificent city of Yang-chou.

Yang-chou was the jewel of China in the eighth century; a man might hope to crown his life by dying there. The city owed its wealth and beauty to its location at the junction of the Yangtze River, which drained all central China, with the Grand Canal (called by the Chinese "River of Transport"), which carried the produce of the whole world to the great cities of the north. Therefore the imperial agent in charge of the national salt monopoly, a very lordly personage, had his headquarters there, and the merchants of Asia congregated there, at the hub of the great network of T'ang waterways, where all goods brought by Chinese and foreign vessels were transshipped to northbound canalboats. The citizens of the city were made rich by its focal position in the distribution of salt (which everyone needed), of tea (which by now had become popular in the north), of precious stones, aromatics, and drugs brought up from Canton, and of costly damasks and tapestries brought down the Yangtze from Szechwan. Moreover, Yang-chou was a banking center and a gold market, where the financier was as important as the merchant. In short, it was a bustling, bourgeois city, where money flowed easily. Yang-chou was also an industrial town, famous for its beautiful metalwork, especially its bronze mirrors, for its felt hats, in the mode among the young men of Ch'ang-an, for its silk fabrics and embroideries and fine ramie linens, for its refined sugar, made here since the seventh century by a process brought from Magadha, for boatbuilding, and for excellent cabinetwork. Yang-chou was a gay city, a city of well-dressed people, a city where the best entertainment was always available, a city of parks and gardens, a very Venice, traversed by waterways, where the boats outnumbered the carriages. It was a city of moonlight and lanterns, a city of song and dance, a city of courtesans. "Yang is first and I is second," went the epigram, placing the reputed elegance and bright frivolity of Ch'eng-tu in Szechwan, along with its solid prosperity, in an inferior position.

It was inevitable that foreign merchants should establish their shops here. We know that their numbers were considerable, for the hordes of the rebel T'ien Shen-kung killed several thousand Arabian and Persian businessmen when they looted the city in 760. Despite this disaster, the city retained its riches and splendor until the last decades of the ninth century, when it was laid waste by such rival captains as Pi Shih-to and Sun Ju, jackals following the trail of the great tiger, Huang Ch'ao. Its glory was partly restored by the new kingdom of Wu, arisen from the ruins of T'ang at the beginning of the tenth century, but it was destroyed again in mid-century by the northern kingdom of Chou, when the latter invaded Wu's successor state, Southern T'ang. The scene of desolation presented by Yang-chou in early Sung times was aggravated by the policy of the emperors of the new dynasty, who encouraged the development of trade, transportation, and finance in the village of Yang-tzu, later called Chen-chou, which was nearer the Long River, and directed the transfer of industries elsewhere. Hung Mai, writing in the twelfth century, expressed astonishment at the enthusiasm for Yang-chou which had been displayed by the poets of the eighth and ninth centuries. In his own day the place could only "sour one's nostrils."

The greatness of Yang-chou and of the Grand Canal alike were the work of the emperors of Sui, but their true flowering came in the eighth century. With the phenomenal increase in population and material wealth in that era, the farmlands of the Yellow River watershed could no longer provide for the two capitals and the other northern cities, so that cereals had to be imported from the Yangtze region. These new demands put an unforseen strain on the old canal system. A remedy was found in 734: granaries were built along the route from Yang-chou to Ch'ang-an at critical points where grain might be properly stored whenever the system could not provide for its transfer beyond such a point. This prevented delays and stoppages, and rot and pilfering, and permitted the transshipment of rice and millet at leisure to vessels of appropriate size. In this way a steady flow northward was assured. Unanticipated, or at least not openly advocated, were the burdens imposed on the boats and waterways of the new relay system by the transfer of increasing quantities of luxury goods from the far South: ivory, tortoise shell, and sandalwood were heaped into lighters originally designed to receive bags of grain.

The traveler then, as well as the barge captain, unaware of these grave economic problems, could leave Yang-chou (unless he preferred to travel by horse or carriage) and proceed north- and westward up the "River of Transport," marveling at the great flocks of ducks and geese which whirred up around his boat. He would pass the barges of the salt bureau, glittering like snow in the sunlight, and stop perhaps at the thriving towns of Sui-yang and Ch'en-liu, both of which had considerable foreign settlements, especially of Persians, and at Pien-chou (K'ai-feng), which also had its temple to the Sacred Fire, a city of more than half a million inhabitants, but whose glory as a metropolis was still in the future. Finally, the traveler came to the Eastern Capital, the ancient city of Lo-yang.

Foreigners who visited China, or settled there, tended to congregate in the vigorous commercial cities of the south, like Canton and Yang-chou. But they also came together in the venerable cities of the north, the centers of political power, the homes of the nobility, where a great bibliophile or a great soldier counted for more than a successful merchant. Of the two great capitals, Lo-yang was the second in rank, and it was the second city of the empire in population, having more than a million inhabitants. It had its holy traditions of a thousand years, was not second in pride even to Ch'ang-an, and was endowed with a spiritual atmosphere somewhat milder and more elegant than its western rival. It was the "Godly Metropolis" of the Empress Wu, well on its way to becoming what it became in the eleventh century, the proudest and most beautiful city of China. It had palaces and parks and throngs of officials. It was noted for its fine fruits and flowers, its patterned damasks and fine silk crepes, and its ceramic wares of all kinds. It had a great market place, the Southern Market, occupying two blocks (*fang*), with a hundred and twenty bazaars, or streets given over to the sale of a single type of ware, and thousands of individual shops and warehouses. For the aliens there on business, there were the usual temples to alien gods, among them three shrines to the Sacred Fire, attesting to the presence of a Persian colony.

In 743 an artificial lake, a transshipment pool, was built east of Ch'ang-an, the Western Capital. In that year, the fascinated northerner, accustomed to speaking the proverb "Boats in the south, horses in the north," could see the boats of every part of the empire gathered on this pool, loaded with the tax goods and local tribute destined for the palace: scarlet felt saddle covers from the north, vermilion bitter tangerines from the south, pink silk-fringed druggets from the east, crimson alum from the west. These goods were transferred to lighters, whose crews were specially garbed in bamboo rain hats, sleeved smocks, and straw shoes, in the fashion of the boatmen of the Yangtze. This was the terminus of a continuous waterway from Canton to the greatest city of the age.

With almost two million taxable residents, Ch'ang-an was ten times as populous as Canton at the other end of this long net of rivers and canals. The capital's foreign population was proportionally large. This international element had a rather different cast from that of the southern port. It was chiefly made up of men from the North and West: Uighurs, Turks, Tocharians, and Sogdians, in contrast to the Chams, Khmers, Javanese, and Singhalese who crowded into Canton. In both places, however, there were many Arabs, Persians, and Hindus. The Iranian population must have been most important. The T'ang government even had an office "of the Sārthavāk" (literally, "of the Caravan Leader") to watch over their interests.

Ch'ang-an had two great markets, the Eastern and the Western, each with scores of bazaars. The Eastern Market was the less crowded of the two, and quieter and richer, being situated near the mansions of the nobles and officials; the Western was noisier, more vulgar and violent (malefactors were punished there), and more exotic. Each bazaar, with its unique kind of merchandise, was surrounded by warehouses, and each had a headman (hang t'ou). Each was required by law to display a sign naming its speciality. Proceeding through the Western Market, where most of the foreign merchants displayed their warès, one might see in succession the butchers' bazaar, the ironmonger's bazaar, the clothing bazaar, the bazaar of saddlers, the silk bazaar, and the bazaar of the druggists. After the middle of the eighth century, the tea merchants were particularly popular. The new vogue for tea drinking was not restricted to the Chinese: it is reported that Uighur visitors to the capital, before doing anything else, spurred their horses to the shops of the dealers in tea. Prominent in the Western Market, among the foreign tradesmen, were the fellow-countrymen of these tea enthusiasts, the Uighur usurers, to whom numberless debt-ridden Chinese businessmen and young Chinese wastrels pledged land, furniture, slaves, and even sacred relics, as security for ready cash. These moneylenders began to be regarded as a plague in the early decades of the ninth century, when prices were rising steadily and everyone was in debt. Indeed, the arrogance of these Turks was limitless: one of them was imprisoned for stabbing a merchant in broad daylight, and was rescued by his chief, without any Chinese inquiry into the event. Popular feeling against them mounted until finally, in the year 836, all private intercourse with the "various colored peoples" was prohibited. The insufferable haughtiness of the Uighurs was an important factor in the outburst of xenophobia in mid-century, and the persecution of foreign religions.

But a citizen could console himself in a hundred ways, and accumulate more debts in so doing. He might, for instance, attend any of a great variety of fetes, dances, and dramatic spectacles at the wealthy Buddhist temples scattered about the city. Among these would be novel entertainments originally devised in the Buddhist nations of India and Turkestan, at once alluring and edifying. Or the citizen might, if lonely, find a different kind of consolation among the whores of the P'ing-k'ang Quarter, between the Eastern Market and the imperial palace. Here he could find famous courtesans, skilled in music, dancing, and flattery, and could expect to enjoy her favors for the night by paying about 1,600 cash to her "stepmother." A young aristocrat, enjoying his father's reputation, or a young scholar seeking success in the examinations as the only road to public office, could easily fall in love with one of these charmers. If he had some literary talent he surrounded her with an aura of glamour in his poems and stories. Less expensive but more exotic were the pleasures of the taverns in a zone extending along the east edge of the city, southward from the "Gate of Spring Brightness," a good place to entertain a friend departing on a trip to Lo-yang and the east. Here an enterprising taverner could better his income by employing an exotically handsome Western girl, a Tocharian or a Sogdian say, to serve rare wines in cups of amber or agate, and to increase sales by means of sweet singing and seductive dancing to the accompaniment of the flutes of Western boys—and especially by means of friendly manners: "a Western houri beckons with her white hand, inviting the stranger to intoxicate himself with a golden beaker." These compliant green-eyed beauties, some golden-haired, confounded the poets, and left their mark on literature. Consider the words of Li Po:

The zither plays "The Green Paulownias at Dragon Gate,"
The lovely wine, in its pot of jade, is as clear as the sky.
As I press against the strings, and brush across the studs,
I'll drink with you, milord;
"Vermilion will seem to be prase-green" when our faces begin to redden.

That Western houri with features like a flower—
She stands by the wine-warmer, and laughs with the breath of spring
Laughs with the breath of spring,
Dances in a dress of gauze!
"Will you be going somewhere, milord, now, before you are drunk?"

Let us leave Ch'ang-an on this pleasant note, and consider briefly the remaining Chinese towns where foreigners were wont to come together. Foreign merchants could, of course, be found anywhere where profits might tempt them. You might find them looking for taffetas in the rich, high valleys of Szechwan, or in the moist lowlands about Tung-t'ing Lake. But of all the regions unconnected with the major cities by water, that in which aliens tended most to settle was the corridor of the caravans, leading westward into Turkestan. Here along the margin of the Gobi were Chinese towns, spaced at regular intervals, and equipped with caravanserais. Iranian fire worshipers and musicians were to be found in all of them, and all were of doubtful allegiance: one year the Chinese mandarins were in residence, quoting the sages and counseling virtue; the next year the Turks rode in, waving their bows; often Tibetan princes were their lords. Typical of these multilingual outposts was the old town of Liang-chou, once subject to the Hsiung-nu and their pastoral successors. Here the regal warlord Ko-shu Han held sway for a time, entertaining fortunate guests with lion pantomines, saber dances, and the thoughtful attentions of red-lipped cupbearers. In the eighth century, Liang-chou had more than a hundred thousand permanent residents, reputed to be of hard and unyielding temperament, since they lived under the influence of the White Tiger and Sign of Metal. Some of these citizens were Chinese, but many were of Indian extraction, surnamed in the Chinese fashion, according to their ethnic origin, *Shindu*, and many could trace their origin to the nations bordering the Oxus and Jaxartes. Here were prime grazing lands for horses, especially along a river which still retained its archaic Mongolian name of Tümigen, meaning "bone marrow" in the Hsien-pi language. It was so named for the fertility of the lands thereabout. Here also were produced fine damasks, mats, and wild horse hides, not to mention an excellent headache remedy. This Liang-chou was a true melting pot, a kind of homely symbol of the exotic to the Chinese, as Hawaii is to the American of the twentieth century. The hybrid music of Liang-chou, at once foreign and familiar, since it was not entirely either, was in fashion in the early Middle Ages of the Far East.

Treatment of Foreigners

Chinese attitudes and policies toward foreigners were not simple. Even at the height of the vogue for the exotic, the best course for an alien was to adopt Chinese manners and habits of thought, as indeed many did. Sometimes, however, the government made it impossible to do this. For instance, an edict of 779 compelled Uighurs resident in the capital, of whom there were then about a thousand, to wear their native costume, and forbade them to "lure" Chinese women into becoming their wives and concubines, or to pass themselves off as Chinese in any way at all. This law may have been the outcome of popular resentment against Uighur usurers, but other such laws may have had no other basis than the zeal of a pious magistrate to protect the purity of Chinese custom, as when Lu Chün, who became governor of Canton in 836, found foreigners and Chinese living together unsegregated, and intermarrying freely. He forced them to separate, forbade further marriages between them, and even prohibited aliens from owning land and houses. Lu Chün regarded himself as a man of upright principles, engaged in policing a dissolute port: he was, in short, a kind of ethnic puritan.

Such Chinese stereotypes as the rich (and therefore enviable) Persian, the black (and therefore ugly) Malay, and the naked (and therefore immoral) Cham belong to the world of vulgar images, and played little part in official policies. And even popular attitudes were ambiguous, to say the least. The same young poets who languished over the pretty Iranian waitresses in the metropolitan wineshops laughed at the little puppets representing drunken Westerners, with their peaked caps, blue eyes, and high noses, with which they played in houses of prostitution—when the ridiculous puppet fell over, the guest at whom it pointed had to empty his cup. The eighth was a century when Central Asiatic harpers and dancers were enormously popular in Chinese cities, but it was also the century of the massacre of thousands of harmless (but wealthy) Persian and Arab traders in Yang-chou. In the ninth century, when exotic things were not so easily and cheaply come by, exotic literature, full of romantic reminiscence, became popular. It is curious that this period when tales about benevolent millionaires from the Far West were being told everywhere, was also an age of suspicion and persecution of foreigners. In this same age of ambivalent attitudes, it was possible for foreigners to rise to high position in the government, especially if they allied themselves with the new gentry, which had been created by the examination system, against the hereditary aristocrats; we have, for instance, the example of an

Arab who gained distinction with the degree of "Advanced Gentlemen" (*chin shih*) in the middle of the ninth century. Many factors were at work, separating the mental image of the "ideal" foreigner from the real one: rising prices, accompanied by resentment against wealthy merchants, and weakening political authority, which allowed foreigners to raid the Chinese soil. Distrust or hatred of foreigners was, in short, not at all incompatible with a love of exotic things. This love was realistic in the fine new days of the seventh and eighth centuries, and embalmed in the literature of the ninth and tenth centuries. Then it recalled the fine old days, when foreigners universally recognized the superiority of Chinese arms and Chinese arts, and when the ordinary Chinese citizen might expect to enjoy the rare goods of distant places. Just so, in our times, a former German soldier might regret the days when he could drink freely of French wines without admitting the equality of the French, or a former English civil servant remember wistfully the treasures of barbaric India under the Empire. Foreign luxuries were too good for foreigners.

There was also something ambiguous about Chinese attitudes toward commerce. Trade was never free from political entanglements. The more necessary the goods were to the general welfare, or the more desirable they were to the upper classes, the more likely it was that the state would take a part in their distribution. Traditional government monopolies on domestic goods, such as those on salt, iron, metal currency, and sometimes on wine and other products of universal consumption, were models for the control of luxury goods from abroad. The new office of "Commissioner for Commercial Argosies," created at Canton in the eighth century, had the ancient office of "Commissioner for Salt and Iron" as its ideal and prototype. Its incumbent bought up such imports as the government desired to control (especially those in demand by the court and by groups favored by the court), prevented smuggling, and followed the pattern of old-style internal monopoly. This attitude had the corollaries that commerce should be entangled with diplomacy and that the gifts of foreign nations to the imperial court, consisting often of great quantities of costly goods and regarded as tokens of submission to the universal authority of the Son of Heaven, should be, in fact, an important part of international trade. To say that "tributary nations" were compelled to offer tribute, is only part of the story. Foreign nations, both those which trembled close at hand and those whose distance made them truly independent of T'ang, sent their goods out of sheer self-interest, and received desirable "gifts" from the Chinese for their trouble. There were certainly drawbacks for the foreign merchant in this system. He was hardly a free agent: he was expected to present certain of his wares formally at the imperial capital, or else to hand them into a government warehouse at the port of entry. If he attempted private enterprise, he was likely to invite official interference or even disaster. A local mandarin was more likely to go too far in the strict interpretation of the government's restraints than to risk his neck by being too liberal. Even those goods which the alien was permitted to sell freely to the public had to be sold in one of the great markets, closely supervised by government agents. To make matters worse, it was precisely those goods which the outlander most desired to take back to his own country which were most jealously watched by the mandarins, lest the government lose its share of the profit. We may judge the nature of these goods from an edict of 714 forbidding the export or the sale to foreigners of tapestries, damasks, gauzes, crepes, embroideries, and other fancy silks, or of yaktails, pearls, gold or iron. Contrariwise, there were erratic government restrictions on the import and sale to Chinese of items conceived to be frivolous and detrimental to the national morals, though these might prove to be the most profitable wares in the merchant's cargo. Indeed, even the sale of counterfeits of luxury goods and adulterated substances, though it made the importer liable to a prison sentence, was, if undetected, a profitable industry, as was discovered by an unlucky Persian priest in Canton, who specialized in manufacturing exotic "rarities" for the sophisticated imperial court. But if he were wise, and knew what could be imported and what could be exported, and under what conditions, even an honest merchant could do very well for himself, as the thousands of foreign merchants on Chinese soil attest. But even the wisest had other hazards to contend with: he was likely, if the local magistrates were not too attentive to the moral principles expected of a Chinese official, to be despoiled of a considerable part of his goods in the name of "customs duty." Even if the inspector at the customs barrier were a person of integrity, the requirements of the goverment were likely to be excessive. An Arab geographer reports that his compatriots were obliged to surrender one-third of their cargo into the imperial warehouses on arrival in China. But nothing was permanent and predictable. Last year's caprice was next year's policy. From time to time relief came in the form of a fiat from the court which made the merchant's condition more bearable and his hope for great profit more reasonable. Such a one was the edict handed down by Wen Tsung in 834, on the occasion of the sovereign's recovery from an illness. This mandate amnestied various classes of criminals, and at the same time expressly extended the imperial protection to strangers from overseas engaged in commerce in Kwangtung, Fukien, and Yangchou, instructing the local magistrates to allow them to trade freely without intolerable tax burdens, since they had placed themselves under the monarch's loving care.

But the foreigner resident in China had other problems. He faced social and economic disabilities unconnected with commerce. If he were unlucky enough to die in China, his goods were sealed and, unless a wife or heir could readily be found, were confiscated by the state. The search for an inheritor could not have extended very far. Moreover, if an alien took a Chinese wife or concubine, he was required to remain in China; in no case could he take a Chinese woman back to his homeland with him. This was ordered in a decree of 628, particularly designated to protect Chinese women from temporary marriages with the envoys of foreign countries and with members of their suites, who required casual comforts while away from home. The rule did not, of course, apply to the gift of a royal princess to a nomadic chieftain. The lady would be sent off to the steppes without a murmur if the good will of her future husband was important to Chinese policy. Such a one was the lady sent to marry the Khan of the Uighurs in the heyday of their power early in the ninth century, in exchange (as it were) for the gifts presented by the envoy sent to fetch her away: camlets, brocades, sable furs, girdles of jade, a thousand horses, and fifty camels. Whether in obedience to the decree, or by free choice, we read of many foreigners of the eighth century who had lived in Ch'ang-an more than forty years, all of them with wives and children. Moreover, as we have noticed, the foreigner was liable to arbitrary segregation laws, which were only partly mitigated by other laws allowing foreign colonies in Chinese cities to elect their own headmen and to settle litigation between members of the colony according to the laws and customs of their native country.

Tribute

Once an ordinary merchant had obtained official permission to trade in the Chinese markets, he took up quarters among his compatriots and went about his business. But an envoy, representing a foreign government, even though he might be primarily interested in commerce or at least in a profitable exchange of lordly gifts, had yet to face the vexatious splendors which awaited all representatives of tribute nations. His nation was bound to be tributary, of course, though the envoy might wink at the deception when closeted with his boon companions. Some cases were exceptional: one cannot guess what token tribute was brought, or what symbols of submission were offered to the Chinese emperor by the fugitive Sāsānid Prince Pērōz, last scion of his house, when he came to Ch'ang-an to seek the protection and assistance of T'ai Tsung against the victorious Arabs. But the average ambassador was an ordinary politician, or a close relative of a king, or a distinguished priest, or perhaps a rich merchant, and ordinarily he made no difficulties about submission. A very distant country interested in encouraging trade might, rather than send its own ambassador, request representation by the envoys of a friendly neighbor. As a case in point, the kingdom of Bali sent an emissary with samples of its native products in the suite of a Cham embassy to the Chinese court in 630.

To gain his rightful privileges when he arrived at the Chinese capital, the envoy needed official credentials. When a foreign potentate sought the favor or protection of T'ang, he would send a petition asking for a golden girdle and a robe of state in many colors, or for a Chinese mandarin to act as his resident adviser, or for a copy of one of the Chinese classics, or for all these things. But most of all he required the gift of a handsome wallet in which his ambassador might carry his official token. This token had the form of a fish of bronze, or rather, of half of such a fish. To each country that maintained regular diplomatic relations with T'ang were assigned twelve such bifurcated fishes, each numbered in sequence, and each inscribed with the name of the nation to which it was allotted. The "male" halves remained in the Chinese palace; the "female" halves were sent to the "tributary" country. An ambassador sent to China had in his brocaded wallet the fish talisman whose number was the number of the month in which he would arrive in Ch'ang-an. If this matched the corresponding piece in the capital, he was accorded those rights and benefits to which he was entitled by nationality. These prerogatives were by no means the same for all envoys. Their food allotments, for instance, were proportional to the distance of their homelands from China. Therefore the representatives of India, Persia, and Arabia were given rations for six months; the envoys from Cambodia, Sumatra, and Java had four-month rations; and the envoys from Champa, whose borders were coterminous with China, got only three. Nor did the agents of great powers yield precedence easily: when, on June 11, 758, the ambassadors of the Uighurs and of the Abbāsid Caliphate arrived simultaneously with "tribute" at the Chinese court, they fought with each other for priority at the palace gate. A special decree from the throne was required to determine the protocol for the occasion: both embassies were allowed to enter at the same time, through gates to right and left.

On first arriving at the capital, the embassy was put up for a while at one of the hostels situated at each of the four major gates of the city, facing the cardinal directions. From this time on, the ambassador's activities were directed by officials of the Hung-lu Office, which was responsible both for the funerals of members of the imperial family and for the reception and entertainment of foreign guests. This important office, quite aside from its basic responsibilities, served also as a clearinghouse of information about foreign countries which was of great value to the nation, especially to the strategists of the army. A special agent of the Department of Arms was sent to interview the envoy immediately upon his arrival. He was interrogated about the geography and customs of his native country, and a map was constructed from the information supplied. The great geographer Chia Tan was head of this office for a period in the second half of the eighth century. It is said that his remarkable knowledge of world geography was derived from personal interviews with visiting diplomats.

The greatest day of the ambassador's period of sojourn in China was the day of his reception by the emperor. On this occasion, everything was calculated to impress the foreigner with the majestic state and awesome power of the ruler of T'ang. If the ambassador was of sufficiently high rank to attend the great reception for tributary princes held on the day of the winter solstice, he found himself face to face with twelve ranks of guards arrayed before the hall of audience. There were swordsmen, halberdiers, lancers, and archers, each group wearing splendid capes of a distinctive color, and each with its appropriate banner—a pennon of parrot or peacock feathers, or a flag embroidered with the image of a wild ass or a leopard, or another symbol of valor. Even a lesser envoy saw before him the household guards, on duty at all audiences. These were divided into five troops, of which four wore scarlet shirts and caps decorated with the tail feathers of the Manchurian snow pheasant, and the fifth wore tabards of scarlet taffeta, embroidered with the figures of wild horses. All carried staves and wore swords at their belts. Dazzled by this spectacle, the foreign delegation approached, and after suitable prostrations had its gifts displayed in front of the audience hall. The chief envoy then approached the throne, and following advice given in whispers by the Chinese official who attended him, bowed toward the sovereign and said, "Your bulwark-vassal so-and-so, of such-and-such a nation, presumes to offer up these oblations from its soil." The emperor continued to sit in stately silence, but the Officer of Protocol accepted the gifts in his name, and received from the ambassador other presents for distribution among his assistants. In return, the tributary king and his ambassador were awarded nominal but resounding titles in the T'ang administration, in accordance with the doctrine that they were vassals of the Son of Heaven, and rich gifts were awarded them as "salary." Thus, when the king of Śrībhoja sent token of tribute to Hsüan Tsung, the monarch handed down a patent of recognition, stating ". . . and it is fitting that there should be a robe-of-state conferred on him, and that he should be awarded, from afar, [the title of] Great Army Leader of the Militant Guards of the Left, and that we should bestow on him a purple caftan and a belt inlaid with gold." After accepting these honors in the name of his lord, the envoy was shown the way out. Now he could expect a more relaxing reward for his labors, as a Japanese ambassador did in the early part of the eighth century:

The Japanese Nation, though far away beyond the seas, has sent its envoys to our levee. Now since they have traversed the glaucous waves, and have also made us presents of articles from their quarter, it is fitting that these envoys, Mabito Makumon and the others, should assemble for a feast at the [Office of] Documents of the Penetralia on the sixteenth day of the present month.

Exotic Taste

Such was the manner of receiving the men who brought the delightful rarities which the aristocrats and their imitators desired. The Chinese taste for the exotic permeated every social class and every part of daily life: Iranian, Indian, and Turkish figures and decorations appeared on every kind of household object. The vogue for foreign clothes, foreign food, and foreign music was especially prevalent in the eighth century, but no part of the T'ang era was free from it. Some individuals, like the poet Yüan Chen, who wrote at the end of the eighth century, lamented these innovations:

Ever since the Western horsemen began raising smut and dust,
Fur and fleece, rank and rancid, have filled Hsien and Lo.
Women make themselves Western matrons by the study of Western makeup;
Entertainers present Western tunes, in their devotion to Western music.

Hsien and Lo are the two capitals Ch'ang-an (under the nominal guise of its vanished precursor Hsien-yang) and Loyang, where these fashions were epidemic.

Some Chinese, at any rate, knew the language of the Turks. There was a Turkish-Chinese dictionary available for serious students, and some Chinese poems of T'ang show the influence of Turkish folksongs in their prosody. Many devoted Buddhists learned some Sanskrit. But the extent of such learning, as also of the study of other foreign languages, such as Korean, Tocharian, Tibetan, or Cham, we do not know.

Fashions in the two capitals tended to follow Turkish and East Iranian modes of dress. In T'ang times, men and women alike wore "barbarian" hats when they went abroad, especially when on horseback. In the early part of the seventh century aristocratic ladies favored a hat and veil combination, a kind of burnoose called a *mi-li*. This mantle enveloped the face and most of the body, and helped a haughty lady to preserve her anonymity and to avoid the curious stares of the vulgar. But modesty suffered a decline after the middle of the century, when the long veil was abandoned for a "curtain hat," a broad-brimmed hat with a hood which fell only to the shoulders, and which might even reveal the face. This hat, originally designed to protect the head on long dusty journeys, was worn both by men and by women, but attracted unfavorable notice to women especially. An edict of 671 attempted to outlaw these brazen-faced equestriennes, who should have traveled in decently covered carriages, but it was ignored, and by the early part of the eighth century women were riding about the city streets wearing Turkish caps, or even bare-headed, and dressed in men's riding clothes and boots. Other exotic fashions of mid-T'ang were leopardskin hats, worn by men, tight sleeves and fitted bodices in the Iranian styles, worn by women along with pleated skirts and long stoles draped around the neck, and even hair-styles and makeup of "un-Chinese" character. Court ladies of the eighth century wore "Uighur chignons." The zeal of colonials for the pure customs of the fatherland, however, inspired the people of Tun-huang in the ninth century to retain Chinese dress under Tibetan rule, when citizens of towns like Liang-chou (notoriously prone to exoticism) freely adopted outlandish dress and manners.

Enthusiasm for Turkish customs enabled some aristocrats to endure the discomfort of living in a tent, even in the midst of the city. The poet Po Chü-i erected two Turkish tents of sky-blue felt in his courtyard, and entertained guests in them, proud to demonstrate how they furnished protection from the winter wind. The most eminent of such urban tent-dwellers was the unhappy prince Li Ch'eng-ch'ien, son of the great T'ai Tsung, who imitated the Turks in everything: he preferred to speak Turkish rather than Chinese, and erected a complete Turkish camp on the palace grounds, where, dressed like a Khan of the Turks, he sat in front of his tent under the wolf's-head ensign, attended by slaves in Turkish dress, and sliced himself gobbets of boiled mutton with his sword.

Though the prince surely had his imitators, it is likely that this barbaric dish had only a limited number of votaries. But other food of foreign parentage was widely admired. Of these the most popular were little "foreign" cakes of various kinds, especially a steamed variety sprinkled with sesame seeds, and cakes fried in oil. The art of making these had been introduced from the West, and though enjoyed by native and foreigner alike, they were ordinarily prepared and sold by Westerners. A popular tale of the age tells of such a cake seller, visited by a young man returning from his mistress' house before dawn, and waiting for the sound of the morning drum to announce that the gate of the quarter was open:

When he came to the gate of the neighborhood, the bar of the gate had not yet been released. Beside the gate was the dwelling of a Westerner who sold cakes, and he was just setting out his lamps, and kindling his brazier. Cheng-tzu sat down under his curtain to rest, and to wait for the drum.

At the other extreme were the elegant viands prepared for the tables of the rich and respectable. Some of these were made with expensive imported ingredients, but may not have been made according to foreign recipes. Especially popular were aromatic and spicy dishes, such as the "cakelets" with grated aromatics, worth a thousand in gold. But some were obviously made according to a foreign formula, as the "Brahman" wheat-paste, "light and high," which was steamed in baskets.

Exotic influences on costume, dwellings, diet, and other aspects of everyday life were paralleled by exoticism in the arts. The foreigners who crowded into T'ang China were pictured by painters and poets alike. There are, of course, exotic artists in every age, since a man may be by temperament out of step with the popular and persuasive cultural trends of his own time. But exoticism flourishes most in eras of new or renewed contact with strange peoples. Therefore it is especially connected with imperialistic conquest and with commercial expansion. The typical exotic artist glorifies his country, and at the same time exposes his guilty conscience, burdened with oppression or exploitation abroad, by glamorizing the oppressed and exploited. The images of Moors and Saracens in the paintings of Gozzoli and Bellini, like those of Algerians and Tahitians in the paintings of Delacroix and Gaughin, are equally symptomatic of an expansive and imperious civilization. They had their counterparts in T'ang. Indeed, even religious exoticism, such as that centered around representations of the Magi in Renaissance art, had its analogue in the idealized arhats, with Indian visages, visible in the Buddhist art of the Far East.

Some medieval critics did not recognize exotic pictures as a special category of painting. The eminent Kuo Jo-hsü, for instance, writing of ninth- and tenth-century art from the vantage point of the eleventh century, classified old paintings under such rubrics as "glimpses of virtue," "heroism," "representations of scenery," and "popular manners and customs," but had no special pigeonhole for pictures of foreigners and their appurtenances, even though he occasionally discussed exotic themes, such as the proper manner of representing deities of Indian origin. Thus, when painting Indra, ". . . one should display a stern and imposing demeanor. . . ."

On the other hand, the anonymous author of the *Hsüan ho hua p'u,* a catalogue of the paintings in the collection of Hui Tsung, imperial Sung connoisseur of the twelfth century, has left us a short essay about paintings showing foreigners. He includes among his examples of distinguished depicters of barbarians of T'ang the painters Hu Kuei and his son, Hu Ch'ien, many of whose works still survived, in Sung times. These men were famous for hunting scenes set in remote countries, and for exotic horses, camels, and falcons. Our unknown cataloguer states that the true value of such pictures is that they illustrate the inferiority of barbarian culture as compared with the Chinese. Such didactic chauvinism was certainly much more common in Sung than in early T'ang. In T'ang the characteristic feeling provoked by a painting of a foreign subject was condescending pride; in Sung it was apprenhensive arrogance. We may be sure in any case that most Sung art collectors, as well as most T'ang art lovers, took the greatest pleasure in these paintings for their style and color, whatever their opinions about the value of the subject matter may have been.

Despite the rarity of generalizations about exoticism and other fashions in critical writings, we can easily create simple pictures of trends and modes in art by synthesizing the critics' statements about the themes best treated by individual artists. If we do this, we find that the great century for the exotic in T'ang paintings was the seventh, when the military might of the T'ang emperors was at its apex, and when overawed barbarians thronged to the T'ang court. Victorious pride made these outlanders seem fit subjects for approved paintings. In contrast, we shall see presently that the great age for the exotic in T'ang literature was the ninth century, an age of reminiscence. Most eminent of the painters of outlandish themes was Yen Li-te, brother of the equally famous Yen Li-pen who had the honor of depicting the martial visage of T'ai Tsung himself. It is said that no painter of exotic subjects of his own or earlier times could touch him. In 629, the scholar Yen Shih-ku introduced a native of the remote mountains of what is now Kweichow Province to the court. "His cap was made of black bearskin, with a gold fillet across the forehead; his outer garments were of fur, and he wore leather leggings and shoes." Shih-ku referred sententiously to appropriate examples from antiquity, and then said, "Today the myriad realms to which the Imperial virtue has extended come to court in their garments of grass and feather ornaments, to meet together in the barbarians' guest quarters. Truly this is a [sight] which might be represented in pictorial form, to exhibit to posterity the far reaching extent of that virtue." Accordingly Yen Li-te was commissioned to paint the flattering scene.

Pictures of foreign countries were once hardly to be distinguished from strategic maps, and were based on the same kind of interrogation. Still, in T'ang times, the practical and aesthetic purposes and results were undoubtedly kept distinct. In 643, Yen Li-pen was commissioned to paint typical scenes of the nations that sent submissive emissaries to the court of T'ai Tsung. Among his productions were two paintings of the "Western Regions." Chou Fang and Chang Hsüan, both of them otherwise famous as painters of women and both active in the late eighth century, more than a century after the Li brothers, made representations of the incredible nation of Prom, or Hrom, or Rome (modern Fu-lin), that is, of some part of the Byzantine realm. We cannot now imagine the character of these scenes, though they would be incomparable treasures if they had survived. Even the great Wang Wei did a landscape from some "Strange Realm," now unidentifiable.

It was usual to picture the inhabitants of such distant places in their native costumes, with their curious features emphasized. Of all representations of foreigners, most of those that we can date with certainty as the works of T'ang craftsmen are the little terra-cotta figurines, among which we can find the images of Uighurs with high hats and haughty manners, Arabs (it may be) with black brows and hawklike noses, and persons with curly hair and toothy grins who, whatever their ethnic type, show the influence of Hellenistic taste. But although exotic peoples were a favorite subject of the great painters as well as of the potters of T'ang, few of the painted images survive. We do not have Yen Li-pen's pictures of tribute bearers bending before the emperor of China, presenting, perhaps, a kingly lion. We can no longer see the mounted barbarian archers, depicted by Li Chien and his son Li Chung-ho, not "The King of Korea Making a Ritual Circumambulation with Incense," painted by Chang Nan-pen, nor Chou Fang's picture of "A Woman of India," nor Chang Hsüan's picture of "A Japanese Equestrienne." But we can see men of several Central Asiatic nations, with strange faces, unusual hats, and exotic haircuts in the frescoes at Tun-huang. The soldier, government clerk, or weary pilgrim passing through one of the oasis cities of Serindia would have seen even stranger beings on the walls of the temples he visited under the protection of the local Chinese garrison: Buddhas in Hellenistic vestment, laics of the purest Iranian type, and nude women straight out of the fervent Indian epics.

Almost equally attractive during those exciting years were the wild beasts of strange lands, especially those sent with missions as gifts to the Chinese court, and also domestic animals, in particular those admired and desired by the Chinese—the famous hawks, hounds, and horses.

Finally, the artists of T'ang loved to show the gods and saints of foreign lands, above all those of the lands where Buddhism thrived: emaciated Hindu arhats with shaggy brows, princely Bodhisattvas glittering with strings of many-colored gems, the ancient gods Indra and Brahma, shown as protectors both of the Law of the Buddha and of palatial Chinese gateways, and other divine guardians—partly assimilated to Northern nomadic and to Chinese—such as Kuvera, Protector of the North, shown bearded and mustachioed, in Chinese armor. Such pictorial amalgams were sometimes the result of the use of a Chinese model by a painter of exotic subjects, as when a geisha in the service of a great lord posed for the figure of a *devi*—a Hindu goddess—in a Buddhist scene, as did the Italian courtesans who loaned their forms to Renaissance madonnas. With these pictures of hybrid beings too must be grouped the elaborate paintings of the ineffable paradises of Buddhism, like distant fairylands. One of the most eminent of painters of Buddhist icons in early T'ang was himself a foreigner, a Khotanese, with the Saka name of Viśa Īrasaṅgä, called in Chinese Yü-ch'ih I-seng. He came to the Chinese court about the middle of the seventh century, recommended by his king, bringing with him a new painting style of Iranian origin, in which modeled and shaded polychrome figures seemed to stand out in relief, or even to float free from their background. A painting of a Devarāja by this master survives to our own day. His manner is said to have influenced the great master Wu Tao-hsüan, and to be traceable in the caves of Tun-huang. He has also been credited with having helped bring the Western technique of using a line of unvarying thickness to outline figures—the "iron-wire" line—to the Buddhist temples of the great cities of China. Not only did this Viśa paint in an exotic manner, but he painted exotic subjects, not disdaining to represent a "Dancing Girl of Kucha."

Exotic Literature

The peak of literary interest in the exotic lagged almost two centuries behind the great period of exoticism in the plastic arts. This new development began late in the eighth century, and was associated with the "old-style" movement in prose writing, a reaction against the "new" (that is, only a few centuries old) formal antithetical prose. But the taste for the strange appears in the poetry as well as in the prose of this era. Rich colors, strange fancies, and romantic images captured the attention of many of the best poets of the ninth century. Typical of the age was Li Ho, a poet of illusions and dream images and vivid coloration, prone to use hyperbole and synecdoche—"amber" for "wine," "cold-reds" for "autumn flowers." It does not surprise us that this young man was devoted to reading the rich old classic *Ch'u tz'u* and the Zen sect's *Laṅkāvatāra-sūtra*, that he died young, and that the Sung critics spoke of his "demoniac talents." Exotic flavors came naturally to him, as in his poem "The Ambassador from Kurung" or in his description of a barbarian boy with curly hair and green eyes. Another like him was Tu Mu, an official also known for his military essay which advocated waging war on the Northern barbarians in the early summer when they were quiescent and unprepared. Whatever his practical talents, Tu Mu was also a poet of the romantic group, and recollections of the splendid past are common in his verses:

Looking back at Ch'ang-an, an embroidered pile appears;
A thousand gates among mountain peaks open each in turn.
A single horseman in the red dust—and the young Consort laughs,
But no one knows if it is the lichees which come.

This poem was suggested by the sight of the deserted palace at the hot springs near Ch'ang-an, where Hsüan Tsung and his

Precious Consort passed the winter months long ago, and refers to the special courier who brought lichees from Canton to satisfy the Consort's whim. A third poet characteristic of the times was Yüan Chen. This great writer longed passionately for the pure and classic standards of the imagined past. He deplored, for instance, the abandonment in the eighth century of the traditional stone from the banks of the Szu River, celebrated in the oldest literature as material for making chimes, in favor of some new stone; alas, few moderns listen to the old music, he says, and though "Hsüan Tsung loved music, he loved *new* music." Even in his stanzas written to popular airs, Yüan Chen laments the rage for new and exotic things. Despite their puritanism, however, these stanzas depend for their effectiveness upon the poet's treatment for such exotic subjects as imported rhinoceroses and elephants, Turkish horsemen, and Burmese orchestras. Yüan Chen was, in short, exotically anti-exotic.

But the history of exoticism in T'ang poetry has yet to be written. The prose tales on exotic themes, constituting an important variety of the T'ang wonder tale, are much better known. These flourished during the two decades on each side of the turn of the century. In particular, fantasy and marvels of every sort were à la mode during the early years of the ninth century. Fortunately many of them have survived into the twentieth. A common type is the tale of the wonderful gem, brought to China or sought by a mysterious stranger. The stone has the power to clear muddy waters, to reveal buried treasures, or to bring fair winds to seafarers, or is endowed with some other equally gratifying property. This taste for the fantastic, which in late T'ang showed itself in astonishingly rugged and awe-inspiring landscape paintings, necessarily also included the romantically foreign in the arts, and was exemplified in its purest form in stories of weird and lovely objects brought from abroad, most particularly the splendid oddities said to have been offered in former years as tribute gifts to the imperial court. We have to deal, then, not with the charm of genuine imports, but with the glamour of wares that existed, nowhere on land or sea, with no truly golden gifts, but with their counterfeits—brummagem of the mind and tensil of the imagination.

Imaginary gifts, which in turn feed the imagination, do not, of course, appear first in T'ang literature. From antiquity, we have the wonderful presents made to Mu, Son of Heaven; since his time, tales of marvelous gifts from abroad have appeared in every age. The two girls presented by the Red Raven people to archaic Mu, King of Chou by divine right, whom he took to be his concubines, are prototypes of the two black maidens sent (or so we are told by a sophisticated thirteenth-century source), as tribute gifts from the Coromandel Coast, whose fiery loins could rejuvenate the least potent of men. The antique charm of such wonders was enhanced by the old belief that foreign travel was full of physical hazards and spiritual perils, and that monstrous adventures were to be anticipated everywhere outside the confines of China. It was readily believed that spirits and monsters waited at every turn in the mountain trail and lurked beneath every tropical wave. People and things from abroad naturally partook of this dangerous enchantment, and even as late as T'ang times it is probable that exotic gods were still invested with the aroma of uncertain magic and perilous witchery. But in every age, even our own, men are willing to credit every quaint superstition if it concerns distant lands. The notion of fantastic tribute, in short, was not novel in the ninth century. The books that told of it simply gave new life to old and natural traditions, but also found raw material in the events of the first half of the T'ang epoch, which had been unusual in the variety of exotic things that could be seen in China. Material and spiritual exoticism had flourished in the taste of the seventh and eighth centuries. Outlanders and their curious trappings were abundantly to be seen, and the vogue for them was everywhere prevalent. In this lively and expansive age, it even became necessary, from time to time, for the Son of Heaven to set an example for his unthrifty and credulous subjects by issuing bans on the submission of the weird, the wild, and the whimsical among articles of tribute. A notable instance of such exemplary simplicity is found in an edict of the founder of the dynasty, handed down in the first year of his reign. This decree had the additional purpose, it should be noted, of pointing up the recklessness of the preceding regime, that of Sui. It concludes, ". . . such things as dwarfs, small horses with short joints, pygmy cattle, strange beasts, odd birds, and all things without actual utility: the presentation of these shall in every instance be discontinued and cut off. Let this be announced and published far and wide! Let everyone hear and understand." This enactment did not remain effective for very long, but similar prohibitions issued from the throne again and again. If not aimed at the odd, like the five-colored parakeets from Java, they were directed against the frivolous, like the snow-white hunting falcons from Manchuria.

But after the troubles of the second half of the eighth century, fewer rarities from overseas and overland could be found in the stricken country. There were even fewer after the depredations of Huang Ch'ao in the ninth century, such as the massacre of the foreign merchants during the sack of Canton. In that same century was the great persecution of foreign religions, which tended to remove from the sight of the average Chinese not only the foreign religions and the foreign priests and worshipers, but also foreign books and the images of foreign gods.

It is not surprising, then, that as the international age, the age of imports, the age of mingling, the golden age, began to pass away at the beginning of the ninth century, and the thirst for wonderful things from beyond the seas and across the mountains—whether for Buddhist manuscripts and medical books, or for costly brocades and rare wines, or perhaps just for the sight of an itinerant juggler from Turkestan—could no longer be readily satisfied, the ancient wonder tale gained new and vigorous life, and furnished to the nostalgic imagination what could not be granted to the senses.

The greatest number of T'ang tales about fictitious imports and fantastic tribute were written in the ninth century, when the authentic marvels had passed beyond reach. So the vogue for the exotic in wares was replaced by the vogue for the exaggerated exotic in literature. To quote a modern critic:

We are no longer in the world of flesh and blood. We are in the Dreamland in which the soul glimmers like the flame of a candle. The landscape has been transformed into an "inscape." The world is drowned in the immeasurable ocean of Darkness, and there remains only "an odorous shade."

Many of the stories pretend to tell of the reign of Hsüan Tsung, the fabulous king, most glorious monarch of a cosmopolitan age, himself a connoisseur of the exotic, and a symbol of everything romantic even before his own death. In *his* day, one could *hear* the lutes of Kucha! In the next century one might only dream of them.

Here are a few examples of this kind of creative reminiscence:

Two white rings, the story tells, were given to an emperor of China by one of his vassals, among other "treasures which make firm the nation." These were the rings of the "Mother who is King in the West," a dim and hoary figure associated with dreams of immortality in the mountains at the summit of the world. They resemble other magic rings well-known in folklore. Their possessor could expect with confidence the submission of all peripheral nations.

Again, from Tongking came a piece of rhinoceros horn, as yellow as gold. This was set on a golden plate in the basilica, and the envoy who brought it explained that it had the virtue of dispelling cold—and indeed warm air radiated from it all around. Similar were the hundred sticks of charcoal called the "charcoal of good omen," said to have been sent from the Western Liang, an ancient state in the Kansu area. These were as hard as iron, and would burn without flame for ten days, unapproachable because of the intensity of the heat.

A royal gift from Kucha was a pillow coarsely wrought from a glossy stone much like agate. The fortunate head which slept on it was blessed with dreams of voyages through all lands and seas, even those unknown to mortal men. The tale tells that the head proved to be that of the upstart statesman Yang Kuo-chung, twice fortunate in being the favored cousin of the Precious Consort of Hsüan Tsung.

The perennial demand for beautiful jade, the most magnificent of minerals, underlies the following story: Hsüan Tsung, midway in his reign, marveled that there was no artifact made from the almost legendary five-colored jade among the gifts recently received from the West, though he had in his treasury a belt decorated with placques of this handsome stone, and a cup carved from it, both submitted long before. He commanded his generals in charge of the "Security of the West" to reprimand the negligent (but anonymous) barbarians who were responsible. The delinquent savages may have been natives of Khotan, the inexhaustible source of jade, and savages they seemed to the Chinese, despite the refinement of their music and the charm of their women. Whoever they were, they did not fail to start a shipment of the pretty polychrome stuff on its way to Ch'ang-an. Alas, the caravan was attacked and robbed of its cargo by the people of Lesser Balūr, turban-wearing lice-eating marauders from the frigid and narrow valleys on the fringes of the snowy Pamirs. When the bad news reached the sacred palace, the Son of Heaven, in his wrath, sent an army of forty thousand Chinese and innumerable dependent barbarians to lay siege to the capital of the marauders and recover his jade. The king of Lesser Balūr quickly surrendered his booty and humbly sought the privilege of sending annual tribute to T'ang. This was refused, and his unhappy city of Gilgit was pillaged. The victorious Chinese general, leading three thousand survivors of the sack, set out for home. He was followed by a prediction of doom, pronounced by a barbarian soothsayer. And indeed the whole multitude was destroyed in a great storm, except for a lone Chinese and a single barbarian ally. The unfortunate Hsüan Tsung, thus finally deprived of his treasure, sent a party to search for the remains of his host. They found an army of transparent bodies, refrigerated prisoners and soldiers of ice, which melted immediately, and were never seen again.

Those had been the magical years, when nothing was impossible. It was this dead glittering world of the eighth century that the writers of exotic fantasy tried to recreate in imagination.

The chief exemplar of this mode in fiction is a book written near the end of the ninth century. Unlike most T'ang wonder books, which exploit every sort of fantasy, this one is almost completely on the subject of exotic marvels. It is called *Assorted Compilations from Tu-yang*, and was written by the scholar Su O in 876. Here are some of the rarities he describes:

The "magic shining beans" were sent from a country called "Forest of the Sun," possibly to be interpreted as "Source of the Sun," which is to say "Japan." This land, far across the seas to the northeast, was most noted for a great shining rock, which reflected the internal organs of a man, like a modern X-ray machine, so that his physician might examine their condition and heal him the more quickly. The beans themselves were of a rich pink color, and radiated light over a distance of several feet. Cooked with leaves of the sweet flag, they would grow to the size of goose eggs. The emperor himself tasted one of these excellent beans, and found them delicious beyond compare. Moreover, they freed him from hunger and thirst for several days.

Another marvelous food came from a country in the mysterious South Seas, which also sent a pillow of crystal, within which could be seen a landscape furnished with buildings and human figures; with the pillow was sent a brocaded coverlet, made of silk of the "water silkworm," which expanded when dampened and contracted when heated. The food sent from this land was a fragrant kind of wheat which made the body light enough to ride with the wind, and some purple rice grains which restored youthful vigor and prolonged life.

Dragons, that is, water spirits, crystallized into miniature concretions, were another favorite gift. Examples are the "dragon horn hairpin" and the "treadwater bead." The wonderful hairpin was a gift that accompanied the "magic shining beans." It was made of a jadelike stone, of a deep plum color, and was carved in dragon shapes with inhuman skill. The Emperor Tai Tsung presented it to his favorite consort, the beautiful Lady Tuku. One day, as he and she were boating on Dragon Boat Pond, a purple cloud formed over the pin. The sovereign took the pin in his palm and spat water on it, whereupon the vapor congealed into two dragons, which leaped into the sky and disappeared in the east. The "tread-water bead" was a black, perforated bead with an oddly scaly surface. Its bearer could pass unharmed through water. The emperor tested it by binding it with a five-colored cord (which poisonous dragons fear) to the arm of a good swimmer. This man walked on the surface of the waves, plunged under the water, and emerged dry. Later, when the women of the palace were playing with the bead in a pool, it turned into a black dragon.

Marvelous birds and bird spirits were desired tribute. One such was the "fire-rejecting sparrow," a black passerine bird, sent as a token tribute on the accession of Shun Tsung. The bird was immune to fire. It was, in short, a true phoenix, unlike the *feng-huang* of Chinese tradition usually miscalled "phoenix" in the West. That is, it was the *samandal* of India (said by the Arabs to be found also in Wāq-wāq) whose skin no flame could consume. A crystal cage in the monarch's bedroom housed this prodigy. There the maidservants amused themselves in vain attempts to burn it with candles. Another country sent two dancing girls, one named "Light Phoenix" and the other "Flying Simurgh," the most ethereal creatures imaginable. On their heads were golden crowns, adorned with the images of the fantastic birds for which they were named, or whose spirits they were. They dined on lichees, gold dust, and "dragon-brain" camphor.

Extraordinary heating devices form a special group. The "ever-burning cauldron" cooked food without fire. This useful object, the tribute of a mythical kingdom, is described in a fantastic narrative that is full of references to countries named in the histories of Han, a millennium before. Related to it was the "fire jade," which was red and could be used like an ember of coal to heat a cauldron.

Contrariwise, sources of cold were equally wonderful and useful. The "ever-hard ice" was found on a great mountain, whose glaciers were a thousand years old. It would not melt in the hottest sunlight. The "pine wind stone" was translucent, and within it could be seen the figure of a pine tree, from whose branches issued a cooling breeze. The sovereign kept it close to him during the summer.

Less desirable, but still to be wondered at, was the "daylight-altering herb." It resembled a banana plant, and was always surrounded by an area of darkness. This uncanny virtue was displeasing to the emperor.

Among these literary marvels were some which could easily have been real, or at least adapted from reality. Such was the "pentachromatic carpet," given to Tai Tsung of T'ang, as were many of these gifts, by the Korean kingdom of Silla. It was marvelously wrought to show the figures of dancers and musicians, and mountains and rivers. Among these things were shown every sort of bird and insect, which fluttered and flitted about when the least breeze blew through the room.

The "mountain of the myriad Buddhas" was a jeweled construction carved from the aloeswood of Indochina, about ten feet high. This too had been sent by Silla. On the mountain were images of all the Buddhas, in a setting of buildings and natural verdure, all done in the minutest detail in pearls and precious stones. The emperor, a pious Buddhist, installed this cosmic symbol in a shrine, and spread the "pentachromatic carpet" on its floor. This wonderful object may not have been entirely imaginary.

The "Chu-lai bird" may also have existed in some form. Though the Emperor Te Tsung was often given trained animals and wonderful fowl, he ordinarily freed such creatures in accordance with Buddhist precept. But he did not release the handsome Chu-lai bird sent by a Southern country in 781. Its bill was red, and its purple-blue tail was longer than its body. It was very clever, and understood human commands. Its voice was high and piercing. This dandy of a bird, apparently a tropical magpie, was much loved by the people of the court, who gave it the most costly delicacies to eat. It passed its nights in a golden cage, and spent its days flying about the courts of the palace, and "neither bold goshawk nor great falcon dared come near." Alas! One day it was caught and murdered by an eagle. The palace mourned it sincerely, and one courtier, a skilled calligrapher, made a copy of the *Prajñāpāramitā-hṛdaya-sūtra* on paper speckled with gold for the good of its soul.

An unknown country in the South Seas sent a girl of fourteen years, called the

"Maiden of the Black Eyebrows," among whose remarkable skills was the talent of embroidering the seven scrolls of the *Lotus Sutra* in tiny, perfectly formed characters on a single foot-length of artist's taffeta. She too may have existed in the flesh.

The wonders just described are only a sampling from the splendid array displayed in Su O's book. As we have seen, some are attributed to such real countries as Japan and Silla, some to ancient nations long since unheard from, and some to lands altogether mythical. But if we survey the tribute records in reliable documents of the T'ang period, we find no mention of any of these gifts, even those from "real countries." The period covered by the narrations of Su O was the last half of the eighth century and the first of the ninth, ranging back over a century before his own lifetime, the later afternoon and the setting of the sun of T'ang's splendor. But the cold, unlovely days of Su O's own time were not yet come. During the years he claims to describe, there actually were horses from the Uighurs, dancing girls from P'o-hai, musicians from Burma, a rhinoceros from Champa, and pearls and amber from some remnant of the dismembered Persian empire. Su O has merely filled the gaps in the record of actual imports for these twilight years with things of magic and delight. His book, in short, deals with fairylands of commerce, and archaic wonder worlds of diplomacy. Its charm lies in its antiquarian exoticism, studded with doubtful gems and forgotten curios. Though conceivably some of these stories may have sprung, fertilized by the imagination, from accounts of actual embassies in the years of waning glory at the end of the eighth century, they are nonetheless delicacies for the use of a poet, not grist for the economist's mill.

E. G. PULLEYBLANK

The Economic Background of the Rebellion of An Lu-shan

From the beginning of the T'ang dynasty an economic revolution of the greatest significance took place. Unity and peace had brought about a great increase in trade between the south and the north and a great agricultural expansion in the south, accompanied by a large-scale migration from the north. Thus we find that there was a great increase in population in the Yangtze Valley and farther south.

From E. G. Pulleyblank, *The Background of the Rebellion of An Lu-shan,* published by the Oxford University Press under the auspices of the School of Oriental and African Studies. Reprinted by permission of the publisher. Footnotes omitted.

A large proportion of the immigrants were peasants who had left the districts in which they were registered to flee from the harsh treatment they had received, including not only natural disasters and invasions, but also taxation, corvée, and military service imposed by the imperial government. With the disappearance of a large number of registered peasants, the whole tax-collecting machinery was in danger of collapse.

Paralleling the large-scale migrations was the increasing phenomenon of estate building. Owners of estates benefited by being able to absorb the labor of these "off the tax-rolls" immigrants. The land-acquiring class often included the local officials whose duty it was to ensure that the peasants were registered. Hence the persons whom the government relied upon to stop the abuses were the same persons who were benefiting from those abuses. That was why in Hsüan-tsung's reign (712–756) many special commissioners were sent from the central government to register unregistered households, and these measures of centralization, most unwelcome to the local provincial officials, caused bad feeling against the government.

As Professor E. G. Pulleyblank, Professor of Chinese History at the University of British Columbia, notes, it has been common to explain many Chinese rebellions as the product of hunger and desperation among oppressed peasants. In Marxist thinking, these rebellions are manifestations of class struggle, and as such have become a favorite subject of study. In the following selection, Dr. Pulleyblank examines the economic factors underlying the rebellion of An Lu-shan. He is concerned to show that the economic policies that the central government adopted during Hsüan-tsung's reign and their repercussions on the economic and political structure of the nation and on military policy may well have contributed to the estrangement of the literati from the court, involved the rise of dictatorship, and exercised a corrupting influence on the emperor and his entourage. Thus conditions arose favoring rebellion by a professional force. Yet Dr. Pulleyblank denies that there was any connection between the men made desperate by the famine and the force that An Lu-shan led southward to attack the Eastern Capital of T'ang. Thus, any theory that connects the rebellion of An Lu-shan and the peasant uprisings is, according to Professor Pulleyblank, quite without foundation.

In order to understand the career of An Lu-shan after he reappears from obscurity in 740 it will be necessary to inquire at some length into the situation in which China found itself at that time, that is, into the historical movements which prepared the way for his rise to power and into the causes which lay behind them. To trace these causes to their origins would unfortunately require a knowledge of many details of the history of the preceding centuries which are as yet obscure. As it has not been possible to go fully into many of these questions—indeed it would have led far beyond the scope of the present study to have done so—some of the conclusions here presented must be provisional in character. Nevertheless, it is hoped that certain main lines have been sketched in which may provide the starting-point for further investigations.

The theory sometimes expressed that the rebellion of An Lu-shan was, at least in part, one of those all-too-frequent peasant uprisings brought about by hunger and desperation, is quite without foundation. It has recently been the fashion to see all the great rebellions of China as motivated by class struggle and some historians have been ready to seize on the slightest hints in order to turn An Lu-shan's rebellion into an agrarian revolt.

It has been easier for these misconceptions to arise because Chinese historiographers have tended to emphasize natural disasters closely preceding troubles in the human sphere, in the belief that they constituted warnings from heaven. We therefore hear a good deal in our sources about various calamities which befell China immediately before the outbreak of the rebellion. The greatest of these was a period of continuous rain in the capital province of Kuan-chung, and to a lesser extent around Lo-yang and T'ai-yüan, in the autumn of the year 754. Considerable hardship is said to have been caused by the destruction of crops, leading to a public distribution of grain from government stores.

Such an excess of *yin* over *yang* was later, and perhaps even at the time, taken as a sign of the dominance exerted over the emperor by his favourite, Yang Kuei-fei, and her family. The evil portent was used to force the resignation of the second Chief Minister, Ch'en Hsi-lieh, who had made himself objectionable to the all-powerful Yang Kuo-chung. After the rebellion the ominous significance of the floods was emphasized. Thus the dismissal of another man from the post of Governor of the Capital was alleged to have been in order to make him a scapegoat for the disaster, but in this case there is good reason for his dismissal. Again we are told in the *Tzu-chih T'ung-chien* that a certain Fang Kuan incurred the displeasure of Yang Kuo-chung by memorializing about the floods, but this incident is not mentioned in Fang Kuan's biographies and is presumably a later anecdote. The displeasure cannot have been very severe for he was soon promoted from the provinces to a post at the capital. Another illustration of the way in which historians discovered portents of disaster in the years before the rebellion is provided by the statement that the spring of 754 when Yang Kuo-chung was invested with the high office of Ssu-k'ung his robes were splashed with mud. Even if such an incident had occurred it would hardly have been recorded at the time and it must have been "remembered" later for its ominous significance.

The question whether the portentous suggestion in the floods and the hardships caused by them affected the mood of the people and helped the rebels must be left for further consideration. We must remember that such disasters were of fairly common occurrence in the best of times and that in this case large-scale measures were taken to relieve famine. The crucial question in the present context must be whether any connexion can be traced between men made desperate by the famine and the forces which An Lu-shan led southward to attack Lo-yang. I have found none. The floods are mentioned only in connexion with Kuang-chung and to a lesser degree Lo-yang and T'ai-yüan. There is no mention whatsoever, there or in any part of the empire, of the sort of small-scale banditry which was usually the first stage in agrarian revolts. Most conclusive of all, the armies of An Lu-shan were by every indication hardened and experienced frontier soldiers, many of them non-Chinese, no ill-trained mob of desperadoes. It was the imperial armies which were often made up of raw recruits. There is no suggestion that the peasants were at all eager to help the rebels, though they are occasionally mentioned as helping the loyalists. They were probably, in general, the victims equally of both armies, intent only on saving their own lives, those of their wives and children, and as much as possible of their crops, houses, and other scanty belongings. It is only towards the end of the rebellion that we hear of banditry of the classic type. In 762 peasants in the lower Yangtze valley were driven to desperation by the exactions of tax-gatherers trying to fill the war-depleted treasury and to supply grain for the armies. They fled to the hills and raised a revolt which demanded the attention of one of the leading generals of the time. But this peasant unrest was the result rather than the cause of the rebellion.

We must look deeper for the genuine economic factors underlying the rebellion. We shall find them in the economic policies which the central government adopted during Hsüan-tsung's reign and their repercussions on the economic and political structure of the nation and on military policy.

When the Emperor Hsüan-tsung ascended the throne in 712, one of his first tasks was to strengthen the finances of the government by eliminating the parasitic horde which had fed upon it during the previous reigns. Especially after the abdication of the Empress Wu in 705, a large part of the revenues had found its way into the pockets of powerful princes, princesses, and other favourites. They had, moreover, further increased their own fortunes at the expense of the state by selling offices in large numbers and procuring the enrollment of Buddhist and Taoist monks and nuns, whereby the persons concerned escaped from the tax-rolls, if they did not actually receive state support. On the accession of Hsüan-tsung the revenues of princes, princesses, and the like were drastically cut, many supernumerary officials were eliminated and large numbers of monks and nuns were laicized. These measures naturally had the approval of the Confucian literati and are given the highest commendation. But the emperor's vigorous policies did not stop there. Throughout the first thirty and more years of his reign measures were introduced and energetically applied to eliminate waste and inefficiency and to increase the flow of taxes to the capital. This centralization soon impinged on the interests of the landed class of the south and east, and aroused bitter opposition which is reflected in the strong disapproval that we find in the histories for these policies and the men who furthered them.

These financial reforms were made possible and necessary by the changed economic situation of China. Since the beginning of the dynasty an economic revolution of the greatest significance had taken place. Unity and peace had brought about both a great increase in trade between south and north and a great agricultural expansion of the south. This latter change was accompanied by large-scale migration from the north. In the process of this revolution much new wealth was created which began to crack the seams of the nation's social structure. Moreover, the assumptions on which the fiscal structure of the empire had been based were no longer valid.

The first problem which attracted the attention of the financial reformers was that of the so-called "runaway households," or "immigrant households." During the last decades of the seventh century and the first decades of the eighth we find many references to this phenomenon—peasants who had left the districts in which they were registered and either disappeared or settled on unoccupied land in other areas. Our sources are unfortunately vague as to the details of this movement, especially as to the geographical areas affected. It would seem that various causes were at work, especially in the north-east and the north-west, encouraging peasants to leave their homes and seek their fortunes elsewhere. In the north-east we know that there were both natural disasters and invasions. In 681 we hear of peasants affected by floods on the lower Yellow River being granted permission to go south. Far more important were the Khitan and Turkish invasions of that region, especially those of 697–8. Not only did peasants flee from the invaders but also from military service in the imperial armies and from the harsh treatment they received at the hands of the imperial commander who repelled the invaders. From Kuan-chung too, and from parts of Ho-nan close to Lo-yang, peasants fled to escape service in the *fu-ping* militia.

We are largely left to infer the destination of these migrants but the great increase in the population of the Yangtze valley and farther south during this period can leave little doubt that a large number found their way to those regions. The attraction of new land remote from the power of the central government and the danger of invasion must have been a positive incentive to the peasants of the north to move, in addition to the pressures we have mentioned. It is clear that a large portion of them found their way to new agricultural land, for when measures were taken to register them, unregistered land "of equal amount" was also recovered. And though there was some incipient banditry in Ho-pei after the troubles of 697–8, there was nothing approaching open revolt. Something of that sort would certainly have resulted from such a large movement of peasantry if there had been nothing to draw them off into productive pursuits.

The concern of the government therefore was not due, or not mainly due, to fear of violent uprising. Their chief anxiety was to keep the peasants enrolled on the local registers so that they should not escape taxation, *corvée,* and military service. Under the basic land law of T'ang, the so-called "equal field" system, the basic taxes and *corvée* were levied per adult male (the land being theoretically equally distributed so that all had equal capacity to pay). This clearly required the keeping of accurate records, and careful provision for this was made in the regulations. There were also severe legal restrictions on the sale of land and the free movement of the peasants. The migrations of which we have been speaking were largely in direct contravention of these regulations and tended to throw the whole tax-collecting machinery into disorder.

Furthermore, it was often in the interests of the local officials responsible for seeing that the peasants were registered, who of course belonged to the landowning, and especially at this time, the land-acquiring class, to fail in their duty and to keep the immigrants off the tax-rolls. While there is much obscurity about the extent to which the "equal field" system ever, even at its beginning under Toba Wei, functioned as an instrument for redistributing land or preventing the encroachment of the large landowners on the small, and it is clear that large land-holdings always existed, it nevertheless appears from the fact of their being displaced that at least in north China there were many independent peasants in the early years of the T'ang dynasty. But around the end of the seventh century and during the first half of the eighth we frequently hear general complaints and particular instances of estate building. It seems to have had the proportions of a vast new movement, induced no doubt by the great increase in wealth which occurred during the long period of internal peace which followed the establishment of T'ang.

Some of the land-grabbing was done within the law—there were convenient loopholes in the rules preventing peasants from disposing of their holdings, and the wealthy person, often a moneylender or local official, could exert many pressures on the peasant to give up his title. Much was completely illegal. Uncultivated land or land vacated temporarily because of invasion or famine might be seized and enclosed or records might be falsified. Thus free peasants were often turned into tenants—and disappeared from the registers—even if they remained on their holdings, and if they left or were driven off, it was even more probable that they would become tenants or hired labourers when they settled elsewhere.

We have only the scantiest indications of the regions in which this development principally took place. One was probably Ho-pei, the province most affected by invasion. Another was undoubtedly Chiangnan, where there was the greatest influx of population and where tenancy had perhaps been more common since the time of the southern dynasties. One of special interest was Kuan-chung, where officials, eunuchs, princesses, and other newly rich were eager to obtain estates near the capital. Such estates tended to be used less for agriculture than for incipient industrial purposes by means of water-mills, or simply as pleasure resorts. This tendency was probably partly responsible for the great decline of Kuan-chung as a food-producing area during T'ang.

The appearance of these newly enriched landlords is undoubtedly connected with a further tremendously important phenomenon. The new examination system was used as a political instrument by the Empress Wu in order to break the power of the old north-western aristocracy which had held power under T'ai-tsung. Through it the literary gentry, chiefly from the east and south, became the dominant element in the officialdom. There can be little doubt that much of the new blood was provided by families enriched through land-grabbing. Thus the new estates, which were seriously interfering with the government's tax-collecting, were to a considerable extent the economic foundation on which depended the very officials whom the government relied upon to stop the abuses.

It was not therefore pure, disinterested love of the peasantry which prompted the great outcry among the literati when in 724 Yü-wen Jung proposed sending out Censors as special commissioners to register unregistered households. We note that he was the first of a series of much condemned financial experts who carried through revenue-increasing schemes on behalf of Hsüan-tsung.

Yü-wen Jung first made proposals concerning the problem of runaway households at the beginning of 721 when he held the post of Examining Censor. As a result of his representations the matter was referred to the officialdom for discussion, after which a decree was issued that all unregistered families should report within one hundred days and be enrolled either where they were or in their former homes. Defaulters were to be sent to frontier districts.

It would appear that the measure of 721 was not really very successful, for in 723 new methods were adopted. Yü-wen Jung was appointed special commissioner with wide powers to travel around the empire and see that registration was carried out. At his request nineteen Assistants (*P'an-kuan*) were appointed and given acting rank in the Censorate. The men chosen were all minor officials of the capital or neighbouring counties. In 724 ten more special Censors were created. The *T'ung-tien* says of the twenty-nine men, "They were all noted scholars. In this affair there was an unparalleled excellence in the men chosen as commissioner's Assistants. Later many of them attained prominent positions." Nevertheless, their efforts did not please the officialdom as a whole.

Besides the creation of special commissioners which gave teeth to the measure, the compulsion of 721 was abandoned in favour of inducement. Persons who voluntarily gave themselves up were offered six years free of all taxes on the payment of a fee of 1,500 cash. It is difficult to estimate with any accuracy the value of this sum at that time. From one decree it appears that payment in kind was accepted. Since we have no information as to how generously this was interpreted and what method was used to compute the value, we cannot easily estimate the special difficulties to the peasant in paying the fee. Nevertheless, it would seem that a good bargain was offered to the peasant. Six years' taxes, including the value of his compulsory labour, were certainly worth much more than 1,500 cash. Moreover, the peasant thus obtained title to the land he was tilling and was freed from the threat of government action and from the illegal exactions of officials and landlords. When families were registered in a new locality their names were to be struck off the lists in their former localities, which would stop the practice of the officials collecting extra taxes from the neighbours of runaways to make up for the loss. Even the strongly biased biography of Yü-wen Jung reports that when he went from place to place proclaiming this edict to the people, many shed tears of gratitude.

This time a considerable success was achieved. Over 800,000 families were registered "with an equal amount of land (*t'ien i ch'eng shih*). Over a million strings of cash were collected. It was decreed that the money should be applied as capital to the Price-stabilizing Granaries (*Ch'ang-p'ing Ts'ang*) which had been newly re-established. The purpose of these granaries was to buy above the market price in times of abundance and to sell below the market price in times of scarcity in order to help the peasants. Though the capital of these granaries often came to be used rather for making loans at extortionate rates of interest, it is likely that at this time, newly re-established, they were functioning to some extent as intended. Thus the money taken from the people was applied to their benefit—at least to a greater extent than if it had merely passed into the treasury or been taken from them in rents and extortions.

Nevertheless, it was 724, not 721, that criticism was first voiced against the activities of the commissioners. It was alleged that this registration was a grievous burden on the people, that it led, for instance, to local officials registering established households as immigrants in order to curry favour, that it was being carried out to feed the superfluous bureaucracy at court. Though this criticism may have been partly justified, the real cause of the complaint clearly seems to have been that these special commissioners, responsible directly to the throne, were able to by-pass the regular officialdom and to prevent them from concealing their own and others' irregularities. Moreover, with the inducements offered in 724 the peasants themselves were enabled and encouraged to escape from the oppression to which they had been subjected. The complaint against taking authority out of the hands of the regular officials is implicit in the memorial sent up by Huang-fu Chiung at this time, but it is most clearly stated in the judgement delivered on Yü-wen Jung's policies by Ssu-ma Kuang, following here the T'ang writer Su Mien: "From this, the hundred officials [i.e. those of the regular bureaucracy] lost their functions." It was a measure of centralization most unwelcome to the provincial officials.

Yü-wen Jung's measures did not end the problem of migrant families. We hear from time to time of measures to deal with them, sometimes with leniency, sometimes with severity. In 730 P'ei Yao-ch'ing, of whom more will be said presently, made proposals which were much harsher than those of Yü-wen Jung. He proposed conscripting the vagrants on to state farms and it would appear that he attempted to carry out this measure in 734 or 735 when he was Chief Minister. No adverse comment is reported but the scheme was dropped after his dismissal in 736. Again we know that vagrants were frequently conscripted as soldiers for the new permanent frontier armies which were being established during this period. There is some indication that the migration had considerably diminished in the years immediately before the rebellion. A decree of 749 has these words: "According to our information, the vagabonds are gradually returning [to their homes] and the number of wandering beggars who have not gone back is not great." Apparently the efficient centralized dictatorship of the latter half of Hsüan-tsung's reign had some success by one means or another in curbing this movement. The pressure to build estates continued undiminished, however, and with the disorders caused by the rebellion the migrations reappeared in aggravated form.

Another problem which was attacked by the financial experts was that of transport. One of the great achievements of the ill-famed Yang-ti of Sui was the construction of the Pien Canal connecting the Yellow River with the Yangtze. The Sui dynasty had other great canals to its credit as well. The importance of this water-transport system in later times has led people to suppose that it had the same importance from the outset and even to consider it the economic foundation on which T'ang power rested. Nevertheless, it appears that the system was largely neglected till near the end of the seventh century and only achieved its great prominence after the reforms introduced in the reign of Hsüan-tsung.

The reason for this comparative neglect was that in the reign of T'ai-tsung (627–49) the needs of the court, which was much smaller than it was a century later, were not so great, and the revenue which could then be obtained from the south was also much less than it later became. The amount of grain shipped into the capital province of Kuan-chung each year during this period was later estimated at only 200,000 *shih*. A hundred years later it was regularly five to ten times that amount and sometimes much more. This being so, the grain obtainable near at hand in Ho-nan and southern Ho-pei was probably sufficient to supply the normal needs of Kuan-chung during T'ai-tsung's reign, and indeed there is evidence to show that during the seventh century cloth was regularly sent from the Yangtze region instead of grain.

In the latter half of the seventh century the needs of the court and the army became more pressing. As a result the government was frequently moved from Ch'ang-an to Lo-yang, since the great productive areas of the lower Yellow River plain and the south were much more easily accessible to the latter city. Nevertheless, no thorough-going attempt was made to improve the transport system. Indeed, the junction of the Pien Canal and the Yellow River was blocked for some years at the beginning of the eighth century and no transport could get through. There are other indications that tax-transport along the Pien Canal was extremely inefficient until well into Hsüan-tsung's reign.

Hsüan-tsung established his main capital at Ch'ang-an but at first found it necessary, as his predecessors had done, to move o Lo-yang from time to time if there was a bad harvest in Kuan-chung. In view of his strong centralizing policies, however, and of the greatly increased wealth of the south it was to be expected that he would make stronger efforts than his predecessors had done to increase the flow of taxes. Early in his reign we hear of various attempts to improve the tax-transport and to put a stop to corruption among officials, who had ample opportunity for peculation on the long slow journey from south to north. Yü-wen Jung himself undertook improvements in the water transport from Ho-pei when he was Prefect of Pien Chou (modern K'ai-feng) in 728. The strongly biased biographer states that he was not very successful in spite of a large expenditure of forced labour, but he must have pleased the emperor for he was soon brought to the capital and made Chief Minister.

The man who was responsible for the fundamental reforms which altered the whole situation was P'ei Yao-ch'ing. This remarkable man has been spared the obloquy attached by the historians to the other financial experts, though in his policies he was certainly one of them, perhaps the greatest. Perhaps because he had been a child prodigy and was rather more of a scholar than the others, perhaps because he was personally incorruptible and was dismissed along with Chang Chiu-ling, the hero of the literati, when Li Lin-fu became dictator, he did not become identified with Yü-wen Jung and his successors. Yet Yü-wen Jung had once recommended him, and his chief assistant in his transport reforms, Hsiao Chiung, was later closely associated with Li Lin-fu.

He first made his proposals for reforming the transport system in 730 when he sent a long memorial describing the inefficiency of the existing system. The chief reason for this inefficiency was, he felt, that each boat had to make the entire journey from its home district to Lo-yang and back again. This resulted in long delays because different parts of the route were navigable at different seasons. It also resulted in much congestion on the waterways in the navigable seasons. Nearly a full year was taken for a boat from south of the Yangtze to reach the Eastern Capital. In this time the living expenses of the boatmen and pilfering along the route had used up most of the cargo. As a remedy he proposed establishing a relay system with granaries at the junctions between each section of the route. Boats would then go only as far as such a junction, discharge their cargoes and return. When the next section of the route became navigable, boats would be hired to continue the journey. This, he felt, would result not only in an increase in the amount of grain transported but also in a saving to the treasury on the "foot-money" (*chüeh-ch'ien*) which people of each district were required to furnish for the transport of taxes.

As an additional means of increasing the revenue, P'ei Yao-ch'ing advocated appropriating the contents of the Public Granaries (*I-ts'ang*) which existed throughout the empire as a precaution against times of need.

They were supplied by an acreage levy of two *sheng* per *mou*, which was not regarded originally as a tax but as a sort of compulsory saving. From time to time during the latter part of the seventh century the contents of these granaries had been appropriated by the government, but early in Hsüan-tsung's reign this practice had been stopped along with other abuses of the previous reigns. P'ei Yao-ch'ing maintained that in the damp climate of the south the grain so stored did not keep long in any case. He proposed exchanging the coarse unrefined grains in these granaries for lighter, more easily transportable, refined grain and shipping it to the capital.

This memorial was not immediately acted upon; but in the autumn of 733, when the emperor was about to move his court to Lo-yang because of a crop failure in Kuan-chung, P'ei Yao-ch'ing made a similar proposal, extending it to transport as far as Ch'ang-an. This received approval, he was made Chief Minister, and granaries to implement the scheme were set up in the following year. In three years' time 7,000,000 *shih* of grain were transported to Ch'ang-an with a saving of 300,000 strings of cash in expenses. In the autumn of 736 the emperor returned to Ch'ang-an and henceforth remained there.

Indeed, the reform was so successful that it was not necessary to continue it in full force. In 737 after the dismissal of P'ei Yao-ch'ing the dangerous "northern transport" along the Yellow River from the mouth of the Lo River to Shan Chou was temporarily abandoned in favour of the safer land route from Lo-yang to Shan Chou. The transport of grain was suspended, first from the most distant regions and, by the sixth month of 737, from all places outside the passes. The price of grain in Kuan-chung had been depressed by the huge influx of grain from the east and two measures were introduced to deal with this surplus. The cloth tax of Kuan-chung, a region not suited to silk production, was henceforth to be converted at market price into grain. To make up for this, the grain tax of inaccessible parts of Ho-pei was to be converted into silk.

Furthermore, in the Administrative Regulations *(Ling)* issued in 737 it was provided that the grain tax of Chiang-nan should be converted to textiles, a reversion to the practice of the seventh century.

In addition public buying of grain was introduced in Kuan-chung and around Lo-yang. This practice, known as "equitable grain-purchase" *(ho-ti)*, became a great abuse in later times when it usually meant forced sales to the government at low prices. At its inception, however, the intention was to help peasants who were adversely affected by the low price. It would appear that it had long been a practice in the north-west for supplying the army and we hear of it also in other frontier regions. It is difficult to say whether it retained its beneficent aspect in all these places and to the end of Hsüan-tsung's reign.

After 737 the budget called for 1,800,000 *shih* of grain to be transported annually to Ch'ang-an. This was found to be more than enough and was reduced by 100,000 *shih*. However, we are also told that after 742 Wei Chien transported 4,000,000 *shih* per year and according to the *T'ung-tien* the yearly amount in 748 was 2,500,000 *shih*. There was now no difficulty in obtaining sufficient food for the capital and the efforts of P'ei Yao-ch'ing's successors were applied more and more to bringing in the silks and other luxury goods of the south.

Further attempts continued to be made to improve the transport system, particularly the costly route from Lo-yang to Ch'ang-an, but the details need not detain us. The policies of the men responsible for filling the exchequer in the latter years of Hsüan-tsung's reign must however be briefly discussed. Three men are singled out by the historians for special condemnation for misleading the emperor into schemes of profit. They were Wei Chien, Yang Shen-ch'in, and Wang Hung.

Wei Chien became Prefect of Shan Chün (Shan Chou) in 742 with the additional office of Commissioner for Land and Water Transport *(Shui-lu Chuan-yün Shih)*. Of his policies the Introduction to the *Monograph on Food and Money* in the *Old T'ang History* says:

Wei Chien modelled himself on the policies of Yü-wen Jung and Yang Shen-ch'in. Accordingly he asked that the tax rice from Chiang-nan should be [again] transported, that the coarse grain in the Public Granaries in the prefectures and counties should be sold for light goods, that rich households should be assigned to look after boats and that if there were any delays or losses it should be charged to the "boat households." In the Kuan-chung Transport canal he dug the Kuang-yün harbourage so as to bring in 4,000,000 *shih* from east of the mountains each year. The emperor considered him able and he too became high and prosperous.

In resuming grain shipments from Chiang-nan and in utilizing the grain of the I-ts'ang for government purposes Wei Chien was following in the footsteps of P'ei Yao-ch'ing and in his improvement of the Wei River channel he likewise merely carried on the work of predecessors. Two innovations are however mentioned in the above passage. One was the conversion of part of the grain of the south into "light goods." This shows on the one hand that the needs of the government for grain were no longer so pressing, and it also illustrates the trend towards an exchange economy which we know was going on in China at this time. But it equally shows a degeneration in the purpose of financial reform from that of providing for essential needs to one of exploiting to the full the new wealth of the east and south in the interests of the government. The other innovation was to make rich households responsible for grain transportation. Previously this responsibility had lain on the tax-paying population as a whole. A fixed sum of money called "foot money" was collected from each taxpayer to pay for transportation costs and furthermore losses or damage *en route* had to be made up by the taxpayers of the district from which the taxes originally came. The details of Wei Chien's reform, which was continued by his successor Wang Hung, are not made clear, but it would appear that the burdens of paying for transportation and of making up losses were transferred from the general population to certain wealthy families. Far from justifying the cry of "oppression" which has been raised against Wei Chien, this measure would seem to have been an alleviation to the peasantry. It was, however, as in the case of Yü-wen Jung's measures, a blow at the newly rich and has accordingly been roundly condemned.

In 743 Wei Chien crowned his achievements with a great pageant of boats from all parts of the empire in his specially prepared artificial lake at Ch'ang-an before the emperor and all his court. Each boat displayed the fine products of its region. This pageant and his success in filling the treasury brought Wei Chien much fame and honours from the emperor. In 744 Li Lin-fu, who was jealous of Wei Chien's prestige, had him promoted to President of the Ministry of Punishments but stripped of his commissionerships.

He was replaced by Yang Shen-ch'in, the son of Yang Ch'ung-li, who had been in charge of the Imperial Treasury (*T'ai-fu*) for many years in the first half of Hsüan-tsung's reign and had distinguished himself for his strictness in demanding the exact quality and quantity of tax goods. When Ch'ung-li retired in 732, Yang Shen-ch'in was appointed to succeed him. He continued his father's strict practices and is criticized for overzealousness by the historians. Conjointly with his treasury office he held ranks in the Censorate and in 743 was made Inspector of the Capital District (*Ching-chi Ts'ai-fang Shih*). His financial policies after he replaced Wei Chien in 744 are not described. He is criticized in general terms for strictness in demanding taxes and for grinding down the people in order to enrich the treasury.

Wang Hung held various posts in the Ministry of Finance and the Censorate in the years 736 to 746 and after the ruin of Wei Chien and Yang Shen-ch'in by Li Lin-fu became the chief financial expert of the government. He is criticized for similar practices to those of Wei Chien. His chief innovation was the paying of revenues directly into the emperor's private purse without passing through the Ministry of Finance. He claimed that these goods had been received in addition to the normal taxes. This wholly deplorable practice is blamed by the Chinese historians for leading Hsüan-tsung into irresponsible extravagance. Such disregard of proper book-keeping naturally also enabled Wang Hung to become a very wealthy man.

Yang Kuo-chung, the cousin of the favourite, Yang Kuei-fei, and dictator after the death of Li Lin-fu, also held many financial commissionerships. He does not however seem to have introduced any important changes in the fields we have been discussing.

How far can we follow those Chinese historians who have laid a large part of the blame for the rebellion on the financial policies of these men? As we have seen, there is no evidence that these policies resulted in actual peasant upheaval, though, of course, it is impossible to estimate how much bad feeling against the government they may have caused. Probably of greater importance was the estrangement of the literati from the court and the rise of Li Lin-fu's dictatorship, of which these financial policies formed one aspect. From the standpoint of the economic life of the country as a whole Hsüan-tsung's centralization was probably beneficial in that it stimulated trade and the growth of an exchange economy. On the other hand, the Chinese historians are probably not altogether wrong in emphasizing the very harmful, corrupting influence it had on the emperor and his entourage.

Many important aspects of the economic life of China at this time have been passed over or only briefly mentioned. If this were intended as an economic history of the period, it would of course be necessary to go into them more fully, but I have confined myself to those matters which seem of crucial importance for an understanding of the background of the rebellion.

GUNGWU WANG

The Military Governors and the Decline of the T'ang Dynasty

One of the pillars of the grand T'ang empire in its early stage was its military system, the fu-ping *(prefecture-soldiers or local militia) system. When the* fu-ping *system was replaced by the* chieh-tu shih *(military governor system), the disintegration of the central power began. As a result, the power structure of the empire shifted in favor of the powerful frontier governors.*

Although the chieh-tu shih *at first exercised primarily military power, they were later given more control over administrative matters, as well as special fiscal rights within their territories. These military governors were first appointed for the specific purpose of frontier defense. But the rebellion of An Lu-shan, from 755 to 763, brought great changes to the system. After the rebellion, the court was forced to concede to the governors greater power and the governors, in return, became increasingly independent. Most of them had large private armies, whose sole loyalty was to their commanders. Thus began the long, painful struggle for control between the T'ang court and its military governors.*

In the following selection, Gungwu Wang, Professor of Chinese History at Australian National University, examines the general history of power struggles between the military governors and the T'ang Court, and among the rival governors themselves. Professor Wang concludes that the basic features of the chieh-tu shih *system had been incorporated into a new type of central government, which continued through the disruptive period of the Five Dynasties (907–960) to the Sung. At the same time, his study suggests the implications of military power for Chinese government, which repeatedly had to grapple with the problem of controlling the very forces that were supposed to defend it.*

During the first half of the 8th century, a number of senior frontier commands were created for the defence of the northern and western borders of the T'ang empire. By 755, there were ten such commands, the commanders being known as *chieh-tu shih*, variously translated as "regional commander," "commissaire impérial au com-

Reprinted from Gungwu Wang, *The Structure of Power in North China During the Five Dynasties* (Kuala Lumpur, Malaysia: University of Malaya Press, 1963), pp. 7–43, 46. By permission of the Publications Committee, University of Malaya. Footnotes omitted.

mandement d'une région" and "military governor." Although the powers of the *chieh-tu shih* were primarily military, the commanders were later given more control over administrative matters. In time, the court conferred upon them several other titles which gave each of them full control of at least one prefecture and supervisory powers over many others. These additional titles also gave them special fiscal rights as well as rights over the local militia and the prefectural garrisons. In this way, they became in fact *governors* with military responsibilities. For this reason, the system of *chieh-tu shih* which became a dominant institution during the second half of the T'ang dynasty is here referred to as the system of military governors.

The military governors were first appointed for the specific purpose of defending the frontiers. There was initially no change in the administrative and fiscal system and the main administrative unit was still the prefecture over which a military governor was allowed only the right of the inspection. But the rebellion of An Lu-shan and his successors (755–763) brought great changes to the system. During the rebellion, several new military governors were appointed by both the central and rebel governments. When the rebellion was checked by the surrender of most of the rebel generals, the T'ang court appointed three of these generals to be governors of new provinces created from the larger provinces in the Ho-pei and Ho-nan region. Other governors were appointed to protect the metropolitan province of Kuan-chung as well as the key economic areas of the Yangtse basin. After the rebellion, the court was

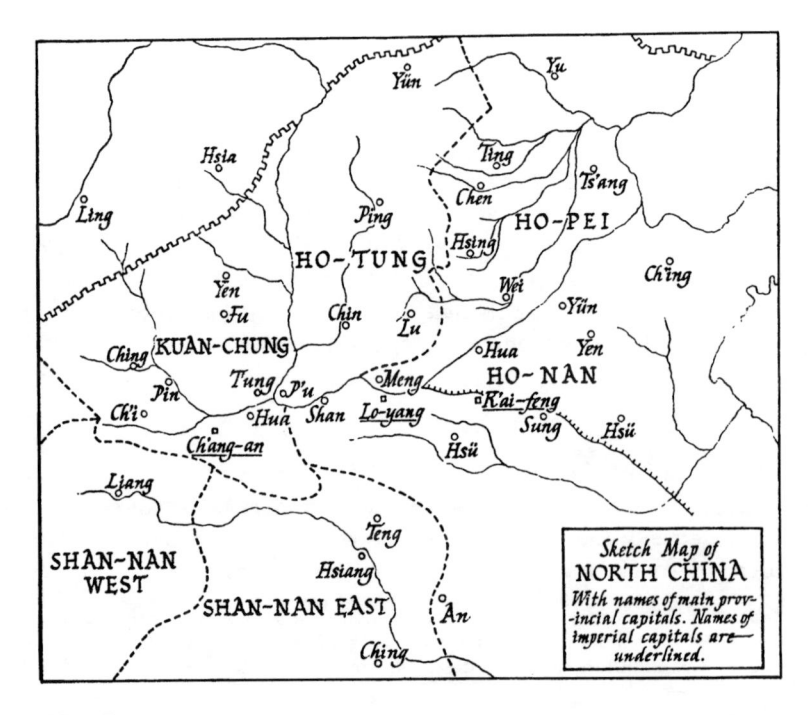

Map I

forced to concede to the governors greater control over the prefectures in their provinces. Most of them had large private armies which dominated the prefectural garrisons, and some even began to appoint their own prefects.

The details of the long struggle for control between the T'ang court through its loyal governors, and the ex-rebels who became increasingly independent, are outside the scope of this study. Briefly, the struggle which lasted for over a century was unresolved, although several important battles were won by the court from time to time. The victories were gained partly by force, but more often by compromise and diplomacy, and by playing off the rebellious governors against one another. Another important factor was the policy of reducing the size of provinces in order to weaken the power of the governors. The emperor Hsien-tsung (806-820) was especially successful in carrying out this policy. By the end of his reign, the number of provinces in the Ho-pei region had increased from three in 762 to six and in the Ho-nan region from five to nine. Some of the governors were further weakened by the return of military authority to the prefects in each of their provinces. This meant that many of the governors had their powers reduced and limited to the prefectures in which their provincial capitals were situated. But the Ho-pei provinces which were in the hands of hereditary governors were unaffected by this policy and these governors continued to appoint their own prefects. After 820, there were at least five such provinces, and although these were reduced to three by 845, the court never succeeded in regaining control over the greater part of the Ho-pei region.

Several imperial victories were won in the years 806-845. They were won chiefly by units of the reorganized imperial armies and the provincial armies bordering on the recalcitrant provinces. The older militia (fu-ping) system had long been abandoned and new professional armies were recruited at the capital and locally in the provinces. The palace armies had been expanded and under the eunuchs the Shen-ts'e (Divine Strategy) Army had become the largest and most privileged. In the provinces, the loyal governors were ordered to build up and maintain armies not only for local defence and garrisoning the frontiers, but also for augmenting any expeditionary army against rebellious governors. Both these developments had important consequences. The new palace armies gave the eunuchs the power to challenge that of the bureaucrats, and the struggle was one of the chief features of ninth-century T'ang history. The eunuchs could directly influence imperial succession, and through the emperors they supported obtained further powers and privileges. They also had control over the provinces either by getting generals of the Shen-ts'e Army appointed as governors or by appointing eunuchs to supervise the governors.

As for the new provincial armies, there were several kinds. There were the armies which the independent governors had built up out of the remnants of An Lu-shan's army and further expanded with fresh recruitment in their provinces. These governors had encouraged professionalism, something not found before outside the imperial capital, and their strength as well as their weakness stemmed from the use of these hereditary officers. The development of this kind of army forced the T'ang court to station permanent armies in the neighbouring provinces. It also forced the court to encourage the same kind of professionalism and hereditary military class. Thus on both sides of a long but fluid frontier, similar types of armies were established. By the middle of the 9th century only the loyalties of the governors and the commanders distinguished the armies built up by the court from those of the independent governors.

There were two other kinds of armies which were also significant. The first of these were frontier garrisons which included units of the palace and other provincial armies. An important feature in these frontier garrisons was the presence of tribesmen whose loyalty could never be taken for granted. The second type were the smaller armies south of the Yangtse which were not large enough to justify the appointment of military governors to supervise them. They were based chiefly on local militia and were in the charge of Inspectors *(kuan-ch'a shih)*. Sometimes these armies also included units from provincial armies in the north. Although they were adequate for defence against local banditry, they were helpless against any large rebellion or invasion. Any such danger would require the despatch of northern armies.

After 820, governors began to be appointed at regular intervals to several provinces in the Ho-nan and Ho-tung regions. The new governors were a mixture of bureaucrats, generals of the imperial armies and surrendered rebels. In 845, regular appointments could be made to all but three provinces in Ho-pei. From 845 to the outbreak of the Huang Ch'ao rebellion in 875, the governors were predominantly important bureaucrats. Table I, for the years 845, 855, 865 and 875, shows the trend of the appointments for twenty-eight provinces north of the Yangtse (the three independent provinces of Ho-pei are not included).

This trend can be a rough gauge of conditions prevailing. There was a relatively peaceful period from 845 to 860 during which the number of bureaucrat governors rose to twenty-four, followed by risings, mutinies and a tribal invasion in the following period from 860 to 875 when the number was halved. It is interesting to note that there was only one non-bureaucrat governor in 855. He was T'ien Mou, the son of a rebel governor who had surrendered, and in 855, was the governor of Hsü province for the second time. He had been called in to control the mutinous provincial army in the one clearly restless area in the empire at that time.

No attempt is made here to survey the events leading to the Huang Ch'ao rebellion in 875. But in order to understand what the rebellion did to the T'ang empire, it is necessary to describe briefly the rela-

Table I

Year	No. of governors known (a)	Aristocratic or literati origins (b)	(c)	Military or rebel origins (d)	(e)	Unclassified (f)
			Not certain		Not certain	
845	25	16	(2)	6	(1)	—
855	26	24	(1)	1	—	—
865	22	18	—	3	(1)	—
875	25	12	(2)	7	(2)	2

tionship between a governor and the court on the eve of it. At this time, the court could rely on most of the governors it appointed and depended on them for the control of the provincial armies. Appointed by the court to help each of the governors in their duties were the eunuch Army Supervisor *(chien-chün)*, the governor's military Deputy *(hsing-chün ssu-ma)* and their assistants. On arrival at the provical capital, the governor could recommend someone to be commander of the army *(tu-chih ping-ma shih)* though he probably always accepted the commander who was already there. He then selected men from the army for a residential garrison, or *ya-chün,* a kind of "governor's guards." The strength of this *ya-chün* varied considerably, but there were always an administrator in charge *(tu-ya-ya)*, an officer in command *(ya-nei tu-chiang)* and several officers *(ya-chiang, ya-hsiao)* and administrative officials *(ya-ya)*.

To help in general administration, the court appointed a number of bureaucrats as

fu-shih (Assistant Governor),
chieh-tu p'an-kuan (Governor's Administrator),
kuan-ch'a p'an-kuan (Inspector's Administrator),
chang shu-chi (Secretary),
kuan-ch'a chih-shih (Inspector's Secretary) and
t'ui-kuan (Law Administrator).

There were also the administrators and secretaries for the prefecture directly under the governor's control, and the magistrates of the counties in the prefecture. A governor could influence the appointment of all these subordinate officials if not actually select the men he wanted.

The relationship between the governor and the prefects in his province varied from province to province. The court appointed the prefects and their staff independently, but they were clearly subject to the governor's supervision and control. Officially, the prefects could memorialize directly to the court, but they would normally hesitate to do so without consultation with their governor. The prefects were mostly bureaucrats (except those in frontier prefectures) whose relationship with a bureaucrat governor was influenced by their ranks in the official hierarchy, and was therefore comparatively straightforward. But the officers of the provincial army probably had undue influence over those of the prefectural garrisons. This was because the provincial officers had a more permanent relationship with the prefectural troops than the bureaucrats who were regularly transferred. With a governor of military and rebel origin, however, the prefects' relations were more complicated. They were allowed the control of their own garrisons, but an army-conscious governor who distrusted bureaucrat soldiers would prefer to have all units in his province under his command. Some of the governors created special garrisons with police and defence duties in strategic counties *(chen-chiang)* within the prefects' territories and either filled the garrisons with their own men or at least sent their officers to command them. Because of this, the prefects' military authority was often negligible.

Many of the above features were changed in the decade after 875, chiefly owing to the ineffective attempts by the court to crush the Huang Ch'ao rebellion. A major factor in Huang Ch'ao's success was the discontent within the provincial armies. Since the P'ang Hsün mutiny, 868–869, was put down with the help of tribal cavalry from outside the Great Wall, this discontent seems to have grown. From 875 onwards, there was at least one mutiny every year. In 877, mutineers in two prov-

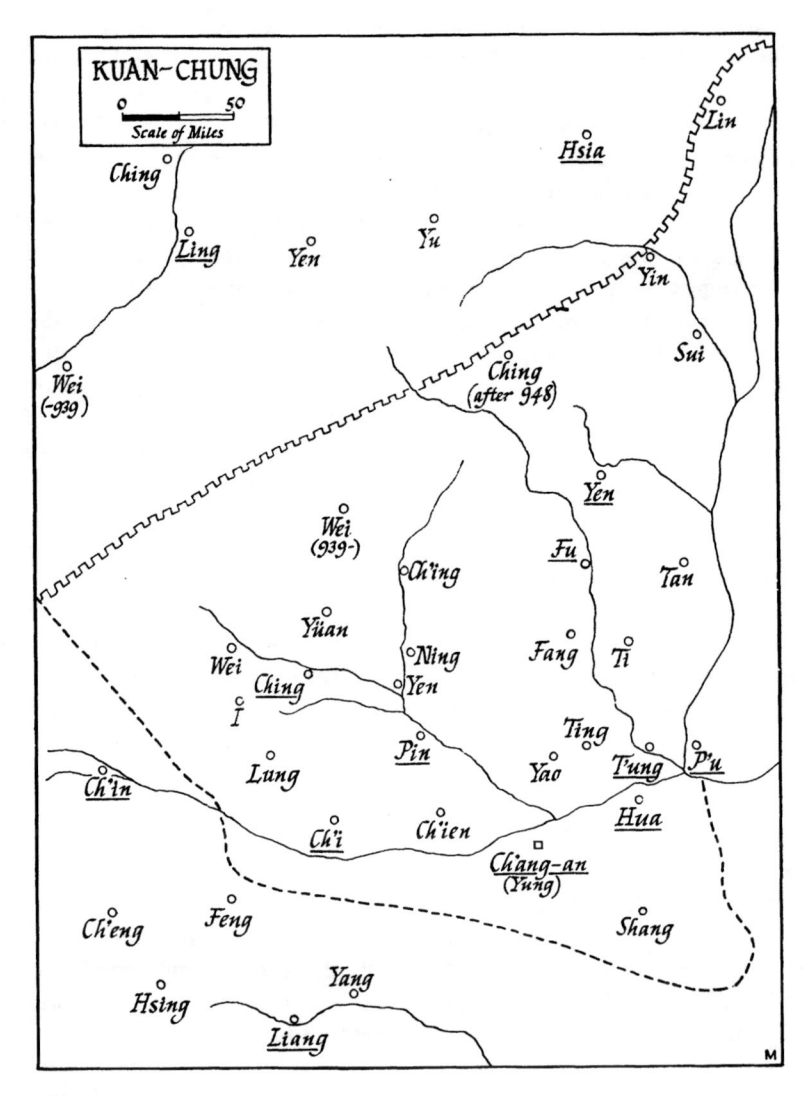

Map II

inces, both within a hundred and fifty miles of Ch'ang-an, removed their governors. The most serious mutinies took place north of the Huang Ho in 878–880 when first the Sha-t'o Turks, the Ping provincial armies and local militia (in Shansi), and finally the reinforcements from Lu province rose against their governors or their commanders and killed them. Although the causes of these mutinies were independent of Huang Ch'ao's rebellion, the mutinies affected it in two ways. Firstly, the court was forced to send to the north most of its reserves from the Eastern Capital and Meng province (in the Ho-nan region) at a critical time and thus forfeited a line of defence east of the vital T'ung-kuan Pass. The result was that when Huang Ch'ao broke through the defences on the Huai River from the south in 880, he could march straight to T'ung-kuan. This shortage of reserves, together with the lenient treatment of mutineers, also aggravated the falling morale of the other provincial armies. There were many incidents to show the court's inability to control these troops. For example, when the governor of Yün province died in 879, an officer of the castle garrison seized power for a few days. Later in the same year, the army defending Ching Chou on the Yangtse went out of control. Part of it returned north as bandit gangs to pillage the canal area, and even managed to engage the provincial armies there till the middle of 880.

This discontent was not limited to the lower ranks of the army. The reasons given by the governor of Hsiang in 879 for not destroying the rebels reflect the extent of discontent among the highest officers. As the governor is recorded to have said, "The empire is wont to be ungrateful. In times of crisis, it nurtures its officers and is not niggardly in its rewards. When the affairs are settled, it rejects them or even punishes them. It is better to leave the bandits there as an investment of our wealth and position." More critical for the empire was the attitude of the commander of the imperial armies himself. He felt the same way about "leaving the bandits there as an investment," and when he decided to let Huang Ch'ao cross the Yangtse and reach the Huai river in 7th/880, all effective resistance came to an end.

From then on, army officers began to take over in their provinces or prefectures, several of them submitting to Huang Ch'ao. Huang Ch'ao in his turn adopted the policy of "indulgence" which the T'ang court had employed before, and kept them on as governors. It would have taken him too long to capture all these provinces and he was eager to reach the capital first. What he did was to leave units of his army behind and an army supervisor to report on each governor, and he was content merely to receive the financial support of the provinces.

The chief redistribution of power took place after the fall of Ch'ang-an to Huang Ch'ao in 12th/880. There were now two emperors, Huang Ch'ao at Ch'ang-an and the boy Hsi-tsung at Ch'eng-tu (in modern Szechuan province). The court at Ch'eng-tu, after the initial losses following the escape there, found that it had retained enough of its authority in the provinces to begin a counter-attack on Ch'ang-an. This was almost successful. It was greatly helped by the defection of the "governors" Huang Ch'ao had appointed. His control over them had been nominal, and the governors did to him what they had done earlier to the T'ang court.

From the military point of view, the most important of the defections was that of the governor of P'u province at the southern bend of the Huang Ho and within striking distance of Ch'ang-an. Together with his brother, the governor of Shan province east of T'ung-kuan pass, he provided the containment of Huang Ch'ao in the Wei valley and made his defeat easier. By 882, Huang Ch'ao held only two prefectures and the metropolitan counties of Ch'ang-an. Then, later in that year, one of Huang Ch'ao's own generals, Chu Wen, surrendered with one of the two prefectures. The court was now eager for a quick victory, and called in thousands of frontier horsemen under Li K'o-yung, the leader of the Sha-t'o Turks to help. In 4th/883, Ch'ang-an was recaptured.

The restoration of the T'ang court, however, was far from complete. The dynastic authority over the provinces had become weaker than ever. The court did directly control Ch'ang-an and the two provinces in Chien-nan (Szechuan) and could still rely on three of the eleven provinces in Ho-nan, three of the nine north of the Huang Ho, the two provinces of Shan-nan and at least four of the eleven on the Yangtse and along the Southern coasts. But the remainder, if not actually defiant or hostile, were in the hands of independent or army-appointed leaders. They were wooed by the court, and were given titles for paying lip-service to the empire.

Table II for the 7th/833 shows what the problem was like in North China in the areas which concern this study of the Five Dynasties. Although all the Yangtse provinces were important to the court in its effort to unify the empire, only the three which had a direct bearing on the developments in the North have been included.

In the thirty-three provinces, the governors of thirteen were court-chosen, those of six court-appointed, and those of nine self-appointed. Of the court-chosen governors, three were bureaucrats and eight were professional soldiers of whom one had already turned away from the court. This compares poorly with the beginning of 880 when probably as many as twenty-nine governors were court-chosen. Of these, about half had been bureaucrats. The contrast in 883 is obvious, especially where direct bureaucratic control of the provinces is concerned. Of the three bureaucrats who were left, two were replaced by the next year, and the third was the governor of the imperial capital itself.

Briefly, comparing the period before and after the Huang Ch'ao rebellion, it may be said that the balance of power between the bureaucrats and the eunuchs which had dominated the history of the sixty years of T'ang rule prior to the rebellion was now upset by the resurgence of the military, whether imperial or rebel in origin. This shift of power led to the loss of central control over most of the empire and was eventually to create the most difficult problems of recovering control over the provinces. . . .

In the past, a policy of "indulgence" towards the independent governors had been followed and this had always given the court time and opportunities to recover. This policy was followed again in 883, not only because it was the only thing the court could do, but also because there was hope that the policy might be made to work again. The situation in 883, however, was very different from any the court had faced before. A great number of provincial and rebel armies had elected governors and prefects whom the court could neither transfer nor dismiss. Larger areas were thus no longer directly subject to any central supervision. Even more important, the court-chosen governor of the important province of Yang (Huai-nan) was defiant and supported rebellions in several provinces south of the Yangtse. This aggravated the rebellious situation in South China which had partly been a hangover from Huang Ch'ao's long campaigns there in 878–880. But the loss to the imperial coffers owing to the imperfect control of these vital economic areas was irremediable. Furthermore, Huang Ch'ao had escaped into Ho-nan in search of another base for his activities. And before he was finally crushed, he had created another rebellion, that of Ch'in Tsung-ch'üan, the governor of Ts'ai province. And this rebellion did even more to isolate the court from the eastern half of the empire.

Lastly, there was a stranglehold on

Table II

Provinces	Status, origins of governors, date appointed

I. *Kuan-chung* (Shensi and areas to its north and west)

1	Ch'ang-an	court-chosen, bureaucrat, 883.
2	Ch'i	self-appointed, leader of mutiny, 881.
3	Pin	court-appointed, leader of defence against Huang Ch'ao, 881.
4	Ching	court-appointed, provincial officer, 882.
5	Fu	court-chosen (?), 882.
6	Hsia	court-appointed, tribal leader and a prefect, 881.
7	Yen *	court-appointed, tribesman frontier officer (?), 883.
8	Hua *	appointed by brother, the governor of P'u, 883.

II. *Ho-tung* (Shansi and areas to its north)

9	P'u	self-appointed, leader of mutiny, 880.
10	Ping	court-appointed, leader of Sha-t'o Turks, 883.
11	Lu	self-appointed, leader of mutiny, 881.

III. *Ho-pei* (Ho-pei and northern Shantung)

12	Yu	son of previous governor, 876.
13	Chên	son of previous governor, 883.
14	Wei	self-appointed, leader of mutiny, 881.
15	Ting	court-chosen, son of a governor, 879.
16	Ts'ang	court-chosen (?), 880.

IV. *Ho-nan* (Honan, Shantung and northern Anhwei and Chiangsu)

17	Shan	appointed by governor of P'u, 881.
18	Mêng	appointed by Huang Ch'ao, surrendered, then court-appointed, 881.
19	Lo-yang	(under control of Mêng governor).
20	Pien	court-chosen, ex-Huang Ch'ao general, 883.
21	Hua	court-chosen, bureaucrat, 882.
22	Yen	court-chosen, imperial officer, 879.
23	Yün	self-appointed after death of governor, provincial officer, 882.
24	Ch'ing	self-appointed, leader of mutiny, 882.
25	Hsü	self-appointed, leader of mutiny, 880.
26	Ts'ai	self-appointed, leader of mutiny, 881; (now supporting Huang Ch'ao).
27	Hsü	self-appointed, leader of mutiny, 881.

V. *Shan-nan* (Northern Hupei and southern Shensi)

28	Hsiang	court-chosen, imperial officer, 879.
29	Liang	court-chosen, protégé of eunuchs and General of Imperial Guards, 880.

VI. *Chien-nan* (Szechuan)

30	I	court-chosen, brother of leading eunuch and General of Imperial Guards, 880.
31	Tzŭ	court-chosen, protégé of eunuchs and General of Imperial Guards, 880.

VII. *The Yangtse provinces*

32	Yang	court-chosen, ex-commander of imperial armies against Huang Ch'ao, 879.
33	Ngo	court-chosen, bureaucrat, 879.
34	Ching	court-appointed, provincial officer chosen by eunuch Supervisor, 882.

* = new province

Ch'ang-an from *within* the Wei valley. This was initially due to the loss of the capital in 880, but later on two mutiny leaders and an adventurous officer had taken over the three nearest provinces and, although they were not hostile, they were not chosen by the court and could not be removed except by force. This was a new situation in T'ang history, for no emperor before Hsi-tsung had been so confined in his capital.

When the recovery of Ch'ang-an was imminent early in 883, the court chose two men to be governors in Ho-nan; Wang To as governor of Hua province and Chu Wen as governor of Pien, both provinces situated to guard against the independent Ho-pei provinces and protect the Grand Canal. And three months after retaking Ch'ang-an, the court-chosen governor of Ping province was recalled and Li K'o-yung, the Sha-t'o Turk, was appointed to replace him. Apart from these three, the court could only confirm the appointments of mutiny leaders and ex-rebels and hope for continued support from previously chosen governors. The three appointments of Wang To, Chu Wen and Li K'o-yung constituted the court's first uncertain steps to regain control over its empire.

Wang To was a successful bureaucrat who had twice been a chief minister of the empire. He had also been twice the commander-in-chief of the expeditionary armies against Huang Ch'ao. The interesting point about his provincial appointment is that the old struggle between the eunuchs and the bureaucrats was probably responsible for it. Wang To was not made governor to try and recover imperial control over the Eastern provinces. He was already quite old by that time, and was not in any case given control of the armies in Ho-nan which were still loyal to the court. Moreover, he was not appointed to the more important Pien province which he had governed before, but to Hua which, though important as a stronghold against the Ho-pei governors, was not vital for the control of the Ho-nan.

The second governor, Chu Wen, had a completely different background. He had been Huang Ch'ao's general and was prefect of T'ung Chou when he surrendered in 9th/882 to the imperial commander. He was the third son of an impoverished teacher. When his father died, he was brought up to be a family retainer or a manor steward in the household where his mother worked as a servant. He became a village tough instead and probably formed his own small bandit gang in the neighbourhood. Some time in 876–877, he and his friends had joined Huang Ch'ao. Chu Wen's surrender in 882 could have hardly been better timed as there was immediate relief to the imperial army. He was appointed governor of the new province of T'ung, became Grand General of the Imperial Guards and a deputy field commander soon afterwards. On 23/3rd/883, only six months after his surrender, he was appointed Military Governor of Pien province, the appointment to take effect after the fall of Ch'ang-an. This was four days before a crucial victory and half a month before the entry into Ch'ang-an. It was already known that Huang Ch'ao planned to escape east to Ho-nan via the Lan-t'ien pass. A reformed rebel with nothing to lose, and with a reputation among other rebels, was probably the man to win the battles still to be fought. A strong recommendation must have come from the P'u governor, Wang Ch'ung-jung, one of the chief architects of the expected victory. He knew of Chu Wen's background and of his experience of the provinces astride the all-important canal route from the southeastern granaries. Chu Wen could be expected to understand both local banditry and the rebel armies that remained with Huang Ch'ao. Further, he had sought the patronage of Wang Ch'ung-jung, and had quickly taken to calling his patron "uncle" because his own mother was of the Wang clan. Now, as a "newphew," he could have asked Wang Ch'ung-jung to press the appointment for him.

The third appointment was again different in its background. Li K'o-yung was not a common rebel but a Turkish aristocrat, son of the hereditary chieftain of the Sha-t'o tribe. His father was an imperial commissioner for three Turkish tribes and the prefect of Shuo Chou. As a boy he had followed his father south to help put down the P'ang Hsün mutiny (869), and when his father was rewarded that year with the imperial surname, he became a member of the imperial family (in the branch of Prince Cheng).

After a stay at Ch'ang-an Li K'o-yung had returned north to be a border officer, and by 877 had become the deputy commissioner of a Turkish garrison. The next year, he led a tribal revolt which developed into a border war. For two years he caused such consternation in Ping province that the court sent six governors in succession to crush his tribal army, but without any success. The seventh governor, a Chief Minister and a former governor of the province, was finally sent with a hand-picked team of officials to deal with him. Reinforcements which could be ill-afforded were brought from the Eastern capital. Eventually in 6th/880, Li K'o-yung was defeated chiefly because he was betrayed by some of his officers. Six months afterwards, Huang Ch'ao captured Ch'ang-an. Li K'o-yung was granted a pardon and invited to join the imperial forces against the rebels. After considerable bargaining which gained him the governorship of a newly created province, he went south. In 4th/883, the rebels were dislodged and he led the imperial armies into Ch'ang-an.

Li K'o-yung's interest in Ping province had dated from 878. That he demanded his appointment as its governor was likely. The demand could be forcibly backed by the presence at Ch'ang-an of thousands of the best horsemen in the empire feasting daily in triumph for three months. Unable to fob them off with titles and to recompense them sufficiently from the strained imperial coffers, the court came around to appointing their leader governor of Ping. It had no illusions about their trustworthiness, nor could it find fault with the present governor who probably argued strongly against his old enemy. The court could only hope to use Li K'o-yung against other enemies at some future date.

These three appointments, so disparate in nature, were no part of any great plan to recover the empire. The three men were unlikely partners and their ability to cooperate with one another was soon put to a test in Ho-nan. The fight against Huang Ch'ao went on for another year. Wang To was completely ineffective from the start and Chu Wen could not cope with the rebels alone. Li K'o-yung had to be called south again and, together with Chu Wen, succeeded in defeating Huang Ch'ao. This seemed to have been the success the court needed. With the help of these two men, it could hope to recover its authority over the rest of Ho-nan and the valuable Huai-nan (Lower Yangtse) region.

But the triumph was short-lived. A quarrel soon occurred between the two governors and a hasty attempt was made by Chu Wen to massacre Li K'o-yung and his bodyguards on the night of 14/5th/884.

The court was then asked by both men to arbitrate on the incident, and when it was unwilling to investigate the matter, it merely gained the mistrust of Li K'o-yung and the contempt of Chu Wen. Chu Wen's act of treachery was not merely historically important as the beginning of the struggle with Li K'o-yung which was to last for forty years through two generations. It had immediate consequences for imperial power in North China. The Ho-nan and Ho-tung regions were now separated by this rivalry, never to co-operate again for the empire. The two governors were left to extend their power in their respective regions. They gathered around themselves territories and resources to oppose each other, and thus built up two centres of power.

An indirect result of this quarrel was the danger to the empire from the new rebellion led by Ch'in Tsung-ch'üan. Had the two continued their co-operation in Ho-nan, they might have prevented the rebellion from being as successful as it was during the next three years. Instead, Chu Wen was left virtually alone to deal with these rebels. If any single event could be said to have blasted all hopes of an imperial restoration, it was probably this quarrel. It had reduced to nothing the court's first steps to regain control. The withdrawal of the tribal cavalry and the Ping provincial army from Ho-nan exposed the Eastern Capital to the rebels and Ch'ang-an was almost completely cut off from Ho-nan until 6th/887. During these years of isolation, Chu Wen survived to defeat the rebels and, by so doing, attained a position of authority in Ho-nan. His loyalty was then so valuable to the court that he was given a free hand and even encouraged to gain further control over the other provinces in the region.

The court still had nominal administrative control over several provinces. It selected the staff of the governors including the chief administrator, legal and financial experts, various secretaries and assistants. These officials, however, were inclined to develop loyalty for their respective governors. Each governor depended on them for efficient administration and was careful to keep them contented. Once they were appointed, the governor would keep those who were efficient and recommend their re-appointment. The officials could remain indefinitely so long as the same governor was still in office. They could be promoted and receive increases in salary without being moved from their posts. Since this was so in most provinces, the officials themselves saw no advantage in leaving unless it was for a promotion to the court. After some time, each governor acquired a team of administrators on whom he could depend without fear of interference from the court. The court's administrative control over the provinces was thus steadily weakened until it merely provided the governors, from time to time, with administrators chosen from some of its ablest officials.

In two other ways, the court was forced to give in to the governors. Firstly they lost direct control over the various prefectures. The appointment of most of the prefects, county magistrates and their immediate staff was still the prerogative of the court. But this, too, had become merely a means of providing the governors with trained administrative personnel. The powers of these prefects and magistrates were restricted as the governors also appointed their own representatives to each prefectural capital and county town. Often, these representatives were backed by the local defence garrisons or were themselves the officers commanding them. In this way, the court-chosen officials tended to be indistinguishable from the governors' own employees. It was only a matter of time before many governors dispensed with court-chosen prefects and magistrates altogether, and recommended their own men for these posts. These men were usually their trusted personal officials or army commanders.

The other loss to the court was in its direction of the military forces in the provinces. While it continued to send eunuch Army Supervisors *(chien-chün)* who were still expected to report on the loyalty of the governors, it was unable to back their admonitions and protests with strong imperial forces. In this way, the supervisors were rendered ineffectual. Instead, the governors could cultivate their friendship and use them for their own benefit. Palace intrigues could thus be better understood by officials in the provinces. The governors could, with the help of friendly eunuchs, participate in these intrigues or take sides more easily in any struggle at the court and thus influence and interfere with court decisions. The appointment of military deputies *(hsing-chün ssu-ma)* by the court also became a contribution to the governor's already large team of trained officials. Not surprisingly, these deputies were not really allowed any authority over the armies which were either directly in the governor's hands or were under his personally selected commanders. In time, two officers became increasingly important and eventually transformed the structure of power in the empire. They were the chief commander of the provincial army and the administrator of the governor's guards. . . .

The court's spheres of control in the provinces were thus systematically reduced. Instead of only three independent governors in Ho-pei, there were now a score of others all over the country. The only way to control the warlordism was probably by efficient diplomacy and intrigue and by playing off the governors against one another. The idea of re-uniting the empire by the assertion of power had to be abandoned and a dynastic duty was thus abrogated. The method of "diplomacy" was already adopted when the newly appointed governors, Chu Wen and Li K'o-yung, urged the court to arbitrate in 5th/884 on Chu Wen's attempted murder of Li K'o-yung and were given an equivocal answer instead. The court pacified Li K'o-yung by making him the most powerful governor in North China while Chu Wen was satisfied that it had turned a blind eye to the whole affair.

The court's relative success was not to be repeated. After its return to Ch'ang-an in 3rd/885, the proximity of three strong governors in the Wei valley itself made interference in court decisions by military pressure much easier and the use of "diplomacy" much more difficult. The formula of the court against the provinces soon proved to be too simple to cope with the increasing difficulties to be faced. There developed political alignments within the court which were backed by powerful governors supporting one or another group. There were defensive alliances between the governors against either the court or other allied governors. The alignments became increasingly complicated, and a study of these alignments would be necessary before any of the stages of the various struggles can be clear. The limitations of our sources make the correct weighing of power both at the court and in the provinces almost impossible. The bias is too much in favour of the groups which survived into the Wu-tai (Five Dynasties) period. An outline of the chief conflicts at Ch'ang-an, however, has been attempted and the remainder of this chapter will deal with the events leading to the fall of the T'ang.

In 885, the emperor returned to Ch'ang-an with a new army of fifty-four regiments, each of a thousand men at full strength. This army was controlled by the eunuch T'ien Ling-tzu. When the army had to be paid and fed, the eunuch put pressure on the nearby governor of P'u to surrender the salt monopoly of the province. He soon found himself fighting against an alliance of the P'u governor and Li K'o-yung. The imperial forces were ignominiously defeated and the court, only nine months after its return, was forced to leave Ch'ang-an again. This was an ominous indication of events still to come.

Some of the chief bureaucrats at this time disassociated themselves from T'ien Ling-tzu's actions. They remained at Ch'ang-an and invited the governors of Pin and Ch'i provinces (both neighbouring Ch'ang-an to the west) to settle the differences at the court. Eventually, the bureaucrats agreed with the governors to depose emperor Hsi-tsung. This was a significant break with the T'ang tradition. Now a new emperor was chosen by an anti-eunuch group. This event shows how an alliance of governors had already begun to dominate the intrigues of the court. The attempt to depose Hsi-tsung, however, did not succeed. This was largely because the alliance of the two western governors broke up at a crucial moment. A compromise was reached in the refugee court and the eunuch T'ien Ling-tzu was dismissed. In 12th/886, the court returned once more to Ch'ang-an. But the situation in the provinces was hardly changed. The new governor of Pin was a provincial officer who had murdered the previous governor, and the governor of Ch'i could no more be trusted than before. The governor of P'u was still supported by Li K'o-yung, the man with the strongest army in the empire.

It was clear that no group of governors could take over all power as long as there was jealousy and the possibility of betrayal among them. No governor was yet strong enough to do so alone, and none of the governors would allow any other to gain more power than he already had. If the court could encourage this vigilance in each of them while rebuilding the imperial armies, it could still hope to regain control over the empire eventually.

The chance soon came to use the armies. In 887, the Ch'i governor was attacked and killed, and Li Mao-chen, the commander who led the expeditionary army, was appointed in his place. This appointment was a major gain for the court at that time but the political effects were to prove disastrous later on.

In 3rd/888, Chao-tsung succeeded to the throne after the death of his brother, Hsi-tsung. He gave the bureaucrats more authority over the imperial armies and tried to get personal control of vital sections of the armies at the expense of the eunuchs who had placed him on the throne. Yang Fu-kuang, the leading eunuch, was finally forced by the emperor to leave Ch'ang-an, but he was able to leave with a section of the imperial armies personally loyal to him. He had in the course of years arranged to have his adopted sons appointed governors and prefects in the Chien-nan region (Szechuan). He now joined the ablest of them, Yang Shou-liang, the governor of Liang province (in northern Szechuan). The regiments which stayed behind with the emperor were too weak to give battle, so Li Mao-chen, the Ch'i governor, offered to help with his provincial army. Thus Yang

Shou-liang and Li Mao-chen, two able ex-commanders of the imperial armies, now fought as rival governors, each with a section of these armies.

In due course, other ex-commanders like Wang Chien of I province (western Szechuan) and Han Chien of Hua (east of Ch'ang-an) also became involved. The struggle of 891–894 was in fact a struggle between various sections of the imperial armies which ended in the removal of eunuch power and in the victory of the governors who had been ex-commanders. But when the imperial armies were drawn into the provinces to serve new governors, imperial power was really near its end.

The emperor for all his efforts had not succeeded in getting any more power for himself. By the middle of 893, he had become frightened even by the presence of army commanders at the capital and replaced several of them with imperial princes. But his attempt to move Li Mao-chen from Ch'i province was unsuccessful and elicited from Li Mao-chen a memorial which clearly expressed the contempt the imperial commanders had for the throne. The memorial comments on the emperor and his court:

His highness in his noble position could not protect the life of his own uncle. With the respect of the empire he could not destroy (Yang) Fu-kuang, a mere eunuch. . . . The court now only observes strength and weakness and does not value right and wrong. . . . (It) exercises the law on those who have failed and offers rewards to those who succeed. . . .

Li Mao-chen then warns, "The mood of the army changes easily and their horses are difficult to restrain except that they fear that your people will suffer the consequences." And finally, he pointedly adds, "I wonder when the imperial retinue leaves the capital where it would go." The memorial had some blunt truths behind its rhetoric, and the imperial response was pathetic. Chao-tsung ordered the recruiting of several thousands of urban youths from Ch'ang-an to fill the greatly depleted fifty-four regiments of the imperial armies and sent them under imperial princes against Li Mao-chen. The latter routed the army without difficulty and threatened Ch'ang-an. The emperor was forced to consent to his demands, which included the execution of Chao-tsung's most trusted chief minister and four leading eunuchs.

There was little that Chao-tsung could do about the governors. Neither could he trust the eunuchs and bureaucrats, most of whom had begun to patronize the governors after Li Mao-chen had brought about the death of their most prominent members in 893. In the following years, the struggle among the governors for influence in the court overshadowed all other developments. With the help of the eunuchs and bureaucrats who had become the tools of the governors they patronized, the governors decided to test their strength in 895.

The governor of Ch'i, Li Mao-chen, was an ally of two other governors in the Kuan-chung region. Li K'o-yung was the ally of the other governor in the Ho-tung region (Shansi), Wang Hsing-yü. When Wang Hsing-yü died in 895, there was a dispute over the succession. His son appealed to the three governors of Kuan-chung to intervene on his behalf while his nephew turned to Li K'o-yung for help. The struggle between the two groups was swiftly settled. Li K'o-yung defeated the Kuan-chung governors, and forced them to withdraw support for the son and to accept his candidate, the nephew. The emperor, seeking a new equilibrium in power, pacified Li K'o-yung with rich rewards and sent him back to his province.

The new position probably pleased Chao-tsung, for a third force had now been formed. In addition to the Kuan-chung and Ho-tung alliances, there was also the powerful governor in Ho-nan, Chu Wen, who decided to support the defeated candidate against his old enemy, Li K'o-yung. Chao-tsung could now hope to use "diplomacy" to maintain a new balance, for none of the groups was as yet strong enough to defy the others. The basic flaw in any equilibrium that could be achieved, however, was unremoved—there was no authority left behind the diplomatic moves. This was accentuated by the fact that all the groups were trying to expand their power. For example, Li Mao-chen was not content with the four provinces in his control but made plans to take two others to his north. Li K'o-yung had extended his control over south-eastern Ho-tung and two provinces in Ho-pei while Chu Wen was still fighting in eastern Ho-nan to add two more provinces to the four he already governed. It was only a matter of time before they turned against each other.

The first to do so were Chu Wen and Li K'o-yung. The bitterness between them upset the balance for which the court had hoped. While they were fully engaged in a bloody struggle for the Ho-pei provinces, Li Mao-chen was able to march to the capital for the second time to stop the emperor from strengthening the imperial armies. This time, the emperor's new armies showed even less resistance, and the court was once again forced to move out of Ch'ang-an.

The problem of where to move to marked the beginning of the final stage of the T'ang "restoration." There were no governors who could be trusted. There was no way open to Ho-nan (Honan) or to Chien-nan (Szechuan) and the governor of Shan-nan East (Hupei) was unreliable. The only route left was the precarious one of getting to Li K'o-yung's capital in Ho-tung through the country of Tangut tribesmen whose loyalty was already uncertain. There was also the danger of being stopped and captured by Li Mao-chen's army. So when Han Chien, the governor of the neighbouring Hua province, turned from his ally Li Mao-chen and offered to be host to the emperor, an offer dangerous to refuse, the emperor accepted.

In doing so, Chao-tsung could only hope for temporary relief. The weakness of Han Chien was obvious to all. He had only two small prefectures in his province and was surrounded by enemies on all sides. His only advantage was his personal wealth and long defensive preparations. The court might have observed that he was in no position to depose the emperor. But the rift between him and Li Mao-chen was also dangerous. There was no longer an alliance to defend Kuan-chung from the governors in the east. It could only be hoped that the feud between Chu Wen and Li K'o-yung would continue indefinitely until they were both exhausted, while adjustments of power could be made in Kuan-chung.

But the harm Han Chien could still do was underestimated. From 1st/897, he reduced the emperor to a mere puppet by disbanding his personal bodyguards, by removing all the princes from military commands and absorbing all their armies, and then by executing the ablest of the emperor's commanders. He also interfered with the emperor's choice of chief ministers and caused the officials he feared to be disgraced. Within a few months, the emperor was stripped of everything he could use to defend himself. In 8th/897, all the imperial princes he had trained were murdered by Han Chien. What Han Chien's purpose was in thus completely enslaving the emperor is not clear. He could not expect to depose the emperor and found a new dynasty on the strength of two prefectures. Neither could he expect to keep the emperor with him indefinitely. Chu Wen had already won his main battles in Ho-nan. Li K'o-yung was preparing to ride south to "save the emperor" and Li Mao-chen was urging that the emperor be returned to Ch'ang-an immediately.

If Han Chien had hoped to bargain with the emperor's person for his own survival against these strong rivals, it soon became evident that his survival depended on his sending the emperor back to Ch'ang-an. One of the chief ministers, Ts'ui Yin, had been persuading Chu Wen to rebuild the palaces of Lo-yang, the Eastern Capital, and take the emperor there. This was the most dangerous threat of all, and both Li K'o-yung and Li Mao-chen insisted that Han Chien release the emperor in order to place him farther from Chu Wen's reach. Han Chien had no alternative but to do so. He undertook the rebuilding of the palaces at Ch'ang-an (burnt by Li Mao-chen in 7th/896) and in 8th/898, sent Chao-tsung back.

The new situation had simplified matters. The three groups of power were reduced to two, with Chu Wen on one side and an uneasy alliance of Li K'o-yung, Li Mao-chen and Han Chien on the other. The issues, too, were simpler—whether the emperor should be at Ch'ang-an or at Lo-yang. In these circumstances, the old struggle between the eunuchs and the bureaucrats returned to the foreground. Once free from the oppressive limits of Han Chien's power, their leading members again took sides among the governors. As neither the eunuchs nor the bureaucrats had any armies of their own, their struggle depended on borrowed strength. The eunuchs sought the support of the Kuan-chung and Ho-tung clique, while Ts'ui Yin, the leading bureaucrat, found support from Chu Wen. In this struggle the balance steadily shifted to Chu Wen's advantage.

The two important events which helped Chu Wen's extension of power were Li K'o-yung's loss of one of his provinces to Chu Wen and the mutinies in western Ho-nan by the T'ung-kuan Pass. The loss of his province exposed Li-K'o-yung's capital to Chu Wen's attack. The mutinies in western Ho-nan brought Chu Wen to the gates of T'ung-kuan Pass and within easy striking distance of the capital.

The shift in power was decisive at the court. Ts'ui Yin, with Chu Wen's support, was too powerful now to be moved. He used Chu Wen's influence to make the emperor kill a rival minister as well as the two eunuch commanders of the newly recruited imperial army. The other eunuchs were so frightened by this that they deposed the emperor five months later in 11th/900 and put up the heir-apparent instead. This was not done to oppose Chu Wen. In fact, they forged a letter from the deposed emperor offering Chu Wen the throne and a new dynastic line. They hoped that Chu Wen would accept them as part of the palace heritage and turn to them instead of the bureaucrats for help in the future. At the same time, they were so afraid of Chu Wen that they did not dare kill Ts'ui Yin, the one man who could have ruined their plans.

It was a desperate attempt, and the motives were so involved that no clear picture can now be drawn. The response of the three governors of Kuan-chung and Ho-tung is vague. The two in Kuan-chung seem to have supported the coup. What explanations the eunuchs gave them are not known. The governors certainly could not have agreed to the offer of the throne to Chu

Wen. As for Chu Wen, he was tempted by the offer, but the fact that the eunuchs had planned the coup made him decide against it. The coup lasted less than two months. On the 1/1st/901, with Chu Wen's backing, Chao-tsung was restored.

The last three years of Chao-tsung's reign were dominated by Chu Wen. . . . The position of the other military governors and their relations with the court can be briefly described. A process of elimination by war and diplomacy among themselves had reduced the number of independent governors. By 904 there were, north of the Yangtse, eight governors who held more than one province, and only four others still independent. During these years, there was no more than a formal reference to the emperor, for example, when providing an excuse for attacking another governor and when asking for the confirmation of a satellite governor of a newly conquered province. The court was also sometimes approached to arrange truces and negotiations in order to gain time for those concerned.

Only a few governors had direct access to the capital where they could make their demands felt. These, too, were reduced in number as they fought among themselves. In 904, there were only three left, with great differences in strength and in the number of provinces ruled. They were Chu Wen, Li K'o-yung, and Li Mao-chen. Table III for 904 may be contrasted with Table II for 883. The province numbers in Table II have been retained while four new provinces have been added.

The table shows how much stronger Chu Wen was compared with others and why he was able, in 901, to march into the Wei valley to get the emperor away from Li Mao-chen. It also shows why he could move the emperor to Lo-yang in 904, and there murder him.

Table III

I. *Territory under Chu Wên*
   a) *directly controlled by him or his men*

20 Pien *	court-chosen, 883
21 Hua (886) *	(court-appointed, 890)
23 Yün (897) *	(court-appointed, 898)
9 P'u (901) *	(court-appointed, 901)
25 Hsü (887)	appointed by Chu Wên, 904
18 Mêng (888)	appointed by Chu Wên, 903
19 Lo-yang (888)	appointed by Chu Wên, 904
27 Hsü (893)	appointed by Chu Wên, 904
22 Yen (897)	appointed by Chu Wên, 903
(35 Hsing (898) **	appointed by Chu Wên, 903)
(26 Ts'ai (899)	reduced to prefecture of Hsü)
17 Shan (899)	self-appointed, 899; (surrendered)
8 Hua (901)	appointed by Chu Wên, 904
1 Yung (901)	appointed by Chu Wên, 904
24 Ch'ing (903)	son of previous governor, 899; (surrendered)

   b) *satellite governors*

13 Chên (900)	son of previous governor, 883; (submitted after siege)
14 Wei (891)	son of previous governor, 898; (submitted after defeat)
15 Ting (900)	uncle of previous governor, 900; (submitted after siege)
(36 Chin (901) **	self-appointed, 899; (submitted voluntarily))

II. *The rest of North China*

   a) *under Li K'o-yung*

10 Ping	court-appointed, 883
(37 Chên-wu (893))**	Li K'o-yung's brother, 903)

   b) *under Liu Jên-kung*

12 Yu	appointed by Li K'o-yung, 895; rebelled in 897
16 Ts'ang (898)	Liu Jên-kung's son, 898

   c) *under Li Mao-chên*

2 Ch'i *	court-chosen, General of Imperial Guards, 887
4 Ching (899) *	(court-appointed, 899)
3 Pin (897)	Li Mao-chên's adopted son, 897
5 Fu (899)	probably also an adopted son, (?)
(38 Ch'in (890))**	Li Mao-chên's nephew, 903)

   d) *under Li Ch'eng-ch'ing*

6 Hsia	nephew of previous governor, Tangut tribal leader, 896
7 Yen (889?)	uncle of Li Ch'eng-ch'ing, 897

   e) *under Chao K'uang-ning*

28 Hsiang	son of previous governor who was an ex-Ts'ai rebel, 893
34 Ching (903)	Chao K'uang-ning's brother, 903

   f) *under Wang Chien*

30 I	court-appointed, General of Imperial Guards, 891
31 Tzŭ (897)	a distant relative of Wang Chien, 897
29 Liang (902)	Wang Chien's adopted son, 903

(Wang Chien also controlled four new provinces created out of the above three. These were mostly under adopted sons.)

   g) *under two other governors*

32 Yang	self-appointed, prefectural officer, 892; (also held Hsüan and parts of Hang province, both south of the Yangtse)
33 Ngo	self-appointed, leader of mutiny, 886

---

* = provinces under Chu Wên (I, a) and Li Mao-chên (II, c) themselves
** = new province

CH'AO-TING CHI

Key Economic Areas in Chinese History: From the Huangho Basin to the Yangtze Valley

The period of disunion from the fourth to the sixth centuries witnessed a tremendous change in the social-economic conditions of China. The "barbarian" settlers, as well as the rebellions of discontented Chinese peasants, drove a vast number of the Chinese landed class to the south of the Yangtze River. When the "barbarian" dynasties established themselves in the north, the Chinese refugees in the lower Yangtze valley prepared for a permanent stay. The result was the beginning of a period of rapid development of the fertile Yangtze Valley, which ultimately became the key economic area in China, replacing the lower Yellow River Valley in this regard. This shifting of the key economic area to the south brought about a sharp transformation of Chinese culture and ushered in the golden era of T'ang civilization.

In the following selection, Dr. Ch'ao-ting Chi (1904–1963) interprets the development of Chinese history from the standpoint of the economic base, or what he terms the key economic areas. According to his point of view, the premodern Chinese empire was an agricultural one in which the decisive factor of political control was based on control over the key economic areas. The shifting of these areas was caused mainly by the rise and decline in water-control development as well as in development of water-routes. Thus, a study of all the water-control activities in each period can illuminate the social and economic history of each age. Clearly, Chi's interpretation is based in general on Marxist assumptions and specifically on the theory of "hydraulic society" advanced particularly by Professor Karl A. Wittfogel and already mentioned in this book.

The fifty years of struggle between the Three Kingdoms (A.D. 221–265) which succeeded the Later Han Dynasty constituted the first period of sustained division in the semi-feudal epoch. Unlike other later periods of division which were complicated by the simultaneous occurrence of barbarian invasions, the period of the Three King-

From Ch'ao-ting Chi, *Key Economic Areas in Chinese History* (New York: Paragon Book Gallery, Ltd., 1963), pp. 96–133. Reprinted by permission of the publisher. Footnotes omitted.

doms was a typical case of division generated by the internal forces of Chinese society.

The material and fundamental factor responsible for such division was the rise of rival economic areas, whose productivity and location enabled them to serve as bases for a sustained challenge of the authority of the overlord who commanded the central or main Key Economic Area. In this case it was the increasing maturity of Shu, or the Szechwan Red Earth Basin, and the adolescent exuberance of Wu, the lower Yangtze Valley, that produced the balance of power politically represented by the Three Kingdoms.

Water-control and Szechwan

Shu, or Szechwan, began to acquire considerable importance in Chinese history after King Chao Hsiang (306–251 B.C.) of the state of Ch'in moved his people from Ch'in (Shensi) to colonize the territory. The colonization of Shu was accompanied by the construction of a remarkable system of irrigation which established the basis for the prosperity of the region. The honour of being the father of the irrigation system in Szechwan fell to Li Ping, the Ch'in governor, whose work has been considered an immortal achievement by Chinese historians.

The central work in the system was the Tuchiang Dam in the Kuan district which divided the Min River into two main streams, each of which branched out into many minor canals. The canals were primarily cut for purposes of transportation, but once cut, they were also extensively used for irrigation. "Small irrigation ditches amounted to hundreds of thousands," and the Ch'engtu plain thus was called "sea-on-land."

The benefit which the people derived from the Tuchiang Dam and the canals was not limited to transportation and irrigation. A stone tablet of the Yüan dynasty definitely states that "water power stations for polishing rice, milling, and spinning and weaving, numbering tens of thousands, were established along the canals and operated for the four seasons of the year."

It is no exaggeration to say that the Ch'engtu plain owes its fertility and economic self-sufficiency to this water-control system. Toward the end of the Earlier Han dynasty, Szechwan had also become sufficiently rich to enable Kung-sun Shu, military chieftain occupying the territory from A.D. 25 to 36, to defy, longer than any other rival group, Liu Hsiu's attempt to unify China. During the period of the Three Kingdoms it provided a base which allowed the Shu Han dynasty (221–265) to hold out against its enemies in North and Central China for nearly fifty years.

Primitiveness of Yangtze Valley During the Han Dynasty

Ssu-ma Ch'ien characterized the lower Yangtze valley, known as Ch'u and Yüeh, as a

> . . . large territory sparsely populated, where people eat rice and drink fish soup; where land is tilled with fire and hoed with water; where people collect fruits and shellfish for food; where people enjoy self-sufficiency without commerce. The place is fertile and suffers no famine and hunger. Hence the people are lazy and poor and do not bother to accumulate wealth. Hence, in the south of the Yangtze and the Hwai, there are neither hungry nor frozen people, nor a family which owns a thousand gold.

This remarkable account, which gives practically all the essential facts for judging the economic development of a region, clearly describes the Yangtze valley during the Han dynasty as a country with a small and scattered population living under a commercial economy, with a primitive agriculture, no exchange of goods, and little sign of class differentiation.

Professor Liu Yi-cheng's researches reveal that, during the Eastern or Later Han, in the region around Huangchow and Tean in Hupei province, and even in some parts of Anhwei, there were a large number of "Southern barbarians," a very primitive people. Even in the period of the Three Kingdoms many districts in Wulin (Changte in Hunan province) were still inhabited by "barbarians." Sun Ch'üan, the founder of the Wu dynasty (229–265), one of the Three Kingdoms, had to force the barbarian inhabitants of his kingdom to serve in the army to make up the shortage of soldiers in the small population.

There was, however, a sufficient number of settlers from the north who, carrying with them all the equipment of an advanced agricultural civilization, could take good advantage of the incomparable natural fertility of the Yangtze valley to establish an independent kingdom under the guiding hand of Sun Ch'üan, who forced the powers in the Yellow River valley and the Ch'engtu plain to treat the new State as their equal.

Water-control as a Weapon in the Three-cornered Struggle

Undoubtedly, military campaigns were the most spectacular aspects of the three-cornered struggle under the Three Kingdoms. But behind the military fronts much effort was spent, especially by Shu Han and Wei, on developing agricultural productivity and water transport as a means of strengthening their military power.

Wu's chief problem was shortage of the man-power needed to develop the virgin fertility of natural resources still within easy reach. History records, however, that the King of Wu, in 226, decreed the establishment of military agricultural colonies, in order to extend the area under cultivation and make up a grain shortage which was then a danger to the kingdom. In 245 the King dispatched his general, Ch'en Hsün, with 30,000 soldiers and workers to cut the Chüyung Canal connecting Hsiaoch'i and Yünyang (the modern Tanyang district in Kiangsu), and made the Ch'ihshan Lake, in the vicinity of Tanyang, for the purpose of irrigating rice-fields.

In Shu Han the brilliant minister, Chu-ko Liang, fearing that the grain supply from his base in Szechwan might be cut off, established military agricultural colonies on the southern bank of the Wei valley in 234, when his attempt to conquer the Yellow River valley was checked by the Wei armies under Ssu-ma Yi. Water-control public works are not expressly mentioned in the records, but taking into consideration the condition of agriculture in the regions involved, it is safe to assume that irrigation developed was an indispensable factor in military agricultural colonization.

In the case of Wei, irrigation as well as military agricultural colonization was carried out most extensively, and the records are most explicit in regard to the relation between the two. Diligent attention was also paid to the extension and improvement of the routes of water transportation. Both kinds of enterprise were, for obvious reasons, centred in the Hwai River Valley. The dams of the Shih Reservoir, the Ju Reservoir, the Seven Gates and the Wu Reservoir were repaired by Liu Fu at the order of Ts'ao Ts'ao, who appointed him governor of Yangchou. In 204 Ts'ao Ts'ao deepened the Pien Canal, cut the Sui Canal to connect the Pien Canal with the Hwai valley, and dammed the Ch'i River (in northern Honan) to force it into the Peik'ai Canal, in order to bring the grain products of Shantung to the centre of his domain in Honan. This was at a time when Ts'ao Ts'ao was engaged in a gigantic scheme of military colonization, storing up grain supplies and developing water-routes of communication. The achievement of the year 204 in the Hwai and Yellow River valleys was followed in the next year by the cutting of the P'inglu Canal in western central Hopei province to lead the water of the Hut'o River into the Sha River, and the Ch'üanchow Canal in central Shansi to use the water of the Lu River for transportation. Ts'ao Ts'ao's victory over the Wuhuan barbarians in the north was largely due to the two canals which were dug as a part of the preparation for this conquest. The Yang Canal in Honan province was cut in 219 to connect the Lo River with the Pien Canal for transporting tribute grain. In 233 the Ch'engkuo Canal which ran from Ch'ents'ang (Paochi district in Shensi province) to Huaili (Hsing-p'ing district in Shensi province) was opened. About the same time the water of the Yen and Lo Rivers was utilized by the construction of the Linchin Reservoir to irrigate about 3,000 *ch'ing* [1] of alkali land.

As pointed out by K'ang Chi-t'ien, these works must have been constructed on the initiative or under the direction of the great Wei general, Ssu-ma Yi, who at that time was defending Wei against the invading Shu Han force led by Chu-go Liang. Ssu-ma Yi was afraid of the military genius of his opponent, but he knew that the Shu Han army's chief weakness lay in its relatively inferior economic base. Therefore he refused to engage in direct combat with the enemy and tried to starve them out, conducting the war with spades, ploughs, irrigation canals, and reservoirs, rather than swords and spears. Chu-ko Liang, after failing to provoke his enemy to battle by all sorts of insults, had to use the same seemingly clumsy but highly effective weapons, and organized military agricultural colonies on the southern bank of the Wei River. Thus the war between Shu Han and Wei was turned into a contest of economic strength and endurance, and by evading the offensive strength of the Shu Han forces and putting his enemies at a great disadvantage, Ssu-ma Yi prepared the ground for the final conquest and the elimination of Shu Han.

Wei wisely adopted the tactics of facing one enemy at a time, and while bent on the conquest of Shu Han, peace and friendship were maintained with Wu. This political accord could be seen even in the field of irrigation development. History records that Chia Ku'ei, the Wei governor of Yü-chow (in Honan province), secured the co-operation of Wu and utilized tools which had been prepared for military purposes to construct a dam on the Ju River (in Southern Honan and Northern Anhwei), as well as to build a reservoir called the Hsin Reservoir, and to cut a transportation canal of over 300 *li*.[2] The canal, a monument of Wei-Wu friendship, was named the Chia-hou Canal.

However, the Wei-Wu partnership

---

[1] *Editor's note:* One *ch'ing* (100 *mou*) was equal to 12.1 English acres at this time.

[2] *Editor's note:* One *li* was equal to 433.56 meters at this time.

proved to be short lived. Even before Shu Han was completely subjugated, Wei made preparations to strengthen its economic base for the conquest of Wu. In 241, military agricultural colonies began to be established in the Hwai Valley; land under cultivation was greatly extended, canals were cut and transportation facilitated; and a large supply of grain was stored up.

In 243, after the campaign against Wu was opened, the army of Wei, under the command of the King himself, defeated the Wu general, Chu-ko Ke, by burning his accumulated supplies. The King planned to strengthen his own economic reserve even further, and made preparation for future campaigns by a further extension of the area under cultivation and a greater accumulation of grain. He ordered his ablest general, Teng Ai, to the territory from the west of Ch'en (the modern Hwaiyang district in Honan) and Hsiang (the modern Hsiangch'en district in Honan) to Shouch'ung (the modern Shou district in Anhwei). General Teng knew that, although the land in that region was good, there was not enough water to take full advantage of the land, and he proposed to cut a canal both for the purpose of irrigation and for transportation. The plan was approved by the King. Camps of sixty soldiers were stationed 5 *li* apart from each other for over 400 *li*, from the bank of the Hwai River, starting at Chungli (the modern Fengyang district in Anhwei province on the southern bank of the Hwai River) to the Pi River (entering the Hwai River at Chenyüan Kuan). The soldiers were both to cultivate the land and to defend the territory; they were also to engage in the work of repairing and widening the Hwaiyang and Peichih Canals. Water from the Yellow River was thus led from the north down to the reservoirs along the Yin, Hwai, and Tachih Rivers. Over 300 *li* of canals were dug both north and south of the Yin River, irrigating about 20,000 *ch'ing* of land.

Thus, "the south and the north of the Hwai were linked. From Shou Ch'ung to the capital in Hsüch'ang (the modern Hsüchou in Honan province) the noise of dogs and chickens in the fields of the government and of the soldiers, and on private farms, could be heard by each other, and the fields of one dove-tailed into those of the others. In times of military emergency in the south-east, when the great army sailed down to the Hwai and Yangtze valleys, there would be food and other supplies stored up and there would be no fear of damage by flood."

The system of irrigation thus established contributed greatly to the agricultural development of the Hwai valley. It represented the culmination of a whole period of energetic competitive increase in agricultural productivity for purposes of military struggle. It added a rich productive area to the kingdom of Wei, and, thenceforth, Wei became so powerful that the balance of power between the Three Kingdoms was resolved, and China was again united under one rule.

Hwai Valley as the Historic Battlefield

But the great military importance of the Hwai valley, which gave impetus to these remarkable water control developments, also prevented the people from enjoying the fruit of this development. It constituted almost a "permanent" check to the economic growth of the whole region between the Yangtze and the Hwai, despite its natural fertility and wealth.

History has it that "during the period of the Three Kingdoms, the region between the Yangtze and Hwai Rivers was a battlefield, and several hundred *li* were not inhabited. . . . It was only after Wu was conquered that the people returned to their homes." This indicates that the major part of the works of this period in the Hwai valley, as enumerated above, were not only built for military purposes, but had to be maintained by military force, and were therefore subject to the quick changes and wanton destruction that characterized all things military.

The military importance of the Hwai valley, unfortunately, was not limited to the period of the Three Kingdoms. Practically throughout Chinese history since the Ch'in dynasty (221–207 B.C.) the Hwai valley has been the battlefield between North and South, and in the intervals between wars it has always been guarded by military colonization.

"From the beginning of the Tsin to the beginning of the Sui (A.D. 265–589), Hwaiyin was guarded by military colonization; reservoirs and dams were constructed and kept in repair, and grain stored for emergencies. Tsu T'i (A.D. 266–321) protected Hwaiyin with 3,000 soldiers, who also worked on government land. . . . Hsieh Hsüan (A.D. 343–388) first colonized Hwaiyin, then Pei and Hsü; and when armed force and food were sufficient, he took the Fei River and proceeded to Loyang. Tsin also subdued Wu by military colonization of the region north of the Yangtze River . . . and military colonization, together with water-control improvements, was also established in the Hwai region during the Ming (1368–1644) dynasty."

The explanations given by various writers and officials of the military importance of the Hwai valley are illuminating. The Tsin (A.D. 265–420) official, Hsün Hsien (A.D. 321–358), says, "The old *Chen* (fort) of Hwaiyin is geographically a very strategic place. With easy communications by land as well as by water, it is a convenient spot to watch for a chance for conquest. The fertile country can be easily developed and colonized, and boats can cross each other's path in the transport of grain tribute and other products."

A Sung (960–1280) official and scholar, Hsü Tsung-yen, puts it even more categorically. He says, "Shanyang is a place over which the north and the south must fight. If we hold it, we can advance to capture Shantung, but if the enemy gets it, the south of the Hwai can be lost in the next morning or evening."

Tung Pu-hsiao of the Yüan dynasty (1260–1368) also said: "Hwaian is the throat between the north and south and the strategic point of Kiang and Che (Kiangsu, Anhwei and Chekiang). If it is lost, the Hwai valley cannot be protected. Now, millions of tons of tribute grain are transported yearly through Hwaian. If the throat is blocked, the capital [in the north] faces the danger of immediate death. Hence, weighty officials are appointed and military colonization established to guard the place."

The secret of this strategic importance was explained by the Sung (960–1280) official, Ch'en Min, who said, "Throughout the 2,000 *li* of the Hwai River, there are five rivers connecting it with the north, the Yin, the Ts'ai, the Ko, the Pien, and the Ssu Rivers; but there is only one avenue southward to the Yangtze, the canal which crosses the Hwai at Ch'u Chou."

Thus its geographic position destined the Hwai valley to the fate of a passageway between the north and south, a centre for military colonization and internal warfare. Under the circumstances, large irrigation constructions were easily reduced to ruins and no enduring constructive development was possible. By being offered on the altar of Mars, the Hwai valley lost the prospect of ever becoming a Key Economic Area, so long as the efforts of men could not change its unenviable position.

Settlement of Yangtze Valley During the Tsin Dynasty

The unity of China under the Western Tsin dynasty (265–317), which succeeded the Three Kingdoms, did not last long. Less than fifty years after its inauguration, the Tsin emperors had to retire to the south of the Yangtze River in the face of victorious rebellions on the part of the peasants in the northern provinces, who were in some districts the descendants of "barbarians" from what is now Chinese Turkistan and Mongolia, who had settled south of the Great Wall several centuries before. This period marks the change from Western Tsin to Eastern Tsin (317–420). In the forty-eight years of the Western Tsin, only two instances of irrigation development are recorded in the annals; the repairing of three canals in the Hwai valley in 274, irrigating 1500 *ch'ing* of land, and the opening up of over ten thousand *ch'ing* of irrigated land along the Chiang and Yü Rivers (in Honan province) in 280.

The transition from Western to Eastern Tsin and subsequent events in the interval before China was unified again under the Sui dynasty in 589 involved a tremendous change in the socio-economic history of the nation. The risings of "barbarian" settlers, who were mostly serfs working on land owned by Chinese "mandarin" lords, as well as the rebellions of discontented Chinese peasants, drove a vast number of Chinese of the upper classes, as well as retinues of their supporters, to the south of the Yangtze River. When the "barbarian" dynasties set up in their northern homes had lasted over a generation, hopes of regaining the northern domain were practically given up in the latter years of the Eastern Tsin, and the Chinese refugees in the lower Yangtze Valley prepared for a permanent stay.

The *Sung Shu* (the history of a minor dynasty, A.D. 420–479) relates the story of the migration in the Hwainan section. It says, "The central domain suffered disturbances, and the *Hu* barbarians frequently invaded the south. Most people in Hwainan, therefore, crossed the Yangtze River. At the beginning of the reign of Ch'eng Ti (326–342), Su Chün and Tso Yao revolted in Kiang-Hwai, and the *Hu* invaders again came in large numbers. Thus even more people crossed the Yangtze River [and migrated to the south]."

The conditions which these and other settlers had to face are set forth very clearly in the following account given in the *History of the Sui Dynasty:*

During the Tsin dynasty, from the time when Yüan Ti moved to the left of the Yangtze River on account of disturbances in the central domain, all those who voluntarily fled to the south were called immigrants. They established districts and prefectures and called them by the place-names of their native land. They scattered and moved about and did not settle at one place. And in the territory south of the Yangtze River [at that time] the custom was to fertilize the land by burning the vegetable overgrowth and, as the seeds were planted, flood the fields with water. The land was low and wet and the people did not save. . . . South of the mountain range, the central government gave official sanction to the authority of local chiefs over their subjects and in return exacted tribute from the chiefs, whose riches consisted of animals, kingfisher feathers, pearls, elephant tusks, and rhinoceros horns. Throughout the various southern dynasties of Sung, Ch'i, Liang, and Ch'en, the system remained unchanged.

It is interesting to compare this account with those quoted above in connection with the study of the kingdom of Wu in the Three Kingdoms. Evidently, the process of colonization in the Yangtze valley was slow, and despite the efforts of the authorities of Wu, the Yangtze Valley still remained sparsely settled and, on the whole, very primitive. The external stimulus of a tremendous social upheaval in the north, which was then still the heart of China, intensified by racial and cultural conflict, provided a powerful impetus as well as a pressing necessity for the Chinese people to settle and develop the south.

Such an impetus and necessity for migration had hitherto never been so keenly felt in the history of the Chinese people. The result, as will be seen, was the beginning of a period of rapid development of the fertile Yangtze valley, which ultimately made it the Key Economic Area in China, replacing the Ching-Wei basin and lower Yellow River Valley. This brought about a sharp transformation of Chinese culture, and ushered in the crowning maturity of Chinese civilization in the T'ang dynasty.

Water-works in Kiangsu During the Southern Dynasties

At the beginning of this southern migration, in 321, the Tsin minister, Chang K'ai, built the Chua and Hsinfeng Reservoirs, which irrigated 800 *ch'ing* of land. Ch'en Min excavated the Lien Lake in the same year. Both were located near the present Chinkiang district in Kingsu province, not far from the Southern bank of the Yangtze. The Lien Lake assumed considerable importance as a reservoir both for purposes of irrigation and transportation, and was repaired several times in practically every one of the succeeding dynasties. During the T'ang dynasty, any one who secretly cut open the dike of the lake without official permission was punishable by death.

These efforts to improve the conditions of agricultural production in the south of the Yangtze were continued after the Tsin under the four following southern dynasties, the Sung, Ch'i, Liang, and Ch'en. During the reign of Ming Ti (465–472) of the Sung dynasty, the Ch'ihshan Reservoir was built by order of the Emperor. Between 494–497 the Ch'angkang Dam was built by a minister of the Ch'i dynasty. Another Ch'i official petitioned the Emperor to open up 8,554 *ch'ing* of abandoned and new land in Tanyang and neighbouring districts. He estimated that 118,000 workers would be needed to work for one spring in order to construct the necessary dams and tanks. Unfortunately, the plan was not carried out, because the official in charge of the work was ordered to another post.

During the Liang dynasty, in 510, the Hsieh Reservoir was constructed; in 528, an imperial edict was issued ordering one of the officials to facilitate the transportation of grain through the Tatu canal; and in 535, the Chün Canal (now called the Liang Canal) was embanked.

During the Ch'en dynasty, the P'okang Canal was put in order. All of these water-control establishments were located in Southern Kiangsu province, where water-control in later years attained the highest development in China.

Forerunners of the Grand Canal

The development of water-routes under the Eastern Tsin dynasty was primarily undertaken for military purposes. During the reign of Mo Ti, from 345 to 361, in order to carry out a military campaign against Mu-yang Lan, who occupied Piench'eng (K'aifeng), a Tsin official ordered the construction of a canal to lead the water of the Wen River from the Huan River, a tributary of the Wen, to Tunga, in the present Yangku district of Shantung province. About the same time, Ch'en Min, who had made the Lien Lake, opened the Shanyang Yuntao (or Shanyang water-route) from Hsiehyang (near the Hsiehyang Lake) to Mok'ou (near Hwaian in northern Kiangsu); thus the avenue of communication connecting the Hwai River with the Yangtze, which was formerly a very devious route, was reduced to a straight line for the first time.

The importance of these two canals is due to the fact that they were both destined to become sectors of the Grand Canal, which was to play such a significant part in Chinese history in providing a vital link between the seat of political power in the north and the emerging new Key Economic Area in the south under the T'ang, Sung, Yüan, Ming, and Ch'ing dynasties.

The Economic Domination of the Yangtze Valley

The Yangtze Valley grew in importance as a productive centre during the Eastern Tsin (317-420), and the other southern dynasties (420-589), definitely assuming the position of the Key Economic Area from the time of the T'ang dynasty (618-907). Politically, the centre of gravity still lay in the north. The constant menace of nomadic invasion on the northern frontier emphasized the strategic importance of the northern provinces. Tradition and political inertia undoubtedly also contributed to the decision to keep the political capital in the north, from the Sui (589-618) to the Ch'ing dynasties (1644-1912), despite the shifting of the Key Economic Area to the south.

This anomalous situation rendered the development and maintenance of a transport system linking the productive south with the political north a vital necessity. The link was provided by the Grand Canal, which engaged the attention of the best minds of China for more than ten centuries, and demanded countless millions of lives and a large portion of the wealth of the country for its improvement and maintenance. Its history is closely intertwined with the whole history of irrigation and flood-control and the development of productive areas, and must be studied as an integral part of the unfolding of the whole process.

History of the Sui Grand Canal

Although traditionally the canal is ascribed to the genius and extravagance of Yang Ti (605-618) of the Sui, it was not built in one period nor by one emperor. Like the Great Wall, it was constructed in disconnected sections at different periods. Yang Ti of the Sui completed it by linking the various waterways running in a north and south direction into a connected system and adding long sectors both in the north and south.

The Grand Canal, thus completed, ran from Ch'angan, or Tahsinch'eng, utilizing the course of the Wei and Pien Rivers, across Honan province to Hwaian, and then turned southward to Kiangtu (Yangchou) and Kuachou, where it crossed the Yangtze River, and finally to Hangchou. Another sector, which branched out from the Hsin River, a tributary of the Yellow River in northern Honan and southern Shansi, terminated at Chochün, near the present Peiping. The Sui Canal, as a whole, was much longer than the present Grand Canal in mileage, and was a north–south as well as an east–west trunk line of communications. It comprised five distinct sections.

The evolution of the canal can best be studied by examining the history of the different sections. The section with the longest history is the Pien Canal, which bridged the distance between the Yellow River and the Hwai River. The date of the beginning of the ancient original canal, which was called Hung Kou, is unknown, but it must have been earlier than the Spring and Autumn period (722–481 B.C.). It was mentioned by the diplomat statesman, Su Ch'in, of the period of the Warring States (481–255 B.C.). Ssu-ma Ch'ien specifically mentions that after the time of the Great Yü "the Yellow River was lead south-eastward from Yungyang (in Honan province) by [the construction of] the Hung Kou Canal, and connected the feudal states of Sung, Cheng, Ch'en, Ts'ai, Ts'ao, and Wei. The Yellow River was thus brought to meet the rivers Ch'i, Ju, Hwai, and Sze."

When Wang Chün (206–285), during the Western Tsin dynasty (265–317), campaigned against Wu, the famous Tsin minister, Tu Yü (222–284), in a letter to Wang Chün, referred to his triumphant return with his troops from the Yangtze valley to the capital at Loyang, through the Pien Canal. Hu Wei (1633–1714), the great authority on historical geography in the Ch'ing dynasty, comments on the grandeur of Wang Chün's fleet and army, saying that they were the best and largest of their kind of history, and if they were able to return through the Pien Canal, "the size of the Pien River could not have been smaller than at present. It also shows that this water-route existed during the Ch'in, Han, Wei, and Tsin dynasties, and did not begin with Yang Ti of the Sui dynasty."

However, the old route was different from that of the Sui Canal of Yang Ti. The pre-Sui Canal, according to the able researches of the Japanese scholar, Sadao Aoyama, ran from east of K'aifeng, near the Ch'i River; while the Sui Canal, which was called the T'ungch'i Canal, followed a much shorter and more direct route. It started from Hsi Wan, near Loyang, by leading the Lo and Ku Rivers into the Yellow River; then from Panchu (in the modern Ch'ishui district in Honan province) it branched out from the Yellow River to run eastward in its own channel, and on approaching K'aifeng from the east, near the Ch'i district, it turned southward from the course of the old canal and entered the Hwai River directly at Szuchou without going through the Szu River.

Aoyama's conclusion agrees with that of the eminent Chinese Scholar, Ku Tsu-yü (1624–1680), author of the famous book, *A Historian's Notes on Geography*. It proves conclusively that the version of the T'ungch'i Canal printed in the *Maps and Gazetteer of Yuanho Chün and Hsien*, the *T'ai-p'ing Yü-lan* and the *Mirrors of History*, which mistook the old route for the new one, was wrong, and that the shorter route, flowing directly into the Hwai without going through the Szu River, as described in the "Biography of Yang Ti" and the "Book on Food and Commodities" in Wei Cheng's *Sui History* and the *T'ung Tien* is correct.

The Pien Canal, or T'ungch'i Canal, which was also called the Yü River, was constructed in 605, and over a million men and women from the prefectures to the south of the Yellow River and north of the Hwai were mobilized for the task. An imperial road was constructed along the bank of the canal and planted with willows. The canal not only combined the navigation facilities of the Yellow River and Hwai River into one system, but wove the tributaries of both rivers into a network of water-routes, covering a section of the North China plain which historically is most important. The economic and military significance of the Pien Canal in Chinese history needs no exaggeration.

The second section of the Grand Canal, which was called the Shanyangtu during the Sui dynasty, ran from Mok'ou, near Hwaian, on the bank of the Hwai River, southward to Kiangtu (Yangchow), thus providing a link between the Hwai River and the Yangtze. The ancient canal bearing the name of Han Kou was dug by King Fu-ch'ai of Wu (495–473 B.C.) in 483 B.C. The original channel ran to the east of the present course, and winding its way through a chain of lakes, especially the Hsiehyang Lake, it was as devious as it was hazardous.

During the reign of Mo Ti (A.D. 345–361) of the Tsin dynasty, the mandarin Ch'en Min cut a more or less straight canal from Hsiehyang to Mok'ou, following a course to the west of the old one, and reducing the distance. It was called the Shanyang Yüntao or Shanyang water-route.

In the time of the Sui dynasty, the canal was silted up, but its course could still be traced. The founder of the Sui Dynasty, Wen Ti, restored the canal in A.D. 587 "to facilitate the transportation of tax grain." In 605, Wen Ti's son, Yang Ti, also ordered improvements of the canal. Over 100,000 inhabitants of the territory south of the Hwai River were mobilized for the work. "From Shanyang (near Hwaian) to the Yangtze River, the water surface of the canal was forty paces wide. Roads were constructed along both banks of the canal and planted with elms and willows. For over 2,000 *li* from the eastern capital (Loyang) to Kiangtu, shadows of trees overlapped each other. A place was built between every two *Yi* [official post stations], and from the capital in Ch'angan to Kiangtu there were more than forty palaces [built to facilitate the travels of the Emperor]."

The length of the Shanyang Tu was over 300 *li*. Traversing the dividing line between North and South China as it did, the key importance of the canal can be easily appreciated. The territory traversed by the canal was the main battlefield between North and South China. For centuries, before railroads changed the situation, the great strategic value of the city of Hwaian, guarding the northern terminus of the canal, was over and over again demonstrated by history, clearly indicating the crucial position which the canal occupied.

The third section of the canal, known as the Kiangnan Ho or River South of the Yangtze, was dug by the order of Yang Ti in 610. It extended "eight hundred *li* from Ch'inkou (Chinkiang in Kiangsu province) to Yühang (Hangchow in Chekiang province). The water surface measured over ten *chang* (about 100 feet)." This section, which completed the southern terminus of the Grand Canal, enabled Yang Ti and his successors for centuries to tap the wealth of the south-eastern coast of China.

The three sections discussed in the foregoing paragraphs covered the distance from Hangchow to Loyang, which was established as a supplementary capital, called the Eastern Capital, by Yang Ti. Loyang was linked with the capital, Ch'angan, by the Yellow River and the Wei River, but navigation on the Wei River was often obstructed by heavy "flowing sand, which subjected the river to sudden changes." This difficulty was avoided by the digging of a canal which could use the water of the Wei for navigation. A complete version of the edict which directed the construction of this canal has been preserved and contains very interesting material:

[People and goods] from five directions converge at the capital [at Ch'angan] which surrounded on four sides by mountain passes and fortresses, faces difficulties in communication by land as well as by water. [Happily] the currents and waves of the Yellow River flow eastward and hundreds of streams facilitate communication for ten thousand *li*. Though there are dangers below the Three Gates (Sanmen), they can be avoided if cargoes are transferred on land at Hsiaop'ing; and after entering Shen (Shensi) by the land route, they could be put back on water and pass from the Yellow River to the Wei River. The Yellow River also dominates the [communications] of the Fen River valley and the territory of Tsin (Shansi). Boats and carts come and go; the benefit [of easy communication] is certainly great. But the force of the water of the Wei changes often, and when the water becomes shallow and sand thick, it obstructs navigation. The distance this river covers only amounts to a few hundred *li*, but when it changes its condition, boats cannot pass and the labour of the men is interrupted.

My rule over the country is dedicated to the promotion of beneficial things and the removal of the harmful. I regret defects both in the realm of public and private life. Therefore, starting from T'ungkwan in the east and leading the water of the Wei from the west, a canal should be cut by human effort. The work is easy and can be accomplished. Artisans and workers have already looked over the site at my order. Adopting the canal to geographical conditions and considering the meaning [and requirements] of permanence, once the canal is cut, it will not be destroyed for ten thousand generations. It will enable the government and private persons to navigate big boats, and from dawn to dusk, grain tribute can be transported ceaselessly upstream and downstream. [Thus] the work of several tens of days would save hundreds of millions. I know that in the hot summer, work easily brings fatigue; but without temporary labour, how could permanent rest be made possible? Proclaim this to the people; they should know my wishes.

The canal which ran from Ch'angan to T'ungkwan was 300 *li* in length and was named the Kwangt'ung Canal. With the completion of this canal, direct water-route communications were established between Ch'angan and Hangchow.

The fifth section of the Grand Canal branched out from the Hsin River, a tributary of the Yellow River in northern Honan and southern Shansi, and ran northward to Chochün (Cho district in northern Hopei). "Over one million men and women from the various prefectures north of the Yellow River were mobilized by imperial edict to undertake the task." Ssu-ma Kuang (1019–1086), in relating the story, added that "men failed to supply the demand, and women began to be used." The canal was completed in 608 and was called Yungchi Canal. It provided a direct link between the Hai Ho basin (Hopei province) and central Yellow River valley, and the Yangtze valley and Ch'ien-t'ang basin, and afforded a direct means of communication from Hangchow to the vicinity of the present city of Peiping.

The Waterway System of the Sui and T'ang Dynasties

In examining the five sections of the Sui Grand Canal as a whole, it is important to note that, except for the two sections from Hangchow to Hwaian which more or less provided the basis of the present Grand Canal, the route from Hwaian northward was entirely different from the present course. The present Grand Canal was primarily the work of the Yüan dynasty (1280–1368) which, for the first time in Chinese history, selected Peiping or Peking as its capital. The Sui Grand Canal was frequently restored and, in places modified during the T'ang (618–907) and Northern Sung (960–1127) dynasties; but on the whole, the system remained practically the same until the Yüan dynasty. . . .

The Cause of the Unpopularity of Large Public Works Construction in China

Sui Yang Ti's extravagance and cruelty were proverbial in Chinese history, and the Grand Canal was frequently cited as a glaring example illustrating both of these tyrannical qualities. However, these historical facts were gradually used by historians, who considered it their thankless task to admonish rulers against becoming tyrants, as lessons in morality. The moral approach of the Chinese historians prevented them from understanding the political meaning of Yang Ti's achievements as well as his crimes.

It is important to realize that, despite the disappearance of a strict caste system in China, the Chinese state was frankly based upon the theory of class rule, and class rule meant the concentration of surplus resources, very often including a large proportion of the necessities of life squeezed from the people, as an instrument of power and to satisfy the extravagant demands of the ruling group. The concentration of resources demanded canal building and canal building in turn demanded a further concentration of resources, which invariably lead to excessive taxation and a cruel and large-scale programme of forced labour.

A convenient system of communication, following the completion of the canals, naturally stimulated the consuming habits of the ruling groups and further enhanced their extravagance. This inevitable connection between public works development and the increase of exploitation and mass misery explains the great unpopularity of Han Wu Ti and Sui Yang Ti, both very energetic and enterprising monarchs, whose achievements in the field of public works development, including canal building and promotion of irrigation, resulted in public discontent and financial disaster in the one case and loss of the empire in the other.

Had Han Wu Ti not stopped in time by proclaiming his famous "confession" and programme of retrenchment, the rule of the Western Han dynasty probably would have ended a hundred years earlier. Sui Yang Ti, on the other hand, as a clever Chinese critic puts it, "shortened the life of his dynasty by a number of years [by his extravagance in public works construction], but benefited posterity unto ten thousand generations. He ruled without benevolence, but his rule is to be credited with enduring accomplishments." It is only necessary to add that practically all enduring accomplishments of the government in the semi-feudal era in China were tainted with lack of benevolence on the part of the rulers and plenty of misery for the masses.

Large-scale public works, like the construction of the Grand Canal, require a mass-mobilization of labour. In the absence of a developed money economy and a free labour market, this meant forced labour assembled and disciplined by authority of the state. Under the conditions of a semi-feudal class society, this cannot be done without cruelty, and the degree of cruelty necessary is usually in direct proportion to the magnitude of the work involved. The exaggerated degree of cruelty resulting from the gigantic scale of the work on the Grand Canal has particularly attracted the attention of historians. A detailed account of labour considerations in the construction of the Pien Canal, the longest section of the Sui Grand Canal, can be found in *The Record of the Opening of the Canal*, by an anonymous author, which contains the following interesting paragraphs:

All men between the ages of fifteen and fifty were ordered to assemble by royal edict. All who tried to hide were punishable by decapitation. . . . The labourers thus assembled numbered 3,600,000. Then each family was required to contribute a child or an old man, or woman, to prepare meals for the workers. Five thousand young and brave soldiers were ordered to be armed with sticks [to maintain discipline]. Together with section chiefs and other administrators, the whole number of people employed in the canal amounted to 5,430,000. . . .

At the beginning of the eighth month of the fifth year of Ta-yeh's reign (609 A.D.), baskets and shovels were put to work; the workers were spread over several thousand *li* in a west–east direction. [After a certain sector of the work was done], when the workers were counted, two million and a half labourers and twenty-three thousand soldiers had been lost.

When the work was all done, . . . the Emperor moved from Loyang to Taliang (K'aifeng) and ordered the various prefectures in the Yangtze and Hwai area to construct with the speed of fire five hundred large boats [for imperial use]. Some families among the people to whom had been assigned the duty of contributing one boat, could not fulfill the order, even by sacrificing the whole of their property. They were punished by flogging and neck weights and were forced to sell their children to satisfy official demands. After the dragon boats were completed, they were sent to Taliang (K'aifeng) for decoration. From Taliang to Hwaikou (perhaps, Hwaian) the boats were lined up one after another, for a thousand *li*. Wherever the silken sails passed, their perfume could be smelled for a distance of a hundred *li*!

The source from which the above quotation is taken, *The Record of the Opening of the Canal*, is considered unreliable by the Ch'ing Imperial Catalogue, because of its "vulgar style," and is regarded as a sort of fictionized history. However, though it may not be accurate in detail, the cruelty of forced labour which it describes is a commonplace of Chinese literature. Even if it gives but a vague indication of the conditions of forced labour, it serves the purpose of contributing to a clearer understanding of the oppressive and unpopular aspect of public works construction in semi-feudal China.

The T'ang Dynasty's Dependence on Kiangnan

However, despite the great suffering which the opening of the Grand Canal must have caused, it provided a link between the two major regional divisions of China, and with its help the capital could successfully tap the resources of the fertile Yangtze valley. Once the Yangtze valley was thus accessible from the capital, a fresh impetus was provided for its rapid development. With its tremendous potentialities released, it soon became the chief producer of grain tribute for the capital, and assumed the position of the Key Economic Area. The *New T'ang History* reveals that

T'ang established its capital in Ch'angan. But, although Kwanchung was known as a fertile country, the territory was too crowded and its products could not support the capital and accumulate reserves to prepare against flood and famine. Hence grain tribute from the south-east was transported.

Dependence on the south increased to such an extent that by the time of Han Yü (768–824), the great writer, the land tax of Kiangnan had already reached the alarming proportion of nine-tenths of the total land tax of the country.

Small wonder that the task of transporting grain tribute assumed greater and greater importance. From the time when Pei Yao-ch'ing (681–743) made his successful contribution to the problem, it became customary to expect leading officials at court to undertake the responsibility of dealing with the transport of tribute grain. Outstanding administrators of the T'ang regime, such as Liu Yen (715–780), were well known for their achievements in this line.

In comparing the T'ang dynasty (618–907) with the Han dynasty (206 B.C. to A.D. 221), which had struggled primarily with problems of transport in the Yellow River valley, it at once becomes obvious that the T'ang administrators were faced with new technical, social and administrative problems, the solution of which was one of the most important contributions of the T'ang dynasty to the history of China. The Sui emperors dug the canal, but the dynasty did not endure long enough to solve the other problems of transport. It was the T'ang dynasty which laid the foundation of the grain transport system between the north and south of China. In three years, during P'ei Yao-ch'ing's administration, about 735, seven million tons of grain were transported. The magnitude of the system involved can easily be imagined.

The problem of transportation involves not only the handling of the transport service, but also the maintenance and improvement of the waterways. The two tasks were tackled jointly by the T'ang officials. In the nineteenth year of K'ai Yüan (731), P'ei Yao-ch'ing (681–743) proposed to establish granaries at Hokou and Kunghsien in the present province of Honan, so that "the boats from Kiangnan would not have to enter the mouth of the Lo River." He also suggested to make use of the granaries at half a dozen places along the water-route for the purpose of facilitating transportation, so that when the waterways were navigable the boats could operate, but whenever the water was too shallow the grain could be stored to avoid loss.

The proposal was adopted three years later, in 733, when a granary was established at Hoyin, where the Pien Canal entered the Yellow River. Two granaries were also built along the course of the Yellow River on the southern border of Shansi, one at each side of Sanmen, the "Three Gates," the stone barrier in the bed of the Yellow River which made navigation extremely dangerous. By using the two granaries, boats could be unloaded at the east side of Sanmen and their cargoes transported by land for 18 *li* (6 miles) and stored in the other granary, to await another convoy of boats for further transport. Thus the dangers of Sanmen, the horror of centuries, were avoided. In the same year, Chi Kan, the governor of Yungchow, opened the Yeiko River, reducing the distance of 60 *li* from Yangtzehsin to Kuachou to 25 *li*.

These improvements culminated in the monumental achievement of Liu Yen, who upon his appointment in 764 as Transport Commissioner of the Yangtze and Hwai Rivers, deepened the Pien River, which was then silted up, and adopted with improvements the system suggested by his predecessor, Pei Yao-ch'ing. Special boats were constructed to suit the different conditions and floating capacities of the various sections of the canal. The Kiang or Yangtze boats were to reach Yangchou, the Pien boats to reach Hoyin, and the Ho boats to reach the mouth of the Wei. The Wei boats would finally carry the cargoes to the Ta Ts'ang, the great granary at the capital. Transit granaries were established along the rivers and canals to facilitate changes of boats and to provide for bad navigation conditions which might necessitate waiting.

The system proved to be safe and efficient and with its help and his own genius for administration, Liu Yen attained the record of over thirty years of uninterrupted service, a very remarkable achievement for his time. Thus in Liu Yen's handiwork culminated the system which "later administrators followed."

Rise of Water-control Works During the T'ang Dynasty

[There was a] sudden rise of irrigation activities in the T'ang dynasty in practically all the provinces except Honan. To follow the method . . . of enumerating all the major works constructed would be superfluous. Ancient irrigation and transport works were fewer in number and were of greater historical importance in shaping the development of the system; hence the different works have been separately enumerated above and the story of the construction of some of them told. Many of the T'ang works were reconstructions of old systems. New works, however, particularly in the south, were numerous, but for the purpose of the present investigation need not be treated individually and in detail.

A feature of the history of the T'ang works which deserves special attention is the fact that according to the great Ch'ing scholar, Ku Yen-wu (1613–1682), seven-tenths of the water-control works recorded in the "Book of Geography" in the *New T'ang History* were constructed before the reign of T'ien Pao (742–756). When it is recalled that T'ien Pao was the reign-style of Hsüan Tsung, after the rebellion of An Lu-shan which plunged the country into years of civil war and destruction, and reduced the financial power and prestige of the T'ang dynasty to a fractional part of its former dimensions, the decline in water-control activities after that period is easily understandable. Ku Yen-wu was right in suggesting that perhaps, after the war, the government, busily engaged in pushing the collection of taxes, had no time to devote to such constructive labour as the encouragement of agriculture and the improvement of waterways.

Neglect of Water-control in the North

The swampy jungle-covered Yangtze valley of ancient China must have offered infinitely greater obstacles to the early settlers than the northern steppes and Huangho or Yellow River delta. But once development began on a large scale, as it did after the great migratory movement of the Eastern Tsin, the potentialities of the region were so great and the return on labour and capital so tempting, that it easily began to outstrip the older and more civilized North.

During the Sui and T'ang dynasties the rate of progress was greatly enhanced by the construction of the Grand Canal, and the South at this period definitely caught up with the North. The North, however, was not entirely neglected at first. The fact that the T'ang arose as a northern dynasty, and that the political inertia which caused the North to be looked on as the centre of gravity of Chinese life was still strong during the T'ang Dynasty, prevented the North from falling in disfavour for some time, despite the dominant economic position which the South had already attained.

The result of the continued care for the North can be seen from an edict issued in 720, which describes Kuanchung as a country where "fertile land spread before one's view and ditches and canals run into each other; where grain is stored in the granaries, and the capital area yields irrigation benefits worth an ounce of gold for each *mu.*" But with the decline of the T'ang and the disturbances of the Five Dynasties (907–960), accompanied by great devastation, particularly in the northern provinces, signs of neglect began to appear. As the Sung dynasty emerged from the struggles in 960 and reunited China, the shift of emphasis became even more evident. This tendency can be clearly seen . . . from the figures below of public works undertakings in the major provinces.

It is significant that even under the Northern Sung, when the Sung dynasty still ruled the whole of China (960–1127), more attention was paid to the development of the South than that of the North.

Sub-regional Divisions in the Yangtze Valley During the Period of the Five Dynasties

But the Yangtze Valley during the T'ang, although contributing a large proportion of grain tribute, had not yet reached a mature stage of development as a consolidated economic area. The topographical character of the country is indicated by the remark of Professor [George B.] Cressey that "all of China south of the Yangtze is a land of hills and mountains."

These hills and mountains cut the region into six distinct sub-regions which made unity difficult under the level of economic development at that time. Barring Szechwan and Yunnan and the two Kwangs (Kwangtung and Kwangsi), whose character as economically self-sufficient and independent regions persisted to a much later date, the four areas that were practically independent regional units were natural geographical regions.

Each of the four regions provided a base for an independent state following the dismemberment of the T'ang dynasty. The T'aihu and Ch'ient'ang valley (present Chekiang and southern Kiangsu) was occupied by Wu Yüeh (907–977). The Hwai valley and lower Yangtze valley (present northern Kiangsu, Anhuei and Kiangsi) was the seat of the dynasty of Wu (907–937), which was later succeeded by Nan-T'ang (937–975). Fukien was for some time the territory of the state of Min (907–945), while the present Hunan province and part of Hupei once comprised the state of Chi (907–922).

Thus, while practically the whole Yellow River valley was dominated by the "Five

Northern Provinces

	Shensi	Honan	Shansi	Chihli
T'ang	32	11	32	24
Northern Sung	12	7	25	20
Kin, contemporaneous with Southern Sung	4	2	14	4

Southern Provinces

	Kiangsu	Chekiang	Kiangsi	Fukien
T'ang	18	44	20	29
Northern Sung	43	86	18	45
Southern Sung	74	185	36	63

Dynasties," in succession (907–960), the Yangtze valley, though economically greatly developed during the T'ang dynasty by water-control undertakings, had not yet advanced far enough to overcome natural and historical barriers between the various independent and self-sufficient constituent units.

In other words, the Yangtze valley, which had contributed a large proportion of the grain tribute under the T'ang dynasty, had, as a whole, in contrast with the Huang Ho or Yellow River valley, assumed the position of the Key Economic Area; but the history of the fifty-three years of the Five Dynasties indicates that the Yangtze valley was still composed of very loose units which had not yet grown into one closely knit homogeneous area. During the period of the Three Kingdoms (221–265), the Yangtze valley had been still too superficially touched by civilization to be territorially differentiated into large, distinct and powerful component areas. After the Sung dynasty, which ended with the Mongol Conquest in 1280, the whole valley, except Szechwan, was sufficiently developed, in regard to communications as well as cultural homogeneity, to allow the major part of the territory to be woven into one regional unit. It is significant that since the Sung dynasty there has been no sustained division in China.

The two outstanding periods of sustained division in Chinese history not primarily caused by invasion were the period of the Three Kingdoms and the period of the Five Dynasties. To state the problem from the standpoint of the economic base, or the Key Economic Area, the former period was due to the rise of rival areas which weakened the relative economic supremacy of the dominant area, while the latter was the manifestation of the fact that the most productive area had not yet become one unit, so that its internal differentiation weakened its potential power.

Thus, during the latter period, the less productive but more homogeneous and organized area, the Huang Ho or Yellow River valley, maintained its dominant position, though it failed for decades to subjugate the South. The Posterior Chou (951–960), the last of the Five Dynasties which occupied the Huang Ho valley, reinforced its economic position by many constructive enterprises, especially water-control works. These achievements strengthened the economic and therefore the military power of the man who succeeded the Posterior Chou dynasty, Chao K'uang-yin, and helped him to bring China once more under one rule and to found the dynasty of Sung.

But the Sung did not persist very long as a united power in China. Wave after wave of Tatar invasion drove the Sung power southward. This contributed greatly to the completion of the development of the Yangtze valley under the technical resources then available. The Yangtze valley toward the end of the Southern Sung was essentially the same as the Yangtze valley on the eve of modern industrialization.

V

LATE IMPERIAL CHINA:

A.D. 960—ca. 1795

E. A. KRACKE, JR.

Sung Society: Change Within Tradition

Traditionally, the Sung dynasty has been viewed as a weak dynasty whose achievements were concentrated in the fields of philosophy and the arts. Only recently have students of history discovered that this period was very significant in the history of Chinese urbanization. In the following selection, Dr. E. A. Kracke, Jr., Professor of Middle Chinese Literature and Institutions at the University of Chicago, vividly describes the tremendous social changes in the Sung period, from the tenth century to the thirteenth. The main goal of Professor Kracke's article is not to explain why the process of urbanization after the thirteenth century failed to go further than it did, but to analyze why the forces of change gathered momentum in the Sung period.

There was a long and continuous process of social development in medieval China. The movement can be traced back through the later period of disunion from the fourth to the sixth centuries. It started with the great migration movement from the northern plains to the Yangtze Valley and the areas along the southeast coast. This striking shift in the population was accompanied by a shifting of key economic areas to the new, rich delta lands of the south. The impact of these changes on every aspect of Chinese life was enormous. Among the new features of the social and economic structures were tremendous growth of commerce, particularly maritime commerce; emergence of new cities and large urban centers; and the rise of a money economy.[1]

The impact of urban growth on the evolution of Chinese culture was also varied. Two developments stood out: As cities stimulated new popular cultural activities, the art of printing flourished. At the same time, new, highly popular literary forms emerged, including stories from which popular novels later grew.

From *The Far Eastern Quarterly*, Vol. 14, No. 4 (Aug. 1955), 479–88. By permission of *The Journal of Asian Studies*. Footnotes omitted.

[1] For a recent comprehensive study of all aspects of the commercial, industrial, and urban development of Sung China, see Shiba Yoshinobu, *Sōdai shōgyō-shi kenkyū* (Commerce and Society in Sung China; Tokyo, 1968). This monumental work analyzes almost every aspect of the changing face of Sung China. An English abstract, entitled *Commerce and Society in Sung Society*, was published in 1970 by the Center for Chinese Studies at the University of Michigan, Ann Arbor, Michigan. See also James T. C. Liu and Peter J. Golas, eds., *Change in Sung China: Innovation or Renovation?* (Boston: D. C. Heath, 1969); Laurence J. C. Ma, *Commercial Development and Urban Change in Sung China (960–1279)* (Ann Arbor, Mich.: Department of Geography, University of Michigan, 1971).

In concluding, Professor Kracke points out that, contrary to general impression, the traditional Chinese social pattern could be significantly modified through the operation of internal forces under favorable conditions.

When we speak of social change in China we most often have in mind one or the other of two pictures. The first is the change that we see today, when radically new ideas, techniques and forces from foreign countries have shaken the traditional social order, altering the old patterns rapidly and sometimes violently. The second picture is that of the dynastic cycle, a concept that we have inherited from the traditional Chinese historian, sometimes adding a few embellishments of our own. The political fortunes of a ruling house are often reflected (and perhaps affected) by a characteristic cycle in the whole political and economic order of the nation: from successful adjustment and control to maladjustment and chaos. The end of each cycle, if we focus our attention only on these factors, leaves Chinese society much as it was at the end of the cycle before. But this perspective tends to omit qualitative changes that occur in Chinese society on a different plane.

The kind of social change to be considered now differs from both of these. It is the long and continuous process of social development that in China as in our own civilization has accompanied the interplay between the traditional ideas and ways of life and the new concepts, techniques, and patterns of activity that evolve at home or enter from abroad. While at times this process of development moved slowly, and at times even retrogressed in some respects, the Chinese way of life nevertheless underwent through the centuries a cumulative alteration that was essentially irreversible. At times the forces of change so interacted that their gathered momentum was almost revolutionary in its social impact. An outstanding example of such rapid and far-reaching change is supplied by the Sung period, from the tenth century to the thirteenth.

The beginnings of the movement that attained so dramatic a tempo in the Sung period can be traced back, in some respects, through several centuries. Perhaps the first clearly perceptible aspect of the movement is the striking shift in the mass of China's population, from the northern plain country to the valleys of the mountainous south and the southeast coast. This migration had begun in the early centuries of our era, impelled both by economic difficulties and by foreign invaders of the old homeland; but as late the middle of the eighth century the Yangtse valley and the areas further south still held only some forty to forty-five percent of China's people. By the end of the thirteenth century this area reported no less than eighty-five to ninety percent of the nation's population, and no less than twenty percent were established in the valleys of Fukien and eastern Chekiang along the southeast coast.

The rich new delta lands of the South became the chief suppliers of China's granaries. Some of the economic consequences of this are already well known, and need only be recapitulated here. To feed the armies guarding the northern border, and to provision the capital in the North, the central administration undertook to expand the canal system and subsidiary land communications from the South on a mammoth scale. Aided by the new facilities, private commerce grew rapidly. The Chinese now living along the remote southern coast no doubt found it necessary to import tools and other goods from the older settlements, and exchanged for these the new products native to the semi-tropical land in which they found themselves, as well as products from the South Seas and the countries of the Indian Ocean. Easier contacts by sea with Persia and Arabia encouraged the growth of foreign commerce, soon bringing to the growing coastal cities settlements of Hindu and Arab merchants. The Chinese also . . . turned to the sea and assumed a leading place among maritime peoples. Internal commerce among the regions of China, at first confined for the most part to luxury items for the few, now expanded in variety and in its significance for larger groups of the nation.

With the growth of inter-regional trade, money came into its own, for many purposes rapidly superseding the old transactions in kind. By the eleventh century, a system of regulated paper currency was in operation, and the coinage of copper money reached proportions never again approached in Chinese dynastic history. Facilities for the transfer of funds and the provision of credit also developed. The various regions of China were no longer self-sufficient economically, but increasingly specialized in their produce—foods or goods or services— and therefore interdependent. These developments brought into being, by the eleventh century, a Chinese economy apparently far more complex than any of earlier times.

Of the social change that accompanied this economic development we have as yet only a very incomplete picture. But certain of its aspects stand out strikingly in the records. One aspect—perhaps of key significance—is the changing role of the great city. In earlier periods the few outstanding cities had achieved their greatness and economic importance only after designation as national capitals. Their symmetrical and regular plan, centered on the principal imperial palace, gave visible evidence of their origin and purpose. From the tenth century to the thirteenth this was not so. In this later period the cities chosen as capitals had already achieved importance as trade centers at strategic points on the lines of communication.

K'ai-feng, the first Sung capital, exemplified this particularly well. Originally a regional administrative seat at a main transfer point on the arterial canal from the South, its access to southern rice supplies recommended it during the troubled years succeeding the T'ang. The city had grown with its commercial importance, as successive new walls inclosed the suburbs that grew spontaneously beyond the older city gates. Within the sixteen-mile circuit of the outer walls, space was at a premium. The second Sung emperor renounced the planned expansion of his palace because it would have forced the demolition of private dwelling quarters. As a result of this history, although the city lay in the level valley of the Yellow River, it lacked the symmetry that had marked earlier national capitals and would later distinguish Peking (also primarily political in its character).

The later Sung capital of Hang-chou was also an important trade center at the time of its political elevation in 1135. Its population was huge: the numbers within its walls during the later years of the dynasty have been estimated as 900,000, and those in its suburbs as some 600,000 more.

While the capitals of the eleventh to thirteenth centuries had thus grown strongly commercial in character, their supremacy among Chinese cities was challenged by other urban centers still more reliant on business activity. By the year 1100 at least four urban areas far surpassed the capital area in population. We have no exact data on the numbers living within the walls of these cities or in their immediate suburbs, but census reports suggest that each of the urban areas held a million or more people within the borders of its prefecture—a space very roughly comparable to the greater metropolitan areas of London or New York. Such population concentrations would seem to out-distance by far the largest urban agglomerations of that time in Europe, even by the largest estimates of the latter.

During the next two centuries the urban growth continued, and in several instances the prefectural populations apparently doubled, tripled, or quadrupled by 1290. Among the most dramatic increases, three were on the southeast coast (Hang-chou, Su-chou, and Fu-chou), and one (Jao-chou) near the inland trade route from the Yangtse to Canton. The prefecture of Fu-chou in 1290 reported approximately 3,875,000 people, suggesting an urban concentration of impressive proportions.

It was just around this time, soon after the Sung downfall, that Marco Polo visited these places as an agent of the Mongol conqueror Kubilai. His descriptions of the magnificence of Hang-chou, the capital, and of the trade metropolis Ch'üan-chou, are well known. But he also observed another phenomenon that is suggested by contemporary census figures—the growth and multiplication of smaller cities and towns. In describing the journey from Hang-chou to Fu-chou (less than three hundred miles as the crow flies), he tells of no less than six "large, noble, and beautiful" or "noble and great" cities, and in the stages of his journey between these he notes no less than seven times "always finding cities and villages enough, very beautiful and very great"; on one two-day ride he remarks that these are "so frequent and continuous that you seem as you ride to go through the middle of a single city." Allowing for the colorful exaggerations we must permit to this oldest of China-hands, the regions that Polo saw along the southeast coast must certainly have been advanced in urban development compared with his native Italy—the most urbanized part of Europe in that day. While most of the terrain was mountainous and poorly adapted to farming, the few lands available had been fully exploited. A Sung writer notes that intensive cultivation had transformed once worthless acres to the most fertile in the empire, and while Marco Polo refers occasionally to the livestock he saw (oxen, buffalo, cows, goats, swine, and fowl) and to certain special plant products, he speaks not of fields but of "fine gardens."

But rich as the fields were, they were still too few. The coastal regions still depended for their prosperity on the income from their mines, commerce, manufactures, tea, and sea produce, and beyond the narrow valley floors must have preserved some of the air of an unsettled borderland. On four stages of his journey Polo mentions the "hunting and chase enough of beasts and birds" and refers as many times to the great and fierce "lions" (tigers?) that molest travellers, to such an extent that in one part of the route at least "it is very dangerous to pass through those regions unless people go in great numbers." In an area seeming thus sparsely settled over much of its extent, and developing rapidly in industry and trade, typifying the new trend, it is difficult not to suspect analogies with the frontier of opportunity that played a vital role in the development of our own civilization.

Who were the people that lived in the growing cities of this area? We have no clear picture of them, but there are at least some clues to their character. As in earlier times, there must have been a considerable number of civil and military officials, stationed there for limited terms by the central government, along with a more or less permanent corps of clerks and official underlings. There were the army garrisons usually stationed in all large places. There were no doubt well-to-do scholars without official employment, and poorer scholars who lived on their earnings as teachers, or from such miscellaneous employments as public letter-writing or story-telling. And there were the merchants and artisans, great and small, blending at the lowest economic level with the unskilled laborers. Considering the indicated sizes of the cities, the last three occupations must have constituted the preponderant group of inhabitants in most cases. The composition of the Sung populations cannot have differed too greatly from that observed by Marco Polo only around a decade after the dynasty's fall: in all his comments on the six larger cities he saw between Hang-chou and Fu-chou, and in four of his comments on the places between, he notes that the inhabitants "live by trade and by crafts," and implies mercantile activities indirectly by repeated references to the "abundance of all things for life," which he notes were very cheap. (To other activities he makes very little reference.)

Surviving records tell us of the merchants' activities and mode of life chiefly at the capitals, but in these respects too different regions may have presented a rather similar picture.

The merchants, artisans, and providers of services were organized in guilds, which had powers of discipline over their own members, although these organizations had no apparent role in the general administration of the cities. The guild members had to some extent emancipated themselves from the close official supervision that existed during the T'ang. Their business activities were no longer confined within the great walled markets, or limited to the hours in which the government permitted the opening of the market portals. Commerce and manufacture were now carried on in shops scattered throughout the city or beyond the city gates, though establishments of the same trade tended to group together.

Long and persistent governmental efforts to regulate trade and control prices were matched by equally persistent and largely successful evasion on the part of the merchants. Attempts of the state to monopolize certain profitable industries had been costly and only partly successful. But in the Sung the state had learned to apply its taxes more flexibly and to restrict its monopolies to certain key operations of an industry; through such policies the state diverted what was perhaps the lion's share of the profits to its treasuries.

Such state controls may well have retarded significantly the growth of commercial activity and power. At the time, however, there must have been little evidence of this. The more successful merchants accumulated great wealth, and their style of living vied with that of the imperial princes. Sumptuary laws had always, before this, restricted the colors that should be used by each class of society. By 995, however, sumptuary laws were unenforceable, and all were repealed but the ban on a certain shade of deep purple reserved for the imperial house and the highest officials. There is evidence that even this color was taken over by commoners within a few years. We read that the families of great merchants wore pearls and jade. Their carriages thronged the roads, and in the words of a contemporary "rubbed hubs with those of distinguished families." In the T'ang, we are told, even a servant who had served in an aristocratic family scorned a master who haggled in person with a merchant. By the eleventh century, even important officials had discovered the attractions of commerce, and many augmented their income by combining business operations with their official journeys. Merchants were socially accepted in elite circles. Through such connections, or through their wealth, some of them secured government office, and served in positions of some importance.

But the professional trader still found certain barriers to his social advancement. He still lacked the approval of more conservative scholars. His indulgence in luxuries elicited complaints very much like those that had been evoked by a more modest commercial expansion a millennium earlier. His pursuit of money was felt to be unworthy. The officials criticized his disposition to make profits by cornering the market; because this was at the expense of the poor—and no doubt because the official preferred that the state monopolies should garner such profits. The grumbling of the conservatives, however, may have been in itself another indication that power of commerce was recognized as a potential threat to the supremacy of the bureaucrat; in fact, specific complaints of the growing influence that merchants exercised over officials are not lacking.

The new social environment created by the cities surely had its impact on the evolution of Chinese culture. The operation of any but the simplest business naturally required at least a certain minimum of literacy, and the city environment gave better opportunities for even the poorest to gain a smattering of the written character. The successful and ambitious tradesman would naturally hope that education would win for his sons an entree into the bureaucracy. When the new urban reader competed with the older scholar for written texts, a new demand for books was created. In the century after 950 the technique of wood engraving, long used to multiply Buddhist charms and texts, suddenly found new uses, and in a short time the art of printing was applied to practically all the existing varieties of literature.

For the relatively unlettered, a multiplicity of entertainments was also devised, ranging from troops of acrobats and displays of fireworks to puppet shows, shadow plays, and simple theatrical presentations. Through the stories that served as themes for such public performances, some parts of the sophisticated culture could reach the illiterate, and facilitate a sharing of the great tradition with larger groups. Particularly important in this respect was the role of the story-teller: unemployed scholars frequently made their living by recounting some of the dramatic episodes of history to audiences in the market place. Through the prompting-books some of them wrote to aid their confreres, they created the prototypes of the later great fictional themes. At the same time the old themes were presented in the language of the people and transmuted to appeal to a more popular audience, until the content itself reflected their viewpoint and their tastes. It could scarcely be accidental that the Chinese popular novel traces back to this period.

The influence of the new city life also had its impact on society beyond the city walls. The growing importance of a money economy must surely have contributed a significant share to the increasing complications of the farm problem. The crops of different regions were becoming more specialized, leaving the farmer often less self-sufficient and more vulnerable in years of crop failure. While the farmer probably relied little on the cities for his basic necessities, it seems that travelling merchants from the cities already came to the country fairs to sell such things as salt, and buy for the city market. The glamor of the city had its weakening effect on the old rural patterns of life in other ways. The wealthy peasant, we are told, tended to emulate the merchant's style of living, and we hear repeatedly that the rewards of commerce tempted the poor farmer to abandon the hard and often unrewarding work on his lands, sell his farm implements, and engage in trade.

Finally, we must note the change that came about in the bureaucratic class itself. It was also in this period that new recruitment procedures opened a governmental career to far wider numbers than before. Competitive recruitment examinations were regularly used from the beginning of the eleventh century on a scale far greater than ever before. Improved through the development of elaborate techniques to make the examinations more objective, the new system helped to break the power monopoly once held by a small group of northern aristocratic families. The social origin of the newcomers who replaced them is not entirely clear. The broader distribution of opportunity was certainly made possible by the increase in literacy and the wider availability of books that we have already noted. Several hundred candidates commonly passed the final stage of the triennial examinations, and we are told that for each of these some hundred candidates had attempted the local preliminary tests. The competition was wide indeed. But the fiercest rivalry and the most numerous successful candidates during most of the dynasty came from the southeast coast, where we have seen the rapid pace of urbanization at this time.

How many of these men came from the great cities? How many traced their educational opportunity to families of ultimately mercantile origin? It is still impossible to say. But data from two lists of graduates that have come down to us from the twelfth and thirteenth centuries show that the regions with more and larger urban concentrations tended to supply not only more graduates in proportion to their area, but also more graduates per family, so that they clearly dominated the field. Moreover the largest proportion of apparently new blood tended to appear in the circuits of most rapid population growth, if we may judge from the numbers of graduates counting no officials among their direct paternal forebears. Conspicuous among these regions of growing population were again those containing the great coastal cities and those on the main inland trade routes. We have here, then, a seeming link between the broadening social base of the bureaucracy and the social mobility that probably characterized the great cities in their period of most rapid expansion.

The political importance of this changing character of the bureaucracy is obvious. Its cultural effect, while less tangible and less calculable, was perhaps none the less real. For while the Sung was a time of beginnings for the more popular literary forms, it was also a time of great vigor, and in some ways a time of culmination, in the intellectual activities practiced or patronized by the bureaucrat: the fine arts, the more sophisticated literary forms, and critical scholarship. In government, it was a time of imaginative reform schemes and experiments. It saw great advances in several fields of technology. In all of these realms the contribution made by men of the Southeast was outstanding.

Thus we have evidence that a genuine alteration of Chinese social patterns accompanied the rise of the great city. The influence of the city extended beyond the bourgeois to the farmer and the bureaucrat. Despite the inhibiting pressures of official conservatism, and at times in disregard of laws and decrees, the merchant had expanded his influence and breached many of the barriers that surrounded him when the period of change began.

The limits of his rise are also apparent. If he achieved a place in government, it was by transforming himself into a bureaucrat; as a merchant he still enjoyed no active political role. The professional official remained supreme, and steadfastly unsympathetic toward the development of private economic interests.

The history of Chinese urbanization after the thirteenth century, and the reasons why the movement failed to go further than it did, are beyond the scope of the present topic. As we contemplate the situation of the thirteenth century bourgeois, however, it is difficult to discern any single insuperable barrier to his further social rise. Most of his disadvantages were also faced by some at least of his European confreres during the later Middle Ages or the Renaissance. In the thirteenth century, the Chinese bourgeois had demonstrated by his will and his resourcefulness that under favorable conditions, the traditional Chinese social patterns could be significantly modified through the operation of internal forces.

JAMES T. C. LIU

Reform in Sung China: Wang An-shih and His New Policies

The Sung dynasty stands out in the history of China as a period of significant reform movements, of which the ultimate goal was an ideal moral society. The scholars of this period were so much involved in these movements, whether for or against them, that there seemed a collective awakening of social consciousness among them. Here the finest Confucian tradition that the scholar should take on the responsibility of ordering the society was exemplified. Al-

Reprinted by permission of the publishers from James T. C. Liu, *Reform in Sung China*. Cambridge, Mass.: Harvard University Press, Copyright 1959 by the President and Fellows of Harvard College. Footnotes omitted.

though almost all reforms failed in practice, later generations have always looked upon the Sung scholars as a source of inspiration.

In the following selection, Dr. James T. C. Liu, Professor of Chinese History at Princeton University, discusses one of the most controversial statesmen and reformers of the Sung period, Wang An-shih (1021–1086). Wang and his ill-fated reforms (1069–1085) have been the subject of heated debates for centuries. Those who opposed him have had a tendency to view him as a Legalist, or at least as a misguided Confucianist who had strayed in the same direction as the Legalists. This judgment was not entirely without foundation; however, prejudices against a radical reformer have also contributed to the opposition.

With fair-mindedness, Professor Liu attempts to present a clear picture of how Wang An-shih came to power and of the nature and content of his reform. He observes that the basic difference between Wang's radical idealism and the conventional Confucianists' belief lay in Wang's emphasis upon the bureaucracy, the government-initiated institution that had always been identified by Confucianists as a symbol of Legalism. Contrary to conventional Confucianists' emphasis on individual officials, Wang stressed the importance of the bureaucracy for reaching a perfect social order. Yet, precisely on this point Wang failed, for he did not obtain strong enough support from the bureaucrats, upon whom he depended principally to carry out his new policies.[1]

The need for reform was recognized time and again in Chinese history, yet comprehensive programs of reform always seemed to generate overwhelming opposition. Professor Liu suggests that at the heart of the problem were the attitudes of the bureaucracy itself.

In the long course of Chinese history few men stand out as prominently as Wang An-shih (1021–1086), the extraordinary reformer and most controversial statesman of the Northern Sung. The unconventional nature of the reform he introduced, the sweeping manner in which it was carried out, and the broad scope it encompassed were almost without precedent and were certainly without parallel until the last century. The specific reform measures, collectively known as the *hsin-fa,* have sometimes been referred to in translation as the New Laws. This translation, however, is unduly restrictive in meaning. The reform measures actually went far beyond the mere promulgation of new laws. They also included the establishing of new systems that brought about institutional changes. Perhaps they can be better described by the term New Policies, a more comprehensive designation which is closer to the facts.

Since Wang has already been made well known through the studies of the Ch'ing

---

[1] For other views on Wang An-shih and his reforms, see John Meskill, ed., *Wang An-shih: Practical Reformer?* (Boston: D. C. Heath, 1963). A more recent comprehensive study of the problem is made by Japanese scholar Higashi Ichio, *Ō Anseki shimpō no kenkyū* (A Study of Wang An-shih's New Policies) (Tokyo, 1970).

scholar Ts'ai Shang-hsiang and of such modern scholars as Liang Ch'i-ch'ao, K'e Ch'ang-i, H. R. Williamson, and several others, there is no need here to give more than a brief account of his life and his reform measures. Wang was a native of Lin-ch'uan, in the prefecture of Fuchou, in the modern province of Kiangsi, an area of rising national significance toward the middle of the Northern Sung period, with its increasing number of leading poets and essayists, esteemed scholars, and statesmen. Wang's family prospered in farming at the time of his great-grandfather. Turning to scholarship, it produced in the next three generations no less than eight holders of the doctorate degree (chin-shih), including Wang himself. Wang's father was a minor official who took his immediate family with him while serving in various local government posts. After his death in 1039 his family did not return to their native place but remained in Kiang-ning, modern Nanking.

Wang An-shih had a strong personality. As a young scholar with deep convictions he tended to choose only a few close friends with similar ideals, usually from the southern areas, specifically from Kiangsi and Fukien. This same tendency persisted throughout his life.

Wang's career began uneventfully. From 1042, when he earned his doctorate, until 1060, he chose to serve in local government posts not very far from Nanking—Yangchou in modern Kiangsu, Chenhsien in modern Chekiang, Suchou in modern Anhwei, and Ch'angchou, also in Kiangsu. He declined the opportunities to serve at the court that would have advanced his career but would not have enabled him to discharge his family and financial responsibilities. Nevertheless, his reputation spread as his scholarship became well known and his administrative ability was proven, especially in connection with irrigation works and financial measures. It was during his early career that he presented to Emperor Jen-tsung, in 1058, his "myriad word memorial" (wan-yen-shu). Though this memorial had no immediate consequences, it became the cornerstone of Wang's political theory, the basis of the reform which he later introduced, and a famous document in the history of Chinese political thought.

Wang's name gradually came to the attention of several high officials of varying political opinions. Through their repeated recommendations came offers of promotion; but he persistently refused them, always on the plea of family considerations. Not until 1060 was Wang finally prevailed upon to serve in the capital. After a brief term as a minor official in the Finance Commission (San-ssu), he was rapidly promoted, first to serve at the Imperial Chi-hsien Library and then to be a special drafting official of the Secretariat (Chih-chih-kao). These positions were among the ones regarded as "pure and respected offices" (ch'ing wang kuan), offices far removed from the "impure" duties involving financial or legal matters; but the holders of these positions were readily accessible to the emperor, not so much in connection with their administrative responsibilities as in the capacity of consultants, a capacity greatly respected by tradition. Such offices were generally reserved for highly recommended and promising scholar-officials.

Wang's advancement was soon interrupted by his observance of the mourning period for his mother from 1063 to 1066. Returning to government service in 1067, he became the governor of Nanking. It seemed as though he would long remain, of his own choice, in local government positions, but destiny dictated otherwise. A new emperor, Shen-tsung, succeeded to the throne in 1067.

An alert and forward-looking man, he sought advice. Upon the recommendation of Han Wei (1017-1098), a former tutor of the Emperor, Wang was summoned to the court in early 1069. The Emperor was so impressed with him that he made him the second privy councilor *(ts'an-chih-cheng-shih)*, a key position in which Wang was responsible for general administration. The Emperor accorded Wang unusual respect and trust and supported the reform which he instituted shortly thereafter.

Many important events and sweeping changes were crowded into the next few years when Wang was in power. Extensive irrigation works were undertaken on the Chang River, the Pien River and a section of the Yellow River, all mainly in the region around the Sung capital or in the modern province of Honan. Successful military campaigns were carried out in the northwest (the modern province of Kansu) around 1072; in the southwest (the modern province of Hunan) in 1073; and in the south (in repelling an invasion from Indochina) in 1076. All of these efforts and accomplishments were certainly noteworthy, but here we shall concentrate on the numerous reform measures that were instituted and that deeply affected government operations and institutions, as well as the livelihood of the people. The following enumeration classifies the New Policies by areas in order to indicate the points of emphasis, and also the points at which complaints and opposition developed. Many of these problem areas, of course, are interrelated and overlap.

Planning of state finance

1. Establishment of the Finance Planning Commission, in the second month of 1069, to study and recommend the reorganization of state finance.

State financing for farmers

2. The Farming Loans, the so-called Young-Shoots Money, instituted in the ninth month of 1069, to be extended to the farmers upon sowing and to be repaid with interest at harvest time.

State revenues and maintenance

3. Tribute revenues. The Tribute Transport and Distribution System, introduced in the seventh month of 1069, governing the transportation, exchange, selling, and buying of the tributary items normally sent to the government from the provinces, in order to anticipate government needs and stabilize prices.

4. Local government maintenance. The Hired-Service System, made effective for the whole nation, after experimentation in the capital, in the tenth month of 1070, assessing a graduated cash tax to pay for the hiring of necessary personnel to render services for the local government, which had previously been carried on by rotating assignment of corvée duties.

5. Maintenance of local order. The *Pao-chia* System, introduced in the twelfth month of 1070, organizing rural inhabitants in basic units of ten families or more, to assume collective responsibility for community policy duties.

6. Land tax. The Land Survey and Equitable Tax, effective in the eighth month of 1072, aiming at the elimination of tax evasion and unfair burdens, especially in the northern areas.

National defense

7. The basic measure. The *Pao-chia* System and its eventual use to raise army reserve units, by a system akin to conscription.

8. Other improvements. The Horse-breeding System, beginning in the fifth month of 1072, assigning a horse with fodder to each family in frontier regions in the north and the northwest; establishment of the Directorate of Weapons, in the sixth month of 1073, to improve the quality of weapons, and other minor measures to strengthen military defense.

Currency

9. Removal of the ban on private shipment and handling of copper, in the seventh month of 1070, and increased government mintage of copper coins on several occasions to meet the demand created by the expanded state financing and the requirements of cash tax payments.

Trade

10. State Trade System, introduced in the third month of 1072, by which the government purchased commodities directly from the smaller merchants and extended loan facilities to them so that they did not have to deal through the guilds. Through this system the government intended to stabilize market prices.
11. Guild Exemption Tax, effective in the ninth month of 1073, a cash assessment of the various guilds, which were thus exempted from the customary burden of contributing supplies to the palace.

Education and civil service

12. Education. Reorganization of the National Academy (sometimes translated as the National University), in the ninth month of 1071, so that it would eventually replace the examination system; establishment of new classes there and schools elsewhere in the capital for training in such specialized fields as military science, law, and medicine; and also the establishment of many prefectural schools, especially in the northern areas where promotion of education has been lacking.
13. Examination system. Placement of emphasis on problems, policy discussions, and interpretations of the classics, rather than on poetry and rhymed prose, in the regular doctoral examinations, beginning in the third month of 1070; and the instituting of law as a new field among those of the lesser degrees.
14. Appointment to offices. Introduction, in the third month of 1073, of a test in law for the holders of the doctorate degree, sponsored candidates, and other persons eligible for appointment.
15. Government clerks. Clerks who had no official rank put on a salary basis, in the twelfth month of 1070, and placed under strict supervision with due punishment for misconduct; also, meritorious clerks promoted to minor officials, after passing a test.

In taking charge of state affairs as the leading court minister and in introducing his New Policies, Wang's greatest difficulty was lack of cooperation among the majority of the bureaucrats. Opposition to his policies came from many prominent officials: to mention but a few, Han Ch'i (1008–1075) and Fu Pi (1004–1083), the venerated elder statesmen who had earlier been responsible for the first, but minor, reform of 1043–1044; Ou-yang Hsiu (1007–1072), another elder statesman who had previously recommended Wang; Lü Kung-chu (1018–1089), a leader among the politically prominent families who had raised and befriended Wang; Ssu-ma Kuang (1019–1086), a greatly respected scholar-official who commanded the support of many conservatives in the northern areas; the Su brothers, Su Shih (1036–1101) and Su Ch'e (1039–1112), the brilliant leaders from the southwestern area of Szechwan; and even Cheng Hsia (1041–1119), who had studied under Wang and supported him at the beginning of the reform. But the widespread opposition deterred neither Wang nor the Emperor. Wang, promoted to first privy councilor (*t'ung chung-shu men-hsia p'ing-chang shih*) in 1071, continued to exercise a dominant influence at the court and persuaded the Emperor to demote his outspoken opponents one after another.

A decisive turn in Wang's career came with his temporary resignation from the court in 1074. The famine in the northern areas aggravated whatever sufferings the people had endured under the reform system. The opposition renewed their attacks with increased vigor, and the Emperor was deeply shocked when Cheng Hsia presented a memorial that gave a dramatic "portrait of the refugees" *(liu-min-t'u)* from the famine areas. At the same time, the State Trade System and the Guild Exemption Tax created discontent in the capital city of K'ai-feng which led the palace people, principally the Empress Dowager Hsüan-jen, and the eunuchs, to warn the Emperor against Wang. Wang's feelings and pride were greatly injured, and he resigned. The Emperor, who still had considerable confidence in him, made him the governor of Nanking, with the honorary rank of titular councilor. On the other hand, the Emperor for the first time expressed some uncertainty about the reform by ordering the temporary suspension of certain controversial measures and asking for frank criticism of them.

Wang was not long absent from the capital; he was restored to his leading place at the court in less than a year, in early 1075. However, his second term in power found him in a much weaker political position than before. Many of his recommendations no longer met with the ready approval of the Emperor. His two principal associates were demoted and left the court, having incurred his displeasure: Tseng Pu (1035–1107) for having exposed, against Wang's wishes, the faults of the state trade system and the guild exemption tax, and thus indirectly contributing to Wang's earlier resignation; and Lü Hui-ch'ing (1031–1111) for having sought to undermine Wang's influence during his absence from the court. The men to whom he now turned for support were much less experimental and, worse, far less trustworthy. The reform continued, but so did the persistent opposition to it. Wang himself became depressed, particularly after the death of his only and much beloved son, Wang Fang.

The Emperor finally allowed Wang to retire in the winter of 1076.

In retirement Wang devoted himself principally to the writing of a book on etymology, *Tzu shuo*. The Emperor honored him highly by making him the Duke of Shukuo, and he had the sustaining satisfaction of seeing his reform system continue without major change for another nine years, until the death of Emperor Shen-tsung in 1085 brought the reform to an end. Wang died the following year, greatly saddened by the sudden turn of the political tide which demolished his reform system.

To complete this brief narrative, one must go beyond the reform phase of 1069–1085 to the antireform of 1085–1093 and the postreform of 1093–1125. The antireform phase occurred under the regency of Empress Dowager Hsüan-jen. One after another, many of the New Policies were rescinded or drastically revised. Prominent reform supporters were formally denounced as the members of an undesirable faction *(tang)*. Even some of the conservatives, like Fan Ch'un-jen, Su Shih, and Su Ch'e, who objected to the swing to the other extreme, were out of favor. The death of Ssu-ma Kuang, who led the conservatives at the beginning of this phase, left the power in the hands of Lü Kung-chu, Lü Ta-fang (1028–1097), and Liu Chih (1030–1097). Their common dislike of the New Policies did not prevent them from disagreeing on other matters and dividing into personal cliques.

The postreform phase began in 1093, when the Empress Dowager died and Emperor Che-tsung took up the reins of government. He recalled to power those who had supported the New Policies, led by Chang Ch'un (1034–1105), Wang An-shih's son-in-law Ts'ai Pien, and his brother Ts'ai

Ching (1046–1126). Most of the New Policies were revived and several were extended in application to additional geographic regions. A revengeful political persecution on a large scale sent hundreds of the conservatives to humiliating local government posts far away. One notable exception to the prevailing political climate occurred in 1100 when Emperor Che-tsung was succeeded by his brother Hui-tsung. Tseng Pu, the only one of Wang's early associates to regain some measure of leadership, introduced a policy of reconciliation and unity by naming the reign "Establishment of a Middle Course" (Chien-chung) and by recommending some conservatives to high offices, in the hope of ameliorating factional antagonism. Unfortunately, this short-lived policy failed to please the other leaders of the postreform or to appease the embittered conservatives. The one who successfully contrived to secure domination over all the rest was Ts'ai Ching. He remained in power, with only brief interruptions, for nearly a quarter of a century, from 1101 to 1125, just two years before the invasion of the Chin army ended the Northern Sung dynasty. Under him the political persecution intensified, corruption increased, and the government administration deteriorated in many ways. The reform went down in history in bad repute as a result of the earlier complaints against it, the unceasing denunciation of the conservatives, and significantly, the criticism that it led directly to the notorious postreform that was identified with the fall of the dynasty.

. . .

This reappraisal has shown Wang An-shih as a bureaucratic idealist who upheld the ideal of a professionally well-trained and administratively well-controlled bureaucracy as the principal instrument for the realization of a Confucian moral society. It has also described him as an institutional reformer, who endeavored not only to change government institutions but also to found new ones in order to guide and shape the behavior of both bureaucrats and the people. Wang's principal emphasis was not upon the promulgation and enforcement of law. Nor did he believe the objective of "enriching the state and strengthening the army" to be of prime importance. His ultimate goal was to improve the social customs of the people, looking toward a perfect social order. For these reasons, he and those who agreed with him at the time, as well as those who admired him in later centuries, denied that he was a Legalist. However, the majority of conventional Confucianists believed that the emphasis should be placed upon individual officials rather than upon the bureaucracy. To them, what Wang meant by regulatory systems—or in our words, government institutions and government-initiated institutions—were of the same nature as law. Consequently, they considered Wang a Legalist or at least a misguided Confucianist who had strayed in the same direction as the Legalists. In all fairness, in terms of the theoretical justifications upon which Wang based his views and in terms of his ultimate goal of a moral society, we may still regard Wang as essentially a Confucianist. He was of course a radical Confucianist, but radical only in comparison with many conservative Confucianists.

Since his idealism was basically bureaucratic, Wang always put the interests of the state, as he interpreted them, above everything else. He did not develop a clear definition of his objectives in terms of their effects upon the various social classes. He thought he was helping the majority of the population; yet the improvement of the state finances which the New Policies brought about was probably far greater than the benefits they brought to the people. While the bureaucratic families and large landowners complained about some features of the New Policies that were objectionable to them, many medium-sized landowners and other less well-to-do people had their share of complaints on other grounds. In short, Wang's policy was neither clearly nor firmly built upon a well-defined social basis.

In Wang's view the bureaucracy was especially important. Yet, precisely on this point he failed, for he did not obtain strong enough support from the bureaucrats. He did not even succeed in inspiring a sustaining loyalty among the executive type of bureaucrats, upon whom he depended principally to carry out the New Policies. What the New Policies did achieve was lost when some of these bureaucrats degenerated into the manipulative type. Furthermore, Wang was theoretical in policy matters rather than practical in politics. He gave far more attention to administration than to the winning over of his opponents, as for example, of the southwestern moderates, who opposed him less vehemently than did the northern conservatives. Thus, though he emphasized the importance of the bureaucracy, he did not really carry the support of the bureaucracy at all.

The bureaucracy performed its service through the government's operations and here Wang's program ran into additional difficulties: growing absolutism, increasing centralization with its attendant danger of power manipulation, greater conformity which was neither politically nor administratively desirable, and the gradually expanding but ever incorrigible clerical sub-bureaucracy which did not carry out the policies as intended. From the reform, through the antireform, to the postreform, these difficulties became steadily greater, to a degree never anticipated by Wang.

China was a bureaucratic state. Wang was indeed outstanding, if not exceptional, in his emphasis upon utilitarian statecraft, upon the bureaucracy, and upon the government institutions and government-initiated institutions. Since his approach did not succeed, the only alternative seemed to be that of conventional Confucianism or what, from the Southern Sung period on, was respected as orthodox Confucianism. Yet this latter approach stressed the moral qualities and the moral influence of the bureaucratic class and disregarded utilitarian policies and manipulative attitudes toward the state machinery.

One cannot help asking whether such a moralistic approach was sufficiently realistic. Did it not gloss over the facts of life in a bureaucratic state and thereby inhibit later Chinese thinking about political institutions?

W. THEODORE DE BARY

A Reappraisal of Neo-Confucianism

Just when Confucianism was in danger of becoming stagnant and stereotyped, T'ang and Sung scholars began their work of systematically instilling a new life into the Confucian school. Sung philosophers, particularly, not only rationalized the Confucian doctrine but also incorporated into it the best of Taoism and Buddhism. Thus they succeeded in formulating a system of thought that has occupied the inquiring mind of the Chinese people until the forceful introduction of Western ideas in modern times.

The rejuvenated Confucianism has been called Neo-Confucianism. Begun in the T'ang dynasty, the movement culminated in the Sung dynasty, represented by Chu Hsi (1130–1200), and continued to the Ming period, represented by Wang Yang-ming (1472–1529). Its impact on early modern China, and to a certain extent also on modern China, was overwhelming. It has since dictated the direction of the intellectual, moral, political, economic, and social lives of the Chinese.

In view of the enormous significance of Neo-Confucianism, its reappraisal is an important task for historians both of the premodern period and of the modern spectrum. The following selection is a major exemplar of this pursuit.

Unlike many other scholars who have been concerned primarily with the metaphysics of Neo-Confucianism, Dr. William Theodore de Bary, Horace Walpole Carpentier Professor of Oriental Studies at Columbia University, has reviewed major Neo-Confucian thinkers in the light of political milieu. Because Ching-shih *(statecraft) has been the major goal of intellectual pursuits and the main focus of living of the traditional Chinese intelligentsia, de Bary's approach is more meaningful and in the end more fruitful. The founding of Sung Neo-Confucianism has been traced to Hu Yüan (993–1059) and Sun Fu (992–1057), as compared to Chou Tun-i (1017–1073), generally recognized by scholars as the chief progenitor of the Confucian revival in the Sung. Both Hu and Sun were acknowledged in their time as the leaders of the Confucian renaissance, presiding over the outstanding private academies where they taught the Confucian classics as guides to moral life rather than as mere texts to be studied for the civil service examinations. The efforts of Hu and Sun were a significant part of the Neo-Confucian movement: returning to the Confucianism of Confucius and redefining the goal of the life of a Confu-*

Reprinted from *Studies in Chinese Thought* by Arthur F. Wright, ed., by permission of The University of Chicago Press. © 1957 by Robert Redfield. All rights reserved. Footnotes omitted.

cian intellectual. To illustrate the further development and impact of this line of the Confucian revival, Professor de Bary gives a revealing analysis of the reform efforts—political programs of such leading Sung Confucian scholars as Shih Chieh (1005–1045), Fan Chung-yen (989–1052), Ou-yang Hsiu (1007–1072), and Wang An-shih (1021–1086). The article succeeds in bringing out some of the main features of the Confucian revival in the Sung, to show what its adherents originally held in common and on what basic issues they ultimately diverged.[1]

From the earliest times Confucianism has been concerned primarily with the problems of men living together. Even questions of individual ethics, upon which it has said much, have been approached largely with a view to political and social requirements. This is because its spokesmen in classical times directed their teachings to prospective officials and because Confucianism in various forms has represented a state creed or cult for centuries. Yet study of the Confucian tradition after the classical period has tended to overlook the development of its political and social doctrines and their relation to those teachings which became the official orthodoxy through incorporation into the civil service examination system. This has been especially true of that vast intellectual movement which was launched in the early years of the Sung dynasty, during the eleventh century A.D., and which continued to exert a preponderant influence in China down to modern times.

There are several reasons for such neglect of this important aspect of Chinese thought in later centuries. The new metaphysical, psychological, and ethical theories of the Sung period, together forming the basis of what we now call "Neo-Confucianism," have been of more lasting significance, since they transcend the time and place of their creation. That Western students of Chinese thought should have been attracted first to this aspect of the revival was natural. Centuries ago the Japanese and Koreans were similarly attracted to the philsophical writings of Chu Hsi and his school and were deeply influenced by them.

Another reason for the greater interest in Neo-Confucianism has been the tendency to attach special importance to whatever seemed new in the thought of a given period. Neo-Confucianism was clearly a new development, borrowing much from Buddhism and Taoism in order to supplement and expand the teachings received from the classical exponents of this school, whereas the more practical thought of the Sung school seemed, on the surface at least, to follow traditional lines, dealing with age-old Chinese institutions and with social problems which had been often met and handled in the same way before.

The study of Confucian political thought has also suffered from the general disfavor in which this school has been held recently by those who have attributed to it all the evils and weaknesses of the old order in China. A reflection of this is the view that Confucianism was inherently reactionary and sterile, so that little of importance was

---

[1] For a similar study of Sung Neo-Confucianism by a distinguished Chinese scholar, see Ch'ien Mu, *Sung-Ming li-hsueh kai-shu* (An Introduction to Sung-Ming Neo-Confucianism), Vol. I (Taipei, Taiwan, 1953).

thought or done in the political and social spheres. Unfortunately this impression has too often been confirmed by the few modern students who have sought to dispel it, since they have been prone, especially in writing for a Western audience, to think of Chinese political thinkers as something of a marvel if only they approximated the ideas of an influential Western writer. Such attempts to rehabilitate Chinese thought have usually been self-defeating. On close examination the thinker in question has proved to be more deeply immersed in his own tradition than was originally supposed, so that the resemblance to Western writers was largely superficial, or else his originality could not be seen in its true proportions so long as the traditions from which he departed remained poorly understood.

Even a cursory study of the Confucian revival in the Sung, however, shows that its leading spokesmen were as vitally concerned with the immediate problems of Chinese society as with the ultimate problems of human life. Moreover, since some of the major problems and institutions of Chinese society have persisted in the same form for centuries and even today have by no means wholly changed, such a study helps to explain why Confucian tradition should have a continued relevance to the understanding of Chinese society. In particular the early Sung Confucianists gave their attention to the validity of the basic ethical doctrines and ideals of their school when applied to the social and political situation confronting them. The answers they gave to some of the questions which arose reveal that a close relationship existed between Neo-Confucian doctrine and important political developments of the Sung period, such as the reforms of Wang An-shih.

In this respect the Sung may be unique, for the scope and diversity of its intellectual life is wider than in some other periods of Chinese history. Yet, despite the Neo-Confucian tendency in later dynasties to regard ethical and metaphysical questions as alone worthy of consideration, the fact remains that Confucianists in office went on grappling with the problems of government, and individual writers of great stature still appeared to take up the challenge which these problems presented. Among the latter Huang Tsung-hsi and Ku Yen-wu may be cited as outstanding examples in the seventeenth century. To study Confucian thought in this sphere involves special difficulties, since in the West particularly we have only begun to study some of the key institutions which were the subject of their discussions, and without such background studies it is difficult to appreciate the significance of their work. But, as we progress along both fronts, institutional and intellectual history can contribute much to each other and in the process enlighten us as to the true range, depth, and vitality of traditional Chinese thought.

In the future, studies of this type should be of increasing importance. For one thing they would throw new light on the original deposit of Confucian teaching, showing how the Classics were interpreted and their doctrines applied in radically different circumstances from those of Confucius and Mencius. Furthermore, in their application to the historical scene in China there may be some lessons which have an indirect bearing on the problems of our own society. For instance, as our own government has expanded its functions in recent decades, it has encountered problems involving civil service, standards of competence and loyalty, corruption and factionalism in office, economic controls and red tape—problems which are not new but have become far more acute in a vast and unwieldy bureaucracy. On these questions the Confucianists are better qualified to speak than many other writers in the past, since they have had to face them for centuries in their own highly centralized, bureaucratic government. Finally, study of the more practical aspects of Chinese thought should be of value as a basis for studies in comparative thought. The same Confucian ideas take on new meaning and significance when adapted to different social requirements in the later Chinese dynasties, in Japan during the Tokugawa period, and in Korea under the Yi dynasty. Only when these divergent experiences are assessed can the social implications of Confucian doctrine be formulated in sufficiently general terms to be of use for broader comparative studies.

The present survey of Sung thought is not the fruit of as close an acquaintance with the period as would be desirable in anyone attempting such an ambitious project. The writer has been led back to this period through his studies in the work of Huang Tsung-hsi, whose history of Confucian philosophy in the Sung and Yüan dynasties (*Sung Yüan Hsüeh-an*) served as the starting point for this investigation. It is to be hoped that others better qualified will pursue the subject to greater advantage.

Han Yü and the Confucian Inheritance of the Sung School

No account of the early Sung school can begin without some mention of the late T'ang writer, Han Yü (786–824), who became the patriarch of this school. Today the influence of Han Yü on Chinese thought is not always appreciated. Often he is regarded as merely a great prose stylist, and in histories of Chinese philosophy his importance is apt to be overlooked because he made no original contribution to the speculative thought which flowered in the metaphysical systems of the Neo-Confucian masters in the Sung. There is some truth in what Fung Yu-lan says about Han Yü's intellectual manifesto, *On the Origin of the Way* (*Yüan Tao*): "Han Yü is primarily famous as one of China's great prose stylists, and there is little of purely philosophical interest in what he says here." Nevertheless, it should be recognized that as an essayist Han Yü was far more concerned with content than with elegance of language and adopted the classical prose style (*ku-wen*) precisely because it enabled him to state his convictions with greater clarity and force than did the elaborate parallel prose style of his day. These convictions may not be of "purely philosophical interest," since they have to do with immediate ethical and political problems, nor are they original with Han Yü. And yet the forceful manner in which he advocated them made an indelible impression on generations of scholars and officials who followed in the main stream of Confucian thought, including many thinkers whose philosophical views differed widely in other respects and many men of affairs who were largely unconcerned with philosophical issues. Among these articles of belief which formed a common legacy for most later Confucianists, the following may be cited in particular:

1. Uncompromising rejection of Buddhism and Taoism as subversive of public morality.
2. Reassertion of Confucian ethics as essential to political stability and social welfare.
3. Confucian ethnocentrism—the rejection of certain ideas as inherently evil because they are foreign.

4. Formulation of Confucian orthodoxy in regard to texts and transmission.
5. The importance of energetically upholding this orthodox tradition and asserting its validity for later times, even against opposition from the court and hostile public opinion.

Of these characteristic features of Han Yü's thought, perhaps only the last requires some explanation here. His role as a defender and definer of Confucian orthodoxy is fairly well known, but it is not usually recognized that in his time to take up this role also put him in the position of a reformer and nonconformist. During the T'ang dynasty Buddhism and Taoism, though to him insidious heresies, had frequently enjoyed the patronage of the court and had also won favor with many intellectuals. To oppose them as Han Yü did sometimes involved paying a heavy price. When, for instance, he remonstrated with the emperor against the latter's intention to venerate publicly a supposed relic of the Buddha, Han Yü narrowly escaped execution for his forthrightness and was subsequently banished from the court.

On the other hand, Confucian orthodoxy as he understood it was by no means generally accepted even by those classed as Confucian scholars. Supposedly the imperial bureaucracy remained a stronghold of Confucianism even during the years when Buddhism and Taoism attained their greatest popularity, since entrance to the civil service was generally limited to those who qualified through the Confucian-style examinations. Yet in actuality the civil service examinations, despite their Confucian provenance, did little to perpetuate the more vital teachings of this school. It is true that one of the many types of examination which candidates might elect to take in the T'ang dynasty was devoted exclusively to the Confucian Classics (that for the *ming-ching* degree), but it stressed memorization of the texts and their commentaries, not an understanding of their teachings. Toward the end of the dynasty scholars naturally enough looked upon this kind of "learning" with some contempt and preferred to seek the degree awarded to those proficient in the composition of prose and poetry (the *chin-shih* degree). The effect of this was to fill the ranks of Chinese officialdom with men skilled at writing the prescribed forms of prose and poetry but not necessarily with able exponents of Confucian doctrine in the political sphere. Other writers in Han Yü's time strenuously criticized this state of affairs and called for a change in the examining procedures so that less emphasis would be put upon memorization or literary skill and greater stress laid on comprehension of the general meaning of the Classics and an appreciation of the Way of the sage-kings—that is, Confucianism as a way of life and a guide to good government.

Han Yü too regarded Confucianism as more a way of life than an academic discipline. Initially he had suffered repeated setbacks in his attempt to win the coveted *chin-shih* degree, which he achieved only after failing three times. Even then he obtained official appointment only long after taking three supplementary examinations, an experience not unusual among candidates for office in the T'ang dynasty. But while his progress in an official career was thus held up, Han Yü devoted himself to writing and teaching, and this was unusual inasmuch as he conceived of himself as more than a mere tutor of reading and writing, being convinced that the business of a teacher was to inculcate the principles of Confucianism as the great classical philosophers had done.

In this way Han Yü established himself as the exponent and exemplar of a new ideal, a new *tao* as it were: the scholar whose worth was not measured in terms of his success in achieving high office and a big salary but rather in terms of his devotion to reviving and reasserting Confucian teachings in a decadent age. At one point he openly declared that pursuit of an official career through the examinations was incompatible with true scholarship. By this he certainly did not mean to rule out government service altogether, for the ultimate aim of any true Confucianist must be to exert some influence on the conduct of government, and eventually Han Yü himself won high honors as an official. But, like his idol Mencius, Han Yü insisted that official employment is not an end in itself. Steadfast devotion to principle, which for Han Yü meant adherence to Confucian tradition, must be the true end of the scholar, and acceptability to the court is no measure of orthodoxy. Regardless of either official disfavor or unpopularity with the general public, the genuine scholar must adhere to the Confucian code and strive to spread it.

In this respect Han Yü's ideal contrasts with another way of life which appealed to men of his time: the monastic ideal of Buddhism and the Taoist ideal of the recluse. These called upon men to "leave the world," withdraw from society and abandon the worldly cares of men. But to a thoroughgoing Confucianist like Han Yü the disappointments of political life and the burdens of one's social obligations could never justify retiring from the field of struggle. Han Yü was a crusader and thought of himself as almost a martyr to his cause. In the past both Mencius and Hsün Tzu had exemplified this ideal, standing fast against the evil tendencies of their times. Han Yü obviously sees himself as their successor in his own day, who is ridiculed or persecuted for his independence of mind and devotion to an ideal. His writings, particularly since his style was so expressive of his innermost personal feelings, eloquently impart this sense of his mission (which was nearly an obsession with him) as a lone defender of the True Way.

Han Yü's biography in the *New T'ang History*, written two centuries later by leaders of the Sung school who regarded him as something of a patron saint, portrays him in this same light:

From the Chin dynasty (A.D. 265–420) through the Sui (590–618), while Taoism and Buddhism were widely practiced, the Way of the Sages (i.e., Confucianism) was carried on without interruption, but the Confucian scholars utilized the orthodox ideas in the world (of Confucianism) to give support to the strange and supernatural. Han Yü alone grievingly quoted the Sages to combat the errors of the world, and, although mocked at by others, he met rebuffs with renewed ardor. In the beginning nobody believed in him, but finally he gained great renown among the people of his generation. Of old, Mencius, who was removed from Confucius by only two hundred years, had refuted Yang Chu and Mo Ti. But Han Yü, who attacked these two schools (of Buddhism and Taoism), came more than one thousand years after (Confucius). In destroying confusion and reviving orthodoxy, his merit is equal to and his energy double (that of Mencius). . . . Since the death of Han Yü, his words have gained wide currency so that scholars now look up to him as if he were Mount T'ai or the Great Dipper.

In view of the tendency in some recent works on China to stress the stereotyped character of Neo-Confucian thought, as if to suggest that later scholars were motivated exclusively by a concern for strict orthodoxy and blind conformity to whatever was sanctioned by the state, it is worth drawing attention to Han Yü as a symbol in this earlier period of the two-sided nature—at once traditionalist and nonconformist—of much Confucian thought in later centuries. No one will deny that there were powerful forces working to compel conformity to the established order or that through the examination system and imperial patronage generations of educated Chinese were wedded to a sterile scholarship. But alongside those whose Confucianism was only a means to office, or a guaranty of their political and intellectual reliability, stood others who took up the challenge of their times and did more with their Confucian inheritance than simply pass it along untouched to others. Among the intellectual pioneers and political reformers were many who withstood the opposition or condemnation of the state. Long before Chu Hsi's commentaries became standard texts in the examination halls of the Ming and Ch'ing dynasties, Chu Hsi himself suffered at the hands of the government for his independence of mind and, when he died, was subjected to further abuse by an annalist of the existing regime who described his funeral as a "gathering of heretics from all over the empire to follow the arch-heretic to the grave." Again, after Chu Hsi's own interpretation of the scriptures was accepted as orthodox by the Ming, others like Wang Yang-ming rejected it and established their own schools, which were likewise subjected to official persecution. Later still, the Tung-lin school, Huang Tsung-hsi, and Ku Yen-wu—to name only a few—carried on this tradition of independent thought and scholarship by standing in opposition to the court, or aloof from it, and by protesting in the name of true orthodoxy against that debased form of Confucian "learning" which had the seal of state approval. That they were dissenters means, of course, that they were not representative of their times. In their own lifetimes they influenced only a few compared to the great number who followed the established pattern and sought their success in serving the ruling power. But it is also true that from these few dissenters came the outstanding contributions to the development of Chinese thought. It was to them that later ages looked for guidance, and it is to them that Confucianism owes its survival as a living tradition instead of simply as a state cult.

Han Yü was not a scholar or classicist in the usual sense. He did not devote himself to the exegetical study of Confucian scripture, as so many commentators did before and after him. What concerned him were the essential teachings of the Classics, reduced to their simplest terms. These were the ethical precepts which underlay good government and social harmony: chiefly the Five Human Relations or Obligations between ruler and subject, father and child, husband and wife, elder and younger brother, and friend and friend, together with the personal virtues proper to each. For Han Yü a return to the Ancient Way involved primarily moral reform and not political reform as we understood it. The reformers of the Sung school, however, pursuing the same ideal of Confucianism as a living faith, extended it to almost every sphere of life and especially to political and social institutions. Thus conservatism and reform were to be united under the banner which proclaimed "Restoration of the Ancient Order" (*fu-ku*).

Origins and General Character of the Sung School

Hu Yüan

The development of Neo-Confucianism in the Sung dynasty is generally traced down through those who contributed most to the impressive synthesis of Chu Hsi, which, to judge only from its lasting influence in Japan and Korea as well as China, must be accounted the crowning achievement of Sung thought. With Chu Hsi as a reference point, it has been customary to work back through intellectual genealogy of the Ch'eng-Chu school to Shao Yung and Chou Tun-i, who in the early years of the dynasty formulated some of the basic principles embodied in this synthesis.

This line of transmission starting with Chou Tun-i is followed, for example, in the biographical section of the *Sung History,* where contributors to the new Ch'eng-Chu orthodoxy are classified under the special designation of *Tao-hsüeh-chia* (roughly: "followers of the True Way"), while other important thinkers of the period are classed simply as *Ju-lin,* "Confucian scholars." It is principally to the teachings of the former group, the *Tao-hsüeh-chia,* that the term "Neo-Confucian" has been applied in the West.

Other intellectual historians of the period, however, have traced the origins of the Sung school in general back to other sources. In their monumental *Survey of Confucian Philosophers in the Sung and Yüan Dynasties (Sung Yüan Hsüeh-an)* the great Ch'ing scholars, Huang Tsung-hsi and Ch'üan Tsu-wang, dispel at the outset the notion that Chou Tun-i was the chief progenitor of the Confucian revival in the Sung. This honor must go instead to Hu Yüan (993–1059) and Sun Fu (992–1057). More than twenty years the senior of Chou Tun-i, Hu Yüan was recognized in his own time as the leader of the Confucian renaissance, presiding over one of the outstanding private academies of his time, where he taught the Confucian Classics as guides to the ethical life rather than as mere texts to be studied for the civil service examinations. In this respect Hu Yüan may be taken as one of the earliest in a long line of teachers who made private academies, in contrast to official schools, the leading intellectual centers of China from the eleventh to the seventeenth centuries. So important was the contribution of these academies to creative thought and independent scholarship that, according to the Ming historian, Wang Ch'i, it is through them that the origins and development of Neo-Confucianism can be traced.

Hu Yüan was above all a teacher who took seriously his duties as a moral preceptor of youth and stressed an appreciation of the teacher–disciple relationship as essential to genuine education. Thus it was regarded as noteworthy in his time that Hu Yüan "adhered strictly to the traditional concept of the master–disciple relationship, treating his students as if they were sons or younger brothers, and being trusted and loved by them as if he were their father or elder brother."

The philosopher Ch'eng Yi, though a student of Chou Tun-i, was himself a protégé and devoted disciple of Hu Yüan and testified to the latter's remarkable moral influence over his students: "You can recognize at a glance anyone who has studied under the Master of An-ting by his purity and sincerity and his calm, amicable disposition."

Hu Yüan's effectiveness as a teacher was also affirmed after his death by one of his leading disciples who, when questioned by the emperor Shen-tsung as to who was superior, Wang An-shih or Hu Yüan, replied:

My master was teaching students in the Southeast about the Way and Virtue, Benevolence and Justice, when Wang An-shih was still busy in the examination halls working for the *chin-shih* degree. It is said that the Way of the Sages has three forms, Principle ($t'i$), Practice (*yung*), and Literary Expression (*wen*). The bond between prince and minister and between father and son, Benevolence, Justice, Rites and Music—these are things which do not change through the ages; they are Principles. The Books of Poetry and History, the dynastic histories, and the writings of the philosophers—these perpetuate the right example down through the ages; they are its Literary Expression. To initiate these principles and put them into practice throughout the Empire, enriching the life of the people and ordering all things to imperial perfection—this is Practice.

Our dynasty has not through its successive reigns made Principle and Practice the basis for the selection of officials. Instead we have prized the embellishments of conventional versification, and thus have corrupted the standards of contemporary scholarship. My teacher (Hu Yüan), from the Ming-tao through the Pao-yüan periods (1032–40), was greatly distressed over this evil and expounded to his students the teaching which aims at clarifying Principle and carrying it out in Practice. Tirelessly and with undaunted zeal, for over twenty years he devoted himself wholly to school-teaching, first in the Soochow region and finally at the Imperial Academy (*T'ai-hsüeh*). Those who have come from his school number at least several thousands. The fact that today scholars recognize the basic importance to government and education of the Principle and Practice of the Sages is all due to the efforts of my Master. Wang An-shih cannot even be compared to him!

This tribute to Hu Yüan suggests several characteristic features of the Confucian revival in the early Sung. Hu Yüan is both a traditionalist and a reformer. He is a moralist, not a metaphysician, and his primary interest is in the application of Confucian ethics to the problems of government and everyday life. Hu Yüan is also an independent scholar, one whose success came through years of private study and teaching, and who gained official recognition only late in life. Echoing criticism of late T'ang writers of the literary examination system, he condemns it as a perverter of scholarship and as productive of a mediocre officialdom. Finally in the threefold conception of the Tao as Principle, Practice, and Literary Expression, which Hu Yüan expounded so effectively among early Sung scholars, we have a concise statement of the aims of the Sung school in their most general terms, amplifying Han Yü's initial reassertion of the Confucian Way and suggesting the broad lines along which it was to be developed by the manifold activities of Sung scholars.

According to this view, the Classics were to be studied as deposits of eternal truth rather than as antiquarian repositories, and the true aim of classical studies was to bring these enduring principles, valid for any place or time, to bear upon both the conduct of life and the solution of contemporary problems. Conversely, no attempt to solve such problems could hope to succeed unless it were grounded on these enduring principles and undertaken by men dedicated to them. Yet neither classical teaching nor a practical program of reform could be furthered, except through the mastery of literature and writing—not the intricacies of form and style with which the literary examinations were concerned but literature as a medium for preserving and communicating the truth in all its forms. Therefore these three concepts, Principle, Practice, and Literary Expression, were seen as essential and inseparable constituents of the Way, which, as the Sung school exemplified it, embraced every aspect of life. In a sense they may be called the Three Treasures of Confucianism, just as Buddha (Truth), Dharma (Law or Scripture), and Sangha (Monastic Discipline) are the Three Treasures of Buddhism which the Sung Confucianists sought to displace.

With this in mind we should be prepared to recognize the many-sided character of both the Confucian revival in the Sung and its individual representatives in this period. The broad current of political reform, most conspicuously promoted by Wang An-shih, and the work of the great Sung historians, such as Sung Ch'i, Ou-yang Hsiu, Ssu-ma Kuang, and Ma Tuan-lin, are as much the products of this revival as Chou Tun-i's Diagram of the Supreme Ultimate or the commentaries of Chu Hsi. And the work of Chu Hsi himself must be appreciated as an expression of the Sung spirit in the fields of history and politics as well as in classical scholarship and metaphysics. The Sung, indeed, has been known for its versatile intellects: Wang An-shih, whose reputation as an outstanding classical scholar in his day has been overshadowed by his fame as a statesman; Ssu-ma Kuang, his chief political antagonist, who is better known today as one of China's great historians; and Su Tung-p'o, perhaps the outstanding literary figure of his time, who was also a man of affairs and played a leading part in the political struggles of that memorable era. These men—to name just a few—are all beneficiaries of the creative and widespreading energy of the Sung revival, and their individual accomplishments, spectacular though they may be, should not be seen in isolation. Their several contributions may have been most significant in one particular sphere of activity, either that of Principle, Practice, or Literary Expression, but both alone and together they exemplify the ideal of unity and universality which the Sung school strove to fulfill.

Especially in its emphasis upon the practical application of Confucian principles to problems of the day, Hu Yüan's threefold formulation points to the fact that political, economic, and social thought were to be as integral a part of the Confucian revival as were classical studies and philosophical inquiry. In his own teaching Hu Yüan exemplified this by his insistence upon practical measures to improve the people's livelihood, to strengthen military defenses against the barbarian menace, to expand irrigation projects in order to increase agricultural production, and also to promote mathematical and astronomical studies. But Hu Yüan never became a practicing politician and cannot himself be called a political reformer. For him a career devoted to teaching was the most effective way of putting classical principles into practice, since the training of able men was a prerequisite to any program of general reform.

Sun Fu and Shih Chieh

Another scholar of the time who distinguished himself as a teacher and must be acknowledged as one of the founding fathers of the Sung school is Sun Fu (992–1057). Like Han Yü and Hu Yüan, he had failed to win recognition in the literary examinations. Retiring to T'ai-shan in Shantung, Sun dedicated himself to the study and teaching of the Classics. In the school he opened there, which became one of the most famous private academies of the time, he affirmed the need for a new appreciation of the Classics and for a return to true orthodoxy. Among the Classics, Sun gave special attention to the *Book of Changes* and the *Spring 'and Autumn Annals*. Of his studies on the latter, Ou-yang Hsiu wrote that Sun sought to express its essential meaning in the simplest terms, without regard to the diverse and confusing commentaries on the work, so as to clarify its ethical implications and the application of the Way of the sage-kings to the problems of his time.

Sun's repudiation of the degenerate intellectual tendencies of the time is reflected in a work by one of his outstanding disciples, Shih Chieh (1005–45), entitled *Strange Teachings (Kuai Shuo)*. Here the Way of the ancient sage-kings and Confucius is upheld as the only true and immutable teaching down through the ages. Specifically condemned as one of three unorthodox paths to learning, along with Buddhism and Taoism, is the mastery of conventional literary forms for the state examinations. Thus, again, a reform in the civil service examinations is pointed to as a first step in the direction of general reform, and it was to become a burning issue in the political debates of the time. Without a change in the examination system, men of character and true learning could find their way into the government only with difficulty. Officials whose accomplishments were purely literary—and that only in a narrow and superficial sense—could not be depended upon to promote the general welfare, to adopt policies based on Confucian principles, or conscientiously to implement such policies if it entailed sacrificing their own interests.

Unfortunately this attempt to rally the serious scholars of the land in support of a new political program, with the aim of bringing into the government a corps of competent officials sympathetic to these objectives, necessarily involved the creation of an organization much like a political party committed to the formation of a government composed of like-minded individuals. Chinese political traditions did not allow for such a development, however. Rulers had always looked with suspicion on any political alignment which might bring pressure upon the throne or threaten its security. Moreover, those in power at court were prone to regard any organized opposition as "factions" or "cliques," bent on serving their own interests rather than those of the state, and therefore potentially subversive. One of the main objectives of the civil service examination system was to prevent "packing" of offices with representatives of any single group or faction through favoritism in the recruitment of officials, and this was in part the reason why the reformers of this period considered the examination system such an obstacle to their plans. Thus the political movements associated with the Confucian revival, in so far as they were aggressive and well organized, were bound to stir up contention and become involved in bitter "factional" struggles. Consequently, the Northern Sung period was torn by intense party strife, which increased rather than abated as the dynasty wore on. Also for this reason many of the reforms attempted in this age of great political activity came to nothing in the end, because each faction, on coming to power, tended to make a clean sweep of policies and personnel associated with the displaced regime.

Proponents of the New Order

Fan Chung-yen

The first steps taken in the government itself to implement a broad program of reform were sponsored by Fan Chung-yen (989–1052), the statesman and general whose patronage of Hu Yüan and Sun Fu had brought them to the capital as lecturers in the Imperial Academy. Something of a self-made man, who had been orphaned at the age of two, Fan was a deep student of the Classics, especially the *Book of Changes* and the *Mean*. He was also known as a staunch defender of the Confucian Way and a vigorous opponent of Buddhism. As a young man he had adopted for himself the maxim, "Before the rest of the world starts worrying, the scholar worries; after the rest of the world rejoices, he rejoices." During the reign of Jen-tsung (1023–56) Fan tried as a prime minister to implement a ten-point program including administrative reforms to eliminate entrenched bureaucrats, official favoritism, and nepotism; examination reform; equalization of official landholdings to insure a sufficient income for territorial officials and to lessen the temptation toward bribery and squeeze; land reclamation and dike repair to increase agricultural production and facilitate grain transport; creation of local militia to strengthen national defense; and reduction of the labor service required by the people of the state.

Of Fan's policies those dealing with education and the examination system had the most significant effect. In his memorial he called for the establishment of a national school system, through which worthy men could be trained and selected for the civil service. Though this would represent a departure from dynastic precedent, Fan justified it as a return to the system set forth in the Classics as obtaining under the benevolent rule of the early Chou kings. He also asked that in the examinations for the *chin-shih* degree more importance be attached to an understanding of the Classics and of political problems than to the composition of poetry. One of his most revealing proposals was to abolish the pasting of a piece of paper over the candidate's name on an examination paper, a practice designed to insure impartial judgment by the examiner. The reasoning behind this suggestion follows from the importance Fan always attached in both teaching and politics to a man's personal integrity. It was just as vital to know the candidate's moral character as his literary and intellectual capacities, which it was impossible to judge except from personal knowledge.

Prompted by Fan's memorial, the emperor called for a general discussion of these questions at court. Fan's proposals were supported by Sung Ch'i and others, who expostulated against the evils of the existing system and urged a "return" to the ancient ideal. As a result a national school system was promulgated by Jen-tsung in 1044, calling for the establishment of a school in each department and district to be maintained and staffed by the local magistrate. At the same time the civil service system was reformed so that the examinations were divided into three parts, with priority given to problems of history and politics, then to interpretation of the Classics, and last to poetry composition. Subsequently instruction in the Imperial Academy was also revamped by Hu Yüan to conform to the methods he had used in his private academy, which Fan had endorsed.

Thus, as the recent historian Ch'ien Mu has put it, "with Fan Chung-yen at court and Hu Yüan in the schools, the whole pattern of the Sung school was laid out."

Ou-Yang Hsiu

Few of Fan's reforms survived when he fell from power as a result of bitter factional struggles. But his influence, and that of Hu Yüan, remained among a number of men who were to dominate the intellectual and political scene for decades to come. First among these stands Ou-yang Hsiu (1007–72), the master of prose and poetry, the historian and statesman whom the brilliant and versatile Su Tung-p'o ranked with the greatest of Chinese writers. "In the discussion of great principles he resembled Han Yü; in the discussion of public questions he resembled Lu Chih; in narrative writing he resembled Ssu-ma Ch'ien; and in the writing of poetry (*shih* and *fu*) he resembled Li Po."

The terms in which Su pays tribute to the extraordinary genius of his master have special significance here. Ou-yang Hsiu has probably been best known as the writer who rediscovered Han Yü and made his "classical prose style" (*ku-wen*) the standard for centuries. But Su says that it is in the "discussion of great principles" (*lun ta tao*) that they resemble each other—that is, as writers on philosophical and moral questions. Ou-yang Hsiu's fame as a historian is well established by virtue of the leading part he took in compiling the *New History of the T'ang Dynasty* and the *New History of the Five Dynasties,* and so the resemblance between him and the great classical historian, Ssu-ma Ch'ien, is understandable. In his own time, however, Ou-yang was equally well known as a writer on public questions and as the statesman who shared with Fan Chung-yen leadership of the Sung school in official circles.

Between these latter activities and his historical studies there was in fact a close connection. Hu Yüan, Sun Fu, and Fan Chung-yen had devoted themselves especially to study of the *Book of Changes* and the *Mean,* as containing the most important truths of the Confucian teaching; and in this way they had opened up the field of classical study which Chou Tun-i and the Ch'eng brothers were later to develop so spectacularly. Ou-yang Hsiu, though an admirer of these earlier scholars and a political ally of Fan Chung-yen, had little interest in the *Book of Changes,* to which he considered the appendixes of dubious authenticity, and he thought the *Mean* much too abstruse and impractical. For him study of the *Spring and Autumn Annals* was of the first importance, since in this history were embodied the essential teachings of Confucius as applied to events in the practical order. The three early commentaries on this work he rejected precisely because they obscured its original ethical import. Thus as a historian and statesman who found in history lessons of practical significance for his own time, Ou-yang Hsiu appears in a role which prefigures that of Ssu-ma Kuang, perhaps the most eminent historian of the period and the great political opponent of Wang An-shih.

As the intellectual heir of Han Yü, Ou-yang Hsiu proved himself a mighty champion of Confucian orthodoxy, who carried on Han Yü's struggle against the twin evils of Buddhist escapism and literary dilettantism. He insisted that "literary activity just benefits oneself, while political activity can affect the situation around us." In him also the Sung school found a vigorous defender of the scholars' right to organize politically for the advancement of common principles, and in him many of the leading figures of the next generation, such as Wang An-shih, Ssu-ma Kuang, and Su Tung-p'o, discovered a patron and sponsor.

Wang An-shih

Wang An-shih himself, though in his later years the arch-enemy of those in the main line of Neo-Confucian succession, was in his early years the protégé of several leaders of the Sung school. He called Fan Chung-yen "a teacher for the whole world" and wrote a poem to Hu Yüan praising him for his steadfast devotion to scholarship. Wang's debt to Ou-yang Hsiu, who helped him to gain recognition at the capital, was such that he has been numbered among the disciples of this great scholar. Han Ch'i (1008–75), another protégé of Fan Chung-yen who was a powerful confederate of Ou-yang Hsiu in the councils of three successive emperors, was Wang's superior during his novitiate in public office, and, though the two later differed sharply on political questions, Wang retained a high personal regard for his former mentor.

Moreover, Wang's relation to the Confucian revival was one which went beyond purely circumstantial associations and acquaintances. His personal outlook too—his approach to classical scholarship, his view of history, and even much of his political philosophy—was strongly influenced by the intellectual climate which the early Sung school produced. This fact has been somewhat obscured by the subsequent course of the Neo-Confucian movement, inasmuch as tradition has followed Wang's opponents in condemning him as unorthodox. In more recent times, owing to the general unpopularity of traditional Confucianism, few have cared to re-examine this judgment; the tendency has been to glorify Wang as a reformer who boldly broke with established tradition. Yet in Wang's own time tradition was by no means so well established, and only when the underlying tendencies of the Sung school are examined can the true relation of Wang's reforms to the Confucian tradition be understood. Only then can we appreciate the extent to which his program was inspired by the same ideal which had stimulated many of his predecessors and how in the end the controversies provoked by his policies served to define more sharply the orthodox tradition.

The Confucian Program for the Sung

It has already been shown that the spread of Buddhism from the fourth to the tenth centuries presented Confucianists with a special problem and a specific occasion for urging a revival of their doctrines. It is also true that the early Sung Confucianists attacked certain established institutions as falling far short of the ancient ideal. This implied, in effect, a conflict between traditions, or perhaps more accurately a conflict between accepted institutions, on the one hand, and, on the other, hallowed ideals never actually established or attained in historical times.

Thus in the Sung dynasty those who advocated a return to the classical order implicitly, and often explicitly, rejected a tradition which had become established through more than twelve centuries of social development and which was in some respects supported by the prestige of the greatest imperial dynasties. It was only natural for later conquerors and statesmen to hope that they might themselves achieve the power and magnificence of the Han and T'ang dynasties and to see in the institutions they had established the key to dynastic success. Yet the Neo-Confucianists could not accept such a view. To follow the Han and T'ang was not enough; indeed, it might be fatal, for both the Han and the T'ang had eventually succumbed to corruption and decay and had left to posterity as vivid an impression of final weakness as of initial strength. Hence the necessity for a complete reappraisal of institutions inherited by the Sung, if it were to avoid their fate. To this was added a special sense of urgency arising from the threat of foreign conquest, an almost constant danger to the life of the dynasty.

As an expression of this view we may cite a memorial on the state of the nation submitted to the emperor Jen-tsung in 1050 by the philosopher Ch'eng Yi (1033–1107) when this disciple of Hu Yüan was only seventeen years of age:

In the Three Dynasties (the era of the Sage Kings) the Way was always followed; after the Ch'in (221–207 B.C.) it declined and did not flourish. Dynasties like the Wei and Chin indeed departed far from it. The Han and T'ang achieved a limited prosperity, but in practicing the Way they adulterated it. . . .

[Thus] for two thousand years the Way has not been practiced. Foolish persons of recent times have all declared that times are different and things have changed, so that it can no longer be practiced. This only shows how deep their ignorance is, and yet time and again the rulers of men have been deceived by their talk. . . . But I see that Your Majesty's heart is filled with solicitude for the people, and if Your Majesty practices the Way of the Sage Kings with such solicitude for the people, how can any difficulties stand in the way?

Of old the Emperor Wu of Han laughed at the failure of Duke Hsüan of Ch'i to heed the counsel of Mencius. But he himself did not act as a true King and failed to adopt the recommendations of Tung Chung-shu. Emperor Wen of the Sui dynasty laughed at Emperor Wu's failure to adopt the recommendations of Tung Chung-shu but he himself did not listen to the advice of Wang T'ung. The folly of these two rulers—I wonder if Your Majesty has not laughed at it sometime. Though your humble servant cannot pretend to the wisdom of these three masters, nevertheless what he studies is the Way of these three masters. Would that Your Majesty could see the present as future generations will, just as we now see the past!

This same view is reiterated and expanded by Ch'eng Yi's elder brother Ch'eng Hao (1032–85) in a memorial to the emperor Shen-tsung (1068–85) which provides a classic exposition of the Principle-and-Practice concept of Hu Yüan:

The laws established by the Sage Kings were all based on human nature and were in keeping with the order of nature. In the great reigns of the Two Emperors and Three Kings, how could these laws not but change according to the times and be embodied in systems which suited the conditions obtaining in each? However, in regard to the underlying principles of government and to the basic doctrines by which the people may be shepherded, these remain forever unalterable in the order of nature, and on them the people depend for their very existence, so that on such points there has been no divergence but rather common agreement among the Sages of all times, early or late. Only if what we call human life should come to an end could the laws of the Sage Kings ever be changed.

Therefore, he explains, "those in later times who practice this Way to the fullest may achieve Ideal Rule, while those who practice only a part will achieve limited success." The T'ang dynasty, for example, achieved such limited success, because it retained some residue of good government as embodied in its administrative codes and attempted to maintain a system of land distribution based on the size of the family. But if the Sung is to succeed where the T'ang failed, it must attempt a general re-establishment of ancient institutions, including a gradual return to the well-field system of equal land distribution, as described by Mencius, a militia of soldier-cultivators to replace the mercenaries of the Sung, and a universal school system, toward which Fan Chung-yen had made an abortive first step. Moreover, since the cost of government has increased enormously over ancient times, expenses must be reduced in order to lighten the tax burden on the people. As it is, the government draws all surplus from the land. "Even the rich and powerful families rarely have a surplus; how much worse off are the poor! Just one bad year and they starve or turn to banditry. In some unfortunate cases the calamity affects thousands of miles of territory or extends over a period of several years." Under such conditions cultivators abandon their land, and the consumers of food far outnumber the producers of it. "In ancient times the four classes of people each had fixed occupations, and eight or nine out of ten were farmers. Therefore food and clothing was provided with no difficulty, and the people knew no want. But today the capital has a floating population of over a million, who are idlers, vagrants or beggars." To correct this, not only must the occupations of the people be fixed and the resources of the land conserved, but the ancient ceremonial regulations, set forth in the *Books of Rites,* must be restored so that people do not waste their substance through competitive extravagance in the satisfaction of their meaner desires.

These recommendations of Ch'eng Hao also reflect the political views of his uncle Chang Tsai (1020–77), known for his insistence upon the adoption of the institutions described in the *Books of Rites.* Chang long cherished the dream of purchasing some land for himself and his disciples and of dividing it up into well-fields in order to demonstrate the feasibility of restoring the system which the early sage-kings had left to posterity, but he died without accomplishing his objective. "If the government of the Empire is not based on the well-field system," he said, "there will never be peace. The Way of Chou is simply this: to equalize." So convinced was he that this system could be re-established in his own time that he asserted, "All the government has to do is issue an order and it can be established without having to resort to flogging even once (the Confucianist's criterion of practicability being whether or not a given measure required coercion for its enforcement)." Chang further looked upon the well-field system as the first step in the gradual restoration of the feudal system which had obtained under the Chou dynasty but had been destroyed by the Ch'in in the third century B.C. "The reason a feudal system must be established is that the administration of the Empire must be simplified through delegation of power before things can be well-managed. If the administration is not simplified [through decentralization], then it will be impossible to govern well. Therefore the Sages insisted on sharing the affairs of the Empire with other men. It was thus that everything was well-administered in their times." "For the government to follow any other way than that of the Three Dynasties will simply mean following the way of expediency."

These two alternatives, the Way of the Sages and the way of expediency, were summed up by Sung writers under the terms *wang* and *pa,* which Mencius had applied to those who were True Kings (*wang*) and those who merely sought power (*pa*). Thus Wang An-shih, like the Ch'eng brothers, emphasized the difference between the ruler who is motivated by a genuine desire to do what is right (*i*) and he who, while making a great display of those virtues expected in a king, is actually motivated by a desire for personal gain (*li*). Despite this pretense the despot or dynast can always be recognized for what he is; he cannot exert that moral influence over his people by which the True King maintains peace and order, and this inner weakness reveals itself in a reliance upon expedient and coercive devices which ultimately fail to achieve the desired end.

At their best the Han and T'ang only achieved the successful overlordship associated with the term *pa.* Lacking the inherent moral power of True Kings, the scions of these dynasties were unable to hold the empire together. This view finds expression, not only in the moral or political essays of the time, but also in historical writings such as Ou-yang Hsiu's *New History of the T'ang Dynasty.* In the prolegomena to his *Treatise on the Army* he writes:

In ancient times it was the moral strength of those who possessed the Empire which determined whether they rose or fell, ruled in peace or gave way to disorder. But since the period of the Warring States, since the Ch'in and Han dynasties, this has been determined almost always by military power. Such being the case we cannot help but recognize how important armies have become.

But military organization has changed with the times, being adopted to obtain some momentary advantage or make the most of an opportune situation, to such an extent that any and all means have been resorted to. And so when we study the systems and regulations adopted in the past, we find many which proved useful at a given time but are not worthy of perpetuation in the present.

However, the T'ang did create a military system which is worthy of praise. In antiquity the military system was based on the well-fields, but since the decline of Chou, the institutions of the Sage Kings were destroyed and never restored. Only with the T'ang militia did soldiers once again become farmers. Their domiciles, their education, their training, their functions and their employment were all governed by regulations, and though it was not possible to conform in all respects to the ancient model, this system did embody the general spirit of the ancient one. For this reason the reigns of Emperors Kao-tsu and T'ai-tsung were glorious ones.

But their descendants in later times were vain and weak; they could not preserve the system and instead changed it repeatedly. Armies are maintained to prevent disorder, but when allowed to deteriorate, they themselves can cause disorder. At their worst they impoverish the Empire by forcing it to feed the forces of disorder, which bring it in the end to utter ruin.

Wang An-shih's "New Deal" as a Restoration of the Ancient Order

In general, then, it may be said that the men of the Sung school, whether they became known as statesmen, historians, poets, or philosophers in the narrow sense, were mindful of the failure of the Han and T'ang to achieve political stability and desirous of inaugurating a new order based on the ancient ideal of the sage-kings. Even Su Tung-p'o, who took some exception to this view, testified to its prevalence: "Everyone who serves in the government chatters about the Way of the Ancient Kings and holds forth on Rites and Music. They all want to restore [the social order of] the Three Dynasties, to follow the ways of Yao and Shun." Wang An-shih, the most determined and perhaps the most dedicated statesman of his time, was no exception to this. In his first audience with the emperor Shen-tsung in 1068 Wang presented his case for reform in these terms:

"What is the most important thing to do in a government?" asked the Emperor.

"To choose the right policy," answered Wang.

"What do you think of the Emperor T'ai-tsung of T'ang?" asked the Emperor again, referring to the most beloved emperor of that dynasty.

"Your Majesty should take the Emperors Yao and Shun as your standard. The principles of Yao and Shun are really very easy to put into practice. Because the scholars of the latter days do not really understand them, they think that the standards of such a government are unattainable."

In an earlier memorial to the emperor Jen-tsung, Wang had explained how these principles were to be understood and put into practice:

I am not arguing that we should revive the ancient system of government in every detail. The most ignorant can see that a great interval of time separates us from those days, and our country has passed through so many vicissitudes since then that present conditions differ greatly. So a complete revival is practically impossible. I suggest that we should just follow the main ideas and general principles of these ancient rulers.

Let us recall the fact that we are separated

from the rule of these great men by over a thousand years of history; that they had their periods of progress and decline; that their difficulties and circumstances differed greatly. But although the measures they devised and adopted to meet their various circumstances varied in character, they were at one in the motives which actuated them, and in their conception of what was fundamental.

Therefore, I contend that we need only follow their principles. I believe that if that could be done, the changes and reforms that would ensue would not unduly alarm the people, or excite undue opposition, but would in the end bring the government of our day into line with that of the Golden Age.

Ever since Wang An-shih's time it has been debated whether or not the measures he enacted were truly in keeping with the basic teachings of the Confucian tradition. But, in spite of his obvious debt to earlier, Legalist-inspired experiments in state capitalism, there is no doubt that Wang himself was inspired by what he considered to be the essential spirit of the Confucian Classics and that the benevolent paternalism ascribed to the sage-kings could easily be construed to justify a vigorous exercise of state power to promote the general welfare. Not only was each of his major reforms prefaced by an appeal to the authority of some classical precedent or principle, but, lest this be regarded as merely conforming to an established convention, it must be said that his entire career, his writings, and the testimony of his contemporaries confirm the deep seriousness—amounting almost to a self-righteous fanaticism—with which he held to his mission of putting Confucian principles into practice in politics.

The close tie between Wang's reforms and classical authority is best shown by his project to bring out a complete revision of the Classics with a modernized commentary, clearly establishing the unity of his policies with the classical teaching. Of these revisions, the most famous was the *New Interpretation of the Institutes of Chou (Chou Kuan, Hsin-i)*, from Wang's own hand, which became a virtual Bible of his political philosophy. For this classical text Wang made the strongest claims in his personal Preface:

When moral principles are applied to the affairs of government . . . the form they take and the use they are put to depend upon laws, but their promotion and execution depend upon individuals. In the worthiness of its individual officials to discharge the duties of office, and in the effectiveness with which its institutions administered the law, no dynasty has surpassed the early Chou. Likewise, in the suitability of its laws for perpetuation in later ages, and in the expression given them in literary form, no book is so perfect as the *Institutes of Chou (Chou-kuan)*.

So effectively did Wang use this book to justify his reforms that his edition of it became one of the most influential and controversial books in all Chinese literature. To deny Wang the support he derived from it, his opponents alleged that the *Institutes of Chou* was itself a comparatively recent forgery. In later times writers commonly attributed the fall of the Northern Sung dynasty to Wang's adoption of this text as a political guide.

Thus Wang's espousal of the *Institutes of Chou* represents the culmination in the political sphere of the long debate in Confucian circles over the applicability of classical institutions, as described in the *Books of Rites,* to conditions obtaining in the Sung dynasty. At the same time, Wang's effort to reinterpret these texts—to discard the Han and T'ang commentaries—and to use a modernized version as the basis for a reformed civil service examination system, stressing the general meaning of the Classics instead of a literal knowledge of them, represents the culmination of the Confucian campaign to cast out the corruptions of the Han and T'ang dynasties, both in the field of classical scholarship and in the form of civil service examinations, in order to return to the essential purity of the classic order. In this respect Wang stands together with the Ch'eng brothers, Chu Hsi, and a host of other Sung scholars in their determination to set aside accepted interpretations and find new meaning in their Confucian inheritance, just as subsequent scholars of a creative or scientific temper were some day to reject the Sung interpretations and press anew their inquiry into the meaning and validity of the Classics.

Finally, in spite of Wang's general condemnation by later Neo-Confucianists, it must be acknowledged that many of the leading scholars of his day were at first sympathetic to his policies, sharing the common outlook of the Sung school. On this point no testimony could be more conclusive than that of Chu Hsi, the final arbiter of Neo-Confucian opinion in the Sung:

> When the New Laws of Wang An-shih were first promulgated, many worthy men were sincerely desirous of cooperating in their promotion, even Ch'eng Hao thinking it right to do so. For in those times such reforms were called for by the circumstances obtaining. Later, however, they found these measures contrary to the general desire, and Ch'eng Hao attempted to remonstrate with Wang on the ground that they could not be made to work in the face of general opposition. But Wang spurned the opinion of the majority and pressed his reforms with greater determination than ever. Only then did these worthy men desert him.

That so many "worthy men" initially should have been sympathetic to the objectives of Wang's reform program is understandable in view of the wide acceptance won for these aims by the earlier reforms and leaders of the Sung school. Kracke testifies to this in concluding his study of civil service reforms during the period:

> Equally noteworthy was the remarkable number of influential officials that in the mid-eleventh century showed a zeal for the improvement of government according to Confucian standards, and a dedication to their task that often courted political eclipse and adversity rather than yield a principle. We need only to think of such men as Fan Chung-yen, Pao Ch'eng, Ou-yang Hsiu, Han Ch'i, Ssu-ma Kuang, Wang An-shih, or (somewhat later) Su Shih. These men differed and sometimes conflicted, but rather through temperament and in questions of immediate method than through any basic disagreement in their ultimate objectives.

In this case the ground upon which many of his earlier supporters eventually broke with Wang—that his measures were contrary to the general desire—had considerable bearing on the subsequent course of Neo-Confucian political thought. Even before the break with Wang this issue had been touched upon in a colloquy among the Ch'eng brothers and Chang Tsai on the feasibility of restoring the ancient well-field system. Ch'eng Hao expressed the opinion that "if land of the people were taken and redistributed so that rich and poor shared alike, then there would be a great majority in favor of the step and only a few against it." Ch'eng Yi dissented: "It is not a question of how much opposition would be put up by the people, but of whether the thing ought to be done or not. Only when everyone, high and low, comes to accept it without nurturing any resentment, can the well-field system be put into effect." Ch'eng Yi accepted the fact that it might take some time to prepare the people for such a big step. "It makes no difference if one's ideas are not carried out in one's own lifetime, so long as they are put into effect by later generations." Chang Tsai, however, insisted upon the necessity for early adoption of the well-fields. Quoting Mencius, he said: "Virtue alone is not sufficient for the exercise of government; laws alone cannot put themselves into effect. . . . Again 'there are those who have benevolent hearts and a reputation for benevoence,' yet they do not achieve good government—'all because they do not practice the ways of the Sage Kings' (Mencius, IVa 1). We must follow the practices of the Sage Kings."

Chang Tsai's attitude is doctrinaire and uncompromising: if the sage-kings maintained a system of well-fields, such a system must also be appropriate for his own time and should be instituted without regard to opposition. Ch'eng Hao, on the other hand, implies that this step should not be taken unless opposition to it is negligible, while Ch'eng Yi stands on principle by maintaining that any opposition at all renders the plan unacceptable, although it might ultimately be achieved if the people as a whole could be educated in its favor. Thus at one extreme Ch'eng Yi holds to the hallowed Confucian doctrine that no act can be justified which involves any coercion, however slight, since it violates the strict standard of virtue as defined by Mencius. At the other extreme Chang Tsai steadfastly maintains that inward virture alone is not enough, that it must be expressed in political action by adopting the institutions of the sage-kings. And he, too, is backed by the authority of Mencius.

Wang An-shih, though a believer in the well-field system, never went so far as to force its adoption but took other measures in the field of taxation, farm credit, and marketing controls which were designed to advance the same ideal of economic equality. Yet, when Wang's reforms encountered strong opposition, this was enough to cause men like Ch'eng Hao to back down, in keeping with the attitudes expressed in his discussion of the well-fields. Meanwhile Wang's position was much like that of the doctrinaire and uncompromising Chang Tsai. Convinced of the rightness of his policies, he overrode all criticism and pressed his program with greater determination than ever. In this light it is not easy to say which party, at that critical juncture in Chinese history, abandoned its Confucian ideals. Indeed, it would be more accurate to say that each party was forced to abandon certain of its ideals in order to remain true to others. Both sides had to face the fact that it was proving far more difficult to "Restore the Ancient Order" than they had originally supposed. Wang held fast to his program, abandoning the strict ethical precepts of Confucius and Mencius in the vain hope that he could still achieve the political ideals of Mencius and the *Chou Li*. His opponents, who balked at coercive methods which violated the ideals of Benevolence and Justice, were thereby compelled to abandon, or rather to postpone indefinitely, achievement of those ends which tradition likewise had led them to accept.

It is more in the light of subsequent, than of earlier, tradition that this question has generally been settled in favor of the Ch'eng brothers, and Wang ostracized from the company of orthodox Confucians. His policies themselves outlasted Wang's tenure of office and, when abolished by Ssu-ma Kuang, were afterward revived for a time, some even enduring into later dynasties. But the fate of his policies had little to do with his standing among later Confucians. After the fall of the Northern Sung the cleavage which had developed in the Sung school over Wang's reforms widened still further, to the point where a great gulf separated those who retained an active interest in political reform and those who had retired to the quiet groves of classical scholarship and metaphysical speculation. The line was now clearly drawn between men like Ch'en Liang (1143–94), who still believed in the possibility and necessity of effecting immediate reforms, and the great Chu Hsi, whose attitude toward politics reflected the disillusionment of his master, Ch'eng Yi. This is not to say that Chu Hsi had lost all interest in politics. He still adhered to the political ideal of the sage-kings and regarded the well-field system as indispensable to the people's welfare. But these ideals were now far more distant. The failure of Wang An-shih had demonstrated that they could only be approached through a long process of education and moral reform, which would prepare the people to accept such changes and bring about a personal reformation in their rulers, since the earlier debacle was seen in great measure to Wang's own defects of character. Therefore among the immediate reforms advocated by Chu those in the field of education took priority, while in the philosophical realm he and his school were led back to the central problems of Confucianism: the problems of human nature, personal cultivation, and man's place in the universe.

A letter to Chu Hsi from his friend Lü Tsu-ch'ien illustrates the prevailing opinion among scholars of the Southern Sung toward political reform. Noting that Chu had written on political questions, urging restoration of the well-fields and making detailed recommendations in regard to taxation and finance, Lü agrees that these are all essential to good government.

But the execution of them involves a step-by-step process. Today the first requirement is to awaken the mind of the ruler. If the ruler possesses that sincerity which leads him to respect virtue and delight in the True Way, then good men will come in great numbers to assist him. Only when everyone, high and low, has full confidence in them, can the necessary steps toward good government be taken in their proper order. But if the people do not have confidence in this program and it is enacted suddenly, then there will be a great furore and it will ultimately fail.

It is this attitude, which reflects Chu Hsi's own point of view, that became dominant in Neo-Confucian circles thereafter and was accepted as orthodox when later dynasties installed Chu Hsi as the official philosopher. It is therefore the point of view from which Wang An-shih has been adjudged a renegade from Confucian tradition. Nevertheless, we should keep in mind that Wang An-shih himself played a leading part in the debates which shaped that tradition and that Neo-Confucian orthodoxy is as much the product of political controversy and experiment in the Sung as it is the fruit of study and speculation in the sanctuaries of Confucian learning.

Conclusion

The purpose of the foregoing discussion has been to bring out some of the main features of the Confucian revival in the Sung in order to show what its adherents originally held in common and on what basic issues they ultimately diverged. Little attention has been given to the considerable diversity of opinion which existed in regard to specific problems of political, economic, and social reform. But it is worth noting that, quite apart from partisan differences involving controversial figures like Wang An-shih, those who subscribed to the same Confucian ideals often differed on their precise applications to conditions obtaining in their own time. Just as one instance we might cite the opinions of Su Hsün, the father of Su Tung-p'o, on the land problem. As we have seen, many scholars of his day had complained about high taxes and demanded a return to the well-field system of feudal times. Su, while asserting that a return to the ancient order was necessary, attempted to show that land taxes in the Sung were not actually much greater than those of the Chou but that they were more oppressive when added to the high rent most cultivators had to pay. Landlordism was the big evil, but the well-field system was not a practical remedy, since the Chinese people would probably perish in the attempt to re-establish so meticulous a system. Instead he urged a simple limitation on landownership to achieve the more equitable distribution which was the essence of the classic order. In the same way, other writers, proceeding from the same general principles, arrived at different practical conclusions on many current problems. It is essential to explore these differences further and to examine Confucian thought more closely in relation to the perennial problems and characteristic institutions of Chinese society if we are to obtain a clear and balanced picture of intellectual life in the Sung or in any other period.

JUNG-PANG LO

The Emergence of China as a Sea Power During the Late Sung and Early Yüan Periods

It is a widely held impression that the Chinese have always been a landbound people oriented toward the land frontier of the north and northwest. Contrary to this popular view, Dr. Jung-pang Lo, Professor of History at the University of California at Davis, points out that China was a naval power during the late Sung, Yüan, and early Ming periods, and that this seaward expansion was the outcome of acute social and environmental changes.

In ancient times North China was not only the political and strategic center of the country but also the economic, cultural, and population center. For many centuries, the attention of the Chinese was occupied with internal problems and with the defense of their land frontier on the north and northwest, the directions from which danger has always come in the past. From the fourth to the sixth centuries,

From *The Far Eastern Quarterly*, Vol. 14, No. 4 (Aug. 1955), 489–503. By permission of *The Journal of Asian Studies*. Footnotes omitted.

the population migrated away from the North, the area most threatened by barbarian invasions. Later the migration intensified when North China was racked by civil strife and economic distress from the tenth to the thirteenth century.

The mass migrations of population were accompanied by a shift of economic power from north to south. The resulting far-reaching social and cultural changes in China culminated in the Sung period, which witnessed the great movement of urbanization, flourishing trade, big cities, and an increasingly important money economy.

Parallel with these social and cultural changes, the need for a navy developed. After being driven out of its capital at K'aifeng (in modern Honan Province) in 1127, the Sung court finally re-established itself in 1138 at Lin-an (modern Hangchow in Chekiang Province), a city exposed to attacks by sea. This stirred the Chinese to adopt measures for self-protection. Moreover, the cultivated area of China was now drastically reduced by the loss of North China and by war. The people had to increase their food supply by intensifying the cultivation of their old fields and by opening new fields, and the huge network of canals and ditches they dug for transportation and irrigation served them also as a means of defense against the Chin attacks. To patrol the waterways of this defensive belt, which covered the region between the Huai River and the Yangtze, and to guard its eastern and western flanks, the Chinese needed a navy. They succeeded in building a strong and mobile one.

Once the shipbuilding business started, the interest of the people in maritime affairs and technological development increased. Thus, with the government paying much attention to the maritime commerce and to the development of a navy, China became a sea power in the sense that the government not only dominated the sea but also viewed the naval strength as a decisive factor in planning national policy.

The naval program continued through Yüan and into the early Ming period, until more urgent internal problems and threats from the northern border again became the center of attention.[1]

One of the topics of Chinese history that deserves greater attention is the nature and direction of the expansion of the Chinese people beyond the geographical confines of China. It is a subject which, for want of more information, is still so cloaked in generalities as to present the misleading impression that the Chinese have always been a landbound people oriented towards the land frontier of the north and northwest. A Western scholar, for example, has written: "China has never been a sea-power because nothing has ever induced her people to be otherwise than landmen, and

[1] In conjunction with this selection, see the following articles by Dr. Lo: "Maritime Commerce and Its Relation to the Sung Navy," *Journal of the Economic and Social History of the Orient*, Vol. XII, 1 (1969), 59–101; and "The Decline of the Early Ming Navy," *Oriens Extremus*, 7 (1958–59), 149–68.

landmen dependent on agriculture with the same habit and ways of thinking drilled into them through forty centuries." In a recent work we find this statement: "Essentially a land people, the Chinese cannot be considered as having possessed seapower. . . . The attention of the Chinese through the centuries has been turned inward towards Central Asia rather than outward, and their knowledge of the seas which washed their coast was extremely small."

These quotations represent views that have wide currency. Sea power, according to the dictionary definition of the term, is the possession and application of naval strength for the control and command of the sea. China in the period from Han to T'ang could not qualify as a sea power although fleets were employed to wage coastal wars and to carry out invasions of Korea and Indo-China, for it was towards Mongolia and Turkestan that the diplomatic and strategic attention was focused. Nor could China qualify as a sea power during recent times, for the navies of foreign powers have held sway over her territorial waters. But can we judge the China of the late medieval period by the China of any other time? Can we say, categorically, that the Chinese were always a continentally-minded people and that China was never a sea power? This is a question of some consequence, basic to our understanding of Chinese civilization.

I have spent some time on the study of this subject and I have arrived at certain conclusions which can be summed up in the thesis that, contrary to popular views, China was a naval power during the late Sung, Yüan and early Ming periods and that this seaward expansion was the outcome of acute social and environmental changes.

Although their history abounds with accounts of battles fought on the rivers, lakes and coastal waters, the early Chinese did not regard the navy as anything more than a subordinate adjunct of the army. There were small standing navies maintained by seaboard states during periods of disunity, there were maritime fleets mobilized for temporary service in overseas campaigns and under centralized control as in the spacious days of Han, Sui and T'ang, and there were navies composed of river units under provincial command as in the Northern Sung period. But until the creation of the Southern Sung navy, China did not have a national sea-going navy established on a permanent basis.

The shock of their defeat by the Chin invaders in 1127, the capture of the emperor and the fall of the capital at K'ai-feng which drove the Sung court to establish itself at Hangchow, a city exposed to attacks by sea, stirred the Chinese to adopt counter-measures for self-protection. With the cultivated area reduced by enemy occupation and by war, the Chinese had to augment their food supply by intensifying the cultivation of their fields, and the huge network of canals and ditches they dug for transportation and irrigation served them also as means of defense. It gave the Chinese a defensive system which invalidated the superiority of the enemy cavalry. To patrol the waterways of this defensive belt which covered the region between the Huai River and the Yangtze and to guard its eastern and western flanks, the Chinese needed a navy and they succeeded in building a strong and mobile one.

Not to be outdone, the Jurchens and later the Mongols both built fleets with which they hoped to outflank the eastern end of the Sung defense line by sailing down the coast. The Jurchen attempt in 1161 failed when their fleet was destroyed by the Chinese off the coast of Shantung. In 1268 the Mongols also gave serious consideration to the idea of an attack on the Sung empire by sea, but abandoned it in favor of the strategy of a powerful drive by river forces down the Han River, the western flank of the Sung defense line. Thus, in the great struggle between the Chinese and their enemies to the north during the Southern Sung period, it was the naval phase of the wars that was the most decisive.

Built upon the remains of the provincial navy of Northern Sung and favored by contemporary technological advances in the art of navigation, naval architecture, and the manufacture and use of fire-arms, the Southern Sung navy reached a high degree of efficiency. It won victories when the army suffered setbacks. It received support from the nation and it had a large merchant marine from which to draw for ships, men and supplies. Its personnel were not landmen called upon to fight at sea but men recruited from the seafaring population of the coast, men who had inherited a naval tradition from their forefathers and who were trained and experienced in naval warfare.

The navy of Southern Sung had the distinction of being the first national navy to be established on a permanent basis and to function as an independent service. It was the first navy to be administered by a special agency of the government, the Imperial Commissioner's Office for the Control and Organization of the Coastal Areas (*Yen-hai chih-chih shih-ssu*) which was established in 1132 with headquarters at Ting-hai, one of the islands of the Chusan group. The fleet steadily grew in strength. In 1130, there were eleven squadrons with three thousand men; in 1174, fifteen squadrons with twenty-one thousand men; and in 1237, the Southern Sung navy had grown to be an effective fighting force of twenty squadrons manned by nearly fifty-two thousand men. The largest base was at Hsü-p'u which guarded the entrance of the Yangtze River and protected a flourishing port, soon to be known as Shanghai. Ting-hai, the second largest base, defended the capital, Hangchow.

By the first half of the thirteenth century, the Sung navy ranged unchallenged over the East China Sea. As a member of the Privy Council (*Shu-mi Yüan*), Wu Ch'ien pointed out in a memorial: "The area of control of our navy extends westward to Hsü-p'u, southward to Fukien, northward to Korea and eastward to Japan, an area of over ten thousand *li*. The navy is used for scouting, the navy is used for patrolling, and the navy is used for the defense of strategic points."

But, he went on, the navy was "only strong enough to check the Japanese and the Koreans," and he and other ministers who shared his views urged the further expansion of the navy and its transformation into a weapon of offense. The adoption of a strong naval policy had been advocated by many Sung officials since 1129 when a bold scheme was conceived for the invasion of Korea by naval forces and the use of Korea as an advance base for seaborne attacks on the Chin empire. Others suggested the extension of Chinese naval power into the South China Sea. But, because of insufficient resources and preoccupation with border wars, the Sung court did not heed these proposals. It remained for the Mongols to take the next step of employing the navy as an instrument of aggression.

The alacrity with which the Mongols, a nation of horsemen unacquainted with the sea, took to naval warfare was amazing. As late as the middle of the thirteenth century, they were still using inflated skins and rafts to cross rivers in their war against the Sung. Two decades later, they were conducting large-scale naval wars against Sung China and Japan, against Tongking, Champa and Java, and sending naval units against Quelpart Island and Formoa. How did they accomplish this feat? The answer is that they took over, wholesale, the navies of Korea and Sung China, but added leadership and imbued the men with energy and *élan*. Thus, the Yüan navy was essentially the Sung navy re-vitalized.

It was a former Sung commander, Liu Cheng, who in 1270 made a suggestion that proved of considerable value to the Mongols. To by-pass the strong Sung defenses established between the Huai and Yangtze Rivers, the Yüan forces had been besieging Hsiang-yang, the gateway of the Han River which Mongol leaders aimed to use as a passage into the heart of the Sung empire, but their efforts were balked by Chinese naval units. This prompted Liu Cheng to say to his Mongol colleagues: "Our strength rests in cavalry which is irresistible, but we are inferior to the Sung in naval warfare. We can nullify their superiority by constructing warships and training men in naval warfare."

Once they decided on the policy of building a naval force, the Mongols carried it through with characteristic vigor and resolution. By building ships and by capturing enemy vessels they expanded their navy from the four "wings" (*i*) they possessed at the time of the siege of Hsiang-yang to forty-one "wings" at the conclusion of the Yangtze campaign in 1275. New ships built in the yards of Kiangsu and Chekiang, ships seized from or contributed by private merchants, pirate ships, and ships of the Sung navy which surrendered or were captured, were welded into a sea-going fleet which in 1279 succeeded in destroying the last of the Sung naval forces in the battle of Yai-shan.

After the collapse of Sung resistance, the Yüan court immediately embarked on a gigantic program of shipbuilding. It ordered the construction of fifteen hundred ships in 1279, three thousand ships in 1281, and four thousand ships in 1283. These were to be built in shipyards as far inland as Changsha, as far south as Canton, as far north as Lung-lu (in northeast Hopei), and as far east as the Korean province of Cholla-do. It ordered the authorities of Quelpart Island and the province of Jehol to supply the lumber. It mobilized an army of 17,000 men to fell trees in the mountains of Jehol and to transport the wood to the shipyards. Sung officers, taken as prisoners in the battle of Yai-shan, were assigned to shipyards in China and Korea to assist in shipbuilding, and former Sung troops were integrated into Mongol and Han (Northern Chinese and Jurchen) units and given training in naval warfare.

Although not all the ships that were ordered built were actually constructed, the Yüan government nevertheless had an impressive navy for its overseas campaigns. The invasion of Japan in 1281 was undertaken with forty-four hundred ships, the invasion of Champa and Tongking from 1283 to 1288 with eight hundred ships, and the expedition against Java in 1293 with a thousand ships. In addition, there was a large coastal defense fleet and a maritime transportation fleet to carry tribute, grain, and imported merchandise from South China to the capital in the north. Thus, by wielding their new weapon, the navy, the Mongols extended the naval domination of China from the East to the South China Sea.

The naval program continued into the early Ming period. Like the Yüan navy, the Ming navy grew out of sanguinary wars on the Yangtze. At its maximum strength during the reign of Yung-lo, it consisted of a central fleet of four hundred ships stationed at Nanking, a coastal defense fleet of twenty-eight hundred ships to ward off raids by *wako* from Japan, a maritime transport fleet of three thousand ships, and, the pride of the Ming navy, a fleet of over two hundred and fifty "treasure ships" (*pao-ch'uan*), each with capacity for five hundred men. The possession and application of naval power not only facilitated the reconquest of Annam but also enabled the Chinese to extend their political control beyond the East and South China Seas into the Indian Ocean. The prestige of the Chinese navy was so great that in 1403, when an Annamese fleet invaded the capital of Champa, the appearance of nine Chinese men-of-war was sufficient to compel the Annamese to withdraw.

If the domination of the sea and the employment of naval strength as an instrument of national policy characterizes a sea power, then China during the late Sung, Yüan and early Ming periods would qualify. Why was it that China emerged as a sea power at this particular period and not at an earlier or later time? To seek an answer, we must take a broad view of sea power. Mere possession of a navy does not, *ipso facto*, make sea power. Sea power is the culmination and the physical expression of a set of geographical and sociological conditions which Admiral Mahan called the "elements of sea power." The maritime expansion of China from the twelfth to the fifteenth century was the result of a fortuitous combination of these conditions.

Geographical environment is one of the basic determining factors of social development. The long coastline of China, large sections of which, as in Shantung, Chekiang, Fukien and Kwangtung, are endowed with harbors and timber-clad mountains, and the adjoining seas enclosed by an island fringe, provide the physiographical conditions which favor and promote maritime activities. But the territorial vastness of China and her cohesion with the continent of Eurasia exercise so profound an influence that for long centuries the attention of the Chinese was occupied with internal problems and the defense of their land frontier on the north and northwest, the directions from which danger had historically threatened. During the ancient period, the hub of China was the inland provinces of Shensi and Honan, which became not only the political and strategic, but also the economic, cultural and population center of the country. The diffusion of population was toward the marginal areas around the heartland, and cultural and commercial relations were primarily carried on over caravan routes with countries of the west. The preoccupation with internal affairs and, to a lesser extent, with the affairs of the northwest frontier was again evident during the Ch'ing period.

The prosperity of China's northwestern provinces depended, however, on a number of factors, chief of which were temperate climate, abundant rainfall and fertile soil. During the medieval period, the climate and geology of the entire region underwent a gradual and profound change. The winters became more severe and the atmosphere drier, rainfall diminished in amount but increased in intensity, the streams became shallower and more saline, and erosion ate steadily into the farmlands. The Cheng-kuo Canal and the Pai Canal, which in Han times irrigated two million *mou* of land in the Wei River Valley, site of the capitals of successive dynasties of the past, by the Northern Sung period watered only a hundred thousand *mou*, or five percent of the former area. As the soil declined in productivity, the struggle to eke out a living began to absorb more and more of the energy of the people.

Coeval with the impoverishment of the Northwest was the prodigious advance of the coastal region of Southeast China as this became the economic center of the nation. In the salubrity of its climate, in the productivity of its soil, and in the potential wealth of its rivers, lakes and mountains, the Southeast far surpasses the Northwest. From the fourth century, when the Northwest was beginning to decline, the progressive peopling of the Southeast and its comparatively peaceful environment led to the extensive development of its resources. The construction of irrigation works was but one example of their already bountiful land. The economy of Southeast China developed to such an extent that by 1119, for example, over seventy percent of the money and goods (*ch'ien-wu*) sent to the court as tribute came from the lower Yangtze Valley.

For a long time, Chinese rulers, cherishing a sentimental attachment for the ancient centers of China's civilization and motivated by strategic considerations, continued to locate their capitals in Shensi or Honan, and they built an elaborate system of waterways to transport supplies from the Southeast to the civilian population in the capital and to the troops on the northwest frontier. But with the progressive desiccation of the Northwest and the frequent wars, these waterways, like the irrigation canals, suffered from shortage of water, damage and lack of repair. Without a continuous supply of food it was impossible to maintain large garrisons and the weakening of the frontier defenses tempted the border peoples to invade.

On one hand, the absence of effective resistance and the attraction of the riches of China; on the other, their own economic distress and population pressure, the appearance of capable leaders and the consolidation of tribal organization were some of the many forces that agitated the nomads and impelled them to erupt periodically in massive tidal waves. The invasions of border peoples have not only had a profound and far-reaching effect on the history and culture of China but also served as a negative factor in turning the attention of the Chinese people to the sea.

The establishment by foreign conquerors of strong militaristic states in Northwest China sealed off Chinese contact with Central Asia, thus obliging the Chinese to carry on cultural and commercial intercourse abroad by sea. This shift in orientation is illustrated by a spot check in the section on foreign countries in the *Sung hui-yao kao* (*Draft of Sung Institutes*). Before the fall of K'ai-feng in 1127, thirty-five percent of the tribute-with-trade missions came to China by land and sixty-five percent by sea. After this date all came by sea. The dislodgment of the Chinese from North China also destroyed much of their attachment for Shensi and Honan as sites for their capital. From 1127 on, their capitals were located near the seacoast.

The invasions from outside, coming at times when China was racked by civil strife, aggravated the economic distress and intensified the migration of the people. This happened from the fourth to sixth centuries and, on a greater scale, from the tenth to thirteenth centuries. During these times the slow drift of the population became a swift stream. The magnitude of the unrest may be seen from the fact that the census takers had to divide the population into two classes, "settled" (*chu*) and "transient" (*k'e*), and that during the Sung period, as the census of 1080 showed, one-third of the population (mostly from North China) was listed as transient.

Instead of spreading more or less evenly into the southern provinces or, as in the eighth century, streaming into Szechwan, from the tenth to thirteenth centuries the people poured into Southeast China as if they were shoved by a gigantic force from the Northwest. This resulted in an abnormal swelling of the coastal population. The six seaboard provinces, with but a tenth of the area of the nation, had, during the Sung and Ming periods, half of the total population, a proportion higher than any in the pre-Sung or post-Ming periods. But if we examine the Yüan census of 1330, taking into account its imperfections and omissions, we find that two-thirds of the tax-paying population resided in the coastal regions.

With the exception of Kiangsu, the coastal provinces are hilly and cannot support a dense population by agriculture alone. Large numbers of people moved into urban areas to find other means of livelihood and the result was the growth of cities. Hangchow, which boasted a population of nearly two million, was but one of the many teeming cities that rose along the southeastern coast. Urbanization led to the development of commerce and industry which, outgrowing the domestic market, sought to expand abroad. The more venturesome spirits sailed out to sea, some to support themselves by fishing or even by piracy and smuggling in nearby waters, others to trade or to colonize distant lands.

The movement of the people into the cities or out to sea was accelerated not only by civil disturbances but also by natural disasters. According to one investigator, the frequency of floods and droughts increased sharply in the Sung period and reached a peak during the Yüan, with Chekiang and Kiangsu the provinces worst hit.

Thus, as the tilting of a table sends articles on the surface sliding to one side and off the edge, so social turmoil and climatic disturbances caused a shifting of the population to the coastal provinces and out to sea. Governments and rulers felt the impact of social and economic forces and were drawn along by the strong currents of popular feeling to turn their attention to the sea. In the creation of the Southern Sung navy under Kao-tsung (1127–1162), the overseas campaigns of Qubilai Qan, and the naval expeditions sent out by Emperor Yung-lo, the aims and ambition of the rulers and the policies of their governments merely supplemented the tendency of the people.

The contraction of the Sung empire and the disruption of normal economic activities, as a result of the inroads of northern peoples on one hand and the rise of money economy and industry on the other, led to another change in Chinese society. This was the participation of the government in monopolistic enterprises and commerce, a practice which the scholar-official class of China was supposed to regard with disdain. But during the Sung period, not only did foreign trade flourish under private management, not only did officials and members of the court hold shares in shipping and manufacturing companies, but the government itself operated monopolies in domestic trade and various productive enterprises. As a result, half of the government's revenue came in the form of returns from monopolies and excise taxes and as much as twenty percent of the cash income of the state came from maritime trade, as was true during the first years of Kao-tsung's reign. Even the Emperor declared:

"The profits from maritime commerce are very great. If properly managed they can be millions [of strings of cash]. Is it not better than taxing the people?"

Under government patronage, Chinese merchants sailed their ships to Southeast Asia and India and succeeded in wresting from their Moslem rivals the monopoly of the freight and passenger business. The merchants not only contributed funds and imported military supplies but also furnished ships and seamen to the Sung navy. Three hundred and thirty-eight huge merchantmen took part in the war of 1161, notably in the battles on the Yangtze. During the Yüan period, when merchants were in control of the government economy and the government needed funds for its armament program, maritime trade flourished. Shipping magnates such as P'u Shou-keng, a man of Persian ancestry, contributed their services and their ships to help in building the Yüan navy. During the early Ming period, maritime commerce was an exclusive monopoly of the state and the government had a large merchant marine to supplement its combat forces.

Maritime commerce and naval wars spurred the development of technology and the expansion of geographical knowledge. They encouraged the opening of ports and dredging of harbors, they advanced the art of navigation by such means as the mariner's compass and star and sea charts, and they furthered the publication of treatises on tides and currents and maps of foreign countries. Most remarkable was the achievement in naval architecture, for it was by the construction of larger and more seaworthy ships that the Chinese were able to capture the shipping business from the Arabs whose vessels at this time were still flimsy craft lashed together with ropes. The ships of the Chinese, by contrast, were ocean liners boasting staterooms, wineshops, and the service of negro stewards. All were sturdily built, with watertight bulkheads, and the larger ones had lifeboats in tow.

The experience acquired in the construction of merchant vessels was utilized in the building of warships. The cash rewards offered by the Sung court as well as the incentive of war inspired the Chinese, officials and commoners alike, to experiment and to design new types of ships. They turned out paddlewheel boats, galleys, rams, and many vessels of strange design, some navigable and some not. The "sea hawk" (*hai-ku*), common type of warship of the Sung period, appears from contemporary description to have been a form of double outrigger. They experimented with square rig and finally evolved the efficient balanced lug sail and, with cotton coming into common use at this time, began to substitute cloth for bamboo mats as sails. Later, when the navy advanced from the thalassic to the oceanic stage, the paddlewheelers and other experimental craft were abandoned in favor of a few basic types of seagoing ships.

Paralleling the achievement in naval architecture was the development of firearms. Incendiary weapons such as flaming arrows, rockets, flame-throwers, and *huo-p'ao*, bombs cast by catapults, made their appearance in the tenth century and were adapted to naval warfare. In the year 1000 a captain of the imperial navy presented to the court some improvements he had made on these weapons, and in 1129 the government decreed that the *huo-p'ao* be made standard equipment on all warships. The next development was in explosive weapons, and the best known was the *p'i-li-p'ao*, rudimentary fragmentation bombs.

Effective use of the *hou-p'ao* and the *p'i-li-p'ao* enabled the Chinese to win naval victories in 1161. The fire-power of the Sung navy is indicated by the fact that half of the fighting men on the warships were archers, crossbowmen and operators of firearms. The Mongols used these weapons in their invasion of Japan in 1273, but in their campaign on the Yangtze against the Sung forces they preferred to use the *hui-hui-p'ao,* giant trebuchets introduced from the Near East.

Already in possession of the *huo-ch'iang,* a flame-thrower, it was but another step for the Chinese to insert a missile into the tube and let the blast of the charge shoot it out. The result was the *t'u-huo-ch'iang,* a prototype of the gun. This weapon appeared in the middle of the thirteenth century, and a hundred years later, iron bombards were in general use. By the beginning of the fifteenth century, there were guns forged out of a brass alloy. In 1393, each Ming warship was required to carry four guns with muzzles the size of rice bowls *(wan-k'ou-ch'ung),* twenty guns of smaller caliber, ten bombs, twenty rockets, and a thousand rounds of shot.

A factor which significantly influenced the technological progress and economic development of the Sung, Yüan and early Ming periods was the mental attitude of the people. The jolt of environmental changes loosened the grip of tradition on the men's minds. Not content with classical learning alone, the Chinese of this period displayed a measure of scientific spirit by their discoveries, and their aptitude for improvisation and invention. Instead of insisting on their own intellectual superiority, they readily accepted the contributions of the Arabs and Hindus in the fields of astronomy, geography and navigation. Instead of opposing foreign trade as unnecessary, they fostered commerce with nations abroad and tried, though unsuccessfully, to import goods needed by and of value to China.

Another manifestation of the broadened outlook of the Chinese of this period was their embarkation on colonial undertakings and voyages of discovery. The spirit of adventure among the Chinese, we are told, is repressed by their attachment to the family and the ideals of filial piety. But wars and unrest shattered family ties and, together with economic stress and population pressure, set in motion the first large-scale emigration by sea and the establishment of the first permanent Chinese settlements in Southeast Asia. "The people depended upon the sea and commerce for their livelihood," states the *Gazetteer of Fukien,* "they would leave their parents, wives and children without a thought to dwell among the barbarians."

The stories of adventure and descriptions of foreign lands current in the literature of the times stirred not only the masses but also many men of the scholar-official class. There was, for example, Mo Chi who, as director of the National Academy (*Kuo-tzu chien*) during the reign of Kao-tsung, may be supposed a staunch Confucianist. But when out of office, he would charter ships and sail out to sea both for the thrill of sailing and to satisfy his curiosity. Once he sailed to the "Northern Ocean" (*Pei-yang*) and when his crew became fearful and mutinous, he drew his sword and compelled them to sail on.

The maritime interest of the officials was reflected in the policy of the government. One of the major policy debates in the Southern Sung court took place between those who advocated a counter-offensive to recover North China and those who favored defense to hold and consolidate South

China. A counter-offensive would necessitate the employment of land forces, especially cavalry, in which the Southern Sung army was weak. So the policy adopted was that of defense and the physiography of Southeast China dictated the use of naval forces. Chang I, president of the Board of Revenue, in one of three memorials on naval preparedness he submitted in 1131, called the sea and the Yangtze River the new Great Wall of China, the warships the watch-towers, and the firearms the new weapons of defense.

Propaganda was used in support of the naval program. A political pamphlet published in 1131 stated: "Our defenses today are the [Yangtze] River and the sea, so our weakness in mounted troops is no cause for concern. But a navy is of value. . . . To use our navy is to employ our strong weapon to strike at the enemy's weakness." Emperor Hsiao-tsung (1163–1189), converted to the naval program, remarked, "The navy is our strong arm and we cannot afford to neglect it."

As the Yüan inherited the Sung navy, so the Ming inherited the Yüan navy. Thus the spirit and tradition of the Sung navy were carried on by the two succeeding dynasties. From a defensive arm the navy developed into an instrument of aggression and political domination, and from the East China Sea the naval power of the Chinese advanced to the South China Sea and into the Indian Ocean.

Broadly speaking, the maritime expansion of China during the late Sung, Yüan and early Ming periods was the cumulative result of changing sociological conditions arising from climatic and geological disturbances, political unrest, and the pressure of alien invaders from the Northwest. The movement of the population to the coastal regions and out to sea, the orientation of the nation towards the Southeast, the interest of the people, even the scholar-official class, in maritime affairs and technological development, and the attention which the government paid to commerce and to the development of a navy, all illustrate the inconstancy of social characteristics commonly attributed to the Chinese and the inconclusiveness of general statements made about them. Social characteristics change under the compelling forces of nature and general statements blur our view of the facts and dynamics of historical change. We cannot discern the zigzags in the course of the historical and cultural development of a people like the Chinese if we remain so close to the ground that we become preoccupied with what Professor Harry Elmer Barnes calls "the episodical aspects of conventional historiography," but we can see them quite clearly if we stand upon an eminence where we can survey the wide sweep of each epoch of Chinese history.

PING-TI HO

Social Composition of Ming-Ch'ing Ruling Class

As the competitive examination system became one of the major channels for recruiting government officials, the scholar-officials became the main body of bureaucracy and the main part of the ruling class. In the following article, Dr. Ping-ti Ho, Jamest Westfall Thompson Professor of History at the University of Chicago, examines the social composition of the degree-holders of the Ming-Ch'ing period.

Professor Ho bases his study on a total of 35,706 cases, which include three categories of degree-holders: chin-shih, chü-jen, *and* kung-sheng. *He analyzes the family origins of these degree-holders and attempts to discern the pattern of their social mobility.*

One of Professor Ho's illuminating observations is that the amount of socio-academic mobility began to become truly substantial in the Sung, reached its maximum in the greater part of Ming, started to level off after the late sixteenth century, and declined steadily thereafter until the final abolition of the examination system in 1905. Whether this persistent downward trend had anything to do with social unrest and rebellions is worth speculation.

In light of the substantial amount of socio-academic mobility throughout the Ming-Ch'ing period, it is difficult to say that the civil service examination system failed to serve an important social and political purpose. But because the examination had degenerated into a mere contest of skill in the composition of a type of mechanical "eight-legged" (Pa-ku) *essay, the Chinese creative genius was impaired. Perhaps this is one reason why the examination system failed to discover as many talents as it should have and finally became a mere instrument of the rich and a mere passport to officialdom.*

Reprinted by permission of the International Association of Historians of Asia and the author from *Second Biennial Conference Proceedings* (Taipei, 1962), pp. 101–17. For a comprehensive treatment of Ming-Ch'ing social mobility, see Ping-ti Ho, *The Ladder of Success in Imperial China, Aspects of Social Mobility, 1368–1911* (New York: Columbia University Press, 1962; paper edition, Science Editions, 1964). Footnotes omitted.

In recent decades few branches of social science have made more progress and exerted more influence over historians than social mobility studies. The reasons are not far to seek. First, much like economic history, social mobility is concerned with the quantification of empirical data and quantification of empirical data is what makes social sciences and history more exact, hence closer to "science." Second, social mobility is aimed at studying quantitatively the movements of individuals and families from one social status to another and the opportunity-structure which accounts for the existence or absence of such movements. In other words, social mobility takes as its main target the investigation of the living organism, or at least the blood circulation, so to speak, of a given society. It is this organic and quantitative approach that opens up new avenues for, and brings fresh meaning to, studies of both contemporary and historical societies.

In using the social mobility concept for the study of the blood circulation of so large and complex a society as that of Ming-Ch'ing China's, four methodological problems merit our attention. First, the period should be sufficiently long to allow an observation of the unchanged aspects as well as the changing trends, and the geographical coverage should be sufficiently broad. Any generalization based on local or regional data of a limited and sometimes special period is likely to be risky. Second, statistical data must be cross-sectional. Any generalization derived from dynastic histories and various biographical series which are inevitably achievement-biased cannot be regarded as conclusive. Third, the criteria for classification must not be based on neat preconceived theory or theories, for historical facts are so complex that they can seldom be reduced to simple patterns.

Fourth, in an age in which there is an insatiable desire to theorize, especially in the Far Eastern field in the West, not all scholars remember that factual control, which requires a laboriously accumulated knowledge of legal, institutional, social, and economic history, is a prerequisite for any responsible generalization.

With these four methodological problems in mind, this paper summarizes the main statistical findings of my recent book, *The Ladder of Success in Imperial China: Aspects of Social Mobility, 1368–1911*, and deals with only one of the several aspects discussed in it, namely, the social composition of the Ming-Ch'ing ruling class. One of the main bodies of sources used is the forty-eight lists of *chin-shih* (those who passed the imperial examinations and almost automatically became middle-ranking officials) of Ming-Ch'ing times available in China and the United States. They yield a total of 12,226 cases. They are supplemented by 23,480 cases from twenty national lists of *chü-jen* (successful candidates of provincial or intermediate examinations) and *kung-sheng* (senior licentiates who much like *chü-jen* had opportunity for minor official appointment). While the *chin-shih* lists cover the entire period from 1371 to 1904 reasonably well, the latter lists are confined to the nineteenth century and used as supplementary data only. The quality of these lists is generally high as they are not only cross-sectional but provide precise information as to whether the candidate's family had produced any officeholder and/or degree-holder during the three preceding generations. Some later Ch'ing lists amount almost to abridged genealogies. These lists are by far the most exact and accurate sources for a study of officials' family background, similar in quality to the two extant Sung lists which form the backbone of professor Edward A. Kracke's illuminating article, "Family vs. Merit in Chinese Civil Service Examinations under the Empire."

It ought to be pointed out, however, that our lists theoretically have two defects, namely, the lack of information in many of them on collaterals and the absence of information on the economic status of candidates' families. But thanks to the standardized practice of conferring honorific titles of officials' ancestors, both living and deceased, those candidates whose direct ancestors were not degree-holders or officeholders but whose close collaterals one or two generations before them were holders of office or higher degrees can as a rule be detected. When detected, they are classified as descendants of officials. As to the second theoretical defect, it may have been serious for the period from the founding of the Ming Empire in 1368 to 1450, when examinations and recommendation were the two only major channels of socio-political mobility. But owing to the serious Mongol invasion of the Peking area in 1449 which resulted in the capture of the reigning emperor, the Ming government from 1451 onwards began to sell minor official titles, offices, and the title of *chien-sheng,* or Imperial Academy studentships. In the course of time it became increasingly common for men of substantial or even limited means to buy such titles. In late Ming and Ch'ing times it may be said that men of above average economic means almost invariably purchased at least an Imperial Academy studentship which cost between one hundred and two hundred taels of silver. For such a small amount of money they could acquire the right of wearing students' gowns and caps and exemption from corvée, thus differentiating themselves from ordinary commoners. For a greater part of the entire Ming-Ch'ing period, therefore, our data in fact imply some information on the economic status of candidates' families.

In the light of the power structure and the peculiar prestige and value system in Confucian China, we adopt three standards for classifying the 35,706 holders of higher degrees. Category A consists of those candidates whose families had failed to produce any officeholder or degree holder in the three preceding generations. From our knowledge of legal, institutional, and social history, and also by implication, these candidates may be regarded as coming from families of humble and obscure circumstances. They thus represent cases of what in contemporary Western societies would be "from rags to riches."

Category B consists of candidates whose families during the three preceding generations had produced one or more *hsiu-ts'ai* or *sheng-yüan* (holders of the elementary degree) but no holder of office or higher degree. Since *sheng-yüan* as a class have been regarded by Dr. Chang Chung-li as members of what he calls "gentry," a brief discussion of their legal, social, and economic status is necessary. Legally and institutionally, as is well known, *sheng-yüan* were undergraduates of county and prefectural schools; as such they were subjected to the periodic tests and reviewing examinations supervised by the provincial educational commissioner and had no right to minor government service, a fact so fundamental that it set them apart from higher degreeholders. Being unable to enter government service, *sheng-yüan* as a class, as revealed in social literature and biographies, were forced to make a meagre living by "ploughing with the writing brush" (that is, teaching in village or private family schools for a mere pittance), or by taking up sundry trades and lowly jobs, many of which were legally prohibited because they were considered as too derogatory to *sheng-yüan's* status as government students. The frequency with which the modern researcher comes across cases in which *sheng-yüan* gave up their metier for trade reflects that even in their subjective "felicific calculus" there was greater comfort in more adequate living than prolonged material privation often entailed upon them by their student's status. When the *sheng-yüan* is viewed not in the abstract but against concrete social realities, it is impossible to agree with Chang that he belonged to the theoretically conceived class of "gentry," albeit an adjective "lower" to qualify it.

Within certain limits it is permissible of course to borrow a foreign term to describe a Chinese social class, but when the difference in the social realities behind Ming-Ch'ing *sheng-yüan* and the English gentry is so great, there is reason to reject the term "gentry" entirely in our study of the Chinese society. For in the sixteenth, seventeenth, and eighteenth centuries an English gentry owned anywhere from 1,000 up to over 10,000 acres of land, usually dominated local administration, and was as a rule Tory in his political sympathy. Some keen seventeenth-century French observers of English society could find no French or European analogy to members of the English gentry, whom they called *nobiles minores,* an appellation with aristocratic aroma. That *sheng-yüan* should be regarded as a socially significant transitional group at all can be justified only because of the premium that the Confucian society attached to bookish learning. Most if not all of the candidates who came from *sheng-yüan* families and constitute our Category B were relatively humble or even poor.

There was yet another category of first degree holders whose status was originally almost the same as a *kung-sheng's*. They were *chien-sheng* or students of the Imperial Academy. In early Ming times hundreds of *chien-sheng* were appointed to offices, some even to high offices, without their having to acquire a more advanced degree. The Imperial Academy was a more important channel for official recruitment than the regular examinations at the beginning of the Ming period. From the 1450's financial reasons forced the government to sell *chien-sheng* title to ordinary *sheng-yüan,* with the long-range result that the *chien-sheng's* prestige and opportunities of actual official appointment steadily deteriorated. But it is important to bear in mind that right down to the end of the Ming dynasty *chien-sheng* were legally and institutionally entitled to minor government offices. After the change of dynasty in 1644 the Imperial Academy had but a nominal existence and the *chien-sheng* title was for sale to anybody, with or without the *sheng-yüan* degree, who could afford to pay between 100 and 200 taels of silver. In the Tao-kuang period (1821-1850) alone the government sold more than 300,-000 *chien-sheng* titles. That the *chien-sheng* title was sold *en masse* to commoners at substantial discounts during and after the Taiping rebellion is common knowledge. A study of Ch'ing statutes reveals that, with the exception of a very small number of *chien-sheng* who were actually enrolled in the Academy in Peking and who through special selective tests could hope to be appointed to the lowest rank of government clerks, the rest of the vast number of *chien-sheng* had no chance of receiving any minor government appointment without further purchase of official ranks or offices. In the light of these changes in *chien-sheng's* status and rights it seems reasonable to include them in the Ming ruling class and to classify them as Category B for the Ch'ing period.

Category C consists of candidates whose

families during the three preceding generations had produced one or more office-holders and/or holders of degrees higher than and including *kung-sheng*. These families may be regarded as official and potential official families. For the Ming period only candidates whose families had produced one or more *chien-sheng* are also to be classified under the same category. To these should be added families with subofficials or ancestors who had purchased official titles and ranks. It ought to be pointed out that, although their legal and social status differed from that of commoners, many families of the lower stratum of this broadly defined ruling class were actually of relatively limited prestige, privilege, and economic means.

Category D, which is a subdivision of Category C, consists of candidates whose families within the three previous generations had produced one or more high officials of the third rank and above. Since officials of the third rank and above had, among other things, the *yin* or hereditary privilege, their families may be regarded as nationally "distinguished." Candidates from families of imperial and non-imperial hereditary nobility are also included in this category.

The criteria for Category A are very strict and those for Category C very lenient. If our criteria must have a certain bias, the bias should be on the safe side, especially when the highest status among the candidate's ancestors for three generations decides the candidate's family status. It must also be emphatically pointed out that our percentage figures based on the above criteria of classification are far from being able to tell the whole story about the long and complex process of socio-academic mobility. Our figures would convey different impressions to those who have gone through these lists themselves and those who are inclined to treat statistics abstractly. While the individual ancestral records often reveal considerable vicissitudes within the families, our figures cannot adequately demonstrate such changes and tend to generalize the family status by the highest status produced in three preceding generations. In other words, the mobility rates shown in the following tables are invariably *minimized*.

The ancestral data of Ming-Ch'ing *chin-shih* are summarized in Table 1.

For the entire Ming-Ch'ing period we find that Category A accounted for 30.2 percent of the total candidates, Category B for 12.1 percent, and Category C for 57.7 percent. The sum of Categories A and B, which by definition represented candidates from commoner families, was 42.3 percent. With the exception of the classes of 1655, 1682, and 1703, candidates from high-ranking official families never exceeded 10 percent of the total and the over-all average of Category D during the whole five and a half centuries was a mere 5.7 percent.

The significant changes in the percentage distribution of Categories A, B, and C during various subperiods are shown in Table 2. Because of its small numbers and relatively few changes, Category D is omitted.

While I must refer the readers to Chapter V of my book for a systematic explanation of the various factors which affected socio-academic mobility rates, it seems pertinent to point out briefly here that the combined circumstances in early Ming were unusually favorable to the humble and obscure, who constituted a majority during our first subperiod, 1371–1496. In the course of time, however, the various advantages enjoyed by members of official families could not fail to prevail. In the sixteenth century Category C steadily gained ground and outnumbered the commoner groups by a small

Table 1
Social Composition of Ming-Ch'ing *Chin-shih* (The Sum of A, B, C—100)

Year	Total number of chin-shih	Category A Number	Category A % of total	Category B Number	Category B % of total	Combined A & B	Category C Number	Category C % of total	Category D Number	Category D % of total
1371	28	21	75.0	—	—	75.0	7	25.0	—	—
1412	106	89	84.0	—	—	84.0	17	16.0	9	8.5
1457	294	182	61.8	—	—	61.8	112	38.2	9	3.0
1469	248	149	60.0	—	—	60.0	90	40.0	11	4.5
1472	250	137	54.8	—	—	54.8	113	45.2	13	5.2
1496	298	140	47.0	—	—	47.0	158	53.0	14	4.6
1505	303	126	41.6	—	—	41.6	177	58.4	12	4.0
1521	330	156	47.3	—	—	47.3	174	52.7	13	3.9
1535	329	154	47.0	—	—	47.0	175	53.0	22	6.9
1538	317	154	48.6	1	0.3	48.9	162	51.1	23	7.3
1544	312	151	48.4	2	0.6	49.0	159	51.0	24	8.0
1553	384	182	47.4	24	6.2	53.6	178	46.6	15	3.9
1562	298	133	44.6	—	—	44.6	165	55.4	17	5.7
1568	405	203	50.1	—	—	50.1	202	49.9	17	4.2
1580	302	134	44.4	—	—	44.4	168	55.6	12	4.0
1586	356	105	29.5	54	15.1	44.6	197	55.4	18	5.0
1610	230	61	26.5	40	17.4	43.9	129	56.1	18	7.8
1652	366	85	23.2	48	13.1	36.3	233	63.7	30	8.2
1655	401	112	28.2	65	16.2	44.2	224	55.8	48	11.7
1658	407	126	30.7	58	14.2	44.9	223	55.1	25	6.1
1659	358	124	34.6	32	8.9	43.5	202	56.5	27	7.5
1661	373	112	29.7	57	15.2	44.9	204	55.1	36	9.6
1673	138	37	26.8	22	15.9	42.7	79	57.3	5	3.6
1682	151	12	8.0	17	11.3	19.3	122	80.7	18	11.9
1685	169	30	17.6	33	19.2	36.8	106	63.2	15	8.9
1703	104	10	9.6	20	19.2	28.8	74	71.2	17	16.3
1822	210	23	10.9	52	24.8	35.7	135	64.3	12	5.3
1829	223	46	20.6	49	22.0	42.6	128	57.4	10	4.4
1833	226	30	13.3	62	27.4	40.7	134	59.3	16	7.1
1835	243	26	10.7	54	22.2	32.9	163	67.1	17	7.0
1844	200	31	15.5	53	26.5	42.0	116	58.2	7	3.5
1859	191	52	27.2	35	18.3	45.5	104	54.5	7	3.6
1860	146	35	24.0	33	22.5	46.5	78	53.5	6	4.1
1865	228	36	15.8	49	21.4	37.2	143	62.8	13	5.7
1868	228	25	10.9	50	21.9	32.8	153	67.2	13	5.7
1871	280	45	16.0	66	23.5	39.5	169	60.5	7	2.5
1874	228	15	6.6	52	22.8	29.4	161	70.6	9	3.9
1876	216	30	13.9	49	22.7	26.6	137	63.4	5	2.3
1877	276	40	14.9	46	16.7	31.6	190	68.4	16	5.6
1880	276	31	11.2	49	17.7	28.9	196	71.1	13	4.7
1883	245	31	12.6	40	16.3	28.9	174	71.1	9	3.6
1886	263	29	11.0	55	20.9	31.9	179	68.1	15	5.7
1889	251	40	15.9	41	16.0	31.9	170	68.1	12	4.8
1890	234	24	10.3	44	18.4	28.7	166	71.3	8	3.5
1892	239	31	12.9	45	18.8	31.7	163	68.3	13	5.4
1895	181	30	16.6	27	14.9	31.5	124	68.5	6	3.2
1898	142	33	23.2	22	15.5	38.7	87	61.3	5	3.5
1904	243	88	36.2	25	10.3	46.5	130	53.5	4	1.7
Total or Average	12,226	3,696	30.2	1,471	12.1	42.3	7,059	57.7	691	5.7

[1] For complete listings of these 48 *chin-shih* lists, see my *The Ladder of Success in Imperial China, Aspects of Social Mobility, 1368–1911* (Columbia University Press, 1962), Bibliography, section 1.

[2] The total numbers of *chin-shih* of various years are those of the candidates whose ancestral records are given. For textual reasons certain numbers of successful candidates have to be excluded from later Ch'ing lists.

[3] For the year 1553 information is available for only two preceding generations instead of the usual three.

Table 2
Changing Social Composition of *Chin-shih* in Various Subperiods
(in Percent)

Period	Category A	Category B	Categories A and B	Category C
1371–1496	58.2	—	58.2	41.8
1505–1580	46.9	0.9	47.8	52.2
1586–1610	28.5	16.0	44.5	55.5
Ming average	47.5	2.5	50.0	50.0
1652–1661	29.2	13.6	42.8	57.2
1673–1703	15.8	16.4	32.2	67.8
1822–1904	15.5	20.0	35.5	64.5
Ch'ing average	19.1	18.1	37.2	62.8

margin. The margin would have been much larger had it not been for the remarkable progress in printing and the mushrooming growth of private academies consequent upon Wang Yang-ming's teachings. The large-scale reproducton of classics, dynastic histories, and literary works provided the poor and humble with the much-needed reference tools. The growth of private academies, which generally provided scholarships for the needy, occurred just at a time when the *she-hsüeh* (private elementary schools) system had begun to decline. The most crucial change occurred from the late sixteenth century onwards, when Category A dropped drastically to below 30 percent, a drop which was partially compensated for by a sharp rise in Category B. These two phenomena seem to indicate that socio-academic mobility was becoming increasingly difficult for the commoners, many of whom required an inter-generation preparation to attain the final goal in mobility. This trend continued for a while shortly after the change of dynasty in 1644, when the Manchu government purposely set up unusually large *chin-shih* quotas in order to attract the services of the newly subjugated Chinese. After the Manchu empire became stabilized under the K'ang-hsi emperor (1662–1722), *chin-shih* quotas were drastically reduced. The reduced quotas, coupled with the persistent fact that academic competition had become increasingly acute, brought about a further drop in Category A percentage. K'ang-hsi's restrictive *chin-shih* quota policy was continued by his grandson, the Ch'ien-lung emperor (1736–1795). Had significant numbers of eighteenth-century *chin-shih* lists been available, it is not unlikely that we should find Category A figures even somewhat smaller than the average of the K'ang-hsi period. This estimate is based on my analysis of several *chü-jen* and *kung-sheng* lists of the Ch'ien-lung period which because of limited space here cannot be tabulated. All in all, therefore, it would appear that because of the lack of data for the eighteenth century the Category A average for the entire Ch'ing period may be slightly too high. If so, the actual Category A average for the entire Ch'ing period should probably be very close to those of the K'ang-hsi era and of the nineteenth century. In other words, the Ch'ing Category A percentage is likely to be slightly over one-fourth of that of the early Ming period. It is important to bear in mind, however, that the drastically lower Category A percentage during the Ch'ing was partially mitigated by a sustained rise in Category B, which, except during the first two decades of the Manchu dynasty, exceeded the percentage for Category A.

The socio-academic mobility at the intermediate level may be shown in Table 3, which, owing to limited space, is necessarily abbreviated.

Although the average percentage figures for Categories A and B of late Ch'ing *chü-jen* and *kung-sheng* are all higher than the corresponding figures for *chin-shih* of the same period, the most remarkable feature of these two independent statistical series is their general compatibility. A comparison of these two series indicates that it was somewhat easier for men of non-official families to acquire the intermediate degrees than the advanced *chin-shih* status. This seems all the more reasonable as competition at the level of the national examination must have been keener and more difficult for the commoners than at the levels of *chü-jen* and *kung-sheng* examinations.

The aspect of socio-academic mobility which is most difficult to ascertain statistically is the entry of commoners of non-scholastic families into the vast *sheng-yüan* body, for these holders of the elementary degree were nowhere socially recognized as being established. Local histories do not as a rule even contain their name lists, let alone any information on their ancestry. Although late in the Ch'ing period special *sheng-yüan* lists were compiled by more than half a dozen lower-Yangtze counties, only three of them yield brief but vital information on *sheng-yüng* ancestry. By way of family background these three useful lists all give two general types of *sheng-yüan*, one with his name only but no other information, one with his name and also a brief reference to his being the great-grandson, grandson, grandnephew, son, or nephew of somebody else. After painstaking checking it has been found that the latter was invariably a holder of the elementary degree or higher degree. Although the information on ancestry is much briefer than that given in the lists of higher degree holders, it actually covers more generations and enables us to establish whether a *sheng-yüan* originated from a scholastic family or from an ordinary commoner family which had not previously produced any degree holder. What enhances the value of these lists is that the information on ancestry extends to collaterals. If quantitatively they do not enable us to generalize on the social composition of *sheng-yüan* for the entire country, they nevertheless yield some invaluable clues on

Table 3
Social Composition of Late-Ch-ing *Chü-jen* and *Kung-sheng* [1]
(The Sum of A, B, and C—100 percent)   (23,480 individuals)

Category A	Category B	Combined % of A and B	Category C	Category D
20.1	25.0	45.1	54.9	2.6

[1] Based on twenty selected national *chü-jen* and *kung-sheng* lists of the years 1804, 1807, 1808, 1816, 1821, 1828, 1831, 1832, 1834, 1835, 1843, 1844, 1849, 1855, 1870, 1879, 1885, 1897, 1906, and 1910. For textual reasons a few similar lists of the 19th century have to be excluded. The total number of individuals is that of those whose ancestral data are given.

Table 4
Percentage of *Shen-yüan* from Families Without Degree Holders
(11,504 individuals)

	Ch'ang-shu County	Haimen County	Nan-t'ung County
Ming period	no information	no information	74.8
Ch'ing period	54.5	48.4	53.0

the socio-academic mobility near its grass-roots levels.

The fact that on the average nearly three-quarters of *sheng-yüan* during the Ming and more than 50 percent during the Ch'ing came from obscure commoner families without previous elementary degree holders would indicate that the social composition of the large *sheng-yüan* body, even more than that of the much smaller *chin-shih* group, was in a constant state of flux. The above figures would also imply a reasonably wide opportunity-structure for ordinary commoners at the broad base of the social pyramid.

The factors which contributed to this substantial socio-academic mobility in Ming-Ch'ing China were many and varied. We can barely mention here in passing the major ones: the unusually sympathetic attitude on the part of early Ming rulers towards the poor and humble; the establishment of government schools at the county, prefectural, and provincial levels; the rudimentary but nationwide scholarship system; the existence in many parts of China in the first half of the Ming period of communal elementary schools; the phenomenal growth since the early sixteenth century of private academies which also offered scholarships to the intelligent and needy; the institution of community chests for the express purpose of subsidizing candidates to travel to provincial and national capitals to take higher-level examinations; the availability in many cases of educational and financial aid from kinsmen and friends; the effect of the continual expansion of printing facilities; and the intellectual and social emancipation as a consequence of the teachings of Wang Yang-ming. All in all, Ming-Ch'ing China approached more closely than any previous period to the true ideal of Confucius that "in education there should be no class distinctions."

It would be one-sided, however, to say that the competitive examination system was the only major channel for social mobility. Wealth, as a matter of fact, was becoming increasingly important since 1451, especially after 1851. This is shown by the analysis of the initial qualifications of Ch'ing officials given in my book. But viewed from the needs of the whole society and from the necessity of maintaining a balance within the officialdom, the sale of offices and titles in later Ming and Ch'ing times, much like the system of *la Paulette* in France under the *ancien régime,* served a not unuseful purpose.

In addition to examinations and sale of offices, descendants of high officials could also enter government service through *yin,* that is, hereditary privilege. In sharp contrast to the T'ang and Sung periods, however, the scope of *yin* was greatly curtailed in Ming-Ch'ing times. By Ming-Ch'ing practice only officials of the three top ranks were entitled to bring one descendant into state service through *yin* as a seventh, sixth, or fifth ranking official. As shown from biographies and genealogies, the *yin* privilege seldom could go beyond two generations. For the entire nineteenth century, for example, those who entered government service through *yin* amounted to only 1,022, as against 12,477 *chin-shih* and a much larger number of *chü-jen* and *kung-sheng*. It does not seem an exaggeration to say that the *yin* privilege in general had very little effect on prolonging the success of high-status families if their descendants were inept.

In order to stimulate general interest and to invite constructive criticism of Asian historians, I wish to utilize this opportunity to present a few broader generalizations of my book.

First, for historians the continuity and changes in the pattern of socio-academic mobility since the permanent institutionalization of the competitive civil service examination system in early T'ang times are worth a brief review. The significance of the examination system on social mobility in T'ang times, though quite obvious, as revealed in Professor Ch'en Yin-k'o's monumental study of T'ang political history, cannot easily be shown statistically because of the lack of sources similar to ours. Actually very little is known of the precise family background of prominent T'ang Chinese who owed their success to the examination. Even when T'ang literature and biographies refer to an individual's social origin as humble and lowly, the adjective must be interpreted in the T'ang social context. It is probable that such adjectives as humble and lowly were used by contemporaries only in comparison with the hereditary aristocracy which, if it was no longer able to monopolize political power from the mid-seventeenth century onwards, remained the dominant political factor and enjoyed unrivalled social prestige down to the very end of the T'ang period.

After the great T'ang clans finally declined amidst the incessant wars of the Five Dynasties (907–60) and the perpetuation of the examination system under the Sung (960–1279), Chinese society definitely became more mobile and the social composition of the ruling bureaucracy more broadened. An excellent recent study by Mr. Sun Kuo-tung shows that of the early Sung (960–1126) officials with biographical entries in the *History of the Sung Dynasty* 46.1 percent may be regarded as coming from *han-tsu* (literally "humble" clans or families); whereas officials of similar social origin constitute a mere 13.1 percent of the late T'ang (756–906) officials with biographical entries in the two *Histories of the T'ang Dynasty*. While within the limitations of dynastic histories the descriptions of the social origin of late T'ang and early Sung officials in the above study are as specific as can be expected, the key word "humble" must be interpreted in the T'ang context. For the Southern Sung period (1127–1279) Professor Kracke's article shows that candidates from non-official families constituted 56.3 percent of the total of the class of 1148 and 57.9 percent of the class of 1256. These figures are highly significant, although they are not strictly comparable to ours for the Ming-Ch'ing period. The main reason is that in Sung times the passing of the provincial examination was merely a requisite for taking the *chin-shih* examination, not a formal degree or qualification for minor official appointment, as it was in Ming-Ch'ing period. A significant portion of Sung *chin-shih* who are technically classified as from non-official families may well fall into our Category C, that is, the broadly and leniently defined official and potential official families.

There is reason to believe that the extant Sung data, if they could be classified by the same criteria used in my study on the Ming-Ch'ing period, would probably yield considerably smaller Category A figures, at least in comparison with the early Ming period. This speculation appears not unreasonable because we know that the number of prefectural and county schools and private academies in Sung times was much smaller than that during the Ming and that printing and other channels, such as the clan organization and community chests, which had a bearing on social mobility, were still in a stage of dormancy towards the end of the Southern Sung period.

In our long-range retrospect, therefore, it may be suggested that the amount of socio-academic mobility began to become truly substantial in the Sung, reached its maximum in the greater part of the Ming, started to level off after the late sixteenth century, and continued its downward trend until the final abolition of the examination system in 1905.

Second, in the light of the substantial amounts of socio-academic mobility throughout the Ming-Ch'ing period, it is difficult to say that the civil service examination system failed to serve an important social and political purpose. Modern students without preconceived theories or prejudice would perhaps rather agree with François Quesnay, a typical eighteenth-century French *philosophe*, who, despite a much idealized picture about China which he acquired from the Jesuits, believed with basically valid reason that by and large the Chinese ruling class was recruited on the basis of individual merit. In fact, the examination system's long history of thirteen centuries is a most eloquent testimonial to its usefulness as a channel of mobility and as a socially and politically stabilizing factor. It is inconceivable for a large nation as pragmatic as China to have perpetuated an institution if it were truly a sham as some modern Western scholars would have us believe.

Third, as a corollary to the preceding generalization, there is no valid reason to believe that Ming-Ch'ing officaldom was a self-perpetuating body. True, the total average of Ming-Ch'ing *chin-shih* from our leniently defined official and potential official families is 57.7 percent, but the social composition of the bureaucracy was constantly changing. The constantly changing social composition of the bureaucracy was well nigh inevitable because academic success and official appointment owed not so much to blood as to intelligence, assiduity, and perseverance. From our study of the genealogies of some of the most prominent Ming-Ch'ing clans and from extensive social literature, we know that it was very difficult for the average official family to maintain that Confucian puritanical spirit which had accounted so much for its early success. But by far the most important reason for the inability of the bureaucracy to be a self-perpetuating body was the absence of primogeniture and the inevitable process of progressive dilution of family property by the typically Chinese clan and family system. This causal relationship is nowhere more poignantly pointed out than by Ke Shou-li, one of the famous censor-generals of the sixteenth century, who, on the occasion of donating some 1,000 *mu* of land as his clan's inalienable common property, remarked: "When the ancient clan system of which primogeniture formed a hard core can no longer be revived, the empire can have no hereditary families; when the empire has no hereditary families, the imperial court can have no hereditary ministers." Small wonder, then, that Ming-Ch'ing China could not have "predestined parliament men" as eighteenth-century England had as a matter of course, for "predestined parliament men" were possible only because through primogeniture and entail the aristocracy had preserved the integrity of its landed states which, in the last analysis, were the most important source of political power before the age of reform. Since Ming-Ch'ing China had more institutionalized channels which promoted the upward mobility of the humble but gifted and determined people but had practically no institutionalized means to prevent the long-range downward mobility of high-status families, the Ming-Ch'ing society was highly competitive in its own peculiar ways.

Fourth, somewhat different from the gradualness of the processes of social mobility in modern Western societies, our Category A figures and a vast amount of biographical material which cannot be presented here would suggest that there were probably more cases of "from rags to riches" in Ming-Ch'ing China than in the modern West.

Last, although the amounts of socio-academic mobility throughout the Ming-Ch'ing period are substantial by any standard, the significance of the downward trend in our Category A figures must be interpreted in the context of Chinese society at that time. For a nation so used to a "Horatio Alger" sort of social myth, though in a strictly academic and political sense, the steady shrinking opportunity-structure for the poor and humble must have engendered a great deal of social frustration. It is worth speculating, therefore, whether the persistent downward trend in our Category A figures has had anything to do with social unrest and revolutions that have characterized nineteenth- and twentieth-century China.

T'UNG-TSU CH'Ü

The Gentry and Local Administration in Ch'ing China

As a social class, the scholar-official was a unique feature of traditional Chinese society. The generally accepted term for this class is gentry, *but the composition of the class has been a subject of debate among historians in the field.*[1]

In the following selection, Professor T'ung-tsu Ch'ü, a senior Chinese scholar who now resides in China, uses gentry *to designate the group of "local elites" who controlled local affairs by means of informal power. Professor Ch'ü specifically emphasizes the gentry's rule in local administration in Ch'ing China.*

Local government at the chou *(department) and* hsien *(district) levels in China under the Ch'ing was highly centralized. The various subdivisions of a province, from the* fu *(prefecture) down to the* chou *and* hsien, *were all under the control of the central government and administered by officials appointed by it. The administrators of the* chou *and* hsien *governments—the magistrates—possessed the least power among all officials, for they had to secure approval from their superiors in regard to most details of administration. But if a magistrate possessed minimum power, the scope of his duties was enormous, covering all matters concerning the common good of the community—welfare, custom, morality, education, agriculture, etc. Moreover, a magistrate was never a native of the province where he held office, and he was therefore likely to have little or no knowledge of the local situation.*[2]

All in all, local government under the Ch'ing was a very peculiar institution. With limited power and resources, the officials who headed the local governments found it necessary to seek help and cooperation from the gentry. The gentry, on the other hand, were a status group that enjoyed certain social, economic, and legal privileges. The law allowed them a particular style of life that distinguished

---

Reprinted by permission of the publishers from T'ung-tsu Ch'ü, *Local Government in China Under the Ch'ing.* Cambridge, Mass.: Harvard University Press, Copyright, 1962 by the President and Fellows of Harvard College. Footnotes omitted.

[1] For example, see the following studies: Chang Chung-li, *The Chinese Gentry* (Seattle: University of Washington Press, 1955), pp. 3–70; and Ho Ping-ti, *The Ladder of Success in Imperial China* (New York: Columbia University Press, 1962), pp. 26–41.

[2] For a recent study of the district magistrate in late Imperial China, see John R. Watt, *The District Magistrate in Late Imperial China* (New York: Columbia University Press, 1972).

them from the commoner. *Naturally, the gentry commanded respect and obedience from the commoner and were treated by local officials with courtesy and respect. However, the intermediary role that the gentry assumed between the magistrate and the people did not give them the authority to issue orders or to make decisions through the governmental apparatus. A gentry member could only exert his influence upon the officials in their decision-making. It is in regard to this that Professor Ch'ü makes the most illuminating observation.*

According to Professor Ch'ü, although the gentry represented the informal power in a local community, they were linked to the formal power at all levels, and it was this link that gave them power to influence the local officials. The gentry's connection with formal power was based primarily upon specific relationships among the persons connected with the imperial examination system, such as teachers (the examiners who passed a candidate in his examinations), students (those who passed the examination, thereby becoming known as the students of the examiner), and fellow degree-holders (those who passed the same examination in the same year). The behavior patterns of the scholar-officials were to a large extent conditioned by these relationships. The scholar-officials were under obligation to be loyal to their teachers, students, and fellow degree-holders, and also to the children of all of them, and to help each other in trouble. Such institutionalized and organized personal relationships were the channel through which the gentry exerted their influence.

In retrospect, we may say that it is in the local government that we find the civil service examination system most influential.

1. The Gentry as an Informal Power

The chou and hsien governments considered all matters concerning the common good of the community—welfare, custom, morality, education, agriculture, and so on —to be within the scope of their activities. Many of these matters, regarded by the Chinese as within the province of governmental "administration," would in other societies have been the responsibility of civil associations. Certainly the government was not in a position to carry out all these functions with equal effectiveness. It was the local gentry that performed some of the functions which the local government was unable or not well qualified to perform. As we shall see, there was a traditional division of function between the local government authority and the gentry. The latter, in fact, were indispensable to the realization of certain of the government's aims.

The gentry were the local elite who shared with the government the control of local affairs. They represented an informal power, in contrast to the formal power invested in the local government. While the two groups depended upon one another, each exercised its power in a different way. The interplay of these two forms of power shaped the power relationship into patterns of coordination, cooperation, and conflict.

An important feature of the Chinese gentry was that it was the only group that could legitimately represent the local community in discussing local affairs with the officials and in participating in the governing process. This privilege was not extended to any other social group or association. The merchants' guild was not powerful enough to have a voice in matters concerning the common good of the community, still less in the governing process. In fact, with the exception of a few wealthy members such as those engaged in the salt business, the merchant class was not treated with courtesy by the government officials and had no access to them. The merchants' strongest means of protest against the authorities was to close their shops. This situation persisted until the latter part of the nineteenth century, when the merchants were allowed to join the gentry in discussions of local affairs (hence the gentry and merchants came to be mentioned together as *shen shang*). But they were still under the domination of the gentry and failed to form an independent power group. Thus, for a long time the gentry's leadership and power went unchallenged, except during a rebellion or other crisis when the *status quo* could not be maintained.

In the sense that the gentry and the officials belonged to the same group, as either members or potential members of the bureaucracy, their power was derived from the political order. Thus, despite the distinction between formal and informal power, it was actually the same power group that controlled society. The same group of men were officials in their public capacity and gentry in their private capacity. The result was that the politically based power was the power that dominated and only those who possessed it, actually or potentially, were admitted into the elite and allowed to participate in the act of governing.

2. Definition of "Gentry"

The term "gentry," borrowed from English history, has been the cause of much confusion and debate when applied to the Chinese scene. To this confusion has been added the fact that the composition of the gentry in China was not the same in all periods.

The early Chinese term, *chin-shen*, which can be traced back to before the Ch'in and Han, was simply a synonym for officials. The term *shen-shih* or *shen-chin* was used in Ming and Ch'ing times, indicating the emergence of a new status group—degree holders (*shih* or *chin*). The Ch'ing inherited both its examination system and the structure of its gentry from the Ming dynasty.

In view of the evolution in the composition of the group, it is misleading to discuss the Chinese gentry without specifying the period. We are concerned here only with the gentry under the Ch'ing. Since the term has no equivalent in English, it would be better either to use the Chinese term or to designate this class in China as the "local elite," meaning a power group which controlled local affairs by means of informal power. While "local elite" might seem rather too general, it does not have the misleading associations that "gentry" has. But, wishing to avoid further confusion through the injection of a new term, I shall keep the commonly accepted term "gentry," emphasizing the rather unique features of the Chinese gentry.

The privileged status of the Chinese gentry was not determined on a purely economic basis. Membership in the gentry did not derive from wealth or the ownership of landed property, as some scholars have assumed. No doubt there was a close connection between wealth and gentry membership and the significance of the former should not be overlooked. The possession of property made possible the leisure necessary for acquiring the education that enabled a person to take the civil service examinations. The characteristic style of life of the gentry was also impossible without some degree of wealth. However, there is a distinction between the conditions facilitating entrance into a privileged class and the actual attainment of privileged status. Wealth or landed property per se was not the qualification for gentry status. The commoner-landlords did not belong to the gentry group, no matter how much land they owned. Probably the connection between wealth and status became closest at times when it was possible to buy from the government an official rank or academic title (student status in the Imperial Academy)—a common practice in the Ch'ing, particularly in the nineteenth century when exigencies forced the government to seek additional revenue. This was the only condition under which wealth could be translated directly into status, bypassing the examinations. But landlords and merchants who did not purchase an official rank or academic title remained commoners.

On the other hand, anyone holding a degree or receiving an official appointment immediately became a member of the gentry, regardless of land ownership. There were poor *sheng-yüan,* holders of the lowest degree, who owned no landed property, and lived on their stipends or incomes from teaching or other occupations. The poorest ones even received relief from the government during a famine. Thus both propertied and propertyless persons belonged to the same status group. While it is true that most gentry members did possess property, particularly landed property, the fact is often overlooked that many of them, as portrayed in the satirical novel, *Ju-lin-wai-shih* (The Scholars), acquired landed property after they had acquired gentry membership. In their case land ownership was the effect rather than the cause of status. All these factors would argue that, although landed property was closely linked with gentry status, it is ambiguous and misleading to define landlords as gentry.

It is also important to keep in mind that a distinction existed between the literati and the gentry, although there was of course a certain degree of overlap. Education was usually a prerequisite to becoming a gentry member, but education alone did not automatically qualify one. It was necessary to pass the civil or military examinations in order to attain this status. For example, a junior student (*t'ung-sheng*) who had passed the preliminary examination given by a magistrate or a prefect (*hsien-shih* or *fu-shih*) was not admitted to the gentry until he had passed the examination given by the provincial director of studies (*yüan-shih*), thus acquiring the First Degree and the status of a student in the government schools. There were learned scholars who never became gentry because they had failed to pass this examination or refused to take it. These men were known as *pu-i* (lit., "wearers of cotton-cloth garments"; that is, commoners). On the other hand, nonliterati might acquire gentry status by purchasing an academic title or official rank.

What, then, were the qualifications for gentry membership? The answer is to be found in the political order; that is to say, membership was based upon the attainment of bureaucratic status or of the qualifications for such status. The gentry class in the Ch'ing period, as it was defined legally, officially, and popularly, was composed of two groups: (1) officials: active, retired, or dismissed, including those who purchased their official titles or ranks; (2) holders of degrees or academic titles, including civil and military *chin-shih* (holders of the Third Degree or those who had passed the metropolitan examination); civil and military *chü-jen* (holders of the Second Degree, or those who had passed the provincial examination); *kung-sheng* (Senior Licentiates, including those who purchased their titles); *chien-sheng* (Students of the Imperial Academy, including those who purchased their titles); and civil and military *sheng-yüan* (students of government schools, who were holders of the First Degree, popularly known as *hsiu-ts'ai*).

These two groups constituted the gentry, known as *shen-shih* or *shen-chin*. But within the gentry, as is indicated in the *Hsien-kang ts'e* (Essentials to government; records prepared by magistrates for their superiors) and other official records in which the names of local gentry were listed, a distinction was made between *shen* and *shih* (or *chin*). *Shen* referred only to the officials (group 1), whereas *shih* referred to the holders of degrees or of academic titles who had not yet entered officialdom (group 2). In other words, a distinction was made between officials and nonofficials, between what may be called, respectively, the "official-gentry" and the "scholar-gentry."

The "scholar-gentry" belonged neither to the ruling class, nor to the ruled; they were an intermediate group. They did not participate in the formal government, but they enjoyed a large measure of the prestige, privileges, and power of the ruling class—a fact which characterized them as the elite and separated them from the masses. As potential candidates for membership in the bureaucracy, they may also be called the potential ruling class.

In view of these factors, I am strongly convinced that the distinction between the official-gentry and the scholar-gentry has considerable sociological significance in the analysis of the Ch'ing power structure. As we shall see, the official-gentry had a superior status, had more privileges, and were more influential than the scholar-gentry. The first group formed the locus of power, where the second was rather on the periphery. The way in which the groups exercised their influence or power was also different.

Both the official-gentry and the scholar-gentry were referred to as *chu-hsiang shih-ta-fu* (scholar-officials living in their home town) because of the close connection between the gentry and their native communities. The degree-holders generally lived in their native places, except when they took employment (for example, as private secretaries) in other areas. The officials, under the "law of avoidance," which prohibited their holding a post in their native province, had a dual status—that of an official in one locality, and that of gentry member in their native province. We might call such an official an "absentee gentry member" because he could assume his role only in an indirect way. He assumed it directly when he was at home on leave, say to observe the mourning period for a parent, or when he had retired or been dismissed. Then he became a *hsiang-huan* or *hsiang-shen* (lit., "official living in his home town").

It was within this territorial sphere that the gentry acted their role and maintained the various forms of interpersonal relations with the local officials. Because their ties with their native places were permanent ones that engendered a sentimental attachment, the gentry seem to have felt that it was their responsibility to guard and promote the welfare of these communities. This sentiment was lacking among the magistrates and other local officials, who were nonnatives.

3. Prestige and Privileges of the Gentry

The gentry had a status superior to that of the rest of society. They had a class consciousness and a sense of belonging to one group. They identified each other as members and shared similar attitudes, interests, and values (specifically, Confucian values). They felt that they were distinct from the rest of the populace. This fact apparently underlay their common sentiments and collective action. An insult to one member, from an outsider, for example, was considered an insult to the whole group. A magistrate once said: "Please one *shih*, and the whole group of *shih* will be pleased; humiliate one *shih*, and the whole group of *shih* will be resentful."

On the whole, the gentry were treated by local officials with courtesy and respect, the extent of which was graded according to the individual's status within the gentry stratum. Only the official-gentry and holders of higher degrees (*chin-shih* and *chü-jen*) were equals of the magistrates; and some among these, having higher official ranks, were considered superior to the magistrates. The holders of the lowest degrees (*sheng-yüan*) were regarded as inferior to the magistrates. The members of this sub-group, having no bureaucratic status, were regarded as merely "heads of the commoners." This status scale was clearly evident in the conventional way in which the gentry referred to themselves before the magistrate and the way in which they were received by him. While the official-gentry or holders of higher degrees had free access to the magistrate, the *sheng-yüan* did not. Under the law, the *sheng-yüan* and those who purchased the titles of *kung-sheng* and *chien-sheng* were under the supervision and control of both the local and educational officials, who were required to report to the provincial director of studies on the conduct of the students. As we shall see later, the students could be and were chastised or dismissed in accordance with a prescribed procedure. In short, while the gentry as a whole enjoyed a status superior to that of the commoners, the status of the *sheng-yüan* and of the *chien-sheng* was inferior to that of the official-gentry and the holders of higher degrees. As Feng Kuei-fen pointed out, it was difficult for a magistrate to inflict hardships on the official-gentry, but easy to inflict them on the *sheng-yüan* and *chien-sheng*. They could be deprived of their titles upon the magistrate's request, or humiliated or ruined by him in some other way.

The gentry enjoyed certain social, economic, and legal privileges. The law allowed them the privilege of a particular style of life. They were entitled to wear a certain kind of hat button, and an official robe and belt. The holder of a higher degree or academic title, from *chin-shih* down to *kung-sheng*, could display on his door a horizontal tablet inscribed with his title, and erect a flagpole in front of his residence to show his superior status. All the gentry had the privilege of observing special ceremonies at weddings, funerals, and sacrifices.

The official-gentry were not placed under the judicial power of their local authority and were not subject to the regular judicial procedures. An official could not legally be tried or given a sentence without the emperor's permission. The same applied to retired or dismissed officials, unless their discharge had been dishonorable.

The scholar-gentry were accorded treatment different from that of the commoners in court. *Sheng-yüan* and purchasers of the title of *kung-sheng* or *chien-sheng* could not be beaten by a magistrate without permission from the educational officials. When corporal punishment was decreed, it was administered by the latter in the presence of the magistrate, in a hall in the government school which was named, literally, "Understand Relations Hall" (*Ming-lun-t'ang*). A magistrate who disregarded this regulation was subject to punishment. When a serious offense was involved, the suspected offender had first to be deprived of his academic title or degree on the recommendation of the magistrate before a trial could be held.

Official-gentry and scholar-gentry were also exempted from punishment short of penal servitude. The law permitted them to cancel a beating by pecuniary redemption. But by mandate, when an offense called for punishment by 100 strokes, an official was to be impeached and a *chin-shih*, *chü-jen, kung-sheng, chien-sheng*, or *sheng-yüan* was to be deprived of his degree or academic title.

When a member of the official-gentry or scholar-gentry was involved with a commoner in a dispute over marriage or landed property, or in any other civil lawsuit, he was permitted by law to send a family member or servant to act as his representative at the trial. A commoner who injured an official, whether active or retired, was punished more severely than if the injured man had been his equal.

All these privileges meant that the gentry received legal protection such as was not enjoyed by the commoners. . . . The common people, including wealthy landlords, were subjected to all kinds of persecution and annoyance by officials and their subordinates. Only when wealth was combined with political power could the people secure protection for themselves and their familes. This helps to explain the eagerness to become degree holders or officials.

4. Gentry Channels of Influence

The gentry's influence in their community was exerted in two spheres. One was the sphere of the commoners, from whom they commanded respect and obedience. As social leaders of the community, they settled disputes, conducted fund-raising campaigns, commanded local defense, and provided other kinds of leadership. The people also expected the gentry to protect them against injustice, to give them relief in time of calamity, and to take an active part in promoting local welfare.

The other sphere of influence was that of the local officials. In this connection, a distinction has to be made between authority and influence. Only an official had the authority to make decisions and to issue orders through the government apparatus. A gentry member, lacking such authority in his native area, could only exert his influence upon the officials in their decision-making—that is, induce the officials to initiate, modify, or withdraw a decision or action. Influence is here defined as operative whenever it induces a change in decisions.

Needless to say, not all the gentry were equally influential. There were prominent members who had influence in a whole province; others had influence only in a prefecture, a hsien, or a village. The degree of influence was determined largely by the local situation. For example, in Kiangsu or Chekiang, where there was a large number of degree-holders, a *chü-jen* was not likely to have a great deal of influence. On the other hand, even the holder of a low degree could be influential in a place where degree-holders were rare; for instance, a *sheng-yüan* might occupy a leading position in a small place, such as a village.

Among the prominent gentry in a community, there were usually a few at the top who were the most influential of all. Their word carried more weight than that of any other gentry members and they often assumed leadership among the group. In general, the official-gentry were more influential than the scholar-gentry, and the holder of a high official post or of a higher degree was more influential than the holder of a lower post or of a lower degree. The reason is obvious. Official-gentry as well as holders of higher degrees had closer connections with the power hierarchy. They invariably had ties with high officials both in the central and provincial governments. They were able to bypass the magistrate and go directly to the provincial or central officials to influence decisions at a higher level. The official-gentry with superior status might even appeal to the monarch directly. Thus, although the gentry represented the informal power in a local community, they were linked to the formal power at all levels, and it was this link that gave them power to influence the local officials. They were by no means an isolated local power.

An important point here is that the gentry's connection with formal power must be examined within the institutional framework, for the connection was based not merely on random and unorganized personal relations, such as between friends or fellow officials; it was based primarily upon specific relationships connected with the examination system. These relationships existed among three groups of people associated with the examinations: (1) teachers (*tso-shih* and *fang-shih*)—the examiners who passed a candidate in his examinations; (2) students (*men-sheng*)—those who passed the examination, thereby becoming known as the students of the examiner; and (3) fellow degree holders (*t'ung-nien*)—those who passed the same examination in the same year.

The behavior patterns of the scholar-officials were to a large extent conditioned by these relationships. Once a relationship of this sort was established, it lasted a lifetime. The scholar-officials were under obligation to be loyal to their teachers, students, and fellow degree-holders, and also to the children of all of them, and to help each other in trouble—an obligation observed by all scholar-officials. This was the kind of particularism that Ku Yen-wu noted as the cause of cliques among the scholar-officials. Such institutionalized and organized personal relationships, then, were the channel through which the gentry exerted their influence.

With this in mind it is not hard to see why retired or dismissed officials could still be influential. While they no longer had the formal power, they were not cut off from the power hierarchy and they usually retained some affiliation with it. On the other hand, officials lacking such affiliation, such as those who entered officialdom through the purchase of a title, were much less likely to be influential. In this connection, it was not so much lack of esteem for purchased titles as lack of proper connections that placed the group at a disadvantage.

As the *sheng-yüan* were outside the power hierarchy, they were the least influential among the gentry. Any power or strength they had derived mainly from group solidarity and collective action—as, for example, in joint petitions, or mass refusals to participate in an examination. At times, acting as a group, they even defied and insulted the local magistrate, who often found it difficult to control or punish them. But as individuals, the *sheng-yüan* had little influence with a magistrate.

Nevertheless, the strength and influence of the *sheng-yüan* should by no means be underestimated. The following statement from an essay by Ku Yen-wu describes some of their activities. Ku's essay dealt with the *sheng-yüan* of the Ming dynasty, yet to a considerable extent his description is applicable to the Ch'ing.

> It is the *sheng-yüan* who visit the yamen and interfere with the administration of the government; it is the *sheng-yüan* who rely upon their influence to be arbitrary in the villages; it is the *sheng-yüan* who associate with the clerks—some of them are even clerks themselves; it is the *sheng-yüan* who get together and riot when the government officials do not comply with their wishes . . . it is impossible for the officials to punish them, or to liquidate them. When they are treated with even slight harshness, they will say: "This is to kill the scholars. This is to bury the scholars."

5. Gentry Families

Strictly speaking, only a man possessing the qualifications described above (section 2) had the status of gentry. But his prestige and privileges were shared by his family members, not merely on a *de facto* basis, but within the provision of the law. Most important, the status of an official might legitimately be transferred to his family members through the system of bestowal (*feng-tseng*)—a system under which an honorary official title was bestowed on an official's father and/or grandfather. An honorary title, such as *fu-jen* or *ju-jen*, was also bestowed on his wife, mother, and/or grandmother. Upon acquisition of such an honorary title, an official's family member attained the legal status of an official, and was entitled to all such privileges as wearing the official hat button and garment, observing the etiquette and ceremonies prescribed for officials, and legal protection.

Technically, the law treated holders of honorary titles (known as *feng-tseng kuan*, bestowed officials) in the same way as regular officials. They could be arrested, tried, and punished only in accordance with the law governing the arrest, trial, and punishment of officials. In fact, such legal privileges were also extended to certain family members not possessing an honorary title. There was a law to the effect that the grandparents, parents, wife, sons, and grandsons of high officials in the category of *pa-i* (lit., "the eight deliberations") could not be arrested or sentenced without approval from the emperor. The parents and wife of an official of the fourth or fifth rank, as well as his son or grandson who was entitled to the privilege of *yin* (that is, holders of the title *yin-sheng*), could be arrested and tried by court, but the sentence had to be approved by the emperor.

An official's father who acquired an honorary title was not himself considered a member of the gentry. While fathers of officials did not participate in such formal gentry activities as meetings, they were not necessarily without influence in the community. They were usually regarded as elders and treated with respect by the local populace and local officials. The form of address used by degree-holders for the father of a fellow degree-holder was *nien-po* (lit., "uncle [who is the father of a] *t'ung-nien*"), a title which implied a sense of kinship and respect. It was not inconceivable for the father of a gentry member to exert a measure of influence on the local magistrate through his son, since sons were expected to be obedient to their fathers. Thus relatives of a gentry member often found it easier to approach him indirectly through his father.

Other relatives of any gentry member—brothers, uncles, nephews, sons, and grandsons—because of their connections with this one gentry member were also often very influential in their community. The higher the gentry member's position, the greater the influence of his relatives. This influence was frequently exerted with greater freedom when the gentry member was away than when he was present to exercise some control. Numerous complaints were made about relatives who used a gentry member's power to oppress the local people, engage in unlawful activities, and interfere with the local administration. Against such practices the local magistrate was helpless.

To deal with this situation, a law was passed to the effect that any relative of an official, other than his father, wife, or son, who relied upon the official's influence to oppress the local people and to insult government authority was to be penalized one degree more severely than commoners guilty of similar offenses. There was also a law holding officials in the capital responsible for the actions of their sons and younger brothers in their home town. The officials themselves were subject to dismissal if their family members used their influence to intimidate the local authority.

In the instructions he left for his children, Wang Hui-tsu warned that the gentry should instruct their family members to abide by the law and not incite them to intimidate or resist the magistrates. For their part, the magistrates were advised in the *Ch'in-pan chou-hsien shih-i* to inform the gentry that punishment would be meted out to their family members if they violated the law.

Women in traditional Chinese society were excluded from membership in the gentry and did not participate in any community activity. However, the wives of gentry members could associate with the wives of magistrates or other local officials, and thus could approach the local officials through their wives.

Even the servants in a gentry family were known to use their master's influence when engaging in unlawful activities. To counter this situation, a law was passed similar to that governing gentry relatives: a slave or servant of an official who relied upon his master's influence to oppress the people or to defy the government authority was to be punished one degree more severely than someone with gentry connections.

All these facts indicate that although the family members of the gentry lacked the formal status of gentry, their activities could not be entirely disassociated from the gentry members themselves. For this reason, they must be included in any survey of the power group; otherwise we see only part of the picture. The point is that the fathers and other close relatives of gentry members were not only more influential than the commoners, but they could actually be as influential as the gentry themselves. Family members of important official-gentry might even be more influential than the low-ranking official-gentry and the scholar-gentry.

As a background factor, we should, of course, keep in mind that the family was the basic unit in Chinese society, and the attitudes and behavior of the gentry were strongly dominated and conditioned by family solidarity. There was a permanent tie between the kinship unit and the local community within which the member's livelihood and the perpetuation of lineage were deeply rooted. Any disturbance in the community naturally threatened the interest of the family. It therefore became the prime responsibility of all family members to protect the collectivity. Similarly it was the obligation of all to help and defend any individual member when he was in trouble, especially when an injustice was done to him by an outsider. An insult to an individual was considered a humiliation to his entire family.

In this environment, one's ability to protect one's self and one's family depended primarily on one's position in the bureaucratic hierarchy. It followed that each family or clan looked upon the gentry member within it as its protector. He in turn accepted this responsibility. Thus, inability to protect the family from encroachment and injustice meant a lack of influence, and group humiliation was equated with personal humiliation.

6. The Gentry's Role in Local Administration

As the magistrate was never a native of the province where he held office, he was likely to have little or no knowledge of the local situation and find it necessary to seek advice from the gentry. In the present context, it is important to note that while regional differences existed in the vast territory of the empire, the administrative code was extremely rigid and contained few provisions for dealing with these differences. The gentry, being more familiar with the local situation, were presumably in a position to offer advice that took the local situation into account.

Information concerning local residents, particularly such undesirable ones as local bullies and pettifoggers, was also sought from the gentry. In this sense, they were considered the "eyes and ears" of the magistrate. It was argued that if the magistrates did not seek information and advice from the gentry, they would have to seek it from another group of natives—the government clerks and runners—who in minds of most officials were people of less integrity and reliability.

As the official-gentry did have some administrative experience, the magistrates often consulted them on administrative matters like public works or local defense, or when a situation was too complicated for the magistrate to make a decision alone. For instance, in 1666 Li Fu-hsing, the magistrate of Lou-hsien, Kiangsu, intended to introduce for taxation purposes a new measure whereby landholdings in the whole district would be grouped into a number of equal units. This required making new records of landholdings and involved many complicated technical problems. The magistrate called a conference with the gentry and got their support for the measure. The book recording this reform attributes success in implementing this new measure mainly to one member of the gentry, a *chü-jen*, on whose advice the magistrate had acted.

In another instance, when the magistrate of Hai-ning, Chekiang, requested that an agent (*li-ts'ui*) be appointed to hasten the collection of land tax in a rural area, the governor, who questioned the suggestion, ordered him to have a conference with the gentry. With the gentry's support the request was finally approved. These examples show that the advice of the local gentry was not only frequently sought by the magistrates voluntarily but at times was required by his superior officials. Sometimes high local officials themselves consulted the gentry on certain administrative matters.

Between the magistrate and the people the gentry assumed an intermediary role, which was facilitated by the traditional respect they commanded from the local populace. Many officials found that it was much easier to pass an order to the people through the gentry than through the formal government channels. At the same time, since they were the only natives who had access to the magistrate, the gentry could make the people's reactions known to the government. Through this channel the magistrate learned, for example, about complaints connected with his administration or his aides.

It is generally assumed that the gentry shared common interests with the local people. Let us see to what degree this was true. In traditional China what the sociologists call community sentiment—that is, a sense of belonging to the same community—was dominant and served to give cohesion to both the gentry and the peasants. Under normal conditions both groups desired a stabilized and orderly society. But such a society was even more important to the gentry because their security and privileges depended upon it. Any great disaster among the peasants would lead to disturbance of the community and thereby threaten the position of the gentry.

On the other hand, as a privileged class the gentry were primarily concerned with the interests of their families and relatives, interests at times necessarily divergent from those of the masses. In times of local crisis community sentiment could emerge forcefully, but in general class interest was more decisive in determining the behavior of the gentry. We conclude that it was only when their own interests were not jeopardized that the gentry took the general interest of the community into consideration and mediated between the magistrate and the local people.

Whether the gentry acted individually or collectively, as a pressure group, on behalf of the community, they were the only group that could voice a protest or exert some pressure on the magistrate or higher officials through recognized channels. One gentry member once addressed a letter to a magistrate stating that the land-and-labor service tax collected from the people was frequently embezzled by government employees and that taxpayers should be treated more leniently. On one occasion the gentry members of Shan-yin and K'uai-chi, Chekiang, complaining about the excessive charges demanded by the clerks for registering the transfer of landed property, held a meeting and decided that only 800 coins should be charged for such a transfer. They forwarded their resolution to the prefect, asking him to authorize this sum as the permanent official charge. The request was granted. When a suggestion or complaint from the gentry was ignored by a local official, they could, as we have suggested above, directly approach his superiors and exert a greater pressure upon him.

In addition to giving advice, the gentry participated in the following aspects of local administration.

Public Works and Public Welfare

The gentry contributed to the building and repairing of dikes, dams, city walls, roads, and bridges, and the establishment of poorhouses, foundling houses, and widows' homes. The magistrate had to depend upon them for help, because, as we said in the preceding chapter, government funds for public works and public welfare were limited. A common procedure was for the government to set up a commission and appoint gentry members as directors to collect and take charge of funds contributed by the local officials, gentry, and commoners. Further, the gentry were often requested by the magistrate to direct or supervise a construction project or manage a charitable organization. Many officials maintained that under the supervision of the gentry the construction work and public services were performed more efficiently and at less expense than in the hands of clerks.

In time of famine or flood, the gentry not only contributed funds for relief but also directed relief commissions in interviewing famine-stricken people and actually distributing food or money. Many community granaries were under the management of the gentry.

The gentry also participated in the attempted construction of provincial railways when China began to modernize her means of communication in the latter part of the nineteenth century. While the merchants were also financially involved in this venture, it was the gentry who took the lead in negotiating with the government officials for the right to build local railways. For this reason, the directors of the railway companies were eventually selected from the gentry members, although in terms of actual accomplishment this meant very little.

Educational Activities

Contributions for repairs to the local Confucian temple, the examination hall, and school buildings came mainly from the gentry, who considered themselves guardians of the Confucian teachings. They also contributed to the establishment of academies (*shu-yüan*), and some of them became chancellors or lecturers in these institutions. They were also expected to assist the magistrates in enforcing the semimonthly lecture system in the rural districts, where the magistrates could not be present themselves.

However, this function was apparently rather nominal. The reader may recall that even in the district seat the lecture system was a formality.

Pao-chia *Administration*

The gentry as a rule were not actually included in the *pao-chia* organization and the commoners who were heads of *pao-chia* were not in a position to supervise them. However, attempts were made by some magistrates to enlist the help of the gentry in such matters as checking the households against the records made by local constables. There was one case where gentry members were appointed as heads of *pao-chia* in the rural district to supervise the heads of minor units (*chia* and *p'ai*) and to visit the magistrate at regular intervals to exchange the rotating *pao-chia* records. Possibly this was not only an attempt to make the *pao-chia* administration more efficient, but also a device to include the gentry in the network of surveillance.

Local Militia

Although the gentry, by and large, did not take an active part in the *pao-chia* administration, they always played a leading role in organizing the local militia in order to protect their native towns, where their homes and properties were located. As a privileged class, they were eager to maintain the *status quo*, opposing any force that might overthrow the established social order. Naturally the task of local defense, which demanded strong leadership and financial support, fell to the gentry, who commanded the respect and obedience of the local residents and had access to the governmental authorities.

The Ch'ing government, since it was too

weak to maintain peace, tolerated, and even depended upon, gentry organization and command of the local militia. A comparable situation had been the organization of local defense by the Ming gentry against the Manchu invaders. This was repeated in the Ch'ing, particularly in the nineteenth century during the Taiping Rebellion. While the regular force was collapsing, the government encouraged the gentry to organize the local militia. Some of the eminent official-gentry on leave in their native provinces, like P'ang Chung-lu (1822–1876) of Ch'ang-shu, Hou T'ung (*chin-shih* 1820) of Wu-hsi, and Tseng Kuo-fan (1811–1872) of Hsiang-hsiang, were ordered by the emperor to organize and command the local militia in their native provinces. Some active officials holding high posts in the central or provincial government—for example, Lu Hsien-chi (1803–1853) and Li Hung-chang (1823–1901)—were sent back to their native provinces to take charge of local defense. During the Sino-French War, Governor-general Chang Chih-tung (1837–1909) also requested the gentry to organize the local militia in Kwangtung to help the government troops resist the invasion.

Often a number of defense corps were organized in the various towns and villages, under the command of a local gentry member. These corps were financed by the gentry themselves, or by voluntary or assigned contributions from the local residents, or by proceeds from a special tax, the likin. Public bureaus were established to collect funds.

In theory the local militia was an auxiliary of regular troops. Most cities were jointly defended by government troops and the local militia, under the over-all command of the magistrate or other local officials. But since the official-gentry often had a status superior to that of the lower-level local officials (in some instances they were the equals of the governor or governor-general), the gentry could sometimes command the local officials. For example, in the defense of Ch'ang-shu and Chao-wen, it was P'ang Chung-lu who directed the defense with the two magistrates under his command.

The gentry activities described in this section were prescribed by law or custom and were generally accepted. The magistrate was expected to accept the role played by the gentry and allow them to participate in community activities. If a magistrate failed to do what the gentry expected him to do or if he denied their established status and role he was faced with opposition. On the other hand, the gentry were expected by the magistrate and by the people to perform their functions in accordance with the established tradition. The failure of any gentry member to meet these expectations usually brought dissatisfaction and complaint from the officials and the local people and even censure from other members of the gentry.

7. Exploitation and Unlawful Activities

So far we have been concerned with the positive contributions of the gentry to their society. Now we must turn to the other side of the coin, to the gentry's exploitation of their privileged position.

In the early Ch'ing, as in the Ming, the practice of land tax evasion among the gentry was widespread. Although the law gave the gentry only limited exemption (two to thirty piculs per person), they sometimes ignored this limit and evaded land tax altogether. This practice continued despite an edict in 1657 which canceled all previous exemptions. A few years after this edict the Ch'ing government ordered investigations in certain areas in Kiangsu and Chekiang where a large number of gentry members appeared to be tax delinquents. It was disclosed in 1661 that in the prefects of Suchou, Sung-chiang, Ch'ang-chou, and Chen-chiang, and in Li-yang hsien, 13,517 gentry members owed tax and their names were reported to the court by the governor. The investigations, together with a generally more rigorous policy toward the gentry members, seem to have been a part of the Manchus' efforts to consolidate their political power over South China during the early days of their rule. Nevertheless, they gave an indication of the extent to which the gentry evaded the land tax in those days.

To cope with the situation, special laws and measures were introduced by the Ch'ing government whereby delinquent taxpayers among the gentry were singled out and their names reported by the magistrate to the provincial authorities. The tax delinquents were penalized by dismissal from office, loss of degree or academic title, beating, or the cangue, depending upon the amount of overdue tax. Their titles could be restored only after they had completed payment.

Such measures, together with a regulation requiring the magistrates to hand in the full amount of tax owed, made it more difficult for the gentry to evade tax payment than had been the case in the Ming dynasty, since magistrates would be risking their own careers if they tolerated tax evasion by the gentry. This does not mean, however, that there were no cases of the gentry refusing to pay land tax and gain tribute, although such cases were comparatively rare during the Ch'ing.

A more serious problem faced by the government in tax collection was the inequality between payments by the gentry and by commoners. In the tax record the gentry households were designated as "official-gentry households" (*shen-hu*), "official households" (*kuan-hu*), "scholar households" (*ju-hu*), or "large households" (*ta-hu*); the commoner households were designated as "people's households" (*min-hu*), or "small households" (*hsiao-hu*). The commoners, who were required to pay the extra surcharges, paid more in tax than the gentry. The latter were reluctant to pay the extra surcharges on the grounds that they were not a part of the legal tax, and that the magistrates and the yamen personnel collected more extra surcharges than were justified to meet the collection cost. Hence it was impossible for the magistrate to collect from them the same amount in extra surcharges as was imposed on the commoner households. In general the gentry paid their land tax and grain tribute at a rate slightly higher than the legal rate. Actually, the taxation rate was not the same among all gentry taxpayers. The extent to which they could avoid the payment of extra surcharges depended upon their status and influence; the more influential the gentry member, the lower the rate of the extra surcharge; and hence the closer his tax payment came to the legal rate.

As the local officials could not argue with the gentry on the legality of collecting extra surcharges or setting a higher conversion rate, they had to accept the lower rate paid by the gentry households in accordance with established usage, and meet the cost of collection and other yamen expenses covered by extra surcharges by shifting the burden onto the commoners, who were unable to protest and protect themselves under the law. Thus the commoner-taxpayers bore the greatest share of the cost of collection and of other yamen expenses. In fact the part of the tax left unpaid by some gentry-landowners was also covered by the extra amounts collected from the commoner-landowners. Therefore the tax burden of the gentry was decreased, while the burden of the commoners was proportionately increased. Throughout the dynasty the tax rates for the gentry households remained different from those of the commoner households—the rate increased as the status and influence of the taxpayer decreased. Governor-general Tso Tsung-t'ang reported to the emperor in 1864 that the gentry in Shan-yin, K'uai-chi, and Hsiao-shan, Chekiang, paid only 1.06 to 1.4 taels for 1 tael of land-and-labor-service tax, whereas the commoners, who were obliged to pay coins in lieu of silver, paid from 2800 to 4000 copper coins for 1 tael of tax. Similar inequality existed in the payment of grain tribute. According to an estimate by Feng Kuei-fen, the gentry paid only 1.2 or 1.3 piculs for 1 picul of tax (at most they paid 2 piculs). Among the commoners, the payment varied from about 2 piculs to 3 or 4 for 1 picul of tax. The governor of Kiangsu, Ting Jih-ch'ang, also reported that the commoner-taxpayers in the Chiang-pei area had to pay 6000 to 7000 coins, or even as much as 15,000 to 16,000 for 1 picul of grain tribute, whereas the gentry paid only 2000 to 3000 coins.

It is obvious that such economic privileges were obtained through political status, and were therefore not extended to commoner-landlords (a fact that again illustrates the impossibility of identifying landlords as gentry, although many of the latter were landlords). The government vainly attempted from time to time to abolish the distinction between the gentry households and commoner households for purposes of tax payment. The gentry refused to give up their special privileges and banded together to defend their common interests.

Another way in which the gentry abused their privileged position was to act as transmitters of tax payments for the commoners (*pao-lan ch'ien-liang*), although a law prohibited such activity and the magistrates were required to investigate any violation of this law. The commoners sometimes sought this arrangement in order to avoid direct dealing with yamen personnel and their numerous techniques of extortion. The gentry stood to profit by collecting tax funds at the commoner-taxpayer's rate (a rate that included the customary extra surcharges) and paying to the government at the lower rate for gentry households, pocketing the difference. Often when the gentry delivered the tax payment to a clerk, the silver contained in the sealed bags was either deficient in amount or inferior in quality. And for grain tribute they often delivered grain of poor quality as payment. An edict declared in 1696 that the large households in Hunan deliberately prevented the small households from paying their taxes directly to the government. In fact, *pao-lan* was so prevalent in the empire that it became a great concern to the government, which was unable to put an end to the practice.

Many gentry members, particularly the *sheng-yüan* and *chien-sheng*, also took advantage of the magistrates' collection of extra surcharges on grain tribute by demanding a share of the profit. In each of the several hsien in Kiangsu as many as 300 or 400 gentry members thus obtained grain tribute fees (*ts'ao-kuei*) from the magistrate. The source of these fees was obviously the commoner-taxpayers; the larger the share of customary fees for the gentry, the more the extra surcharges levied upon the people.

The gentry were exempted from the labor-service tax, the revenue from which was used to hire men to render services to the government. In the earlier days of the Ch'ing dynasty this exemption was extended to the gentry's family members, who might number from two to thirty persons, depending upon the status of the particular gentry member. In 1657 the exemption became limited from "miscellaneous labor service" (*tsa-fan ch'ai-yao,* or simply, *ch'ai-yao*) not covered by the labor-service tax, for example, labor service in connection with public works, government transportation, and the *pao-chia* administration. As a result, the burden of such labor service, which sometimes was rendered in money, was borne by the commoners. It was for this reason that Ku Yen-wu maintained that the official-gentry, scholar-gentry, and clerks and runners, who were all exempted from labor service, were the groups that caused the people to suffer. He suggested that only "the abolition of the *sheng-yüan*" could alleviate the suffering of the people.

Although the law limited labor-service exemption to the gentry members themselves, in practice it was frequently extended to their relatives as well. In many instances, the gentry made arrangements with commoner-landowners, permitting them to register their landed property under the names of the gentry. By this arrangement the commoners could avoid rendering miscellaneous labor service while the gentry profited, in the method described above, by keeping part of the commoner's tax money. Thus a member of the official-gentry in the northern provinces, according to a magistrate's report, often had several tens of such persons under his protection (these were known as *kung-ting*), and a member of the scholar-gentry could also have several. Once a commoner became thus attached to a gentry member, the government agent in the villages did not dare to assign miscellaneous labor service to him. Consequently all the burden of miscellaneous labor service was borne by the commoner-villagers who had no way to appeal, and as more households or land came under the "protection" of the gentry members, fewer households or landowners were left to share the burden.

In general, in the words of one magistrate, "when a project planned by the hsien government is disadvantageous to the gentry, they advance arguments to prevent it from being carried out." Conversely, something useful, like newly reclaimed land or irrigation facilities, would be monopolized by some of the gentry for their own use.

The influence that the gentry was frequently able to exert over the local magistrate was also applied in judicial affairs. True, there were gentry members who helped the innocent for the sake of justice. But more frequently their actions were motivated by nepotism or by financial gain. Some gentry members, according to an imperial edict, presumed upon their position and frequently interfered with the administration of justice. While *chien-sheng* and *sheng-yüan* could not see the magistrate freely, they often had connections with clerks and runners. Thus they were able to become pettifoggers, prompting litigation, handling lawsuits on behalf of others, and making arrangements for their "clients" with the yamen personnel.

That such corruption was prevalent among the *sheng-yüan* is suggested by the fact that one of the eight imperial instructions engraved on a stone tablet (*wo-pei*) placed in all government schools warned the students to keep away from the yamen, not to get involved in lawsuits, and not to appear in court as witnesses. Further, they were instructed to send a deputy instead of going to court personnally, even when they were directly involved. Laws were also promulgated to impose punishment on *sheng-yüan* who appeared in court as witnesses, wrote complaints for others, or engaged in pettifoggery.

Gentry members were often accused of being overbearing and tyrannical in their community and of being a menace to local residents, who dared not offend them. An imperial edict of 1747 reads:

> Previously the official-gentry in the various places relied upon their influence and were arbitrary and tyrannical in their native places, bullied their neighbors, and constituted a great source of harm to the local area. After an effort was made in the Yung-cheng period to rectify this situation and to strictly prohibit [their unlawful activities], the official-gentry and the scholar-gentry began to obey the law and dared not be involved in affairs not concerning them. Yet recently the old habit has revived. They do not heed the laws but act arbitrarily.

Some gentry members engaged in unlawful activities in an even more flagrant manner—falsely accusing innocent people, seizing the landed property or graveyards of others, beating their own tenants, assaulting others, and swindling. An edict stated that a number of *sheng-yüan* collected fees from boats navigating on rivers, and taxes from people trading at country fairs. The gentry commanding the local militia were even more abusive, for they could make arrests freely. They were accused of disturbing the local communities, and of killing arbitrarily.

Realizing the potential threat posed by the gentry to the peace and security of the local community, the Ch'ing government passed special laws to deal with it. These laws ruled that officials on leave at home who interfered with local government business or engaged in unlawful activities were to be dismised. Retired and dismissed officials and degree-holders who interfered with government affairs, controlled government officials, or brought harm to the people or to the administration, were to receive eighty strokes. Another law authorized the local officials to impeach any member of the official-gentry or scholar-gentry who was found to be interfering with yamen affairs or oppressing the local people. At the same time the government placed the responsibility for supervising and investigating the gentry on local officials, that for the *sheng-yüan* on the educational officials in particular. The local authorities were to be punished if they connived in or failed to report any gentry wrongdoing to their superiors.

Despite these laws, the imperial government failed to prevent the gentry from exploiting their privileged position and engaging in unlawful activities. The law leaving the responsibility of supervising them to the local officials remained ineffective. In general these officials were not in a position to control the gentry, especially those of superior status and great influence. Moreover, normally the local officials had a tendency to maintain friendly relations with the gentry, avoiding any offense to them. Nor could the honest and upright gentry members be expected to go out of their way to use their influence to check the activities of the gentry of bad repute, except by expressing their disapproval and dissociating themselves from the group. Under these circumstances, it is no exaggeration to say that the presence in any community of the oppressive gentry, customarily referred to as *lieh-shen* (the bad gentry) constituted a menace to the populace who were at their mercy.

8. Cooperation and Conflict Between Magistrate and Gentry

Cooperation and conflict between local officials and the gentry were manifested in various ways and in varying degree. In general, conflict of interests occurred between the magistrate and individual members of the gentry rather than the local gentry as a whole. Only occasionally did a conflict involve all or the majority of the group—either because the interest of the whole group was involved or because the group sentiment was so strong that all the gentry members felt obliged to participate.

The magistrate and the gentry, of course, had interests in common. The magistrate needed the gentry's cooperation and support, without which his administration could not be carried out smoothly. Even his career and reputation depended to a large extent, if not entirely, upon the gentry. As one magistrate, Ho Keng-sheng, put it: "As the gentry are leaders of a locality, the good or bad reputation of the official often hinges on their opinion." Sometimes the gentry even helped the magistrates to make up deficits in government funds by claiming to the government that the local people were willing to contribute money. Actually, as an edict by the Yung-cheng emperor in 1724 indicated, these so-called "voluntary contributions" were a means to force the local residents to share the financial burden. For these reasons, the magistrates treated the gentry with special favor and maintained friendly relations with them.

On their part, the gentry depended upon the magistrate to maintain both their influence in the local community and such special privileges as paying tax at a favorable rate and sharing customary fees collected by the magistrate. A profit-seeking gentry member and a corrupt magistrate often cooperated closely for mutual benefit. The gentry could also cooperate with the magistrate's relatives, private secretaries, personal servants, and yamen clerks. Through these connections the gentry could ask favors of the magistrate either for themselves or on behalf of others.

However, this pattern of cooperation or collusion between the gentry and the magistrate was reversed whenever there was a clash of interests between the two—for example, when the magistrate insisted on enforcing laws that the gentry customarily violated, or when he prevented them from seeking personal gain. There were magistrates who adopted a policy of showing no weakness toward the gentry:

> Those who dare to overstep the bounds by making trouble, to slander the officials by submitting complaints, or to contemn them orally in public, must be disciplined, and their errors must be emphatically rectified. They should never be given a chance to get their wish lest they become overbearing in the future.

Conflicts also arose when the gentry had military power in their hands. Some of them only treated officials with contempt, but often went beyond the traditional bounds of informal power and intruded into the area of formal power. In other words, they ceased to observe the customary way of exercising their influence, and were inclined to strive for superiority, usurp the power of the local authorities, and take the law into their own hands, even making arrests and meting out punishments. Tseng Kuo-fan, who himself had been a gentry member in charge of local militia and an expert in gentry-official power relations, described the situation in his warning to the gentry in 1860:

> First [the gentry] request from magistrates an appointment as commissioners of the local militia bureau to obtain honor. Then the power goes down [from the officials to them], and they have nothing to fear. The yamen is dependent upon them for its food and other needs. They bestow rewards and inflict punishment at will, and contemn the officials. Now I want to warn the gentry that they should respect and stand in awe of the officials and observe this rule as a first principle.

Under the circumstances, it was inevitable that the gentry came into direct conflict with the local authorities, magistrates as well as higher officials. Several instances were reported by Hsüeh Fu-ch'eng (1838–1894), who was aware of the problems involved in authorizing the gentry to organize the local militia. Obviously there were tensions between the local officials and the gentry. To a magistrate, the maintenance of harmonious relations with and proper control of the gentry was a very difficult problem. He was always under the threat of fault-finding, intimidation, slander, and accusations on the part of the gentry.

The gentry were likewise subject to stresses and strains because of their uncertainty as to the attitudes of the magistrate, who might not tolerate their exploitation of privileges and their unlawful activities. Open conflict with the magistrate could ruin them, particularly in the case of the scholar-gentry, whose status was less secure than that of the official-gentry.

While there were sometimes clashes of interest between individual gentry members and individual local officials, they seem never to have been serious enough to cause a change in the power structure and the established social and political order. Such conflicts should be interpreted as conflicts within the same power group or social class, not between two different groups or social classes. Since both the gentry and the officials belonged to the same privileged class, they depended upon each other for the *status quo,* with the result that they remained entrenched in their perpetuation of their common interests; they permitted them to maintain a position of privilege and power for a long period in China's history.

PING-TI HO

The Population of China in Ming-Ch'ing Times

Historically, the Chinese population—both China's strength and its weakness—has grown in response to favorable economic and political conditions. But the details of this growth have been blurred by the government's incomplete and undependable official population data. Moreover, general historical documents and literature do not provide much help, for the traditional Chinese scholar-official was often vague about figures and economic matters and his judgments tended to be impressionistic rather than quantitative.

In his remarkable population studies, Dr. Ping-ti Ho has attempted to suggest ways of reconstructing China's historical population data for the period 1368–1953. The following selection states the conclusion of his studies.

According to Professor Ho, the Chinese population slightly more than doubled in the two hundred years from the beginning of the fifteenth to the end of the sixteenth century. In the seventeenth century, the social unrest caused by misgovernment and peasant rebellions led to severe losses in population, the exact extent of which cannot be determined. The unification under the Ch'ing Empire and the benevolent despotisms of K'ang-hsi (1662–1722) and Yung-cheng (1723–1735) in the late seventeenth and early eighteenth century stimulated the growth of population, which more than doubled in one century, from 1683 to around 1794, thus reaching the peak of population growth rate. The rate of growth has since declined. By the middle of the nineteenth century the population increased only one-third over the 1794 figure, and from 1850 to 1953 it increased only another one-third over the 1850 figure.

This persistent trend of a declining rate of growth tallies well with our knowledge of the changing economic and political conditions. It seems that the high prosperity of economic growth in the eighteenth century was coincident with the rapid growth of population. But when the population outgrew the economic growth, the situation deteriorated and the economic strain and population pressure started to show. These factors, combined with the corruption and inefficiency of the late Ch'ing government, not only led to the fall of the Manchu empire, but also to a certain extent account indirectly for the difficulties of modern China.

Reprinted by permission of the publishers from Ping-ti Ho, *Studies on the Population of China, 1368–1953*. Cambridge, Mass.: Harvard University Press, Copyright, 1959, by the President and Fellows of Harvard College. Footnotes omitted.

An attempt will be made here to suggest certain ways of reconstructing China's historical population data—a most difficult undertaking. For one thing, none of the long series of Ming, Ch'ing, and modern population figures was based on censuses in the technical sense of the term. Data for the years 1776–1850 seem better than the data of any other periods, but some annual totals contain regional omissions which are not clearly explained. Secondly, unlike European historians who can approach eighteenth-century population problems in the light of detailed modern censuses, students of Chinese history at most can have only the summaries of the imperfect 1953 census for reference. A third difficulty lies in the long intervals between the three periods that yield the comparatively more reliable population figures—the Ming T'ai-tsu era, the mid-Ch'ing period between 1776 and 1850, and the census year of 1953–54. Furthermore, traditional China failed to produce political arithmeticians of the caliber of Gregory King, let alone founders of economic and demographic science like Adam Smith and T. R. Malthus. With regard to figures and economic matters the traditional Chinese scholar-official is often vague, and his testimony impressionistic rather than quantitative.

For these reasons it is impossible for any modern student to suggest definite numbers in his attempt at historical reconstruction. The best that he can do is to suggest ranges and limits within which, to the best of his knowledge, China's population is likely to have grown or fluctuated through the last five and three-quarter centuries. Such ranges should be ascertained by correlating all major economic and institutional factors which had important bearing on population movements and which varied from one period to another. Broad demographic theories must therefore be resisted until all available facts and factors peculiar to each period have been examined.

I

The official Ming population data, though indicating relatively little change in the national totals for households and mouths throughout the two and three-quarter centuries of the dynasty, nonetheless show important changes in the geographic distribution of population which are summarized in Table 1. These data show that the five northern provinces registered an increase of 11,230,000 mouths, or 73 percent, in the course of 150 years, while the population of the southern provinces, excepting Szechwan, Yunnan, and Kweichow, declined by 12,000,000. When the increase of the southwestern provinces is included, the total population of China increased by a mere 3.3 percent.

These changes as shown in the official data, however, are probably more apparent than real. The gains in population in the northern provinces cannot be explained simply by the moving of the national capital from Nanking to Peking in 1421, nor can the extraordinarily large percentage gains registered by Yunnan and Szechwan be accounted for by immigration alone. It seems reasonable to assume that these regional increases reflect a general growth of population throughout China. But, because some of the northern provinces, particularly those of the low plain area, had suffered most from the devastation of the wars that attended the downfall of the Mongols, they were at first assigned much smaller landtax and labor-service quotas, and at lower rates than those of the southeastern provinces. The abundance of land, together with do-

Table 1
Changes in the Geographic Distribution of Population

Province	1393	1542	Increase or Decrease (Number)	Increase or Decrease (Percent)
Nan-Chihli	10,755,938	10,402,198	—353,740	—3.3
Pei-Chihli	1,926,595	4,568,259	2,641,664	137.1
Chekiang	10,487,567	5,108,855	—5,378,712	—51.3
Kangsi	8,982,481	6,098,931	—2,883,550	—32.1
Hu-kuang	4,702,660	4,436,255	—266,405	—5.7
Shantung	5,255,876	7,718,202	2,462,326	46.8
Honan	1,912,542	5,278,275	3,365,733	176.0
Shansi	4,072,127	5,069,515	997,388	24.5
Shensi	2,316,569	4,086,558	1,769,989	76.4
Fukien	3,916,806	2,111,027	—1,805,779	—46.1
Kwangtung	3,007,932	2,052,343	—955,589	—31.8
Kwangsi	1,482,671	1,093,770	—388,901	—26.2
Szechwan	1,466,778	2,809,170	1,342,392	91.5
Yunnan	259,270	1,431,017	1,171,747	452.0
Kweichow	—	266,920	—	—
Total	60,545,812	62,531,295	1,985,483	3.3

Source: *Hou-hu chih.*

mestic peace and government retrenchment in the early fifteenth century, presumably stimulated the growth of population. The increasing population of the north was required to share a greater portion of taxes and labor services, since the demands for the lightening of the fiscal burden by the people and officials of the southeast had always been highly vocal.

In addition, the soil of north China, being less fruitful than that of the rice area, could not be expected to bear much more than its own share of the combined fiscal burden; whereas in the rice area there had been a gradual, and indeed inevitable, shift of the incidence of the labor services from the people to the land. In north China services for the most part had to be assessed directly on the people; therefore the original system of population registration was maintained longer than in the south. For these reasons the natural growth of the population in the northern provinces was substantially reflected in the official population returns. Immigration and the choice of Peking as the natural capital were other, but probably comparatively minor, factors contributing to the growth of the population in north China.

The reasons for the high percentage-increase of recorded population in Yunnan and Szechwan may have been political and cultural. That there had been some natural growth of population in these two provinces cannot be doubted, but the unusually high percentage gains probably can be attributed to unusual under-enumerations in early Ming times. It was not until 1420 that Yunnan and Kweichow were made into provinces. It was not until Chinese cultural influence gradually spread to the rich basins and valleys of Yunnan that the ordinary civil administration was set up and population was registered in these districts. Despite the abnormally high percentage-increases, the 1542 returns for these southwestern provinces were still far too low, for some districts in these provinces remained outside the pale of Chinese civilization down to the eighteenth century. Because of very large aboriginal populations all pre-1953 population figures for the southwestern provinces of Yunnan, Kweichow, and Kwangsi were too low.

While the northern and southwestern provinces registered population gains, the official population data show a general decline of population in the southern provinces, particularly Chekiang and Fukien. When the prefectural breakdowns are studied, it is found that, although the recorded population of Nan-Chihli declined but slightly, the populations of Su-chou and Sung-chiang, two prefectures that bore the heaviest fiscal burden in the country, substantially declined. Northern Chekiang and parts of Fukien were also among the heavily taxed areas. Since a decline of population meant a reduction of fiscal burden, the decline of registered population in these heavily taxed areas was often connived at, and at times even endorsed by, provincial and local authorities. The memorials urging tax reduction for the southeast are voluminous. The compiler of a famous sixteenth-century encyclopedia commented: "South of the Yangtze the household often does not have actual ting, for the household is assessed to its [landed] property. The laws punishing the evasion of household and ting registration cannot be strictly enforced." A scholar and fiscal expert of the late sixteenth century also said: "When the labor services and taxes are heavy, there are bound to be evasions." K'uai-chi county, a part of modern Shao-hsing in Chekiang, testified that among the local population only those liable to labor services were entered into the official registers and that those who were outside the registers were probably three times the official population figure.

A Fukien local history is most revealing:

From 1391 to 1483, in a period of 92 years, the number of households in our locality had declined by 8,890 and that of mouths by 48,250. This means a loss of between 60 and 70 percent. Why is it that after a long period of peace and recuperation there should be such a decline? It was probably due to the fear [on the part of local officials] that an increase would mean a further burden to the people and they therefore connived at the evasions and omissions without bothering to check.

It is clear that in the heavily taxed areas a decline of registered population was not infrequently regarded as a convenient means of redressing fiscal inequities.

While most counties in the southeastern provinces registered a declining population, some recorded a slightly increasing, and others a stationary population. Whatever the type of return, few if any can have reflected the actual changes in population. Under-registration was probably common even in those prefectures and counties that registered an increasing population. For instance, the population of Ch'ang-chou prefecture in southern Kiangsu nearly doubled between 1377 and 1602, yet a well-informed native scholar and fiscal expert remarked that the prefectural population had been in fact considerably under-registered because of the common practice by the well-to-do of avoiding the division of clan property, in order to lighten or evade the labor-service assessment. The editor of the 1629 edition of the history of Fukien went so far as to say that "neither the numbers of households nor those of mouths are authentic."

The 1613 edition of the history of Fu-chou prefecture not only explains the reasons behind under-registration but throws light on the general question of population growth, at least in the southeastern provinces:

I have gathered from my studies that usually towns and villages were partially deserted at the beginning of a dynasty, because the people had just gone through a period of turmoil and suffering. During a long period of peace, population could not but grow and multiply. Our old prefectural history recorded that in the Cheng-te period (1506–1521) the population had increased but two-tenths or three-tenths since the beginning of the reigning dynasty. Our present population remains more or less the same as that of the Cheng-te period. The empire has enjoyed, for some two hundred years, an unbroken peace which is unparalleled in history. During this period of recuperation and economic development the population should have multiplied several times since the beginning of the dynasty. It is impossible that the population should have remained stationary. This may have been due to the intrigues of government underlings and the failure of the authorities to get at the truth, but more probably to the old convention that at the time of decennial assessment little should be done beyond the fulfilment of the old quotas.

The evidence from southeastern local histories accords well with the impressions of contemporary observers. Unfortunately, although a fair amount of qualitative evidence can be gathered to bear witness to a continual growth of population, none yields a reliable quantitative statement. To mention an extreme statement, an official said in a memorial of 1614, "the present population is probably five times that at the beginning of the dynasty." Exaggerated as this and other vague guesses are, they seem to substantiate the observations and theory of population put forth by Hsieh Chao-che, who served as the governor of Kwangsi in the early seventeenth century and was one of the most widely traveled and best informed persons in the country. In his famous *Wu-tsa-tsu,* a miscellany on China in five parts which was widely read in Tokugawa Japan for its valuable information on Ming China, he advanced the theory that population growth is slow and difficult except under very favorable human and material conditions. The slow increments during periods of peace were often more than offset by the effects of wars and epidemics that attended the end of certain dynasties. He was therefore of the opinion that population movements had always been cyclical from ancient times to the end of the Yüan dynasty, a generalization with which most traditional commentators on China's population concurred. But, he was convinced through his travels and observations that, since the founding of the Ming dynasty in 1368, the population had had a continual, and perhaps linear, growth. He said of the population of the Ming period: "During a period of 240 years when peace and plenty in general have reigned, people have no longer known what war is like. Population has grown so much that it is entirely without parallel in history." If a leader's merit was to be judged by the conditions which he had created for the multiplication of the human race, then in Hsieh's opinion the founder of the Ming dynasty deserved equal ranking with P'an-ku, the Creator in ancient Chinese mythology; and if the greatness of an age was to be measured by the extent to which mankind was allowed to rest, nourish and reproduce, then he was certain that the Ming period should outclass all the previous glorious dynasties—Shang, Chou, Han, and T'ang.

Although such statements argue for a continual and more or less linear and uninterrupted growth of population during Ming times, we have yet to find a relatively safe clue whereby we can reconstruct the population of Ming China. The only clue we have so far is that the aggregate recorded population of the five northern provinces increased from roughly 15,500,000, recorded in 1393, to about 26,700,000 in 1542—an apparent gain of 73 percent in almost 150 years, at an average annual rate of growth of 0.34 percent. But, since the growth of population in these northern provinces was not entirely reflected in the official returns, this is not a satisfactory statistical guide. In all likelihood the under-registration of northern population in the early Ming was proportionately less serious than that in the middle and late Ming periods. The actual growth of the population of north China, therefore, must have been somewhat greater than is revealed in the official data. Even estimated at the above rate, perhaps the population of north China should have at least doubled itself by 1600.

North China, of course, is not representative of the whole country. For one thing, an unusually large extent of land was available for agricultural settlement in the low plain of north China. It was so large that the founder of the Ming dynasty granted permanent tax exemption to settlers of certain areas in Pei-Chihli, Shantung and Honan, which was revoked in the fifteenth century. For another, in north China there seemed to be fewer institutional impediments to population growth. Generally speaking, north China was a land of small landowning peasants who bore a lighter fiscal burden than their southern counterpart. The effects of landlordism, if not entirely absent in the north, were certainly far weaker than those of the lower Yangtze area, northern Chekiang, and greater parts of Fukien and Kwangtung. These are the main arguments for the occurrence of a more rapid growth of population in north China.

On the other hand, various factors seem to favor the opposite view. In the first place, if the south suffered more from a heavier fiscal burden and from the evils of landlordism, it benefited greatly by an expanding and more varied economy. The effects of landlordism on population growth, particularly during a period when the total population of the country was small as compared with the modern population, were probably far less important than some have judged. Concentration of landed property in an age of increasingly labor-intensive agriculture had little adverse bearing on employment. The southeast had been allotted the heaviest fiscal burden precisely because of its ability to bear it. Hsieh Chao-che was right in saying that it was the gainful opportunities created by a many-sided economy that made the lower-Yangtze area prosperous, despite a fiscal load so heavy that it would have crushed any other region. Agriculturally, the inland-Yangtze provinces remained to be fully developed and plenty of good land was reported as available all along the Huai River and the lowlands of Hupei and Hunan. Kwangtung, Yunnan, and central and southern Hunan, with their natural abundance, and small populations, made up what Hsieh called a "land of paradise." Even the common Ming impression of congestion in the southeast must be read in its context and measured by the standard then prevailing.

When all factors are weighed, it seems that the population of south China was increasing somewhat more rapidly than the population of north China. It was by no means coincidental that the writers who testified to a continual and fairly rapid growth of population were in general southerners, while northern local histories were often full of complaints about the heavy labor-service burden which, though lighter than that of the lower Yangtze, was a cause of rural depopulation in some northern localities. On these assumptions one may guess that China's population had increased from some 65,000,000 in the late fourteenth century to the neighborhood of 150,000,000 by 1600. Even assuming that the southern population had been increasing at the same moderate rate revealed in official figures for the northern population, it may be hazarded that China's population had exceeded 130,000,000 by the turn of the sixteenth century.

There are strong reasons for favoring the higher estimate. In the first place, the extent of officially registered land reached 176,000,000 acres in 1602, which is 86 percent of the lowest, or 75.8 percent of the highest, estimate made by Professor J. L. Buck for the entire cultivated area in China Proper in the 1930's. Secondly, the continual dissemination of early-ripening rice throughout the Ming must have contributed heavily to the growth of population, particularly the population of the rice belt. It was during the Ming that the lowlands of Hupei and Hunan, along with the lower-Yangtze delta, ranked as the nation's main rice baskets. In fact, as early as 1002, within one century of the introduction of the Champa rice into China, the Northern Sung government registered over 20,000,000 households. Since evasion of population registration was rampant in the Sung period, 20,000,000 households seems to indicate a national population on the order of 100,000,00 at a time when the clan and compound family system had just been strengthened. On this basis, had it not been for the subsequent political division of China, the serious agricultural retrogression suffered by the Huai River region and Hupei (which became a much contested theater of war between the Chinese and the Jurchen), and the unusually oppressive government and vested interests of the Mongol period (1260–1368), the population of the country would probably have reached our assumed height of 150,000,000 much earlier.

By about 1600, however, the effects of Ming misgovernment apparently outweighed the benefits of commercial and agricultural expansion. Although the fiscal burden of the nation had been steadily increasing since the middle of the sixteenth century, the increases had been moderate compared with those of the early seventeenth century. There is no way of knowing how the nation adjusted itself, during the first quarter of the seventeenth century, to the apparently worsening economic and political conditions. In all likelihood the adjustment was slow and painful and the population was still increasing. But the second quarter of the seventeenth century witnessed the outbreak of great peasant rebellions. It was reported that the population of the densely settled Red Basin of Szechwan was nearly exterminated and that relatively few counties in Szechwan escaped from the scourge of Chang Hsien-chung and the conquering Manchus. Chang and other bandit leaders also exacted a heavy toll in human lives in Shansi, Shensi, Honan, Hupei, northern Hunan, the Huai River valley, and parts of Shantung and Hopei. It is impossible to estimate even approximately the number of people who perished directly in the two decades of peasant wars and indirectly from famine, pestilence, and economic dislocation. But one thing is clear: in terms of life destruction these wars must be compared with the Thirty Years' War in Europe and the Taiping wars in nineteenth-century China. Overpopulation, a factor believed by some Chinese demographers to have caused the social upheavals toward the end of every dynastic cycle, is conspicuously absent in the recorded discussions and data on late Ming China.

II

Despite the abolition of all late Ming surtaxes after the enthronement of the first Manchu emperor in 1644, the benefit of a reduced fiscal burden was not immediately evident. Wars against the various groups of Ming loyalists were still going on in central and south China and occasionally the conquering Manchus vented their wrath by widespread slaughter of loyalist Ming forces and civilian populations in a number of localities. It was not until the Prince of Kuei, the last Ming pretender, was driven to Burma in 1659 that the conquest of the Chinese mainland was completed. Formosa remained in the hands of Ming loyalists who from time to time harassed the southeast coast. Consequently, there was considerable economic dislocation along the coast; some of the coastal population was forced to move to inland districts and thus was deprived of its normal agricultural pursuit and its lucrative trade with foreigners. In 1673 the new Ch'ing empire was shaken by the rebellion of the powerful southern feudatories, which were pacified only after seven years of bitter fighting and heavy taxation. Not until the conquest of Formosa in 1683 did China see the beginning of an era of real peace, government retrenchment, and prosperity. It is true that the military campaigns, with the exception of the war against the feudatories, were of limited scale; possibly the population of the areas unaffected by wars began to increase at moderate rates shortly after the change of the dynasty, for some contemporaries were of the impression that by the 1690's the population of the provinces, except Szechwan, had exceeded that of the middle seventeenth century. Yet the second half of the seventeenth century as a whole must be regarded as a period of slow and gradual recovery from previous heavy losses. One cannot be certain whether by 1700 the population of China was as large as that of 1600, for the return of favorable economic and political conditions may have been too late for the seventeenth century to register any net gain in population.

We may further hypothesize as follows: combined economic and political conditions became most favorable after 1683. The last years of the seventeenth century were a prelude to the unique chapter of population growth that did not end until the outbreak of the Taiping Rebellion in 1851. The tone of early eighteenth-century observers on population differs drastically from that of late seventeenth-century writers. In fact, one of the main reasons for the K'ang-hsi Emperor's freezing of the national ting payment in 1711 was his idea of a rapidly increasing population, an idea that was the outcome of his personal tours of the empire and interviews with the common people. The plains, valleys, and easily worked agricultural land of the greater parts of the country must have been densely settled by the Yung-cheng period (1723–1735), when a series of edicts exhorted the nation to practice more intensive farming, to improve the crops, and to discourage the cultivation of non-cereal commercial plants like tobacco. Li Fu, while governor of Kwangsi in 1724–25, was of the impression that the population of the whole country had nearly doubled during the sixty years of the reign of K'ang-hsi. Although his statement cannot be taken as an accurate estimate, there can be little doubt as to the unusual rate of population growth during the last years of the seventeenth century and the first quarter of the eighteenth century.

One phenomenon of this period was the steady rise in the price of rice throughout the first half of the eighteenth century. By 1743 the young Ch'ien-lung Emperor was so puzzled by this phenomenon in years of bumper harvests that he ordered the provincial authorities to discover the reason for the high prices. Neither the exemption of taxes on rice nor the reduction of public purchase of rice could halt this upward swing in agricultural prices. Finally in 1748 Yang Hsi-fu, governor of rice-rich Hunan and a native of Kiangsi, who had a firsthand knowledge of rice production and marketing, offered perhaps the most satisfactory explanation. He attributed the rising rice prices to the higher standard of living for the nation as a whole, the increasing extravagance of the people, rice hoarding and price manipulation by the rich and cunning, large-scale public purchase of rice, and the rapid multiplication of the population. The last factor he considered the most basic. He said in a much-cited memorial:

> I was born and brought up in the countryside and my family had been for generations engaged in farming. I can recall from personal memory that prices of one *shih* of rice ranged between two-tenths and three-tenths of a tael during the K'ang-hsi period. By the Yung-cheng period such low prices were no longer possible and they rose to four-tenths or five-tenths of a tael. Nowadays the prices can never be lower than five-tenths or six-tenths of a tael. This is because a large population consumes large quantities of rice. Despite the considerable cultivated area that has been developed during the past few decades, in many regions there is no more room for agricultural expansion. It is inevitable that a rapidly increasing population should have caused a steady rise in the price of rice.

Although Yang referred probably only to the changing price structure in Kiangsi and Hunan, his generalization is supported by scattered official reports on rice prices for various provinces. By about 1750 the surplus rice of lowland Hupei and those districts of Hunan and Kiangsi easily reached by rivers was no longer sufficient to meet the demand of the southeast coast. At times even Hupei became partially dependent on Szechwan for the supply of rice, although in the remoter districts of Hupei, Hunan and Kiangsi, inaccessible to cheap water transportation, there was still surplus rice. It is helpful in estimating the eighteenth-century population to recall that when the population was presumably in the neighborhood of 150,000,000 around the turn of the sixteenth century, Hupei, Hunan, and Kiangsi, the traditional rice-bowl of China, were far from fully developed agriculturally. The filling-up of the important rice-producing lowlands and low hills is one of the indications that China's population may have considerably exceeded 150,000,000 in the early decades of the eighteenth century.

To mitigate the increasing regional pressure of population, the central and provincial officials repeatedly exhorted the nation to experiment with various new crops, particularly the sweet potato. A series of laws issued in the late 1730's granted permanent tax exemption to small plots of cultivable land, at varying sizes for various provinces, to prospective cultivators. It was during the first half of the eighteenth century that extensive interregional migrations took place and dry hills and mountains began to be systematically developed into maize and sweet potato fields. Szechwan, the inland Yangtze highlands, the Han River drainage, and even southwestern aboriginal districts were invaded by millions of migrant farmers and the forested mountains were opened upon a truly national scale. By the end of the eighteenth century the hilly and mountainous areas had been so intensively exploited that soil erosion and diminishing agricultural returns were reported to have become a serious problem.

The population growth throughout the eighteenth century assumed above was presumably connected with a standard of living. The benefit of the freezing of the national ting payment and of the merger of the ting payment with the land tax seems to have been passed on to the common people. The famous fiction writer P'u Sungling (1640-1715) testified that the average peasant household in his native Shantung had ample storage of grains, fresh and salted meats, vegetables and dried fruits, chickens and eggs, and home brewed wine for the lunar new year. This description need not have been an exaggeration or a portrayal of the standard of living for a comparatively well-to-do family. Although he himself was from a small landowning family, he received only twenty mou of land at the time of division of the family property, while many tenants in his novel worked on at least forty mou. Some of the peasants in Shantung, by no means one of the rich provinces, were so well off in the late K'ang-hsi period that they spent relatively freely and wasted a great deal of grain in good years.

The rising standard of living and general increase in wealth are attested to by various eighteenth-century local histories. A rapidly increasing population and a prolonged economic prosperity were said to be responsible for a manifold increase in land values in northeastern Hunan. The hilly and backward southeastern corner of Hunan bordering Kwangtung had never been reported as richer than during the second half of the eighteenth century, when the area could boast of a number of fortunes ranging from scores of thousands to over a million taels. Whereas Ying-ch'eng county in Hupei had been poor and sparsely populated in the 1660's, the county was not only densely populated but had several hundreds of inhabitants with a fortune of 10,000 taels by the turn of the eighteenth century. Of even a relatively poor district in Shensi it was testified in 1762:

Our old local history [1557 edition] said that the people were so frugal that sometimes they failed to comply with the customary standards of propriety. Previously even at a banquet there were but few courses, now people vie with each other in offering more. Wine, silk and meat have become common articles of local consumption. . . . The prices of cotton and silk fabrics, vegetables and fruits, meats and fuel have consequently increased several fold.

The lower Yangtze area probably established a new standard of extravagance during the eighteenth century. Such cities as Nanking, Yang-chou, Su-chou, and Hang-chou became great centers of consumption and luxurious living. Many contemporaries deplored this trend toward more wasteful and extravagant living. There must have been a substantial gap between the newly acquired standards of living in the late seventeenth and early eighteenth century and the subsistence living for a large part of the population during the first half of the nineteenth century.

A continuous rapid growth of population was reflected in the official figures for the years 1779-1794, the first years of improved *pao-chia* population registration without noticeable regional omissions. The average rate of increase during these fifteen years is 0.87 percent, as compared with 0.63 percent for the entire period 1779–1850 and 0.51 percent for the years 1822–1850. This may be comparable with the average rate of 0.771 percent for the population of pre-industrial Eastern Europe in the period 1800–1850. The population of China, which was presumably in the neighborhood of 150,000,000 around 1700 or shortly after, probably increased to 275,000,000 in 1779 and 313,000,000 in 1794. If so, it had more than doubled itself within a century that offered uniquely favorable conditions for growth.

III

Although it is often difficult to determine exactly when and where population pressure increases, there is reason to believe that in the case of Ch'ing China, the optimum condition (the point at which "a population produces maximum economic welfare") at the technological level of the time, was reached between 1750 and 1775. Up to the third quarter of the eighteenth century contemporaries had viewed the continual rapid increase of population as an almost unqualified blessing; the generation of Chinese who reached maturity during the last quarter of the century, however, began to be alarmed by the noticeable lowering of the standard of living that had become "customary" since the earlier decades of the eighteenth century. If the transition from high prosperity to growing economic strain was relatively abrupt, it may be accounted for by the fact that the optimum population, probably in the neighborhood of 250,000,000 in the middle of the third quarter of the eighteenth century, was already large and any further proportionate growth brought about a formidable increase in the total numbers. Granted that the deterioration of economic conditions occurred in various places at different times, the generalizations and the analysis of the economic situation made by Hung Liang-chi (1746–1809), "The Chinese Malthus," toward the end of the eighteenth century seem applicable to large areas of the nation. In his two famous essays, "Reign of Peace" and "Livelihood," written in 1793 while serving as educational commissioner of Kweichow, five years before the appearance of the first edition of Malthus' *Essay on Population,* he expounded many ideas similar to those of Malthus. Hung's theory of population is summarized and paraphrased by a modern Chinese scholar:

1. The increase in the means of subsistence and the increase of population are not in direct proportion. The population within a hundred years or so can increase from five-fold to twenty-fold, while the means of subsistence, due to the limitation of the land-area, can increase only from three to five times.
2. Natural checks like flood, famine and epidemic, cannot diminish the surplus population.
3. There are more people depending on others for their living than are engaged in productive occupations.
4. The larger the population, the smaller will be the income *pro rata;* but expenditure and the power of consumption will be greater. This is because there will be more people than goods.
5. The larger the population, the cheaper labor will be, but the higher will be the prices of goods. This is because of the over-supply of labor and over-demand for goods.
6. The larger the population, the harder it will be for the people to secure a livelihood. As expenditure and power consumption become greater than the total wealth of the community, the number of unemployed will be increased.
7. There is unequal distribution of wealth among the people.
8. Those who are without wealth and employ-

ment will be the first to suffer and die from hunger and cold, and from natural calamities like famine, flood and epidemics.

As to the possible remedies for overpopulation and their effectiveness, Hung says:

> Some may ask: "Do Heaven and Earth have remedies?" The answer is that their remedies are in the form of flood, drought, sicknesses and epidemics. But those unfortunate people who die from natural calamities do not amount to more than 10 to 20 percent of the population. Some may ask: Does the government have remedies? The answer is that its methods are to exhort the people to develop new land, to practice more intensive farming, to transfer people from congested areas to virgin soils, to reduce the fiscal burden, to prohibit extravagant living and the consumption of luxuries, to check the growth of landlordism, and to open all public granaries for relief when natural calamities strike. . . . In short, during a long reign of peace Heaven and Earth could not but propagate the human race, yet their resources that can be used to the support of mankind are limited. During a long reign of peace the government could not prevent the people from multiplying themselves, yet its remedies are few.

Like Malthus, Hung could not foresee the effect of technological inventions and scientific discoveries on agricultural and industrial production. Unlike Malthus, who, while expounding his abstract theory, analyzed practically all available material concerning the population problem, Hung misread, or at least did not bother with, the exact meaning of official population data. Whereas Malthus in the revised edition of his *Essay* and especially in his later economic writings succeeded in formulating a system, Hung's ideas are fragmentary and his quantitative statements irresponsible. But by far the most serious drawback in Hung's theory of population is his failure to understand the law of diminishing returns, which Malthus belatedly understood and which saves his arithmetical ratio of food increase from being a pure fallacy. To do him justice, however, Hung's ideas are original; among his bookish contemporaries he had the keenest grasp of the changing economic condition.

Although the tempo of population growth may have slackened because of a series of regional disturbances after 1796, the nation continued to register large net gains in population after peace was restored. In 1820 Kung Tzu-chen, a gifted scholar profoundly disappointed by the traditional cultural and institutional system, viewed the situation as a lull before the storm:

> Since the late Ch'ien-lung period the officials and commoners have been so distressed and slipping fast. Those who are neither scholars and farmers nor artisans and traders constitute nearly one-half of the population. . . . In general the rich households have become poor and the poor hungry. The educated rush here and there but are of no avail, for all are impoverished. The provinces are at the threshold of a convulsion which is not a matter of years but a matter of days and months.

Kung's alarmist view seems largely justified in the light of evidence from ninteenth-century local histories. Many local histories of Hunan and Kiangsi, the rice bowl of China, give the impression that by the first half of the nineteenth century the urgent economic problem was no longer how to maintain the customary living standards but how to maintain bare subsistence. Some traditional rice-exporting areas had only a small surplus in years of bumper harvests and became partially dependent on other regions for their food supply in bad years. Although an area of intensive farming, southern Kiangsi by the 1840's could not cope with the problem of rural unemployment, which had become more and more serious. With Szechwan almost entirely filled up, there was no more room for agricultural expansion in China Proper. Even the comparatively newly developed Yangtze highlands and the Han River drainage had begun to suffer from diminishing returns and soil erosion. Because of the silting-up of the Yangtze, its tributaries, and the lakes, which acted as its reservoirs, there was also an increasing incidence of flood. Yet the growing population of the Hupei and Hunan lowlands defied the law and the public interest and reclaimed and expanded the newly formed sandbanks and islets. A Hupei local history stated that the locality had become so congested by about 1850 that even after the successive Taiping and Nien wars, which somewhat relieved the local pressure of population, "still there can only be idle adults in the households but no untilled land in the fields." There is reason to believe that in the middle of the nineteenth century the Yangtze region was even more crowded than it is today.

"It was precisely in this situation," says a modern economic historian, "when a growing population was straining at resources and a large part of it living near the margin of subsistence, that a society was particularly vulnerable." So vulnerable was the Chinese society that in 1851 the world's greatest civil war, the Taiping Rebellion, broke out. It lasted fourteen years and affected nearly all provinces of China Proper, but most of all the densely populated central and lower Yangtze regions. Although the factors contributing to the rebellion were many, there can be little doubt that the pressure of population was one of the most basic.

The most frighteningly realistic discussion of the population question was made by Wang Shih-to (1802–1889), whose *I-ping jih-chi*, a diary written in 1855–56 while he was a Taiping captive, is an important source for the study of the background and early events of the rebellion. He was one of the millions who were innocent victims of the process of progressive impoverishment brought about by continual increase of population. Although his great-grandfather had been a rich merchant, by his lifetime the family had become so poor that he was sent out as a boy to apprentice in stores. The necessity for putting aside a little in order to marry off his daughters made it impossible for him to provide sufficient medical care for his consumptive first wife, which caused him deep sorrow for the rest of his life. Among his five daughters and three sons only two girls reached adulthood, and both of these met with tragic deaths in the 1850's. His bitter experience made him a misanthropist. He said of over-population in general:

> The harm of over-population is that people are forced to plant cereals on mountain tops and to reclaim sandbanks and islets. All the ancient forestry of Szechwan has been cut down and the virgin timberland of the aboriginal regions turned into farmland. Yet there is still not enough for everybody. This proves that the resources of Heaven and Earth are exhausted.

As far as he could diagnose, the ills of nineteenth-century China were due neither to misgovernment nor to the nation's lack of ingenuity and diligence. They were primarily accounted for by an increasing disproportion between population and economic resources. The remedy that he suggested was to relax the prohibition against female infanticide, or rather to encourage such a practice en masse, to establish more nunneries and to forbid the remarriage of widows, to propagate the use of drugs that would sterilize adult women, to postpone the age of marriage for both sexes, to impose heavy taxation on families having more than one or two children, and to drown all surplus infants of both sexes except the physically fittest. The problem of overpopulation and mass poverty which has plagued modern China had come into full existence by 1850.

In retrospect, it seems a great irony that the benevolent despotism of K'ang-hsi and Yung-cheng, one of the stimulants to population growth, sowed the seeds of the decline and fall of the Manchu empire and to a large extent accounted indirectly for the economic difficulties of modern China.

IV

Although it is difficult to suggest any definite figure for the net loss in population during the fourteen years of Taiping wars, our detailed local evidence testifies very clearly that a figure of twenty or thirty million, estimated by contemporary Western residents of the treaty ports, was too low. The Nien wars, which ravaged the Huai River area of northern Anhwei and parts of the north China plain, did not come to an end until the early 1870's. The Moslem rebellion, which greatly reduced the population of Shensi and Kansu, lasted until the late 1870's. It seems as though a readjustment between population and land resources could not be effectively brought about by nature's routine revenge alone but had to be supplemented by unprecedented man-made disasters.

The readjustment between population and land resources may best be evidenced by post-Taiping interregional migrations. Ironically it was the historically most densely settled lower Yangtze area that played the role of the pre-1850 Szechwan as the leading recipient of immigrants for about a generation. The sudden and unexpected lessening of population pressure could not entirely fail to have a certain beneficent, if transient, effect on the living standard of the people in the lower Yangtze region. The abundance and cheapness of good agricultural land, together with the government's eagerness to attract immigrants, helped many tenants to become small landowners. Even without the opportunity of climbing up the agricultural ladder, tenant farmers benefited for a while from the lenient tenurial terms that the acute shortage of labor had forced owners to offer.

The unusually observant Hu Ch'uan, father of Dr. Hu Shih, testified:

> I personally witnessed in 1866–67 that within the several-hundred-*li* stretch between Hui-chou and Ning-kuo and T'ai-p'ing [in southern Anhwei] the survivors had surplus grain in their storerooms, meat in their kitchens, and wine in their pitchers. They were well fed, occasionally got drunk, and enjoyed to the full what a restored peace could offer. On the roads practically no one would care to pick up something dropped by others and at night one did not have to shut his gate.

But the civil wars of the third quarter of the nineteenth century at best conferred upon the nation a brief breathing spell and failed to redress the old population–land balance. While the growth of the lower Yangtze population was definitely halted by the Taiping wars, the population of the low plain provinces of north China seems to have been increasing even faster than it had been before 1850. Emigration must have had comparatively little effect on provinces like Honan, whose population, as Richthofen observed, was apparently increasing rapidly due chiefly to the custom of early marriage. We may surmise that in all likelihood China's total population surpassed the 1850 peak sometime in the last quarter of the nineteenth century. The opening-up of Manchuria and overseas emigration, though having regional alleviating effects, failed to bring about a more favorable population–land ratio for the nation at large.

The absence of a major technological revolution in modern times has made it impossible for China to broaden the scope of her land economy to any appreciable extent. It is true that, after the opening of China in the 1840's, the moderately expanding international commerce, the beginnings in modern money and banking, the coming of steamers and railways, the establishment by both Chinese and foreigners of a number of light and extractive industries have made the Chinese economy somewhat more variegated, but these new influences have been so far confined to the eastern seaboard and a few inland treaty ports. There has not been significant change in the basic character of the national economy. In fact, for a century after the Opium War the influence of the West on the Chinese economy was as disruptive as it was constructive.

While the Chinese economy failed to make a break-through, the ideal of benevolent despotism was dead once and forever. The reduction of the land tax in the lower Yangtze region was only temporary, and very soon the financial straits of the central and provincial governments made large increases in surtaxes and perquisites inevitable. The people's fiscal burden was made even heavier by nationwide official perculation. With the lower Yangtze region partially recovered from war wounds, land tenure once more became a serious factor aggravating the peasants' economic difficulties. But the worst days did not come until China was ushered into an era of warlordism, at a time when the nation had so little economic reserve that natural calamities exacted disproportionately heavy tolls of human lives. Even under the twenty-two years of Nationalist rule the nation hardly enjoyed a year without war. All in all, therefore, the combined economic and political condition in post-1850 China was such that the nation seems to have barely managed to feed more mouths at the expense of further deterioration of its living standard.

Small wonder, then, that China's population has been computed as having increased only 35.5 percent between 1850 and 1953, giving an average annual rate of growth of 0.3 percent. If we take into account the probable net loss in population during the greater part of the third quarter of the nineteenth century and take 1865 instead of 1850 as the datum, then the average assumed rate of growth was between 0.4 and 0.5 percent, which is substantially lower than the average of 0.63 percent assumed for the period 1776–1850. It is even slightly lower than the average rate of 0.51 percent assumed for the period 1822–1850, when the basic population–land pattern had fully assumed its modern characteristics. Whatever the margin of error in the pre-1850 population figures, the evidently persistent trend of a declining rate of growth tallies well with our knowledge of the changing economic and political conditions.

In conclusion, it may be guessed that China's population, which was probably at least 65,000,000 around 1400, slightly more than doubled by 1600, when it was probably about 150,000,000. During the second quarter of the seventeenth century the nation suffered severe losses in population, the exact extent of which cannot be determined. It would appear that the second half of the seventeenth century was a period of slow recovery, although the tempo of population growth was increased between 1683 and 1700. The seventeenth century as a whole probably failed to register any net gain in population. Owing to the combination of favorable economic conditions and kindly government, China's population increased from about 150,000,000 around 1700 to perhaps 313,000,000 in 1794, more than doubling in one century. Because of later growth and the lack of further economic opportunities, the population reached about 430,-000,000 in 1850 and the nation became increasingly impoverished. The great social upheavals of the third quarter of the nineteenth century gave China a breathing spell to make some regional economic readjustments, but the basic population–land relation in the country as a whole remained little changed. Owing to the enormous size of the nineteenth-century Chinese population, even a much lowered average rate of growth has brought it to its reported 583,-000,000 by 1953.

Today the population of China is again increasing rapidly, even more rapidly than during the eighteenth century. The return of peace and order, the removal of some institutional barriers, the beginnings of large-scale industrialization, and especially the nation-wide health campaign cannot fail to stimulate population growth. Historically the Chinese population has been responsive to favorable economic and political conditions and has had a tendency toward prolonged growth even at the expense of progressive deterioration of the national standard of living. Whether history will repeat itself or whether the new China can achieve a rate of economic growth greater than her current rate of population growth remains to be seen. But the existence of a population of 600,000,-000—which is both China's strength and weakness—has already compelled the pragmatic Communist state to adopt a policy of limiting future population growth.

Bibliographical Note

My *Premodern China: A Bibliographical Introduction,* published in 1971 by the Center for Chinese Studies at the University of Michigan, Ann Arbor, Michigan, covers all major fields of premodern China, and includes various types of scholarly works—books, monographs, articles, pamphlets, and theses and dissertations. Combining a bibliography with a syllabus of traditional Chinese history and civilization, it has three parts. The first part is an introduction to the field of Chinese studies. The second part contains lists of selected Western-language reference works, including bibliographies of various disciplines, periodicals and newsletters, research aids, and suggested style sheets. The last part is a selected bibliography of Western-language sources on all aspects of traditional China, concentrating on the history and civilization of China from prehistoric times to about the beginning of the nineteenth century. The bibliography is the most up-to-date and comprehensive of its kind at this time. Refer to it for further readings and research materials on premodern China.

Other reference bibliographies include the following:

ASSOCIATION FOR ASIAN STUDIES, *Bibliography of Asian Studies.* Ann Arbor, Mich.: Association for Asian Studies, 1956–. (Annual bibliography of Asian studies, since 1956.)

CORDIER, HENRI, *Bibliotheca Sinica* (5 vols., reprint). New York: Burt Franklin, 1968. (Works on China published before 1922.)

ÉCOLE PRATIQUE DES HAUTES ÉTUDES, *Revue bibliographique de Sinologie.* Paris: École Pratique des Hautes Études, 1955–. (Annual abstracts of current books and articles in Oriental and Western languages on China.)

FAR EASTERN ASSOCIATION, *Far Eastern Bibliography.* Ithaca, N.Y.: Cornell University Press, 1941–1955. (Annual bibliography of Far Eastern Studies.)

GORDON, LEONARD H. D., and FRANK J. SHULMAN, *Doctoral Dissertations on China: A Bibliography of Studies in Western Languages, 1945–1970.* Seattle: University of Washington Press, 1972. (Lists 2,217 dissertations on China, completed at institutions throughout North America, Europe, the Soviet Union, Australia, and India.)

HUCKER, CHARLES O., *China: A Critical Bibliography.* Tucson: University of Arizona Press, 1962. (With annotations and critical comments.)

LUST, JOHN, *Index Sinicus: A Catalogue of Articles Relating to China in Periodicals and Other Collective Publications, 1920–1955.* Cambridge, England: Heffer, 1964.

SHUMAN, FRANK J., "Doctoral Dissertations," in *Association for Asian Studies Newsletter,* Vol. XIV, No. 4 (May 1969–). (Includes titles of dissertations already completed as well as works in progress both in the United States and abroad.)

STUCKI, CURTIS W., *American Doctoral Dissertations on Asia, 1933–June 1966,* 2nd ed. Ithaca, N.Y.: Department of Asian Studies, Cornell University, 1968. (Lists 750 dissertations on China.)

YÜAN, T'UNG-LI, *China in Western Literature.* New Haven, Conn.: Yale University Far Eastern Publications, 1958. (Works on China published between 1921 and 1957.)

For a review of recent research trends in and major works on the study of Chinese civilization, see John K. Fairbank, *New Views of China's Tradition and Modernization* (Washington, D.C.: American Historical Association, 1968).

BIBLIOGRAPHY
WTR-195 / 2002
HIST-352
MB&S/Imperial China

Chun-shu Chang   763-2294

1. Chang, Chun-shu (prof. of course) (1975). Entire out of print text. <u>Making of China, The</u>, ix-347, Upper Saddle River: Prentice Hall, Inc..

(c) 1990-1996, David H. Crawshaw Inc.

Program: CPY_BIB   (Bibliography Listing)